Lecture Notes in Computer Science 3578

Commenced Publication in 1973
Founding and Former Series Editors:
Gerhard Goos, Juris Hartmanis, and Jan van Leeuwen

T0189858

Marcus Gallagher   James Hogan
Frederic Maire (Eds.)

Intelligent
Data Engineering and
Automated Learning –
IDEAL 2005

6th International Conference
Brisbane, Australia, July 6-8, 2005
Proceedings

 Springer

Volume Editors

Marcus Gallagher
University of Queensland
School of Information Technology and Electrical Engineering
Brisbane Qld 4072, Australia
E-mail: marcusg@itee.uq.edu.au

James Hogan
Frederic Maire
Queensland University of Technology
School of Software Engineering and Data Communications
GPO Box 2434, Brisbane Qld 4001, Australia
E-mail: {j.hogan,f.maire}@qut.edu.au

Library of Congress Control Number: 2005928541

CR Subject Classification (1998): H.2.8, F.2.2, I.2, F.4, K.4.4, H.3, H.4

ISSN   0302-9743
ISBN-10   3-540-26972-X Springer Berlin Heidelberg New York
ISBN-13   978-3-540-26972-4 Springer Berlin Heidelberg New York

Springer is a part of Springer Science+Business Media

springeronline.com

© Springer-Verlag Berlin Heidelberg 2005
Printed in Germany

Typesetting: Camera-ready by author, data conversion by Olgun Computergrafik
Printed on acid-free paper   SPIN: 11508069   06/3142   5 4 3 2 1 0

Preface

The ongoing success of the Intelligent Data Engineering and Automated Learning (IDEAL) conference series reflects the continuing need for intelligent approaches to understanding relationships in the massive data sets which confront the modern researcher.

From its origins in Hong Kong in 1998, this focus upon the nature of the data has been the unifying theme of the conference, allowing it to become a key forum for researchers to present novel approaches to data engineering and learning, and to provide a particularly valuable opportunity for cross-disciplinary exchange of ideas in emerging application areas. This breadth and continual evolution may be seen in this year's programme, with sessions devoted to data mining and knowledge engineering, bioinformatics, agent technologies and financial engineering, together with the traditional focus on learning algorithms and systems.

This volume in the Lecture Notes in Computer Science series contains accepted papers presented at IDEAL 2005, held in Brisbane, Australia, during July 6–8, 2005. The conference received 167 submissions from throughout the world, which were subsequently refereed by the Programme Committee and additional reviewers. The vast majority of submissions received three independent reviews, and for some borderline submissions an additional, fourth review was commissioned prior to the decision being made.

In the end, 76 papers were judged to be of sufficient quality for acceptance and inclusion in the proceedings, with a smaller set of these articles to be considered for inclusion in planned special issues of a number of major journals – continuing a practice from recent IDEAL conferences. At the time of writing, this arrangement had been confirmed with the International Journal of Neural Systems, and discussions were well advanced with two other publications.

Happily, IDEAL 2005 also enjoyed a fine list of keynote speakers, with talks by Adam Kowalczyk, Geoff McLachlan, and Mehran Sahami bringing an ideal mix of theoretical innovation and application focus.

We would like to thank the International Advisory Committee and the Steering Committee for their guidance and advice, and we would particularly like to acknowledge the work of our Programme Committee members and additional reviewers who performed admirably under tight deadline pressures. It has been a pleasure to work with a publisher such as Springer, and we thank them for their ongoing professionalism and attention to detail.

We were fortunate to receive support from two Australian research organizations for paper prizes (The Australian Research Council Centre for Complex Systems) and student travel grants (The Australian Research Council Network in Complex Open Systems). This support allowed us to recognize outstanding contributions to the programme, and to give opportunities to young researchers that they might not otherwise receive, and we are grateful to these sponsors.

Finally, we would like to acknowledge the efforts of our colleagues on the conference Organizing Committee, administrative support from the University of Queensland, and our respective institutions for allowing us the time to undertake this task. We trust that you will enjoy the papers in this volume.

May 2005   Marcus Gallagher
                                                James Hogan
                                               Frederic Maire

Organization

General Co-chairs

Tom Downs	University of Queensland, Australia
Hujun Yin	University of Manchester, UK

International Advisory Committee

Lei Xu	Chinese University of Hong Kong (Chair)
Yaser Abu-Mostafa	Caltech, USA
Shun-ichi Amari	RIKEN, Japan
Michael Dempster	University of Cambridge, UK
Nick Jennings	University of Southampton, UK
Erkki Oja	Helsinki University of Technology, Finland
Latit M. Patnaik	Indian Institute of Science, India
Burkhard Rost	Columbia University, USA

IDEAL Steering Committee

Hujun Yin	University of Manchester, UK (Co-chair)
Laiwan Chan	Chinese University of Hong Kong, China (Co-chair)
Nigel Allinson	University of Manchester, UK
Yiu-ming Cheung	Hong Kong Baptist University
Marc van Hulle	K.U.Leuven, Belgium
John Keane	University of Manchester, UK
Jimmy Lee	Chinese University of Hong Kong, China
Malik Magdon-Ismail	Rensselaer Polytechnic Institute, USA
Zheng Rong Yang	University of Exeter, UK
Ning Zhong	Maebashi Institute of Technology, Japan

Organizing Committee

Marcus Gallagher	University of Queensland, Australia (Chair)
Tom Downs	University of Queensland, Australia
Mikael Boden	University of Queensland, Australia
Jennifer Hallinan	University of Queensland, Australia
James Hogan	Queensland University of Technology, Australia
Frederic Maire	Queensland University of Technology, Australia
Gordon Wyeth	University of Queensland, Australia

Programme Committee

James Hogan (Co-chair) (Australia)
Frederic Maire (Co-chair) (Australia)

Nigel Allinson (UK)
Martyn Amos (UK)
Jiyuan An (Australia)
Alan Blair (Australia)
Mikael Boden (Australia)
Matthew Casey (UK)
Sheng Chen (UK)
Songcan Chen (China)
Sungzoon Cho (Korea)
Emilio Corchado (Spain)
David Corne (UK)
Robert Dale (Australia)
Zhao Yang Dong (Australia)
Tom Downs (Australia)
Richard Everson (UK)
Marcus Frean (New Zealand)
Colin Fyfe (UK)
Marcus Gallagher (Australia)
John Qiang Gan (UK)
Mark Girolami (UK)
Jennifer Hallinan (Australia)
Tony Holden (UK)
David Holye (UK)
Paul Jackway (Australia)
Gareth Jones (Ireland)
Ata Kaban (UK)
Samuel Kaski (Finland)

Irwin King (China)
Jimmy Lee (China)
Kwong S. Leung (China)
Paulo Lisboa (UK)
Simon Miles (UK)
Ajit Narayanan (UK)
David Powers (Australia)
Jose Principe (USA)
Omer Rana (UK)
Magnus Rattray (UK)
Vic Rayward-Smith (UK)
Shazia Sadiq (Australia)
Michael Small (China)
P.N. Suganthan (Singapore)
David Taniar (Australia)
Peter Tino (UK)
Marc van Hulle (Belgium)
Lipo Wang (Singapore)
Dong-Qing Wei (China)
Ian Wood (Australia)
Gordon Wyeth (Australia)
Zheng Rong Yang (UK)
Yong Xu (UK)
Hujun Yin (UK)
Du Zhang (USA)
Ning Zhong (Japan)

Additional Reviewers

Jonathan Gabbai (UK)
Nic Geard (Australia)
James Gordon (Australia)
Hisashi Handa (Japan)
John Hawkins (Australia)
Geir Hovland (Australia)
Arto Klami (Finland)
Kin Lun Law (Hong Kong, China)
Wai Yie Leong (Australia)
Carla S. Möller Levet (UK)

Bicheng Li (UK)
Jin Li (UK)
Wenye Li (Hong Kong, China)
Yong Liang (Hong Kong, China)
Brian Lovell (Australia)
Stefan Maetschke (Australia)
Janne Nikkilä (Finland)
Jaakko Peltonen (Finland)
David Rohde (Australia)
Jarkko Salojärvi (Finland)

X   Organization

Table of Contents

Data Mining and Knowledge Engineering

EXiT-B: A New Approach for Extracting Maximal Frequent Subtrees
from XML Data 1
    Juryon Paik, Dongho Won, Farshad Fotouhi, and Ung Mo Kim

Synthetic Environment Representational Semantics
Using the Web Ontology Language 9
    Mehul Bhatt, Wenny Rahayu, and Gerald Sterling

New Rules for Hybrid Spatial Reasoning 17
    Wenhui Li and Haibin Sun

Using Pre-aggregation for Efficient Spatial Query Processing
in Sensor Environments 25
    Soon-Young Park and Hae-Young Bae

Model Trees for Classification of Hybrid Data Types 32
    Hsing-Kuo Pao, Shou-Chih Chang, and Yuh-Jye Lee

Finding Uninformative Features in Binary Data 40
    Xin Wang and Ata Kabán

Knowledge Reduction of Rough Set Based on Partition 48
    Xiaobing Pei and Yuanzhen Wang

Multiresolution Analysis of Connectivity 56
    Atul Sajjanhar, Guojun Lu, Dengsheng Zhang, and Tian Qi

Kernel Biased Discriminant Analysis Using Histogram Intersection Kernel
for Content-Based Image Retrieval 63
    Lin Mei, Gerd Brunner, Lokesh Setia, and Hans Burkhardt

Unsupervised Image Segmentation
Using Penalized Fuzzy Clustering Algorithm 71
    Yong Yang, Feng Zhang, Chongxun Zheng, and Pan Lin

Multi-attributes Image Analysis for the Classification
of Web Documents Using Unsupervised Technique 78
    Samuel W.K. Chan

Automatic Image Annotation Based on Topic-Based Smoothing 86
    Xiangdong Zhou, Jianye Ye, Lian Chen, Liang Zhang, and Baile Shi

A Focused Crawler with Document Segmentation 94
    Jaeyoung Yang, Jinbeom Kang, and Joongmin Choi

An Intelligent Grading System Using Heterogeneous Linguistic Resources . 102
    Yu-Seop Kim, Woo-Jin Cho, Jae-Young Lee, and Yu-Jin Oh

Probabilistic Data Generation for Deduplication and Data Linkage 109
    Peter Christen

Mining Job Logs Using Incremental Attribute-Oriented Approach 117
    Idowu O. Adewale and Reda Alhajj

Dimensional Reduction of Large Image Datasets
Using Non-linear Principal Components.............................. 125
    Silvia S.C. Botelho, Willian Lautenschlger,
    Matheus Bacelo de Figueiredo, Tania Mezzadri Centeno,
    and Mauricio M. Mata

Classification by Instance-Based Learning Algorithm 133
    Yongguang Bao, Eisuke Tsuchiya, Naohiro Ishii, and Xiaoyong Du

Analysis/Synthesis of Speech Signals
Based on AbS/OLA Sinusoidal Modeling Using Elliptic Filter 141
    Kihong Kim, Jinkeun Hong, and Jongin Lim

Robust Model Adaptation Using Mean and Variance Transformations
in Linear Spectral Domain 149
    Donghyun Kim and Dongsuk Yook

Using Support Vector Machine for Modeling of Pulsed GTAW Process 155
    Xixia Huang and Shanben Chen

Design of Simple Structure Neural Voltage Regulator for Power Systems .. 164
    Mahdi Jalili-Kharaajoo

EEG Source Localization for Two Dipoles in the Brain
Using a Combined Method 171
    Zhuoming Li, Yu Zhang, Qinyu Zhang, Masatake Akutagawa,
    Hirofumi Nagashino, Fumio Shichijo, and Yohsuke Kinouchi

Intelligent Control of Micro Heat Exchanger with Locally Linear Identifier
and Emotional Based Controller 179
    Mahdi Jalili-Kharaajoo

Identification of Anomalous SNMP Situations Using a Cooperative
Connectionist Exploratory Projection Pursuit Model 187
    Álvaro Herrero, Emilio Corchado, and José Manuel Sáiz

Learning Algorithms and Systems

Neural Networks: A Replacement for Gaussian Processes? 195
 Matthew Lilley and Marcus Frean

A Dynamic Merge-or-Split Learning Algorithm on Gaussian Mixture
for Automated Model Selection 203
 Jinwen Ma and Qicai He

Bayesian Radial Basis Function Neural Network 211
 Zheng Rong Yang

An Empirical Study of Hoeffding Racing for Model Selection
in k-Nearest Neighbor Classification 220
 Flora Yu-Hui Yeh and Marcus Gallagher

Designing an Optimal Network Using the Cross-Entropy Method......... 228
 Sho Nariai, Kin-Ping Hui, and Dirk P. Kroese

Generating Predicate Rules from Neural Networks 234
 Richi Nayak

Improving Ensembles with Classificational Cellular Automata 242
 Petra Povalej, Mitja Lenič, and Peter Kokol

A Gradient BYY Harmony Learning Algorithm on Mixture of Experts
for Curve Detection 250
 Zhiwu Lu, Qiansheng Cheng, and Jinwen Ma

A Novel Anomaly Detection Using Small Training Sets 258
 Qingbo Yin, Liran Shen, Rubo Zhang, and Xueyao Li

Induction of Linear Decision Trees
with Real-Coded Genetic Algorithms and k-D Trees 264
 Sai-cheong Ng and Kwong-sak Leung

Intelligent Predictive Control of a 6-Dof Robotic Manipulator
with Reliability Based Performance Improvement 272
 Ahmet Akbas

Sequential Search for Decremental Edition 280
 José A. Olvera-López, J. Ariel Carrasco-Ochoa,
 and José Fco. Martínez-Trinidad

Bearing Similarity Measures for Self-organizing Feature Maps........... 286
 Narongdech Keeratipranon and Frederic Maire

Efficient Spatial Clustering Algorithm Using Binary Tree............... 294
 Mohsin Ali, Xue Li, and Zhao Yang Dong

Cluster Analysis of High-Dimensional Data: A Case Study 302
  Richard Bean and Geoff McLachlan

Universal Clustering with Family of Power Loss Functions
in Probabilistic Space 311
  Vladimir Nikulin

Circular SOM for Temporal Characterisation
of Modelled Gene Expressions 319
  Carla S. Möller-Levet and Hujun Yin

Recursive Self-organizing Map as a Contractive Iterative Function System . 327
  Peter Tiňo, Igor Farkaš, and Jort van Mourik

Differential Priors for Elastic Nets.................................... 335
  Miguel Á. Carreira-Perpiñán, Peter Dayan, and Geoffrey J. Goodhill

Graphics Hardware Implementation
of the Parameter-Less Self-organising Map 343
  Alexander Campbell, Erik Berglund, and Alexander Streit

Weighted SOM-Face: Selecting Local Features for Recognition
from Individual Face Image 351
  Xiaoyang Tan, Jun Liu, Songcan Chen, and Fuyan Zhang

SOM-Based Novelty Detection Using Novel Data 359
  Hyoung-joo Lee and Sungzoon Cho

Multi-level Document Classifications with Self-organising Maps 367
  Huilin Ye

Bioinformatics

Predictive Vaccinology: Optimisation of Predictions
Using Support Vector Machine Classifiers 375
  Ivana Bozic, Guang Lan Zhang, and Vladimir Brusic

Evolving Neural Networks for the Classification
of Malignancy Associated Changes 382
  Jennifer Hallinan

Matching Peptide Sequences with Mass Spectra........................ 390
  K.W. Lau, B. Stapley, S. Hubbard, and H. Yin

Extraction by Example: Induction of Structural Rules for the Analysis
of Molecular Sequence Data from Heterogeneous Sources 398
  Olivo Miotto, Tin Wee Tan, and Vladimir Brusic

A Multi-population χ^2 Test Approach to Informative Gene Selection 406
  Jun Luo and Jinwen Ma

Gene Selection of DNA Microarray Data
Based on Regularization Networks 414
    Xin Zhou and Kezhi Mao

Application of Mixture Models to Detect Differentially Expressed Genes .. 422
    *Liat Ben-Tovim Jones, Richard Bean, Geoff McLachlan,
    and Justin Zhu*

A Comparative Study of Two Novel Predictor Set Scoring Methods 432
    Chia Huey Ooi and Madhu Chetty

Deriving Matrix of Peptide-MHC Interactions in Diabetic Mouse
by Genetic Algorithm 440
    Menaka Rajapakse, Lonce Wyse, Bertil Schmidt, and Vladimir Brusic

SVM Based Prediction of Bacterial Transcription Start Sites 448
    James Gordon and Michael Towsey

Exploiting Sequence Dependencies in the Prediction
of Peroxisomal Proteins... 454
    *Mark Wakabayashi, John Hawkins, Stefan Maetschke,
    and Mikael Bodén*

Protein Fold Recognition Using Neural Networks
and Support Vector Machines 462
    Nan Jiang, Wendy Xinyu Wu, and Ian Mitchell

Agents and Complex Systems

Support Tool for Multi-agent Development 470
    Hyunsang Youn, Sungwook Hwang, Heeyong Youn, and Eunseok Lee

A Hybrid Agent Architecture for Modeling Autonomous Agents
in SAGE... 478
    *Amina Tariq, Amna Basharat, H. Farooq Ahmad, Hiroki Suguri,
    and Arshad Ali*

Toward Transitive Dependence in MAS 486
    *Bo An, Chunyan Miao, Lianggui Tang, Shuangqing Li,
    and Daijie Cheng*

An Architecture for Multi-agent Based Self-adaptive System
in Mobile Environment 494
    Seunghwa Lee, Jehwan Oh, and Eunseok Lee

Autonomous and Dependable Recovery Scheme
in UPnP Network Settings 501
    Youngsoo Choi, Sanguk Noh, Kyunghee Choi, and Gihyun Jung

A Transitive Dependence Based Social Reasoning Mechanism
for Coalition Formation 507
    Bo An, Chunyan Miao, Lianggui Tang, Shuangqing Li,
    and Daijie Cheng

A Multi-agent Based Context Aware Self-healing System 515
    Jeongmin Park, Hyunsang Youn, and Eunseok Lee

Combining Influence Maps and Cellular Automata
for Reactive Game Agents 524
    Penelope Sweetser and Janet Wiles

Patterns in Complex Systems Modeling 532
    Janet Wiles and James Watson

Global Optimization Using Evolutionary Algorithm
Based on Level Set Evolution and Latin Square 540
    Yuping Wang, Jinling Du, and Chuangyin Dang

Co-evolutionary Rule-Chaining Genetic Programming 546
    Wing-Ho Shum, Kwong-sak Leung, and Man-Leung Wong

A Dynamic Migration Model for Self-adaptive Genetic Algorithms 555
    K.G. Srinivasa, K. Sridharan, P. Deepa Shenoy, K.R. Venugopal,
    and Lalit M. Patnaik

Financial Engineering

A Multicriteria Sorting Procedure for Financial Classification Problems:
The Case of Business Failure Risk Assessment 563
    Ceyhun Araz and Irem Ozkarahan

Volatility Modelling of Multivariate Financial Time Series
by Using ICA-GARCH Models 571
    Edmond H.C. Wu and Philip L.H. Yu

Volatility Transmission Between Stock and Bond Markets:
Evidence from US and Australia 580
    Victor Fang, Vincent C.S. Lee, and Yee Choon Lim

A Machine Learning Approach to Intraday Trading
on Foreign Exchange Markets 588
    Andrei Hryshko and Tom Downs

Author Index 597

EXiT-B: A New Approach for Extracting Maximal Frequent Subtrees from XML Data[*]

Juryon Paik[1], Dongho Won[1], Farshad Fotouhi[2], and Ung Mo Kim[1]

[1] Department of Computer Engineering, Sungkyunkwan University,
300 Chunchun-dong, Jangan-gu, Suwon,
Gyeonggi-do 440-746, Republic of Korea
quasa277@gmail.com, dhwon@dosan.skku.ac.kr, umkim@ece.skku.ac.kr
[2] Wayne State University, Detroit, MI, USA

Abstract. Along with the increasing amounts of XML data available, the data mining community has been motivated to discover the useful information from the collections of XML documents. One of the most popular approaches to find the information is to extract frequent subtrees from a set of XML trees. In this paper, we propose a novel algorithm, EXiT-B, for efficiently extracting maximal frequent subtrees from a set of XML documents. The main contribution of our algorithm is that there is no need to perform tree join operation during the phase of generating maximal frequent subtrees. Thus, the task of finding maximal frequent subtrees can be significantly simplified comparing to the previous approaches.

1 Introduction

Along with the rapidly increasing volume of XML data, it becomes a new challenge to find useful information from a set of XML trees. In order to make the information valuable, it is important to extract frequent subtrees occurring as common trees embedded in a large collection of XML trees. In this paper, we present a novel algorithm *EXiT-B* (*Ex*tract ma*Xi*mal frequent sub*T*rees with *B*inary code) for efficiently finding frequent subtrees, especially maximal frequent subtrees, from a set of XML documents. The proposed algorithm not only reduces significantly the number of rounds for tree pruning, but also simplifies greatly each round by avoiding time-consuming tree join operations. Toward this goal, our algorithm represents each node label of a XML tree as binary coding, stores them in a specially devised data structure, and correctly finds all maximal frequent tree patterns by expanding frequent sets incrementally.

The rest of this paper is organized as follows. We begin by reviewing some related works in Section 2. We continue in Section 3 with a description of some notations and definitions used throughout the paper. Then, we present our new algorithm EXiT-B in Section 4, and report experimental results in Section 5. Finally, Section 6 concludes the paper.

[*] This research was supported by the MIC(Ministry of Information and Communication), Korea, under the ITRC(Information Technology Research Center) support program supervised by the IITA(Institute of Information Technology Assessment)

2 Related Works

The various works for mining frequent subtrees are described in [2, 7–9]. Wang and Liu [8] considered mining of paths in ordered trees by using Apriori [1] technique. They propose the mining of wider class of substructures which are subtrees called schemas. Asai et al. [2] proposed FREQT for mining labeled ordered trees. FREQT uses rightmost expansion notion to generate candidate trees by attaching new nodes to the rightmost edge of a tree. Zaki [9] proposes two algorithms, TreeMiner and PatternMatcher, for mining embedded subtrees from ordered labeled trees. PatternMatcher is a level-wise algorithm similar to Apriori for mining association rules. TreeMiner performs a depth-first search for frequent subtrees and uses the scope list for fast support counting. Termier et al. [7] developed TreeFinder which uses a combination of relational descriptions for labeled trees and θ-subsumption notion to extract frequent subtrees. Other recent works describe how to mine frequent graph patterns [3, 4]. Such graph mining algorithms are likely to be too general for tree mining as pointed out in [9].

The common problems of the previous approaches are identified as follows: They represent each node of a XML tree as a labeled character string. This causes increasing the number of tree pruning operations greatly, thus generating large number of candidate sets during the mining phase. Furthermore, each tree pruning round during generating candidate sets requires to perform expensive join operations. Therefore, as the number of XML documents increases, the efficiency for extracting frequent subtrees deteriorates rapidly since both the cost of join operations and the number of pruning rounds add up.

3 Preliminaries

In this section, we briefly introduce some notions of tree model for mining XML data.

Definition 1 (Subtree). *We denote a tree as $T = (N, E)$ where N is a set of labeled nodes and E is a set of edges. We define that a tree $S = (N_S, E_S)$ is a* **subtree** *of T, denoted as $S \preceq T$, iff $N_S \subseteq N$ and for all edges $(u, v) \in E_S$, u is an ancestor of v in T.*

Definition 1 preserves the ancestor relation but not necessarily the parent relation.

Let $D = \{T_1, T_2, \ldots, T_i\}$ be a set of trees and let $|D|$ be the number of trees in D. Then, we define minimum support and maximal frequent subtree as follows:

Definition 2 (Minimum Support). *Given a set of trees D, and a subtree S in D, the frequency of S in D, $freq_D(S)$, is defined as $\Sigma_{T \in D} freq_T(S)$ where $freq_T(S)$ is 1 if S occurs in T and 0 otherwise. The* **support** *of S in D, $supp_D(S)$, is the percentage of the trees in D that contain S. We denote it by $supp_D(S) = \frac{freq_D(S)}{|D|}$. Then,* **minimum support** *σ is defined as the percentage which satisfies $supp_D(S) \geq \sigma$.*

Definition 3 (Maximal Frequent Subtree). *Given some minimum support* σ, *a subtree S is called* ***maximal frequent*** *iff:*

i) *the support for S is not less than a value of σ, i.e., $supp_D(S) \geq \sigma$.*
ii) *there exists no any other σ-frequent subtree S' in D such that S is included in S'.*

The subtree S is just called a σ-**frequent subtree** if it satisfies only the first property. Note that every frequent subtree can be derived from the maximal frequent subtrees by the fact that all subtrees of maximal frequent subtrees are also frequent.

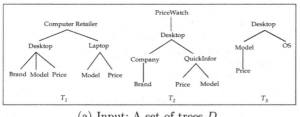 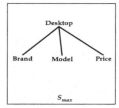

(a) Input: A set of trees D

(b) Output: A maximal $\frac{2}{3}$-frequent subtree

Fig. 1. Maximal Frequent Subtree Extracted from D

Example 1. An example of a set of input trees D with various nesting of labels is shown in Fig. 1(a). For instance, the nesting of the Desktop differs in trees T_1, T_2 and T_3. Fig. 1(b) shows an example of maximal frequent subtrees extracted from D. Its minimum support σ is $\frac{2}{3}$.

4   Overview of EXiT-B

In this section, we present a new algorithm EXiT-B for efficiently extracting maximal frequent subtrees from a given set of trees. EXiT-B algorithm is outlined in Fig. 2. It consists of three functions; The first function is to represent each tree by a set of bit sequences through assigning an n-bit binary code to each node label and concatenating the codes on the same path. The second function is to create and maintain a specially devised data structure called PairSet to avoid join operations entirely and reduce the number of candidates. The third function is to extract maximal frequent subtrees incrementally based on the n-bit binary codes stored in the PairSet. We omit the pseudo codes of three functions due to lack of space.

4.1   Representing Tree as Bit Sequences

Typical methods of representing a tree are an adjacency list [3], adjacency matrix [4], or character string [2, 5, 9]. Extracting frequent subtrees by using those

---

Algorithm EXiT-B

Input :
    D: *set of trees*
    L: *set of labels*
    σ: *minimum support*
Output :
    MFT: set of *all maximal frequent subtrees*
Method:
    // *convert each tree into a set of bit sequences*
    (1)   minsup = | D | * σ
    (2)   **for** each tree $T \in D$
    (3)   BS := ***genBitSeq***(T, L)
    // *collect all sets of bit sequences*
    (4)   SBS := $\cup_{T \in D}$BS
    // *calculate set of all frequent sets*
    (5)   FS := ***calFreSet***(SBS, minsup)
    // *construct maximal frequent subtrees*
    (6)   MFT := ***maxSubtree***(FS, minsup)
    (7)   return MFT

Fig. 2. Algorithm EXiT-B Consisting of Three Functions

methods requires expensive join operations. Thus, to avoid the unnecessary join expense, we adopt binary coding method for representing the tree.

Let L be a set of labeled nodes in a set of trees D. A function *genBitSeq* works as follows; First, it assigns an unique n-bit binary code randomly to each labeled node. Note that it must assign the same n-bit code to the nodes labels with the same name. Let $|L|$ be a total number of labeled nodes in L. Then, the value of n is $\lceil \log_2 |L| \rceil$. Secondly, it concatenates sequentially all the n-bit binary codes on the same path from the root to each leaf node in a tree. We call the concatenated n-bit binary codes for each path by a *bit sequence* (*bs*). Referring Fig. 2 again, BS denotes a set of bit sequences derived from a single tree in D. Similarly, SBS denotes a collection of BSs derived from a set of trees D.

4.2   Generating PairSets

Definition 4 (Key). *Given a SBS, let K_d be a collection of n-bit binary codes assigned on the nodes at depth d in every tree in D. We assume that depth of root node is 0. We call each member in K_d by a **key**.*

At this point, note that there may exist some nodes labeled with the same names in D. Thus, for each key, we need to correctly identify the list of trees to which the key belongs.

Definition 5 (PairSet). *A **PairSet**, $[P]^d$, is defined as a set of pairs (k_d, t_{id}) where k_d is a key in K_d and t_{id} is a list of tree indexes to which k_d belongs.*

According to some minimum support, a collection of PairSets is classified into two sets.

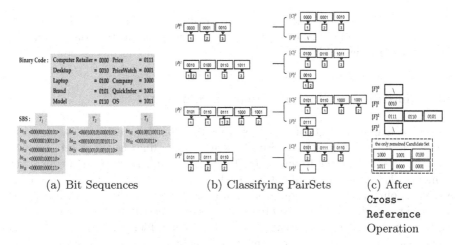

Fig. 3. Binary Code Representation and PairSets

Definition 6 (Frequent Key). *Given some minimum support σ and a pair (k_d, t_{id}), the key k_d is called* **frequent** *if $|t_{id}| \geq \sigma \times |D|$.*

Definition 7 (Frequent Set). *Given a PairSet, $[P]^d$, a pair in $[P]^d$ is called* **frequent set** *if its key is frequent. Otherwise, it is called* **candidate set**. *We denote frequent set and candidate set by $[F]^d$ and $[C]^d$, respectively.*

The initial frequent sets correspond to the frequent subtrees with only one node commonly occurring in D. Thus, we need to further extend these frequent sets incrementally to find final maximal frequent subtrees. For this purpose, we introduce an operation called `cross-reference`.

`Cross-Reference`: Let $\mathcal{FS} = \{[F]^0, [F]^1, \ldots, [F]^d\}$ be a set of initial frequent sets and $\mathcal{CS} = \{[C]^0, [C]^1, \ldots, [C]^d\}$ be a set of initial candidate sets. The ith round (for $i = 1, 2, \ldots d$) of the `cross-reference` consists of the following two steps:

– *Step 1 (Pruning phase). $Difference$ ($[C]^{i-1}$ vs. $[F]^i$) and*
  $([C]^i$ *vs. $[F]^{i-1}$ through $[F]^0$)*

– *Step 2 (Merging phase). $Union$ ($[C]^i$ vs. $[C]^{i-1}$)*

We refer to the reader to the paper [6] for a detailed explanation of `cross-reference` as well as for the efficiency of using PairSet structure in order to mine XML documents.

Example 2. Fig. 3(a) shows a collection of BSs derived from a set of trees D in Fig. 1(a). Fig. 3(b) presents all three kinds of PairSets generated from SBS. For instance, we know that the key 0010 in $[P]^1$ corresponds to the 'Desktop' nodes at depth 1 in both T_1 and T_2. The frequent set and candidate set placing in right side of Fig. 3(b) are derived from all PairSet $[P]^d$. The last picture Fig. 3(c) shows the final results after applying cross-reference operation over the two sets in Fig. 3(b).

4.3   Constructing Maximal Frequent Subtrees

To derive maximal frequent subtrees from the final frequent sets, we need to notice the following two facts: Firstly, some of the final frequent sets may be empty. For example, the frequent set $[F]^0$ and $[F]^3$ in Fig. 3(c) do not have any elements. An empty frequent set at depth d indicates that there does not exist any n-bit binary code satisfying the minimum support at depth d. Thus, we do not need to consider those empty frequent sets for constructing maximal frequent subtrees. Secondly, although each frequent set has a hierarchical structure, not every key in the frequent set has connected each other in tree structures. In other words, some n-bit binary codes in different frequent sets have edges between them and some have not. It is required to decide whether an edge exists between two keys being in different frequent sets. A minimum support is used to make an edge between them. The following theorem shows that our algorithm EXiT-B correctly extracts all the frequent subtrees from a given set of trees.

Theorem 1 (Correctness of EXiT-B) *Given a set of trees D, EXiT-B always generates **all the frequent subtrees** from D.*

Proof. Let $[F]^i$ and $[F]^j$ be arbitrary nonempty frequent sets, for $i < j$. Let (k_i, t_{k_i}) be a pair in $[F]^i$ and $(k_j, t_{k_j}), (e_j, t_{e_j})$ pairs in $[F]^j$. Let x and y be a tree-id in t_{k_j} and t_{e_j}, respectively, for $x \neq y$. We assume that either $|t_{k_i} \cap t_{k_j}|$ or $|t_{k_i} \cap t_{e_j}|$ are greater than $\sigma \times D$. Then, we can consider the following three cases:

- **case I** ($x \in t_{k_i}$ and $y \notin t_{k_i}$): k_j *is the only child node of k_i. Then,*
    A subtree $S_{f1} = (N_{S_{f1}}, E_{S_{f1}})$ is built,
        where $N_{S_{f1}} = \{k_i, k_j\}$ and $E_{S_{f1}} = \{(k_i, k_j)\}$.

- **case II** ($y \in t_{k_i}$ and $x \notin t_{k_i}$): e_j *is the only child node of k_i. Then,*
    A subtree $S_{f2} = (N_{S_{f2}}, E_{S_{f2}})$ is built,
        where $N_{S_{f2}} = \{k_i, e_j\}$ and $E_{S_{f2}} = \{(k_i, e_j)\}$.

- **case III** ($x \in t_{k_i}$ and $y \in t_{k_i}$): *Both k_j and e_j are children nodes of k_i.*
    Then,
        A subtree $S_m = (N_{S_m}, E_{S_m})$ is built with all pairs of $[F]^i$ and $[F]^j$,
            where $N_{S_m} = \{k_i, k_j, e_j\}$ and $E_{S_m} = \{(k_i, k_j), (k_i, e_j)\}$.

In each case, the built subtree is frequent because all of its paths are frequent. However, not every subtree is maximal since it does not satisfy the second condition of Definition 3.   ■

5   Evaluation

Experimental Setting. Our experiments were run on a AMD Athlon 64 3000+ 2.0 GHz, with 1GB RAM running Windows XP. The algorithm was implemented in Java.

Two synthetic data set, S15 and T10K, were tested. These data sets were generated by using the method, tree generator, described in [7]. The generator mimics three target frequent trees reflecting predefined parameters. The parameters used in the tree generation include number of labels $N = 100$, the parameter of probability $\rho = 0.2$ including a target frequent tree at each node, the maximum number of perturbation $\delta = 25$, the maximum fanout of a node in a tree $f = 5$, and the maximum depth $d = 3$, the minimum support σ ($\sigma = 0.15$ for S15) and the total number of trees in the data set T ($T = 10000$ for T10K).

We evaluated EXiT-B over the most generic algorithm for tree mining, FSM (Frequent Structure Mining) termed in [9]. The basic idea behind FSM is to identify frequent subtrees through a repeated process of enumerating and pruning candidate subtrees. Two variations of EXiT-B algorithm were compared to examine the effect of binary code representation.

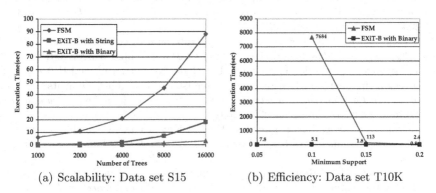

(a) Scalability: Data set S15   (b) Efficiency: Data set T10K

Fig. 4. Execution Time

Performance Comparison. The execution time for data set S15 with varying number of input trees is shown in Fig. 4(a). It can be seen that EXiT-B algorithm demonstrates a dramatic improvement over the generic frame FSM. This is because the bottlenecks of FSM, which are generations of thousands of candidate subtrees and expensive join operations, are significantly reduced in EXiT-B. Both variations of EXiT-B outperform the FSM, however, EXiT-B with binary representation shows much better execution time than EXiT-B with string representation. Fig. 4(b) shows the execution time for data set T10K with changing minimum support. The execution time decreases as the minimum support increases in two graphs, but there is significant time difference between EXiT-B and FSM. We stopped to run FSM after minimum support 0.1 since the running time exceeds several hours.

6   Conclusion

We presented an efficient algorithm, EXiT-B, for extracting all maximal frequent subtrees from a collection of XML trees. Unlike the previous approaches, the EXiT-B represents each node of a XML tree as binary coding, stores them in a specially devised structure, and correctly finds all maximal frequent subtrees by expanding frequent sets incrementally. The beneficial effect of the EXiT-B is that it not only reduces significantly the number of rounds for tree pruning, but also simplifies greatly each round by avoiding time consuming tree join operations.

References

1. R. Agrawal and R. Srikant. Fast algorithms for mining association rules in large databases. *In Proc. of the 12th International Conference on Very Large Databases*, pp487–499, 1994.
2. T. Asai, K. Abe, S. Kawasoe, H. Arimura, H. Sakamoto, and S. Arikawa. Efficient substructure discovery from large semi-structured data. *In Proc. of the 2nd SIAM International Conference on Data Mining (ICDM'02)*, 2002.
3. A. Inokuchi, T. Washio, and H. Motoda. An Apriori-based algorithm for mining frequent substructures from graph data. *In Proc. of the 4th European Conference on Principles of Data Mining and Knowledge Discovery (PKDD'00)*, pp.13–23, 2000.
4. M. Kuramochi, and G. Karypis. Frequent subgraph discovery. *In Proc. of IEEE International Conference on Data Mining (ICDM'01)*, pp.313–320, 2001.
5. T. Miyahara, T. Suzuki, T. Shoudai, T. Uchida, K. Takahashi, and H. Ueda. Discovery of frequent tag tree patterns in semistructured web documents. *In Proc. of the 6th Pacific-Asia Conference of Advances in Knowledge Discovery and Data Mining (PAKDD'02)*, pp.341–355, 2002.
6. Juryon Paik, Dong Ryeol Shin, and Ungmo Kim. EFoX: a Scalable Method for Extracting Frequent Subtrees. *In Proc. of the 5th International Conference on Computational Science (ICCS'05), Atlanta, USA, May 22–25, 2005*, to appear
7. A. Termier, M-C. Rousset, and M. Sebag. TreeFinder: a First step towards XML data mining. *In Proc. of IEEE International Conference on Data Mining (ICDM'02)*, pp.450–457, 2002.
8. K. Wang, and H. Liu. Schema discovery for semistructured data. *In Proc. of the 3rd International Conference on Knowledge Discovery and Data Mining (KDD'97)*, pp.271–274, 1997.
9. M. J. Zaki. Efficiently mining frequent trees in a forest. *In Proc. of the 8th ACM SIGKDD International Conference on Knowledge Discovery and Data mining (KDD'02)*, pp.71–80, 2002.

Synthetic Environment Representational Semantics Using the Web Ontology Language

Mehul Bhatt[1], Wenny Rahayu[1], and Gerald Sterling[2]

[1] Department of Computer Science
La Trobe University
Melbourne, Australia 3086
+61-3-94791280
{mbhatt,wenny}@cs.latrobe.edu.au
[2] Air-Operations Division, DSTO
PO Box 4331 Melbourne
Australia 3001
+61-3-96267728
Gerald.Sterling@dsto.defence.gov.au

Abstract. The application of Ontologies for the definition and interoperability of complementary taxonomies has been well-recognised within the Modelling & Simulation (M&S) community. Our research pertaining to the specification of *Synthetic Environment* (SE) representational semantics has proposed the use of an *Synthetic Environment Data Representation Ontology* (***sed*Onto**), which is modeled using W3C's *Web Ontology Language*(OWL). The vocabulary specified in *sed*Onto is based the SEDRIS Data Representation Model (DRM), which is a technological framework for SE data interchange and interoperability.
In this paper, we present STOWL – *SEDRIS To OWL Transform* that automates the transformation of a SEDRIS based SE to a Web-Ontology based representation scheme in the OWL language. The target representation scheme, which shall be based on *sed*Onto, is in actuality an instantiation of the SE data representation terminology as specified by *sedOnto*. Such a transformation has many perceived advantages: It enhances SE interoperability by utilizing a Web-Ontology based approach for the specification of SE representation data, is consistent with existing industry based SE representation standards, namely SEDRIS, and that the representation scheme facilitates ontological reasoning over SE objects; a facility that is not directly supported by the SEDRIS DRM.

1 Introduction

The application of Ontologies for solving interoperability problems has been widely recognised across multiple domains. Ontologies, by virtue of the shared conceptualization that they provide, may be communicated between people and application systems thereby facilitating interchange, interoperability and common understanding. An ontology typically consists of a hierarchical description of important concepts in a domain, along with descriptions of the properties of each concept. The degree of formality employed in capturing these descriptions can be quite variable, ranging from natural language to logical formalisms, but increased formality and regularity clearly facilitates

M. Gallagher, J. Hogan, and F. Maire (Eds.): IDEAL 2005, LNCS 3578, pp. 9–16, 2005.

machine understanding [1]. Ontologies are increasingly being applied in the Modelling & Simulation (M&S) domain, with the eXtensible Modelling and Simulation initiative (XMSF) recommending the use of ontologies to allow the definition and approval of complementary taxonomies that can be applied across multiple XMSF application domains. As specified in the XMSF charter, this would involve the use of such XML based technologies such as XML Schema, RDF, OWL etc. [2]

In this paper, we propose the use of Ontological formalisms as the basis of Synthetic Environment (SE) representational semantics. The work reported herein is in continuum with our previous research pertaining to the construction of a SE representation ontology called *sed*Onto [3]. *sed*Onto is based on a ISO/IEC standard, namely SEDRIS, which is a technological framework for the successful *representation* and *interchange* of environmental data sets. In this paper, we propose and implement a necessary extension to *sed*Onto called **STOWL – SEDRIS TO OWL** *Transform*, which is the automation of the transformation of a SEDRIS based SE to a OWL ontology based form. More precisely, the resulting OWL representation scheme shall be based on *sed*Onto and will consist of instance data relevant to the vocabulary defined in it. Such a transformation has many perceived advantages: (a) Utilisation of the OWL/RDF (XML) serialisation syntax enables web-based sharing of SE data semantics thereby contributing toward the XMSF goal of web-enabled simulation systems. (b) Since the representation scheme is based on a ISO/IEC standard, it is practically applicable in industrial settings such as Defence and/or Environmental simulation systems where SEDRIS is mostly used. (c) Most importantly and in line with our envisaged application, existing OWL based reasoners may be applied so as to perform ontological reasoning in the SE domain.

2 *sed*Onto: A Synthetic Environment Data Representation Ontology

*sed***Onto** – *Synthetic Environment Data Representation* **Onto***logy* [3] is an ontology to be used within the M&S domain for the representation of data pertaining to a SE. We leverage existing standards for SE representation by '*web-enabling*' the SEDRIS Data Representation Model (DRM), which is widely adopted within the M&S community for the representation of SE data. The DRM is an object-oriented model, and provides a unified method for describing all data elements, and their logical relationships, needed to express environmental data in a seamless manner across all environmental domains. *sed*Onto is represented using the the *Web Ontology Language* [4]. More specifically, we utilize the OWL DL subclass of the OWL language for the representation of *sed*Onto; driven by the fact that tool builders have already developed powerful reasoning systems that support ontologies constrained by the restrictions required by OWL DL, the best example here being RACER [5]. It must be emphasized that *sed*Onto formalizes the same terminology for SE representation as is specified in the SEDRIS DRM. Whereas the SEDRIS DRM is a UML based specification of the various SE representation classes (and their relationships), *sed*Onto is a mapping of the same in the OWL language.

Fig. 1, an extract from sedOnto, consists of OWL statements necessary for the definition of the DRM class *Model*. Models within the DRM are used to represent some generic environmental entity that can be referenced many times in a *transmittal* (a SE

```
<owl:Class rdf:about="#Model">
  <owl:Restriction>
      <owl:onProperty>
        <owl:FunctionalProperty rdf:ID="hasDynamicModelProcessing"/>
      </owl:onProperty>
      <owl:cardinality rdf:datatype="http://www.w3.org/2001/XMLSchema#int"
      >1</owl:cardinality>
    </owl:Restriction>
  </rdfs:subClassOf>
  <owl:Class rdf:about="#SEDRIS_DRM_CLASS"/>
  </rdfs:subClassOf>
  <rdfs:comment rdf:datatype ="http://www.w3.org/2001/XMLSchema#string"
  >SEDRIS DRM Ref: Sheet 2</rdfs:comment>
  <rdfs:subClassOf>
    <owl:Restriction>
      <owl:maxCardinality rdf:datatype ="http://www.w3.org/2001/XMLSchema#int"
      >1</owl:maxCardinality>
      <owl:onProperty>
        <owl:ObjectProperty rdf:about="#hasClassificationData"/>
      </owl:onProperty>
    </owl:Restriction>
  </rdfs:subClassOf>
</owl:Class>
```

Fig. 1. Definition For *Class Model* in *sed*Onto

database) to create many instances of representations of similar environmental entities [6]. The class definition in Fig. 1 makes a number of important assertions such as: (a) *Model* has a certain attribute (*datatype property*), (b) *Model* is a subclass of another class (*subsumption relationship*), (c) *Model* aggregates objects of other classes (*aggregation relationship*) etc. Note that not all properties, both datatype or object, have been specified in the Model class definition in Fig. 1. The actual definition in *sed*Onto for a *Model* is too large to be included in its entirety in Fig. 1. For an in depth coverage of *sed*Onto, we direct interested readers to [3], which presents the *sed*Onto construction methodology along with potential applications of our proposed approach, namely – Terminological reasoning over SE objects and Web-based Sharing of SE transmittal semantics.

3 *STOWL*: Sedris to OWL Transform

In this section, we present the design and implementation of **STOWL** – SEDRIS *To OWL* Transform, which is the automation of the transformation of a SEDRIS based SE or SEDRIS transmittal to a Web-Ontology based form. The resulting OWL based representing scheme will be based on *sed*Onto and in actuality shall be an instantiation of it. Specifically, *sed*Onto represents the 'Terminology' or TBOX whereas the automatically transformed SEDRIS transmittal represents the 'Assertions' or ABOX[1]. To make things clear, the precise situation is illustrated in Fig. 2. Note that although in different forms, the shaded boxes in Fig. 2 represent the same terminology for SE representation.

---

[1] The formal semantics of OWL are based on Description Logic (DL), which distinguishes between an ontology (the TBox) and instance data (the ABox) relevant to the ontology

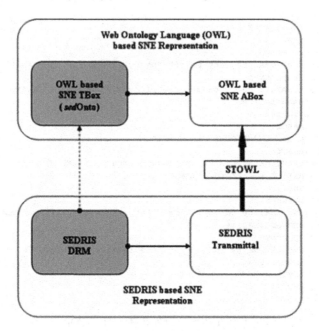

Fig. 2. *sed*Onto & *STOWL* – A Unified View

3.1   Restricted Views from the DRM

The DRM is massive in that it encompasses every structural element likely to be used for the representation of a SE pertaining to any domain. Indeed, applications with differing requirements would be interested in different aspects of a SE transmittal. For instance, an application with a task to reason about the topology or connectedness of the various objects present in the transmittal would be interested in the *FeatureTopologyHierarchy* present in it whereas one concerned with visualisation of those objects in the *GeometryHierarchy*.

STOWL uses the concept of a *Restricted View* so as to extract and transform the relevant information of interest. This is achieved by the specification of a DRM class factory that maintains a repository of the various DRM classes currently within the required view. With this setup, the actual transformer simply performs a depth-first traversal of the DRM class hierarchy whilst delegating object extraction and initialisation to the DRM class factory, which conditionally performs the necessary extraction and initialisation.

3.2   A Transformation Walkthrough

Providing a Web-Ontology based view of a SEDRIS DRM based transmittal is the essence of STOWL. In Fig. 2, it can be seen that the input to STOWL consists of a SEDRIS transmittal, which is semantically coupled to the SEDRIS DRM, whereas its output is a OWL document consisting of instance data for the terminology defined in *sed*Onto. In this section, we present a illustrative walkthrough of the transformation process for sample transmittal data. We utilize the definition for *class Model* from se-dOnto, previously discussed in section 2 (see Fig. 1).

STOWL Input. Various SE transmittals freely available from [6] have been used for testing STOWL. For the purposes of this walkthrough, we use one such transmittal, namely *anywhere_ruby.stf*. Whilst the details being unimportant here, it must be added *anywhere_ruby.stf* is a fictitious Model for a town square that could exist anywhere.

STOWL Output Extract. The output of the transformation process is a valid OWL/ RDF document expressed using the XML serialization syntax. It basically consists of two inseparable parts – the *Instance Ontology Template*, which is the document preamble consisting of the ontology definition and *Instance Data*, which consist of the actual instance data for the terminology present in *sed*Onto. Fig. 3 consist of an extract from the output generated by STOWL for input *anywhere_ruby.stf*.

Instance Ontology Template. All output instance data is associated to a OWL ontology model. The instance ontology template is the generic specification for such a ontology. Loosely speaking, the Instance Ontology Template consists of the standard namespace declarations required in any OWL ontology and a *OWL:imports* statement asserting the fact that the instance ontology in question imports the vocabulary defined in *sed*Onto. The namespace declarations and the ontology itself is required to be embedded inside a *RDF element*[2]. Other instance data (such as the one in Fig. 3) would follow the namespace declarations and *import directive*.

Instance Data (ABox). The OWL extract in Fig. 3 consists of instance data for the *class Model* defined in *sed*Onto (see Fig. 1). The Model instance, which corresponds to one of the models present in the transmittal *anywhere_ruby.stf*, makes the following assertions: (a) **hasGeometryModel**: The Model has a *GeometryModel* instance (given by the relative URI *"#instance_GeometryModel_57404368"*)associated with it. Note that *hasGeometry* is a *subproperty* of a another object property called *hasComponent* thereby giving it the intended interpretation of a *aggregation relationship*, i.e., Model aggregates objects of class GeometryModel. (b) **hasDynamicModelProcessing**: This Model represents something that can move within the environment defined by the transmittal in which it is present. (c) **hasClassificationData**: This Model aggregates an instance of the class *ClassificationData* (given by the relative URI *"#instance_ClassificationData_57405136"*). Instances of this class are used within the source transmittal to provide *thing-level* semantics for the Models being represented. In this case, it can be seen in Fig. 3 that the ClassificationData associated to this Model has an attribute (given by the *hasEDCSClassification* relationship) that assign a EDCS[3] code of *145* to this Model. Within SEDRIS, this code has been defined to be a building; using the symbolic constant *ECC_BUILDING*.

---

[2] Since every valid OWL document has a valid RDF model

[3] The Environmental Data Coding Specification (EDCS) provides a mechanism to specify the environmental *"things"* that a particular data model construct (from the DRM) is intended to represent

```
<sedOnto:Model rdf:about="#instance_Model_57122976">
  <sedOnto:hasMovingParts rdf:datatype="XMLSchema#boolean"
  >false</sedOnto:hasMovingParts>
  <sedOnto:hasName rdf:datatype="XMLSchema#string"
  >/apartment_bldg</sedOnto:hasName>
  <sedOnto:hasGeometryModel>
    <sedOnto:GeometryModel
    rdf:about="#instance_GeometryModel_57404368"/>
  </sedOnto:hasGeometryModel>
  <sedOnto:hasUnits rdf:datatype="XMLSchema#boolean"
  >true</sedOnto:hasUnits>
  <sedOnto:hasDynamicModelProcessing rdf:datatype="XMLSchema#boolean"
  >false</sedOnto:hasDynamicModelProcessing>
  <sedOnto:hasClassificationData>
    <sedOnto:ClassificationData
    rdf:about="#instance_ClassificationData_57405136">
      <sedOnto:hasEDCSClassificationCode rdf:datatype="XMLSchema#int"
      >145</sedOnto:hasEDCSClassificationCode>
    </sedOnto:ClassificationData>
  </sedOnto:hasClassificationData>
  <sedOnto:hasModelReferenceType rdf:resource="#SE_MDL_REF_TYP_ROOT"/>
</sedOnto:Model>
```

Fig. 3. *Model* Extract: Apartment Building

Unique Instance Names. As can be seen in Fig. 3, the Model instance itself and every object related to Model through a object property has a resource name that is unique. This is necessary because most instance objects are related to many other objects through various relationships. By having unique instance names, such references can be resolved to the same instance object instead of having to reproduce instance data multiple times under different heads (ie., URI's). Such instance names are generated by concatenating the string *"instance_$DRM_CLASS_NAME_"* with a unique *Sort ID* that is maintained by the SEDRIS implementation for every object present in the transmittal. Uniqueness and absence of redundant data is therefore guaranteed.

Data Completeness and Validation. Within the scope of the *restricted view* that STOWL is working on, the resulting OWL instance data generated by it is *Complete*. This means that every *defining element* of a certain DRM *Class* – all its attributes and relationships with other classes in the DRM – is transformed into the target representation scheme. The transformation is complete so that a two way transform would in principle be possible. The only exception to this is a scenario in which one of the classes defining elements (say its attribute or another component object) lies outside of the restricted view. Validation here refers to the process of performing the following three types of tests on the transformed model (and *sed*Onto): (a) **Maintenance Tests**: Check whether or not facet (property) constraints are being maintained. (b) **OWL DL Tests**: Perform OWL DL language tests to determine whether or not all OWL language elements in use belong to its DL class so as to qualify the resulting ontology as a OWL DL one. (c) **Sanity Tests**: Check the integrity of the ontology by performing tests such as whether or not redundant classes have been used in the range of a property, domain of a sub-property has only narrowed the one in its super-property etc. Note that all the three tests are being performed through the Protege Ontology development environment in use by the Protege-OWL plugin.

3.3 Design Overview

STOWL Phases. The design overview for STOWL is shown Fig. 4. STOWL basically involves the use of SEDRIS and Semantic Web based technologies. Implementation has been done using both C++ and Java, with integration involving the use of Java Native Interface. The following are the important components that make up STOWL: (a) **Transmittal Import**: Involves import of the synthetic environment represented in the SEDRIS Transmittal Format (STF) using the SEDRIS read API. The import layer constructs a object-oriented view, similar to the DRM, of the imported transmittal.(b) *sed*Onto **Import**: Import our SE representation ontology, sedOnto, using the Jena 2 Ontology API. (c) **JNI Bridge**: Data imported from a transmittal is provided to the transformer as input with the JNI bridge acting as link between the two. (d) **OWL Transform**: This refers to the actual transformation engine. Starting at the root of the DRM class hierarchy, this involves a depth-first traversal of the input transmittal. (e) **Instance Ontology Export**: This again involves use of the Jena Ontology API, albeit not directly, for serialisation of the transformed model.

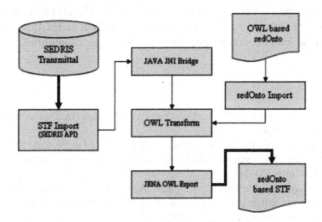

Fig. 4. STOWL – Design Overview

Implementation Details. For the construction of *sed*Onto, we have utilised version 3.1 of the SEDRIS DRM and *Protege*, which is a open-source development environment for ontologies and knowledge based systems[4]. We utilize the C++ based SEDRIS SDK (release 3.1.2) [6] for importing SEDRIS transmittals. For purposes of importing sedOnto and exporting the transformed transmittal to the OWL serialization syntax, we

---

[4] *Protege*: http://protege.stanford.edu

have utilized the JENA 2.1 Ontology API [5]. The export layer also utilizes Kazuki[6], which is a library for generating an object oriented interface for instance objects from an OWL Ontology file.

4   Conclusion and Further Work

We propose a novel approach involving the use of ontological primitives for the specification of Synthetic Environment Representational Semantics. A prototype, namely STOWL, has been implemented to automate the creation of the desired representation scheme. The paper also presented the design and implementation details for STOWL alongwith a illustrative walkthrough of the transformation.

The use of a industry based standard (SEDRIS) as the basis of our SE ontology makes our approach practically applicable in industrial settings such as Defence and/or Environmental Simulation systems where SEDRIS is generally used. Moreover, sedOnto and STOWL are also in line with the broader research goals within the Modeling & Simulation community for the development of Web-Enabled Simulation systems (XMSF). By mapping the SEDRIS DRM to the OWL language, we make explicit the SE representational semantics of the DRM using a language, which unlike UML is inherently suitable to do so. The logical basis of the language means that automated reasoning procedures can be utilized to perform ontological reasoning over SE objects – *subsumption, satisfiability, equivalence, retrieval* [7] etc. Currently, work pertaining to the applications of sedOnto and STOWL, viz Web based sharing of SE representational semantics and Terminological reasoning over SE objects [3], is in progress. We are extending a description logic based reasoner, namely RACER [5], so as to be able to provide synthetic environment specific query answering capabilities.

References

1. Horrocks, I.: DAML+OIL: A Reasonable Ontology Language. In: Proceedings of EDBT-02, Volume 2287 of LNCS. (2002) 2–13
2. Brutzman, D., Zyda, M., Pullen, M., Morse, K.: XMSF 2002 Findings and Recommendations Report: Technical challenges workshop and strategic opportunities symposium. Technical Report: XMSF Basis (2002)
3. Bhatt, M., Rahayu, W., Sterling, G.: sedOnto: A Web Enabled Ontology for Synthetic Environment Representation Based on the SEDRIS Specification. In: Proceedings of the Fall Simulation Interoperability Workshop. (2004)
4. W3C: OWL Web Ontology Language Guide. http://www.w3.org/TR/owl-guide/ (2004)
5. RACER: (Renamed ABox and Concept Expression Reasoner)
   http://www.sts.tu-harburg.de/ r.f.moeller/racer/.
6. SEDRIS: (The Source for Environmental Representation and Interchange)
   http://www.sedris.org.
7. Baader, F., Calvanese, D., McGuinness, D.L., Nardi, D., Patel-Schneider, P.F.: The description logic handbook: theory, implementation, and applications. Cambridge University Press (2003)

---

[5] *JENA Ontology API*: http://www.hpl.hp.com/semweb/jena.htm
[6] *Kazuki*: http://projects.semwebcentral.org/projects/kazuki/

New Rules for Hybrid Spatial Reasoning

Wenhui Li and Haibin Sun

Key Laboratory of Symbol Computation and Knowledge Engineering
of the Ministry of Education,
College of Computer Science and Technology, Jilin University
Changchun 130012, China
liwh@public.cc.jl.cn

Abstract. In this article, we investigate the problem of checking consistency in a hybrid formalism, which combines two essential formalisms in qualitative spatial reasoning: topological formalism and cardinal direction formalism. Instead of using conventional composition tables, we investigate the interactions between topological and cardinal directional relations with the aid of rules that are used efficiently in many research fields such as content-based image retrieval. These rules are shown to be sound, i.e. the deductions are logically correct. Based on these rules, an improved constraint propagation algorithm is introduced to enforce the path consistency.

1 Introduction

Combining and integrating different kinds of knowledge is an emerging and challenging issue in Qualitative Spatial Reasoning (QSR), content-based image retrieval and computer vision, etc. Gerevini and Renz [1] has dealt with the combination of topological knowledge and metric size knowledge in QSR, and Isli et al. [2] has combined the cardinal direction knowledge and the relative orientation knowledge.

To combine topological and directional relations, Sharma [3] represented topological and cardinal relations as interval relations along two axes, e.g., horizontal and vertical axes. Based on Allen's composition table [4] for temporal interval relations, Sharma identifies all of the composition tables combining topological and directional relations. But his model approximated regions with Minimal Boundary Rectangles (MBRs), and if a more precise model (e.g., in this paper) is used, his composition tables will not be correct. We base our work on the same topological model as Sharma's, and a different directional model from his, which is more general and thereby, is more practical.

In this paper, we detail various interaction rules between two formalisms and we are also devoted to investigating the computational problems in the formalism combining topological and cardinal directional relations.

In the next section, we give the background for this paper. The interaction rules are introduced in section 3, which are used to implement our new path consistency algorithm in section 5 after some definitions and terminologies are prepared in section 4. In section 6, the conclusion is followed.

M. Gallagher, J. Hogan, and F. Maire (Eds.): IDEAL 2005, LNCS 3578, pp. 17–24, 2005.

2   Background

We first introduce the two formalisms of topological and cardinal directional relations, respectively. The region considered in this paper is a point-set homeomorphic to a unit disk in Euclidean space $\mathbb{R}^2$.

2.1   Topology Formalism

Topology is perhaps the most fundamental aspect of space. Topological relations are invariant under topological transformations, such as translation, scaling, and rotation. Examples are terms like *neighbor* and *disjoint* [6]. RCC8 is a formalism dealing with a set of eight jointly exhaustive and pairwise disjoint (JEPD) relations, called basic relations, denoted as DC, EC, PO, EQ, TPP, $NTPP$, $TPPi$, $NTPPi$, with the meaning of DisConnected, Extensionally Connected, Partial Overlap, EQual, Tangential Proper Part, Non-Tangential Proper Part, and their converses. Exactly one of these relations holds between any two spatial regions. In this paper, we will focus on RCC8 formalism.

2.2   Cardinal Direction Formalism

Goyal and Egenhofer [8] introduced a direction-relation model for extended spatial objects that considers the influence of the objects' shapes. It uses the projection-based direction partitions and an extrinsic reference system, and considers the exact representation of the target object with respect to the reference frame. The reference frame with a polygon as reference object has nine direction tiles: north (N_A), northeast (NE_A), east (E_A), southeast (SE_A), south (S_A), southwest (SW_A), west (W_A), northwest (NW_A), and same (O_A, i.e., the minimum bounding rectangle). The cardinal direction from the reference object to a target is described by recording those tiles into which at least one part of the target object falls. We call the relations where the target object occupies one tile of the reference object *single-tile* relations, and others *multi-tile* relations. We denote this formalism by CDF(Cardinal Direction Formalism) for brevity. It should be noted that Sharma [3] did not consider the kind of *multi-tile* relation and the intermediate relations, i.e., *NW*, *NE*, *SE* and *SW*.

3   Interaction Rules Between RCC8 and CDF

The internal operations, including converse and composition, on RCC8 can be found in [10]. The internal operations on CDF have been investigated in [9] and [11]. In order to integrate these two formalisms, we must investigate interaction rules between them. These rules are very useful to improve the spatial reasoning and can be the complement of the present composition tables. The spatial reasoning based on rules is more efficient and extended easily in the future as Sistla et al. [5] indicated.

The notation and representation of these rules are similar to [5], i.e. each rule will be written as $r :: r_1, r_2, \cdots, r_k$, where r is called the head of the rule, which is deduced by the list $r_1, r_2, \cdots, r_k$ called the body of the rule.

To facilitate the representation of the interaction rules, we denote a basic cardinal direction (i.e., single-tile or multi-tile relation) relation by a set SB, which includes at most nine elements, i.e. the nine single-tile cardinal direction relations. For example, a relation $O{:}S{:}SE{:}SN$ (multi-tile relation) can be denoted by $\{O,S,SE,SN\}$. The general cardinal direction relation (i.e., a basic cardinal direction relation or the disjunction of basic cardinal direction relations) can be regarded as a superset GB, whose element is the kind of set SB. So we have the relation: $SB \in GB$. The universal relation is the set $BIN = \{O, N, NE, E, SE, S, SW, W, NW\}$, and the universe, i.e. the set of all possible cardinal relations, is denoted by U.

Now, we present a system of rules for deducing new spatial relations from existing ones.

3.1 Rules for Deducing CDF Relations from RCC8 Relations (RCC8 → CDF)

Assume that there exists some RCC8 relation between two regions A and B and we want to know the potential cardinal direction relations between them, we show the deduction rules in three cases and give their proofs if necessary.

From the RCC8 relation A DC B, we can not specify the CDF relation between them, i.e.,

$$A \ U \ B :: A \ DC \ B, \tag{1}$$

where U is the universe of possible CDF relations between two non-empty and connected regions.

This rule is obvious, because the DC relation is the least restricted relation between two regions.

Let x denote any relation symbol in $\{EC, PO, TPPi, NTPPi\}$. We have the following rule for each x. Because this rule is difficult to represent, we adopt first-order logic and the notations for CDF.

$$\forall SB \in GB(A, B), O \in SB :: A \ x \ B \tag{2}$$

Let x denote any of the relation symbols in $\{TPP, NTPP, EQ\}$. We have the following rule for each such x.

$$A \ O \ B :: A \ x \ B \tag{3}$$

3.2 Rules for Deducing RCC8 Relations from CDF Relations (CDF → RCC8)

In this section, we will investigate the rules deducing RCC8 relation between any two regions A and B from the CDF relation between them in three cases.

Let y denote any relation symbol in $\{DC, EC, PO, TPP, NTPP, EQ, TPPi\}$ (i.e., $\overline{NTPPi}$). We have the following rule.

$$A \; y \; B :: A \; O \; B \tag{4}$$

Let x denote a cardinal direction relation which is a multi-tile relation at least including O and another single-tile relation, for example $\{O:N:NE\}$. Let y denote the relation set $\{DC, EC, PO, TPPi, NTPPi\}$, which means y can be anyone of these relations. We have the rule below.

$$A \; y \; B :: A \; x \; B \tag{5}$$

Let x denote any of the cardinal direction relations which do not contain O. Another rule can be described as follows.

$$A \; DC \; B :: A \; x \; B \tag{6}$$

3.3   Rules for Deducing Relations from the Composition of RCC8 and CDF Relations (RCC8 ∘ CDF)

We will discuss these rules in three cases.

Let x denote any of the relation symbols in $\{TPP, NTPP\}$, y any CDF relation and z the induced CDF relation. The rule is described as follows.

$$A \; z \; C :: A \; x \; B, B \; y \; C, \tag{7}$$

Where, if y is a single-tile CDF relation, z equals y, and if y is a multi-tile CDF relation, z is any subset of y.

This rule is similar to the above except that x is anyone of the relation symbols in $\{TPPi, NTPPi\}$. So we have the relation A⊇B. It follows that the rule can be described as follows.

$$A \; z \; C :: A \; x \; B, B \; y \; C, \tag{8}$$

where z is any superset of y, i.e. y is the subset of z.

This rule is obvious, so we present it directly.

$$A \; y \; C :: A \; EQ \; B, B \; y \; C \tag{9}$$

The rules for deducing RCC8 relations from the composition of RCC8 and CDF relations can be derived by combining the above rules (7)-(9) and rules (4)-(6).

3.4   Rules for Deducing Relations from the Composition of CDF and RCC8 Relations (CDF ∘ RCC8)

The rules are presented in three cases as follows

Let x denote any single-tile CDF relation and y denote the deduced CDF relation. The rule is described as follows.

$$A \; y \; C :: A \; x \; B, C \; \{TPP, NTPP\} \; B, \tag{10}$$

Where, if x is any of the relation symbols in {NW, NE, SE, SW}, y equals x, and if x is N (respectively S, E or W), y is any subset of {NW, N, NE} (respectively {SW, S, SE}, {NE, E, SE} or {SW, W, NW}).

Using the above methods, we can also verify the following rule.

$$A\ y\ C :: A\ x\ B, C\ \{TPPi, NTPPi\}\ B, \tag{11}$$

Where, if x is SW (respectively NW, NE or SE), y is any subset of {W, SW, S, O} (respectively {N, NW, W, O}, {N, NE, E, O}, or {E, SE, S, O}), and if x is N (respectively S, E or W), y is any subset of {N, O} (respectively {S, O}, {E, O} or {W, O}).

Let x denote any CDF relation. This rule is obvious. We just describe it directly as follows.

$$A\ x\ C :: A\ x\ B, B\ EQ\ C \tag{12}$$

The rules for deducing RCC8 relations from the composition of CDF and RCC8 relations can be derived by combining the above rules (10)-(12) and rules (4)-(6).

3.5 Composite Rules

The advocation of the rules in this section is motivated by such situations where given the relations A N B, B PO C, C N D, what is the relation between A and D? We can not find the answer using the above rules and we should find more powerful rules.

Sharma [3] verified and extended [?]'s inference rule:

$$A\ x\ D :: A\ x\ B, B\ y\ C, C\ x\ D\ .$$

In this paper, we adapt this rule to our model and investigate its properties. Let R denote any of the RCC8 relation symbols in {*EC, PO, TPP, NTPP, TPPi, NTPPi, EQ*}, x and y denote any single-tile CDF relation and z denote the deduced CDF relation, respectively. These rules are discussed in three cases.

$$A\ z\ D :: A\ x\ B, B\ R\ C, C\ y\ D, \tag{13}$$

where x is N (respectively S, W, or E), y is any of the relation symbols in {NW, N, NE} (respectively {SW, S, SE}, {NW, W, SW}, or {NE, E, SE}) and then z is any subset of {NW, N, NE} (respectively {SW, S, SE}, {NW, W, SW}, or {NE, E, SE}).

Using the above methods, we can validate the following two rules.

$$A\ z\ D :: A\ x\ B, B\ R\ C, C\ y\ D, \tag{14}$$

where x is any of the relation symbols in {NW, NE} (respectively {SW, SE}, {NW, SW}, or {NE, SE}), y is N (respectively S, W, or E) and then z is any subset of {x, N} (respectively {x, S}, {x, W}, or {x, E}), i.e., when x is NE and y is N, then z is any subset of {NE, N}.

$$A\ z\ D :: A\ x\ B, B\ R\ C, C\ y\ D, \tag{15}$$

where x is NW (respectively SW, NE, or SE), y equals x, and then z is NW (respectively SW, NE, or SE).

4   Preliminary

Definition 1. *Binary Constraint Satisfaction Problem (BCSP)*
If every one of the constraints in a Constraint Satisfaction Problem (CSP) in-volves two variables (possibly the same) and asserts that the pair of values as-signed to those variables must lie in a certain binary relation, then the constraint satisfaction problem is called Binary Constraint Satisfaction Problem.

Definition 2. *We define an RCC8-BCSP as a BCSP of which the constraints are RCC8 relations on pairs of the variables. The universe of a RCC8-BCSP is the set $\mathbb{R}^2$ of regions anyone of which is a point-set homeomorphic to a unit disk. Similarly we can define CDF-BCSP as a BCSP of which the constraints are CDF relations on pairs of the variables and the universe is the set $\mathbb{R}^2$ of regions anyone of which is a point-set homeomorphic to a unit disk, and RDF-BCSP as a BCSP of which the constraints consist of a conjunction of RCC8 relations and CDF relations on pairs of the variables and the universe is the set $\mathbb{R}^2$ of regions anyone of which is a point-set homeomorphic to a unit disk.*

A binary constraint problem with n variables and universe U can be simply viewed as an n-by-n matrix M of binary relations over U: the relation M_{ij} (in row i, column j) is the constraint on $< x_i, x_j >$.

Let M and N be n-by-n matrices of binary relations. We have definitions as follows:

Definition 3.

$$(M \circ N)_{ij} = (M_{i0} \circ N_{0j}) \cap (M_{i1} \circ N_{1j}) \cap ... \cap (M_{in-1} \circ N_{n-1j}) = \underset{k<n}{\cap} M_{ik} \circ N_{kj} \quad .$$

Let $M^2 = M \circ M$.

Definition 4. *An n-by-n constraint matrix M is path-consistent if $M \leq M^2$.*

M is path-consistent just in case $M_{ij} \subseteq M_{ik} \circ M_{kj}$. We must note that path consistency is the necessary, but not sufficient, condition for the consistency of a BCSP.

5   Path Consistency in RDF-BCSP

To enforce the path consistency in RDF-BCSP, we must consider the interactions between the RCC8 component and CDF component in RDF-BCSP in addition to the internal path consistency in RCC8-BCSP and CDF-BCSP, respectively.

We devise a constraint propagation procedure $Dpc()$ for enforcing path con-sistency in RDF-BCSP, which is adapted from the path consistency algorithm described in [4]. Our algorithm employs two queues RCC8-Queue and CDF-Queue, which are initialized to all pairs (x, y) of the RCC8-BCSP and CDF-BCSP variables, respectively, verifying $x \leq y$ (the variables are supposed to be ordered). The algorithm removes pairs of variables from the two queues in parallel or in turn. When a pair $\langle X, Y \rangle$ of variables of RCC8-BCSP (respectively CDF-BCSP) is removed from RCC8-Queue (respectively CDF-Queue), firstly the RCC8 (respectively CDF) relation on $\langle X, Y \rangle$ is converted to the CDF (respectively RCC8) relation on $\langle X, Y \rangle$ according to the rules (1)-(3) (respectively (4)-(6)). If the resulting CDF (respectively RCC8) relation on $\langle X, Y \rangle$ is different from the original relation on $\langle X, Y \rangle$, the pair of variables will be entered to the CDF-Queue (respectively RCC8-Queue); Then this CDF (respectively RCC8) relation on the pair $\langle X, Y \rangle$ is used to update the CDF (respectively RCC8) relations on the neighboring pairs of variables (pairs sharing at least one variable) according to the prerequisites in the rules provided by section 3. If a pair is successfully updated, it is entered into RCC8-Queue (respectively CDF-Queue), if it is not already there, in order to be considered at a future stage for propagation. This propagation procedure is common with Allen's algorithm, what's different is that the RCC8 (respectively CDF) relation on every pair of variables will be used to refine the relevant relations according to these rules provide by section 3.

The algorithm loops until it terminates if the empty relation, indicating inconsistency, is detected, or if RCC8-Queue and CDF-Queue become empty, indicating that a fixed point has been reached and the input RDF-BCSP is made path consistent.

Theorem 1. *The constraint propagation procedure Dpc() runs into completion in $O(n^3)$ time, where n is the number of variables of the input RDF-BCSP.*

Proof. The number of variable pairs is $O(n^2)$. A pair of variables may be placed in queue at most a constant number of times (8 for a pair of RCC8 variables, which is the total number of RCC8 atoms; and 218 for a pair of CDF variables, which is the total number of CDF basic cardinal direction relations. Every time a pair is removed from queue for propagation, the procedure performs $O(n)$ operations. □

6   Conclusions

In this paper, we have combined two essential formalisms in qualitative spatial reasoning, i.e., RCC8 and cardinal direction formalism. The interaction rules have been given and they can be embedded into the propagation algorithm to enforce the consistency of BCSP based on the new hybrid formalism. The other combinations of formalisms in QSR should be investigated in the future, and the modeling and computational problems in Fuzzy QSR should be also interesting.

References

1. A. Gerevini and J. Renz. Combining Topological and Size Constraints for Spatial Reasoning. *Artificial Intelligence (AIJ)*, vol. 137(1-2): 1-42, 2002
2. A Isli, V Haarslev and R Moller. Combining cardinal direction relations and relative orientation relations in Qualitative Spatial Reasoning. Fachbereich Informatik, University Hamburg, Technical report FBI-HH-M-304/01, 2001
3. J. Sharma. Integrated spatial reasoning in geographic information systems: combining topology and direction. Ph.D. Thesis, Department of Spatial Information Science and Engineering, University of Maine, Orono, ME, 1996
4. James F. Allen. Maintaining knowledge about temporal intervals. *Communications of the ACM*, vol. 26(11): 832-843, November, 1983
5. A. Prasad Sistla, Clement T. Yu and R. Haddad. Reasoning About Spatial Relations in Picture Retrieval Systems. In: *20th International Conference on Very Large Data Bases*, pp. 570-581, Morgan Kaufmann, 1994
6. M. Egenhofer. A Formal Definition of Binary Topological Relations. In *Third International Conference on Foundations of Data Organization and Algorithms (FODO)*, Vol. 367, pp. 457-472, Paris, France: Lecture Notes in Computer Science, Springer-Verlag, 1989
7. Randell D, Cui Z and Cohn A. A spatial logic based on regions and connection. In: Nebel B, Rich C, Swartout W, (eds.) *Proc. of the Knowledge Representation and Reasoning*, pp. 165~176, San Mateo: Morgan Kaufmann, 1992
8. R. Goyal and M. Egenhofer. Cardinal Directions between Extended Spatial Objects. *IEEE Transactions on Knowledge and Data Engineering* (to be published), 2000
9. S. Skiadopoulos and M. Koubarakis. Composing cardinal direction relations. *Artificial Intelligence*, vol. 152(2): 143—171, 2004
10. D. A. Randell, A. G. Cohn and Z. Cui. Computing Transitivity Tables: A Challenge For Automated Theorem Provers. In *11th International Conference on Automated Deduction*, pp.786-790, Berlin: Springer Verlag, 1992
11. Serafino Cicerone and Paolino Di Felice. Cardinal directions between spatial objects: the pairwise-consistency problem. *Information Sciences*, vol. 164: 165-188, 2004

Using Pre-aggregation for Efficient Spatial Query Processing in Sensor Environments

Soon-Young Park and Hae-Young Bae

Dept. of Computer Science and Information Engineering, Inha University
Yonghyun-dong, Nam-ku, Inchon, 402-751, Korea
sunny@dblab.inha.ac.kr, hybae@inha.ac.kr

Abstract. Many applications using sensing data require the fast retrieval of aggregated information in sensor networks. In this paper, distributed spatial index structure in sensor networks for time-efficient aggregation query processing is proposed. The main idea is to logically organize sensors in underlying networks into distributed R-Tree structure, named Sensor Tree. Each node of the Sensor Tree has pre-aggregated results which are the collection of the values of aggregated result for sensing data of the same type of sensors within Minimum Bounding Rectangle (MBR). If a spatial region query is required, the processing of the query searches the location of the target sensor from the root of the Sensor Tree. And then it finally sends the values of pre-aggregated result of that sensor. By the proposed Sensor Tree aggregation query processing on any region, response time and energy consumption can be reduced since it avoids flooding query to the leaf sensor or non-relevant sensors in the sensor networks.[*]

1 Introduction

In the past few years, smart sensor devices have matured to the point that it is now feasible to realize a large, distributed sensor networks. Sensors are connected to the physical world which they monitor and collect data from. Sensors are connected to other sensors through a wireless network, and they use multi-hop routing protocol to communicate with sensors that are spatially distant apart [11, 13]. Sensors of the same type, for example temperature sensors, light sensors result in the sensing data of the same type which has the same schema. Sensor network consists of lots of sensors and provide opportunities for monitoring information about a spatial region of interest. Sensor data might contain noise, and it is often possible to obtain more accurate result by aggregation of data from several sensors. Summaries and aggregates of sensing data are thus more useful than individual sensor readings [1].

Sensors in the sensor networks are usually not connected to a fixed infrastructure, they use batteries as their main power supply, and saving of power is one of the design issues of a sensor network [12]. But sensor networks can be embedded in a variety of environments. Different applications usually have different requirements from

---

[*] This research was supported by the MIC (Ministry of Information and Communication), Korea, under the ITRC (Information Technology Research Center) support program supervised by the IITA (Institute of Information Technology Assessment).

M. Gallagher, J. Hogan, and F. Maire (Eds.): IDEAL 2005, LNCS 3578, pp. 25–31, 2005.

accuracy, power consumption to time-efficient processing. In many spatial applications, for example rescue region control system, spatial query which gather sensing data within a specific region is an essential functionality and requires the fast retrieval of aggregated information in sensor networks.

In this paper, distributed spatial index structure in sensor networks for time-efficient aggregation query processing is proposed. The main idea is combining inter-network distributed spatial index with the pre-aggregated results, named Sensor Tree. It is to cover the underlying sensors distributed R-tree using the location of the same type of sensors and to store for each Minimum Bounding Rectangle (MBR), the values of the aggregation function for sensing data of the same type of sensors that are enclosed by MBR [5, 7]. If a region query is required, the processing of the query is started to search the location of the target sensor from the root of the Sensor Tree and finished by sending the pre-aggregation value of the finding sensor to server which requires the query.

By using pre-aggregation technique of the proposed Sensor Tree region query processing can reduce response time and energy consumption since it avoids flooding query to the leaf sensor or non-relevant sensors in the sensor networks.

The remainder of the paper is structured as follows. Section 2 provides some related work. Section 3 proposes Sensor Tree which is a distributed index with pre-aggregated results in sensor networks and presents efficient aggregation query processing using Sensor Tree. Section 4 evaluates the proposed approach by comparison with others. Finally section 5 has concluding remarks of this paper.

2   Related Work

Traditionally, sensors are used as data gathering instruments, which continuously feed a database on the server. Each sensor can produce a stream of data about its surroundings. If queries are posed at a powered server, they are flooded to sensors in the networks. Most of all queries over sensor networks are simple and repeatable. In particular, since a message sending operation may spend at least 1000 times more battery than a local operation (e.g. sense operation), query processing in sensor network should avoid unnecessary communication as much as possible [3].

There has been much previous work on query processing in sensor networks [6, 9, 10, 11, 13]. Due to the geographical distribution of sensors in a sensor network, each piece of data generated in the sensor network has geographic a location. And hence to specify the data of the interest over which a query should be answered, each query in a sensor network has a geographical region associated with it. It seems that any kind of index on distributed data requires a hierarchical structure that aggregates information from different region of the networks. Prior work in range query for sensor networks has addressed a number of important issues in constructing such hierarchies. More detailed information can be accessed by top down traversal of the hierarchy to visit the sensors holding the relevant information [2, 4, 7, 8]. These researches noted the importance of power consumption. They focus on in-network query processing to reduce communication cost and power consumption.

Therefore, there is a need for making an efficient access structure on sensor networks in order to contact only the relevant sensor nodes for the execution of a query and hence achieve real time response and an accurate result.

3   Efficient Spatial Query Processing
Using Sensor Tree with Pre-aggregated Results

In this section, distributed index structure in sensor networks for time-efficient aggregation query processing is proposed. The main idea is to cover the underlying sensors in networks distributed R-Tree with pre-aggregated results, named Sensor Tree. Sensor Tree stores for each Minimum Bounding Rectangle (MBR), the values of the aggregation function for sensing data of the same type of sensors within the MBR. Sensor Tree is built on the sensor of the spatial dimension, therefore its structure is a hierarchical partitioning of the sensor network into rectangle-shaped clusters.

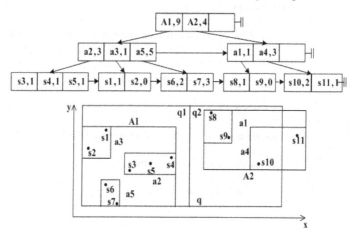

Fig. 1. The Structure of Sensor Tree

It is assumed that every sensor nodes in sensor networks lie in (x, y) coordinate space and have been deployed and arranged into a connected topology. Protocols for routing of the messages, and the cost of communication between nodes that are distance d apart takes $O(d)$ amount of energy.

Fig. 1 logically depicts a Sensor Tree which indexes a set of 5 road segments $r1, r2, \ldots, r5$, with MBR is $a1, a2, \ldots, a5$ respectively when we assume the virtual road is in the rectangle. There are 3 sensors on the road $r2$, sensing data of sensor $s3$, $s4$, $s5$ are 1, 1, 1 respectively. Therefore the total number of sensing data in $r3$ is 3 and there is an entry $(a2, 3)$ in the internal node of the Sensor Tree. Moving one level up, MBR $A1$ contains three roads, $r2$, $r3$, $r5$. The total number of sensing data in these roads is 9, and therefore there is an entry $(A1, 9)$ at level one of the Sensor Tree.

Each sensor node has a unique identifier, id. Each node has a field of communication, which is capable of sending/receiving messages. All nodes within this boundary are its immediate neighbors by duplex link. For a node v, we denote v's r-neighborhood, $Nbr(v, r)$, as the set of nodes within a radius r of v. Every node v maintains a variable $l.v$, level of v denoting the highest level of the Sensor Tree that v has participated in. Every node in sensor networks cooperates at level 0 of Sensor Tree, only clusterheads of level i cooperate for construction of level $i + 1$ of the Sensor Tree. To minimize communication cost, the choice of clusterhead should be tiered into the routing structure. We use a simple clusterhead selection procedure as follows.

For every level i, v maintains a variable p, parent node ptr to denote v's clusterhead for level i. Dually, v maintains c, children node ptr, That means, v is the clusterhead of the MBR that contains $c.v(i)$, children of v for level i. Using this doubly linked structure, any node can query the Sensor Tree. The pseudo code of joining cluster for node v at a level i is as follows.

```
join_cluster()
{
    if (l.v = i and p.v(i) = nil)
    {
        r <- 1;
        while (Nbr(v, r) < m or p.v(i) != nil)
        {
            if (there exists an i such that both u ∈ Nbr(v, r) and l.u = i+ 1)
            {
                p.v(i) <- u;
                c.u(i) <- c.u(i) ∪ {v};
            }
            r <- r + 1;
        }
        if (p.v(i) = nil and (if u ∈ Nbr(v, r) is true than so is p.u(i) = nil))
        {
            calculate mbr.v(i) using Nbr(v, r);
            p.v(i) <- v; l.v <- i + 1;
            c.v(i + 1) <- Nbr(v, r);
        }
    }
}
```

A node v with $l.v = i$ executes the join_cluster() if it is not included in the cluster of level $i + 1$, that is $p.v(i) = $ nil. In this case v first tries to contact a neighboring node u with $l.u = i + 1$ by searching increasingly larger radii, r, and join u's cluster by setting $p.v(i) = u$. if no such u exists and v encounters n nodes in level i within its r-neighborhood, and become the clusterhead of these n nodes in one step. If v is contacted by another node u with $l.u = i + 1$, v simply joins u's cluster.

During the concurrent executions of join operation by multiple nodes, a clusterhead may end up havng more than N children. In the splitting cluster, a clusterhead v with more than N children at level i splits its cluster into clusters with number of children greater than or equal to n but less than N. Split operation is the same in based R-tree. The pseudo code of splitting cluster for node v at a level i is as follows.

```
split_cluster()

{
    if (c.v(i) > N) split(mbr.v(i));
}
```

As an example consider a simple window query q of the form, "find the total number of cars sensing by sensors on all road segments inside a query window". Using proposed Sensor Tree, the processing of this query starts from the root of the tree and proceeds recursively to the leaf nodes. Let X_i be a pointer a node of Sensor Tree, and

AG() be the aggregation function. The pseudo code for aggregated window queries is as follows.

```
aggregation()
{
    for (every entry x ∈ Xᵢ)
    {
        if (q contains x)
                then result <- AG(result, x.pre_aggr);
        else if (q intersects x)
        {
                partial_result <- aggregation(x.subtree_ptr, q);
                result <- AG(result, partial_result);
        }
    }
}
```

The algorithm is similar to the query algorithm for based R-trees. However, there is fundamental difference. For common window queries, if the query window is large the use of the index does not pay off and the optimizer uses sequential search on the MBR of the sensors. For aggregates queries, on the other hand, there are two cases. First, if the query window q is large, then many nodes in the intermediate level of the tree will be contained in q so the pre-calculated results are used and there is no visiting of the individual sensors. Second, if the query window is small, Sensor Tree of this case is used as a spatial index in sensor networks and it is allowed to select the qualifying sensors.

4 Comparison with Other Approaches

Given a query over a sensor network, a naive way to run the query will be to simply flood all of the relevant sensors in sensor network with a query. Each sensor node in the network broadcasts the query message exactly once and also remembers the id of the sensor node it receives the query from. If there are n sensors whose sensing regions intersect with the query's region, then using about n message transmissions, a communication routing tree spanning the n sensor could be built within the network. Each node built in the routing tree responds to the query. The responses propagate upwards in the tree towards the root of the query source. This again incurs a cost of n message transmissions, assuming the responses are aggregated at each tree node. Thus, the total communication cost incurred in answering q such queries over the same region is $2qn$ using the naive flooding approach.

Case of in-network query processing to visit only the sensors holding the relevant information, if there are m relevant sensors of the total n sensors, the total communication cost incurred in answering q such queries over the same region is $C + 2qm$, where $C, m \leq C \leq n$, is the communication cost incurred in composing the routing tree by m relevant sensors.

Consider Sensor Tree with pre-aggregated results composed of m sensor. The total cost incurred in executing q queries over the same region will be $D + m$, where $D, m \leq D \leq n$, is the communication cost incurred in composing the Sensor Tree and m is the cost of propagating information from leafs to root of the Sensor Tree in the worst

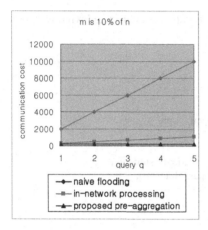 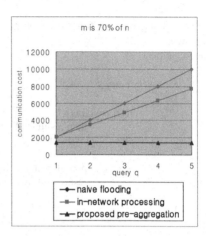

Fig. 2. Comparison of Communication Cost

case. If m is substantially less than n, constructing Sensor Tree could result in large savings in communication cost. If there are n sensors, n is 1000, whose sensing regions intersect with the query's region, communication cost incurred in answering query q is as Fig. 2.

5 Conclusion

In this paper, the focus is made upon the efficient execution of region query for aggregation distributed information in sensor networks. A distributed spatial index structure on sensors of the same type in sensor networks, which is called Sensor Tree, is established. Each node of the Sensor Tree has pre-aggregated result which is the collection of the values of aggregated results for sensing data of the same type of sensors within MBR. Therefore, an aggregation query does not need to access all sensors in networks, since part of the answer is found in the intermediate sensor nodes of the tree.

By using pre-aggregation of the proposed Sensor Tree the query can be answered much more efficiently without processing of aggregation and reduces response time and energy consumption and achieves an accurate response since it avoids flooding query to the leaf sensor or non-relevant sensors in the sensor networks. Our method allows efficient range query in sensor networks.

References

1. J. Considine, F. Li, G. Kollios, and J. Byers, Approximate Aggregation Techniques for ensor Databases, Proceedings of ICDE 2004.
2. H. Cupta, S. R. Das, and Q. Gu, Connected Sensor Cover: Self-Organization of Sensor Networks for Efficient Query Execution, Proceedings of MobiHoc 2003.
3. N. Demirbas and H. Ferhatosmanoglu, Peer-to-Peer Spatial Queries in Sensor Networks, Proceedings of P2P 2003.

4. J. Gao, L. J. Guibas, J. Hershberger, and L. Zhang, Fractionally Cascaded Information in a Sensor Network, Proceedings of IPSN 2004.
5. A. Guttaman, R-trees: A Dynamic Index Structure for Spatial Searching, Proceedings of SIGMOD 1984.
6. C. Intanagonwiwat, R. Govindan, and D. Estrin, Directed Diffusion: A Scalable and Robust Communication Paradigm for Sensor Networks, Proceedings of MobiCom 2000.
7. I. Lazaridis and S. Mehrotra, Progressive Approximate Aggregate Queries with a Multi-Resolution Tree Structure, Proceedings of SIGMOD 2001.
8. X. Li, Y. J. Kim, R. Govindan, and W. Hong, Multi-dimensional Range Queries in Sensor Networks, Proceedings of SenSys 2003.
9. S. Madden and M. J. Franklin, Fjording the Stream: An Architecture for Queries over Streaming Sensor Data, Proceedings of ICDE 2002.
10. S. Madden, M. J. Franklin, J. M. Hellerstein, and W. Hong, TAG: a Tiny AGgregation Service for Ad-Hoc Sensor Networks, Proceedings of OSDI 2002.
11. S. Madden, M. J. Franklin, J. M. Hellerstein, and W. Hong, The Design of an Acquisitional Query Processor For Sensor Networks, Proceedings of SIDMOD 2003.
12. S. Madden, R. Szewzyk, M. J. Franklin, and D. Culler, Supporting Aggregate Queries Over Ad-Hoc Wireless Sensor Networks, Proceedings of WMCSA 2002.
13. Y. Yao and J. Gehrke, Ouery Processing for Sensor Networks, Proceedings of CIDR 2003.

Model Trees
for Classification of Hybrid Data Types*

Hsing-Kuo Pao, Shou-Chih Chang, and Yuh-Jye Lee

Dept. of Computer Science & Information Engineering,
National Taiwan University of Science & Technology, Taipei, Taiwan
{pao,M9115009,yuh-jye}@mail.ntust.edu.tw

Abstract. In the task of classification, most learning methods are suitable only for certain data types. For the hybrid dataset consists of nominal and numeric attributes, to apply the learning algorithms, some attributes must be transformed into the appropriate types. This procedure could damage the nature of dataset. We propose a model tree approach to integrate several characteristically different learning methods to solve the classification problem. We employ the decision tree as the classification framework and incorporate support vector machines into the tree construction process. This design removes the discretization procedure usually necessary for tree construction while decision tree induction itself can deal with nominal attributes which may not be handled well by e.g., SVM methods. Experiments show that our purposed method has better performance than that of other competing learning methods.

1 Introduction

In the real world, the datasets usually include both of the (unordered) *nominal* (or discrete) attributes and the *numeric* (or continuous) attributes. We name this kind of datasets as *hybrid* datasets. Most learning algorithms for classification are only suitable for certain specified data types. When the undesired data types are encountered in the dataset, conventionally we transform them into appropriate types so that the learning algorithm can be proceeded [1–4]. E.g., numeric data need a discretization process before the typical decision tree induction can be applied and SVM works on the space of numeric data only. Sometimes the type transformation is artificial and results in changing of the dataset nature.

To overcome this problem we employ a novel model tree approach which a decision tree (DT) framework, combining with SVMs [5, 6] will be used for the classification of hybrid sets. During the tree construction, the SVMs play a role of replacing the discretization procedure and providing a possible way of extending a univariate decision to a multivariate decision. In an internal node, before the tree splitting, SVM will help to generate a synthetic Boolean attribute based on the numeric attributes of current training examples in this node, rather

---

* Research partially supported by Taiwan National Science Council Grant # 93-2213-E-011-036

M. Gallagher, J. Hogan, and F. Maire (Eds.): IDEAL 2005, LNCS 3578, pp. 32–39, 2005.
© Springer-Verlag Berlin Heidelberg 2005

than discretize the numeric attributes regardless of their interdependencies [1,3]. When we choose the "best" splitting attribute we consider the original nominal attributes as well as the synthesized Boolean attribute. If the synthetic Boolean attribute is chosen as the splitting attribute, it means that the decision node has a multivariate decision implicitly. Therefore, this strategy extends the ability of DTs to include multivariate decisions. On the other hand, SVM itself can not naturally deal with nominal data without creating any artificial encodings. Thus, our proposed model tree, combining the power of DT and SVM, will be suitable to solve the classification problem for hybrid datasets.

2 Decision Tree Induction with Hybrid Data Types

DT methods [7,8] are used widely in the fields of machine learning and data mining. A DT consists of internal and external nodes where an internal node with several branches represents alternative choices to make based on the (discrete) values of selected attribute and an external node (a leaf) is usually associated with a single class label. A prediction is done following the path from the tree root to a leaf, by several branch choices according to given attribute values. The typical DT construction adopts the top-down, divide-and-conquer strategy to recursively build the classification tree [8]. DTs have some advantages such as easy to interpret, efficient to generate and capable of coping with noisy data [9,10]. However, DTs are notorious to be unstable (i.e., high variance). Often a small change in the training set results in different trees and produces inconsistent classification results for the same test set. The instability is inherent because the effect of an error on a top split will be propagated down to all of the splits below [11]. Some approaches have been proposed by combining multiple models to improve the accuracy and stability of DT prediction, such as *bagging* or *boosting* [12–14]. Some examples of DT induction are ID3, C4.5[1], C5.0[2] [8,12] and CART [7]. We shall discuss two issues related to DT induction.

2.1 Incorporating Continuous-Valued Attributes

Many real world classification tasks involve nominal and numeric attributes. For numeric attributes, DT can not be adopted directly unless they are discretized in advance, i.e., partitioning each of the continuous attributes into disjoint intervals [1]. E.g., an attribute X can be separated as $X \leq c$ and $X > c$ for the binary DT. The strategies of discretization are usually categorized by (1) being supervised or unsupervised, (2) being global or local, and (3) being static or dynamic, three options [1,2,4,8,3]. Most choices are heuristically or empirically decided. Also, for many of the discretization approaches, the number of intervals is decided arbitrarily. These can lead to low prediction accuracies or inefficient tree structures, for datasets with hybrid data types or only the numeric data

---

[1] Some MDL-based discretization for continuous attributes is adopted in certain versions

[2] A variant of AdaBoost is implemented

type [15,1,4,8]. While many DT inductions are more satisfied with discrete attributes than continuous ones, we adopt SVM for classification in the subspace spanned by those continuous attributes. In Sec. 4, a combined classifier from DT and SVM will be introduced to deal with datasets with hybrid types.

2.2 Univariate and Multivariate Decision Trees

The classical approach for building a DT, such as C4.5, uses an orthogonal (or axis-parallel) partition at each decision node, so called *univariate* method [8]. Opposite to that, CART [7] allows for the option of *multivariate* decisions. For instance, one check simultaneously involving two attributes X_1 and X_2, such as $X_1 + X_2 \leq 6.5$, may be operated in a decision node. Clearly, there are cases where multivariate approach can work efficiently (producing trees with few nodes), but not for the univariate approach[3] [17,7,9,18–21,10]. We introduce SVM for being capable of multivariate consideration at a node. Other than using a SVM in each decision node in [17], we adopt the machine *only* for continuous attributes. For discrete attributes, the regular ID3 algorithm is applied. By that, we take advantage of powerful SVM for classification, while not losing the readability of DT induction. Further discussion is in Sec. 4.

3 Support Vector Machines

We are given a training dataset $S = \{(\mathbf{x}^1, y_1), \ldots, (\mathbf{x}^m, y_m)\} \subseteq R^n \times R$, where $\mathbf{x}^i \in R^n$ is the input data and $y_i \in \{-1, 1\}$ is the corresponding class label. The aim of SVM is to find the optimal separating hyperplane with the largest margin from the training data. Here, "optimal" is used in the sense that the separating hyperplane has the best generalization for the unseen data based on statistical learning theory [6]. This can be achieved by solving a convex optimization problem given as follows:

$$\min_{(w,b,\xi) \in R^{n+1+m}} C \sum_{i=1}^{m} \xi_i + \frac{1}{2} \|w\|_2^2$$
$$\text{s.t. } y_i(w'x^i + b) + \xi_i \geq 1 \tag{1}$$
$$\xi_i \geq 0, \quad for \; i = 1, 2, \ldots, m,$$

where C is a positive control parameter and weights the tradeoff between the training error and the part of maximizing the margin. We have to point out here, due to the nature of SVM it is more suitable for numeric data type.

In smooth support vector machine (SSVM) [22], the SVM model (1) is changed slightly and converted into a unconstrained minimization problem by utilizing the optimality conditions. These give the SVM reformulation defined as follows:

$$\min_{(w,b) \in R^{n+1}} \frac{C}{2} \sum_{i=1}^{m} (1 - y_i(w'x^i + b))_+^2 + \frac{1}{2}(\|w\|_2^2 + b^2), \tag{2}$$

---

[3] For the multivariate case, the separating hyperplane do not need to be linear [16]

where the *plus* function x_+ is defined as $x_+ = \max\{0, x\}$. In SSVM, the plus function x_+ is approximated by a smooth p-function, $p(x, \alpha) = x + \frac{1}{\alpha} \log(1 + e^{-\alpha x}), \alpha > 0$. By replacing the plus function with a very accurate smooth approximation p-function gives the smooth support vector machine formulation:

$$\min_{(w,b) \in R^{n+1}} \frac{C}{2} \sum_{i=1}^{m} (p(1 - y_i(w'x^i + b), \alpha))^2 + \frac{1}{2}(\|w\|_2^2 + b^2), \tag{3}$$

where $\alpha > 0$ is the smooth parameter. The objective function in problem (3) is strongly convex and infinitely differentiable. Hence, it has a unique solution and can be solved by using a fast Newton-Armijo algorithm [22]. This formulation can be extended to the nonlinear SVM by using the kernel trick. We will not use the nonlinear SSVM in our proposed method because the nonlinear SSVM tends to overfit the small portion of training dataset in the training process.

In next section, we employ the linear SSVM to deal with the numeric attributes and to generate the corresponding synthetic Boolean attribute for the training examples at each node.

4 Model Trees

With the description in the previous sections, we know DTs and SVMs have their own characteristics to deal with different classification problems:

1 Most DTs require a discrete feature space. When a DT encounters numeric attributes, a discretization procedure is applied beforehand to divide each single numeric attribute into many distinct intervals.
2 On the other hand, SVMs are suitable for the classification of numeric data. If datasets contain the nominal attributes, some strategies such as encoding (usually artificial) are applied to transform the nominal attributes into a series of binary attributes and SVMs treat the values of binary attributes as the integers, 0 and 1.

To flexibly choose the most appropriate method for different types of attributes and to overcome the limitation of univariate decision for numeric attributes in DT induction, we propose a new approach which adopts SVM training in the process of DT construction. At each node, we use a SVM classification in the subspace spanned by the (whole) numeric attributes to replace the used-to-be-necessary discretization procedure. Simultaneously, the SVM represents the possible multivariate decision to improve the efficiency of univariate method. After the SVM is built, this "multivariate" decision can be considered and competed with the other nominal attributes, based on information gain, gain ratio or other goodness criteria. Below, we give the modeling process in detail.

4.1 Building Model Trees

Suppose an example in the hybrid dataset is expressed as the form $(\mathbf{x}_{NOM}, \mathbf{x}_{NUM}, y)$, where $\mathbf{x}_{NOM}, \mathbf{x}_{NUM}$ and y represent all of the nominal attributes, all of the numeric attributes and the associated class label, respectively. Moreover, we use the notation, x_{SVMB}, to represent the synthesized Boolean attribute whose value is assigned at each node by the SSVM classifier, built from the part of numeric attributes and training labels. Afterwards, the gain ratio criterion is employed to decide the best attribute among all of the nominal ones and the synthesized SVM attribute. That is, *in each node*, we do the following steps:

Step 1 Using $(\mathbf{x}_{NUM}, y)$ to build x_{SVMB}. The process consists of three parts. The first work is to search the appropriate weight parameter for the linear SSVM classifier. That is to say, we split $\mathbf{x}_{NUM}$ of training examples into training set and validation set following the stratification and then decide the appropriate weight parameter by them. The second work is to retrain the SSVM classifier by means of the chosen parameter and $(\mathbf{x}_{NUM}, y)$ of training examples. Finally, we use the retrained SSVM classifier, denoted by $f(\mathbf{x}_{NUM})$, to generate the corresponding x_{SVMB} according to $\mathbf{x}_{NUM}$ of each training example. If $f(\mathbf{x}_{NUM}) > 0$, the value of x_{SVMB} is True; otherwise is False. After the process is finished, training examples are transformed to the new form, $(\mathbf{x}_{NOM}, x_{SVMB}, y)$.

Step 2 Using the gain ratio to select the most appropriate splitting attribute from $\mathbf{x}_{NOM}$ or x_{SVMB}. The split with the highest value of gain ratio will be selected as the attribute. After the splitting attribute is decided, the dataset is partitioned into two or more subsets accordingly. Note that in order to avoid the case that our method always chooses the synthetic Boolean attribute generated via the SSVM, we confine ourselves in the *linear* SSVM. Besides, the weight parameter used in SSVM is determined by a tuning procedure to avoid the overfitting risk.

If one attribute of $\mathbf{x}_{NOM}$ is selected, it means that not only the nominal attribute is more distinguishing than x_{SVMB} but also the decision is univariate. Oppositely, if x_{SVMB} is selected, it shows that the linear combination of all numeric attributes has better chance to separate the examples and the decision node is multivariate implicitly. The process is repeated recursively until any stopping criterion is met.

5   Experiments

In this section, we test our method on three benchmark datasets from the UCI repository[4] to evaluate its performance. In order to get a fair result, we repeat four rounds tenfold cross-validation procedure for each experiment. Furthermore, two popular classification methods, Naive Bayes (NB) and k-nearest-neighbor (k-NN), are employed to provide the baseline accuracies. Three series of experiments are performed. First, the classification error rates from different *views* (different parts of attributes) are presented. Then we present the final comparison results from NB, k-NN, C4.5, SSVM and our model tree method. In our experiments, we

---
[4] http://www.ics.uci.edu/~mlearn/MLRepository.html

choose three hybrid datasets, Cleveland heart disease, Australian and German that include both of the nominal and numeric attributes from the UCI repository. They are summarized in Table 1.

Table 1. Summary of Datasets

Dataset	Instances	# of nominal attr.	# of numeric attr.	Majority error
Heart	270	7	6	44.44%
Australian	690	8	6	44.49%
German	1000	13	7	30%

In NB approach, for nominal attributes, NB counts the frequencies as the probabilities $P(y)$ and $P(x_i|y)$, for attribute value x_i and class label y; and for numeric attributes, it assumes that the data follows a Gaussian distribution, hence; the probability of the attribute value can be estimated by the probability density function. Finally, the class of the test example is assigned by the posterior probability. In k-NN, for nominal attributes, the distance is zero if the attribute value is identical, otherwise the distance is one; for numeric attributes, the Euclidean distance is applied directly. We discuss three series of experiments.

Different views: nominal attributes. In the first series, only nominal attributes are extracted from the dataset. Three learning methods, NB, k-NN and C4.5 are performed. Appropriate parameter tuning is done for each learning algorithm if there is a need. In this series, k-NN is the most questionable method. Because it can not reflect the actual distance among different nominal values. The result is shown in Table 2(a).

Different views: numeric attributes. In the second series, only numeric attributes are extracted. There are five learning methods, NB, k-NN, C4.5, linear SSVM and Nonlinear SSVM performed. Appropriate parameter tuning is done if there is a need. In C4.5, the values of the numeric attributes are divided into two intervals in the local discretization procedure. The result is shown in Table 2(b). From the first two series, we discover that the results of nominal attributes are significantly better than the numeric counterparts. Also, it shows that the linear SSVM performs better than all other methods.

Different methods: all attributes. In the third experiment, we compare the error rates of different methods for hybrid datasets. Because SSVM can only deal with the numeric attributes, we encode the nominal attributes into a series of Boolean attributes for SSVM. For example, if the nominal attribute has three possible values, we encode them as 001, 010 and 100. In model trees, we use the minimum instances as the early stopping criterion. The number of minimum instances is determined by a tuning procedure. The final results are shown in Table 3. The model tree and linear SSVM have the similar accuracies. Moreover, comparing model trees with C4.5, we find that model trees outperform C4.5 in the Heart and German, and have the similar accuracy in the Australian.

Table 2. Classification based *only* on nominal or numeric attributes (error rates %)

Dataset	Classification Method			Classification Method				
	Naive k-NN Bayes		C4.5	Naive k-NN Bayes		C4.5	Linear SSVM	Nonlinear SSVM
Heart	21.02	19.81	24.54	23.33	22.87	25.83	21.76	29.63
Australian	13.73	13.33	14.42	28.55	25.83	23.80	23.04	24.35
German	25.68	28.20	27.25	29.08	33.70	30.13	28.77	28.90
	(a) only nominal attributes			(b) only numeric attributes				

Table 3. Classification for hybrid datasets (error rates %)

Dataset	Classification Method					
	Naive Bayes	k-NN	C4.5	Linear SSVM	Nonlinear SSVM	Model trees
Heart	16.02	17.78	21.67	13.98	29.81	*15.65*
Australian	22.90	13.33	13.26	13.38	23.88	*12.61*
German	25.25	25.95	26.55	24.38	28.98	*24.67*

6   Conclusion

We employed DT as the classification framework and incorporated the SVM into the construction process of DT to replace the discretization procedure and to provide the multivariate decision. The main idea of our proposed method was to generate a synthetic Boolean attribute according to the original numeric attributes and the synthetic Boolean attribute represented the discriminability of the numeric attributes. Hence, the multivariate decision could be taken into account during the selection of next splitting attribute. Finally, the experiment results showed that model tree has better accuracy than the conventional DT C4.5. We noted that our method can not avoid the inherent instability of DTs.

Our model tree was not just designed for the SVM method only. Any learning methods appropriate to apply to numeric attributes such as Fisher's linear discriminant function or neural networks could be adopted to form a synthetic Boolean attribute and the rest induction procedure is the same. We could also accept more than one such synthesized attribute; thus, more than one learning algorithm at a time under the framework of DTs. We have to point out that designing a good tuning process to avoid the overfitting risk is extremely important. Otherwise, DTs tend to choose the synthetic Boolean attribute induced by the learning algorithm which has the overfitting drawback as the splitting attribute. One design is to apply MDL principle to balance between nominal attributes and the synthetic attribute(s), or between the synthetic attributes generated from different learning methods. With the help from characteristically different learning methods, we could build a classifier which can deal with data of hybrid types successfully.

References

1. Dougherty, J., Kohavi, R., Sahami, M.: Supervised and unsupervised discretizations of continuous features. In: Proceedings of the 12th International Conference on Machine Learning, New York, Morgan Kaufmann (1995) 194–202

2. Fayyad, U.M., Irani, K.B.: Multi-interval discretization of continuous valued attributes for classification learning. In: Proceedings of the 13th International Joint Conference on Artificial Intelligence. (1993) 1022–1029

3. Gama, J., Torgo, L., Soares, C.: Dynamic discretization of continuous attributes. In: Proceedings of the Iberoamericam Conference on AI (IBERAMIA-98), Springer-Verlag (1998) 160–169

4. Kohavi, R., Sahami, M.: Error-based and entropy-based discretization of continuous features. In: Proceedings of the Second International Conference on Knowledge Discovery and Data Mining (KDD-96), AAAI Press (1996) 114–119

5. Burges, C.J.C.: A tutorial on support vector machines for pattern recognition. Data Mining and Knowledge Discovery 2 (1998) 121–167

6. Vapnik, V.N.: The Nature of Statistical Learning Theory. Springer-Verlag, New York (1995)

7. Breiman, L., Friedman, J.H., Olshen, R.A., Stone, C.J.: Classification and Regression Trees. Wadsworth, Belmont, CA (1984)

8. Quinlan, J.R.: C4.5 Programs for Machine Learning. Morgan Kaufmann (1993)

9. Brodley, C.E., Utgoff, P.E.: Multivariate decision trees. Machine Learning 19 (1995) 45–77

10. X.-B. Li, Sweigart, J.R., Teng, J.T.C., Donohue, J.M., Thombs, L.A., Wang, S.M.: Multivariate decision trees using linear discriminants and tabu search. Systems, Man and Cybernetics, Part A, IEEE Transactions on 33 (2003) 194–205

11. Hastie, T., Tibshirani, R., Friedman, J.: The Elements of Statistical Learning. Springer-Verlag, New York (2001)

12. Freund, Y., Schapire, R.E.: A decision-theoretic generalization of online learning and an application to boosting. J. of Comp. and Sys. Sciences 55 (1997) 119–139

13. Quinlan, J.R.: Bagging, boosting, and c4.5. In: Proceedings of the Thirteenth National Conference on Artificial Intelligence and Eighth Innovative Applications of Artificial Intelligence Conference, AAAI 96, AAAI Press (1996) 725–730

14. Breiman, L.: Bagging predictors. Machine Learning 24 (1996) 123–140

15. Quinlan, J.R.: Improved use of continuous attributes in C4.5. Journal of Artificial Intelligence Research 4 (1996) 77–90

16. Ittner, A., Schlosser, M.: Non-linear decision trees - NDT. In: Machine Learning, Proc. of the 13th Inter. Conf. (ICML '96), Morgan Kaufmann (1996) 252–257

17. Bennett, K., Blue, J.: A support vector machine approach to decision trees (1997)

18. Heath, D., Kasif, S., Salzberg, S.: Induction of oblique decision trees. In: Proceedings of the 13th Inter. Joint Conf. on AI, San Mateo, CA, Morgan Kaufmann (1993) 1002–1007

19. Murthy, S.K., Kasif, S., Salzberg, S.: A system for induction of oblique decision trees. Journal of Artificial Intelligence Research 2 (1994) 1–33

20. Murthy, S.K., Kasif, S., Salzberg, S., Beigel, R.: OC1: Randomized induction of oblique decision trees. In: Proceedings of the Eleventh Nat. Conf. on AI, Washington, DC, MIT Press (1993) 322–327

21. Utgoff, P.E., Brodley, C.E.: Linear machine decision trees. Technical report, University of Massachusetts (1991) COINS Technical Report 91-10.

22. Y.-J. Lee, Mangasarian, O.L.: SSVM: A smooth support vector machine. Computational Optimization and Applications 20 (2001) 5–22 Data Mining Institute, University of Wisconsin, Technical Report 99-03.

Finding Uninformative Features in Binary Data

Xin Wang and Ata Kabán

School of Computer Science, The University of Birmingham,
Birmingham, B15 2TT, UK
{xcw,axk}@cs.bham.ac.uk

Abstract. For statistical modelling of multivariate binary data, such as text documents, datum instances are typically represented as vectors over a global vocabulary of attributes. Apart from the issue of high dimensionality, this also faces us with the problem of uneven importance of various attribute presences/absences. This problem has been largely overlooked in the literature, however it may create difficulties in obtaining reliable estimates of unsupervised probabilistic representation models. In turn, the problem of automated feature selection and feature weighting in the context of unsupervised learning is challenging, because there is no known target to guide the search. In this paper we propose and study a relatively simple cluster-based generative model for multivariate binary data, equipped with automated feature weighting capability. Empirical results on both synthetic and real data sets are given and discussed.

1 Introduction

In text mining tasks, such as Information Retrieval (IR), classification and clustering, text data or documents are usually represented as high-dimensional vectors over a global vocabulary (a bag of words). This representation brings the problem of high dimensionality and in addition, the observation features may be of uneven importance. However, high dimensionality and uninformative features typically deteriorate the performance of machine learning methods.

A lot of research has been devoted to dimensionality reduction, feature selection and feature weighting techniques for high-dimensional data, such as text [2–4]. This is, how to decide which attributes of the data are relevant or important under some criterion. However, these works consider a supervised setting, namely text classification. In this case, class labels are available and these can be used in the formulation of a criterion for selecting good features. Information Gain (IG) and Mutual Information (MI) are widespread term-goodness criteria that work well with text classification [3, 5]. However class labels are indispensable.

Clustering is arguably the most important unsupervised learning problem, the goal of which is to discover a natural grouping in a set of patterns or points without knowledge of any class labels. Class labels are not given, at the same time not all features are important, some features may be redundant, some may even harm the clarity of the structure in the data.

M. Gallagher, J. Hogan, and F. Maire (Eds.): IDEAL 2005, LNCS 3578, pp. 40–47, 2005.
© Springer-Verlag Berlin Heidelberg 2005

Filter methods such as principal component analysis (PCA) [11], factor analysis and random projection [10] select features prior to clustering. They are in fact dimensionality reduction methods involving some kind of feature transformation prior to clustering. However, these are completely unrelated to the clustering objective.

There are very few approaches that build feature assessment as an integral part of an unsupervised objective. Law *et al.* [1] estimated feature saliency by modeling relevant features as conditionally independent Gaussians given the class variable, while common features are assumed to be identically distributed for all clusters. Due to the Gaussian building block, this is not directly applicable to discrete data such as text. Dy and Brodley [8] introduced a wrapper framework incorporating model selection with feature selection by a cross-projection criterion normalisation scheme. Vaithyanathan and Dom [9] construct a hierarchical model by making assumptions that noise and useful features are conditionally independent and all parameter sets are independent on each level. In fact these two assumptions are rather limited. The hierarchical aspect models by Barnard *et al.*[6], closely related to Hofmann's Cluster-Abstraction Model (CAM) [7], propose that components are modeled by the horizontal structure while features are modeled by the vertical structure (aspects). They don't consider this model for analysing the individual data attributes however.

We propose a generative model for cluster-based feature analysis, specifically formulated for multivariate binary data. There is no previous work in this setting. Binary data arises in several domains including those where digital repositories are involved. Our model is in principle somewhat related to both [1] and [6], however it is simpler than those. The selection of a common distribution component is assumed to depend neither on the cluster index as in [6] nor on the features themselves as in [1]. Under this simplified framework, a multivariate Bernoulli is employed as a discrete data representation. The data conditions which favour good generalisation are systematically examined. Empirical results are given on both synthetic and real data, showing that the algorithm is able to find uninformative attributes simultaneously with clustering the data.

2   Model Formulation

2.1   Notation

Let y_n denote a T-dimensional multivariate binary observation, and y_{tn} its t-th component, $t = 1, \cdots, T$. θ_k is the set of parameters of the k-th of K cluster components of the model, further λ denotes a common component. The probability that an observation comes from any of the K clusters is denoted by ρ, and $\alpha_1, \ldots, \alpha_K$ will denote the individual prior probabilities of these clusters. Let $\Theta \equiv \{\alpha_1, \ldots, \alpha_K, \theta_1, \ldots, \theta_K, \lambda, \rho\}$ denote the full parameter set.

2.2   Model

The proposed model assumes the following generative process for each data point y_n:

1. Choose $z_n \sim$ Multinomial $(\boldsymbol{\alpha})$;
2. For each of the T features w_t:
   - Choose $\phi \sim$ Bernoulli (ρ);
   - If $\phi = 1$, choose either a presence (1) or an absence (0) event for w_t from $\theta_{tk} \equiv P(y_{tn}|z_n, \phi = 1)$; Else $(\phi = 0)$ from $\lambda_t \equiv P(y_{tn}|z_n, \phi = 0)$.

The likelihood of a datum point $\boldsymbol{y}_n$ under the above model is the following:

$$p(\boldsymbol{y}_n|\boldsymbol{\Theta}) = \sum_{k=1}^{K} \alpha_k \prod_{t=1}^{T} p(y_{tn}|\boldsymbol{\Theta})$$

$$= \sum_{k=1}^{K} \alpha_k \prod_{t=1}^{T} \left[\rho\theta_{tk}^{y_{tn}} (1 - \theta_{tk})^{1-y_{tn}} + (1 - \rho)\lambda_t^{y_{tn}} (1 - \lambda_t)^{1-y_{tn}} \right] \quad (1)$$

2.3   Model Estimation

For estimating (1), the EM algorithm is used. This produces a sequence of estimates using the two alternating steps below.

- E-step: the posteriors, that is the expected value of the latent variables $(z_n$ and $\phi)$ associated with each observation given the current parameter estimates are calculated

$$r_{kn} \equiv P(z_n = k|\boldsymbol{y}_n)$$

$$\propto \alpha_k \prod_{t=1}^{T} \left[\rho\theta_{tk}^{y_{tn}} (1 - \theta_{tk})^{(1-y_{tn})} + (1 - \rho)\lambda_t^{y_{tn}} (1 - \lambda_t)^{(1-y_{tn})} \right] \quad (2)$$

$$r_{tkn} \equiv P(z_n = k, \phi = 1|y_{tn})$$

$$= \frac{\rho\theta_{tk}^{y_{tn}} (1 - \theta_{tk})^{(1-y_{tn})}}{\rho\theta_{tk}^{y_{tn}} (1 - \theta_{tk})^{(1-y_{tn})} + (1 - \rho)\lambda_t^{y_{tn}} (1 - \lambda_t)^{(1-y_{tn})}} \times r_{kn} \quad (3)$$

$$r'_{tkn} \equiv P(z_n = k, \phi = 0|y_{tn}) = r_{kn} - r_{tkn}$$

- M-step: the parameters are re-estimated as follows,

$$\hat{\alpha}_k = \frac{\sum_n r_{kn}}{\sum_{nk} r_{kn}} = \frac{\sum_n r_{kn}}{N} \propto \sum_n r_{kn} \quad (4)$$

$$\hat{\theta}_{tk} = \frac{\sum_n y_{tn} r_{tkn}}{\sum_n r_{tkn}} \quad (5)$$

$$\hat{\lambda}_t = \frac{\sum_n y_{tn} \sum_k r'_{tkn}}{\sum_{nk} r'_{tkn}} = \frac{\sum_n y_{tn} - \sum_k \sum_n y_{tn} r_{tkn}}{N - \sum_n \sum_k r_{tkn}} \quad (6)$$

$$\hat{\rho} = \frac{\sum_n \sum_k \sum_t r_{tkn}}{\sum_n \sum_k \sum_t (r_{tkn} + r'_{tkn})} = \frac{\sum_n \sum_k \sum_t r_{tkn}}{N \times T} \quad (7)$$

2.4   Feature Saliency Definition

Here, feature saliency is defined as the probability of a feature being informative for clustering, averaged over N data points:

$$\frac{1}{N}\sum_{n=1}^{N} P(\phi = 1|y_{tn}) = \frac{1}{N}\sum_{n=1}^{N}\sum_{k=1}^{K} r_{tkn} \tag{8}$$

Algorithm analysis and efficiency. Similarly to all other Bernoulli mixtures, the scaling of the algorithm is $O(N \times T \times K)$. The algorithm has some limitations, one is that the ρ may be over-estimated because in general, it is easier to explain the distribution of a feature by a mixture rather than a single common distribution. Secondly, it may inherit the limitation of mixture models, whose impressive performance is restricted to low dimensional data. A more thorough experimental study is presented in the sequel.

3   Experiments

3.1   Results on Synthetic Data

We generated several synthetic data sets of varying size and varying proportion of uninformative features. In each generated data set, 4 clusters were present, over a vocabulary of 100 features.

Structure identification. In this experiment, 100 data points have been generated over 100 features, out of which 60 are uninformative. To avoid local optima, the model estimation was repeated 40 times and the estimated model with the best in-sample log likelihood was selected. Fig.1 shows the estimated feature saliencies – indeed the 40 informative features, that define the four true clusters, have been identified. It can also be seen that the frequency of occurrences in the original data set would have been misleading for determining which features are important. Further, for completeness, different densities of 1-s in the uninformative features from 0.2 to 0.8 were also tested, all provided similar satisfactory results.

Generalisation. Here we use the out-of-sample data likelihood as a criterion. This is a measure of how good a probabilistic model is in terms of estimating the probability of the data under the assumption that the model is the true generator of both the training data and the testing data.

In this experiment, datasets of the same vocabulary size but varying proportion of uninformative features, and varying training size are generated. Further, at the generation, $K = 4$, vocab_size=100, the proportion of uninformative features ranges across $0.2, 0.4, 0.6, 0.8$.

- *Large training set*: This dataset contains $N = 10,000$ points. A number of 7,000 of the total points are used for training, the remaining 3,000 are for testing. Out-of-sample likelihood, as calculated on testing data, is shown in the right plot of Fig.2.

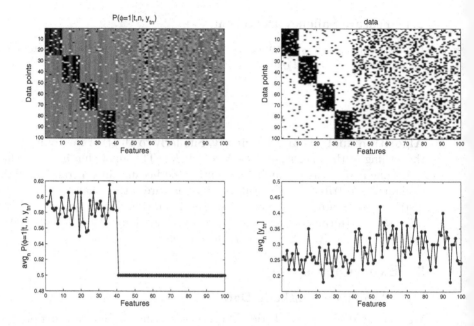

Fig. 1. The upper left plot is the posterior probability of informativeness for each observation y_{tn}. Darker means higher probability. The lower left plot is the Feature Saliency of each feature computed by averaging $P(\phi = 1|t, n, y_{tn})$ over data points. The upper right plot is the data itself containing clear structures as well as uninformative features. The lower right plot is the average frequency of presences of each feature across the data points

- *Medium and small training set*: The setting is similar to that in the previous experiment, but the number of points is, 1,000 and 100 respectively. Ten fold cross-validation is used. Mean±1 standard error are reported vs. different model orders and these can be seen in the middle and left plots of Fig.2 respectively.

Observations from the experiment. From the comparative assessment of the proposed approach with a simple Bernoulli mixture, we see that both models are able to recognize the correct number of clusters, except in the case when too few data points are available. On the large training set, the performance of these two models is comparable. On medium size training set, the advantage of the proposed approach becomes noticeable and the difference in performance becomes statistically significant in the experiment with the small sample size. So it appears that the proposed model has the potential to handle the limited training data settings better than the simple mixture. When training data is abundant, the proposed model may not have any advantage in terms of generalisation, however, as we have seen earlier, its built-in feature-weighting mechanism offers an additional data explanatory ability that simple mixtures do not have.

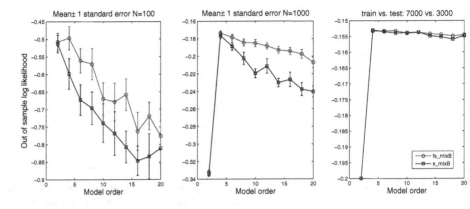

Fig. 2. Comparison of generalisation performance of the proposed model (fs_mixB) and simple Bernoulli mixture (s_mixB), on generated data sets of varying size

3.2   Results on Real Data

Generalisation. Two binary data sets are chosen for testing the proposed model on real data.

- *5 Newsgroups*: We apply the model on text document data from five newsgroups of the 20 Newsgroups corpus[1]: alt.atheism, sci.crypt, sci.med, sci.space and soc.religion. christian. 3,750 documents over a vocabulary of 1,218 words were taken. These documents were indexed by removing stop words and applying Porter Stemming. Infrequent terms were also removed. The data has been split into a training set of 3,250 documents and an independent test set of 1,500 documents.
- *Advertisement data*[2]: This data was collected to predict whether or not images are advertisements. Each data point represents an image. The data for our experiment consists of 3,279 images over 1,554 binary attributes. This is split into a training set of 1,640 and a test set of 1,639 instances.

As we can see from Fig.3, the proposed model outperforms the simple Bernoulli mixture on both these data sets. Indeed, from the data characteristics it is clear that we have relatively sparse training set in both real cases, compared to the dimensionality of the data. Also we have noticed that in both cases the out-of-sample data likelihood of the two models peak at a model order higher than the true number of components. Finally, it can be noticed that the difference in performance appears to be greater in the case of the Adverts data, compared to that observed on the Newsgroups data set. In the light of the observations made from the synthetic data experiments, this may be caused by the smaller training set size in the case of the Adverts data.

---

[1] Available from http://www.cs.cmu.edu/~textlearning
[2] Available from UCI machine learning repository

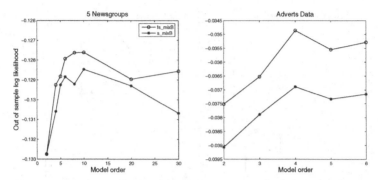

Fig. 3. Comparison of generalisation performance on real data: 5 newsgroups and adverts data. In both cases, the proposed model performs better than the simple mixture of Bernoulli

Finding non-discriminative terms. Now, we apply the model on a small text document collection in order to visually illustrate in more details the workings of our approach on text data. We use four newsgroups of the 20 Newsgroups corpus: sci.crypt, sci.med, sci.space and soc.religion. christian. In this experiment, there are 384 documents over a dictionary of 100 terms selected with the aid of class labels, using Infogain feature selection.

It can be seen from the Fig.4 that most of the 100 features are found to be informative, even though, some less informative terms can also be recognised. The top 10 most uninformative term presences selected by our algorithm are: peopl, word, system, accept, space, faith, love, agre, kei, comput, govern. Obviously, words such as people, system can appear in any topic and are not necessarily specific to just one.

It can also be noted, that interestingly, for text data, in average, term presences have been found more informative than term absences (See Fig.4, lower left, first two plots). This is a novel insight that motivates the study of event models that concentrate on term presences only, such as the multinomial event model. There are also uninformative term absences, meaning terms whose omission is not due to the topical content.

4   Conclusions and Future Work

We have presented a simple cluster based generative model for multivariate binary data, equipped with automated feature weighting capability. The model is able to improve over the Bernoulli mixture model in the case of two medium size real-world data sets considered. A number of extensions are currently under study. The combination of feature selection with model selection will be investigated in the future. Comparisons with a multinomial version of the model for ad-hoc retrieval and classifications are also underway. Finally, the extension of the model by introducing a continuous (Dirichlet) prior will hopefully endow the proposed model with the ability to deal with really high dimensional data sets.

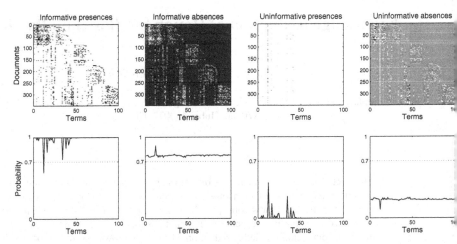

Fig. 4. The Posterior of $P(\phi = 1|y_{tn})$ broken up to presence and absence observations. Darker encodes higher probability. The bottom plots contain the terms of the saliency estimates averaged over data points that contain those presences or absences. The estimated ρ is traced with dotted lines

References

1. M. Law, M. Figueiredo, and A.K.Jain (2004). Simultaneous feature selection and clustering using a mixture model. IEEE Transaction on Pattern Analysis and Machine Intelligence **26** (9), pp. 1154–1166.
2. Daphne Koller, Mehran Sahami (1996). Toward Optimal Feature Selection. Proc. 13-th International Conference on Machine Learning (ICML-96), pp. 284–292.
3. Yiming Yang and Jan O. Pedersen (1997). A comparative study on feature selection in text categorization. Proc. ICML-97, pp. 412–420.
4. David D. Lewis, Feature Selection and Feature Extraction for Text Categorization (1992). Proc. of Speech and Natural Language Workshop, pp. 212–217.
5. Tao Liu, Shengping Liu, Zheng Chen and Wei-Ying Ma (2003). An Evaluation on Feature Selection for Text Clustering. Proc. ICML-2003.
6. Kobus Barnard, Pinar Duygulu, Nando de Freitas, David Forsyth, David Blei and Michael I. Jordan (2003). Matching Words and Pictures. Journal of Machine Learning Research 3, pp. 1107–1135.
7. T. Hofmann. The cluster-abstraction model: Unsupervised learning of topic hierarchies from text data (1999). In Proceedings of 16th International Joint Conference on Artificial Intelligence IJCAI-99, pp. 682–687.
8. Jennifer G. Dy and Carla E. Brodley (2004). Feature Selection for Unsupervised Learning. Journal of Machine Learning Research 5, pp. 845–889.
9. S. Vaithyanathan and B. Dom (2000). Model-based hierarchical clustering. Proc. of 6-th Conf. on Uncertainty in Artificial Intelligence, pp. 599–608.
10. Dmitriy Fradkin and David Madigan (2003). Experiments with random projections for machine learning. Proc. of the 9-th ACM SIGKDD Int. Conf. on Knowledge Discovery and Data Mining, pp. 517–522.
11. George H, Dunteman (1989). Principal components analysis (Quantitative Applications in the Social Sciences Series, No. 69). Sage Publications.

Knowledge Reduction of Rough Set Based on Partition

Xiaobing Pei and Yuanzhen Wang

Department of computer science, HuaZhong University of Science & Technology,
Wuhan, Hubei 430074, China
xiaobingp@tom.com

Abstract. Knowledge reduction is one of the basic contents in rough set theory and one of the most problem in knowledge acquisition. The main objective of this paper is to introduce a new concept of knowledge reduction based on partition. It is referred to as partition reduction. The partition reduction is to unify the definitions of classical knowledge reductions. Classical knowledge reductions such as absolute attribute reduction, relative reduction, distribution reduction, assignment reduction and maximum distribution reduction are special cases of partition reduction. We can establish new types of knowledge reduction to meet our requirements based on partition reduction.

1 Introduction

The rough set theory, which was first proposed by professor Pawlak in 1982, is an excellent mathematics tool to handle imprecise and uncertain information. It has been successfully applied in many fields such as data mining, decision support etc [2–4].

Knowledge reduction is one of the major concerns in research on rough set theory and one of the most problems in knowledge acquisition. It is well known that an information system or a decision table may usually have irrelevant and superfluous knowledge, which is inconvenient for us to get concise and meaningful decision. When reducing attributes, we should eliminate the irrelevant and superfluous knowledge without losing essential information about the original data in information system. Nowadays many types of knowledge reduction have been proposed, such as attribute reduction [1–4], relative reduction [1–4], distribution reduction [5], assignment reduction [5], maximum distribution reduction [6] and VPRS [7] etc. Attribute reduction, relative reduction, distribution reduction, assignment reduction and maximum distribution reduction are most common types of knowledge reduction, which have been studied by many researchers. Many good results have been obtained [3–10], but there are limitations in these works as follows: they did not unify the measure of classification ability and the definition of the concepts with respect to classical knowledge reductions.

The main objective of this paper is to unify the measure of classification ability and present a general method for establishing new types of knowledge reductions. Therefore we introduce a new concept of knowledge reduction based on partition, called partition reduction. The partition reduction is to unify the concept of classical knowledge reductions, from which we can establish new types of knowledge reductions to meet our requirements based on partition reduction.

M. Gallagher, J. Hogan, and F. Maire (Eds.): IDEAL 2005, LNCS 3578, pp. 48–55, 2005.

2   Basic Concepts of Rough Set Theory

In this section, we introduce only the basic notations from rough set approach used in the paper.

An information system S is defined as follows: S=<U, A, V, f>, where A is a set of attributes, $U=\{x_1, x_2, ..., x_n\}$ is a non-empty finite set of objects called universe. $V=\bigcup_{a\in A} V_a$, and V_a is value set of attribute a. f: $U\times A\rightarrow V$ is a total function such that $f(x_i, a)\in V_a$ for each $a\in A$, $x_i\in U$.

Any subset B of A defines a binary relation ind(B) on U, which will be called an indiscernibility relation and is defined as below: ind(B)=$\{(x,y): f(x, a_k)=f(y, a_k)$, $\forall a_k\in B\}$.

It can be seen that ind(B) is an equivalence relation. Thus U/ind(B) is a set of equivalence classes as defined below: U/ind(B)=$\{[x]_B : x\in U\}$, where $[x]_B=\{y: (x,y)\in ind(B)\}$ is a equivalence class for an example x with respect to concept B.

Any attribute subset $B\subseteq A$ and any objects subset $X\subseteq U$. The B-lower approximation and the B-upper approximation of X are defined respectively as follows: $B_*(X)=\bigcup\{Y\in U/ind(B) \mid Y\subseteq X\}$, $B^*(X)=\bigcup\{Y\in U/ind(B) \mid Y\cap X\neq \Phi\}$.

$bnd_B(X)=B_*(X)-B^*(X)$ is called the B-boundary region of X.

We say B is an absolute attribute reduction on U if and only if the following conditions are satisfied:

(1) ind(B)=ind(A); (2) $\forall b\in B$, follows that ind(B-{b})$\neq$ ind(B);

Let P and Q be attribute sets, the P-positive region of Q is denoted by POS$_P$(Q), and is defined as: POS$_P$(Q)= $\bigcup_{X\in U/ind(Q)} P_*(X)$

We say $R\subseteq P$ is a reduction of P relative to Q iff the following conditions are satisfied:(1)POS$_R$(Q)=POS$_P$(Q);(2) $\forall r\in R$, follows that POS$_{R-\{r\}}$(Q)$\neq$ POS$_R$(Q);

The mark RED$_Q$(P) denotes the reductions set of P relative to Q.

Let S=<U,A,V,f> be an information system, A=C$\bigcup$D, where C and D are condition attributes set and decision attributes set respectively, U/ind(D)=$\{D_1, D_2, ..., D_r\}$, for any x$\in$ U, we denote

(1) $\mu_C(x)=\{P(D_1 /[x]_C), P(D_2 /[x]_C), ..., P(D_r /[x]_C)\}$; (2) $\gamma_C(x)=\{D_k : P(D_k /[x]_C)=Max\{P(D_j /[x]_C), j=1,2,...,r\}\}$; (3) $\eta_C(x)=\{D_j : D_j \cap [x]_C \neq \Phi\}$;

where $P(D_j /[x]_C)=\dfrac{|D_j \cap [x]_C|}{|[x]_C|}$.

Let B be attributes subset of attributes C: (1)if $\mu_C(x)=\mu_B(x)$ for any x$\in$ U, we say that B is a distribution consistent set of <U,A,V,f>. If B is a distribution consistent set, and no proper subset of B is distribution consistent set, then B is referred to as a distribution reduction of <U,A,V,f>. (2)If $\gamma_C(x) = \gamma_B(x)$ for any x∈ U, we say that B is a maximum distribution consistent set of <U,A,V,f>. If B is a maximum distribution consistent set, and no proper subset of B is maximum distribution consistent set, then B is referred to as a maximum distribution reduction of <U,A,V,f>. (3)If $\eta_C(x)=\eta_B(x)$ for any x∈ U, we say that B is a assignment consistent set of <U,A,V,f>. If B is a assignment consistent set, and no proper subset of B is assignment consistent set, then B is referred to as a assignment reduction of <U,A,V,f>.

3   Partition Reduction

From the above discussion, rough set theory gives a method to use the subset to express the set. Therefore, we think the most natural definition of the rough sets is expressed with partition. The following is the definition.

Definition 1: Let S =<U, A, V, f> be an information system, $U_1, U_2, ..., U_m$ is a U's partition, defined as follows:

$$1. U_k \cap U_t = \Phi \, (k \neq t),; \, 2. U = \bigcup_{i=1}^{m} U_i \,; 3.\text{if}(x,y) \in \text{ind}(A) \text{ and } x \in U_k \text{ then } y \in U_k.$$

It is easy to conclude that U/μ_C, U/γ_C and U/η_C are partitions on U respectively, where U/μ_C={$[x]_{\mu_C}$: x∈ U}, $[x]_{\mu_C}$ ={y: $\mu_C(x)=\mu_C(y)$, y∈ U }; U/γ_C={$[x]_{\gamma_C}$: x∈ U}, $[x]_{\gamma_C}$ ={y: $\gamma_C(x) = \gamma_C(y)$, y∈ U }; U/$\eta_C$ ={$[x]_{\eta_C}$: x∈ U}, $[x]_{\eta_C}$ ={y: $\eta_C(x)=\eta_C(y)$, y∈ U }.

Definition 2: Let S=<U, A, V, f> be an information system, C is a attribute subset of A, $U_1, U_2, ..., U_m$ is a U's partition. Let R be a attribute subset of C, if 1)f(x, R) ≠ f(y, R) for any x∈ U_k , y∈ U_t (k ≠ t); 2)for any a∈ R, there exist x∈ U_k , y∈ U_t (k ≠ t) such that f(x, R-{a})=f(y, R-{a}), then it can be said that R is a partition reduction of U_1, U_2, ..., U_m with respect to concept C.

There may be more than one partition reductions of U_1, U_2, ..., U_m with respect to concept A.

Remark 1: f(x, R) = (f(x, r_1),f(x, r_2),..., f(x, $r_{|R|}$)), where R={$r_1, r_2, ..., r_{|R|}$ }.

Proposition   1: Let   S=<U,A,V,f>   be   an   information   system, U/ind(A)={$U_1, U_2, ..., U_m$ }is a U's partition, the set of all partition reductions of {$U_1, U_2, ..., U_m$ } with respect to concept A is denoted by $PRED$, the set of all absolute attribute reductions on U is denoted by $ARED$ .Then $PRED = ARED$.

Proof: If $\alpha \in PRED$ then $f(x, \alpha) \neq f(y, \alpha)$ for any $x \in U_k$, $y \in U_t$ $(k \neq t)$, so we can conclude that U/ind(α)=U/ind(A). Suppose that there is a $\in \alpha$ such that U/ind(α-{a})=U/ind(A), then we have $f(x, \alpha -\{a\}) \neq f(y, \alpha -\{a\})$ for any $x \in U_k$, $y \in U_t$ $(k \neq t)$, which contradicts $\alpha \in PRED$. Thus we conclude U/ind(α-{a})$\neq$U/ind(A) for any a$\in \alpha$, that is $\alpha \in ARED$.

On the other hand, if $\beta \in ARED$ then U/ind(β)=U/ind(A), that is $f(x, \beta) \neq f(y, \beta)$ for any $x \in U_k$, $y \in U_t$ $(k \neq t)$. Suppose that there is a$\in \beta$ such that $f(x, \beta -\{a\}) \neq f(y, \beta -\{a\})$ for any $x \in U_k$, $y \in U_t$ $(k \neq t)$, then U/ind(β-{a})=U/ind(A), which contradicts $\beta \in ARED$. Therefore there are $x \in U_k$, $y \in U_t$ $(k \neq t)$ such that $f(x, \beta -\{a\})=f(y, \beta -\{a\})$ for any a$\in \beta$, that is $\beta \in PRED$.

Thus we conclude that $PRED = ARED$. □

Proposition 2: Let S=<U,A,V,f> be an information system, $P \subseteq A$, $Q \subseteq A$, U/ind(Q)=$\{Q_1, Q_2, ...Q_m\}$, $\{$U-POS$_P(Q), B_*(Q_1), B_*(Q_2), ... B_*(Q_m)\}$ is a U's partition. Let U_0=U-POS$_P(Q)$, $U_i = B_*(Q_i)(1 \leq i \leq m)$, $PRED$ denotes the set of all partition reductions of $\{U_1, U_2, ..., U_m\}$ with respect to concept P, RED$_Q(P)$ denotes the set of all relative reductions of P relative to Q. Then $PRED = RED_Q(P)$.

Proof: If $\alpha \in PRED$ then $f(x, \alpha) \neq f(y, \alpha)$ for any $x \in U_k$, $y \in U_t$ $(k \neq t)$, So we conclude that POS$_\alpha(Q)=$POS$_P(Q)$. Suppose that there exist a$\in \alpha$ such that POS$_{\alpha-\{a\}}(Q)=$POS$_P(Q)$, then $f(x, \alpha -\{a\}) \neq f(y, \alpha -\{a\})$for any $x \in U_k$, $y \in U_t$ $(k \neq t)$, which contradicts $\alpha \in PRED$. Thus we conclude that POS$_{\alpha-\{a\}}(Q) \neq$ POS$_P(Q)$, that is $\alpha \in$ RED$_Q(P)$.

On the other hand, if $\beta \in$ RED$_Q(P)$, then POS$_\beta(Q)=$ POS$_P(Q)$, that is $f(x, \beta) \neq f(y, \beta)$ for any $x \in U_k$, $y \in U_t$ $(k \neq t)$. Suppose that there is a$\in \beta$ such that $f(x, \beta -\{a\}) \neq f(y, \beta -\{a\})$ for any $x \in U_k$, $y \in U_t$ $(k \neq t)$, hence we have POS$_{\beta-\{a\}}(Q)=$POS$_P(Q)$, which contradicts $\beta \in$ RED$_Q(P)$. Thus $\forall$ a$\in \beta$, follows that there are $x \in U_k$, $y \in U_t$ $(k \neq t)$ such that $f(x, \beta -\{a\})=f(y, \beta -\{a\})$, that is that $\beta \in PRED$.

Therefore we conclude that $PRED = RED_Q(P)$. □

By the same method as proof proposition 1, we have the proposition as follows:

Proposition 3: Let S=<U,A,V,f> be an information system, A=C$\bigcup$D, where C and D are condition attributes and decision attributes respectively.

(1) $U / \gamma_C = \{U_1, U_2, ..., U_m\}$ is a U's partition, the set of all partition reductions of $\{U_1, U_2, ..., U_m\}$ with respect to concept C is denoted by $PRED$, the set of all maximum distribution reductions of <U,A,V,f> is denoted by $MRED$. Then $PRED = MRED$.

(2) $U / \mu_C = \{U_1, U_2, ..., U_m\}$ is a U's partition, the set of all partition reductions of $\{U_1, U_2, ..., U_m\}$ with respect to concept C is denoted by $PRED$, the set of all distribution reductions of <U,A,V,f> is denoted by $DRED$. Then $PRED = DRED$.

(3) $U / \eta_C = \{U_1, U_2, ..., U_m\}$ is a U's partition, the set of all partition reductions of $\{U_1, U_2, ..., U_m\}$ with respect to concept C is denoted by $PRED$, the set of all assignment reductions of <U,A,V,f> is denoted by $ARED$. Then $PRED = ARED$.

By proposition 1, 2, and proposition 3, we conclude that attribute reduction, relative reduction, distribution reduction, assignment reduction and maximum distribution reduction are special cases of partition reduction, and they are the measure of classification abilities with respect to concrete U's partition. It shows that the concept of partition reduction in this paper is valuable and it extends the classical knowledge reductions. In other words, partition reduction is uniform description of measure of classification abilities and definition of the concept with respect to classical knowledge reduction.

As partition reduction is a measure of classification abilities for any U's partitions, we can choose appropriate partitions to obtain a type of knowledge reduction that we need according to our requirement. Now we will present a method for establishing a new type of knowledge reduction as follows:

Algorithm 1: establish a new type of knowledge reduction
 1. Calculate U's partition according to user's requirements;
 2. The partition reduction of $\{U_1, U_2, ..., U_m\}$ is a new type of knowledge reduction.

4   Calculation Method for Partition Reduction

In this section, we will give the calculation method for partition reduction.

Definition 3: Let S=<U,A,V,f> be an information system, where $U = \{x_0, x_1, \Lambda, x_{n-1}\}$ is a non-empty finite set of objects, $A = \{a_1, \Lambda, a_m\}$ is a set of attribute, C is a attribute subset of A, Par=$\{U_1, U_2, ..., U_m\}$ is a U's partition. We denote:

$$D_{ij} = \begin{cases} \{a : f(x_i, a) \neq f(x_j, a), a \in C\}, there.is.no.U_k such.that.x_i, x_j \in U_k. \\ \Phi, otherwise \end{cases}$$

Then D_{ij} is referred to as discernibility attributes set of x_i and x_j, $D=[D_{ij}]$ is referred to as to partition discernibility matrix of partition $\{U_1, U_2, ..., U_m\}$, with respect to concept C.

We denote $M = \bigwedge_{i,j} \{\vee\{a_k : a_k \in D_{ij}\}\}, i, j \leq n$.

Then M is referred to as partition discernibility function with respect partition discernibility matrix D.

Theorem 1: Let S=<U,A,V,f> be an information system, $U_1, U_2, ..., U_m$ is a U's partition, $B \subseteq C \subseteq A$. Let $D=[D_{ij}]$ be partition discernibility matrix of partition $\{U_1, U_2, ..., U_m\}$ with respect to concept C, then for any $x \in U_k, y \in U_t$ ($k \neq t$), f(x, B) $\neq$ f(y, B) is satisfied $\Leftrightarrow D_{ij} \cap B \neq \Phi$ (where $D_{ij} \neq \Phi$).

Proof: Suppose that there exist $D_{ij} \neq \Phi$ such that $D_{ij} \cap B = \Phi$, then there are $x \in U_k$, $y \in U_t$ ($k \neq t$) such that $\{a \mid f(x,a) \neq f(y,a), a \in A\} \cap B = \Phi$, we have f(x, B)=f(y, B),which contradicts f(x,B) $\neq$ f(y,B) for any $x \in U_k, y \in U_t$ ($k \neq t$). Thus we can conclude that $D_{ij} \cap B \neq \Phi$ for any $D_{ij} \neq \Phi$.

Suppose that there are $x \in U_k$, $y \in U_t$ ($k \neq t$) such that f(x, B)=f(y, B). Denotes d={a $\mid$ f(x, a) $\neq$ f(y, a), a $\in$ A }, hence d $\cap$ B= Φ,which contradicts $D_{ij} \cap B \neq \Phi$ for any $D_{ij} \neq \Phi$. Thus we conclude that f(x, B) $\neq$ f(y, B) for any $x \in U_k, y \in U_t$ ($k \neq t$).

Theorem 2: Let S =<U,A,V,f> be an information system, $U_1, U_2, ..., U_m$ is a U's partition $C \subseteq A$. Let $D=[D_{ij}]$ be partition discernibility matrix of partition $\{U_1, U_2, ..., U_m\}$ with respect to concept C, M be partition discernibility function with respect to $[D_{ij}]$. The minimal disjunctive normal form of discernibility function M is

$$M = \bigvee_{k=1}^{r} (\bigwedge_{s=1}^{q_k} a_{ks}).$$ We denote $R_k = \{a_{ks} : s=1, ..., q_k\}$, then $\{R_k : k=1, ..., r\}$ are just the set of all partition reductions of $\{U_1, U_2, ..., U_m\}$ with respect to C.

Proof: It follows directly from theorem 1 and the definition of minimal disjunctive normal forms of the discernibility functions.

From the above discussion, we will present algorithm for the set of all partition reductions as follows:

Algorithm 2:

1. Calculate partition discernibility matrix $D=[D_{ij}]$ of partition $\{U_1, U_2, ..., U_m\}$;

2. Calculate partition discernibility function $M = \bigwedge_{i,j} \{\vee\{a_k : a_k \in D_{ij}\}\}, i, j \leq n$;

3. Calculate minimal disjunctive normal form $M = \bigvee_{k=1}^{r} (\bigwedge_{s=1}^{q_k} a_{ks})$;

4. Output partition reductions of $\{U_1, U_2, \ldots, U_m\}$ with respect to concept C;

Example 1: Consider the following information system in table 1, A=\{a, b, c, d\}, U=\{#1,#2,#3,#4,#5,#6\}, $\{U_1 = \{\#1, \#2\}, U_2 = \{\#3, \#4\}, U_3 = \{\#5, \#6\}\}$ is a U's partition:

Table 1.

U	a	b	c	D
#1	2	2	0	1
#2	1	2	0	0
#3	1	2	0	1
#4	0	0	0	0
#5	1	0	1	0
#6	2	0	1	1

The partition discernibility matrix of partition $\{U_1, U_2, U_3\}$ is

$$
D=[D_{ij}]=
\begin{vmatrix}
0 & & & & & \\
0 & 0 & & & & \\
a & d & 0 & & & \\
a,b,d & a,b & 0 & 0 & & \\
a,b,c,d & b,c & b,c,d & a,c & 0 & \\
b,c & a,b,c,d & a,b,c & a,c,d & 0 & 0
\end{vmatrix}.
$$

Then, $M = \bigwedge_{i,j}(\vee D_{ij}) = a \wedge d \wedge (b \vee c)$, it represents the fact that only attributes a, d and one of b or c is required to discern partitioned objects.

Thus, both \{a, d, b\} and \{a, d, c\} are all partition reductions of $\{U_1, U_2, U_3\}$.

5 Conclusions

In this paper, a new concept of knowledge reduction is introduced, which is referred to as partition reduction, and the calculation method for partition reduction is obtained. The partition reduction is to unify the definitions of concept of classical knowledge reductions. Classical knowledge reduction such as attribute reduction, relative reduction, distribution reduction, assignment reduction and maximum distribution reduction are special cases of partition reduction. We can establish new types of knowledge reduction to meet our requirements based on partition reduction.

References

1. Pawlak Z.Rough sets,.International Journal of Computer and Information Science, 11(5)(1982): 341-356
2. Skowron A,Rauszer C, 1992. The discernibility matrics and function in information system.In: Slowinski R ed.Intelligent Decision Support Handbook of Application and Advances of the Rough sets Theory.Dordreecht:Kluwer Academic Publishers.331-362

3. Liu Q. Rough Set and Rough Reasoning.Beijing, 2001: Science Press.
4. Zhang W. X. etc. Rough set Theory and Methods.Beijing (2001) Science Press.
5. Kryszkiewicz M..Comparative studies of alternative type of knowledge reduction in inconsistent systems.International Journal of Intelligent Systems, 16(1), 2001:105–120
6. Zhang wenxiu etc. Knowledge reduction in inconsistent information systems, Chinese journal of compuers, 26(1),2003:12-18
7. M. Beynon. Reducts within the variable precision rough sets model: a further investigation, European Journal of Operational Research 134, 2001:592 – 605.
8. Wang Jue,Wang Ren,Miao Duo-Qian et al.Data Enriching based on rough set theory.Chinese Journal of Computer, 21(5),1998:393-395
9. Liu Shao-hui etc..Research on Efficient Algorithms for Rough Set Methods.Chinese Journal of Computers, 26(5),2003: 524-529
10. Wang J.,Wang J.. Reduction algorithm based on discernibility matrix:The ordered attributes method. Journal of Computer Science & Technology, 16(6),2001:489–504

Multiresolution Analysis of Connectivity

Atul Sajjanhar[1], Guojun Lu[2], Dengsheng Zhang[2], and Tian Qi[3]

[1] School of Information Technology, Deakin University
221 Burwood Highway, Burwood, VIC 3125, Australia
atuls@deakin.edu.au
[2] Gippsland School of Computing & Information Technology
Monash University, Northways Road, Churchill, VIC 3842, Australia
{guojun.lu,dengsheng.zhang}@infotech.monash.edu.au
[3] Media Division, Institute for Infocomm Research
21 Heng Mui Keng Terrace, Singapore 119613
tian@i2r.a-star.edu.sg

Abstract. Multiresolution histograms have been used for indexing and retrieval of images. Multiresolution histograms used traditionally are 2d-histograms which encode pixel intensities. Earlier we proposed a method for decomposing images by *connectivity*. In this paper, we propose to encode centroidal distances of an image in multiresolution histograms; the image is decomposed a priori, by connectivity. Multiresolution histograms thus obtained are 3d-histograms which encode connectivity and centroidal distances. The statistical technique of Principal Component Analysis is applied to multiresolution 3d-histograms and the resulting data is used to index images. Distance between two images is computed as the *L2*-difference of their principal components. Experiments are performed on Item S8 within the MPEG-7 image dataset. We also analyse the effect of pixel intensity thresholding on multiresolution images.

1 Introduction

Multiresolution histogram is a family of histograms obtained for multiple resolutions of an image. Multiresolution histogram overcomes the inability of a single histogram to encode the spatial features of images [7]. Multiresolution histogram of image intensities have been used extensively for retrieval of images and video from visual databases [2][7]. Multiresolution histogram is robust to noise. We use the concept of multiresolution histogram to encode centroidal distances of an image. Centroidal distance histogram is obtained by discretising the centroidal distance of each point in an image into a bucket. Centroidal distance of a point is obtained as the distance of the point from the centroid. Before obtaining centroidal distance histograms, however, images need to be normalised for scale. The method is inherently invariant to rotation and translation. Multiresolution histogram based on centroidal distances is the ground truth against which we compare the proposed approach. Based on the previously proposed concept of *connectivity* [1], we show how multiresolution histograms which encode centroidal distances and connectivity can be used effectively for shape-based retrieval of images. We evaluate the proposed method against the traditional approach (described above) which does not use connectivity. The proposed method is described in Section 2. Experimental Results are presented in Section 3. Finally, Discussion and Conclusion are presented in Sections 4 and 5 respectively.

M. Gallagher, J. Hogan, and F. Maire (Eds.): IDEAL 2005, LNCS 3578, pp. 56–62, 2005.
© Springer-Verlag Berlin Heidelberg 2005

2 Proposed Method

In this section, we describe the proposed method for image retrieval. The proposed method is based on *connectivity* [1]. First, we briefly explain connectivity. Connectivity is used to decompose images based on the state of the nearest 8-neighbour pixels. Consider a sample image shown in Fig. 1(a), we refer to the dark pixels as *OFF*. The state of the nearest 8-neighbours is computed for each *OFF* pixel. Connectivity of an *OFF* pixel is obtained as the number of *OFF* pixels amongst the nearest 8-neighbours. Figure 1(b) provides additional information for the image in Figure 1(a). For each *OFF* pixel within the image, the connectivity can take values 0 through 8. A connectivity of 0 indicates that none of the nearest 8-neighbours are *OFF*. A connectivity of 8 indicates that all of the nearest 8-neighbours are *OFF*.

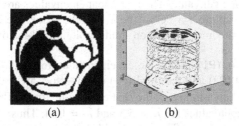

(a)   (b)

Fig. 1. Image decomposition by connectivity

Consider the image in Fig. 1(a); multiresolution images for the image are shown in Fig. 2. These are obtained by convolving the original image with a Gaussian filter. Centroidal distances are obtained for each resolution of an image which is decomposed by connectivity. 3d-histograms are computed which encode centroidal distances and connectivity. Multiresolution histograms h_τ is a family of 3d-histograms for multiple image resolutions τ. Feature vector for an image consists of a family of 3d-histograms. The dimensionality of the feature vector will depend on the number of resolutions used for an image.

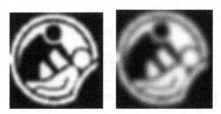

Fig. 2. Multiple resolutions of sample image

Principal Component Analysis (PCA) is a statistical approach for reducing the dimensionality of data [3][4][5]. We apply PCA to feature vectors and the resulting low dimensional data is used to index images. PCA involves a mathematical procedure that transforms a number of (possibly) correlated variables into a (smaller) number of uncorrelated variables called *principal components*. The first principal component accounts for as much of the variability in the data as possible, and each succeeding component accounts for as much of the remaining variability as possible.

We briefly explain the theory behind PCA. Performing PCA is the equivalent of performing Singular Value Decomposition (SVD) on the covariance matrix of the data. Singular value decomposition for the data matrix A is computed as U S V'. Matrices U and V are such that they are orthogonal. The columns of U are called left singular values and the rows of V' are called right singular values. Eigenvectors and eigenvalues of A.A' and A'.A need to be calculated to obtain matrices U and V. Multiplications of A by its transpose results in square matrices. The columns of V are made from the eigenvectors of A'.A and the columns of U are made from the eigenvectors of A.A'. The eigenvalues obtained from the products of A.A' and A'.A, when square-rooted, make up the columns of S. The diagonal of S is said to be the singular values of the original matrix, A. Each eigenvector described above represents a principle component. PC1 (Principle Component 1) is defined as the eigenvector with the highest corresponding eigenvalue. The individual eigenvalues are numerically related to the variance they capture via PC's - the higher the value, the more variance they have captured. The outcome of PCA on multiresolution 3d-histograms for image in Fig. 1 is shown in Fig. 3.

The first eigenvector (P1) has the largest eigenvalues to the direction of the largest variance. The second (P2) and the third (P3) eigenvectors are orthogonal to the first one. In the example shown in Fig. 3, the first eigenvalue for the first eigenvector is λ_1 = 81.65. The other eigenvalues are λ_2 = 5.3 and λ_3 = 1.54. Thus, the first eigenvector contains almost all the energy. The data could thus be approximated in one-dimension.

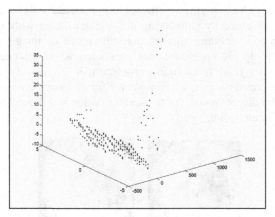

Fig. 3. Principal components of multiresolution histograms

Consider the sample image shown in Fig. 4(a). This image has only two pixel intensities, 0 and 255. Centroidal distances are computed for pixel intensities of 255 only. The corresponding 3d-histogram is shown in Fig. 4(b).

The image in Fig. 5(a) is a Gaussian blurred image and has pixel intensities ranging from 0-255, as shown in Fig. 5(b). The distance histogram in Fig. 5(c) is obtained by computing the centroidal distances for all pixel intensities in the range 1-255; only the black pixels (intensity=0) are ignored.

The pattern in Fig. 5(c) is significantly different from that in Fig. 4(b). This is because of the fineness of the shape [2]. Rates of change of histogram densities are significant for images with fine regions. Hence, we consider pixel intensity *thresholding*. The 3d-histogram when using pixel intensity thresholding is shown in Fig. 5(d). In Fig. 5(d), pixels which have intensity less than 55 are ignored i.e. their centroidal distances do not contribute to the histograms. The generic process of indexing is illustrated in the diagram below.

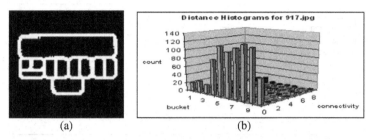

(a)   (b)

Fig. 4. (a) Sample image (b) Distance histogram for Sample Image

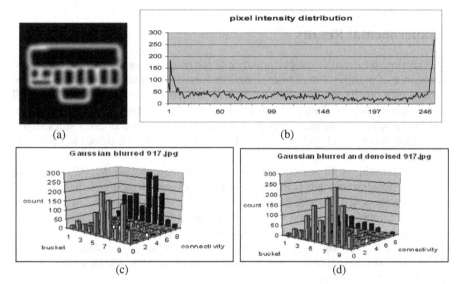

Fig. 5. (a) Image after Gaussian blur (b) Pixel intensity distribution (c) 3d histogram for Gaussian blurred image (d) 3d histogram after pixel intensity thresholding

Multiple resolutions of each image is obtained using Gaussian filters. Each resolution of the image is decomposed by connectivity. The family of 3d-histograms is obtained for each image. Within the histogram family each histogram encodes the connectivity and the centroidal distances for a particular resolution of the original image. The process of obtaining histograms is preceded by pixel intensity thresholding. Pixel intensity thresholding is especially useful for fine shapes which would otherwise have significant rates of change in histogram densities. Principal components are obtained for the histogram family and used as an index for each image. During querying, the distance between two images is computed as the *L2*-difference of their principal components.

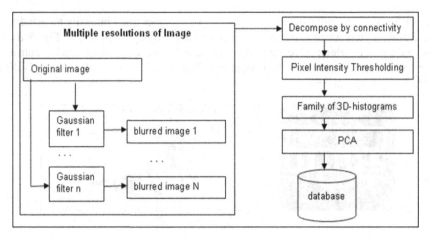

Fig. 6. Image Indexing

3 Experimental Results

In this section, we evaluate the performance of the proposed method. We compare the performance of multiresolution histograms obtained by the traditional method and the proposed method. Experiments are performed on Item S8 within the MPEG-7 Still Images Content Set [6]. This is a collection of trademark images and originally provided by the Korean Industrial Property Office. Item S8 consists of 3621 still images. It is divided into Sets A1, A2, A3, A4 to test the robustness of methods to geometric and perspective transformations.

Fig. 7 below shows the results of retrieval experiments on Sets A1, A2, A3, A4 of the dataset. Experiments are performed for the proposed method and the traditional method. The proposed method, based on connectivity is prefixed with '3d mra' in the legend. The traditional approach which is based on 2d-histograms is prefixed with '2d mra' in the legend. When computing histograms for multiple resolutions of an image, pixel intensity thresholding may be required. Results for Set A1 are obtained with and without pixel intensity thresholding. Results for Sets A2, A3, A4 are obtained after pixel intensity thresholding.

4 Discussion

Improvement of the proposed method when compared with the traditional method is conclusive. The reason for the improvement of the proposed method is attributed to additional information captured by connectivity; descriptors which encode connectivity are able to discriminate better between shapes [1]. We note that the dataset does not contain fine contours. In Fig. 1, we see that the pixel density is high for connectivity=0 and connectivity=8. We believe that the relative improvement in the effectiveness of the proposed method will be more with an increase in pixel densities for intermediate values of connectivity. In the future, we will perform experiments on different datasets to test the veracity of the statement above.

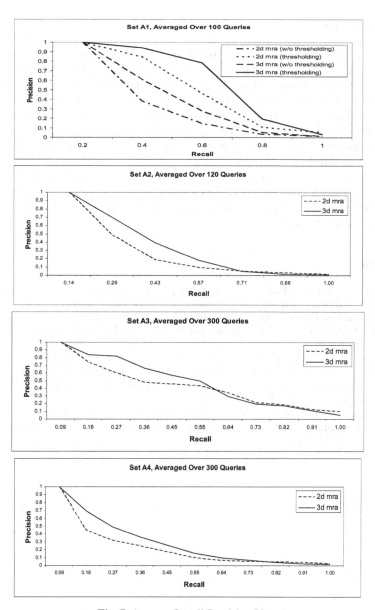

Fig. 7. Average Recall-Precision Plots

Computational expense of the proposed method also needs to be addressed. The proposed method requires more processing compared with the traditional approach. Additional processing is required for decomposition of images by connectivity. Computational complexity for obtaining connectivity of an image is $O(n)$ where n is the number of foreground pixels in the image. In applications where accuracy of retrieval is important, the improvement in effectiveness may outweigh the additional processing cost.

5 Conclusion

We have proposed a novel method for shape representation and retrieval based on combination of connectivity and multiresolution histograms. We propose to use 3d-histograms which encode connectivity and centroidal distances of images. Experiments performed show the effectiveness of the proposed method. We also show the sensitivity of pixel intensity thresholding on the accuracy of retrieval. The degree of sensitivity to pixel intensity thresholding will depend on the image database and the nature of queries. A large number of *fine* shapes will require careful computation of pixel intensity threshold.

In this paper, multiple image resolutions are each decomposed by connectivity and then encoded using 3d-histograms. Given multiple image resolutions which are decomposed by connectivity, the feature space can be encoded in any conventional technique for image indexing.

References

1. Sajjanhar, A., Lu, G., Zhang, D.: Discriminating Shape Descriptors Based on Connectivity, IEEE International Conference on Multimedia and Expo, Taipei, Taiwan (2004)
2. Hadjidemetriou, E., Grossberg, M. D., Nayar, S. K.: Multiresolution Histograms and their Use for Texture Classification, International Workshop on Texture Analysis and Synthesis, Nice, France (2003)
3. Gonzalez, R. C., Woods, R. E.: Digital Image Processing, Prentice Hall (2002)
4. Jolliffe, I. T.: Principal Component Analysis, Springer Verlag (1986)
5. Vranic, D.: 3D Model Retrieval, University of Leipzig, PhD Thesis (2004)
6. http://ipsi.fraunhofer.de/delite/Projects/MPEG7/
7. Hadjidemetriou, E., Grossberg M. D., Nayar, S. K.: Multiresolution Histograms and their Use for Recognition, IEEE transactions on Pattern Analysis and Machine Intelligence, Vol. 26, No. 7 (2004), 831-847

Kernel Biased Discriminant Analysis
Using Histogram Intersection Kernel
for Content-Based Image Retrieval

Lin Mei, Gerd Brunner, Lokesh Setia, and Hans Burkhardt

Chair of Pattern Recognition and Image Processing
Computer Science Department
Albert-Ludwigs-University
79110 Freiburg, Germany
{mei,gbrunner,setia,burkhardt}@informatik.uni-freiburg.de

Abstract. It is known that no single descriptor is powerful enough to encompass all aspects of image content, i.e. each feature extraction method has its own view of the image content. A possible approach to cope with that fact is to get a whole view of the image(object). Then using machine learning approach from user's Relevance feedback to obtain a reduced feature. In this paper, we concentrate on some points about Biased Discriminant Analysis / Kernel Biased Discriminant Analysis (BDA/KBDA) based machine learning approach for CBIR. The contributions of this paper are: 1. using generalized singular value decomposition (GSVD) based approach solve the small sample size problem in BDA/KBDA and 2. using histogram intersection as a kernel for KBDA. Experiments show that this kind of kernel gets improvement compare to other common kernels.

1 Introduction

Content-Based Image Retrieval (CBIR) has gained more and more attention in the last few years. The main aim of CBIR is to search for similar images in a given database based on an expressive representation of its images. The process of finding these expressive information is known as "Feature Extraction". It is known that no single descriptor is powerful enough to encompass all aspects of image content, i.e. each feature extraction method has its own view of the image content. A possible approach to cope with that fact is to get a whole view of the image(object).

Relevance feedback (RF) [16] has been proven as an effective solution to improve performance of CBIR. Relevance feedback with only positive (i.e., relevant) examples can be cast as a density estimation. While with both positive and negative training examples it becomes a classification problem, but with the following characteristics: 1) Small sample issue. 2) Asymmetry in training sample. 3) Real time requirement [16]. Because of small sample size, it is difficult to get a *true* distribution of the negative (irrelevant) images from such few negative samples. Biased discriminant analysis (BDA) [15] has been proven successful to deal with this problem. This approach assumes that image retrieval is a $(1 + x)$-class problem, which means there are an unknown number of classes in the database, but use is only interested in the relevant class, rather than a 2-class problem which assumes all the irrelevant images belong to the same class. It is reasonable

M. Gallagher, J. Hogan, and F. Maire (Eds.): IDEAL 2005, LNCS 3578, pp. 63–70, 2005.

while it is difficult or inconvenient to get plenty of both, positive and negative samples for training. Kernel biased discriminant analysis (KBDA) [15] is a kernel version of BDA, which extend the application of BDA using a nonlinear kernel mapping.

To solve the BDA or KBDA, one always meets the Small-Sample-Size (SSS) problem, because the number of samples is always far smaller than the dimensionality of the feature. There are many methods to solve SSS problem [3, 7]. In this paper, we use the generalized singular vector decomposition method [6] to solve it.

The choice of kernel function for KBDA is another important problem. Some kernel functions also need several parameters. Zhou [14] proposed a kernel alignment based approach to get the optimal parameters, but parameter tuning still makes the online learning unfeasible. In this paper, we use histogram intersection kernel which needn't use any parameters, and compare the performance with other common kernels (such as RBF kernel, Linear kernel, etc...)

2   Feature Combination from Histograms of Local Features

2.1   Haar-Integral Feature

Siggelkow et al. [10, 11] used rotation- and translation-invariant color and texture feature histograms for image retrieval. These features are based on the invariant integration described in [9]. Experimental results have shown that these features demonstrate a very good capability in retrieving images.

The idea of constructing invariant features is to apply a nonlinear kernel function $f(\mathbf{I})$ to the gray value image, $\mathbf{I}$, and to integrate the result over all possible rotations and translations (Haar integral over the Euclidean motion), i.e.,

$$IF(\mathbf{I}) = \frac{1}{2\pi MN} \int_{r=0}^{M} \int_{c=0}^{N} \int_{\theta=0}^{2\pi} f(g(r,c,\theta)\mathbf{I})d\theta dr dc \qquad (1)$$

where $IF(\mathbf{I})$ is the invariant feature of the image, M, N are the dimensions of the image and g is an element in the transformation group G (which consists in our case of rotations and translations).

The above equation suggests that invariant features are computed by applying a nonlinear function, f, on the neighborhood of each pixel in the image, then summing up all the results to get a single value representing the invariant feature.

Much of the local information is lost by summing up the local results. This makes the discrimination capability of the features very weak. In order to preserve the local information, Siggelkow et al. [10, 11] replaced the integration ($\int_{r=0}^{M} \int_{c=0}^{N}$) by histogramming.

We can construct our overcomplete feature set of histogram features from different color space(in this paper, we use RGB,rgb,HSV,HMMD) and different local invariant features(such like histogram of gradient magnitude, histogram of morphological filtered image, etc.). The dimensionality of the feature we used in this paper is 4567.

3 BiasMap Revisited

[14, 15]

3.1 Biased Discriminant Analysis (BDA)

BDA wants to solve an optimal discriminative transform matrix W_{opt}:

$$W_{opt} = \arg\max_w \frac{|W^T S_y W|}{|W^T S_x W|}, \qquad (2)$$

where S_x and S_y are the scatter matrix estimates:

$$S_x = \frac{1}{N_x} \sum_{i=1}^{N_x} (x_i - m_x)(x_i - m_x)^T, S_y = \frac{1}{N_y} \sum_{i=1}^{N_y} (y_i - m_x)(y_i - m_x)^T \qquad (3)$$

$\{x_i, i = 1, \ldots, N_x\}$ are the positive examples, and $\{y_i, i = 1, \ldots, N_y\}$ are the negative examples. Each element of these sets is a vector of length n, which is the dimension of the feature. m_x is the mean vector of the sets $\{x_i\}$.

3.2 Kernel BDA

We can apply the original linear algorithm in a *feature space*, $\mathcal{F}$. Using nonlinear mapping

$$\phi : \mathcal{C} \longrightarrow \mathcal{F} \quad | \quad x \longrightarrow \phi(x), \qquad (4)$$

where $\mathcal{C}$ is a compact subset of $\mathbb{R}^n$, linearly non-separable configurations become separable in $\mathcal{F}$.

Using ϕ to denote quantities in the new *feature space*, we rewrite the objective function in (2) as:

$$W_{opt} = \arg\max_w \frac{|W^T S_y^\phi W|}{|W^T S_x^\phi W|}, \qquad (5)$$

where

$$S_x^\phi = \frac{1}{N_x} \sum_{i=1}^{N_x} (\phi(x_i) - m_x^\phi)(\phi(x_i) - m_x^\phi)^T, S_y^\phi = \frac{1}{N_y} \sum_{i=1}^{N_y} (\phi(y_i) - m_x^\phi)(\phi(y_i) - m_x^\phi)^T \qquad (6)$$

Through the evaluation of a kernel matrix K with components $k(x_i, x_j) = \phi(x_i)^T \phi(x_j)$, we can avoid the huge computing. More details may be found in [15].

4 Generalized Singular Value Decomposition (GSVD) Method to Solve the BDA/KBDA

It is well known that, the optimal solution w to BDA corresponds to the largest eigenvalue for the eigenvalue problem

$$S_x^{-1} S_y w = \lambda w. \qquad (7)$$

However, in RF the size of the training set is much smaller than the dimension of the feature vector, thus the scatter matrix S_x becomes singular. It may cause the SSS problem. There are several methods to solve this problem, such as the regularization method, the null-space method, etc.

In this paper, we use the generalized singular value decomposition (GSVD) method to solve the problem [5, 6].

Regardless of the singularity of S_x, GSVD solves a generalized eigenvalue problem

$$S_y w = \lambda S_x w \tag{8}$$

and without forming the products S_x, S_y explicitly.

The scatter matrices defined in (2) can be expressed as

$$S_y = H_y H_y^T \quad and \quad S_x = H_x H_x^T, \tag{9}$$

where

$$H_x = [x - m_x e_x^T] \in \mathbb{R}^{n \times N_x}, H_y = [y - m_x e_y^T] \in \mathbb{R}^{n \times N_y},$$
$$x = [x_1, x_2, \dots, x_{N_x}] \in \mathbb{R}^{n \times N_x}, y = [y_1, y_2, \dots, y_{N_y}] \in \mathbb{R}^{n \times N_y},$$
$$e_x = [1, 1, \dots, 1] \in \mathbb{R}^{1 \times N_x}, e_y = [1, 1, \dots, 1] \in \mathbb{R}^{1 \times N_y} \tag{10}$$

We can get an optimal solution of w using GSVD method. Details may be found in [6].

For, KBDA, we define

$$K_y^\Phi = (K_y - K_x I_{N_x}^y), K_x^\Phi = (K_x - K_x I_{N_x}^x) \tag{11}$$

Then we can get the solution using the algorithm introduced in [5].

5   Kernel Selection

There are many types of kernel functions. Table 1. are some common kernels used for SVM [13].

Table 1. Common kernels used for SVM

Linear Kernel	$k(x, x') = \langle x, x' \rangle$
Laplacian RBF Kernel	$k(x, x') = \exp(-\gamma \|x - x'\|)$
Gaussian RBF Kernel	$k(x, x') = \exp(-\gamma \|x - x'\|^2)$
Polynomial Kernel	$k(x, x') = (\langle x, x' \rangle + 1)^d$

Kernels can be viewed as similarity measures [8]. We can use any kind of similarity measure to define our own kernel for a specific problem.

5.1 Histogram Intersection

Recently [1], proposed a kernel function of histogram intersection. The performance is better than other kernel functions used in SVM in image classification. Histogram intersection can be defined as follows [12]. We denote with A and B the histograms of images A_{im} and B_{im}. Both histograms consist of m bins, and the i-th bin for $i = 1, \ldots, m$ is denoted with a_i and b_i, respectively. Let us assume that A_{im} and B_{im} have the same size (N pixels); by construction we have $\sum_{i=1}^{m} a_i = N$ and $\sum_{i=1}^{m} b_i = N$. Then,

$$k_{int}(A, B) = \sum_{i=1}^{m} \min\{a_i, b_i\} \tag{12}$$

In [1], the authors proved that histogram intersection k_{int} is a Mercer's kernel [4] by represent A with an $N \times m$-dimensional binary vector $\mathbf{A}$ defined as

$$\mathbf{A} = (\overbrace{1, 1, \ldots, 1}^{a_1}, \underbrace{0, 0, \ldots, 0}_{N-a_1}, \overbrace{1, 1, \ldots, 1}^{a_2}, \underbrace{0, 0, \ldots, 0}_{N-a_2}, \ldots, \overbrace{1, 1, \ldots, 1}^{a_m}, \underbrace{0, 0, \ldots, 0}_{N-a_m})$$

and similarly B with $\mathbf{B}$. Then the histogram intersection $k_{int}(A, B)$ in (12) can be readily seen to be equal to the standard inner product between the two corresponding vectors $\mathbf{A}$ and $\mathbf{B}$:

$$k_{int}(A, B) = \mathbf{A} \cdot \mathbf{B}. \tag{13}$$

6 Experiments

6.1 Image Database

We choose WANG1000 database[1] [2] for our experiments. It is a subset of the Corel database of 1000 images which have been manually selected to be a database of 10 classes(e.g. 'Africa', 'beach', 'monuments', 'food'...) of 100 images each. The images are subdivided into 10 classes such that it is almost sure that a user wants to find the other images from a class if the query is from one of these 10 classes. This is a major advantage of this database because due to the given classification it is possible to evaluate retrieval results.

We selected 20 queries randomly from the image database. Each query consists of 3 positive and 3 negative samples. We compare the performances of using different kernel functions in KBDA and BDA. For KBDA, we choose histogram intersection, linear, laplacian RBF kernel, gaussian RBF kernel and polynomial kernel.

6.2 Performance Evaluation

For each query we can get groundtruth data from the class they belong to. That means, each positive training samples have 100 images from the same class as their groundtruth

---

[1] http://wang.ist.psu.edu

data. We must mention here that some images from the same class are visually dissimilar but semantically belong to the same class. The precision P and recall R are defined as:

$$P = \frac{\text{Number of relevant images retrieved}}{\text{Total number of images retrieved}},$$

$$R = \frac{\text{Number of relevant images retrieved}}{\text{Total number of relevant images}}.$$

These two values are often combined into a so called PR-graph. But we cannot get a averaged PR-graph of the total 20 queries easily because different queries may have different recall values. If we use N_{ret}-R-graph, we can cope with it. N_{ret} is the number of the first N returned images. This graph shows the recalls as a function of N_{ret}. We can also use another performance measure normalized area under the N_{ret}-R-graph ($NAUG$):

$$NAUG = \frac{\text{Area under the } N_{ret}\text{-}R\text{-graph}}{\text{Area under the groundtruth } N_{ret}\text{-}R\text{-graph}}$$

Because the area under the groundtruth N_{ret}-R-graph is not 1, we use the equation above to get a normalized area.

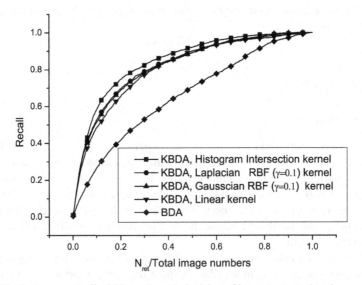

Fig. 1. Average recall of 20 queries as a function of images returned to the user

6.3   Retrieval Results

The retrieval results are shown in Table 2. and Fig. 1. From the results we can see that, the performance using histogram intersection kernel is better than the other kernel types. KBDA based approach always better than BDA based approach.

In this paper, we only give the results using different kernel types for KBDA. In [15], the authors gave the comparison results between KBDA and SVM.

Table 2. Results of normalized area under the N_{ret}-R-graph($NAUG$) of different BDA/KBDA methods

Kernel type	$NUAG(\%)$
KBDA,histogram intersection kernel	88.95
KBDA,linear kernel	85.01
KBDA,2-nd deg polynomial kernel	84.92
KBDA,4-th deg polynomial kernel	84.72
KBDA,Laplacian RBF kernel($\gamma = 0.1$)	86.36
KBDA,Laplacian RBF kernel($\gamma = 1$)	85.84
KBDA,Gaussian RBF kernel($\gamma = 0.1$)	86.13
KBDA,Gaussian RBF kernel($\gamma = 1$)	86.17
BDA	69.42

7   Conclusion

In this paper, we construct a overcomplete feature set using different histogram-based invariant features. Using BDA/KBDA based feature fusion approach to reduce the feature dimensionality. To solve the SSS problem, we use GSVD based approach. A histogram intersection kernel is used for KBDA. Experiment results show that this kind of kernel has advantage than other common kernels for image retrieval.

Acknowledgement

This research was supported by the BMBF I-Search project (project No.: 01 IR B02 B).

References

1. Annalisa Barla, Francesca Odone, Alessandro Verri: Histogram intersection kernel for image classification. In International Conference on Image Processing, volume 2, pages III-513-516, Sep. 2003.
2. James Z. Wang, Jia Li, Gio Wiederhold: SIMPLIcity: Semantics-sensitive Integrated Matching for Picture LIbraries.IEEE Trans. on Pattern Analysis and Machine Intelligence, 23(9):947–963, 2001.
3. L. F. Chen, H.Y. Liao, M. T. Ko, J. C. Lin, and G. J. Yu: A new lda-based face recognition system which can solve the small sample size problem. IJPR, 33:1713–1726, 2000.
4. J. Mercer: Functions of positive and negative type and their connection with the theory of integral equations. Philos. Trans. Roy. Soc. London, A 209:415–446, 1909.
5. Cheong Hee Park and Haesun Park: Kernel discriminant analysis based on generalized singular value decomposition. Technical report, Department of computer science and engineering, University of Minnesota, 2003.
6. Peg Howland, Haesun Park:Generalizing discriminant analysis using the generalized singular value decomposition. IEEE Transactions on Pattern analysis and machine intelligence, 26(8):995–1006, 2004.
7. Rui Huang, Qingshan Liu, Hanqing Lu, Songde Ma: Solving the small sample size problem of lda. pages 29–32, 2002.

8. B. Schoelkopf and A. J. Smola: A short introduction to learning with kernels. In LNAI, volume 2600, pages 41–64, 2003.
9. Hanns Schulz-Mirbach: Invariant Features for Gray Scale Images. In G. Sagerer, S. Posch, and F. Kummert, editors, 17th DAGM - Symposium "Mustererkennung" pages 1–14, Bielefeld, 1995. Springer.
10. Sven Siggelko: Feature Historgrams for Content-Based Image Retrieval. PhD thesis, Albert-Ludwigs-Universität, Freiburg, December 2002.
11. Sven Siggelkow and Marc Schael and Hans Burkhardt:SIMBA - Search IMages By Appearance. In B. Radig and S. Florczyk, editors, Proceedings of 23rd DAGM Symposium, number 2191 in LNCS Pattern Recognition, pages 9–16. Springer, September 2001.
12. M. J. Swain and D. H. Ballard: Color indexing. International Journal of Computer Vision, 7(1):11-32, 1991.
13. Vapnik, V: The nature of statistical learning theory. Springer, New York, 1995.
14. Xiang Sean Zhou, Ashutosh Garg, and Thomas S. Huang: A discussion of nonlinear variants of biased discriminants for interactive image retrieval. In CIVR 2004,LNCS 3115, pages 353–364, 2004.
15. Xiang Sean Zhou, Thomas S. Huang: Small sample learning during multimedia retrieval using biasmap. In IEEE Int'l Conf Computer Vision and Pattern Recognition, volume 1, pages 11-17, December 2001.
16. Xiang Sean Zhou, Thomas S. Huang: Relevance feedback in image retrieval: A comprehensive review. Multimedia Systems, (8):536–544, 2003.

Unsupervised Image Segmentation
Using Penalized Fuzzy Clustering Algorithm

Yong Yang, Feng Zhang, Chongxun Zheng, and Pan Lin

Key Laboratory of Biomedical Information Engineering of Education Ministry,
Institute of Biomedical Engineering, Xi'an Jiaotong University, Xi'an 710049, P.R. China
greatyang@mail.xjtu.edu.cn

Abstract. Fuzzy c-means (FCM) clustering algorithm as an unsupervised fuzzy clustering technique has been widely used in image segmentation. However, the conventional FCM algorithm is very sensitive to noise for the reason of incorporating no information about spatial context while segmentation. To overcome this limitation of FCM algorithm, a novel penalized fuzzy c-means (PFCM) algorithm for image segmentation is presented in this paper. The algorithm is realized by incorporating the spatial neighborhood information into the original FCM algorithm by a penalty term, which is employed to take into account the spatial dependence of the objects. Experiments demonstrate the proposed algorithm is effective and more robust to noise and other artifacts than the standard FCM algorithm.

1 Introduction

Image segmentation is the first essential and important step of low-level computer vision as well as the bottleneck of the development of image processing technology. Many different segmentation techniques have been developed and detailed surveys can be found in references [1]-[3]. Thanks to the fuzzy set theory [4] was proposed, which produced the idea of partial membership of belonging described by a membership function, fuzzy clustering as a soft segmentation method has been widely studied and successfully applied in image segmentation [6]-[10] in the last decades. Among the fuzzy clustering methods, fuzzy c-means (FCM) algorithm [5] is the most popular method used in image segmentation because it has robust characteristics for ambiguity and can retain much more information than hard segmentation methods. Although the conventional FCM algorithm works well on most noise-free images, it has a serious limitation: it dose not incorporate any information about spatial context, which cause it to be sensitive to noise and imaging artifacts.

Many algorithms have been proposed to overcome the above drawback of FCM [6]-[8], [10]. Tolias *et al.* [6] proposed a fuzzy rule-based scheme called the rule-based neighborhood enhancement system to impose spatial continuity by postprocessing on the clustering results obtained using FCM algorithm. In their another approach [7], spatial constraint is imposed in fuzzy clustering by incorporating multiresolution information. Recently, some approaches [8], [10] were proposed for increasing the robustness of FCM to noise by directly modifying the objective function. In [8], a new dissimilarity index that considers the influence of the neighboring pixels on the centre pixel was presented to replace the conventional normed distance

M. Gallagher, J. Hogan, and F. Maire (Eds.): IDEAL 2005, LNCS 3578, pp. 71–77, 2005.

in the FCM algorithm. However, this method can handle only a small amount of noise [9]. In [10], a regularization term was introduced into the standard FCM to impose neighborhood effect. Although this method is promising, it is computational complexity.

In this paper, a novel fuzzy clustering method, called penalized FCM (PFCM) algorithm is presented for image segmentation. The penalty term takes the spatial dependence of the objects into consideration, which is inspired by the Neighborhood EM (NEM) algorithm [11]. Minimizing this new objective function according to the zero gradient condition, the PFCM algorithm is then proposed. Experimental results show the method is effective.

2 Fuzzy C-Means Algorithm

The fuzzy c-means (FCM) algorithm was first introduced by Dunn [12] and later was extended by Bezdek [5]. The algorithm is an iterative clustering method that produces an optimal c partition by minimizing the weighted within group sum of squared error objective function J_{FCM} [5]:

$$J_{FCM} = \sum_{k=1}^{n} \sum_{i=1}^{c} (u_{ik})^q d^2(x_k, v_i) \tag{1}$$

where $X = \{x_1, x_2, \cdots, x_n\} \subseteq R^p$ is the data set in the p-dimensional vector space, n is the number of data items, c is the number of clusters with $2 \le c < n$, u_{ik} is the degree of membership of x_k in the ith cluster, q is a weighting exponent on each fuzzy membership, v_i is the prototype of the centre of cluster i, $d^2(x_k, v_i)$ is a distance measure between object x_k and cluster centre v_i. A solution of the object function J_{FCM} can be obtained via an iterative process, which is carried as follows:

$$v_i = \frac{\sum_{k=1}^{n} (u_{ik})^q x_k}{\sum_{k=1}^{n} (u_{ik})^q} \tag{2}$$

$$u_{ik} = \frac{1}{\sum_{j=1}^{c} \left(\frac{d_{ik}}{d_{jk}} \right)^{2/(q-1)}} \tag{3}$$

3 Penalized FCM Algorithm

It is noted from (1) that the objective function of the traditional FCM algorithm does not take into account any spatial information; this means the clustering process is related only to gray levels independently on pixels of image in segmentation. This limitation makes FCM be very sensitive to noise. The general principle of the technique presented in this paper is to incorporate the neighborhood information into the FCM algorithm during classification. In order to incorporate the spatial context into FCM algorithm, the objective function of (1) is penalized by a regularization term, which is inspired by the NEM algorithm [11] and modified based on the criterion of FCM algorithm. The new objective function of the PFCM is defined as follows:

$$J_{PFCM} = \sum_{k=1}^{n}\sum_{i=1}^{c}(u_{ik})^q d^2(x_k, v_i) + \gamma \sum_{k=1}^{n}\sum_{j=1}^{n}\sum_{i=1}^{c}(u_{ik})^q (1-u_{ij})^q w_{kj} \qquad (4)$$

where w_{kj} is defined as $w_{kj} = \begin{cases} 1 & if\ x_k\ and\ x_j\ are\ neighbors\ and\ k \neq j, \\ 0 & otherwise \end{cases}$. The pa-

rameter $\gamma\ (\geq 0)$ controls the effect of the penalty term. The relative importance of the regularizing term is inversely proportional to the signal-to-noise (SNR) of the image. Lower SNR would require a higher value of the parameter γ, and vice versa. When $\gamma = 0$, J_{PFCM} equals to J_{FCM}. The major difference between NEM algorithm and PFCM algorithm is that the penalty term in the NEM is maximized to get the solutions while in the PFCM it should be minimized in order to satisfy the principle of FCM algorithm. This new penalty term is minimized when the membership value for a particular class is large and the membership values for that class at neighboring pixels is also large, and vice versa. In other words, it constrains the pixel's membership value of a class to be correlated with those of the neighboring pixels.

The objective function J_{PFCM} can be minimized in a fashion similar to the standard FCM algorithm. An iterative algorithm for minimizing (4) can be derived by evaluating the centroids and membership functions that satisfy a zero gradient condition. The constrained optimization in (4) will be solved using one Lagrange multiplier:

$$\eta_q = \sum_{k=1}^{n}\sum_{i=1}^{c}(u_{ik})^q d^2(x_k, v_i) + \gamma \sum_{k=1}^{n}\sum_{j=1}^{n}\sum_{i=1}^{c}(u_{ik})^q (1-u_{ij})^q w_{kj} + \lambda\left(1 - \sum_{i=1}^{c}u_{ik}\right) \qquad (5)$$

Taking the partial derivate of (5) with respect to u_{ik} and setting the result to zero yields:

$$\left[\frac{\partial \eta_q}{\partial u_{ik}} = q(u_{ik})^{q-1} d^2(x_k, v_i) + \gamma q(u_{ik})^{q-1}\sum_{j=1}^{n}(1-u_{ij})^q w_{kj} - \lambda\right]_{u_{ik}=u_{ik}^*} = 0 \qquad (6)$$

Solving for u_{ik}^*, we have

$$u_{ik}^* = \left(\frac{q\left(d^2(x_k, v_i) + \gamma\sum_{j=1}^{n}(1-u_{ij})^q w_{kj}\right)}{\lambda}\right)^{-1/(q-1)} \qquad (7)$$

Since $\sum_{l=1}^{c} u_{lk} = 1, \forall k$, this constraint equation is employed, thus the zero-gradient condition for the membership estimator can be written as:

$$u_{ik}^{*} = \frac{1}{\sum_{l=1}^{c} \left(\frac{d^2(x_k, v_i) + \gamma \sum_{j=1}^{n} (1 - u_{ij})^q w_{kj}}{d^2(x_k, v_l) + \gamma \sum_{j=1}^{n} (1 - u_{lj})^q w_{kj}} \right)^{1/q-1}} \tag{8}$$

Since the penalty function does not depend v_i, the necessary conditions on the centroids for (4) to be minimized is identical to that of FCM. Thus the PFCM algorithm is given as follows:

PFCM algorithm

Step 1: Set the cluster centroids v_i, fuzzification parameter q, the values of c and ε.

Step 2: Calculate membership values using (8).

Step 3: Compute the cluster centroids using (2).

Step 4: Go to step 2 and repeat until convergence.

When the algorithm has converged, a defuzzification process then takes place in order to convert the fuzzy partition matrix U to a crisp partition. A number of methods have been developed to defuzzify the partition matrix U, among which the maximum membership procedure is the most important. The procedure assigns object k to the class C with the highest membership:

$$C_k = \arg_i\{\max(u_{ik})\}, \quad i = 1, 2, \cdots, c. \tag{9}$$

With this procedure, the fuzzy images are then converted to crisp image that is segmentation.

4   Experimental Results

In this section, the results of the application of the PFCM algorithm are presented. The performance of the proposed method is compared with that of the standard FCM algorithm. For all cases, unless otherwise stated, the weighting exponent $q = 2.0$ and $\varepsilon = 0.0001$. Here we set the parameter $\gamma = 400$, which is selected experimentally in order to provide appropriate results. A 3×3 window of image pixels is considered in this paper, thus the spatial influence on the centre pixel is through its 8-neighborhood pixels. All the algorithms are coded in Microsoft Visual C++ Version 6.0 and are run on a 1.7GHz Pentium IV personal computer with a memory of 256 MB.

In the first example, we generate a synthetic image with intensity values 0, 255 and 128, and the image size is 256×256. Additive 10% Gaussian noise was added to the image. To get a better insight, the image is segmented by FCM and PFCM into three corresponding classes with intensity values 255, 0, and 128 representing class 1, class 2 and class 3, respectively. Fig. 1 (a) shows the test degraded noisy images. The results of FCM algorithm and PFCM algorithm are displayed in Fig. 1 (b) and (c), respectively. We observed that the three regions are well brought out by these two algorithms. However, with the FCM algorithm, the segmentation result still has much noise especially in class 1 and class 3, while the result used by PFCM algorithm is less speckled and smoother. The number of misclassified pixels with the two methods is counted during the experiments and is listed in Table 1. It can be seen from Table 1. that the total number of misclassification pixels for the FCM algorithm is nearly 63 times than that of the proposed method. This demonstrates the incorporation of the spatial neighborhood constraints into the FCM algorithm can significantly improve the segmented result in presence of noise.

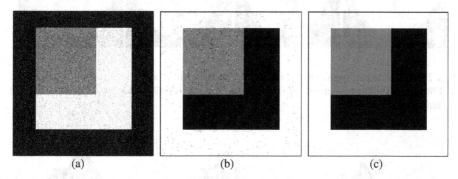

(a)   (b)   (c)

Fig. 1. Comparison of segmentation results on a synthetic image corrupted by 10% Gaussian noise. (a) The original image. (b) FCM result. (c) PFCM result

Table 1. Number of misclassified pixels with FCM and PFCM methods

Segmentation method	FCM	PFCM
Class 1	185	1
Class 2	42	1
Class 3	337	7
Total	564	9

The second example is a simulated magnetic resonance (MR) brain image obtained from the BrainWeb Simulated Brain Database [13]. This brain image was simulated with T1-weighted contrast, 1-mm cubic voxels, 7% noise and no intensity inhomogeneity. Before segmentation, the non-brain parts of the image have been removed. The class number of the image was assumed to be four, corresponding to gray matter (GM), white matter (WM), cerebrospinal fluid (CSF) and background. Fig.2 (a) shows a slice from the simulated data set, Fig.2 (b) and (c) shows the segmentation results obtained by applying FCM and PFCM, respectively and the ground truth is given in Fig.2 (d). It is clearly seen that our segmentation result is much closer to the ground truth. The result of PFCM is more homogeneous and smoother than that of the FCM algorithm, which again indicates our method is effective and robust to noise.

In the last example, there is a real standard test image named *camerman* without adding any type of noise. In this experiment, the class number c is set to be 2. Fig.3 (a) illustrates the original image. The results of the FCM algorithm and PFCM algorithm are presented in Fig.3 (b) and (c), respectively. As can be seen, both the FCM and PFCM algorithms can extract the object from the background. However, it is important to note the proposed method performs better for segmenting the object from background with least spurious components and noise particularly in the grass ground area. This example proves that our method is capable of coping with not only noises but also artifacts in the image.

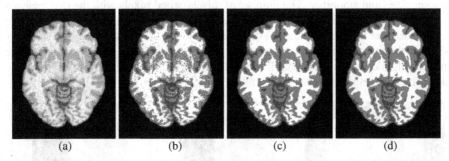

(a)   (b)   (c)   (d)

Fig. 2. Comparison of segmentation results on a MR phantom corrupted by 7% Gaussian noise and no intensity inhomogeneity. (a) The original image. (b) FCM result. (c) PFCM result. (d) Ground truth

(a)   (b)   (c)

Fig. 3. Comparison of segmentation results on a real standard image named *cameraman*. (a) The original image. (b) FCM result. (c) PFCM result

5   Conclusions

We have presented a novel penalized fuzzy c-means (PFCM) algorithm that is able to incorporate both local spatial contextual information and feature space information into the image segmentation. The algorithm is developed by modifying the objective function of the standard FCM algorithm by a penalty term that takes into account the influence of the neighboring pixels on the centre pixels. A variety of images, includeing synthetic, simulated and real images were used to compare the performance of FCM and PFCM algorithms. Experimental results show the proposed method is effective and more robust to noise and other artifacts than the conventional FCM algorithm in image segmentation. Future work will focus on compensating for intensity inhomogeneity while segmenting the image data.

References

1. S. K. Fu, J. K. Mui: A survey on image segmentation, Pattern Recognition, Vol. 13, (1981) 3-16.
2. R. M. Haralick, L. G. Shapiro: Image segmentation techniques, Comput.Vision Graphics Image Process., Vol. 29, (1985) 100-132.
3. N. Pal, S. Pal: A review on image segmentation techniques, Pattern Recognition, Vol. 26, (1993) 1277-1294.
4. L. A. Zadeh: Fuzzy sets, Inform. and Control, Vol. 8, (1965) 338-353.
5. J. C. Bezdek: Pattern Recognition with Fuzzy Objective Function Algorithms. New York: Plenum Press, 1981.
6. Y. A. Tolias, S. M. Panas: On applying spatial constraints in fuzzy image clustering using a fuzzy rule-based system, IEEE Signal Processing Letters, Vol.5, (1998) 245-247.
7. Y. A. Tolias and S. M. Panas: Image segmentation by a fuzzy clustering algorithm using adaptive spatially constrained membership functions, IEEE Trans. Systems, Man, Cybernet. A, Vol. 28, (1998) 359-369.
8. A.W. C. Liew, S. H. Leung, and W. H. Lau: Fuzzy image clustering incorporating spatial continuity, IEE Proc. Visual Image Signal Process. Vol. 147, (2000) 185-192.
9. M. J. Kwon, Y. J. Han, I. H. Shin, H. W. Park: Hierarchical fuzzy segmentation of brain MR images, International Journal of Imaging Systems and Technology, Vol. 13, (2003) 115-125.
10. M. N. Ahmed, S. M. Yamany, N. Mohamed, A. A. Farag, and T. Moriarty: A modified fuzzy C-means algorithm for bias field estimation and segmentation of MRI data, IEEE Trans. on Medical Imaging, Vol. 21, (2002) 193-199.
11. C. Ambroise, G. Govaert: Convergence of an EM-type algorithm for spatial clustering, Pattern Recognition Letters, Vol.19, (1998) 919-927.
12. J.C. Dunn: A Fuzzy Relative of the ISODATA Process and its Use in Detecting Compact Well separated Clusters, Journal of Cybernetics, Vol. 3, (1974) 32–57.
13. D. L. Collins, A. P. Zijdenbos, V. Kollokian, J. G. Sled, and N. J. Kabani, et al.: Design and construction of a realistic digital brain phantom, IEEE Trans. Med. Imaging, Vol. 17, (1998) 463-468.

Multi-attributes Image Analysis for the Classification of Web Documents Using Unsupervised Technique

Samuel W.K. Chan

Dept. of Decision Sciences, The Chinese University of Hong Kong
Hong Kong SAR, China
swkchan@cuhk.edu.hk

Abstract. The aim of this research is to develop a system based on multi-attributes image analysis and a neural network self-organization feature map (SOFM) that will facilitate the automated classification of images or icons in Web documents. Four different image attribute sets are extracted. The system integrates different image attributes without demanding any particular primitive to be dominant. The system is implemented and the results generated show meaningful clusters. The performance of the system is compared with the Hierarchical Agglomerative Clustering (HAC) algorithm. Evaluation shows that similar images will fall onto the same region in our approach, in such a way that it is possible to retrieve images under family relationships.

1 Introduction

The common technique for content-based image retrieval systems is to extract a signature for every image based on its pixel values, color, or shape, and to define a classification mechanism for image comparison [1, 5]. Two major classes of signatures are commonly found. First, with the increasing availability of devices supporting acquisition and visualization of color images, a mounting interest is being focused on color as a key feature in the signature to characterize the content of archived images [4, 8]. Its major tradeoff is that spatial features are completely lost and the spatial relations between parts of an image cannot be thoroughly utilized. Different from color histogram techniques, image features have been semantically interpreted with domain knowledge to recognize conceptual objects [2]. More recent work attempts to combine semantic interpretation of data in different media including different annotations [10]. In this research, we advocate the integration of multi-attributes image features into a high-level cognition classification model using a self-organization feature map (SOFM). We describe a framework that encompasses color, line segment, texture, and region fragment, without demanding any particular image features to be dominant. Different levels of abstraction and high level features, such as the image domain knowledge based on a set of image templates, are employed. In addition, since different users may perceive image patterns of the same objects differently and, consequently, may categorize the same objects into different groups, we provide an interactive user interface to capture the user preferences on different image features. These high-level user preferences with a set of image templates encapsulated with a wide range of low level image attributes are most appropriately viewed as complementary in the Web document classification. The overview of the system architecture is first discussed in Section 2. The technical details in extracting image signatures are

M. Gallagher, J. Hogan, and F. Maire (Eds.): IDEAL 2005, LNCS 3578, pp. 78–85, 2005.

described in Section 3. Details on how the images can be compared and similarity measures can be deduced are also explained. Experimental results on different composition of image features are discussed in Section 4 with a comparison with the traditional Hierarchical Agglomerative Clustering (HAC) technique, followed by a conclusion.

2 System Architecture

The system architecture, as shown in Figure 1, consists of four main classes of operation objects to provide the multi-attributes image classification capabilities. The four classes of objects include image partition objects, feature extraction objects, classification objects, and user interface objects.

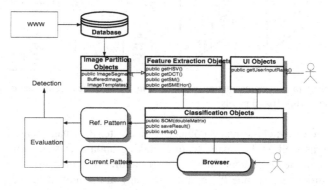

Fig. 1. System architecture of the image classifier

In order to have an efficient image classifier, we first partition all the images which extract from the World Wide Web into a quad-tree image representation in our image partition objects. The quad-tree which is a pyramidal image partition has been introduced as a spatial decomposition technique, without regard to the representation of gray-scale intensities at each level. It is on the basis of successive subdivision of the image into quadrants hierarchically as shown in Figure 2. The most obvious spatial information can be found from the image pads at the upper half of the pyramid, i.e., with significantly lower resolution, while significant details are obtained at the lower half. In our simulation using the WWW images or icons which are usually small in size, we partition all the input images or icons into two different levels of resolution A_1, A_2 with total 20 image pads each having 16×16 pixels.

Before proceeding to the image classification objects using the Self-Organization Feature Map (SOFM), we restrict ourselves, among many possible features that can be extracted from an image, to ones that are global but low-level image attributes. Our image signatures involve attributes from color, edge, region and texture as shown in Figure 3. An algorithm is also devised to calculate their similarities. The algorithm is not on the basis of Euclidean distance which only provides a displacement insensitive measure in image comparison. By using the image similarity algorithm, each input image pad in the partition P is compared with the corresponding image pad in the n template images. The comparison will be repeated for each image pad in order to identify the image similarity measures for color-, edge-, region- and texture-based images. As a result, there will have $4n$ similarity values which reflect the resemblance between the target image and the n templates. Each of these image signatures encompasses the different aspect of the image.

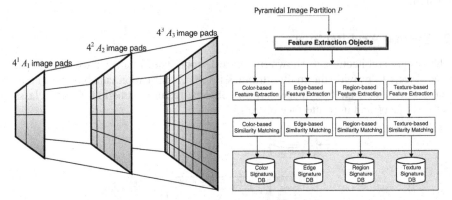

Fig. 2. Pyramidal image representation with each image pad having 16×16 pixels

Fig. 3. Image feature extraction objects

The objective of the classification objects is to cluster the images based on the image signatures as well as the image feature ranking upon user selection. The image feature ranking in the UI objects allows users to modify the composition of the image signatures in order to fine-tune the relative saliency in the human image perception. By using a self-organization feature map (SOFM) model proposed by Kohonen [6], the image signatures which usually have more than a few hundred dimensions are then clustered in the classification objects. The SOFM is on topological feature-preserving basis. It compresses the input signature vector in its connection weights, of which greatly reduce the size of the input. It is more sophisticated in dimension reduction particularly for the input vectors having a large dimension as in our image classification. As a result, similar images will form clusters on the map according to their similarity. Further discussion on the algorithms used in the multi-attributes image classifier can be found in the following section.

3   Image Signature Extraction

While we adopt the traditional HSV components in extracting the color attributes from the images, Discrete Cosine Transformation (DCT) is used to extract the texture similarity. Loosely speaking, DCT reflects the overall structure of the images and provides details regarding their spatial frequency content. Our DCT method, which is a lossy operation, starts by breaking the images into 16×16 pixel blocks or 32×32 pixel blocks. All the pixel blocks are analyzed separately in the feature extraction objects. The low frequency components in the DCT reflect the coarseness of the images. The larger the coefficients, the more alike the transformed image are to the original image. In addition to the color and texture attributes, edge- and intensity-based region images are also involved to compare the similarity measures with a set of pre-defined image templates. An edge detector is a high pass filter which outputs an edge image using convolution kernels. A convolution kernel is a discrete approximation to a two-dimensional convolution integral. In this research, we employ the Sobel and Isotropic kernels, which look for edges in both horizontal and vertical directions, and then combine into a single metric. As opposed to the edge detection, region-based approaches which attempt to segment an image into regions according to similarity (or dissimilarity) are applied in our multi-attributes image analysis. Images containing light objects on a dark background or dark objects on a light background can be segmented by means of a simple threshold operation. The following relationship exists between the input image $f(m, n)$ and the output image $g(m, n)$:

$$g(m,n) = \begin{cases} I_1 & 0 \le f(m,n) < S \\ I_2 & S \le f(m,n) \le f_{max} \end{cases} \tag{1}$$

where I_1 and I_2 are two arbitrary values with $I_1 \ne I_2$ (usually $I_1 = 0$, $I_2 = 1$ are selected) and S is the intensity threshold to be used. In addition, a region growing technique, called *pixel aggregation*, in identifying the possible regions in the gray-scale images is also devised. Our pixel aggregation starts with a set of seed points. Regions are grown by appending those similar neighboring pixels to the seeds. Seeds are selected from the gray level histogram with the most predominant values. Although typical region analysis must be carried out with a set of descriptors based on intensity and spatial properties, such as moments, only intensity-based regions are used in our simulations to compare with the existing templates.

Table 1. Image Similarity Measure Algorithm

```
INPUT Image A and Image B gray-level matrices
DETERMINE size of window, N
COMPUTE difference matrix based on A and B
SEARCH the intensity center as described in (2) & (3)
INITIALIZE sum
DO WHILE pixel (i, j) within the window
       COMPUTE
```
$$f(i,j) \leftarrow \frac{\partial g(i,j)}{1+\lambda}\{\lambda^2(i-\mu_r)^2 + \lambda^2(j-\mu_s)^2 + \partial g^2(i,j)\}^{\frac{1}{2}}$$
```
       CALCULATE  sum ← sum + f²(i,j)
ENDDO
OUTPUT
```
$$ISM(A,B) \leftarrow \frac{1}{N}\sqrt{sum}$$

While most of the measures in comparing multi-attributes between two image pads heavily rely on the Euclidean distance, we employ an Image Similarity Measure (ISM) which makes use of intensity center of an image as the key parameter for computing the similarity values [3]. The algorithm provides a displacement insensitive measure in our multi-attributes image comparison. An intensity center $\mu = (\mu_r, \mu_s)$ of an image is first defined as shown in (2) and (3).

$$\mu_r = \min\left(\sum_{i=1}^{\mu_r}\sum_{j=1}^{m}\partial g(i,j) - \sum_{i=\mu_r}^{m}\sum_{j=1}^{m}\partial g(i,j)\right) \tag{2}$$

$$\mu_s = \min\left(\sum_{i=1}^{m}\sum_{j=1}^{\mu_s}\partial g(i,j) - \sum_{i=1}^{m}\sum_{j=\mu_s}^{m}\partial g(i,j)\right) \tag{3}$$

where $\partial g(i,j)=\left|g_a(i,j)-g_b(i,j)\right|$ is the absolute difference between the two images a and b, calculated pixel by pixel. The ISM algorithm shown in Table 1 takes two image matrices as input. The difference image matrix is calculated for every pixel in image A relative to the same pixel in image B. Based on the difference matrix, comparison between the surrounding pixels within a predefined window surrounding the intensity center (μ_r, μ_s) is performed. This process is repeated until all the pixels of the difference image within the predefined window have been processed.

4 Experiments and Evaluation

It is not difficult to realize the dimension of the multi-attributes image signature vectors is very huge. In most cases, the dimension of our image signature is more than six hundred. It is out of the capacity of most clustering algorithms. On the other hand, it has been postulated that human brain uses spatial mapping to model complex data structure. Much of the cerebral cortex is arranged as a two-dimensional plane of interconnected neurons but it is able to deal with concepts in much higher dimensions. In our experiment, the self-organization feature map is used to categorize the image signature vectors in such a way that their topological features and relations are both preserved [6]. To study the performance of our image classifier, we have implemented a prototype system with a hundred target images. The images from seven categories are retrieved through the Web. Images P01-P16, P17-32, P33-P48, P49-P56, P57-P70, P71-P85, and P86-P100 are under the classes of fruit, scenery, mobile phone, Clinton, flower, airplane and cartoon respectively. Each target image downloaded from the WWW is 64×64 in size with maximum gray level of 256. All the images or icons are in GIF format. One target image is selected from each domain as an image template. As shown in Figure 2, the size 64×64 target image is first partitioned into four A_1 image pads which are then further subdivided into sixteen A_2 image pads.

Different users may perceive image patterns on the same objects differently and, consequently, may categorize the same objects into different clusters. In our prototype, in addition to implement a more generic displacement insensitive measure in image comparison with a wide variety of low level image features, we allow users to incorporate their own preferences in each image attribute so that they can tailor-make their own profiles in their perception. An interactive user interface to capture the user preferences on different image attributes is provided. This is one step forward towards the stimulation of human-like image classification and replication of human performance. These high-level user preferences with a set of image templates encapsulated with a set of low level image attributes are regarded as complementary in our domain of image analysis for the classification of Web documents.

In the training of SOFM, the weight factors for color and texture similarity are assigned to be three and one respectively while the other is set to be zero in the image pads of A_1. However, the weight factor for color is set to be three and the rest is set to be one in high-resolution level as in 4^2 A_2 image pads. The SOFM with 1,600 neurons organized on a two-dimension lattice with 40×40 grid is used for the training. The number of neurons used is empirically determined by considering the number of similar clusters in the training sets. Each 636-dimension image signature vector is presented to the network and the connection weights are stabilized after 5750 epochs. As shown in Figure 4, the images are clustered in a way that emphasizes the grouping between images. The SOFM captures the family relationships among the images which are likely to be grouped together under the same category.

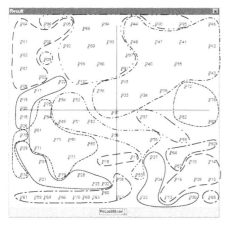 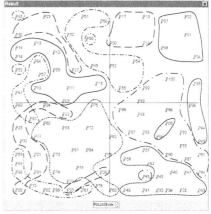

Fig. 4. Image clusters formed after the training in SOFM in 40×40 grid

Fig. 5. Clusters formed in SOFM while the weights of color attribute are reduced

As shown in Figure 4, it is not difficult to realize that images with light background, such as the images from mobile phone and cartoon categories are grouped together while the opposite corner corresponds to the images with dark background. The images from the category fruit are further split into two parts located at the upper left-hand and lower right-hand side in the map. The subdivision is mainly due to different texture appeared in these images. The complexity of scenery-categorized image signatures makes them be positioned at different regions in the map. Generally speaking, images with brighter background are located at the upper portion of the map with further subdivision relied on their categories. Compared with the result shown in Figure 5 with the color attributes downgraded, Figure 4 shows a clear and distinct classification. It is postulated that color seems to be most dominant attribute in clustering WWW images which are iconic-based and have a relatively low resolution. On the other hand, in order to justify our approach of utilizing a wide range of image attributes, we repeat the experiment for one single image attribute. Figure 6 shows the SOFM generated solely from line segments. All hundred images are clustered into 43 image groups. More than half of the clusters have only one image. While it is possible that same set of images might come up with slightly different clusters, our experiment indicates that the classification using a single image attribute is unsatisfactory, if not unacceptable. This comparison shows our attribute-rich image classifier provides an efficient classification, particularly for Web based documents.

In order to evaluate the performance of the SOFM, we compare our result with the classical Hierarchical Agglomerative Clustering (HAC) algorithm. HAC is an iterative procedure in which clusters are merged into one bigger cluster according to a distance function. Two clusters with least discrepancy are first identified and merged together. In our research, we start with some trivial clusters in which each cluster represents a single image. Two closest clusters according to the distance function are first identified and are merged into a single cluster. The process repeats until the desired number of clusters is reached.

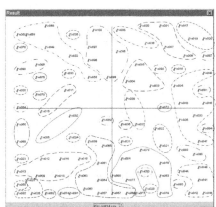

Fig. 6. Clusters generated in SOFM with a sole image attribute from line segments

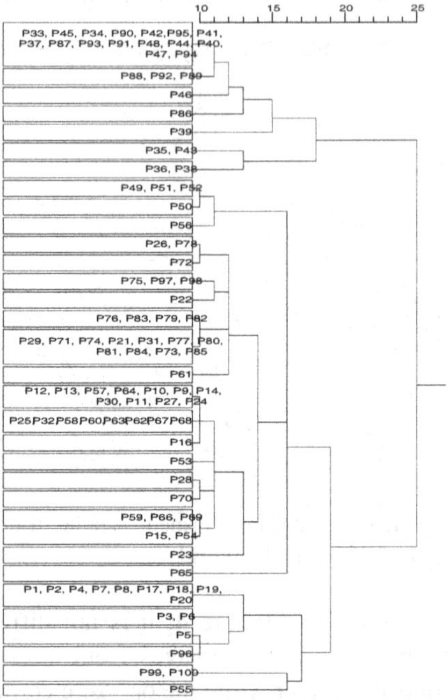

Fig. 7. Dendrogram using between-groups linkage cluster method

In fact, there are many different measures for the merging. The one that we employed in the evaluation is group-average clustering in which the combined dissimilarity of two clusters is the average of all dissimilarities between members of each cluster [7, 9]. This function measures the cluster dissimilarity using a weighted squared distance between the two cluster centers μ_i and μ_j

$$\frac{2n_i n_j}{n_i + n_j} \left\| \mu_i - \mu_j \right\|^2 \qquad (4)$$

where n_i and n_j represent the cardinalities of clusters i and j. Figure 7 shows dendrogram produced by the HAC algorithm using the between-groups linkage cluster method. In the HAC dendrogram, the images in categories mobile and cartoon are grouped together at the upper branch. The main reason behind is their bright background. Images of Clinton P49, P50, P51, P52 and P56 are clustered together. However, images under the category scenery are scattered into different branches of the tree. Same situation occurs in the flower images. When the two results obtained in SOFM and HAC are compared, it can be observed that the image under categories mobile phone and cartoon can't be distinguished sharply in both algorithms. While the fruit images are under examined, we can find out that both algorithms separate the images into two major clusters by differentiating their image background. However, the result in SOFM seems to be much better than the ones in HAC.

5 Conclusion

With the proliferation of WWW documents, image classification will certainly be an important issue in content-based information retrieval. In this research, we have presented an approach to classify images based on various attributes. The system integrates multi-attributes of an image into the classification procedure without demanding any particular ones to be dominant. We have evaluated the approach and compared our result with other clustering algorithm. The system implemented and the results generated provide discrimination clusters. This approach suggests one of the possible ways to classify WWW documents, in which the embedded images are usually small in size.

Acknowledgement

The work described in this paper was partially supported by a grant from the Research Grants Council of the Hong Kong Special Administrative Region, China (Project No. CUHK4171/01E).

References

1. Chang, S.F., Smith, J.R., Beigi, M., and Benitez, A. (1997). Visual information retrieval from large distributed on-line repositories. *Communications of the ACM*, 40, 12, 63-71.
2. Chu, W.W., Hsu, C.C., Cardenas, A.F., Taira, R.K. (1998). Knowledge based image retrieval with spatial and temporal constructs. *IEEE Transactions on Knowledge and Data Engineering*, 10, 6, 872-888.
3. Cios, K.J., and Shin, I. (1995). Image recognition neural network: IRNN. *Neurocomputing*, 7, 159-185.
4. Corridoni, J.M., Del Bimbo, A., & Pala, P. (1999). Image retrieval by color semantics. *Multimedia Systems*, 7, 175-183.
5. Flickner, M., Sawhney, H., Niblack, W., Ashley, J., Huang, Q., Dom, B., Gorkani, M., Hafner, J., Lee, D., Petkovic, D., Steele, D., & Yanker, P. (1995). Query by image and video content: The QBIC system. *Computer*, 28, 9, 23-32.
6. Kohonen, T. (1990). The self-organization map. *Proceedings of the IEEE*, 78, 1464-1480.
7. Ripley, B.D. (1996). *Pattern Recognition and Neural Networks*. Cambridge University Press.
8. Vinod, V., & Murase, H. (1997). Focused retrieval of color images. *Pattern Recognition*, 30, 10, 1787-1797.
9. Ward, J.H. (1963). Hierarchical grouping to optimize an objective function. *Journal of the American Statistical Association*, 58, 236-244.
10. Zhou, X.S., & Huang, T.S. (2002).Unifying keywords and visual contents in image retrieval. *IEEE Multimedia*, 9, 2, 23-33.

Automatic Image Annotation
Based on Topic-Based Smoothing

Xiangdong Zhou, Jianye Ye, Lian Chen, Liang Zhang, and Baile Shi

Department of Computing and Information Technology
Fudan University
Shanghai, China, 200433
xdzhou@fudan.edu.cn

Abstract. Automatic image annotation has attracted much attention recently, due to its wide applicability (such as image retrieval by semantics). Most of the known statistical model-based annotation methods learn the joint distribution of the keywords and the image blobs decomposed by segmentation or gride approaches. The effects of these methods suffer from the sparseness of the image blobs. As a result, the estimated joint distribution is need to be "smoothed". In this paper, we present a topic-based smoothing method to overcome the sparseness problems, and integrated with a general image annotation model. Experimental results on 5,000 images demonstrate that our method can achieves significant improvement in annotation effectiveness over an existing method.

1 Introduction

In traditional image databases, image queries are evaluated based on manually obtained annotations. With the increasing amount of images, manual annotation, which suffers from low efficiency, high labor intensity and human perception subjectivity, can hardly guarantee the labelling integrity. Since, users are more familiar with semantic queries (semantic labelling-based) than content-based queries. Therefore, automatic image semantic annotation is attracting more and more research interest [1–11].

Most known statistical model-based image annotation techniques assume that each image can be described by a small vocabulary of blobs, which are the sub regions of images decomposed by segmentation [6] or grid [10] approaches. Similar to using words to describe documents in text retrieval, blobs can be used as the basic units to describe images. Based on this a statistical model between the semantic labels and the blobs can be established to perform the automatic annotation [6, 7, 10].

Generally, the number of blobs of an image is small [6, 7]. The sparsity of blobs will lead to the problem of "zero" probability in the process of the modelling, causing lower precision of the annotation model. In statistical modelling, "smoothing" techniques are usually exploited to solve the zero probability problem. In this paper, we propose a smoothing method based on a layered topic image model. The basic idea is that the probability of the events observed in a training image can be reinforced by evaluating the probability of the events

M. Gallagher, J. Hogan, and F. Maire (Eds.): IDEAL 2005, LNCS 3578, pp. 86–93, 2005.

$$P(w|J) = \lambda_1 \frac{\#(w, J)}{|W_J|} + \lambda_2 \frac{\#(w, C(J))}{|W_{C(J)}|} + (1 - \lambda_1 - \lambda_2) \frac{\#(w, T)}{|W_T|} \qquad (7)$$

where $\#(w, J)$ represents the number of occurrences of w in W_J (the value is 0 or 1) and $|W_J|$ represents the number of keywords of W_J.

Correspondingly, with respect of the topic layer, we have:

$$\#(w, C(J)) = \sum_{X \in C(J)} \#(w, X) \qquad |W_{C(J)}| = \sum_{X \in C(J)} |W_X|$$

and with respect of general layer, we have:

$$\#(w, T) = \sum_{X \in T} \#(w, X) \qquad |W_T| = \sum_{X \in T} |W_X|$$

Let $P(b|J)$ denote the probability of blob b occurred in the topic image model of J. Then:

$$P(b|J) = \mu_1 \frac{\#(b, J)}{|B_J|} + \mu_2 \frac{\#(b, C(J))}{|B_{C(J)}|} + (1 - \mu_1 - \mu_2) \frac{\#(b, T)}{|B_T|}, \qquad (8)$$

where $\#(w, J)$ denotes the number of occurrence of b in B_J (in terms of individual image layer) and $|B_J|$ represents the number of elements of B_J.

Accordingly, with respect to topic layer, we have:

$$\#(b, C(J)) = \sum_{X \in C(J)} \#(b, X) \qquad |B_{C(J)}| = \sum_{X \in C(J)} |B_X|$$

and with respect of general layer:

$$\#(b, T) = \sum_{X \in T} \#(b, X) \qquad |B_T| = \sum_{X \in T} |B_X|$$

According to equ.7 and equ.8, we can calculate the $P(w, B_D)$ for $\forall w \in W$ by equ.5. Thus, the top N keywords with the largest probabilities $P(w, B_D)$ are used to form W_D, namely the corresponding image of D will be labelled by W_D.

5   Experiment and Analysis

5.1   Experiment Data Set

The data set of [6, 7] is used to compare the performance of different models. The data set consists of 5,000 images from 50 Corel Stock Photo cds. Each cd includes 100 images on the same topic. Normalized cut segmentation is used to construct the image document. Each image was also assigned with 1-5 keywords. Overall there are 371 words and 500 blobs in the data set. We divided the data set into 2 parts – with 4,500 images as the training set, and 500 images as the test set.

For the CMRM, we used the parameters provided in [7](keyword parameter is 0.9, blob parameter is 0.1). There are 4 parameters used in our topic-based smoothing method, $\lambda_1 = 0.1$ and $\lambda_2 = 0.9$ are keywords smoothing parameters, which represent the weights of the individual layer and the topic layer respectively; $\mu_1 = 0.1, \mu_2 = 0.9$ are blobs smoothing parameters respectively. The number of keywords annotated in the experiment is set to 5 for all the annotation models.

5.2   Experiment Result

As the authors stated that the CMRM model [7] was more effective than some of the known methods. The experimental methods of [7] is adopted in this paper to make the experimental results comparable. The 500 images used as the test data set are divided into 50 topics, 10 images per topic. The CMRM [7] and our method are used to perform annotations. After annotation, the keywords-based image retrieval is performed [7] to estimate the effectiveness of the image annotation. Among the 273 possible keywords, only some of them can retrieve more than one relevant image. The number of such type of keywords varies for different models. Specifically, CMRM model that can retrieve multiple relevant images has 65 keywords that can retrieve multiple relevant images, topic-based smoothing has 77, The union of the above 2 keyword sets has less than 90 unique keywords. table 2 shows the retrieval precision and recall of 10 keywords randomly selected from the 90 keywords in the corresponding models.

Table 1. The comparisons of annotation models by precision and recall

	The number of success keywords	Average precision	Average recall
CMRM	65	25.56%	27.53%
LaM	77	32.93%	40.98%

Precision = (auto annotation ∩ manual annotation)/(auto annotation)
Recall = (auto annotation ∩ manual annotation)/(manual annotation)

The average performance of the 90 keywords based image retrieval using the corresponding image annotation methods is given in Table 1. The experimental results show that the annotation performance of topic-based smoothing method is better than CMRM [7]

6   Conclusion

To overcome the spareness problem of the relevance language model based image annotaion, we proposed the topic-based smoothing method based on the layered image model. Experimental results show that compared with the CMRM model, our method can improve the annotation effectiveness significantly.

Acknowledgement

This work was supported in part by the NSF of China under grant number 60403018 and NSF of Shanghai of China under grant number 04ZR14011. We would like to thank Prof. Weiyi Meng for his helpful advice and comments.

References

1. Barnard, K., P. Duygulu, and D. Forsyth. Clustering Art. in Proceedings of IEEE ICPR. 2001.
2. K. Barnard, P. Duygulu, N. de Freitas, D. Forsyth, D. Blei, and M. I. Jordan. Matching words and pictures. Journal of Machine Learning Research, 3:1107-1135, 2003.
3. A.Benitez and S.-.F. Chang. Semantic knowledge construction from annotated image collections. In Proc IEEE ICME, Lausanne, July. 2002
4. D. Blei, and M. I. Jordan. (2003) Modeling annotated data. In Proc. of the 26th Intl. ACM SIGIR Conf., 127-134, 2003
5. Cusano, C., G. Ciocca, and R. Schettini. Image Annotation Using Svm. in Proceedings of Internet imaging IV, Vol. SPIE 5304. 2004.
6. P. Duygulu, K. Barnard, N. de Freitas, and D. Forsyth. Object recognition as machine translation: Learning a lexicon for a fixed image vocabulary. 7th European Conference on Computer Vision, pp IV:97-112, 2002.
7. J. Jeon, V. Lavrenko, R. Manmatha. Automatic Image Annotation and Retrieval using Cross-Media Relevance Models. Proc.of the 26th ACM SIGIR conference, pages 119-126, 2003
8. R. Jin, J.Chai and L. Si,Effective Automatic Image Annotation Via A Coherent Language Model and Active Learning, ACM MM2004
9. F. Monay and D. Gatica-PerezOn. On image auto-annotation with latent space models. In Proc. of the ACM Int'l Conf. on Multimedia 2003.
10. Y.Mori, H. Takahashi, and R. Oka. Image-to-word transformation based on dividing and vector quantizing images with words. In First Int'l Workshop on Multimedia Intelligent Storage and Retrieval Management, 1999.
11. J. Shi and J. Malik. Normalized cuts and image segmentation. IEEE Transactions on Pattern Analysis and Machine Intelligence, 22(8):888-905, 2000.

A Focused Crawler
with Document Segmentation

Jaeyoung Yang, Jinbeom Kang, and Joongmin Choi

Hanyang University
Department of Computer Science and Engineering
1271 Sa-1 Dong, Ansan, Korea
{jyyang,jbkang,jmchoi}@cse.hanyang.ac.kr
http://islab.hanyang.ac.kr/

Abstract. The focused crawler is a topic-driven document-collecting crawler that was suggested as a promising alternative of maintaining up-to-date Web document indices in search engines. A major problem inherent in previous focused crawlers is the liability of missing highly relevant documents that are linked from off-topic documents. This problem mainly originated from the lack of consideration of structural information in a document. Traditional weighting method such as TFIDF employed in document classification can lead to this problem.

In order to improve the performance of focused crawlers, this paper proposes a scheme of locality-based document segmentation to determine the relevance of a document to a specific topic. We segment a document into a set of sub-documents using contextual features around the hyperlinks. This information is used to determine whether the crawler would fetch the documents that are linked from hyperlinks in an off-topic document.

1 Introduction

Traditional Web crawlers have been faced with problems in collecting documents mainly due to dynamic changes in the structure and the size of Web documents, which makes it difficult to maintain up-to-date document indices in search engines. Current Web crawlers heavily rely on classical search algorithms such as breadth-first or depth-first search, and as a result, it takes a fair amount of time for search engines to periodically index all linked Web pages. In order to reduce this time, many technical tricks are applied, but most of them are ad-hoc.

Some search engines dealing with specific topics, such as CiteSeer and yellow page search in Yahoo, are not interested in the entire Web documents but a subset of them relating to the topics. In contrast to the exhaustive crawler that is interested in collecting the entire documents, focused crawlers aim to collect a subset of documents that are relevant to specific topics. While traversing the Web, focused crawlers assign a relevance score to each document. If the score is below the threshold value, the Web page is thrown away and the hyperlinks in this document are not used in subsequent traversal. This prevents focused crawlers from wasting time with irrelevant documents.

M. Gallagher, J. Hogan, and F. Maire (Eds.): IDEAL 2005, LNCS 3578, pp. 94–101, 2005.

However, there are some problems in current focused crawlers. Proper assignment of credit to Web documents becomes more critical for focused crawlers. Without a reliable credit assignment mechanism, the volume of Web documents that a focused crawler can gather would be small. Existing focused crawlers adopt the method of text classification to assign a proper credit to a document. But since the current focused crawlers use text classifiers that are not considering Web document structure, the crawlers can miss some relevant documents linked by hyperlinks from an off-topic document.

In this paper, we propose a new focused crawler adopting a scheme of document segmentation to overcome this problem. Document segmentation divides a document into several sub-documents using hyperlinks. Text classifier analyzes documents not as a whole but as a set of small documents. In our point of view, a document consists of sub-topics, which have implicit relations among them. A set of these sub-topics is combined to explain a more general topic. The overall topic of a document is not always the same as sub-topics in the document. In this paper we use this intuitional fact for extracting on-topic hyperlinks from off-topic documents.

2   Related Work

Early studies on focused crawler including FishSearch[1], SharkSearch[2], and the work in[3] use traditional information retrieval algorithms such as term frequency (TF) and/or inverse document frequency (IDF). In addition, [3] uses some heuristics such as the page rank and the number of in-links. A key characteristic of these studies is the re-ordering of document fetching that assigns the rank to each page based on its degree of relevance. These systems have one thing in common that they do not employ any classification algorithm to identify on-topic documents.

Charabati[4] is the first to adopt a classification algorithm in focused crawler. This study assigns a class score to every URL extracted from a page. But its major problem is that the focused crawler is unable to reach on-topic pages that are linked from off-topic pages. Context graph-based crawler [5] and Cora [6] try to solve the problem by generating context graphs that are used to calculate distance and by developing a reinforcement learning algorithm, respectively, but the results are not satisfactory.

3   Problem Statement

Focused crawlers extract relevant hyperlinks from an on-topic document and pursue them in order to collect interesting documents only. Current focused crawlers assign a credit to a document, and extract all hyperlinks from it to follow up if the credit exceeds the predefined threshold. But this might lead to a problem as shown in Fig. 1.

Figure 1 shows an off-topic document which is classified as an irrelevant document by the classifier but linked to a set of on-topic documents. In this case we

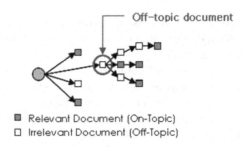

Fig. 1. Off-topic document which leads to relevant documents

may miss some on-topic documents linked from the off-topic document. Existing focused crawlers have not solved this problem. We claim that the assignment of a credit to a document as a whole causes this problem. A document may consist of several sub-topics which have implicit relations among themselves. Current classifiers that are employed in most focused crawlers ignore sub-topic structure and assume that a document deals with a single explicit topic. But this assumption is not always true especially for a Web page that contains various link information.

A Bayesian Approach to Filtering Junk E-Mail - Sahami, Dumais, Heckerman.. (1998)   (Correct)   (44 citations)
we can not only employ traditional **document classification** techniques based on the text of
research.microsoft.com/~heckerman/spam98.ps

Distributional Clustering of Words for Text Classification - Baker, McCallum (1998)   (Correct)   (44 citations)
of Distributional Clustering [20] to **document classification**. This approach clusters words into
aggressively, while still maintaining high **document classification** accuracy. Experimental results obtained
www.cs.cmu.edu/~mccallum/papers/clustering-sigir98.ps.gz

Concept Based Query Expansion - Yonggang Qiu Department (1993)   (Correct)   (42 citations)
useful [Min 72, Pea 91, Spa 91]2) Use of **document classification**. Documents are first classified using a
Documents are first classified using a **document classification** algorithm. Infrequent terms found in a
72, Pea 91, Spa 91]2) Use of **document classification**. Documents are first classified using a document
www.ubilab.org/publications/print_versions/ps/qiu93.ps.gz

Building and Maintaining Analysis-Level Class Hierarchies Using .. - Godin, Mili (1993)   (Correct)   (31 citations)
conceptual distance measurements [5]and **document classification** and browsing [10]Building such
ftp.crim.ca/igloo/privee/publications/Reuti-RG-galois-lattice-OOPSLA93.ps.gz

SPIRIT: Sequential Pattern Mining with Regular.. - Garofalakis, Rastogi.. (1999)   (Correct)   (29 citations)
topics and the inherently fuzzy nature of **document classification**, there are numerous cases in which
www.bell-labs.com/project/serendip/Papers/vldb99-cam.ps.gz

Fig. 2. An example of an off-topic document

As an example, consider a document shown in Fig. 2. This document shows a list of papers for the topic of *document classification*. But each paper description represents a different type of classification methods. A focused crawler which is interested in the topic of *Bayesian method* tries to determine whether this document is relevant to the topic using an existing classifier that employs TFIDF or some other statistical methods. If we use TF as measurement of feature extraction, we get the features such as *Document(11)*, ..., *Classification(9)*, and *Bayesian(1)*. Even though this document contains an on-topic hyperlink, the focused crawler would regard this page as an off-topic document because the target term *Bayesian* occurs only once and other features prevail in terms of TF.

This phenomenon is due to ignoring the structure of Web documents and lump all features together in a document. Web documents dealing with a topic may consist of some related sub-topics as shown in Fig. 2. Note that all sub-topics in a document do not necessarily explain the same theme. In the focused crawling, features that are lumped together as a bag of words affect the performance of a classifier. A motivation of this paper is that the consideration of Web document structure by properly segmenting a document into sub-topics can enhance the performance. In Fig. 2, there are five sub-topics denoting different document classification approaches. A crucial problem of current focused crawlers can be reduced if we can properly segment a document and assign a credit not to the whole document but to each of the hyperlinks in a document.

4   Classification and Crawling

4.1   Document Segmentation

The purpose of document segmentation is to identify useful segments around a hyperlink. A useful segment is a set of words or phrases which well represent the content of a page associated with a hyperlink. Segmenting a document is a difficult task, and we use some heuristics in which useful segments are located using contextual information around the hyperlinks and the anchor texts in them.

Our task of documentation segmentation proceeds in two phases. In the first stage, the sentence containing a hyperlink is extracted as complete as possible. We do not use the technique of NLP to analyze the sentence, but use simple method of stacking tokens until the sentence period or one of predefined HTML tags is reached. In the second phase, a set of tokens occurred before and after the hyperlink are extracted. The number of tokens that need to be extracted is specified manually. We set this number to 10 in this paper.

4.2   Collecting a Set of Features

We collect features from two different sources. The first source is the training examples. To select features from the training examples, we assess the usefulness of a feature by the χ^2-measure [8] which is a well-known statistical value used in document classification. In our experiment the χ^2-measure extracts better features than other measures such as TFIDF, entropy, or mutual information. The χ^2-measure can be written as

$$\chi^2 = \frac{N(N_{r+}N_{n-} - N_{r-}N_{n+})^2}{(N_{r+} + N_{r-})(N_{n+} + N_{n-})(N_{r+} + N_{n+})(N_{r-} + N_{n-})} \tag{1}$$

where N is the total number of training examples, N_{r+} and N_{n+} are the number of relevant and irrelevant documents in which the term occurs, respectively, and N_{r-} and N_{n-} are the number of relevant and irrelevant documents in which the term does not occur, respectively. We use top 5% features to stand for a class.

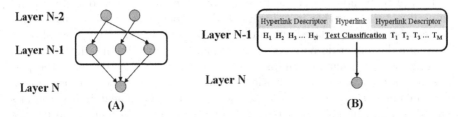

Fig. 3. Range of parent nodes, and the anchor text and HDs in a parent node

The second source of feature extraction is the anchor text of a hyperlink that links to a training document and the hyperlink descriptors in a parent node. Figure 3 shows a graph explaining the relation between training examples and their parent nodes which point to training examples by using hyperlinks. We collect features from the layer N(training examples) and the layer N-1(parent nodes). Each parent node is comprised of the hyperlink descriptors(HD) and the anchor text that are used as features. In order to collect features from the parent nodes, the crawler should perform backward visiting. We use google's page-specific search service to obtain pages which point to the training examples.

4.3   Classifier and Parameter Estimation

The Naive Bayes classifier is commonly used in text categorization because it is easy to implement and provides well-studied mathematical background. This classifier predicts the most-likely class with the maximum posterior value by using the features extracted from a new instance that are compared with the given features extracted from the training examples. An instance (a document in this case) is represented by a vector of extracted features as $\vec{d_i} = <f_1, f_2, \cdots, f_n>$. With a set of extracted features from instances, the Naive Bayes classifier can be written as

$$C_{est} = \arg\max_{c_j \in C} P(c_j) \prod_k P(f_k|c_j) \qquad (2)$$

where c_j is a class from a set of predefined classes $C = \{c_1, c_2, \cdots, c_m\}$.

$P(c_j)$ and $P(f_k|c_j)$ are calculated by using term frequencies from the training examples. In this paper we use *m-estimate* [7] instead of classical and robust maximum likelihood estimation to prevent the probability from being zero. The *m-estimate* can be written as

$$\frac{n_c + tp}{n + t} \qquad (3)$$

where n denotes the total frequency of feature occurrences in the training examples, n_c represents the frequency of feature occurrences in a class, t is the sample size, and p is a weight for the sample size.

4.4 Crawling

After learning and gathering a set of topics, the focused crawler starts traversing with classifiers from seed pages. In the initial stage, the focused crawler put seed pages for each class to the class stack. To identify on-topic hyperlinks, the focused crawler pops a page from the stack and fragmentizes it into a set of sub-documents using the document segmentation heuristics. Each segment is comprised of a hyperlink, its anchor text, and HDs. Classifiers evaluate each sub-document using the anchor text and HDs to determine if the extracted hyperlink in the sub-document is on-topic. Classifiers use a predefined threshold as the criterion to evaluate sub-documents. The sub-document which does not satisfy the predefined threshold is not associated with any class. The document satisfying the threshold is assigned a class with the maximum class score. If a hyperlink is assigned a class, it is pushed into the class stack and processed in subsequent cycles. The crawler repeats the task of downloading and classification until the class stack becomes empty.

5 Experimental Results

Performance evaluation of the focused crawler is difficult and subjective since there are no test-beds to evaluate the performance. Typically the precision and recall measures that are popular in information retrieval are used. In this paper we claim that the focused crawler using document segmentation reduces the loss of on-topic Web pages, which means that the recall is higher than traditional focused crawlers.

To show the improvement of performance, we have implemented three different focused crawlers and carried out experiments to compare them: (1) traditional focused crawler using naive classifier, (2) focused crawler using document segmentation without extracting features from parent Web pages, and (3) focused crawler using document segmentation with extracting features from parent Web pages. The third experiment is done to examine the impact of the anchor text and HDs in parent Web pages.

We have used 10 Web documents related to the topic of CORBA for training the classifier. A seed page is "http://www.omg.org/gettingstarted/corbafaq.htm". Our focused crawler gathered 8822 documents on the net. The threshold is set to 0.76 based on experiments. A segmented document that is assigned the credit above the threshold by the classifier is accepted as a link to an on-topic document. If the credit of a segmented document is under the threshold, our crawler does not use a hyperlink in the segmented document to download a linked document.

Figure 4 shows that as the number of features increases, the precision is getting low due to impure features that interfere with the classifier. But our crawler

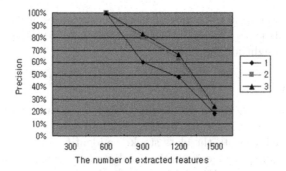

Fig. 4. Experimental result: Precision

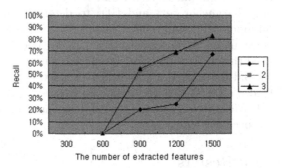

Fig. 5. Experimental result: Recall

shows better performance than traditional crawlers. Figure 5 shows the recall measure according to the number of features. Our focused crawler also shows better performance than traditional crawler that mainly resulted from the fact that our crawler identifies on-topic documents linked from off-topic documents. In short, these results support our claim that the document segmentation affects the classification performance.

6 Conclusions

In this paper we have proposed a focused crawler with document segmentation to reduce the loss of on-topic Web pages. Our experiment shows that the model we proposed improves the performance of focused crawler by evaluating on-topic segment by considering the anchor text and contextual information around hyperlink. Since we analyze each hyperlink and its contextual information, we can reduce the loss of on-topic hyperlinks in an off-topic document. Without the consideration of features in a parent node, our focused crawler is more efficient than traditional focused crawler using naive classifier.

To increase the classifier accuracy, we plan to investigate other credit assignment functions and feature selection methods for naive classifier.

References

1. P. De Bra et al.: Information Retrieval in Distributed Hypertexts. Proc. 4th Int'l Conf. Intelligent Multimedia Information Retrieval System and Management, Center of High Int'l Studies of Documentary Information Retrieval (1994) 481-491
2. M. Hersovici et al.: The SharkSearch Algorithm-An Application: Tailored Web Site Mapping, Proc. 8th Int'l World Wide Web Conf. (1998) 213-225
3. J. Cho et al.: Efficient Crawling through URL Ordering, Computer Networks and ISDN Systems, vol. 30 (1998) 161-172
4. S. Chakrabarti, M.H. Van den Berg, and B.E. Dom.: Focused Crawling: A New Approach to Topic-Specific Web Resource Discovery, Computer Networks, vol. 31, nos. 11-16 (1999) 1623-1640
5. M. Diligenti et al.: Focused Crawling Using Context Graphs, Proc. 26'th Int'l Conf. Very Large Data Bases, Morgan Kaufmann (2000) 527-534
6. A. McCallum et al.: Building Domain-Specific Search Engines with Machine Learning Techniques, Proc. AAAI Symp. Intelligent Agents in Cyberspace, AAAI Press (1999) 28-39
7. Tom M. Mitchell.: Machine Learning, McGraw-Hill (1997) 154-199
8. Yang, Y., Pedersen J.P.: A Comparative Study on Feature Selection in Text Categorization, Proceedings of the Fourteenth International Conference on Machine Learning (1997) 412-420

An Intelligent Grading System
Using Heterogeneous Linguistic Resources

Yu-Seop Kim[1], Woo-Jin Cho[1], Jae-Young Lee[1], and Yu-Jin Oh[2]

[1] Division of Information Engineering and Telecommunications, Hallym University,
Gangwon, Korea 200-702
{yskim01,woojini,jylee}@hallym.ac.kr
[2] Department of Economics, Korea University,
Seoul, Korea 136-701
ouj@ewha.ac.kr

Abstract. In this paper, we propose an intelligent grading system using heterogeneous linguistic resources. We used latent semantic kernel as one resource in former research and found that a deficit of indexed terms gave rise to performance bottleneck. To solve this, we expand answer papers, written by students and instructors, by utilizing one of widely used linguistic resources, WordNet. We supplement the papers with words semantically related to indexed terms of papers. The added words are selected from the synonyms and hyponyms on WordNet. And to get rid of the criterion decision problem, we use partial score of each question and evaluate the correlation coefficient between grading results of the proposed approach and human instructors. The proposed approach in this research achieves maximally 0.94 correlation coefficient to instructors, which is 0.06 higher than that of the former research.

1 Introduction

Bang et al. [1] developed a short essay-typed exam grading system running in an Internet environment. However, the system must employ human instructors to grade the answer papers submitted, and it requests high cost and unpredictable response time. Kim et al. [2] hired information retrieval based methodologies, called as latent semantic kernels [3], to mark the papers automatically and promptly. Even though they reported a promising sign of performance results, a deficit of indexed terms, used for constructing the semantic kernel, brought about performance bottleneck, which captures a half out of total grading errors. So we utilize another heterogeneous linguistic resources to supplement above researches.

In this research, we expand the answer papers written by students and instructors, by supplementing the papers with words similar to those existing in the papers. The similar words are defined as those located in the same and/or the nearest nodes on WordNet, known as the most widely used ontology information of word meaning. By utilizing WordNet information as well as existing linguistic knowledge discovered by latent semantic kernel, and by employing partial scores

M. Gallagher, J. Hogan, and F. Maire (Eds.): IDEAL 2005, LNCS 3578, pp. 102–108, 2005.

of each answers, which alleviates exertion to find out the optimum criterion, the correlation coefficient between the grading results from instructors and the suggested system, was grown up to 0.94 from 0.88.

The rest of this paper is composed of the following way. Section 2 explains the existing intelligent grading system based on the latent semantic kernel. WordNet and its application for this system are described in section 3. Section 4 shows the experimental results and its evaluation, and concluding remarks are given in section 5.

2   Intelligent Grading System

The intelligent grading system of the research [2] was based on the latent semantic kernel proposed by [3]. Similarity between papers written by students and instructors is estimated after replacing a student paper with a query, q, and instructor papers, a model paper, with documents, d, on the following model.

$$sim(d, q) = cos(P^T d, P^T q) = \frac{d^T PPq}{|P^T d||P^T q|}, \tag{1}$$

where P is a matrix transforming documents from an input space to a feature space. A kernel function $k(d, q) = < \phi(d), \phi(q) >$ uses the matrix P to replace $\phi(d)$ with $P^T d$. To find P, the term-document matrix A is first built and then the matrix is transformed by singular value decomposition (SVD) like

$$A = U\Sigma V^T, \tag{2}$$

where Σ is a diagonal matrix composed of nonzero eigenvalues of AA^T or $A^T A$, and U and V are the orthogonal eigenvectors associated with the r nonzero eigenvalues of AA^T and $A^T A$, respectively. The original term-document matrix (A) has size of $m \times n$. One component matrix (U), with $m \times r$, describes the original row entities as vectors of derived orthogonal factor value, another (V), with $n \times r$, describes the original column entities in the same way, and the third (Σ) is a diagonal matrix, with $r \times r$, containing scaling values when the three components are matrix-multiplied, the original matrix is reconstructed. The singular vectors corresponding to the k $(k \leq r)$ largest singular values are then used to define k-dimensional document space. Using these vectors, $m \times k$ and $n \times k$ matrices U_k and V_k may be redefined along with $k \times k$ singular value matrix Σ_k. It is known that $A_k = U_k \Sigma_k V_k^T$ is the closest matrix of rank k to the original matrix A. And U_k is replaced with P. Landauer et al. [4] explains more details of above SVD-based methods, latent semantic analysis (LSA).

After receiving answer papers from students, the system transforms answer papers into vectors. And then it estimates the similarity between the vectors for answer papers and stored vectors representing model papers written by instructors, by using the above Latent Semantic Kernel. Finally the system determines the correctness of the papers by using a criterion which is determined heuristically. The whole structure of the grading system is described in figure 1. More details are explained in [2]

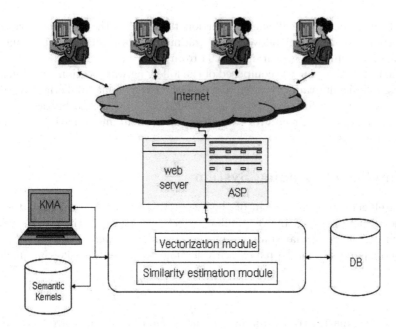

Fig. 1. Whole structure of intelligent grading system

3   Paper Expansion with WordNet

WordNet is an online lexical reference system whose design is inspired by current psycholinguistic theories of human lexical memory [5]. We expanded both answer papers written by students and instructors by Hangul (Korean characters) WordNet [6]. Figure 2 shows the structure of paper expansion module by using WordNet.

For paper expansion, the system extracts noun terms from input papers with a Hangul morphological analyzer[7]. The extracted terms are used to search their synonym and hyponym words from WordNet. The synonym words are included in their own synsets and the hyponym words are located in the nodes only adjacent to themselves. 'hyponym' is a subordinate categorization of a given

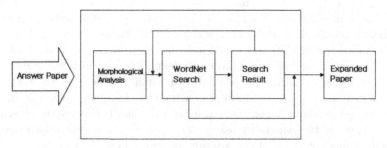

Fig. 2. Structure of Paper Expansion Module with WordNet

term. For example, a term 'car' has a same synset with 'automobile' and is also hyponym word of 'vehicle'. Table 1 shows examples of expanded terms by using Hangul WordNet.

Table 1. Examples of Term Expansion. The first column shows input terms to be expanded and the second column shows their synonym and hyponym terms. The words in parenthesis are English-translated terms of given Korean terms

given terms	expanded terms
moon-je (problem)	bool-oon (misfortune), bool-haeng (unhappiness)
go-nan (trouble)	go-saeng (privation), jae-nan (misfortune)
yo-ri (cooking)	goop-gi (roasting), tui-gi-gi (frying)
gyung-young (management)	ji-hui (command), gwan-ri (management)

Figure 3 shows the whole structure of the proposed intelligent grading system in this research. When a question is given to the student, model papers for the question, which are written by instructors, are prepared to be transformed into vectors (d_i). And after receiving a student paper, the system also transforms the paper into a vector (q). The student and model papers, then, are ready to be expanded by using WordNet. The system retrieves words similar to noun terms in the vectors from WordNet and the retrieved words are inserted into the paper vectors. The Expanded vectors in this phase are represented as 'Expanded q' and 'Expanded d_i' in figure 3. And finally the semantic kernel helps to calculate the similarities between the student paper and the model papers expanded.

4   Experimental Results

4.1   Data and Methods

For the experiments, we extracted thirty descriptive questions from a book named 'Proverbs' (in Korean 'Ko-Sa-Seong-Eo') [8]. One hundred students were connected to the grading system and took exams and about 3,000 descriptive exam answer papers were built. We collected 38,727 articles from a Korean newspaper site, one of the largest newspaper companies in Korea, for corpus data, which will be used for construction of the semantic kernels. And we extracted 40,376 indexed terms from the corpus by using the Hangul morphological analyzer. And for the construction of U_k of section 2, we decided k to 200 empirically.

Kim et al. [2] used a criterion to determine whether an answer paper is correct or not. And the criterion was decided heuristically. However, instead of criterion, we employ the similarity value. In detail, for each student, we calculate the similarity value of each question, partial scores, then compare the total scores with total scores marked by instructor itself. To check out performance improvement, we employ three methods to compare each other. At first, LSA1 means the methods exactly same as [2], giving 1 points to the answer if the similarity is higher than criterion and 0 point otherwise. And LSA2 employ the partial score

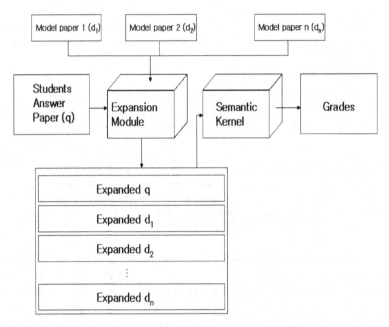

Fig. 3. An Intelligent Grading System using Semantic Kernel and WordNet

of each answer. The partial score comes from the similarity value itself. And finally, ELSA (Expanded LSA) employs paper expansion using WordNet and it also uses the partial scores. And for the evaluation of similarity between grading results from instructor and the three methods, we consider both an answer sheet for thirty questions and an answer for one question as base units of data.

Figure 4 shows an user interface of an intelligent grading system. The system gives a question randomly selected out of thirty questions and outputs scores for the question after receiving an answer from a student.

4.2 Evaluation

We evaluate the similarity of scoring results from instructors and three methods, that is, LSA1, LSA2, and ELSA. Pearson's correlation coefficient [9] is used to evaluate similarity between two variables. The coefficient ranges from -1.0 to 1.0. Positive coefficient reflects a direct relationship between two variables, and a negative coefficient reflects an inverse.

In table 2, ELSA, combination of latent semantic kernel and WordNet, shows the highest similarity to instructors. It shows up to 0.94 coefficient value, when each answer paper sheet of one student is considered as a data unit. However, when the data unit is broken down into each answers for a question, the coefficient value was decreased to 0.66. From the fact, we can infer that the intelligent grading system can make better display of its human-like grading capability when the final scoring results are computed by summing up scores of large num-

Fig. 4. An user interface of an intelligent grading system

Table 2. Correlation coefficient between score by instructors and those by three methods. Each number in the cell means the correlation coefficient value. In the second row, the experimental data are answer papers of 100 students, and each paper has thirty questions, that is the score of each paper is up to thirty points. On contrary, the data of the third row mean 3,000 answers, which have up to 1 point

	LSA1	LSA2	ELSA
100 answer paper sheets	0.88	0.91	0.94
3,000 questions	0.57	0.62	0.66

ber of answers. And human instructors gave only 0 or 1 point to each answer and this made score differences more.

We can classify the reason of failure of 0.06 into three categories. One is from the failure of Hangul morphological analysis, 12%, the second 20% is caused from the deficit of the indexed terms, decreased from about 50% before, and the final 68% is from the limitation of the methodologies used in this research. And we also found out the main reason of last category is from very humble answer papers. Many of student papers were seemed to leave out noun keywords containing main ideas of given proverbs and had just predicates and their modifier words instead.

5   Concluding Remarks

This research proposed an intelligent grading system trying to recover a deficit of indexed term problem caused in the former researches. The system integrated the former latent semantic kernel and WordNet. By combining two heterogeneous methodologies and by employing partial scoring, the system could improve its correlation coefficient from 0.88 to 0.94. It also shows that if data are bundles of answers than the system plays a role very similar to human beings.

For the future work, we should extend types of examinations. The questions of this research need just one-sentence answers. We should find the way to test the similarity when the question needs multiple sentences, even to a letter. And we should find out the way to reflect the syntactic structure of answers to grading, and finally integrate semantic structure and syntactic structure, in order to make the system to be elaborate.

Acknowledgments

This work was supported by Korea Science and Engineering Foundation, 2004 (R05-2004-000-10376-0) and the Brain Korea 21 Project in 2005.

References

1. Bang, H., S. Hur, W. Kim, and J. Lee: A System to Supplement Subjectivity Test Marking on the Web-based. Proceedings of KIPS (2001) (in Korean).
2. Kim, Y., J. Oh, J. Chang, and J. Lee: A Supplement Subjectivity Test Marking System using Latent Semantic Kernels. Proceedings of Asia Information Retrieval Symposium (AIRS 2004), (2004) 225–228.
3. Cristianini, N., J. Shawe-Taylor, and H. Lodhi: Latent Semantic Kernels. Journal of Intelligent Information System, Vol. 18 No. 2 (2002) 127–152.
4. Landauer, T. K., P. W. Foltz, and D. Laham: An introduction to latent semantic analysis. Discourse Processes, No. 25 (1998) 259–284.
5. Miller, G. A.: WordNet: An On-Line Lexical Database. International Journal of Lexicography, (1999).
6. Lee, E. and S. Lim: Korean WordNet ver. 2.0. Korean Language Processing Laboratory, Pusan National University, (2004).
7. Kang, S.: Gerneral Purposed Morphological Analyzer HAM Ver. 6.0.0. http://nlp.kookmin.ac.kr, (2004).
8. Kim, W.: Ko-Sa-Seong-Eo (Proverbs) Encyclopedia. Eu-Yu Inc. (2003) (in Korean).
9. Bain, L. and M. Engelhardt: Introduction to Probability and Mathematical Statistics. Thomson Learning. 179–190 (1987).

Probabilistic Data Generation
for Deduplication and Data Linkage

Peter Christen

Department of Computer Science, Australian National University,
Canberra ACT 0200, Australia
peter.christen@anu.edu.au
http://datamining.anu.edu.au/linkage.html

Abstract. In many data mining projects the data to be analysed contains personal information, like names and addresses. Cleaning and pre-processing of such data likely involves deduplication or linkage with other data, which is often challenged by a lack of unique entity identifiers. In recent years there has been an increased research effort in data linkage and deduplication, mainly in the machine learning and database communities. Publicly available test data with known deduplication or linkage status is needed so that new linkage algorithms and techniques can be tested, evaluated and compared. However, publication of data containing personal information is normally impossible due to privacy and confidentiality issues. An alternative is to use artificially created data, which has the advantages that content and error rates can be controlled, and the deduplication or linkage status is known. Controlled experiments can be performed and replicated easily. In this paper we present a freely available data set generator capable of creating data sets containing names, addresses and other personal information.

1   Introduction

Finding duplicate records in one, or linking records from several data sets are increasingly important tasks in the data preparation phase of many data mining projects, as often information from multiple sources needs to be integrated, combined or linked in order to allow more detailed data analysis or mining. The aim of such linkages is to match all records related to the same entity, such as a patient or customer. As common unique entity identifiers (or keys) are rarely available in all data sets to be linked, the linkage process needs to be based on the existing common attributes.

Data linkage and deduplication can be used to improve data quality and integrity, to allow re-use of existing data sources for new studies, and to reduce costs and efforts in data acquisition. In the health sector, for example, linked data might contain information that is needed to improve health policies, and that traditionally has been collected with time consuming and expensive survey methods. Businesses routinely deduplicate and link their data sets to compile mailing lists, while in taxation offices and departments of social security data

M. Gallagher, J. Hogan, and F. Maire (Eds.): IDEAL 2005, LNCS 3578, pp. 109–116, 2005.

Table 1. Data sets used in recent publications

Data set	Publication
Cora [16]	[16] (2000), [7] (2002), [2, 3] (2003), [12] (2004)
Restaurant [22]	[7, 22] (2002), [2, 3] (2003), [20] (2004)
Citeseer [2]	[21] (2002), [2, 3] (2003)
Proprietary or confidential	[24] (2000), [7, 10, 21, 22] (2002), [20, 23] (2004)
Artificially generated data [1, 6, 14]	[14] (1995), [10] (2002), [1] (2003), [12] (2004)

linkage can be used to identify people who register for benefits multiple times or who work and collect unemployment money. Another application of current interest is the use of data linkage in crime and terror detection, which increasingly rely on the ability to quickly bring up files for a particular individual that may help to prevent crimes or terror by early intervention.

As data linkage and deduplication is often dealing with data sets that contain (partially) identifying attributes (like names, addresses, or dates of birth), it can be difficult for a researcher to acquire standard data for testing and evaluation of new linkage algorithms and techniques. For a user, it is challenging to learn how to use and customise data linkage systems effectively without data sets where the linkage status is known. An alternative is the use of artificially generated data, which we will discuss in the following section.

2   Data Linkage, Deduplication and Artificial Data

Computer-assisted data (or record) linkage goes back as far as the 1950s, and the theoretical foundation has been provided by [11] in 1969. The basic idea is to link records by comparing common attributes, which include person identifiers (like names and dates of birth) and demographic information (like addresses).

In recent years, researchers started to explore machine learning and data mining techniques to improve the linkage process. Clustering [5, 10, 16], active learning [21, 22], decision trees [10, 22], graphical models [20], and learnable approximate string distances [2, 3, 8, 17, 23, 24] are some of the techniques used.

In these publications various data sets (some publicly available, others proprietary or even confidential) were used in experimental studies, as shown in Table 1. This variety makes it difficult to validate the presented results and to compare new deduplication and linkage algorithms with each other. Tuning of parameters can result in high accuracy and good performance for a certain algorithm on a specific data set, but the same parameter values might be less successful on other data or in different application areas.

There is clearly a lack of publicly available real world data sets for deduplication and data linkage, which can be used as standard test beds (or test decks) for developing and comparing algorithms, similar to data collections used in information retrieval (TREC) or machine learning (UCI repository [4]). However, because many real world data sets contain personal information, privacy and confidentiality issues make it unlikely that they can be made publicly available. Using de-identified data, where e.g. names and addresses are encrypted or removed, is not feasible either, as many linkage algorithms specifically work on name and address strings [6, 11].

Artificially generated data can be an attractive alternative. Such data must model the content and statistical properties of comparable real world data sets, including the frequency distributions of attribute values, error types and distributions, and error positions within these values. Typographical errors have been analysed in a number of studies [9, 13, 19], and are important issues in the areas of error correction in text [15] and approximate string matching [13]. One of the earliest studies [9] found that over 80% of typographical errors were single errors, either an insertion, deletion or substitution of a character, or transposition of two adjacent characters. Substitutions were the most common errors, followed by deletes, then inserts and finally transpositions, followed by multiple errors. Similar results were reported by others [13, 15, 19].

Names and addresses are especially prone to data entry errors. Different error characteristics will occur depending upon the mode of data entry [15], for example manually typed, scanned, or via automatic speech recognition. Optical character recognition [13, 19] (scanning) will lead to substitution errors between similar looking characters (e.g. 'q' and 'g'), while keyboard based data entry can result in wrongly typed neighbouring keys. Data entry over the telephone will mainly lead to phonetical errors, which seem to occur more likely towards the end of names [19]. While for many regular words there is only one correct spelling, there are often different written forms of proper names, for example 'Gail' and 'Gayle'. Additionally, names are often reported differently by the same person depending upon the organisation they are in contact with, resulting in missing middle names, initials only, or even swapped name parts.

Artificially generating duplicate records based on real world error distributions will result in data sets that have characteristics similar to real world data. A first such data generator (called *DBGen* or *UIS Database Generator*)[1] that allows the creation of databases containing duplicates records was presented in [14]. It uses lists of names, cities, states, and postcodes, and provides a large number of parameters, including the size of the database to be generated, percentage and distribution of duplicates, and the amount and types of errors introduced. An improved generator is described in [1], that allows for missing attribute values and increased variability in the set of possible values generated.

3   A Probabilistic Data Set Generator

We have developed a data set generator based on ideas from [14] and improved in several ways. Our generator can create data sets containing names and addresses (based on frequency tables), dates, telephone and identifier numbers (like social security numbers). It is implemented as part of the *Febrl* [6] data linkage system, and freely available under an open source software license. A user can easily modify and improve the generator according to her or his needs.

---

[1]   Available from: http://www.cs.utexas.edu/users/ml/riddle/data.html

A user specified number of *original* records are generated in the first step, and in the second step *duplicate* records are created based on these original records by randomly introducing errors. Each record is given a unique identifier as can be seen in Figure 1. This allows the evaluation of error rates (false linked non-duplicates and non-linked true duplicates).

Original records are randomly created using frequency look-up tables for name and address attributes (like given- and surname; street number, name and type; locality, postcode, state or territory). These frequency tables can be compiled for example by using publicly available electronic telephone directories, or by extracting frequencies from data sets at hand, as shown in Section 4. For date, telephone and identifier number attributes, a user can specify the range (e.g. start and end date, or number of telephone digits).

Duplicate records are generated next based on the original records and according to the following parameters.

- The total number of duplicate records to be generated.
- The maximum number of errors to be introduced into one attribute in a record.
- The maximum number of errors to be introduced into one record.
- The maximum number of duplicate records to be created based on one original record.
- The probability distribution (either uniform, Poisson, or Zipf) of how many duplicates are being created based on one original record.

Duplicate records are created by randomly selecting an original record (which has so far not been used to create duplicates), followed by randomly choosing the number of duplicates to be created for it, and then randomly introducing errors according to user specified probabilities. A additional probability distribution specifies how likely attributes are selected for introducing errors (it is possible to have attributes with no errors at all). The following types of errors can be introduced.

- If an attribute value from an original record is found in a look-up table with misspellings (for example of real typographical errors), then randomly choose one of it's misspellings.
- Insert a new character at a random position into an attribute value.
- Delete a character at a random position from an attribute value.
- Substitute a character in an attribute value with another character. Substitution is based on the idea of keying errors, where the substituted character will more likely be replaced with a randomly chosen neighbouring character in the same keyboard row or column, than with another character (that is not a keyboard neighbour).
- Transpose two adjacent characters at a random position in an attribute value.
- Swap (replace) the value in an attribute with another value (similar to when a value was randomly created when the original records were generated).
- Insert a space into an attribute value and thus splitting a word.
- Delete a space in an attribute value and merge two words (this is obviously only possible if an original attribute value contains at least two words).
- Set an attribute value to missing (with a user definable missing value).
- Given an original attribute value is missing (or empty), insert a randomly chosen new value (similar to when creating the original records).
- Swap the values of two attributes in a record (e.g. surname with given name).

```
REC_IDENT,    GIVEN_NAME, SURNAME,  STR_NUM, ADDRESS_1,        ADDRESS_2, SUBURB,    POSTCODE
rec-0-org,    james,      whiteway, 2,       maribyrnong ave,  aird,      red hill,  2611
rec-1-org,    mitchell,   devin,    26,      knox st,          chelvy,    holder,    2606
rec-2-dup-0,  james,      sayl,     73,      chauncy cres,     ,          watson,    2913
rec-2-dup-1,  jame,       ,         73,      chauncy cres,     ,          watson,    2913
rec-2-dup-2,  jaems,      salt,     73,      chauncy pl,       ,          watson,    2913
rec-2-org,    james,      salt,     73,      chauncy cres,     ,          watson,    2913
rec-3-org,    mitchell,   polmear,  341,     fitchett st,      ,          o'connor,  2605
rec-4-dup-0,  isaad,      white,    15,      tyrrell circ,     tagarra,   rivett,    2906
rec-4-dup-1,  isaac,      wiglht,   15,      tyrrell circ,     ,          rivett,    2906
rec-4-org,    isaac,      white,    15,      tyrrell circ,     ,          rivett,    2906
rec-5-dup-0,  elle,       webb,     5,       burnie pl,        ,          bruce,     2617
rec-5-org,    elle,       webb,     3,       burnie pl,        ,          evatt,     2617
```

Fig. 1. Generated example data set with 6 original and 6 duplicate records, a maximum of 3 duplicates per record, and maximum 2 errors per attribute and per record

Following studies on real world typographical errors [15, 19], single character errors (inserts, deletes, etc.) are more likely introduced in the middle or towards the end of attribute values when the duplicate records are created.

4 Experimental Study

In order to evaluate the generation of artificial data, we conducted a study using the New South Wales Midwives Data Collection (MDC) [18]. We extracted 175,211 records from the years 1999 and 2000. The eight attributes used in our study were the mother's name (given- and surname), address (street number and name, locality and postcode) and date of birth, as well as the baby's date of birth. The data set contained 5,331 twin and 177 triplet births (which were assumed to be duplicates in the attributes describing the mother). Additional duplicates were from mothers giving birth twice (or even three times) within the two years period (possibly recorded with changed names and addresses). Unfortunately we did not have access to the duplication status.

We first extracted frequency tables for the attributes listed above, and then generated three artificial data sets using these tables, containing 5%, 10% and 20% duplicates, respectively. Table 2 shows the average frequencies and standard

Table 2. Average frequencies and standard deviations of attribute values in MDC data sets (original and generated with given percentage of duplicates)

Attribute	Original	Generated 5%	Generated 10%	Generated 20%
Surname	3.5 / 16.6	4.3 / 17.6	3.9 / 16.4	3.4 / 14.4
Given name	5.0 / 45.9	6.3 / 49.8	5.8 / 46.4	5.2 / 41.8
Street number	12.3 / 125	15.9 / 138	16.1 / 139	3.4 / 137
Street name	2.4 / 5.4	3.0 / 5.7	2.9 / 5.8	2.6 / 5.1
Postcode	224 / 337	167 / 294	154 / 284	138 / 267
Locality	55.7 / 123	30.5 / 91.6	21.9 / 76.8	14.7 / 60.7
Mother date of birth	16.6 / 12.1	16.6 / 12.1	16.6 / 12.1	16.6 / 12.1
Baby date of birth	240 / 42.1	225 / 62.8	225 / 63.8	224 / 64.4

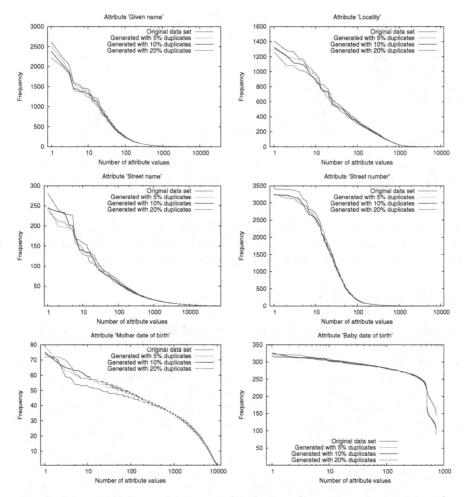

Fig. 2. Selected MDC sorted frequency distributions (log-scale on horizontal axis)

deviations of the attributes in the original and generated data sets, and Figure 2 shows a selection of the corresponding sorted frequency distributions.

As can be seen all three generated data sets have frequency distributions as well as standard deviations similar to the original data set. Different error types were introduced into the various attributes. These were mainly typographical errors in the attributes containing name strings, while in the date attributes values were mainly swapped with another value from the corresponding frequency table (resulting in nearly consistent average frequencies and standard deviations). For most attributes an increased percentage of duplicates resulted in smaller average frequencies and standard deviations, as the number of different attribute values was increased by the introduction of typographical and other errors.

5 Discussion and Outlook

We have discussed the issues and problems associated with real world test data for deduplication and data linkage, and presented a freely available data set generator. Improvements on our generator include the relaxation of the independent assumption, i.e. instead of creating attribute values independently, use frequency distributions for value combinations. Similarly, the introduction of errors and modifications could be based on statistical dependencies between attributes. For example, if a person moves, most of her or his address attributes (like street number and name, postcode and locality) will change. Another interesting extension would be to generate groups of records representing households (useful for generating census style data). Further fine-tuning the methods of how errors and modifications are introduced (for example character substitution based on scanning errors of handwritten forms) is another area of possible improvements. We are also planning to do further comparison studies, specifically we are interest in comparing the deduplication and linkage outcomes for real world and artificially created data, to see if similar error rates are achieved. Artificially generated data can also be useful for research in the areas of approximate string comparisons as well as correcting errors in text.

Acknowledgements

This work is supported by an Australian Research Council (ARC) Linkage Grant LP0453463 and partially funded by the NSW Department of Health. The author would like to thank William Winkler, Tim Churches and Karl Goiser for their valuable comments.

References

1. Bertolazzi, P., De Santis, L. and Scannapieco, M.: Automated record matching in cooperative information systems. Proceedings of the international workshop on data quality in cooperative information systems, Siena, Italy, January 2003.
2. Bilenko, M. and Mooney, R.J.: Adaptive duplicate detection using learnable string similarity measures. Proceedings of the 9th ACM SIGKDD conference, Washington DC, August 2003.
3. Bilenko, M. and Mooney, R.J.: On evaluation and training-set construction for duplicate detection. Proceedings of the KDD-2003 workshop on data cleaning, record linkage, and object consolidation, Washington DC, August 2003.
4. Blake, C.L. and Merz, C.J.: UCI Repository of machine learning databases. University of California, Irvine, Dept. of Information and Computer Sciences, http://www.ics.uci.edu/~mlearn/MLRepository.html
5. Chaudhuri, S., Ganti, V. and Motwani, R.: Robust identification of fuzzy duplicates. Proceedings of the 21st international conference on data engineering, Tokyo, April 2005.
6. Christen, P., Churches, T. and Hegland, M.: A parallel open source data linkage system. Proceedings of the 8th PAKDD, Sydney, May 2004.

7. Cohen, W.W. and Richman, J.: Learning to match and cluster large high-dimensional data sets for data integration. Proceedings of the 8th ACM SIGKDD conference, Edmonton, July 2002.
8. Cohen, W.W., Ravikumar, P. and Fienberg, S.E.: A comparison of string distance metrics for name-matching tasks. Proceedings of IJCAI-03 workshop on information integration on the Web (IIWeb-03), pp. 73–78, Acapulco, August 2003.
9. Damerau, F.: A technique for computer detection and correction of spelling errors. Communications of the ACM, vol. 7, no. 3, pp. 171–176, March 1964.
10. Elfeky, M.G., Verykios, V.S. and Elmagarmid, A.K.: TAILOR: A record linkage toolbox. Proceedings of the ICDE' 2002, San Jose, USA, March 2002.
11. Fellegi, I. and Sunter, A.: A theory for record linkage. Journal of the American Statistical Society, December 1969.
12. Gu, L. and Baxter, R.: Adaptive filtering for efficient record linkage. SIAM international conference on data mining, Orlando, Florida, April 2004.
13. Hall, P.A.V. and Dowling, G.R.: Approximate string matching. ACM computing surveys, vol. 12, no. 4, pp. 381–402, December 1980.
14. Hernandez, M.A. and Stolfo, S.J.: The merge/purge problem for large databases. Proceedings of the ACM SIGMOD conference, May 1995.
15. Kukich, K.: Techniques for automatically correcting words in text. ACM computing surveys, vol. 24, no. 4, pp. 377–439, December 1992.
16. McCallum, A., Nigam, K. and Ungar, L.H.: Efficient clustering of high-dimensional data sets with application to reference matching. Proceedings of the 6th ACM SIGKDD conference, pp. 169–178, Boston, August 2000.
17. Nahm, U.Y, Bilenko M. and Mooney, R.J.: Two approaches to handling noisy variation in text mining. Proceedings of the ICML-2002 workshop on text learning (TextML'2002), pp. 18–27, Sydney, Australia, July 2002.
18. Centre for Epidemiology and Research, NSW Department of Health. New South Wales Mothers and Babies 2001. NSW Public Health Bull 2002; 13(S-4).
19. Pollock, J.J. and Zamora, A.: Automatic spelling correction in scientific and scholarly text. Communications of the ACM, vol. 27, no. 4, pp. 358–368, April 1984.
20. Ravikumar, P. and Cohen, W.W.: A hierarchical graphical model for record linkage. Proceedings of the 20th conference on uncertainty in artificial intelligence, Banff, Canada, July 2004.
21. Sarawagi, S. and Bhamidipaty, A.: Interactive deduplication using active learning. Proceedings of the 8th ACM SIGKDD conference, Edmonton, July 2002.
22. Tejada, S., Knoblock, C.A. and Minton, S.: Learning domain-independent string transformation weights for high accuracy object identification. Proceedings of the 8th ACM SIGKDD conference, Edmonton, July 2002.
23. Yancey, W.E.: An adaptive string comparator for record linkage RR 2004-02, US Bureau of the Census, February 2004.
24. Zhu, J.J., and Ungar, L.H.: String edit analysis for merging databases. KDD-2000 workshop on text mining, held at the 6th ACM SIGKDD conference, Boston, August 2000.

Mining Job Logs
Using Incremental Attribute-Oriented Approach

Idowu O. Adewale and Reda Alhajj

Department of Computer Science, University of Calgary, Calgary, Alberta, Canada
{adewale,alhajj}@cpsc.ucalgary.ca

Abstract. With the emergence of grid computing, researchers in different fields are making use of the huge computing power of the grid to carry out massive computing tasks that are beyond the power of a single processor. When a computing task (or job) is submitted to the grid, some useful information about the job is logged in the database by the Scheduler. The computing infrastructure that makes up the grid is expensive; hence, it is of great importance to understand the resource usage pattern. In this paper, we propose an incremental attribute-oriented approach that mines data within a given time interval. We test our approach using a real life data of logs of jobs submitted to Western Canada Research Grid (WestGrid). We also develop an incremental attribute-oriented mining tool to implement the proposed approach. Our approach uncovers some hidden patterns and changes that take place over a period of time.

1 Introduction

Computing grids are geographically separated computers or computer clusters; they are linked so that their processing power can be combined to act as one massive computer. They may spread out over provinces, countries or around the world, depending on how computers are set up to communicate with one another. Grid computing fosters the creation of "collaboratories" where researchers and scientists interact, process, transfer, and share large amounts of data within the scientific research community regardless of their geographical location [1]. Western Canada's powerful new grid computing system called WestGrid [3] (Western Canada Research Grid) is helping University of Calgary biomedical engineers reduce the cost and time involved in developing new heart-healing drugs and devices. There are some simulations that would have taken some researchers weeks to perform, but it took an hour on the WestGrid; therefore, researchers could perform hundreds of simulations. WestGrid is a collaborative project of the University of Alberta, University of Calgary, University of Lethbridge, University of British Columbia/TRIUMF (Canada's National Laboratory for Particle and Nuclear Physics), Simon Fraser University, and The Banff Center that provides high performance computing and multimedia/visualization resources to researchers and educators.

Users submit jobs to the grid and the Scheduler (i.e., a system that orders tasks/jobs on compute resources and communication between tasks) keeps logs of the jobs submitted. The logs contain information about submitted jobs like the job owner (user), user's accounting group, job expected completion time, submission time, completion time, and resources needed to run the job (number of nodes and CPUs). The resources

M. Gallagher, J. Hogan, and F. Maire (Eds.): IDEAL 2005, LNCS 3578, pp. 117–124, 2005.

used in grid computing environments are very expensive. For example, many clusters of machines in grid computing environment are networked via fiber optics links. A nationwide, multi-10-Gbps fiber optics network capability can be built for the cost of a typical university building or two; hence, it is of great importance to understand the job submission and resource usage pattern.

The most appropriate data mining technique for discovering the resource usage and job submission pattern in this scenario is the attribute-oriented approach to data generalization and summarization-based characterization. In this project, we propose an incremental attribute-oriented approach that uses time in the mining process. This approach reveals the patterns and changes that take place over time. We test our approach using a real life data of logs of jobs submitted to the WestGrid. We also develop an incremental attribute-oriented mining tool to implement the proposed approach. Our approach uncovers some hidden patterns and changes that take place over a period of time.

The rest of this paper is organized as follows. Section 2 covers related work. Section 3 discusses the proposed incremental attribute-oriented approach and presents the results obtained using the developed data mining tool. Section 4 is conclusions.

2 Related Work

The attribute-oriented induction approach was first proposed in 1989, a few years prior to the introduction of the data cube approach [7]. The work described in [5] gives an overview of multi-level data generalization, summarization, and characterization data mining technique. The two methods for efficient and flexible generalization of large data sets, namely the data cube approach and the attribute-oriented approach are discussed in details in [5]. The generalization-based data mining approach was used in studying the general characteristics of NSERC (Natural Science and Engineering Research Council of Canada) research grant database. In [2], the power of data mining is examined in two aspects: 1) attribute-oriented induction for mining different kinds of rules, including characteristic rules, discriminant rules, association rules, and cluster description rules; and 2) extension of the method for data mining in advanced database systems. An efficient induction method for learning quantitative rules in relational databases has been developed in [4], for learning both characteristic rules and classification rules [4].

DBMiner is a data mining system developed by DBMiner Technology Inc. located in Victoria, Canada. The system is used for interactive mining of multiple-level knowledge in large relational databases. The system implements a wide spectrum of data mining functions, including generalization, characterization, association, classification, and prediction [6]. DBMiner [2, 4, 5, 8] was used for implementing the attribute-oriented approach.

None of the previous work on the attribute-oriented approach mined transactions within a time interval but our approach does. Also, most of the previous work on the attribute-oriented induction approach needs a knowledge engineer or domain expert to develop or define concept hierarchies. Some previous work used synthetic data to test their implementation, but we use a real life data. Finally, the proposed approach will reveal the job submission and resource usage patterns in the log database which is useful in both grid computing and high-performance-computing environments.

3   Incremental Attribute-Oriented Approach

The implementation of the attribute-oriented induction approach in this paper is based on the original work of Han and Kamber described in [7]. Data Mining Query Language (DMQL) [6] is used in their work and can only be specified and interpreted in the DBMiner. In our work, we specify our queries in the standard SQL which is universal and supported in all existing relational database management systems. We have tested our approach using a real life data set, and we have implemented the approach using the incremental attribute-oriented mining tool developed in Java.

In our approach, a time attribute (window) is used in the mining process in order to reveal the changes that take place over a period of time. It is assumed in our implementation that the transaction or log database has a timestamp or date attribute which could be used in the characterization of data sets. Our program prompts the user for the window size: which may be specified as weekly, monthly or yearly. The window size determines the range of data that would be selected for analysis. If the database has two or more attributes with data type "DATE", the user has the choice of using any of the date fields in specifying the data mining window size. It should be noted that only one date attribute can be used at a time.

Our implementation and approach is not hard-coded to a particular database or some kind of databases. After specifying the window, the user enters the database name and path. The program lists all the tables in the database, their fields (attributes or columns) and their corresponding field type (data or column types). This gives the end user an idea of the kind of data stored in each table and which table is likely to be the transaction or log table. Our incremental attribute-oriented data mining tool is user friendly and analyzes any transaction or log database using the attribute-oriented induction approach.

In our work, we use a job log database which contains log of jobs submitted to the WestGrid research infrastructure. The database contains 15 tables and the transaction table Jobs contain about 1.6 million records of job logs. Each tuple has a Job ID which is unique to each job submitted to the WestGrid.

Based on the properties of the tables in the database, the user is allowed to select a transaction or log table to be mined. This option is available so that the data mining process will be interactive because some databases may have two or more transaction or log tables at different levels. The tool is a generic incremental attribute-oriented data mining system; hence, the tool is flexible to use and works for all databases with one or more transaction tables. Though, it should be noted that only one of the transaction or log databases can be mined at a time.

Since the system has a full knowledge of the database metadata, concept hierarchies are generated for some attributes in the job log. The detail of how the schema concept hierarchy is generated is beyond the scope of this study, but it is similar to the discussion in [7]. Our approach makes most of the relationship among the tables in the database, which can be deduced from the metadata information. Our method of generating concept hierarchy is not rigid, but flexible and user-friendly.

Numerical attributes can be organized as discrete hierarchical concepts and the hierarchies can be constructed automatically based on database statistics [8]. In our work, the concept hierarchies for numerical fields are generated by retrieving the number of distinct counts, the minimum and maximum values for the numeric fields.

The user has the choice of generating the concept hierarchy automatically or manually. Using the automatic method, the user supplies the interval and the lower bound for the first class. In this method, each class has the same width, but in the manual method the user sets the upper and lower bounds for each class. The groups formed using the manual method may have same or unequal widths, but the user need to supply the label for each class or number range in both methods.

For fields containing text, the distinct values and their corresponding counts are presented to the user. The user could generate a concept hierarchy for the text attribute by supplying the label for each text, though two or more text attributes could belong to the same class at the same level.

Considering the job log database, the *user id* includes user a_1, user a_2, user a_3, ..., user a_n. Each user can be mapped to an accounting group to which she/he belongs. For example user $a_1, b_1, c_1, ..., z_1$ can be mapped to an accounting group a_i. The accounting groups in turn can be mapped to an institution to which they belong, such as University of Calgary, Simon Fraser University, University of British Columbia, Banff Research Center, and so on. The mappings form a concept hierarchy for the dimension *user id* maps a set of low-level concepts *accounting group* to higher level, more general concepts *institutions*.

Our concept hierarchy generation method can generate a concept hierarchy for any field in the transaction table in a database. In our implementation, the end user does not necessarily need to be an expert in the field of study before he/she can generate a concept hierarchy for an attribute. Though, it is important for the end user to have a basic knowledge of the field where the data set was collected. This would help in the generation of concept hierarchies and the interpretation of results.

Table 1 shows the initial relation at the beginning of the data mining process, though some attributes are omitted due to space constraints. At this stage, generalization is performed on the smallest decomposable components (or attributes) of a data relation. Generalization on the smallest decomposable components instead of generalization on composite attributes ensures that the smallest possible chance is considered in the generalization, which enforces commitment to minimally generalized concepts and avoids over-generalization [4, 8].

Table 1. A relation Job in a Job log database

Job id	System id	User id	Account group	Queue id	Number of Nodes	Executable	State	Submission time	Completion time
1444534	1	19	16	35	1	CoRun83.pbs	15	2004-01-01 08:07:49	2004-01-01 08:08:06
1444535	1	15	4	35	1	test5	15	2004-01-01 10:21:20	2004-01-01 10:22:42
1444542	1	15	4	36	2	test5	7	2004-01-01 10:23:39	2004-01-01 15:24:05
...	...	...	...	...	...	...	...	...	...
2702591	3	106	81	48	16	gh3d_bhs1	7	2004-12-03 00:28:31	2004-12-04 03:35:59
2703061	3	13	3	48	8	P_h_w_pH3	7	2004-12-03 09:28:31	2004-12-04 10:31:20
...	...	...	...	...	...	...	...	...	...
1833636	3	106	81	62	64	gh3d_hc	15	2004-01-12 18:17:10	2004-01-12 20:17:45
1833637	3	106	81	62	64	gh3d_hc	7	2004-01-12 19:22:19	2004-01-12 20:27:19
...	...	...	...	...	...	...	...	...	...
2468064	3	153	69	48	504	gaussian2.sh	7	2004-08-16 11:49:19	2004-08-17 18:28:59

User → Accounting Group → Institution

{user a_1, user a_2, user a_3, ..., user a_n} ⊆ accounting group a_i

{user b_1, user b_2, user b_3, ..., user b_n} ⊆ accounting group b_i

{account group a_1, account group b_1, account group c_1,..., account group z_1} ⊆ institution 1

{account group a_2, account group b_2, account group c_2, ..., account group z_2} ⊆ institution 2

{institution 1, institution 2, institution 3, ..., institution n} ⊆ ANY (institution)

User — Institution

{user i_1, user i_2, user i_3, ..., user i_n} ⊆ institution 1

{user j, user j, user j, ..., user j} ⊆ institution 2

{institution 1, institution 2, institution 3, ..., institution n} ⊆ ANY (institution)

Queue — System

{queue a, queue b, queue c, ..., queue z} ⊆ system 1

{system 1, system 2, system 3, ..., system n} ⊆ ANY (system)

Range of nodes → {small, average, huge} → Number of nodes

{0 - 16} ⊆ small

{17 - 64} ⊆ average

{65 - 1024} ⊆ huge

{small, average, huge} ⊆ ANY (number of processors)

Fig. 1. A concept hierarchy table of Job log database

Generalization is performed on each attribute in the initial data relation shown in Table 1. Generalization is performed on each attribute in the initial data relation. By examining the task relevant attributes in sequence, there is no higher level concept specified on the attributes *job id*, *job number*, *wall limit*, *executable*, *state*, *submission time*, *dispatch time*, *start time*, and *completion time*. The attributes are removed in the generalization, which shows that the general properties of jobs cannot be characterized by those attributes.

Attributes with a large set of distinct values but no higher level concept are removed in the generalization process. Since an attribute-value pair represents a conjunct in the logical form of a tuple, the removal of a conjunct eliminates a constraint and thus generalizes the rule [4, 8]. Table 2 shows the distinct counts for the fields in the Jobs table. The attributes *job id, job number, wall limit, number of processors, executable, state, submission time, dispatch time, start time*, and *completion time* have high distinct counts. These attributes except *number of processors* (which is relevant in the data mining task) are removed from the relation because they have a large set of distinct values and no higher level concept. Attributes *queue id* and *state* have small distinct counts, but both are not relevant in the data mining task therefore, they could be removed from the initial relation. The remaining attributes are *system id, user id, accounting group id*, and *number of nodes*; but, *accounting group id* is removed because its concept hierarchy ascends to Institution which is same for *user id*. In order to avoid duplicates in the final relation, we drop *accounting group id* attribute in our data mining task. The result of steps 1 and 2 is shown in Table 3.

Table 2. Distinct counts of fields in Jobs table

Table 3. The generalized Relation after the Generalization process and Attribute removal

Attribute	Distinct Count	Have concept Hierarchy?
Job id	1458553	No
System id	3	No
Job number	888342	No
User id	321	Yes
Accounting Group id	147	Yes
Queue id	39	Yes
Wall limit	888	No
Number of nodes	113	No
Number of Processors	159	No
Executable	132017	No
State	16	No
Submission time	692946	No
Dispatch time	658421	No
Start time	657012	No
Completion time	1006225	No

System id	User id	Number of Nodes
1	19	1
1	15	1
1	15	2
...	...	...
3	106	16
3	13	8
...	...	...
3	106	64
3	106	64
...	...	...
3	153	504

Table 4. Initial relation for the month of November 2004

System id	User id	Number of nodes
2	2	small
2	2	small
3	5	small
1	1	small
3	1	small
...	...	...
3	9	huge
3	1	average
3	null	0
3	5	small
2	9	small
3	9	average

3	5	small
...	...	...
3	1	small
1	1	small
...	...	...
3	5	small
3	null	0
3	5	average
3	2	small
...	...	...
2	9	small
3	9	average
...	...	...

For an attribute value of a tuple with a higher level concept in the concept hierarchy, the substitution of the value with its higher level concept generalizes the tuple. Minimal generalization is enforced by ascending the tree one level at a time. Hence, ascending the concept hierarchy one level at a time ensures that the generalization follows the least commitment principle and thus reduces the chances of over generalization.

From concept tree ascension, different tuples may generalize to an identical tuple, where two tuples are identical if they have the same corresponding attribute values without considering the special attribute *vote*. By generalizing the attributes *user id* and *number of nodes*, a new relation emerges as shown in Table 4.

Further generalization is performed on the relation if the number of tuples of a generalized relation in the target class is larger than the specified generalization threshold value [4, 8]. The size of the generalized relation is reduced by further generalization on selected attribute(s) and merging of identical tuples.

The final generalized relation consists of a small number of tuples, which can be transformed into logical formula. A special attribute *vote* is added to each generalized relation in order to incorporate quantitative information in the learning process [4]. Two tuples in the generalized relation are identical if they have the same corresponding attribute values without considering the special attribute *vote*. The value of each tuple is carried to its generalized tuple and the votes are accumulated in the preserved tuple, while other identical and redundant tuples are removed from the generalization [4]. A generalized table for November 2004 is shown in Figure 5.

Table 5. A generalized relation for the month of November 2004

System id	User id	Number of nodes	Vote (count)
1	1	small	2332
1	2	small	61
1	3	small	38
1	8	small	28
1	9	small	240
1	Null	0	245
2	1	small	214
2	2	small	867
2	9	small	165
2	null	0	126

3	1	average	16
3	1	small	32767
3	2	small	595
3	3	small	671
3	5	average	4
3	5	huge	3
3	5	small	16515
3	8	small	11
3	9	average	12
3	9	huge	6
3	9	small	2831
3	null	0	2661

Table 6. Summary of generalized relation

Time	System name	Institution	Number of nodes
AUGUST, 2003	lattice	University of Calgary	small
SEPTEMBER, 2003	lattice	University of Calgary	small
OCTOBER, 2003	glacier	University of British Columbia	small
Between NOVEMBER, 2003 and NOVEMBER, 2004	glacier	University of Calgary	small

In the proposed Incremental attribute-oriented mining approach, the tuple with the highest vote in the final relation is transferred to the summary relation. The time attribute is added to each tuple in the summary relation. The time attribute indicates the time interval or window where the target class emerged as the class with the highest vote or count. The summary relation shown in Table 6 gives the end user a very good idea of the changes that took place from one window to another.

4   Conclusions

This work proposes a new approach known as incremental attribute-oriented approach for data generalization, summarization and characterization. Our approach allows the user to specify the data mining window size which in turn determines the range of data for data that would be used in the generalization. Our approach uncovers some patterns that are hidden in the existing approach. The change that takes place over a period of time is obvious by moving from one window to another. The incremental data mining tool is capable of mining any well designed log or transaction database. Unlike most of the existing data mining tools, our tool is not hard-coded to mine a particular database or kind of databases. The incremental attribute-oriented mining tool is interactive, flexible and user friendly. Our approach negates the assumption in the previous work that a knowledge engineer or domain expert is needed to provide the concept hierarchies. We use a real life data of logs of jobs submitted to the West-Grid over a period of 16 months to test the proposed approach. This work would be the first study on Job logs in grid computing and high performance computing environments. Also, the first work to mine job logs in data mining research area. The results obtained show that some computing resources are used more than others and some users or group of users tend to submit jobs often than others at different windows (times). This information would help system administrators and chief technology Officers (CTO) in knowing the resource usage and job submission patterns in their computing environments.

Acknowledgements

Our sincere gratitude goes to Dr. Rob Simmonds of the Grid Research Center for giving us access to the job logs. We also thank Mark Fox for organizing the job logs.

References

1. GRID RESEARCH CENTRE. http://grid.ucalgary.ca/resources.html.
2. J., Han and Y. Fu, Attribute-Oriented Induction in data Mining, *Advances in Knowledge Discovery and Data Mining*, pp.399-421, 1996.
3. WESTERN CANADIAN RESEARCH GRID. http://www.westgrid.ca/home.html.
4. J. Han., Y. Cai and N. Cercone, Data-Driven Discovery of Quantitative Rules in Relational Databases, *IEEE TKDE*, Vol.5, No.1, pp.29-40, 1993.
5. M.-S. Chen, J. Han and P.S. Yu, Data Mining: An overview from Database perspective, *IEEE TKDE*, Vol.8, No.6, pp.866-883, 1996.
6. J. Han, et al, A System for Mining Knowledge in Large Relational Databases, *Proceedings of ACM-KDD*, 1996.
7. J. Han and M. Kamber, Data Mining Concepts and Techniques, Morgan Kaufmann Series in Data Management Systems, Morgan Kaufmann Publishers, 2000.
8. J. Han, Y. Cai and N. Cercone, Knowledge Discovery in Databases: An Attribute-Oriented Approach, *Proceedings of VLDB*, pp. 547-559, Vancouver, 1992.

Dimensional Reduction of Large Image Datasets Using Non-linear Principal Components

Silvia S.C. Botelho[1], Willian Lautenschlger[1], Matheus Bacelo de Figueiredo[2], Tania Mezzadri Centeno[2], and Mauricio M. Mata[1]

[1] FURG, Fundação Universidade Federal do Rio Grande, Dept. de Física
Av. Itália, Km 8, Carreiros, 96201-900 Rio Grande, RS, Brazil
silviacb@ee.furg.br, wirlau@yahoo.com.br, mauricio.mata@furg.br
[2] CPGEI, CEFET-PR, Av. Sete de Setembro, 3165, CEP:80230-901 Curitiba, PR, Brazil
{matheus,mezzadri}@cpgei.cefetpr.br

Abstract. In this paper we apply a Neural Network (NN) to reduce image dataset, distilling the massive datasets down to a new space of smaller dimension. Due to the possibility of these data have nonlinearities, traditional multivariate analysis, like the Principal Component Analysis (PCA), may not represent reality. Alternatively, Nonlinear Principal Component Analysis (NLPCA) can be performed by a NN model to fulfill that deficiency. However, when the dimension of the image increases, NN may easily saturate. This work presents an original methodology associated with the use of a set of cascaded multi-layer NN with a bottleneck structure to extract nonlinear information of the large set of image data. We illustrate its good performance with a set of tests against comparisons using this methodology and PCA in the treatment of oceanographic data associated with mesoscale variability of an oceanic boundary current.

Keywords: neural network, image processing, cascaded-NLPCA.

1 Introduction

A general problem faced in computer science is to reduce the dimensions of a large datasets, like image datasets, in order to make sense of the bulk information contained in them. The artificial Neural Network approach, called Nonlinear Principal Component Analysis (NLPCA), has been applied by several authors as a tool to try to overcome the limitations imposed by linear PCA (Principal Component Analysis) [4,5,7]. The main advantage besides being able to take nonlinearity into account is that the computational process can occur unbiased by our knowledge about the variability aspects that ultimately control the study case.

However, NLPCA brings together an important limitation: saturation phenomena presented in Neural Networks (NN) prevents the use of this approach to handle large datasets. Hence, dataset forming large matrices (or data units), like images, can not be treated by Neural-based NLPCA.

When the dimension of image is much bigger with respect to the number of temporal samples available to analyze, a pre-processing stage is thus necessary to extract the relevant information backbone prior to the NN run. For instance, a PCA can be used as a dimension reduction, leaving the NN to work over a few modes only [2]. In this case, NLPCA runs with linearly reduced input patterns, thus limiting the method's potentials.

M. Gallagher, J. Hogan, and F. Maire (Eds.): IDEAL 2005, LNCS 3578, pp. 125–132, 2005.

Hence, this work presents an original approach, called Cascaded-NLPCA (C-NLPCA), whose main purpose is to eliminate the pre-filtering stage, allowing the nonlinear PCA of the whole image. Our approach does not impose limitations associated with the original dimensions of the image, allowing important result gains. The C-NLPCA can be used in a set of different domains. Particularly, we are interested in evaluating the potential of the approach to investigate the satellite image variability in oceanic areas dominated by strong mesoscale dynamics. The results presented here are compared with the classical PCA technique and NLPCA, highlighting the advantages and disadvantages of C-NLPCA from the computational and physical sense.

2 Feature Extraction Problem and the Theory of NLPCA

Independently of their nature, temporal data samples can be viewed as a vector, $\vec{X}(t)$, with a particular variability behaviuor.Principal Components Analysis (PCA) is a multivariate procedure which rotates the data such that maximum variabilities are projected onto the axes. Essentially, a set of correlated variables are transformed into a set of uncorrelated variables, $u(t)$, which are ordered by reducing variability. The uncorrelated variables are linear combinations of the original variables, and the last of these variables can be removed with minimum loss of real data.

PCA only allows a linear mapping from $\vec{X}(t)$ to $u(t)$ [2]. On the other hand, NLPC is obtained using a multi layer Neural Network, see figure 1 [3]. To perform NLPCA, the NN contains 3 hidden layers of neurons between the input and output layers. Hidden layers have nonlinear activation functions between the input and bottleneck layers and between the bottleneck and output layers. Hence, the network models a composition of functions. The five-layer NLPCA network has p nodes in the input layer, r nodes in the third (bottleneck) layer, and p in the output layer. Output layer must reproduce the input signals presented to the network. NLPCA network allows data compression/reduction because the p-dimensional inputs must pass through the r-dimensional bottleneck layer before reproducing the inputs. Once the network has been trained, the bottleneck node activation values give the scores.

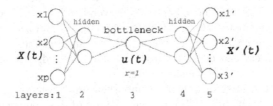

Fig. 1. NLPCA: Neural Network to map Nonlinear Components

The weights in the NLPCA network are determined under the following objective function:

$$\min \sum_{t=1}^{n} \|\vec{X}(t) - \vec{X}'(t)\|, \tag{1}$$

where $\vec{X}'(t)$ is the output of the network for the sample t. The residual $\|\vec{X}(t)-\vec{X}'(t)\|$, can be input into the same network to extract the second NLPCA mode, and so on for the higher modes [7].

3   C-NLPCA: Cascaded Non-linear Principal Component Analyses

When it is necessary to run NLPCA with large dimension datasets, like images, there is a noticeable increase of parameters (weights) associated with the neurons of the NN, thus leading to the necessity to have a bigger number of temporal samples, so that this value can be near to the parameters of the NN. It is known that sometimes it is not possible to attend this requirement even if one accepts the saturation and poor dimensional reduction risks. Moreover, the addition of more samples increases in an expressive way the computational overhead to conclude the analyses.

Thus, when the original dataset have many dimensions, several authors opt to filter the data before the NLPCA analyses, like the use of PCA reduction techniques [1,2]. Using the former approach, the simplification introduced by the use of linear PCA analyses can lead to erroneous outputs or, at least, can produce coarser results.

Our C-NLPCA has the aim to allow the direct and totally nonlinear analyses of high dimension dataset, using a cascaded set of successive NLPCAs, see figure 2. The architecture is composed by two main stages: reduction and expansion.

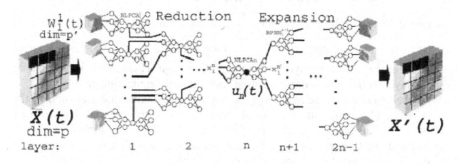

Fig. 2. C-NLPCA: a set of layers grouped in Reduction and Expansion Stages. The pointed out neuron gives the pattern associated to the reduction of the original dataset

3.1   Obtaining the C-NLPC – The Reduction Process

C-NLPCA assumes that p' is the ideal dimension for the input data. The ideal concept is associated with the relationship between parameters number (weights) and the number of temporal samples (see [2] for details). Thus, we divide the original input image with dimension p into smaller windows with dimension p'. Each window receives a set of p' random pixels of $\vec{X}(t)$. These windows are used directly as input of a first layer of NLPCAs. Each NLPCA, constrained by the saturation requirements, finds a local principal component (local reduction) of one window. The number of obtained reductions of the first layer is giving by $m_1=p/p'$. The resulting patterns (reductions) are used as input to a new layer i of NLPCAs. Each new layer i will have a new set of reductions calculated, $m_i=m_{(i-1)}/p'$. This process is repeated n times until only one pattern is left, $m_n=1$, thus giving the final reduction, $u(t)$, nonlinear principal component, of whole original dataset.

3.2 Obtaining C-NLPCAs – The Expansion Stage

The second role of the Principal Component Analyses, called expansion, is to obtain the data associated with each principal component reduction (PC, C-NLPC) in the original dimension of the image (PCA, C-NLPCA). Moreover, each time when a principal component k is calculated and we desire to obtain the next $(k+1)$, the expansion process is also necessary to calculate the residues associated with k, which will be the input to the $(k+1)$ C-NLPC analyses.

Hence, due to the cascading process, we have lost the original dimension of the input image, it is then necessary a method to obtain the expansion of the reduction. Expansion Stage is trained to expand the nonlinear principal component, $u_n(t)$, in a set of nonlinear expanded images. In fact, we propose a bottleneck layered structure to obtain the reduction/expansion of NLPCs.

Expansion layers are symmetric with reduction layers, resulting in a total of $(2*n-1)$ layers. They are composed by simple back-propagation networks *BPNN* (without bottleneck neuron). The input of each *BPNN* is an output of the last layer. We use the original propagated image to train the desired outputs of *BPNN* networks.

Training BPNNs: Each resulting output $x_i^{'n}$ of the bottleneck NLPC layer n is used as input to train its respective $BPNN_i^{(n+1)}$ in the next layer $(n+1)$. The desired output is the input of the respective layer $(n-1)$ in reduction stage. This process is repeated up to $(2n-1)$ layer, which has as desired output each pixel of original image.

Thus, the expanded image represents the original input taking into account only the current principal component. We use all components of the original dataset, their neighbors relations and temporal variability. The method can be applied independently of the dataset dimension size. It also maintains the nonlinearity associated with NN, avoiding the saturation restriction associated with them.

4 Tests and Results

We intend to compare both methods, PCA and C-NLPCA, looking to show the advantages of C-NLPCA utilization. In high dimension data sets cases, the C-NLPCA method is applied directly in data, without the necessity of a dimension reduction like the one used at NLPCA method [2]. This way, a set of synthetic images with 2 modes known variation ways was produced, like the pre-set functions. It was increased the importance of the first mode looking for highlight the results.

The data set is formed by 128 points in time and images with 3.600 pixels (60 x 60), with three set of points (X1, X2 and X3, random dispersion) varying according to the pre-set functions showed in figure 3. The images set variation happen in a non-linear way. The first variation mode is described by:

Fig. 3. Synthesized produced images

$$X1 = 10(t-0.3t^2), \quad X2 = 10(t+0.3t^3) \ e \ X3 = 10(t^2), \qquad (2)$$

and the second variation mode is described by:

$$X1' = s-0.3s^2, \quad X2' = s-0.3s^3 \ e \ X3' = -s^4, \qquad (3)$$

where the magnitude of the first mode is ten times the second mode.

PCA method captured the two variations modes according to the method limitations, generating the principal components showed in figure 4. The application of the C-NLPCA method, applied directly on data, as expected, capture two variation modes. The first mode captures almost all the variability of the set, leaving only one residue in the second mode, showed on figure 5, possibly because of the difference of importance (10 times) imposed between the two modes.

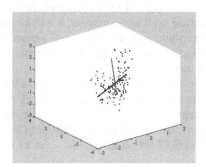

Fig. 4. Principal components captured by PCA (first mode in blue and second mode in pink).

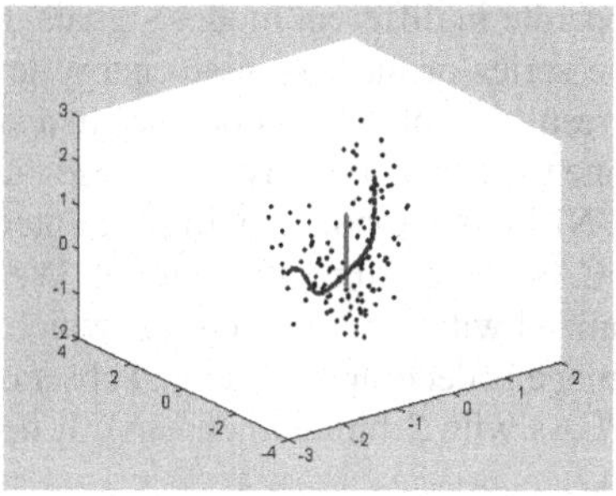

Fig. 5. Principal components captured by C-NLPCA (first mode in blue and second mode in pink).

In opposition to other works [2,7], where a pre-filter stage is necessary to apply NLPCA method, here the C-NLPCA is able to extract the images principal components, being applied directly on the data. The method C-NLPCA is applied in high dimension data sets (3600 pixels, in this case) without only pre-processing, proving the method efficiency.

Applying C-NLPCA in SST Satellite Images Series. We have tested our approach in a set of Sea Surface Temperature (SST). In order to analyze these data, researchers have generally adopted classical multivariate statistical methods, like PCA. However, related methods may produce an oversimplification of the dataset being analyzed by assuming that linear phenomena are dominant. Thus, if the data contain nonlinear lower-dimensional structure, it can not and will not be detectable by the PCA. Moreover, these images compose a large dataset, saturating and preventing the usual NLPCA methods. Thus, SST satellite images seem to be an ideal application to justify and test C-NLPCA approach.

The data used are a series of three and a half years Sea Surface Temperature (SST) satellite images (from 1991 to 1994) of the southwestern Pacific Ocean. These images have been derived from the full resolution images (1 km x 1 km) recorded by the Advanced Very High Resolution Radiometer (AVHRR) on board of the National Oceanic Atmospheric Administration (NOAA) polar orbiting satellites. Data have a 9 km x 9 km spatial and 10 days temporal resolution (enough for the study of mesoscale dynamics).

The dataset dimension is 60 x 60 pixels [6] and 128 time points. In this area, one can expect that the first 2 or 3 principal components would be enough to explain almost the totality of the data variance. Indeed, that is confirmed by computing the PCA modes from the dataset, which revealed that the eigenvalues associated to spatial modes 1, 2 and 3. Thus, we are going to search/analyze only the firsts mode 1 and 2.

The first PCs (time series) computed shown an ample dominance of the first mode variability over the higher ones. Having a frequency of about 1 year, the first mode has a clear physical meaning in oceanography, which is related to the seasonal heating and cooling of sea surface waters following the annual cycle of solar radiation input. The second and third modes are not that straightforward to interpret. They seem to be dominated by a higher than seasonal frequency, however, this signal seems also contaminated by a long term component. This is a clear sign of the inability of the PCA to separate in different modes signals that either are typically nonlinear, not dominant in the series or have similar energy levels (contribute equally to the total variance). The result is a blend of processes in a single mode and thus making almost impossible for one to extract any physical sense out of this mode.

C-NLPCA method was implemented to avoid local minimum. Thus a set of 20 C-NLPCAs process the same dataset. We eliminate the worst results. Each C-NLPCA is initialized with random weights, which are changed in 40.000 iterations. Each temporal image is decomposed into a subset of windows to feed C-NLPCA network ($p'=24$, NLPCAs with 2 hidden neurons). It needs 5 layers (2 for reduction and 2 for expansion).

As the solution of the first PCA mode is linear, and it dominates unquestionably the dataset variability (the seasonal oscillation pattern of the sea surface temperature), one would expect that the first principal component of the C-NLPCA network would have quite a similar pattern. Indeed, that is confirmed in figure 6, where it is clear the excellent agreement between the PC1 and C-NLPC1 functions.

Conversely, one can expect different patterns when comparing the PCA solution for the higher modes (mode 2 for example) with the correspondent C-NLPCs.

After computing C-NLPC2, it is plotted together with PC2 in figure 7. One can see how different they look and, taking advantage of the use of normalized units, it is clearly notable that PC2 contains a combination of a higher frequency phenomenon (about 140 days) with a lower frequency one (about 3 years). The 140 days signal should be basically composed by marine mesoscale phenomena while the 3 years one should be related to a residual of the interannual signal in the sea surface temperatures due to El Niño events, which can be quite intense in this part of the ocean. The blend of signals of such a different nature in only one PCA mode is related to the fact that

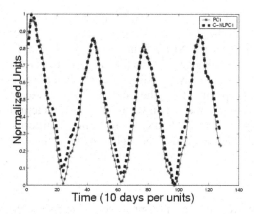

Fig. 6. First PC from the PCA (with *) and from C-NLPCA (dashed line). Due to linearity of the first mode, both method present the same results

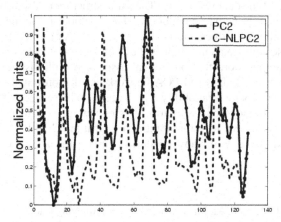

Fig. 7. PC2 from the PCA (with *) and C-NLPC2 (dashed line) computed using the C-NLPCA network

those phenomena are essentially nonlinear and also contribute similarly to the total variance, hence making the PCA linear approach only a crude approximation of the observed variability.

In other hand, C-NLPC2 describes a pattern with only some isolated peaks that have frequency of about 120-180 days, and showing no clear evidence of another signal being superimposed (low frequency phenomena). The latter reinforces the hypothesis that NLPCA deals better with the higher mode variability due to an enhanced capability in isolating the signals of higher modes, and thus suggests that C-NLPC2 may be representing a single oceanographic process. Indeed, several studies support the above assertion as they have found that besides the seasonal variability, the mesoscale dynamics is a quite important feature in that ocean area [6]. These authors also emphasize that the measoscale variability is basically due to the shedding of large eddies by the East Australian Current to the south of 33. S. During those times the Current would leave from its "normal" state and move about the study domain (mainly retract to the north), thus creating a sea surface temperature anomaly possible to be captured by the NLPCA analysis. The NLCP2 function depicts quite well this pattern, as it remains most of the time around the zero line and shows spikes that may well represent the eddy shedding events. The above studies about the East Australian Current also point out that the Current sheds between 2 – 4 eddies per year, but can also experience periods of lower activity [6], pattern also matched by the NLPC2. Thus, we believe that C-NLPC is producing significantly better results than the linear PCA, further assessment of the higher modes is underway.

5   Conclusions

In the present study, we propose an original method to reduce the dimension of large image dataset, obtaining principal components of them. We use a cascaded Neural Network in a bottlenecked structured to obtain dimension reduction, giving the principal components of the data variability. The same structure is also used to expand the data from obtained principal component. The method is applied to study the mesoscale variability of an oceanic boundary current. As results, the PCA can not fully isolate those low frequency modes from others and the computation leads to time series containing more that one signal associated with distinct physical processes. On the other hand, the C-NLPCA network has demonstrated the capability of isolating the second mode of variability which seems to be related with the mesoscale variability of the oceanographic scenario, thus encouraging further investigation on others application domains. It is important to note that the C-NLPCA is tested in synthesized produced images with known patterns to assess the method efficiency.

References

1. S. Botelho, R. de Bem, M. M. Mata, and I. Almeida. Applying neural networks to study the mesoscale variability of oceanic boundary currents. *Lectures Notes in Artificial Inteligence*, 2871:684-688, 2003.
2. W. Hsieh. Nonlinear principal component analysis by neural network. *Tellus*, 53A:599-615, 2001.
3. M. Kirby and L. Sirovich. Application of karhunen-loeve procedure for the caracterization of human faces. *IEEE On pattern analysis and machine intelligence, 1990.*
4. M Kramer, Nonlinear Principal Component Analysis Using Autoassociative Neural Networks, *AIChE Journal, 37, 233-243, 1991.*
5. S. Lek and J. Guegan. Artificial neural networks as a tool in ecological modelling an introduction. *Ecological Modelling*, 120:65-73, 1999.
6. M. Mata. *On the mesoscale variability of the East Australian Current at subtropical latitudes.* PhD thesis, Flinders University, 2000.
7. A. Monahan. *Nonlinear principal component analysis of climate data.* PhD thesis, University of British Columbia, 2000.
8. R. W. Preisendorfer. *PCA in Metereology and Oceanography. Developments in Atmospherics Science*, volume 17. Elsevier, 1988.
9. S. Romdhani, A. Psarrou, and S. Gong. Multi-view nonlinear active shape model using kernel pca. *In Tenth British Machine Vision Conference, 1999.*

Classification by Instance-Based Learning Algorithm

Yongguang Bao[1], Eisuke Tsuchiya[2], Naohiro Ishii[2], and Xiaoyong Du[3]

[1] Aichi Information System, Japan
baoyg@yahoo.com.cn
[2] Department of Information Networking Eng., Aichi Institute of Technology, Japan
eisuke@hm.aitai.ne.jp, ishii@in.aitech.ac.jp
[3] School of Information, Renmin University of China, China
duyong@mail.ruc.edu.cn

Abstract. The basic k-nearest-neighbor classification algorithm works well in many domains but has several shortcomings. This paper proposes a tolerant instance-based learning algorithm TIBL and it's combining method by simple voting of TIBL, which is an integration of genetic algorithm, tolerant rough sets and k-nearest neighbor classification algorithm. The proposed algorithms seek to reduce storage requirement and increase generalization accuracy when compared to the basic k-nearest neighbor algorithm and other learning models. Experiments have been conducted on some benchmark datasets from the UCI Machine Learning Repository. The results show that TIBL algorithm and it's combining method, improve the performance of the k-nearest neighbor classification, and also achieves higher generalization accuracy than other popular machine learning algorithms.

1   Introduction

Classification is a primary data mining method. Given a set of classes, it assigns an input vector x to one of those classes. Classification has been applied in many applications, such as the credit approval, pattern recognition, part classification in computer vision, and so on. Many inductive learning algorithms have been proposed for classification problem. For example, ID3, C4.5, k-Nearest Neighbor (KNN), Naive-Bayes, IB, T2, Neural-network, association rules etc are developed. However, improving accuracy and performance of classifiers are still attractive to many researchers. In this paper, we focus on the k-nearest-neighbor classification method. The k-nearest neighbor method is one of the most common instance-based learning algorithms. To classify an unknown object, it ranks the object's neighbors among the training data and then uses the class labels of the k nearest neighbors to predict the class of the new object.

In this paper, we use tolerant rough set and GA to create the suitable mode and feature weight for kNN based on the training data firstly, and then apply kNN to classification. Specifically, we use tolerant rough set to measure the quality of the training objects and the classification power of a subset of attributes,

M. Gallagher, J. Hogan, and F. Maire (Eds.): IDEAL 2005, LNCS 3578, pp. 133–140, 2005.

and GA algorithm to find the optimal tolerant rough relation, i.e. determine the optimal weights for each attribute and similarity threshold. It also means that we find the optimal tolerant rough relations between objects that provide as small classification error as possible.

2   Tolerant Rough Sets

Let $R = (U, A \cup \{d\})$ be a decision table, where U is a set of elements (objects, examples), A is a set of condition attributes, d is the decision attribute. Each attribute $a \in A$ has a set of values V_a, called domain of the attribute, and let $r(d)$ be the number of decision values.

We say that two objects x and y are similar with respect to the subset Q of attributes when the attribute values $Q(x)$ and $Q(y)$ satisfy $Q(x) R_Q Q(y)$, denoted as $x R_Q y$. Furthermore, we say that two objects x and y are similar with respect to all attributes A, if $Q = A$, $x R_Q y$, denoted as $x \Gamma_A y$.

A tolerance set $TS(x)$ of an object x with respect to subset Q is defined as follows:

$$TS(x) = \{y \in U : x R_Q y\}$$

$TS(x)$ contains all objects which has tolerant relation with x.

Now we use a distance function and a similarity threshold to define a tolerant relation. Let the distance with respective to the subset Q of attributes between two objects x and y be $D_Q(x, y)$. We define the tolerance relation as

$$x R_Q y \quad iff \quad D_Q(x, y) \leq t(Q)$$

where $t(Q)$ is a similarity threshold with respect to the subset Q, whose value is in the interval of [0,1].

The k-nearest neighbor algorithm is based on assumption that *similar objects have similar classes*. This assumption means the objects in the tolerant set have the same class in the opinion of tolerant rough sets. By the definition of tolerant set, we can get the four different cases as shown in Figure 1. In the cases of (a) and (b), we say the object x is *center point*, which is consistent with the assumption of kNN, that is the objects in the tolerant set $TS(x)$ have the same class. In the case of (c), the most of objects in the $TS(x)$ have the same class as x, we say the object x is *good border point*. In the case of (d), the most of objects in the $TS(x)$ have the different class from x, we say the object x is *noise point*, which is unsuitable to use for kNN.

3   Genetic Algorithm

When we apply the GA to determine the optimal feature weighting/selection and similarity threshold, the inputs into the GA are the information table $R = (U, A \cup \{d\})$ and the distance type. The output from the GA is a set of optimal features weight w_i and threshold values $t(A)$.

For constructing the fitness function, let's see the different case of tolerant set in Figure 1. The positive region consists of trivial lower approximation set (Figure

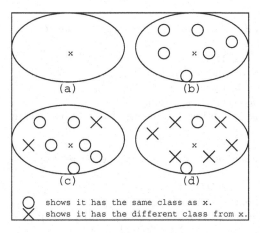

Fig. 1. Four different cases of tolerant set

1(a)) and untrivial lower approximation set (Figure 1(b)). If we take $\gamma(\Gamma_A, \{d\})$ as fitness simply, that will lead $t(A)$ near to 0, then it is meaningless. So we divide $\gamma(\Gamma_A, \{d\})$ into two parts as follows and denote it as $Criterion1(\Gamma_A)$.

$$\frac{card(\cup\{TS(x) : \exists i s.t. TS(x) \subseteq Y_i and card(TS(x)) > 1\})}{card(U)}$$

$$+\epsilon \times \frac{card(\cup\{TS(x) : \exists i s.t. TS(x) \subseteq Y_i and card(TS(x)) = 1\})}{card(U)}$$

where ϵ is a coefficient, $0 \leq \epsilon < 1$, and $card()$ denotes the cardinality of a set. We can see $Criterion1(\Gamma_A) \leq \gamma(\Gamma_A, \{d\})$.

If two chromosomes have the same $Criterion1((A)$ value, we prefer the one with many untrivial positive region. And based on [2], we hope the center points of untrivial positive region are as many as possible. That will be valuable to the accuracy. In the last, we hope $t(A)$ is as larger as possible. Considering the above discussion, we use a ranking technique, which is one of a number of ranking criteria, instead of an absolute fitness. The first criterion in ranking chromosomes is $Criterion1(\Gamma_A)$.

4   A Tolerant Instance-Based Learning Algorithm (TIBL)

We use tolerant rough set to measure the classification power of attributes and GA algorithm to find the optimal tolerant rough relation, i.e. determine the optimal feature weighting/selection and similarity threshold. Then we use the tolerant rough set to select a set of objects from the initial training data. Finally, we use the KNN to classify new objects. Now, we describe our algorithm in detail in Figure 3. For convenience, we denote $DTS(x) = \{y \in TS(x) : d(x) = d(y)\}$ in the following. Let U be all of training instances and PRUNE be the flag of pruning for reduction points (RP).

Step 1   Determine the optimal tolerant relation using GA.

(1) Read training data;
(2) Define the distance function type;
(3) Generate initial population;
(4) Perform the genetic algorithm;
(5) Determine the optimal feature weight/selection and similarity threshold value.

Step 2   Determine the objects based on tolerant relation

$CP = \{x \in U : card(DTS(x)) = card(TS(x))\};$
/* Center Point: Figure 1(a, b) */
$DTO(x) = max_{d' \neq d(x)}\{ card(\{y \in TS(x) : d(y) = d'\}) \};$
$BP = \{x \in U : 1 > \frac{card(DTS(x)) - DTO(x)}{card(DTS(x))} > \frac{1}{r(d)}$
/* Good Border Point: Figure 1(c) */
If PRUNE
    $CP = \{x \in CP : no \quad y \in CP s.t. DTS(x) \subseteq DTS(y)\};$
    $BP = \{x \in BP : no \quad y \in CP \cup BP s.t. DTS(x) \subseteq DTS(y)\};$
End if
$RP = CP \cup BP.$

Step 3   Classification based on KNN

For an unseen object u, we use the smallest k as possible to classify u by using k-nearest neighbor. That means, if there is only one instance x with the minimal value $D_A(x, u)$ in RP, then set u to class $d(x)$. And if there are two instances with the minimal value $D_A(x, u)$ in different class, we should check instances with th secondary minimal value $D_A(x, u)$ in RP. If we still cannot determine class, the process should be continued until the class of the object u is determined.

Fig. 2. Tolerant instance-based learning algorithm

5   Experimental Results for TIBLs

For evaluating the classification generalization accuracy of our algorithm, the TIBL algorithm was implemented and tested on 30 benchmark datasets from the UCI Machine Learning Repository [3].

In the process of simulation, the most common normalized Euclidean distance (the absolute distance) is used for linear or continuous attributes and the *overlap metric* is used for nominal attributes.

$$D_A(X, Y) = \sqrt{\sum_{i=1}^{n} \omega_i \times d(x_i, y_i)^2} \; (\sum_{i=1}^{n} \omega_i = 1, \omega_i \geq 0)$$

5.1   Comparison of TIBLs with KNN

The KNN algorithm is a basic k-nearest neighbor algorithm that uses k=3 and majority voting. The KNN algorithm uses the same type of distance function type as TIBL, and its accuracy is shown in column "KNN" of Table 1.

The "FS" column shows what percent of the features A is retained and subsequently used for actual classification of the test set. For the analysis of TIBL, we give the results of TIBL in the case of using all instances, center points, center points and good border points, respectively. The "ALL" column shows the accuracy using 100% of the instances in the training set for the classification.

The "CP" column and the following "size" column show the accuracy and storage requirements using center points only. Other "size" columns show what percent of the training set is retained and subsequently used for actual classification of the test set. For the "KNN" column, 100% of the features and 100% of the instances in the training set are used for the classification.

The "CP/p" column means the accuracy of using the pruned center points, the "CBP" column means the accuracy of using center points and good border points, and the "CBP/p" column means the accuracy of using pruned center points and good border points. The average of storage requirements of all datasets, which considers the feature reduction and object reduction simultaneously, are shown near the bottom of the table.

As can be seen from Table 1, each case raises the average generalization accuracy on these datasets when compared with the basic KNN. In the case of ALL, TIBL reduces storage requirements from 100% to about 60.97% and increases the average accuracy 79.72% to 83.48%. This indicates that the feature weighting/selection determined by GA is very efficient. In most cases, center points and good border points are the only parts of all objects. On the average, in the case of CP, TIBL uses the 58.80% objects (center points), reduces storage to about 33.81%, and gets 85.14% accuracy. After pruning, CB/p reduces objects to about 28.27%, reduces the storage to about 18.43%, and gets 84.99% accuracy. When using the center points and good border points (CBP), TIBL gets the highest average generalization accuracy 85.03% by using 89.24% objects. And in the case of CBP/p, TIBL uses the 41.38% objects, reduces storage to about 27.17%, and gets 84.82% accuracy.

6   A Combined Algorithm of TIBLs

To Improve the accuracy in the classification, the operation of classifiers as a decision committee, is needed. A committee as the final classifier, here, is composed of TIBL classifiers as committee members, each of which makes its own classifications that are combined to create a single classification result of the whole committee. A combined algorithm flow of the TIBLs is shown in Fig.4. The TIBL computations are carried out for 10 times, in which the weights are computed by the GA algorithm.

Table 1. Generalization accuracy of TIBL and the basic KNN

DataSet	FS	ALL	CP	(size)	CP/p	(size)	CBP	(size)	CBP/p	(size)	KNN
Bridges	74.33	**62.75**	62.25	36.37	62.03	21.61	59.94	68.37	60.67	33.22	52.47
Flag	55.40	54.14	60.22	50.87	58.78	36.27	**61.80**	74.35	59.61	47.11	50.01
Glass	54.95	76.46	76.89	65.36	77.09	44.72	**78.89**	90.52	78.19	51.49	70.10
Heart	72.43	77.91	80.67	40.73	80.60	29.28	81.12	83.31	**81.38**	54.38	79.43
Cle	74.05	76.65	82.29	39.42	**82.35**	28.68	80.37	82.40	80.91	55.37	78.97
Hun	44.46	91.27	92.74	72.02	**93.12**	14.77	91.74	93.74	91.83	18.26	78.45
LB	48.57	83.81	87.96	57.79	87.84	27.08	89.29	89.16	**89.50**	44.59	73.42
Swi	44.54	95.21	**96.49**	77.04	**96.49**	25.18	**96.49**	97.97	**96.49**	33.95	92.07
Hepat	62.59	80.60	82.52	60.36	**83.08**	34.58	81.88	89.16	81.70	50.87	80.50
Iris	78.27	95.56	95.96	70.01	**96.40**	25.62	95.16	96.11	95.64	33.75	96.00
Promo	21.60	**82.93**	82.20	65.28	81.98	39.99	82.71	92.07	82.18	52.96	79.88
Voting	71.18	95.74	95.64	35.95	95.64	17.29	**96.12**	95.72	95.97	37.53	93.35
Wine	66.89	97.46	**98.39**	61.90	97.65	34.87	97.36	98.31	96.68	50.00	96.29
Zoo	68.47	**98.17**	97.77	90.09	96.76	15.77	97.51	98.18	96.76	15.86	95.10
Average	59.84	83.48	85.14	58.80	84.99	28.27	**85.03**	89.24	84.82	41.38	79.72
Storage			60.97	33.81	18.43		53.08		27.17		100.0

Table 2. Example of combined result in Promol

instance	1	2	3	4	5	6	7	8	9	10	11	12	13	14	15	16
0	0.0	0.0	0.0	0.0	1.0	0.0	0.0	0.0	1.0	0.0	0.0	1.0	1.0	1.0	1.0	1.0
1	1.0	1.0	1.0	1.0	0.0	1.0	1.0	1.0	0.0	1.0	1.0	0.0	0.0	0.0	0.0	0.0
result	1	1	1	1	0	1	1	1	0	1	1	0	0	0	0	0
correct	1	1	1	1	1	1	1	1	0	0	0	0	0	0	0	0
error					×					×	×					

The values in the columns in Fig.4(a), show the classes of instances by TIBL computations. The classes are summed and voted as shown in Fig.4(b); 3 for the class 0, 7 for the class 1 and 0 for the class 2. Then, the class 1 is determined for the instance 1 as shown in Fig.4(c) are summed as shown in Table. 2, as an example.

The data is composed of 16 instances in Table. 2. The TIBL computations with 10 times are combined in the classification of the 0 class with 3 times, and that of the 1 class with 7 times. Thus, the final classification in the instance 1, becomes the 1 class by voting the majority of 7 times of 1. The class of the instance 1, is given as the class 1 in the data which is shown in the column, "correct" in Table. 2. Then, the there is no error between the classified result, class 1, and the given class 1 in the data. But, in the instance 5, the TIBL computations with 10 times, are combined in the classification of the 0 class with 6 times and that of the 1 class with 4 times. Thus the final classification in the instance 5, becomes the 0 class by voting the majority of 6 times of 0. In this instance, we have error × in Table. 2.

The combined results in the UCI data, are shown in Table. 3. The bold numerals show the maximum value among the combined computation results

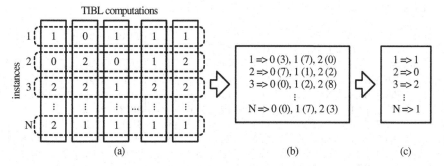

Fig. 3. Flow of combined algorithm

Table 3. Accuracy by the combined algorithm

DataSet	ALL	CP	CP/p	CBP	CBP/p
Bridges	**0.6457**	0.5982	0.6046	0.5872	0.5816
Bupa	**0.6314**	0.5829	0.5833	0.6115	0.6023
Echoc	0.8858	**0.8975**	0.8958	0.8750	0.8883
Flag	0.5335	0.5858	0.5860	0.5943	**0.5991**
Glass	0.7697	0.7980	**0.7985**	0.7890	0.7948
Heart	0.7840	**0.8293**	0.8269	0.8160	0.8141
Heartcle	0.7672	**0.8247**	0.8233	0.8171	0.8149
Hearthun	0.8840	**0.8957**	0.8950	0.8914	0.8922
Heartlb	0.8376	0.8829	0.8795	**0.8862**	0.8839
Heartswi	0.9508	**0.9680**	**0.9680**	**0.9680**	**0.9680**
Hepat	0.8020	0.8317	0.8317	**0.8350**	0.8337
Iris	0.9533	**0.9600**	0.9573	**0.9600**	0.9573
Promo	0.8850	**0.8935**	0.8930	**0.8935**	0.8930
Wine	0.9783	0.9846	**0.9858**	0.9846	**0.9858**
Zoo	0.9838	**0.9844**	0.9698	**0.9844**	0.9698

by the combined algorithm of TIBLs. These values by the combined algorithm show that the accuracy is improved than the respective TIBL computations.

6.1   Comparison of TIBLs with Other Machine Learning Algorithms

In order to see how TIBL compares with other extensions of the nearest neighbor algorithm, we compare TIBL with IB1-4 [5] (four instance-based learning algorithms) and IDIBL system [7]. IB1 is a simple nearest neighbor classifier with k = 1. IB2 prunes the training set.

The results of these comparisons are presented in Table 4. For C4.5 we give the result of using tree, pruned tree and rules. For IDIBL, we just use the results reported by Wilson [5].The average values of the combined computations by TIBLs, are shown in Table 3, in which, the average are computed among ALL, CP, CPP, CBP and CBPP in Table 4.

The highest accuracy achieved for each dataset is shown in bold type.

Table 4. Generalization accuracy of TIBL and several well-known algorithms

DataSet	C4.5			IB			Bayes	BP	IDIBL	(size)	CBP	Comb.
	Tree	P-Tree	Rule	IB1	IB2	(size)						
Bridges	68	65.3	59.5	53.8	45.6	38.94	66.1	**67.6**	63.2	34.89	59.9	60.4
Flag	59.2	61.3	60.7	**63.8**	59.8	21.21	52.5	58.2	57.7	32.07	61.8	57.8
Glass	68.3	68.8	68.6	70	66.8	14.3	71.8	68.7	70.6	38.68	78.9	**79**
Heart	73.3	72.1	80	76.2	68.9	13.5	75.6	82.6	**83.3**	24.28	81.1	81.4
Hepat	77.7	77.5	78.8	80	67.8	14.41	57.5	68.5	81.9	18.43	81.9	**82.7**
Iris	94.7	94.7	94.7	96	92.7	3.85	94.7	96	96	10.15	95.2	**95.8**
Promo	73.3	71.9	79.1	81.5	72.9	7.34	78.2	87.9	88.6	21.8	82.7	**89.2**
Voting	95.4	**97**	96.1	92.3	89.9	5.49	95.9	95	95.6	11.34	96.1	95.8
Wine	94.1	94.1	92.9	96	91.6	4.44	94.4	98.3	93.8	8.74	97.4	**98.4**
Zoo	91	91	91.4	96.4	97.5	20.05	**97.8**	95.6	92.2	22.22	97.5	**97.8**
Average	79.1	79.54	80.07	81.09	75.49	15.41	78.46	77.84	82.33	24.55	83.33	**83.83**

7   Conclusions

The proposed method TIBL in this paper is a tolerant nearest neighbor algorithm, which improves the performance of the k-nearest neighbor. It is based on genetic algorithm, tolerant rough sets and the k-nearest neighbor algorithm. For the better classification, it is important to find the optimal tolerant relation between objects that provide as a small classification error as possible.

References

1. Z.Pawlak, ROUGH SETS: Theoretical Aspects of Reasoning about Data (Kluwer, 1991).
2. T.M. Cover and P.E. Hart, "Nearest Neighbor Pattern classification", IEEE Transactions on Information Theory, Vol. 13, No.1, pp. 21-27, 1967.
3. C.J. Merz and P. M. Murphy, 1998, UCI Repository of Machine Learning Databases, Irvine, CA: University of California Irvine, Department of Information and Computer Science, Internet: http://www.ics.uci.edu/ mlearn /MLRepository.html.
4. H.A. Guvenir and A. Akkus, "Weighted K-Nearest Neighbor Classification on Feature Projections", Proc. 12th Intel. Symposium on Computer and Information Sciences (ISCIS'97), Antalya, Turkey, pp. 44-51, 1997.
5. D.W. Aha, D. Kibler and M.K. Albert, "Instance-Based Learning Algorithms", Machine Learning, 6, pp. 37-66, 1991.
6. D.W. Aha, "Tolerating Noisy, Irrelevant and Novel Attributes in Instance-Based Learning Algorithm", International Journal of Man-Machine Studies, 36(1), pp. 267-287, 1992.
7. J.Rachlin, S. Kasif , S.Salzberg and D.W. Aha, "Towards a Better Understanding of Memory-Based and Bayesian Classifiers", Proc. Eleventh International Machine Learning Conference, New Brunswick, NJ: Morgan Kaufmann, pp. 242-250, 1994.
8. D.R.Wilson and T.R. Martinez, "An Integrated Instance-Based Learning Algorithm", Computational Intelligence, 16(1), pp. 1-28, 2000.

Analysis/Synthesis of Speech Signals Based on AbS/OLA Sinusoidal Modeling Using Elliptic Filter

Kihong Kim[1], Jinkeun Hong[2], and Jongin Lim[1]

[1] Graduate School of Information Security, Korea University,
1, 5-Ka, Anam-dong, Sungbuk-ku, Seoul, 136-701, Korea
hong0612@etri.re.kr, jilim@korea.ac.kr
[2] Division of Information & Communication, Cheonan University,
115 Anseo-dong, Cheonan-si, Chungnam, 330-704, Korea
jkhong@cheonan.ac.kr

Abstract. The analysis-by-synthesis/overlap-add (AbS/OLA) sinusoidal model has been applied to a broad range of speech and audio signal processing, such as coding, analysis and synthesis, fundamental frequency modification, time and frequency scale modification. This model uses an iterative analysis-by-synthesis procedure to estimate the sinusoidal parameters {amplitudes, frequencies, and phases}. However, one drawback of this model is that the analysis frame length is generally fixed in analyzing the signal. As a result, since each sinusoidal parameter has different frequencies, an analysis frame with fixed length cannot an optimal spectral resolution to each sinusoidal parameter. In this paper, in order to overcome this drawback and to estimate sinusoidal parameter more accurately, an AbS/OLA sinusoidal model using an elliptic filter is presented and evaluated against the performance of conventional AbS/OLA sinusoidal model. Our proposed AbS/OLA sinusoidal model is found to achieve better performance, in terms of spectral characteristics, phase characteristics, and the synthetic speech quality, than conventional model.

1 Introduction

The AbS/OLA sinusoidal model has been applied to a broad range of speech and audio signal analysis/synthesis, coding, modification, and various other fields since it was first proposed [1][2][3][4]. This model uses an iterative analysis-by-synthesis procedure to estimate the sinusoidal parameters {amplitude, frequencies, and phases}. At each step the AbS algorithm finds a sinusoid that will minimize the mean square error between the original and synthetic speech signals reconstructed with parameters estimated in previous steps. Synthesis system uses an inverse fast Fourier transform (FFT) and overlap-add method [1][2].

However, in the conventional AbS/OLA sinusoidal model, the analysis frame length is generally fixed to a size of about two times or more of the average pitch period [1][2][3]. As a result, since each sinusoidal parameter has different frequencies, an analysis frame with fixed length cannot guarantee an optimal spectral resolution to each sinusoidal parameter, and thus it results in reconstruction artifacts. To overcome this problem, several different previous approaches have been suggested. One approach is to use a wavelet filter bank, wherein subband filtering is followed by sinusoidal modeling of the channel signals with long analysis frames for low frequency band and short analysis frames for high frequency bands [5][6]. Another approach is adaptive windowing method in which the analysis frame length is varied

M. Gallagher, J. Hogan, and F. Maire (Eds.): IDEAL 2005, LNCS 3578, pp. 141–148, 2005.

based on the signal characteristics [7][8]. A third approach to sinusoidal modeling is to use a parallel bank of constant-Q filters as a front end [9]. Then, one can perform sinusoidal modeling on filter output. In this approach, the amount of data storage and complexity increases linearly with the number of filters.

This paper focuses on the first, in which long analysis frames are used to estimate lower frequency sinusoidal parameters, which improves frequency resolution, and short analysis frames are used to estimate higher frequency parameters, which improves time resolution.

In this paper, in order to overcome this drawback and to estimate the sinusoidal parameters more accurately, an AbS/OLA sinusoidal model using elliptic filter [10][11] is presented and its performance is evaluated against that of convectional model. This approach applies a variable-length analysis frame to the filtered speech signal analyzed by the elliptic band pass filter. That is, after decomposing an input speech signal into some filtered signals using the elliptic band pass filter, conventional AbS/OLA sinusoidal models with different analysis frame length are applied to each filtered signals, respectively. Experimental results show that the proposed model achieves better performance, in terms of spectral characteristics, phase characteristics, and synthetic speech quality, than conventional model.

Hereinafter, section 2 reviews a detailed description of the conventional AbS/OLA sinusoidal model. Then, section 3 examines a proposed AbS/OLA sinusoidal model using an elliptic filter. Some experimental results are presented in section 4, and conclusions are provided in section 5.

2 Conventional AbS/OLA Sinusoidal Model

The sinusoidal model represents a speech signal as a linear combination of sinusoids with time-varying amplitudes, frequencies, and phases. That is, the speech signal is represented as the sum of a finite number of corresponding sinusoidal parameters at the fundamental frequency and its harmonics during voiced speech regions, and is represented as numbers of corresponding sinusoidal parameters at peaks in the spectral domain during unvoiced speech regions [1][2][3]. In estimating the sinusoidal parameters, the peaks peaking method [12] and AbS/OLA is widely used, and the latter provides better estimation of the sinusoidal parameters than the peaks peaking method [1].

The conventional AbS/OLA sinusoidal model is a method that reduces the computation load of sinusoidal model based on discrete Fourier transform (DFT). It finds its parameters to minimize the mean square error between original and synthetic speech signals. In the AbS/OLA sinusoidal model, the speech signal can be represented as follows in Eq. (1).

$$\tilde{s}(n) = \sigma(n) \sum_{k=-\infty}^{\infty} w_s(n-kN_s) \tilde{s}^k(n-kN_s) \qquad (1)$$

Here, N_s is the synthesis frame length, and the modulating envelope sequence $\sigma(n)$ is a moving weighted average of the amplitude of $s(n)$. $w_s(n)$ is a synthesis frame obeying the following constraint

$$\sum_{k=-\infty}^{\infty} w_s(n - kN_s) = 1 \qquad (2)$$

If the amplitudes, frequencies, and phases that are estimated for the k th frame are denoted by A_l^k, ω_l^k, and ϕ_l^k, the synthetic speech signal $\tilde{s}^k(n)$ can be represented as follows in Eq. (3)

$$\tilde{s}^k(n) = \sum_{j=1}^{l^k} A_j^k \cos(\omega_j^k n + \phi_j^k) \qquad (3)$$

Here, L is the number of sinusoidal parameter in the frame. These parameters are estimated iteratively and the parameters to minimize the mean square error between the original and synthetic speech signals given by Eq. (4) are optimal.

$$\tilde{s}(n+kN_s) = \sigma(n+kN_s)(w_s(n)\tilde{s}^k(n) + \\ w_s(n-N_s)\tilde{s}^{k+1}(n-N_s),\ 0 \le n \le N_s \qquad (4)$$

The modeling error E is given by

$$E = \sum_{n=-\infty}^{\infty}(s(n)-\tilde{s}(n))^2 \qquad (5)$$

Figure 1 shows an analysis and synthesis system of the conventional AbS/OLA sinusoidal model. In the analysis system, sinusoidal parameters to minimize the mean square error E between the original and synthetic speech signal are found. Then, in the synthesis system, synthetic speech signal is synthesized using these parameters.

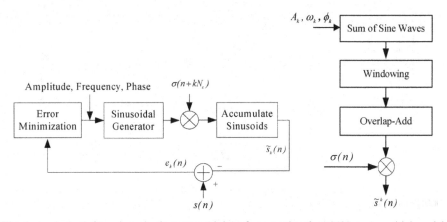

Fig. 1. Analysis (left) and synthesis system (right) of conventional AbS/OLA sinusoidal model

3 Proposed AbS/OLA Sinusoidal Model Using Elliptic Filter

In the conventional AbS/OLA sinusoidal model, an analysis frame has fixed length and is about two times or more of an average pitch period [1][2][3]. However, since each sinusoidal parameter has different frequencies, this approach is not very effective in terms of achieving an optimal spectral resolution to each sinusoidal parameter. Another problem caused by the fixed length frame in the AbS/OLA sinusoidal model is difficulty in modeling noise-like components and time-localized transient events. Then, these result in pre-echo distortion in the synthetic speech signal [5][6][7][8]. In order to overcome this drawback and to estimate sinusoidal parameters more accurately, we propose and implement an AbS/OLA sinusoidal model using elliptic band pass filter in the conventional AbS/OLA sinusoidal model.

The elliptic filter, also called a Cauer filter, has equi-ripple passband, an equi-ripple stopband, a sharp cuff off, obtained by use of transmission zeros on the frequency axis. It offers steeper roll-off characteristics than Butterworth and Chebyshev filter, and is the filter of choice stringent magnitude response requirements. In addition, of the conventional filter types, elliptic filter usually meet a given set of filter performance specification with the lowest filter order [10][11]. Fig. 2 shows the example of frequency response of 4th order elliptic band pass filter.

In the proposed AbS/OLA sinusoidal model, first the input speech signal is decomposed into some filtered signals using an elliptic band pass filter. Lower frequency sinusoidal parameters are then calculated over a greater length of time and have higher fine frequency resolution. Higher frequency parameters are estimated with poor frequency resolution but high time resolution. Fig. 3 shows a block diagram of the proposed AbS/OLA sinusoidal. In this model, the input speech signal is decomposed into filtered signals using an elliptic band pass filter. These filtered signals are then independently analyzed and synthesized with the conventional AbS/OLA sinusoidal model.

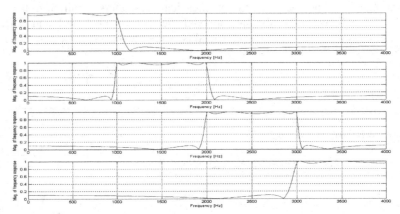

Fig. 2. Example of frequency response of 4th order elliptic band pass filter : 1 to 1000Hz (top), 1000 to 2000Hz (second from the top), 2000 to 3000Hz (third from the top), and 3000 to 4000Hz (bottom)

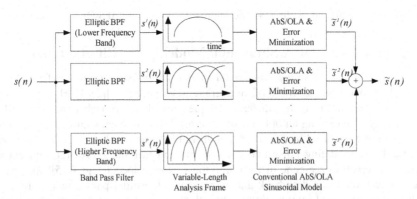

Fig. 3. Block diagram showing analysis and synthesis of proposed AbS/OLA sinusoidal model

4 Experimental Results

In this paper, to prove the performance of the proposed AbS/OLA sinusoidal model, we compared and analyzed the waveform, spectrum characteristics, and phase characteristics of our proposed model with conventional model. The synthetic speech quality of the proposed AbS/OLA sinusoidal has been evaluated in terms of the perceptual evaluation of speech quality (PESQ) [13][14] test based on objective speech quality measures.

Sixteen speech signals were sampled at 8KHz with 16 bits quantization per sample. In the conventional AbS/OLA sinusoidal model, the analysis frame length is set to 20ms. Hamming window was used in the analysis system, and a triangular window was used in the synthesis system. For the elliptic filter, we used a 4th order elliptic band pass filter. We decomposed input speech signals into 3 filtered signals, 1 to 2000Hz band, 2000 to 3000Hz band, and 3000 to 4000Hz band, using an elliptic band pass filter. Ranging from the lowest to highest band, the proposed AbS/OLA sinusoidal model uses analysis frame length of 30ms, 20ms, and 10ms respectively. The number of subbands was experimentally fixed to 3.

The one division of original and synthetic speech signal waveform reconstructed with the conventional and the proposed AbS/OLA sinusoidal model is presented in Fig. 4. The spectral and phase characteristics of the original and synthetic speech signals synthesized using conventional and proposed AbS/OLA sinusoidal model are illustrated in Fig. 5 and Fig. 6. In these figures, we can see that the synthetic speech signals waveform using the proposed AbS/OLA sinusoidal model is similar to that using the conventional model. However, the spectral characteristics of the synthetic speech signals indicate that the proposed AbS/OLA sinusoidal model achieves better performance than the conventional model. It is also demonstrated that the phase characteristics of the synthetic speech signals from the proposed model accurately approximates that of the original speech signal.

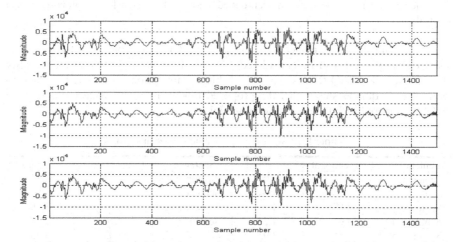

Fig. 4. Waveform between original and synthetic speech signal : original signal (top), synthetic signal using conventional model (middle), synthetic signal using proposed model (bottom)

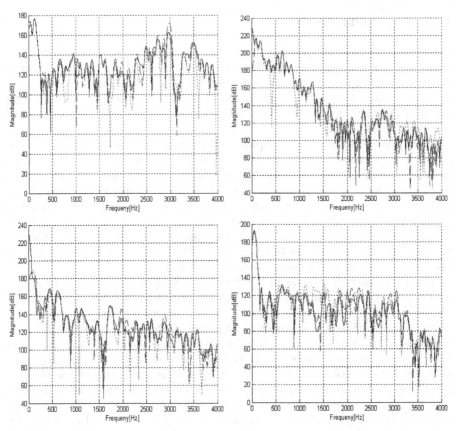

Fig. 5. Spectrum between original and synthetic speech signal : original signal (solid line), synthetic signal using conventional model (dotted line), synthetic signal using proposed model (dashed line)

To evaluate the performance of proposed AbS/OLA sinusoidal model, synthetic speech quality must also be considered. The result of the objective speech quality assessments, the PESQ test, is shown in Table 1. Simulation for comparison of synthetic speech quality shows that the proposed model improves mean opinion score (MOS) compared with the conventional model.

Table 1. PESQ test of the synthetic speech signal

Sentences	Conventional	Proposed	Sentences	Conventional	Proposed
Sentence 1	3.91	4.00	Sentence 9	4.14	4.15
Sentence 2	3.93	4.04	Sentence 10	4.02	4.02
Sentence 3	3.89	4.11	Sentence 11	3.68	3.79
Sentence 4	4.01	4.24	Sentence 12	4.16	4.18
Sentence 5	3.85	3.95	Sentence 13	4.05	4.23
Sentence 6	3.97	4.00	Sentence 14	3.87	4.01
Sentence 7	4.13	4.21	Sentence 15	4.15	4.15
Sentence 8	4.07	4.17	Sentence 16	4.11	4.25

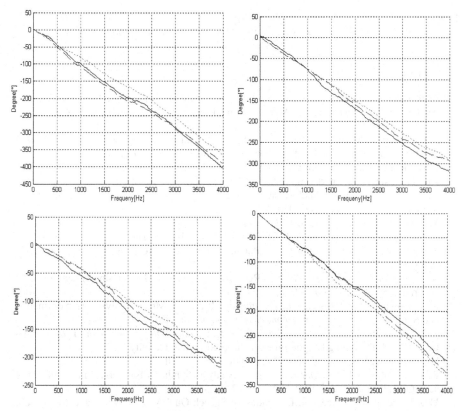

Fig. 6. Phase between original and synthetic speech signal : original signal (solid line), synthetic signal using conventional model (dotted line), synthetic signal using proposed model (dashed line)

5   Conclusions

One drawback of AbS/OLA sinusoidal model is that the analysis frame length is generally fixed in analyzing the signal. As a result, since each sinusoidal parameter has different frequencies, an analysis frame with fixed length cannot an optimal spectral resolution to each sinusoidal parameter. In this paper, in order to solve this drawback and to enhance performance of the parameters estimation in the conventional AbS/OLA sinusoidal model, an AbS/OLA sinusoidal model using an elliptic filter is presented and evaluated against the performance of conventional AbS/OLA sinusoidal model. In the proposed model, after decomposing an input speech signal into filtered signals using the elliptic band pass filter, conventional AbS/OLA sinusoidal models with different analysis frame length are applied to each filtered signals respectively. Experimental results showed that the proposed model achieved better performance in the spectral characteristics, phase characteristics, and synthetic speech quality.

The proposed AbS/OLA sinusoidal model provides natural speech signal decomposition, high quality output, and a combination of modification flexibility. The proposed model can be applied to many applications including text-to-speech (TTS) systems, audio signal processing, and time and frequency scale modification.

References

1. E. B. George and M. J. T. Smith. Speech Analysis/Synthesis and Modification Using an Analysis-by-Synthesis/Overlap-Add Sinusoidal Model. *IEEE Trans. on SAP*, Vol.5, pp.389-406, 1997.
2. S. Furui and M. M. Sondhi. Advances in Speech Signal Processing. *Dekker Inc.*, NY, 1992.
3. W. B. Kleijn and K. K. Paliwal. Speech Coding and Synthesis. *Elsevier*, 1995.
4. E. B. George. Practical High-Quality Speech and Voice Synthesis Using Fixed Frame Rate AbS/OLA sinusoidal modeling. *IEEE ICASSP*, pp.301-304, 1998.
5. D. V. Anderson. Speech Analysis and Coding Using a Multi-Resolution Sinusoidal Transform. *IEEE ICASSP*, pp1037-1040, 1996.
6. M. Rodriguez-Hernandez and F. Casajus-Quiros. Improving Time-Scale Modification of Audio Signals Using Wavelets. *IEEE ICASSP*, pp.1573-1577, 1994.
7. M. Goodwin. Multiresolution sinusoidal Modeling Using Adaptive Segmentation. *IEEE ICASSP*, pp.1525-1528, 1998.
8. K. H. Kim and I. H. Hwang. A Multi-Resolution Sinusoidal Model Using Adaptive Analysis Frame. *EURASIP EUSIPCO*, pp.2267-2270, 2004.
9. M. Goodwin and M.Vetterli. Time-Frequency Models for Music Analysis, Transformation, and Synthesis. *Time-Frequency Time-Scale Symposium*, 1996.
10. T. W. Parks and C. S. Burrus. Digital Filter Design. *John Wiley & Sons*, NY, 1987.
11. C. A. Corral. Designing Elliptic Filters with Maximum Selectivity. http://www.web-ee.com/primers/files/Elliptical_Filters.pdf.
12. R. J. McAulay and T. F. Quatieri. Speech Analysis/Synthesis Based on Sinusoidal Representation, *IEEE Trans. on SAP*, Vol.34, pp.744-754, 1986.
13. ITU-T Rec. P.862, Perceptual Evaluation of Speech Quality (PESQ) an Objective Assessment of Narrowband Telephone Networks and Speech Code. 2002.
14. A. W. Rix et al. Perceptual Evaluation of Speech Quality(PESQ) – a New Method for Speech Quality Assessment of Telephone Networks and Code, *ASSP*, pp.749-752, 2001

Robust Model Adaptation Using Mean and Variance Transformations in Linear Spectral Domain

Donghyun Kim and Dongsuk Yook

Speech Information Processing Laboratory
Department of Computer Science and Engineering
Korea University, Seoul, Korea
{kaizer,yook}@voice.korea.ac.kr

Abstract. In this paper, we propose robust speech adaptation technique using continuous density hidden Markov models (HMMs) in unknown environments. This adaptation technique is an improved maximum likelihood linear spectral transformation (ML-LST) method, which aims to find appropriate noise parameters in the linear spectral domain. Previously, ML-LST and many transform-based adaptation algorithms have been applied to the Gaussian mean vectors of HMM systems. In the improved ML-LST for the rapid adaptation, the mean vectors and covariance matrices of an HMM based speech recognizer are transformed simultaneously using a small number of transformation parameters. It is shown that the variance transformation provides important information which can be used to handle environmental noise, in the similar manner that the mean transformation does.

1 Introduction

When a speech recognizer is used in an unknown environment, the performance of the system may be degraded due to the mismatch between the training and testing conditions. Also most adaptation algorithms have focused on the problem to modify a large number of model parameters with only a small amount of adaptation data. Previously, transformation-based adaptation methods have been proposed to handle the problem. One such method is maximum likelihood linear regression (MLLR) [1], which estimates a set of linear transformations for the Gaussian mean vectors of hidden Markov model (HMM) systems. Another method, a maximum likelihood linear spectral transformation (ML-LST) [2] was proposed for rapid channel adaptation. This approach also uses the mean transformation to compensate for the channel noise in the linear spectral domain. While the channel noise causes a shift of the cepstrum mean vectors, the additive noise gives rise to a change in the cepstrum covariance matrices. Therefore, when there are both the additive noise and the channel noise, the mean vectors and the covariance matrices of the HMM have to be transformed simultaneously in order to better match the testing environment. In this paper, we propose an improved ML-LST that uses a mean and variance transformation in linear spectral space to handle the problem of additive noise more efficiently, in addition to dealing with the channel noise. In the study of [3], the mean and variance transformations are also used with MLLR framework, but it is dealt in the cepstral domain and it has a little increase of recognition rate in comparison with MLLR. By applying the linear spectral transformation principle [2], the number of transformation parameters required for the mean and variance transformation is reduced, thereby allowing rapid

M. Gallagher, J. Hogan, and F. Maire (Eds.): IDEAL 2005, LNCS 3578, pp. 149–154, 2005.

adaptation. The proposed method is evaluated empirically using a far-field micro-phone TIMIT (FFMTIMIT) speech corpus.

In Section 2, we review the theory of the ML-LST. The training procedure is explained in Section 3. The experimental results are presented in Section 4, followed by some conclusions in Section 5.

2   Maximum Likelihood Linear Spectral Transformation

As discussed in [2], noisy speech affected by additive noise such as background sounds, and convolutional noise such as microphone differences, can be characterized by the following equation:

$$\psi = N_\otimes[\chi + N_\oplus],\tag{1}$$

where χ is the clean speech, ψ is the noisy speech, and $N_\otimes$ and $N_\oplus$ are the convolutional and additive noise, respectively. Usually, if we consider the channel distortion to be stationary and the additive noise to be random, the statistics of the noisy speech may be expressed by the following equation:

$$E[\psi] = N_\otimes E[\chi] + N_\otimes E[N_\oplus].\tag{2}$$

This is the motivation for performing the transformation of the variance in the linear spectral domain. The linear spectral noisy mean vector, $\widetilde{\mu}$, and covariance, $\widetilde{\Sigma}$, can be represented by the following equations:

$$\widetilde{\mu} = \mathbf{A}\cdot\mu + \mathbf{b},\tag{3}$$

$$\widetilde{\Sigma} = \mathbf{A}\cdot\Sigma\cdot\mathbf{A}^T + \mathbf{D},\tag{4}$$

where $\mathbf{A}$ is a diagonal matrix of the convolutional noise parameters, μ is the corresponding clean linear spectral mean vector, and $\mathbf{b}$ is a vector of additive noise parameters. $\mathbf{D}$ is the product of the additive noise covariance and the convolutional noise parameters. $\mathbf{D}$ can be simplified to a diagonal matrix assuming that each frequency bin of additive noise is independent.

2.1   Domain Transformation

Equations (3) and (4) form the basis of the ML-LST method of mean and variance adaptation. However, speech recognition systems use models expressed in the cepstral domain, so we need to perform domain transformation on the model parameters. Speech waveforms are typically converted to mel-frequency cepstral coefficients (MFCC). Also, the statistics of the feature vectors are obtained in the cepstral domain. The clean linear spectral mean, μ_i, and covariance, Σ_{ij}, can be expressed in terms of the cepstral domain statistics as follows, assuming a log-normal distribution [4]:

$$\mu_i = \exp\left[\sum_k c_{ik}^{-1}\mu_k^c + \frac{1}{2}\sum_k\sum_l c_{il}^{-1}\Sigma_{lk}^c c_{ik}^{-1}\right],\tag{5}$$

$$\Sigma_{ij} = \mu_i\mu_j\left[\exp\left[\sum_k\sum_l c_{il}^{-1}\Sigma_{lk}^c c_{jk}^{-1}\right]-1\right],\tag{6}$$

where c_{ik} is an element of the I by K discrete cosine transformation (DCT) matrix, I is the dimensionality of the cepstrum mean vector, $\boldsymbol{\mu}^c$, K is the number of filter-banks, and Σ_{lk}^c is an element of the cepstrum covariance matrix. Then, the noisy cepstral mean, $\tilde{\mu}_i^c$, can be obtained as follows, by applying equation (3) and converting back to the cepstral domain:

$$\tilde{\mu}_i^c = \sum_k c_{ik}\left[\log(a_{kk}\mu_k + b_k) - \frac{1}{2}\log\left(\frac{a_{kk}^2\Sigma_{kk} + d_{kk}}{(a_{kk}\mu_k + b_k)^2} + 1\right)\right], \tag{7}$$

where, a_{ii}, b_i, and d_{ii} are the i-th components of $\mathbf{A}$, $\mathbf{b}$, and $\mathbf{D}$, respectively. Similarly the noisy cepstral covariance, $\tilde{\Sigma}_{ij}^c$, is derived using equation (4) in the linear spectral domain and then going back to the cepstral domain, as follows:

$$\tilde{\Sigma}_{ij}^c = \sum_k \sum_l c_{il} \log\left[\frac{a_{ll}a_{kk}\Sigma_{lk} + d_{lk}}{(a_{ll}\mu_l + b_l)(a_{kk}\mu_k + b_k)} + 1\right]c_{jk}. \tag{8}$$

2.2 Time Derivatives

The first and the second order time derivatives of MFCC, called as "delta" and "accel", respectively, also can be used for adaptation with linear spectral transformation. The delta and accel of noisy cepstral mean vectors are estimated from static portions (i.e., the first 13 dimensions) of the noisy cepstral mean and covariance. The delta is derived as follows:

$$\Delta\tilde{\mu}_i^c = \sum_j c_{ij}\left(-\frac{1}{\tilde{\mu}_j}\frac{\partial\tilde{\mu}_j}{\partial t} - \frac{\partial\tilde{\Sigma}_{jj}^l/2}{\partial t}\right), \tag{9}$$

where $\tilde{\Sigma}^l$ is the noisy log covariance matrices. The accel is estimated as follows:

$$\Delta^2\tilde{\mu}_i^c = \sum_j c_{ij}\left(-\frac{1}{\tilde{\mu}_j^2}\left(\frac{\partial\tilde{\mu}_j}{\partial t}\right)^2 + \frac{1}{\tilde{\mu}_j}\frac{\partial^2\tilde{\mu}_j}{\partial^2 t} - \frac{\partial\tilde{\Sigma}_{jj}^l/2}{\partial^2 t}\right). \tag{10}$$

3 Estimation of the ML-LST Parameters

The ML-LST finds the noise parameters, a, b, and d which maximize Baum's auxiliary function. This can be done by using the EM algorithm [5]. If we just consider the mean transformation, the auxiliary function can be simplified to $Q_{\tilde{\mu}}$:

$$Q_{\tilde{\mu}} = -\sum_t \sum_s \sum_g \gamma_{s,g}^{(t)}[(\mathbf{o}^{(t)} - \mathbf{C}\tilde{\boldsymbol{\mu}}_{s,g}^l)^T \Sigma_{s,g}^{c-1}(\mathbf{o}^{(t)} - \mathbf{C}\tilde{\boldsymbol{\mu}}_{s,g}^l)], \tag{11}$$

where $\gamma_{s,g}^{(t)}$ is the posterior probability of the Gaussian distribution g, in state s, at time t_s, $\mathbf{o}^{(t)}$ is a cepstrum vector, $\tilde{\boldsymbol{\mu}}_{s,g}^l$ is the noisy mean vector of the Gaussian g, in state s in the log domain, and $\mathbf{C}$ is the DCT matrix. If the state of the HMM is modeled with a mixture of Gaussian distributions with diagonal covariance matrices, equation (11) is rewritten as follows:

$$Q_{\tilde{\mu}} = -\sum_t \sum_s \sum_g \sum_i \frac{\gamma_{s,g}^{(t)}}{\Sigma_{s,g,ii}^c} \left(o_i^{(t)} - \sum_j c_{ij} \log \frac{(a_{jj}\mu_j + b_j)^2}{\sqrt{(a_{jj}\mu_j + b_j)^2 + (a_{jj}^2\Sigma_{jj} + d_{jj})}} \right)^2. \tag{12}$$

In fact, since the modification of the mean values affects the distribution of the variance, the mean and the variance transformations have to be performed at once for the purpose of variance adaptation. The auxiliary function denoted by $Q_{\tilde{\mu},\tilde{\Sigma}}$ represents the portion of the objective function which is affected by the mean and variance transformation:

$$Q_{\tilde{\mu},\tilde{\Sigma}} = -\sum_t \sum_s \sum_g \gamma_{s,g}^{(t)}[\log|\mathbf{C}\tilde{\Sigma}_{s,g}^l\mathbf{C}^T| + (\mathbf{o}^{(t)} - \mathbf{C}\tilde{\mu}_{s,g}^l)^T \mathbf{C}\tilde{\Sigma}_{s,g}^{l^{-1}}\mathbf{C}^T(\mathbf{o}^{(t)} - \mathbf{C}\tilde{\mu}_{s,g}^l)], \tag{13}$$

$$= -\sum_t \sum_s \sum_g \gamma_{s,g}^{(t)} \cdot \left[\left(\sum_i \log\mathbf{G}_{ii}[\mathbf{C}\tilde{\Sigma}_{s,g}^l\mathbf{C}^T] \right) \right.$$
$$\left. + \left(\sum_j \sum_i (o_i^{(t)} - \tilde{\mu}_{s,g,i}^c)\tilde{\Sigma}_{s,g,ij}^{c^{-1}}(o_j^{(t)} - \tilde{\mu}_{s,g,j}^c) \right) \right] \tag{14}$$

where $\mathbf{G}[.]$ is a matrix using Gauss-Jordan elimination, which efficiently calculates a matrix determinant, and $\tilde{\mu}_{s,g,i}^c$ and $\tilde{\Sigma}_{s,g,ij}^c$ are from equations (7) and (8), respectively. The modified Powell's algorithm [6] may be used to maximize equations (12) or (14).

4 Evaluation of the ML-LST

To evaluate the ML-LST method, an automatic speech recognition system that uses the Viterbi decoding algorithm was implemented. In a supervised manner, the noise parameters are estimated using labeled adaptation data. The baseline models are speaker-independent, tied state, cross-word triphone HMMs with 10 Gaussian distributions per state. The 3,696 training utterances from the TIMIT data were used for training. The 1,296 testing utterances from the FFMTIMIT data were used for testing, which are measured to have average 10dB SNR with 35dB of additive noise. For each speaker, we used each word from one sentence for the adaptation, and performed the recognition test on the remaining sentences of the same speaker. When the training and testing environments were the same (i.e., TIMIT training and TIMIT testing), the phone error rate (PER) was 26.4%. The PER was increased to 47.0% when the testing was performed with the FFMTIMIT data.

4.1 Mean Adaptation

We first compared ML-LST and MLLR. Figure 1 shows that ML-LST is consistently better than MLLR regardless the amount of the adaptation data. The ML-LST is especially effective when only one or two words are used for the adaptation.

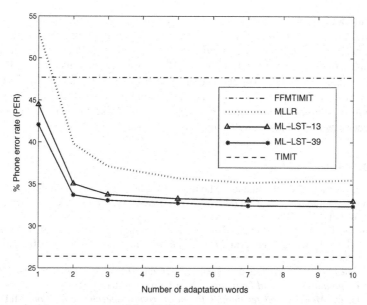

Fig. 1. Average phone error rates (%) of ML-LST and MLLR for various amounts of adaptation data. ML-LST has two kind of the transformation dimensionality; static only (ML-LST-13) and addition of delta and accel (ML-LST-39)

It has been also observed that the time derivatives help the ML-LST. The ML-LST using the delta and the accel, ML-LST-39 in Figure 1, is better than the ML-LST using only the static portion of the MFCCs, ML-LST-13.

4.2 Mean and Variance Adaptation

In this section, the adaptation of the mean and variance are performed at the same time. We focus on the one or two words adaptation which are approximately 0.25 and 0.5 second long. During the domain transformation of the variances, full covariance calculations are typically required. To reduce the computational complexity, we used the 13-dimensional linear spectral transformation. Table 1 shows that the ML-LST mean and variance adaptation (ML-LST-MV) has a lower error rate than the MLLR or the ML-LST mean adaptation (ML-LST-M).

Table 1. Average phone error rates (%) of the MLLR, ML-LST mean adaptation (ML-LST-M), and ML-LST mean and variance adaptation (ML-LST-MV)

Word	MLLR	ML-LST-M	ML-LST-MV
1 (0.25 sec)	51.2	44.3	39.1
2 (0.50 sec)	37.1	35.1	33.5

5 Conclusions

In this paper, we proposed a mean and variance adaptation algorithm that uses a maximum likelihood linear spectral transformation to handle unknown environments.

The linear spectral transformation has the effect of performing a nonlinear transformation in the cepstral domain. Since the ML-LST uses a small number of transformation parameters, it requires only a small amount of adaptation data compared to other adaptation methods. From the results of the adaptation experiments on the TIMIT and FFMTIMIT data, it has been observed that the error rate of speech recognizer can be decreased by 16.8% using only 0.25 seconds of adaptation data, and by 28.7% using 0.5 seconds of adaptation data. Finally, it was concluded that the variance transformation is necessary and handles environmental noise effectively.

References

1. C.J. Leggetter and P.C. Woodland, "Maximum likelihood linear regression for speaker adaptation of continuous density hidden Markov models", *Computer Speech and Language*, vol. 9, pp. 171-185, 1995.
2. D. Kim and D. Yook, "Fast channel adaptation for continuous density HMMs using maximum likelihood spectral transform", *IEE Electronics Letters*, vol. 40, no. 10, pp. 632-633, May 13, 2004.
3. M.J.F. Gales and P.C. Woodland, "Mean and variance adaptation within the MLLR framework", *Computer Speech and Language*, vol. 10, pp. 249-264, 1996.
4. M.J.F. Gales, *Model-based techniques for noise robust speech recognition*, Ph.D. thesis, Cambridge University, 1995.
5. L. Baum. "An inequality and associated maximization technique in statistical estimation of probabilitic functions of a Markov process", *Inequalities*, vol. 3, pp. 1-8, 1972.
6. W. Press, S. Teukolsky, W. Vetterling, and B. Flannery, *Numerical recipes in C++*, pp. 398-460, Cambridge University Press, 2002.

Using Support Vector Machine
for Modeling of Pulsed GTAW Process

Xixia Huang and Shanben Chen

School of Materials Science and Engineering, Shanghai Jiao Tong University
Shanghai 200030, P.R. China
merryhuang@sjtu.edu.cn

Abstract. This paper investigates modeling of the pulsed gas tungsten arc welding (GTAW) process using support vector machine (SVM). Modeling is one of the key techniques in the control of the arc welding process, but is still a very difficult problem because the process is multivariable, time-delay and nonlinear. We analyze the characteristics of SVM for solving the challenge problem and give the main steps of modeling, including selecting input/output variables, kernel function and parameters according to our specific problem. Experimental results of the SVM, neural network and rough set methods show the feasibility and superiority of our approach.

1 Introduction

Modeling of the pulsed gas tungsten arc welding (GTAW) is one of the key techniques in automated welding. In order to obtain the fine formation of the weld seam, the sizes of the weld pool should be exactly dominated in real time, i.e. the backside width and the topside width. The control of the weld pool shape is a critical issue in automated welding, including robotic welding. Appropriate modeling of the welding process is the foundation for designing the control system, and therefore an essential work for transferring welders' operating experience to automatic welding.

However, it is very difficult to obtain a practical model of the process by classical modeling methods. The arc welding process involves many uncertain factors, such as metallurgy, heat transfer, chemical reaction, arc physics, and magnetization. As a result, it is characterized as inherently nonlinear, time-delay and strong coupling in its input/output relationships.

Recently, several artificial intelligence approaches have been proposed to obtain the model of the GTAW process, i.e. neural network (NN), fuzzy set (FS) and rough set (RS) methods[1-3]. Some researches show that the above methods can obtain the model of the process under certain conditions. However, the NN approach needs to determine network structure and the solution maybe local minima. For FS method, it directly depends on the operator's experience, which is hard to obtain. Moreover, the number of inputs, outputs and their linguistic variables could not be too large, or it will lead to "rule explosion". As to RS theory, it is not so effective for the task of prediction, which is more like a tool for data description. Therefore, it is necessary to develop more practical modeling methods for some complex welding processes.

The goal of this study is to use support vector machine (SVM) for the modeling of the arc welding process. SVM, developed by Vapnik[4], is gaining popularity due to

M. Gallagher, J. Hogan, and F. Maire (Eds.): IDEAL 2005, LNCS 3578, pp. 155–163, 2005.

many attractive features and promising empirical performance. Originally, SVM is developed for pattern recognition problems. Recently, with the introduction of ε-insensitive loss function, SVM has been extended to nonlinear regression estimation, time-series prediction, system nonlinear identification and control[5, 6].

The remainder of this paper is organized as follows. In Section 2, we give the basic theory of SVM for regression estimation and analyze SVM for modeling of the GTAW process. In Section 3, we demonstrate how to obtain the model of the process using SVM. In Section 4, we compare our method with the NN and RS methods on predicting ability. Finally, some discussion and conclusions are given in Section 5.

2 Brief Description of SVM for Regression Estimation

In this section, we give the basic theory of SVM for regression estimation[7]. Besides, some analysis about SVM is presented for the modeling of the arc welding process.

According to statistical learning theory, the actual risk $R(\varpi)$ is the sum of the empirical risk $R_{emp}(\varpi)$ (training error) and the confidence interval. The confidence interval is related to VC dimension, which can be regarded as a measurement of diversity, complexity and learning capability of the learning machine. In order to obtain the good generalization performance, the goal of learning is to minimize actual risk $R(\varpi)$, which means that empirical risk (training error) as well as VC dimension is minimized. This is the basic idea of structure risk minimization (SRM) principle.

We describe the linear function using the form $\langle \varpi \bullet x \rangle + b$. In the non-linear case, we map a nonlinear problem in an input space to a linear problem in a higher-dimensional feature space via a nonlinear mapping $\phi(x)$. SVM approximates the function using the following form:

$$f(x) = \langle \varpi \bullet \phi(x) \rangle + b \tag{1}$$

The optimization problem is

$$\min \quad \frac{1}{2}\|\varpi\|^2 + C\sum_{i=1}^{l}(\xi_i + \xi_i^*)$$

$$s.t. \quad \begin{cases} y_i - \langle \varpi^T \bullet \phi(x_i) \rangle - b \leq \varepsilon + \xi_i \\ \langle \varpi^T \bullet \phi(x_i) \rangle - b - y_i \leq \varepsilon + \xi_i^* \\ \xi_i, \xi_i^* \geq 0 \end{cases} \tag{2}$$

where, minimizing $\|\varpi\|^2/2$ means minimizing VC dimension[4], and at the same time $f(x)$ approximates pairs (x_i, y_i) with ε precision. Thus, the above optimal problem is a realization of SRM principle. Therefore, the obtained regression estimation possesses good generalization ability. C>0 is cost coefficient, which represents a balance between the model complexity and the approximation error. When the constraint conditions are infeasible, slack variables ξ_i, ξ_i^* are introduced[4].

In order to solve the optimization problem more easily, by utilizing Lagrange multipliers the dual formulation is obtained:

$$\min_{\alpha,\alpha^*} \frac{1}{2}(\alpha-\alpha^*)^T Q(\alpha-\alpha^*)+\varepsilon\sum_{i=1}^{l}(\alpha_i+\alpha_i^*)+\sum_{i=1}^{l}y_i(\alpha_i-\alpha_i^*)$$

$$s.t. \quad \sum_{i=1}^{l}(\alpha_i-\alpha_i^*)=0, 0\le\alpha_i,\alpha_i^*\le C, i=1,...,l,$$

(3)

Where, $Q_{ij}=K(x_i,x_j)\equiv\phi(x_i)^T\phi(x_j)$ is the so-called kernel function.

By solving (3), the approximate function is obtained:

$$f(x)=\sum_{i=1}^{l}(\alpha_i-\alpha_i^*)K(x_i,x)+b$$

(4)

The motivation of using SVM in modeling of the GTAW process is as following:

1. SVM can perform very well in modeling of the welding process because it has good generalization ability, even for relatively few samples. Small data sets are common in practical applications in welding field because acquirement of large numbers of raw data is costly or even impossible.
2. The nonlinear problem in modeling of the process will be well solved. Nonlinear solutions can be calculated efficiently due to the usage of inner products in SVM.
3. SVM can solve the high-dimension problem in the modeling of the GTAW process. The model may contain a number of inputs because many factors affect the process. The influences on the process involve welding parameters, experiment conditions, welding conditions and so on. This will be explained in more detail in Section 3.

3   Modeling for the Pulsed GTAW Process Using SVM

In this section, we obtain the model using SVM for the pulsed GTAW process. Note that different welding technologies may lead to different models, which can be obtained using similar methods.

3.1   Select Input/Output Variables

In the GTAW process, two metals are joined by melting or fusing their adjoining surfaces. We first give the following analysis about the input/output variables for modeling of the welding process, using a sketch of a weld pool (Fig. 1):

1. The input variables should include the welding parameters because they have great influence on the weld pool. When weld current feeds, the arc between the tungsten electrode (nonconsumable) and the workpiece is initiated. The arc develops intense heat that melts the surfaces of the metals to form the weld pool; the filler metal is melted into the weld pool. Weld current and weld speed affect the heat input, therefore weld current (I), weld speed (V) and wire feeding rate (R) are main influences on the weld pool. In manual welding a skilled operator can make a near-perfect weld by regulating these welding parameters.
2. The geometry parameters of the weld pool should be contained in the input variables because the weld pool can indicate the formation of the weld seam. When the arc, i.e. the intense heat, moves away, the weld pool solidifies to form the weld seam. So, the weld pool can provide accurate and instantaneous information about the weld seam forming. In fact, skilled welders can estimate the bead forming by observing the weld pool so as to dominate the welding process perfectly.

3. The history information (including welding parameters and size parameters) should also be included in the model inputs. The arc welding process is a process of accumulating heat. Because of the heat inertia, the weld pool responds to welding parameters with a delay. So the weld pool is affected by the history parameters.

4. The output of the model should be the backside weld width because it is the quality target. Weld joint penetration has a direct influence on weld strength, so full penetration is an essential factor for ensuring weld quality. Figure 1 shows that the backside weld width is a major indicator for full penetration. Therefore, the backside weld width is a main quality index in the GTAW process.

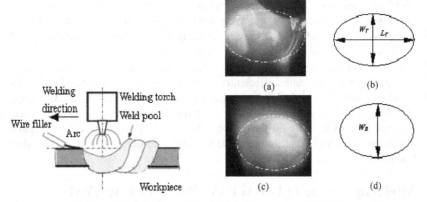

Fig. 1. A sketch of the weld pool. The welding process is multivariable (I, R, V). It is affected by the history information (due to heat inertia). The backside weld width is the major indicator of full penetration

Fig. 2. Images and definitions of geometry parameters of the weld pool. (a)Topside image; (b) Definition of geometry parameters of the topside; (c) Backside image; (d) Definition of geometry parameter of the backside

We adopt the system in [8] to acquire images and define the geometry parameters of the weld pool. The double-side visual sensor system captures the topside and backside vision images of the weld pool simultaneously. The topside and backside sizes of the weld pool are acquired by a real-time image processing algorithm. A complete weld pool image is shown in Fig.2, in which (a) is topside image and (c) is the backside image. Define the pool characters as: the backside maximum width (W_B), the topside maximum width (W_T) and the topside maximum length (L_T), shown in Fig. 2. These parameters could be used to describe the pool characters in full penetration.

In short, we need the data of welding parameters, R, V, I, and geometry parameters, W_T, L_T, W_B (W_B in the previous periods) to predict the backside weld width. Formally, the t-th time datum will be denoted as a vector $d_t = \begin{bmatrix} R^t & V^t & I^t & L_T^t & W_T^t & W_B^t \end{bmatrix}$. Considering the influence of the history information, we extend raw data d_t to D_t, where $D_t = \begin{bmatrix} R^{t-k} & V^{t-k} & I^{t-k} & L_T^{t-k} & W_T^{t-k} & W_B^{t-k} \dots R^t & V^t & I^t & L_T^t & W_T^t & W_B^t \end{bmatrix}$. In our experiments, when the t-th time weld pool begins to form, the $(t-4)$th time weld pool has solidified and it has almost no influence on the t-th weld pool. So it is appropriate that $k=3$ and the model includes 23 inputs (first 23 entries of D_t) and 1 output (last entry of D_t).

3.2 Acquire the Raw Data

To form a valid method to monitor weld joint penetration, the major welding parameters that vary during welding are considered in the experiment designing. Based on the analysis about the welding process I, R and V are selected as the input signals. Random signals are considered as the optimal input signals to the welding process. The size parameters of the weld pool are measured on-line with the double-side visual sensing system. The welding conditions are listed in Table 1. The experimental data of I, R, V, W_T, L_T, W_B is shown in Fig. 3. Note that W_T, L_T and W_B vary widely, from 4mm to 9mm, from 6mm to 13mm, from 2mm to 7mm, respectively. The variations of the size parameters are caused by the different welding parameters or conditions.

Table 1. Welding conditions

welding joint	closed flat butt joint	duty cycle of pulse duration	0.5
size of workpiece	280mm×80mm×2mm	peak value of the pulse current	variable
base metal	A3 steel	welding speed	variable
protective atmosphere	argon gas(99%)	wire feeding rate	variable
welding current	pulse alternating current	diameter of tungsten electrode	3.2mm
pulse frequency	50Hz	arc length	3.0mm
base value of the pulse current	100A	diameter of welding wire	0.8mm

3.3 Select Model

3.3.1 Select Kernel Function

We adopt RBF kernel as the kernel function of SVM. The arc welding process is inherently nonlinear. The RBF kernel nonlinearly maps samples into a higher dimensional space, so it can handle the case when the relation between inputs and outputs is nonlinear. Therefore, the RBF kernel can achieve better performance than the linear kernel in the modeling of the pulsed GTAW process.

3.3.2 Select Parameters

While using RBF kernels, the parameters (C, γ and ε) must be appropriately selected so that the regression estimate can accurately predict unknown data.

We use a "grid-search" on C and γ using cross-validation because the optimal values of (C and γ) are data dependent. Basically pairs of (C and γ) are tried and the one with the lowest cross-validation train error (mean square error) is picked. We try exponentially growing sequences of C and γ because the values of C and γ vary in a wide range.

We choose the best ε according to our problem because the optimal value of ε is problem dependent. We start from a very small value (for example 0.05, which means about 1% error for our problem), and we try the best (C, γ), then the mean absolute error is obtained (about 0.35). From the result we know that it is impossible and unnecessary for the model to approximates samples with precision ε=0.05. Therefore,

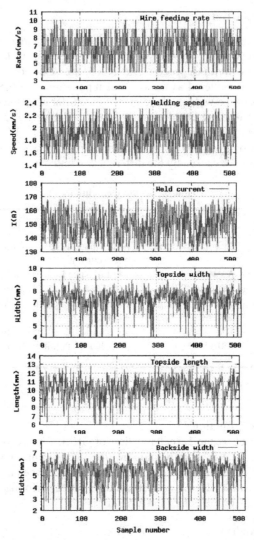

Fig. 3. Experimental data. Top to bottom: wire feeding rate, welding speed, weld current, topside width, topside length, backside width of the weld pool

we search the best ε in the range [0.05, 0.5]. The precision keep almost changeless when ε is less than 0.3, so we choose ε=0.3 in order to obtain a model with a high precision as well as less computing time.

3.4 Obtain the Model

From the description in Section 2, we know that solving regression estimation problem using SVM method is actually an optimization problem. In order to perform the optimization more efficiently, we use the sequential minimal optimization (SMO) algorithm here, see [9-11] for more information.

4 Experiments

We compare our method with the NN method and the RS method[3] upon generalization performance. We construct our support vector regression function using the package LIBSVM[12].

A standard three-layer BP neural network is used as a benchmark. There are 23 nodes in the input layer and one node in the output layer. The number of hidden nodes and the learning rate is determined based on the validation set. The hidden nodes use the sigmoid transfer function and the output node uses the linear transfer function. The stochastic gradient descent method is used for training the BP neural network, which could give better performance than the batch training for large and nonstationary data sets. Standard Matlab toolboxes have been used for the calculations of the BP neural network.

Generally, main steps of the RS-based knowledge modeling method are as follows[3]: Firstly, the raw data can be regarded as a decision table. The condition attributes are the input variables of the model and the decision attribute is the output variable. Secondly, continuous attributes need discretization. Intervals of values of I, R, V, W_T, L_T and W_B are equally divided into 5 subintervals. Then we in turn compute the attribute reduction, attribute value reduction and rule reduction. At last, we get the minimum set of decision rules.

For the purpose of validating the models, the data set is randomly split into 390 training samples and 130 test samples. The partitioning is repeated 10 times independently. The precisions (mean square error) of the three methods are listed in Table 2. Figure 4 shows the error curves of the three methods for the same data.

Table 2. The precision (mean square error) of the three methods

times	SVM	NN	RS
1	0.660	1.241	3.090
2	0.599	1.055	1.528
3	0.396	0.842	1.630
4	0.223	0.754	1.350
5	0.204	0.781	2.828
6	0.534	0.735	1.420
7	0.573	1.156	2.320
8	0.563	1.183	1.380
9	0.46	1.380	1.532
10	1.02	1.246	2.319
Average	0.524	1.038	1.940

The experimental results show that the SVM model has the best performance and the BP neural network model outperforms the RS model. The SVM method exhibits the best generalization ability because SVM adopts the SRM principle and a global optimal solution is obtained. The reason the NN model performs worse is that it is plagued with the problem of local minima and overfitting. As for the RS method, the basic idea is to compute reduction if only the decision rules can classify the training data correctly, so the decision rules are data description only for the training set.

Therefore, the decision rules may not classify the test data. This is depicted in Figure 4(c), in which the large errors are caused by misclassification. Besides, the modeling for the welding process is a regression problem, but the RS theory is based on classification.

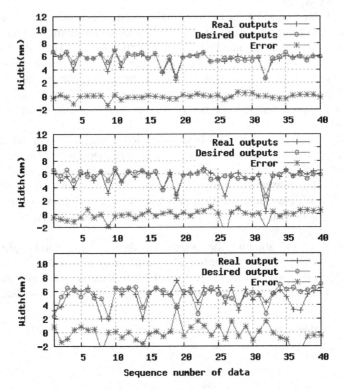

Fig. 4. The error curves of the SVM, NN and RS methods (top to bottom)

5   Conclusion and Future Work

This paper proposes a SVM-based modeling method for the pulsed GTAW process. Experimental results indicate that the method is effective. Comparing with the NN method and RS methods, our method is more precise.

However, evaluating a modeling technique is a complex problem. As for the SVM method and the NN method, the poor comprehensibility has a negative effect on wider applications to some extent. A fuzzy modeling method based on SVM will be investigated in our future work to improve the comprehensibility of SVM.

Acknowledgement

We would like to thank Dr. Chih-Jen Lin in National Taiwan University for his patient help. This work is supported by the National Natural Science Foundation of China under Grand No. 60474036.

References

1. Chen SB, L.Y., Wu L, Zhao DB, Intelligent methodology for sensing, modeling and control of pulsed GTAW: part1-band-on-plate welding. Welding Journal, 2000. **79**(6): p. 151-163.
2. Chen SB, Z.D., Wu L, Lou YJ, Intelligent methodology for sensing, modeling and control of pulsed GTAW: part2-butt joint welding. Welding Journal, 2000. **79**(6): p. 164-174.
3. B. Wang, S.B.C., J.J. Wang, Rough set based knowledge modeling for the aluminum alloy pulsed GTAW process. The International Journal of Advanced Manufacturing Technology, in press.
4. Vapnik, V., The Nature of Statistical Learning Theory. 1995.
5. Abhijit Kulkarni, V.K.J., B.D. Kulkarni, Control of chaotic dynamical systems using support vector machines. Physics Letters A, 2003. **317**(5-6): p. 429-435.
6. U. Thissena, R.v.B., A.P. de Weijerb, W.J. Melssena, L.M.C. Buydensa, Using support vector machines for time series prediction. Chemometrics and Intelligent Laboratory Systems, 2003. **69**: p. 35-49.
7. Smola AJ, S.B., A tutorial on support vector regression. Statistics and Computing, 2004. **14**(3): p. 199-222.
8. Wang JJ, L.T., Chen SB, Obtaining of weld pool vision information during aluminum alloy TIG welding. The International Journal of Advanced Manufacturing Technology, in press.
9. Platt, J., Fast training of support vector machines using sequential minimal optimization. In B. Scholkopf, C. Burges, and A. Smola, editors, Advances in Kernel Methods - Support Vector Learning. 1998.
10. Platt, J., Using sparseness and analytic QP to speed training of support vector machines. In M. S. Kearns, S. A. Solla, and D. A. Cohn, editors, Advances in Neural Information Processing Systems 11. 1999.
11. Flake GW, L.S., Efficient SVM regression training with SMO. Machine Learning, 2002. **46**(1-3): p. 271-290.
12. Chih-Chung Chang, C.-J.L., LIBSVM: a library for support vector machines. 2004. Available at http://www.csie.ntu.edu.tw/~cjlin/libsvm

Design of Simple Structure Neural Voltage Regulator for Power Systems

Mahdi Jalili-Kharaajoo

Young Researchers Club, Islamic Azad University, Tehran, Iran
mahdijalili@ece.ut.ac.ir

Abstract. This paper presents a simple neural Automatic Voltage Regulator (AVR) for power systems. By representing the proposed neuro-controller in s-domain, its parameters can be obtained analytically to ensure system stability. Results of simulation studies on a nonlinear third order generator model with the proposed neuro-controller using calculated parameters are given. Results of simulation studies demonstrate the effectiveness of this simple neuro-controller.

1 Introduction

A power system must be modeled as a nonlinear system for large disturbances. Although power system stability may be broadly defined according to different operating conditions, an important problem, which is frequently considered, is to maintain steady acceptable voltage under normal operating and disturbed conditions, which is referred as the problem of voltage regulation [1,2].

The Artificial Neural Network (ANN) technology has matured enough to be applied successfully in many control fields [3-6]. However, its success will eventually depend on its ability to remove a major obstacle, i.e. the lake of a firm theory. There is no general theory available to assist the developer to design neural networks [7]. As a first step towards a solution for many problems that face practical applications of neural network in control field, an s-domain model of a simple neuro-controller is developed in this paper.

Training of the proposed neuro-controller is on-line by the back propagation (BP) algorithm using a modified error function. By representing the neuro-controller learning equations in the s-domain, the controller parameters can be determined analytically. Using the calculated parameters, applications of the neuro-controller as a field excitation controller for a synchronous generator in a single-machine infinite-bus power system are illustrated by simulation studies.

2 Model of Power System

In this paper, a simplified dynamic model of a power system, namely, a Single-Machine Infinite-Bus (SMIB) power system is considered [8]. This model consists of a single synchronous generator connected through a parallel transmission line to a very large network approximated by an infinite bus (Fig. 1). The classic third order single-axis dynamic model of the SMIB power system Fig. 1 can be written as follows [2]:

M. Gallagher, J. Hogan, and F. Maire (Eds.): IDEAL 2005, LNCS 3578, pp. 164–170, 2005.

- *Mechanical equations*

$$\dot{\delta}(t) = \omega(t) - \omega_o \tag{1}$$

$$\dot{\omega}(t) = -\frac{D}{2H}(\omega(t) - \omega_o) - \frac{\omega_0}{2H}(P_e(t) - P_m) \tag{2}$$

The mechanical input power P_m is treated as a constant in the excitation controller design, i.e., it is assumed that the governor action is slow enough not to have any significant impact on the machine dynamics.

- *Generator electrical dynamics*

$$\dot{E}'_q(t) = \frac{1}{T'_{do}}(E_f(t) - E_q(t)) \tag{3}$$

- *Electrical equations (Assumed $x'_d = x_q$)*

$$E_q(t) = E'_q(t) + (x_d - x'_d)I_d(t) \tag{4}$$

$$E_f(t) = k_c u_f(t) \tag{5}$$

$$P_e(t) = \frac{E'_q(t)V_s}{x'_{ds}}\sin\delta(t) \tag{6}$$

$$I_d(t) = \frac{E'_q(t) - V_s\cos\delta(t)}{x'_{ds}} \tag{7}$$

$$I_q(t) = \frac{V_s}{x'_{ds}}\sin\delta(t) \tag{8}$$

$$V_t(t) = [(E'_q(t) - x'_d I_d(t))^2 + (x'_d I_q(t))^2]^{\frac{1}{2}} \tag{9}$$

More details about power system modeling and the definition of the parameters are [2,8].

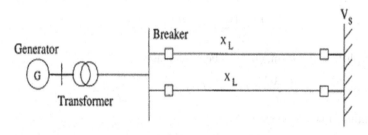

Fig. 1. A single machine infinite bus power system

3 Structure of Neural Voltage Regulator

The overall control system with the proposed neuro-controller consisting of one neuron is shown in Fig. 2. The neuro-controller uses a linear hard limit activation function and a modified error feedback function.

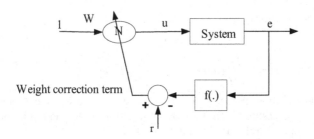

Fig. 2. Overall control system with simple neuro-controller

The neuro-controller uses a simple procedure to update its weight on-line. There is no need for any off-line training. There is no need for parameter identification or reference model. The neuro-controller is trained directly, in an on-line mode, from the system output and there is no need to determine the states of the system. The neuro-controller uses the sampled values of the system output to compute the error using the modified error function. This error is back propagated through the single neuron to update its weight. Then the output of the neuro-controller is computed, which is equal to the neuron weight.

The neuro-controller output can be derived as

$$u(t) = W(t) \tag{10}$$

$$W(t) = W(t-1) + \eta \times WCT(t) \tag{11}$$

where WCT is the neuron weight correction term based on the modified error function. $W(t)$, $u(t)$, η are neuron weight, neuron output and the learning rate respectively.

Based on equations (10) and (11), the neuro-controller model in s-domain can be obtained. In time domain, (11) can be written as

$$W(t) - W(t-\Delta t) = \eta \times WCT(t) \tag{12}$$

Dividing (12) by Δt:

$$\frac{W(t) - W(t-\Delta t)}{\Delta t} = \frac{\eta \times WCT(t)}{\Delta t} \tag{13}$$

Using the differential form, (13) can be written as:

$$\frac{dW(t)}{dt} = \eta_1 \times WCT(t) \quad ; \quad \eta_1 = \frac{\eta}{\Delta t} \tag{14}$$

Representing (14) in s-domain:

$$sW(t) = \eta_1 \times WCT(t) \tag{15}$$

From (10) and (15):

$$U(s) = \frac{\eta_1 \times WCT(t)}{s} \tag{16}$$

The general form of the weight correction term is:

$$WCT(s) = R(s) - C(s)f(s) \tag{17}$$

where $R(s)$, $C(s)$ and $f(s)$ are reference input, system output and feedback function respectively.

Complete model of the proposed neuro-controller in s-domain is shown in Fig. 3, where $G(s)$ represents the controlled system.

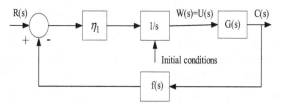

Fig. 3. Neuro-controller model in s-domain

In order to obtain the best parameters of the controller, first a simplified linear model of the synchronous generator is used. The neuro-controller as an automatic voltage regulator (AVR) with the simplified machine model is shown in Fig. 4.

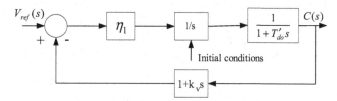

Fig. 4. Neuro-controller as an AVR for simple model of synchronous generator

The proposed modified feedback function in this case is:

$$f(s) = 1 + k_v s \qquad (18)$$

Assuming that $k_v = 0$ (unity feedback), the system response to a 0.05pu step change in reference input for two values of η_1 is shown in Fig. 5 ($\eta_1 = .5, \eta_1 = 2$).

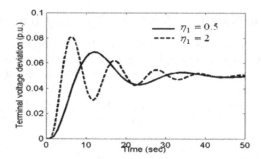

Fig. 5. Neuro -controller performance using unity feedback function for the simple model of the synchronous generator

As shown in Fig. 5, the overall system behaves as a stable second order system. But as η_1 increases, the system is more oscillatory. This is an expected result even for a complicated structure neural network [4].

To improve the performance of a neuro-controller, which is trained on-line by the BP algorithm, a modified function was introduced in [4]. Assuming that the neuro-controller uses the proposed feedback function f(s), equation (18), in its training, a critically damped response to a step change in reference input can be obtained for [9]:

$$k_v = \frac{2\sqrt{\eta_1 T'_{do}} - 1}{\eta_1} \tag{19}$$

For $\eta_1 = 500$, $T'_{do} = 6.9$, then $k_v = 0.23$ for a critically damped response. This critically damped response is shown in Fig. 6 for a 0.05pu step change in reference input. Also, other values for η_1 and k_v for a critically damped response can be obtained. These values are: $\eta_1 = 200, k_v = 0.37, \eta_1 = 10, k_v = 1.56$.

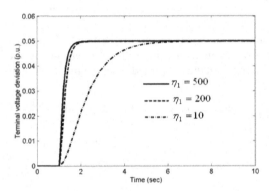

Fig. 6. Neuro-controller performance using modified error function for the simple model of the synchronous generator

The system response corresponding to these values is also shown in Fig. 6. It is clear from this figure that as η_1 increases the response is better. So, the proposed values for η_1 and k_v are: $\eta_1 = 500, k_v = 0.23$.

4   Application to Nonlinear Model of Power Systems

The proposed neuro-AVR is used to simulate the dynamic behavior of the generating unit connected to a constant voltage bus through two parallel transmission lines [3]. The parameters of the model mentioned in section 2 and the initial conditions of the system are as the following

$x_d = 1.863$ $x'_d = 0.257$ $x_T = 0.127$ $x_L = 0.4853$ $x_{ad} = 1.712$ $H = 4$

$D = 5$ $\omega_o = 314.159$ $k_c = 1$ $x_{ds} = 2.23265$ $x'_{ds} = 0.62665$ $x_s = 0.36965$ $T'_{do} = 6.9$

$$\delta_o = 34.2^o \qquad P_{mo} = .8 p.u. \qquad V_{to} = 1 p.u.$$

In case of $k_v = 0$, the system response to a 0.05pu step change in reference voltage is shown in Fig. 7 for different values of η_1. As it is clear from this figure, this controller is not suitable to control the generator terminal voltage.

In case of $k_v = 0.23$ and $\eta_1 = 500$, system response to a 0.05pu step increase in reference voltage at 1sec is depicted if Fig. 8. It is seen from Fig. 8 that the terminal voltage response is excellent. It also demonstrates that the parameters obtained based on a simplified linear model can be used for the non-linear model as well.

With the function $f(s) = 1 + kvs$, the neuro-controller is designed to control the generator terminal voltage only. It can be seen from Fig. 8 that the system still needs a supplementary signal to enhance stability. As proposed in [5], including an additional term in $f(s)$ based on the generator speed deviation can enhance system stability. The performance of the proposed NAVR is compared with the commercial AVR (the AVR obtained from MATLAB toolbox). The results are shown in Fig. 9. As it can be seen the performance of the NAVR is much better than that of AVR in response to 0.05pu step disturbance in voltage reference.

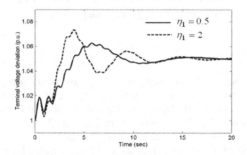

Fig. 7. Neuro-controller performance using unity feedback function for the third-order model of the synchronous generator

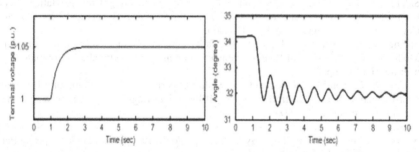

Fig. 8. Neuro-controller performance using modified error function for the third-order model of the synchronous generator

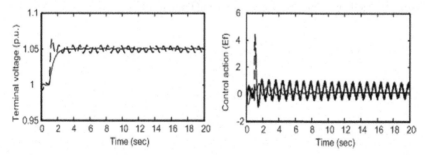

Fig. 9. System response to 0.05pu step disturbance in voltage reference using NAVR (solid line) and commercial AVR (dashed line)

5 Conclusions

In this paper, a neuro-controller with a simple structure for a synchronous generator was presented. The Neuro-controller is trained on-line based on a modified function. The neuro-controller consists of one neuron, one weight, hard limit activation function, and a constant input. Having the neuro-controller in s-domain, its stability analysis with a simplified generator linear model was presented. The neuro-controller parameters were obtained analytically to ensure system stability. The controller parameters, which were calculated, based on a simplified linear model, can be used for a nonlinear model. The proposed controller was used to function as an AVR for a SMIB power system. Results showed that the neuro-controller acts as an adaptive controller with better performance than the commercial AVR.

References

1. Zhu C., Zhou R., Wang Y., A new nonlinear voltage controller for power systems, International Journal of Electrical Power and Energy Systems, 19, pp. 19-27, 1996.
2. Jalili-Kharaajoo, M. and Moezi-Madani, K., Optimal Nonlinear Transient Controller for a Single Machine-Infinite Bus Power System, in Proc. IEEE International Conference on Control Applications (CCA'03), Istanbul, Turkey, pp.306-311, 2003.
3. Shamsollahi, P. and O. P. Malik, An Adaptive Power System Stabilizer Using On-Line Trained Neural Networks, IEEE Transactions on Energy Conversion, 12(4), pp. 382-387, 1997.
4. Salem, M., E. Abu El- Zahab, and O. P. Malik, Generating Unit Excitation Neuro- Controller. Proceedings, in Proc. IFAC Symposium on Power Plants and Power Systems Control, Brussels, Belgium, pp. 97-102, 2000.
5. Salem, M., E. Abu El- Zahab, and O. P. Malik, On-Line Trained Neuro-Controller with a Modified Error Function, in Proc. Canadian Conference on Electrical and Computer Engineering, Halifax, pp. 83-87, 2000.
6. Salem, M., E. Abu El- Zahab, and O. P. Malik, Experimental Verification of a Generating Unit Excitation Neuro- Controller, in Proc. IEEE Power Engineering Society Winter Meeting, Singapore, pp.22-27, 2000.
7. El-Sharkawi, M. A. and Niebur, D. (Editors), A Tutorial Course on Artificial Neural Networks with Applications to Power Systems, IEEE Power Engineering Society Special Publications, no. 96TP112-120, 1996.
8. Kundur, P., Power system stability and control, In the EORI Power System Engineering Series, New York, Mc Grow Hill, 1994.
9. Ogata, K., Modern Control Engineering. Second Edition, 1990.

EEG Source Localization for Two Dipoles in the Brain Using a Combined Method

Zhuoming Li[1], Yu Zhang[2], Qinyu Zhang[3], Masatake Akutagawa[1],
Hirofumi Nagashino[4], Fumio Shichijo[5], and Yohsuke Kinouchi[1]

[1] Department of Electrical and Electronic Engineering, Faculty of Engineering,
The university of Tokushima, Minami-josanjima, Tokushima 770-8506, Japan
{lzm,makutaga,kinouchi}@ee.tokushima-u.ac.jp
[2] Department of Information Science and Intelligent, System Faculty of Engineering
The university of Tokushima, Minami-josanjima, Tokushima 770-8506, Japan
zhangyu@is.tokushima-u.ac.jp
[3] Shenzhen Graduate School of Harbin Institute of Technology, Shenzhen, China
zqy@hit.enu.cn
[4] School of Medical Sciences, The University of Tokushima, Tokushima, Japan
[5] Suzue Hospital, Tokushima 770-0028, Japan

Abstract. Estimating the correct location of electric current source
with the brain from electroencephalographic (EEG) recordings is a challenging analytic and computational problem. Specifically, there is no
unique solution and solutions do not depend continuously on the data.
This is an inverse problem from EEG to dipole source. In this paper we
consider a method combining backpropagation neural network (BPNN)
with nonlinear least square (NLS) method for source localization. For inverse problem, the BP neural network and the NLS method has its own
advantage and disadvantage, so we use the BPNN to supply the initial
value to the NLS method and then get the final result, here we select the
Powell algorithm to do the NLS calculating. All these work are for the
fast and accurate dipole source localization. The main purpose of using
this combined method is to localize two dipole sources when they are
locating at the same region of the brain. The following investigations are
presented to show that this combined method used in this paper is an
advanced approach for two dipole sources localization with high accuracy
and fast calculating.

1 Introduction

A pervasive problem in neuroscience is determining active regions of the brain,
given potential measurements at the scalp . The computer era allowed the development of method for quantifying brain electrical signals and thus further
refining our investigative tools. So it gives a way to find the active regions of
brain source. In the process of detecting the active regions of the human brain,
it is often required to estimate the location and strengths of biopotential sources
inside a volume of tissue, based on the potential field measured over the periph-
ery of that volume (inverse problem of electrophysiology).

M. Gallagher, J. Hogan, and F. Maire (Eds.): IDEAL 2005, LNCS 3578, pp. 171–178, 2005.

To calculate the source parameters from the potential field measured over the scalp, some advanced methods have been used, such as Moving Dipole, Music, Dipole Tracing, and LORETA. But most of these methods have several limitations. First, it is computationally expensive, and suffers from model complexity. It may take long computational time. Second problem with these iterative methods is their being model dependent. Their needing large number of electrodes to avoid local minima can be pointed out as the third shortcoming of these methods. Due to restrictions mentioned above, recently, artificial neural networks are introduced in source localization as an optimization tool. However, in the case of two dipoles global source localization, using neural work to do the computation is not a good choice and the classical technique has its own disadvantage, it needs long calculating time and suitable initial value to get accuracy solution. So in this paper a combined method is given, her the method combined the BP neural network with Nonlinear Least Square Method [1, 2].

Our study is to set up a method to localize the brain source when there are two dipoles in the same region of human brain, the method is combining BPNN with nonlinear least square method. It is to improve the disadvantage of BPNN introduced above and avoid the long calculating time. In this paper, we do the computation with the EEG data from 32 electrodes arrangement of a 10-20 system, discuss how to combine the BPNN and nonlinear least square method, explain the simulation EEG data generation, and also investigate the localization accuracy from combined method. Moreover, the noise signal influence and calculation time are illustrated at last.

2   Method

The results reported in this paper are based on the following models commonly found in literature: (a) the human brain is represented by the four-concentric-shell model , and (b) the biopotential sources are represented by moving current dipoles [3]. Each dipole is parameterized by its location vector and the dipole moment vector. In order to do localize sources in global human brain, we set up the combined method. The block diagram of the system employed in this study is shown in Fig. 1.

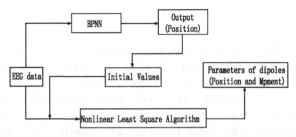

Fig. 1. System of the combined method. The output of BPNN is used as the initial values for the NLS algorithm

2.1   Forward Calculating Method

Quasistatic approximations of Maxwell's equations gave the relationship between neural current dipole sources and the EEG data they produced. Generally, for m sensors and n current dipoles, the vector of measured data at one time can be expressed as:

$$\mathbf{V} = \begin{bmatrix} V_1 \\ \vdots \\ V_m \end{bmatrix} = \begin{bmatrix} \mathbf{g}(\mathbf{q}_1, \mathbf{r}_1) & \cdots & \mathbf{g}(\mathbf{q}_1, \mathbf{r}_n) \\ \vdots & \ddots & \vdots \\ \mathbf{g}(\mathbf{q}_m, \mathbf{r}_1) & \cdots & \mathbf{g}(\mathbf{q}_m, \mathbf{r}_n) \end{bmatrix} \begin{bmatrix} \mathbf{m}_1 \\ \vdots \\ \mathbf{m}_n \end{bmatrix} \tag{1}$$

Where $\mathbf{V}$ is the column vector of the surface potential $V_j (j = 1 \ldots m)$, which is the measured potential in jth electrode. $[\mathbf{q}_1 \ldots \mathbf{q}_m]$ is locations for m electrodes, here m is 32. $[\mathbf{r}_1 \ldots \mathbf{r}_n]$ and $[\mathbf{m}_1 \ldots \mathbf{m}_n]$ are both concatenations of the parameters for n dipoles (n = 2), locations and moments. In Eq.1, the vector $\mathbf{q}_j$ $(j = 1 \ldots m)$ represents the 3-dimensional location of the jth electrode. The vector $\mathbf{r}_L$ $(L = 1 \ldots n)$ represents the 3-dimensional location of the Lth current dipole, and mL represents the corresponding 3-dimensional dipole moment. The $\mathbf{g}(\mathbf{q}_j, \mathbf{r}_L)$ represents the gain transfer vector for n dipoles, relating the dipole point to the electrode point and $\mathbf{g}(\mathbf{q}_j, \mathbf{r}_L)$ is defined from the head model. Note that the dipole location parameters are nonlinearly related to measurement potential [4].

First of all, theoretical calculation described in (1) is computed for current dipoles placed in a hemisphere brain of concentric 4-phere head model with 32 EEG channels. But before this step, the source model, head model and electrode configuration method must be set up.

2.2   Source Model, Head Model and Electrode Configuration

The current dipole, because of its simplicity and physical appropriateness, is adopted in this study as a source model. Each dipole is composed of six parameters, i.e. the position parameter: r = [rx ry rz]T and the moment parameter: m = [mx my mz]T. In this study, the human brain is represented by concentric 4-sphere model with the radii and conductivities for the inner brain, cerebrospinal fluid layer, the skull layer and the scalp layer respectively, as shown as Fig. 2(a). 32 EEG electrodes are placed on the surface of the scalp with the radius of 8.8 cm, where the locations of 32 sensors are indicated as shown as the figure. Fig. 2(b) shows the coordinate system used for the basic EEG formulas. When a dipole on z-axis, the potential on the surface of concentric 4-sphere head model referenced infinity is given by Cuffin and Cohen(1979). Other dipole locations are found by applying rotation transform to the basic formulas [5].

2.3   Inverse Calculation Method

In the following we briefly describe the inverse computation methods used in our work, i.e. the BPNN and the Powell algorithm.

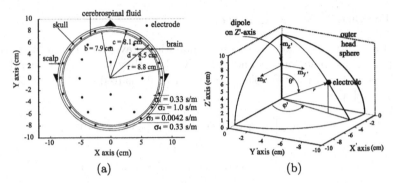

Fig. 2. (a): 4 - concentric spheres head model with radii b, c, d and r and conductivities σ_1, σ_2, σ_3 and σ_4 (Cuffin and Cohen 1979). (b): EEG coordinate system for a dipole on z'-axis in a spherical head model. An arbitrary dipole location can be generated with standard coordinate transformations

Neural Network Based Techniques. When a source model and a head model have been assumed, the nest step is to calculate the inverse solution for the location of the source in the model. If there are two dipole sources in the hemisphere brain, BPNN is not a good choice to localize the brain source when two dipole sources are in the same region. To get better location accuracy, the brain has to be divided into two regions (left and right) and each region is assumed to hold one dipole source to get better location accuracy. In this study the purpose is to localize the global brain source in the hemisphere, so the BPNN is not used to get the final source locations but only to be selected to supply the initial value to the nonlinear least square algorithm. Fig. 3 describes the general strategy used in this paper to train/test neural networks and also shows the structure of neural network. To get better results for the initial values, we set the training

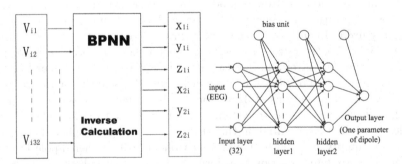

Fig. 3. Strategy used in neural network source localization and the structure of neural network. The left is the Strategy used in neural network source localization. Input vector $\mathbf{V} = \{V_{i,j}|j = 1, 2, \ldots m\}$ denotes potentials calculated at m = 32 electrode locations for the dipole pair $'i'$. The output vector $\mathbf{r} = [x_{1,i}y_{1,i}z_{1,i}x_{2,i}y_{2,i}z_{2,i}]$ parameterized the location of ith dipole pair. And the right figure is the structure of neural network

region in head model with the radius of b ($b = 7.9$cm), and then make a smaller region as the testing region, it is 6.9cm [6].

Classical Technique (Powell Algorithm). The classical method for the inverse problem is a direction set method, used to minimize the cost function in order to get the global minimum, and then calculates the correct solutions. Same as other minimization algorithms, Powell algorithm is also used to minimize the cost function. In order to estimate the location of dipole sources in the brain from EEG data, we assume $\mathbf{V}_{meas}$ and $\mathbf{V}_{cal}$ express the measured potential and theoretical potential calculated by (1). Then the n dipoles at chosen location can be estimated from a standard nonlinear minimization of the sum-squared residual, as the following:

$$J_n = (\mathbf{V}_{meas} - \mathbf{V}_{cal})^T (\mathbf{V}_{meas} - \mathbf{V}_{cal}) \tag{2}$$

The moments of dipoles are given by the so-called "normal equation":

$$\mathbf{M}_n = \mathbf{G}^+ \mathbf{V}_{meas} \tag{3}$$

Where $\mathbf{G}^+$ is known as "Moore-Penrose pseudoinverse" of the matrix $\mathbf{G}$.

$$\mathbf{G}^+ = (\mathbf{G}^T \mathbf{G})^{-1} \mathbf{G}^T \tag{4}$$

From (2) (3) and (4), the residual J_n can be expressed as:

$$J_n = \mathbf{V}_{meas}^T (\mathbf{I} - \mathbf{G}\mathbf{G}^+) \mathbf{V}_{meas} \tag{5}$$

Here $\mathbf{I}$ denotes the $m \times m$ identify matrix [7].

3   Results and Discussion

In the simulation using the method combining BPNN with Powell algorithm, there are three steps: simulation data generation, initial value calculating with BPNN and finial dipole parameters computation using Powell algorithm with the initial value from BPNN.

In the following EEG data generation, two restrictions are imposed. Firstly, the pairs of dipole are placed randomly in the head model, and the distance between each pair of dipole is set to be large than 2cm. Secondly, the angles of moments are generated randomly and the constant strength is 0.8. For EEG data used in the simulation, we generate five groups, without noise, with 5%, 10%, and 30% white noise respectively. Here 5%, 10%, 30% white noise means the same percent of root mean square value of the EEG data.

In the BPNN implementation, we trained neural networks with 2 hidden layers, first hidden layer having 72 neurons and the second having 60 neurons. The number of neurons in the input and output layers were fixed by the number of electrodes (32) and the parameters of the dipole model (6: the location parameters of two dipoles). During the net works training and testing, we find it is better to use BPNN to calculate one parameter of dipole than to use net works to calculate the total dipole parameters in the same time. In our study, two dipoles are placed in the brain and only use BPNN to get the position parameters of dipoles, so we apply 6 same net works for two dipole positions calculating, one net work will work for one location parameter. The sizes were chosen by a trial-and-error process, aiming to get the maximum possible generalization results. The training procedure was done until the minimum error rate to a test data set was observed. In Table 1, the position error of BPNN output is shown, gotten from different EEG data (without noise, with 5%, 10% and 30% white noise). From the result of BPNN, we can know that the position error between the calculated and the target location is big, so this result is not suitable to be as the finial solution for two brain sources localization in our study. Here the BPNN is only used to get the initial value for the following Powell algorithm.

Table 1. Location accuracy from BPNN with different noise

	non-noise	5%	10%	30%
Position Error(cm)	3.3144	3.3298	3.3315	3.3337

After getting the initial value from BPNN, in order to bring the location accuracy up and find the correct moment result, we insert initial value to the Powell algorithm for the final solution of two brain sources localization from the same BPNN testing EEG data generated before. The two dipoles localization accuracy from combined method is shown in Table 2, including position error and moment error. From the final results, we can conclude that the accuracy of location and direction localization by the combined method used in this paper is taken to a higher level than only by BPNN. On the other hand, the noise in EEG signal also affects the localization accuracy, where larger noise makes bigger position and moment error. Comparing the results from BPNN and the combined method, we find that the noise signal in EEG data make the bigger influence over the calculating by Powell algorithm than by BPNN. That is because that the computing process of neural network is only to set up the relationship between the input and output signal. But the classical non-linear algorithm is the iteration computation, the intruder in the input signal will make the direct effect on the accuracy of finial result.

Table 2. Location accuracy from BPNN with different noise

	non-noise	5%	10%	30%
Position Error(cm)	0.7433	0.7957	0.8095	0.9772
Moment Error(deg)	0.2458	0.2446	0.2635	0.3043

Next let us discuss the distribution of error for localization as shown as Fig. 4. About the location accuracy gotten from combined method, average position error is 0.8cm around and max error is about 10cm. The combined gets the

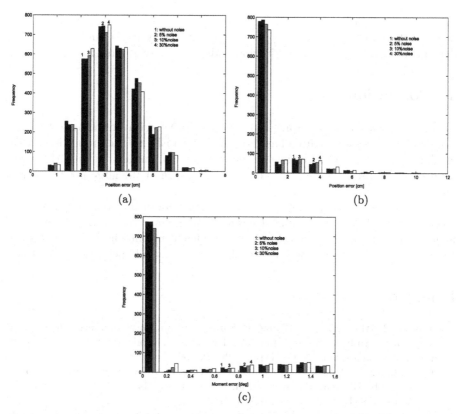

Fig. 4. The distribution of position errors and moment errors. (a) shows the distribution of position errors by BPNN from different EEG signal (without noise, with 5%, 10%, 30% insert noise). (b) and (c) show the distribution of localization accuracy using the combined method, including the position errors and moment error

average moment error about 0.25 degree and max error about 1.5 degree. In BPNN calculating, some pairs of dipoles locating near the brain boundary cause the large position error. For Powell algorithm, some conditions will make the finial localization accuracy go down, such as the distance between the initial value and target position, noise percent in EEG signal and the location of brain sources. Bad initial value, high percent noise signal and pairs of dipole locating near the brain boundary will produce large position and moment errors.

In training the BPNN used here, long computing time is needed. But for the trained networks, it can output the results within few milliseconds. Using the combined method to obtain the localization results, it takes about 25 seconds (DELL PC with Pentium4 1.5GHz CPU). But this time is still much less then using Powell algorithm to do the computing with random initial value or from other initial value calculating methods.

In our work, BPNN can not localize multiple brain sources successfully. How to extend neural networks method for multi-dipoles is therefore become important, because it will save much calculating time. On the other hand, how to increase the localization accuracy is a important study in the future, maybe it depends on EEG signal noise reduction and complex head models.

4   Conclusions

In this paper, we proposed a method combing BPNN with Powell algorithm for two dipole sources localization based on 32 channel EEGs. The properties of this combined method were investigated. The accuracy of initial value and the finial localization result are given. Also discuss the reason of the large position error appearance.

The average position error and moment error obtained from computer simulation proved that this combined method can localize the brain sources with high accuracy for two dipole case. And the calculating time in the simulation is acceptable. Maybe the method used in this paper is useful in clinical application.

References

1. Udantha R. Abeyratne, G. Zhang, P. Saratchandran: EEG source localization: a comparative study of classical and neural network methods. International Journal of Neural Syatems, vol. 11, no. 4, pp. 349-359, 2001
2. Qinyu Zhang, H. Nagashino, Yohsuke Kinouchi: Accuracy of single dipole source localization by BP neural networks from 18-channel EEGs. IEICE TRANS. INF. & SYST., vol. E86-D, no. 8, pp. 1447-1455, 2003
3. Zhou H and van Oosterom A.: Computation of the potential distribution in a four-layer anisotropic concentric spherical volume conductor. IEEE Trans Biomed Eng., vol. 39, no. 2, pp.154-158, Feb. 1992
4. B.N. Cuffin: A comparison of moving dipole inverse solutions using EEG's and MEG's. IEEE Trans. Biomed. Eng., vol. 11, no. 2, pp. 905-910, Jan. 1985
5. Stok, C.J.: The influence of model parameters on EEG/MEG single dipole source estimation. IEEE Trans. Biomed. Eng., vol. 34, pp. 289-296, 1987
6. Zhang Q, Bai X, Akutagawa M, Nagashino H, Kinouchi Y et al.: A method for two brain sources localization by combining BPNN and nonlinear least squares method. Proc. Of 7th Inti. Conf. On control, automation, robotics and vision, pp. 536-541, Singapore, 2002
7. Zhuoming Li, X. Bai, Q. Zhang, M. Akutagawa, F. Shichijo, Y. Kinouchi, U. R. Abeyratne: Multi Dipole Source Identification From EEG/MEG Topography, The Eighth International Conference on Control, Automation, Robotics and Vision, pp. 953 - 957, Kunming, China, December, 2004

Intelligent Control of Micro Heat Exchanger with Locally Linear Identifier and Emotional Based Controller

Mahdi Jalili-Kharaajoo

Young Researchers Club, Islamic Azad University, Tehran, Iran
mahdijalili@ece.ut.ac.ir

Abstract. In this paper, an intelligent controller is applied to electrically heated micro heat exchanger. First, the dynamics of the micro heat exchanger, which is a highly nonlinear plant, is identified using Locally Linear Model Tree (LOLIMOT) algorithm. Then, an intelligent controller is applied to the identified model. The performance of the proposed intelligent controller is compared with that of classic controllers like PID. Our results demonstrate excellent control action, disturbance handling and system parameter robustness for the intelligent controller.

1 Introduction

Electrically heated micro heat exchangers have been developed to accelerate the fluid and gas heating in a reduced space [1,2]. This system consists of a diffusion bonded metal foil stack with many grooves, the heating element are placed between the foils. We have used BELBIC [3,4], the recently developed neuromorphic controller based on emotional learning model elaborated in [5,6], to produce the control action. Biologically motivated intelligent computing has been successfully applied to solving complex problems in recent years. Model-based approaches to decision making are being replaced by data-driven and rule-based approaches in recent years [7].

A cognitively based version of reinforcement learning has been developed in which a critic constantly assesses the consequences of actuating the plant with the selected control action in any given state in terms of the overall objectives or performance measures and produces an analog reinforcement cue which in turn directs the learning in the controller block [8]. This cognitive version of the reinforcement signal has been denoted as an emotional cue, for it is indeed the function of emotions like stress, concern, fear, satisfaction, happiness, etc. to assess the environmental conditions with respect to goals and utilities and to provide cues regulating action selection mechanisms [8,9]. Whether called emotional control or merely an analog version of reinforcement learning with critic (evaluative control), the method is increasingly being utilized by control engineers, robotic designers and decision support systems developers and yielding excellent results [4-11].

In this paper, an intelligent controller will be applied to temperature control in a micro heat exchanger. First, the nonlinear behavior of the plant is identified using Locally Linear Model Tree (LoLiMoT) algorithm for training of neurofuzzy network [12,13] and then Brain Emotional Learning Based Intelligent Controller (BELBIC) is applied to the plant. The performance of the proposed controller is compared with that of a PID controller, which simulation results show better match for BELBIC.

M. Gallagher, J. Hogan, and F. Maire (Eds.): IDEAL 2005, LNCS 3578, pp. 179–186, 2005.

2 Electrically Heated Micro Heat Exchanger

Electrically heated micro heat exchangers have been developed to accelerate the fluid and gas heating in a reduced space [1,2]. This system consists of a diffusion bonded metal foil stack with many grooves, the heating element are placed between the foils (Fig. 1). In a small volume, powers to 15 kW can be converted with the advantages of

- Fluids and gas heated by electrical power and not by additional flow cycle
- Efficient transformation of electrical energy in thermal energy
- Fast temperature change of the media and temperature fit for sensitive media
- Compact construction due to micro system technology

Also, the results of that are

- Production of 45 °C warm water by an electric power of 14 kW and a flow of about 6 l/min
- Complete evaporation of water with a flow of 5 l/h
- Heating of an air stream in only 1 millisecond from 25 °C to 850 °C with an electrical power of 400 W and a flow of 2000 l/h

Its characteristics is listed in below

- Heat transmission coefficient: 17500 W m-2 K-1 (for water)
- Yield higher than 90%
- Ultimate electric power: 15 kW
- Pressure drop: 100 mbar for 5 l/h water-flow
- Dimensions: 95 mm * 30 mm * 35 mm

For the identification of the plant, the input-output data is used. For this plant, the voltage in the system input and the output temperature is the output.

Fig. 1. Electrically heated micro heat exchanger

3 Locally Linear Model Tree Identification of Nonlinear Systems

In the following, the modeling of nonlinear dynamic processes using LOLIMOT models is described. The network structure of a local linear neuro-fuzzy model [11,12] is depicted in Fig. 2. Each neuron realizes a local linear model (LLM) and an associated validity function that determines the region of validity of the LLM. The validity functions form a partition of unity, i.e., they are normalized such that

$$\sum_{i=1}^{M} \varphi_i(\underline{z}) = 1 \tag{1}$$

for any model input $\underline{z}$. The output of the model is calculated as

$$\hat{y} = \sum_{i=1}^{M} (w_{i,o} + w_{i,1}x_1 + \ldots + w_{i,n_x}x_{n_x})\varphi_i(\underline{z}) \tag{2}$$

where the local linear models depend on $\underline{x} = [x_1, \ldots, x_{n_x}]^T$ and the validity functions depend on $\underline{z} = [z_1, \ldots, z_{n_z}]^T$. Thus, the network output is calculated as a weighted sum of the outputs of the local linear models where the $\varphi_i(\cdot)$ are interpreted as the operating point dependent weighting factors. The network interpolates between different Locally Linear Models (LLMs) with the validity functions. The weights w_{ij} a are linear network parameters. The validity functions are typically chosen as normalized Gaussians as

$$\varphi_i(\underline{z}) = \frac{\mu_i(\underline{z})}{\sum_{j=1}^{M} \mu_j(\underline{z})} \tag{3}$$

with

$$\mu_i(\underline{z}) = \exp(-\frac{1}{2}(\frac{(z_1 - c_{i,1})^2}{\sigma_{i,1}^2} + \ldots + \frac{(z_1 - c_{i,n_z})^2}{\sigma_{i,n_z}^2})) \tag{4}$$

The centers and standard deviations are *nonlinear* network parameters. In the fuzzy system interpretation each neuron represents one rule. The validity functions represent the rule premise and the LLMs represent the rule consequents. One-dimensional Gaussian membership functions

$$\mu_{i,j}(z_j) = \exp(-\frac{1}{2}(\frac{(z_j - c_{i,j})^2}{\sigma_{i,j}^2})) \tag{5}$$

can be combined by a t-norm (conjunction) realized with the product operator to form the multidimensional membership functions in (3). One of the major strengths of local linear neuro-fuzzy models is that premises and consequents do not have to depend on identical variables, i.e. $\underline{z}$ and $\underline{x}$ can be chosen independently.

The LOLIMOT algorithm consists of an outer loop in which the rule premise structure is determined and a nested inner loop in which the rule consequent parameters are optimized by local estimation. For the termination criterion various options exist, e.g., a maximal model complexity, that is a maximal number of LLMs, statistical validation tests, or information criteria. Note that the *effective* number of parameters must be inserted in these termination criteria.

Fig. 3 illustrates the operation of the LOLIMOT algorithm in the first four iterations for a two-dimensional input space and clarifies the reason for the term "tree" in the acronym LOLIMOT. Especially two features make LOLIMOT extremely fast. First, at each iteration not all possible LLMs are considered for division. Rather, Step 2 selects only the worst LLM whose division most likely yields the highest performance gain. For example, in iteration 3 in Fig. 3 only LLM 3-2 is considered for further refinement. All other LLMs are kept fixed. Second, in Step 3c the local estimation approach allows to estimate only the parameters of those two LLMs which are newly generated by the division. For example, when in iteration 3 in Fig. 3 the LLM 3-2 is divided into LLM 4-2 and 4-3 the LLMs 3-1 and 3-3 can be directly passed to the LLMs 4-1 and 4-3 in the next iteration without any estimation.

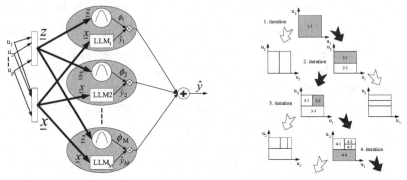

Fig. 2. Network structure of a local linear neurofuzzy model with M neurons for nx LLM inputs x and nz validity function inputs z

Fig. 3. Operation of the LOLIMOT structure search algorithm in the first four iterations for a two-dimensional input space ($p = 2$)

4 Brain Emotional Based Learning Intelligent Controller

Motivated by the success in functional modeling of emotions in control engineering applications [5,6,8,10,11], the purpose of this research is to use a structural model based on the limbic system of mammalian brain, for decision making and control engineering applications. A network model have been adopted which is developed by Moren and Balkenius [5,6], as a computational model that mimics amygdala, orbi-tofrontal cortex, thalamus, sensory input cortex and generally, those parts of the brain thought responsible for processing emotions. There are two approaches to intelligent and cognitive control. In the indirect approach, the intelligent system is used for tuning the parameters of the controller and in the direct approach; the intelligent system itself functions as the controller. While in our past utilizations of BELBIC the direct approach was taken [4], here we have used BELBIC for tuning an existing controller. As a result, the basic performance of the system is determined by our choice of the controller block in ideal situation, and BELBIC is responsible for tuning the parameters of the controller and, generally, to improve its performance. Excellent perform-ance at the expense of more reasonable levels of control effort has thus been achieved.

The model is illustrated in Fig. 4. BELBIC is essentially an action generation mechanism based on sensory inputs and emotional cues. In general, these can be vec-tor valued, although in the benchmark discussed in this paper for the sake of illustra-tion, one sensory input and one emotional signal (stress) have been considered [4]. The emotional learning occurs mainly in amygdala. The learning rule of amygdala is given in formula (6):

$$\Delta G_a = k_1 . \max \left(0, EC - A\right) \tag{6}$$

where G_a is the gain in amygdala connection, k_1 is the learning step in amygdala and EC and A are the values of emotional cue function and amygdala output at each time.

The term max in the formula (6) is for making the learning changes monotonic, implying that the amygdala gain can never be decreased as it is modeled to occur in biological process in amygdala [5,6]. This rule is for modeling the incapability of unlearning the emotion signal (and consequently, emotional action), previously learned in the amygdala [5,6]. Similarly, the learning rule in orbitofrontal cortex is shown in formula (7).

$$\Delta G_o = k_2.(MO - EC) \tag{7}$$

which is completely based on the original biological process. In the above formula, G_o is the gain in orbitofrontal connection, k_2 is the learning step in orbitofrontal cortex and MO is the output of the whole model, where it can be calculated as formula (8):

$$MO = A - O \tag{8}$$

in which, O represents the output of orbitofrontal cortex. In fact, by receiving the sensory input S, the model calculates the internal signals of amygdala and orbitofrontal cortex by the relations in (9) and (10) and eventually yields the output.

$$A = G_a.SI \tag{9}$$

$$O = G_o.SI \tag{10}$$

Since amygdala does not have the capability to unlearn any emotional response that it ever learned, inhibition of any inappropriate response is the duty of orbitofrontal cortex.

Controllers based on emotional learning have shown very good robustness and uncertainty handling properties [4,10,11], while being simple and easily implementable. To utilize our version of the Moren-Balkenius model as a controller, it should be noted that it essentially converts two sets of inputs (sensory input and emotional cue) into the decision signal as its output. A closed loop configuration using this block (termed BELBIC) in the feed forward loop of the total system in an appropriate manner have been implemented so that the input signals have the proper interpretations. The block implicitly implemented the critic, the learning algorithm and the action selection mechanism used in functional implementations of emotionally based (or generally reinforcement learning based) controllers, all at the same time [10,11]. The structure of the control circuit we implemented in this study is illustrated in Fig. 6. The implemented functions in emotional cue and sensory input blocks are given in (11) and (12),

$$EC = MO.(-W_1.\dot{e}.e + W_2.e) \tag{11}$$

$$SI = W_3.e + W_4.\dot{e} + W_5.\int edt \tag{12}$$

where EC, MO , SI and e are emotional cue, controller output, sensory input and output error and the W_1 through W_5 are the gains must tuned for designing a satisfactory controller. In the choice of these two signals some principles are taken into consideration as following:

1. Sensory input is a kind of control signal which in BELBIC is reinforced or punished based on Emotional cue so it should be chosen as a function of error just like a PID controller. This choice has some advantages such as existence of a systematic

way to tune the gains. In this way one can set the Emotional cue equal to zero at first and then tune the gains of Sensory input as a simple PID controller and then proceed to tune the gains of the other parts of BELBIC in the direction of improving the performance of primary sensory input signal. This method can solve the main problem of BELBIC which was the tuning of the gains. In addition to this point the controller now has more reliability because of being based on a classic controller (PID). Also PID controller has some other advantages such as robustness to some extend which is very desirable especially in this work with possible uncertainties in estimated model including less than enough neurons. Besides, using this signal selection it does not need to concern on effect of noises on identification. So an identification using less numbers of neurons can easily filter the noises while could be used in tuning of controller and it will accelerate the online control process certainly.

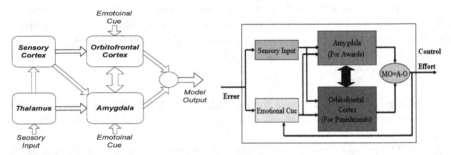

Fig. 4. The abstract structure of the computational model mimicking some parts of mammalian brain

Fig. 5. Control system configuration using BELBIC

2. When the Emotional cue is a positive number, the gain of amygdala connection will be increased and when the Emotional cue is a negative number, the gain of orbitofrontal connection will be increased and the bigger Emotional cue causes the bigger reinforcement or punishment so the Emotional cue should increase when the absolute value of error decreases. In order to avoid the offset error the Emotional cue should include error in addition to its derivative but with a very smaller coefficient. Finally the Emotional cue is compared with the control signal (MO) therefore it should have the same dimension with (MO). So, one can define the Emotional cue like equation (9).

5 Simulation Results

In this section, the simulation results of the output voltage tracking problem using BELBIC with LOLIMOT identifier will be presented. The closed-loop system response using BELBIC is shown in Fig. 6. In order to investigate the performance of BELBIC, we will provide another simulation using conventional PID controller. The closed-loop system response using PID controller with above parameters is shown in Fig. 7. Comparing Fig. 6 with Fig. 7, we can see that the performance of the system using BELBIC is much better than that of PID controller. The system response using BELBIC is faster with less distortion.

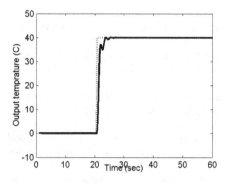

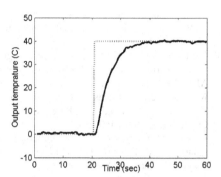

Fig. 6. Closed-loop system response using BELBIC with LOLIMOT identifier

Fig. 7. Closed-loop system response using PID with LOLIMOT identifier

6 Conclusion

In this paper, a Brain Emotional Based Learning Intelligent Controller (BELBIC) was applied to electrically heated micro heat exchanger, which is a highly nonlinear plant. To this end, the dynamics of the system was identified using Locally Linear Model Tree (LOLIMOT) algorithm. Then, BELBIC was applied to the system to tackle the output temperature tracking problem. The closed-loop system performance using BELBIC was compared with that of PID controller, which the result of BELBIC was much better that PID controller. BELBIC could settle faster with less distortion.

References

1. Stief, T., Langer, O.U. and Schuber, K., Numerical investigations on optimal heat conductivity in micro heat exchangers. In Irven, R. [Hrsg.] Micro reaction Technology: 4th International Conference; AIChE Spring Nat. Meeting, Atlanta, Ga., March 5-9, 2000.
2. Brander, J., Fichtner, M., Schygulla, U. and Schubert, K., Improving the efficiency of micro heat exchangers and reactors. In Irven, R. [Hrsg.] Micro reaction Technology: 4th International Conference; AIChE Spring Nat. Meeting, Atlanta, Ga., March 5-9, 2000.
3. J R. Neese, Emotional Disorders in Evolutionary Perspective, British Journal Of Medical Psychology, 71, pp. 397-415, 1998.
4. C. Lucas, D. Shahmirzadi, N. Sheikholeslami, "Introducing BELBIC: Brain Emotional Learning Based Intelligent Controller," International Journal of Intelligent Automation and Soft Computing, 10(1), 2004.
5. J. Moren, C. Balkenius, "A Computational Model of Emotional Learning in The Amygdala: From animals to animals," in Proc. 6th International conference on the simulation of adaptive behavior, Cambridge, Mass., The MIT Press, 2000.
6. C. Balkenius, J. Moren "A Computational Model of Emotional conditioning in the Brain," in Proc. workshop on Grounding Emotions in Adaptive Systems, Zurich, 1998.
7. K. Miyazaki, N. Araki, E. Mogi, T. Kobayashi, Y. Shigematsu, M. Ichikawa, G. Matsumoto, "Brain Learning Control Representation in Nucleus Accumbens," in Proc. Second International Conference on Knowledge-Based Intelligent Electronic Systems, Australia, April, 1998, 21-23.
8. C. Lucas, S. A. Jazbi, M. Fatourechi, M. Farshad "Cognitive Action Selection with Neurocontrollers," in Proc. Third Irano-Armenian Workshop on Neural Networks, August 2000, Yerevan, Armenia.

9. K. Inoue, K. Kawabata, and H. Kobayashi "On a Decision Making System with Emotion," in Proc. 5th IEEE International Workshop on Robot and Human Communication, 1996, 461-465.
10. M. Fatourechi, C. Lucas, A. Khaki Sedigh "Reducing Control Effort by means of Emotional Learning," in Proc. 9th Iranian Conference on Electrical Engineering, (ICEE2001), , May, 2001, Tehran, Iran, 41-1 to 41-8.
11. M. Fatourechi, C. Lucas, A. Khaki Sedigh "Reduction of Maximum Overshoot by means of Emotional Learning," in Proc. 6th Annual CSI Computer Conference, February, 2001,Isfahan, Iran, 460-467.
12. O. Nelles, "Orthonormal Basis Functions for Nonlinear System Identification with Local Linear Model Trees (LoLiMoT)," in Proc. IFAC Symposium on System Identification, Kitakyushu, Fukuoka, Japan, 1997.
13. O. Nelles, "Local linear model tree for on-line identification of time variant nonlinear dynamic systems," in Proc. International Conference on Artificial Neural Networks (ICANN), Bochum, Germany, 1996, 115-120.

Identification of Anomalous SNMP Situations Using a Cooperative Connectionist Exploratory Projection Pursuit Model

Álvaro Herrero, Emilio Corchado, and José Manuel Sáiz

Department of Civil Engineering, University of Burgos, Spain
escorchado@ubu.es

Abstract. The work presented in this paper shows the capability of a connectionist model, based on a statistical technique called Exploratory Projection Pursuit (EPP), to identify anomalous situations related to the traffic which travels along a computer network. The main novelty of this research resides on the fact that the connectionist architecture used here has never been applied to the field of IDS (Intrusion Detection Systems) and network security. The IDS presented is used as a method to investigate the traffic which travels along the analysed network, detecting SNMP (Simple Network Management Protocol) anomalous traffic patterns. In this paper we have focused our attention on the study of two interesting and dangerous anomalous situations: a port sweep and a MIB (Management Information Base) information transfer. The presented IDS is a useful visualization tool for network administrators to study anomalous situations related to SNMP and decide if they are intrusions or not. To show the power of the method, we illustrate our research by using real intrusion detection scenario specific data sets.

1 Introduction

Connectionist models have been identified as a very promising method of addressing the intrusion detection problem due to two main features: they are suitable to detect day-0 attacks (new and modified intrusion strategies) and they have the ability to classify patterns (attack classification, alert validation). IDS are hardware or software systems that monitor the events occurring in a computer system or network, analyzing them to identify computer security problems in an automate way. IDS have become a necessary additional tool to the security infrastructure of most organizations as the number of network attacks has increased very fast during the last years.

IDS try to identify any attack that may compromise the integrity, confidentiality or availability of a system, which are the three computer security principles [1]. Intrusions are produced for example by attackers accessing to the system from networks as Internet, for authorized users who attempt to obtain more privileges for which they are not authorized and authorized users who misuse the privileges given to them. The complexity increases in the case of distributed network-based systems and insecure networks.

Up to now, there have been several attends to apply artificial neural architectures (such as Self Organising Maps [2, 3], Elman Network [4]) to the network security field [5, 6]. This paper presents an IDS based on a novel neural EPP architecture.

M. Gallagher, J. Hogan, and F. Maire (Eds.): IDEAL 2005, LNCS 3578, pp. 187–194, 2005.

EPP [7, 8, 9, 10] is designed for analyzing high-dimensional data using low-dimensional projections. The aim of EPP is to reveal possible interesting structures hidden in the high-dimensional data so that a human can investigate the projections by eye. This technique can be very interesting for a network administrator to visualize the traffic travelling along the network and use it to detect anomalous situations.

The remainder of this paper is structured as follows:

Section 2 introduces the developed IDS model. Section 3 provides an overview of the unsupervised connectionist method used by the IDS model. Section 4 describes the problem and Section 5 describes the data set used. Finally, we present the results in Section 6 and the conclusions and future research in Section 7.

2 A Novel IDS Model

The aim of this work is the design of a system capable of detecting anomalous situations for a computer network. The information analysed by our system is obtained from the packets which travel along the network. So, it is a Network-Based IDS. The necessary data for the traffic analysis is contained on the captured packets headers. This information can be obtained using a network analyser.

When we talk about anomaly detection models we refer to IDS which detect intrusions by looking for abnormal network traffic. Anomaly detection is based on the assumption that misuse or intrusive behaviour deviates from normal system use [5, 11]. In many cases, as in the case of the attacker who breaks into a legitimate user's account, this is a right assumption.

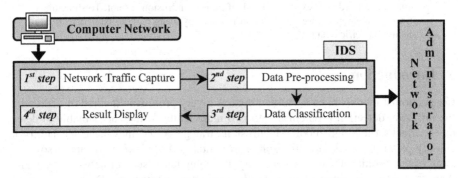

Fig. 1. Graphical Description of the proposed IDS

The structure of this novel IDS is showed in Fig.1 and it is described as follows:

- **1st step.** Network Traffic Capture: one of the network interfaces is set up as "promiscuous" mode. It captures all the packets travelling along the network.
- **2nd step.** Data Pre-processing: the captured data is pre-processed as it is described in section 5 and later, it is used as the input data to the following stage.
- **3rd step.** Data Classification: once the data has been pre-processed, the connectionist model (section 3) analyses the data and identifies the anomalous patterns.
- **4th step.** Result Display: the last step is related to the visualization stage. At the end, the output of the network is presented to the administrator or person in charge of the network security.

3 The Unsupervised Connectionist Architecture

EPP [7, 8, 9, 10] is a statistical method for solving the difficult problem of identifying structure in high dimensional data. The method used here is based on the projection of the data onto a lower dimensional subspace in which we search for its structure by eye. It is necessary to define an "index" that measures the interestingness of a projection. After that, the data is transformed by maximizing the index in order to maximize the interest according to that index. From a statistical point of view the most interesting directions are those which are as non-Gaussian as possible.

The Data Classification and Result Display steps (Fig. 1) performed by this IDS model are based on the use of a neural EPP model called Cooperative Maximum Likelihood Hebbian Learning (CMLHL) [12, 13, 14]. It was initially applied to the field of Artificial Vision [12, 13] to identify local filters in space and time. Here, we have applied it to the computer security field [6]. It is based on Maximum Likelihood Hebbian Learning (MLHL) [9, 10, 13]. Consider a N-dimensional input vector, x, and a M-dimensional output vector, y, with W_{ij} being the weight linking input j to output i.

MLHL can be expressed as:

$$y_i = \sum_{j=1}^{N} W_{ij} x_j, \forall i. \tag{1}$$

The activation is fed back through the same weights and subtracted from the input.

$$e_j = x_j - \sum_{i=1}^{M} W_{ij} y_i, \forall j. \tag{2}$$

And finally, the weight update:

$$\Delta W_{ij} = \eta . y_i . sign(e_j) | e_j |^{p-1}. \tag{3}$$

Lateral connections [12, 13] have been derived from the Rectified Gaussian Distribution [15] and applied to the negative feedback network [16]. The resultant net will be shown to be a network which can find the independent factors of a data set but do so in a way which captures some type of global ordering in the data set.

We use the standard MLHL but now with lateral connections (which act after the feed forward but before the feedback).

Thus we have a feed forward step (Eq. 1) follows by:

Lateral activation passing: $y_i(t+1) = [y_i(t) + \tau(b - Ay)]^+.$ (4)

Feedback: $e_j = x_j - \sum_{i=1}^{M} W_{ij} y_i$. (Eq. 2) (5)

Weight change: $\Delta W_{ij} = \eta . y_i . sign(e_j) | e_j |^{p-1}$. (Eq. 3) (6)

Where:
- τ is the "strength" of the lateral connections.
- b is the bias parameter.
- A is a symmetric matrix used to modify the response to the data based on the relation between the distances among the output neurons.

- η is the learning rate.
- p is a parameter related to the energy function [9, 10, 13].

4   Problem Description

A protocol in a network context is a specification that describes low-level details of host-to-host interfaces or high-level exchanges between application programs. Among all the implemented network protocols, there are several of them that can be considered quite more dangerous (in terms of network security), such as SNMP, ICMP (Internet Control Message Protocol), TFTP (Trivial File Transfer Protocol) and so on.

We have focused our effort in the study of SNMP anomalous situations because an attack based on this protocol may severely compromise the systems security. CISCO [17] found the top five most vulnerable services in order of importance, and SNMP was one of them. Initially, SNMP was oriented to manage nodes in the Internet community [18]. It is used to read and write a wide variety of information about the device: operating system, version, routing tables, and so on. Some of this data can be extremely sensitive and the MIB is used to store this information. The MIB can be roughly defined as a database which contains information about some elements or devices that can be network-controlled.

One special feature of the traffic travelling along the network is that SNMP packets are generated and sent inside the own network. It is an internal protocol and any host out of the network can not introduce any packets of this type in the network.

There are some anomalous situations related to SNMP implementations. Among those we have chosen the two most dangerous ones: a SNMP port sweep and a MIB information transfer. This kind of transfer is considered a quite dangerous situation because a person having some free tools, some basic SNMP knowledge and the community password (in SNMP v. 1 and SNMP v. 2) can come up with all sorts of interesting and sometimes useful information.

The study of SNMP is the reason why the system selects packets based on UDP (User Datagram Protocol) in the Data Pre-processing step. This means that in terms of the TCP/IP (Transmission Control Protocol/Internet Protocol) protocol stack, the model captures only the packets using UDP at transport layer and IP at network layer.

5   Real Intrusion Detection Scenario Specific Dataset

In the Data Pre-processing step, the system performs a data selection of all the information captured: we used the following 5 variables extracted from the packet headers:

- **Timestamp:** time (in milliseconds) when the packet was sent (difference in relation to the first captured packet).
- **Protocol:** we have codified all the protocols contained in the data set, taking values between 1 and 40.
- **Source Port:** port number of the source host which sent the packet.
- **Destination Port:** port number of the destination host where the packet was sent.
- **Size:** total packet size (in bytes).

As it is said before, we study two anomalous situations related to SNMP. Therefore the used data set contains examples of those situations:

- **SNMP port sweep:** it consists of a scanning of network hosts for the SNMP port using sniffing methods. The aim is to make a systematic sweep in a group of hosts to verify if SNMP is active in some ports. We have used default [18] port numbers (161 and 162) and also a random port number (3750) as a test random element.
- **MIB information transfer:** the previous situation is followed by a MIB transfer. The data set contains a transfer of some information stored in the SNMP MIB.

In addition to the SNMP packets, this data set contains traffic related to other protocols installed in the network, like NETBIOS and BOOTPS.

6   Results

Fig. 2 shows the best projection displayed by the model for this data set, where it is easy to identify some anomalous groupings of packets. Just by looking, a strange behaviour can be identified in Groups 1, 2 and 3. After a visual analysis of these groups, the following characteristics can be identified:

- Group 1 (Fig. 2) is subdivided in three subgroups. Packets belonging to each one of these subgroups (S1, S2 and S3) progress in a direction (Abnormal direction) different from the one in which the rest of the packets ("normal") groups progress (Normal direction).
- Groups 2 and 3 (Fig. 2) have a very high temporal concentration of packets. Moreover, packets contained in these groups do not progress in a unique direction, they progress in two different ones, while the rest of the packets ("normal") groups progress in only one direction (Normal direction).

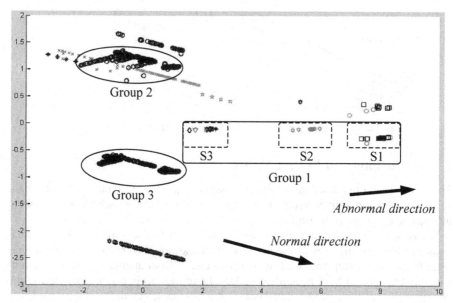

Fig. 2. Data projection displayed by the model

After the study of these graphical characteristics and the analysed data set, we have came to the following conclusions:

− Group 1 (Fig. 2) contains packets related to the SNMP sweep presented in the data set. Each one of the subgroups in it are associated to each port number included in the sweep (161, 162 and 3750 in this case). This is, the first subgroup starting from the right side (S1) includes packets sent to port number 161, the second subgroup (S2) includes packets sent to port number 162 and so on.

− Groups 2 and 3 (Fig. 2) are related to the SNMP MIB transfer mentioned above. They contain packets sent and received during the transfer embedded in the data set. Group 2 contains all the traffic in one way (from destination to source), while Group 3 contains all the traffic in the other way (from source to destination). One of the main axes identified in the visual analysis can be related to the packet size and the protocol while the other one is related to the timestamp.

We have compared the results provided by CMLHL (Fig. 2) with MLHL (Fig.3.a) and Principal Component Analysis (PCA) (Fig.3.b). CMLHL is able of identifying both anomalous situations while PCA [16, 19] is just identifying the sweep (Group 1, Group 2 and Group 3 in Fig.3.b) by means of normal/abnormal directions. Fig.3.a shows how MLHL is capable of detecting the MIB transfer (Groups 2 and 3) but the port sweep (Group 1) is not detected as clearly as by using CMLHL.

CMLHL highlights anomalous situation more clearly because the projections are more spread out so it is easier to analyse them. The anomalous situations are detected due to the different traffic directions or the high temporal density. CMLHL shows both features better than other methods as MLHL or PCA.

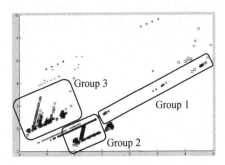

Fig. 3a. MLHL Projection

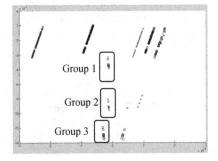

Fig. 3b. PCA Projection

7 Conclusions and Future Work

The visualization tool used in the Result Display step, displays data projections highlighting anomalous situations clearly enough to alert the network administrator, taking into account aspects as the traffic density or "anomalous" traffic directions.

It has been showed how the proposed model is able to identify anomalous situations by means of the eyes of the network administrator. In this case, the system has identified a port sweep followed by a MIB transfer. Both anomalous situations contained in the data set have been identified by the model. So in performance terms, the systems achieves very good results because it is able to detect all the anomalous situations contained in the data set.

We can not consider a simple packet as an anomalous one, because it is considered anomalous with respect to the rest of packets (both normal and anomalous ones) traveling along the network.

Further work will be focused on:

- Application of GRID [20, 21] computation. This increase of the system power will be used in such a way that the system can be able to capture, process, classify and display the data in real time.
- Study of different distributions and learning rules.
- Application to more complex data sets, trying to extend the model to cover several different situations, including other SNMP anomalous situations and protocols, until to cover all of them.

Acknowledgments

This research has been supported by the McyT projects: TIN2004-07033.

References

1. Myerson, J.M.: Identifying Enterprise Network Vulnerabilities. International Journal of Network Management, Vol. 12 (3) (2002) 135–144
2. Hätönen, K., Höglund, A.,Sorvari, A.: A Computer Host-Based User Anomaly Detection System Using the Self-Organizing Map. International Joint Conference of Neural Networks, Vol. 5 (2000) 411–416
3. Zanero S., Savaresi S.M.: Unsupervised Learning Techniques for an Intrusion Detection System. ACM Symposium on Applied Computing (2004) 412-419
4. Ghosh, A. Schwartzbard A., Schatz A.: Learning Program Behavior Profiles for Intrusion Detection. Workshop on Intrusion Detection and Network Monitoring (1999) 51-62
5. Debar, H., Becker, M., Siboni, D.: A Neural Network Component for an Intrusion Detection System. IEEE Symposium on Research in Computer Security and Privacy. Oakland, California (1992)
6. Corchado, E., Herrero, A., Baruque, B., Saiz J.M.: Intrusion Detection System Based on a Cooperative Topology Preserving Method. International Conference on Adaptive and Natural Computing Algorithms. Lecture Notes in Computer Science. Springer-Verlag, Berlin Heidelberg New York (2005) 454-457
7. Friedman J., Tukey. J.: A Projection Pursuit Algorithm for Exploratory Data Analysis. IEEE Transaction on Computers, Vol. 23 (1974) 881-890
8. Hyvärinen A.: Complexity Pursuit: Separating Interesting Components from Time Series. Neural Computation, Vol. 13(4) (2001) 883-898
9. Corchado, E., MacDonald, D., Fyfe, C.: Maximum and Minimum Likelihood Hebbian Learning for Exploratory Projection Pursuit. Data Mining and Knowledge Discovery, Vol. 8(3). Kluwer Academic Publishing, (2004) 203-225
10. Fyfe, C., Corchado, E.: Maximum Likelihood Hebbian Rules. European Symposium on Artificial Neural Networks (2002)
11. Denning, D.: An Intrusion Detection Model. IEEE Transactions on Software Engineering, Vol. SE-13(2) (1987)
12. Corchado, E., Han, Y., Fyfe, C.: Structuring Global Responses of Local Filters Using Lateral Connections. Journal of Experimental and Theoretical Artificial Intelligence, Vol. 15(4) (2003) 473-487
13. Corchado, E., Fyfe, C.: Connectionist Techniques for the Identification and Suppression of Interfering Underlying Factors. International Journal of Pattern Recognition and Artificial Intelligence, Vol. 17(8) (2003) 1447-1466

14. Corchado, E., Corchado, J.M., Sáiz, L., Lara, A.: Constructing a Global and Integral Model of Business Management Using a CBR System. First International Conference on Cooperative Design, Visualization and Engineering (2004) 141-147
15. Seung, H.S., Socci, N.D., Lee, D.: The Rectified Gaussian Distribution. Advances in Neural Information Processing Systems, Vol. 10 (1998) 350-356
16. Fyfe, C.: A Neural Network for PCA and Beyond. Neural Processing Letters, Vol. 6(1-2) (1997) 33-41
17. Cisco Secure Consulting: Vulnerability Statistics Report (2000)
18. Case, J., Fedor, M.S., Schoffstall, M.L., Davin, C.: Simple Network Management (SNMP). RFC-1157 (1990)
19. Oja, E.: Neural Networks, Principal Components and Subspaces. International Journal of Neural Systems, Vol. 1 (1989) 61-68
20. Foster I., Kesselman C.: The Grid: Blueprint for a New Computing Infrastructure. 1st edn. Morgan Kaufmann Publishers (1998)
21. Kenny, S.: Towards a Grid-wide Intrusion Detection System. European Grid Conference. Lecture Notes in Computer Science. Springer-Verlag, Berlin Heidelberg New York (2005)

Neural Networks:
A Replacement for Gaussian Processes?

Matthew Lilley and Marcus Frean

Victoria University of Wellington, P.O. Box 600,
Wellington, New Zealand
marcus@mcs.vuw.ac.nz
http://www.mcs.vuw.ac.nz/~marcus

Abstract. Gaussian processes have been favourably compared to back-propagation neural networks as a tool for regression. We show that a recurrent neural network can implement exact Gaussian process inference using only linear neurons that integrate their inputs over time, inhibitory recurrent connections, and one-shot Hebbian learning. The network amounts to a dynamical system which relaxes to the correct solution. We prove conditions for convergence, show how the system can act as its own teacher in order to produce rapid predictions, and comment on the biological plausibility of such a network.

1 Introduction

Multi-layer Perceptron (MLP) neural networks are powerful models of broad applicability, able to capture non-linear surfaces of essentially arbitrary complexity. However such networks have their drawbacks, two of which we highlight here. Firstly, the learning algorithm is generally believed to be implausible from a biological point of view, for example in requiring synapses to act bi-directionally, and being very slow to train. Secondly, there is no uncertainty model in a neural network implemented in this way: given an input, the network produces an output directly, and nothing else. This is undesirable – the real world is dominated by uncertainty, and predictions without uncertainty are of limited value.

Gaussian process regression is not based on any biological model, but provides an explicit uncertainty measure and does not require the lengthy 'training' that a neural network does. While techniques for obtaining uncertainty from a neural network exist [9], [6] they are additions to the architecture, whereas Gaussian processes have uncertainty as a fundamental component arising naturally from a Bayesian formulation. Indeed, predictions made by neural networks approach those made by Gaussian processes as the number of hidden units tends to infinity. There are good arguments for Gaussian processes being considered a replacement for supervised neural networks [7].

Here we show that neural networks can themselves implement Gaussian process regression, in a way that has interesting parallels with neural circuitry.

M. Gallagher, J. Hogan, and F. Maire (Eds.): IDEAL 2005, LNCS 3578, pp. 195–202, 2005.

2   Gaussian Process Regression

Suppose we are given training data D consisting of input patterns $\{\mathbf{x}_1, \mathbf{x}_2 \ldots \mathbf{x}_n\}$, each of which is a vector, paired with their associated scalar output values $\mathbf{t} = \{t_1, t_2 \ldots t_n\}$. MLP networks can be thought of as imperfectly transforming this data into a set of representative weights. The actual data is not directly involved in making predictions for a new target t given a new input vector $\mathbf{x}$. The process of training the network (setting the weights) is slow, but the predictions are fast.

Gaussian processes make predictions in a way that is fundamentally different to MLP networks. Rather than capturing regularities in the training data via a set of representative weights, they apply Bayesian inference to explicitly compute the posterior distribution over possible output values t given all the data D and the new input x. This process involves $\mathbf{C}$, a covariance matrix generated using a covariance function $Cov(x, x'; \Theta)$ where Θ are hyper-parameters. Although a variety of other alternatives are possible [13], a typical form for the covariance function is

$$Cov(\mathbf{x}, \mathbf{x}') = \theta_1 \exp\left(-\frac{(\mathbf{x} - \mathbf{x}')^2}{2\theta_2^2}\right) + \theta_3\, \delta_{\mathbf{x}, \mathbf{x}'}\,.$$

θ_1 determines the relative scale of the noise in comparison with the data. θ_2 characterises the distance in x over which t is expected to vary significantly. θ_3 models white noise in measurements and δ is the delta function.

Essentially, the covariance matrix determines the scale and orientation of a Gaussian distribution amongst the variables $\mathbf{t}$. The task of regression is to find the distribution $P(t|D, \mathbf{x}, \mathbf{C}, \Theta)$, conditioning on the n input-output pairs corresponding to the training data, together with the new input. For a Gaussian process this conditioning process can be done analytically, resulting in a 1-D Gaussian distribution characterised by the following (see e.g. [2] for a derivation):

$$\texttt{mean} = \mathbf{k}^T \mathbf{C}^{-1} \mathbf{t}, \quad \texttt{variance} = \kappa - \mathbf{k}^T \mathbf{C}^{-1} \mathbf{k}\,. \tag{1}$$

Here $\mathbf{C}_{ij} = Cov(\mathbf{x}_i, \mathbf{x}_j)$ and $\mathbf{k}$ is the vector of individual covariances $\mathbf{k}_j = Cov(\mathbf{x}_j, \mathbf{x})$ between the new input $\mathbf{x}$ and each of those in the data set. κ is $Cov(x, x)$, a constant for stationary convariance functions. For the above it is $\theta_1 + \theta_3$.

3   Gaussian Processes as Neural Networks

In this section we show how relatively simple neural circuitry could carry out the operations required for Gaussian process inference.

Firstly, notice that the vector $\mathbf{k}$ can be thought of as the output of a layer of radial basis function (RBF) units, given input pattern $\mathbf{x}$. Each RBF unit arises from a previously observed input vector, and calculates its response to the new input using a Gaussian receptive field centered on the original vector, just as so-called "grandmother cells" [4] show peak activity for a particular input pattern, and progressively less response the greater the difference between the current stimulus and this pattern.

The primary task appears at first to be inversion of $\mathbf{C}$, but this is not strictly necessary - it is sufficient to find $\mathbf{k}^T\mathbf{C}^{-1}$. Thus the problem can be reformulated as follows: given a matrix $\mathbf{C}$ and a vector $\mathbf{k}$, we wish to find $\mathbf{C}^{-1}\mathbf{k}$. Supposing that $\mathbf{C}^{-1}\mathbf{k} = \mathbf{g}$, pre-multiplying by $\mathbf{C}$ gives $\mathbf{k} = \mathbf{Cg}$. The problem then reduces to iteratively improving $\mathbf{g}$ until the difference between $\mathbf{Cg}$ and $\mathbf{k}$ is sufficiently small. Gibbs [2] defines a measure $Q = \mathbf{g}^T.(\mathbf{k} - \frac{1}{2}\mathbf{Cg})$, the gradient of which is:

$$\nabla_g Q = (\mathbf{k} - \mathbf{Cg}) . \tag{2}$$

This gradient is zero at the solution to our problem. Gibbs uses a conjugate gradient routine to locate the solution. However for our purposes note that since $\nabla_g^2 Q = -\mathbf{C} < 0$, $\mathbf{g}$ can be iteratively improved by simply taking a small step in the direction of the gradient,

$$\Delta\mathbf{g} = \eta(\mathbf{k} - \mathbf{Cg}) . \tag{3}$$

In the Appendix we show that this algorithm converges on the exact solution, and we derive an optimal value for η.

The change to each component of $\mathbf{g}$ is a linear function of itself at a previous time-step, which suggests a network of linear neurons that integrate their inputs over time. The input needs to be $\mathbf{k} - \mathbf{Cg}$, so we have direct input of $\mathbf{k}$ together with inhibitory recurrent connections between all the $\mathbf{g}$ neurons, with weights $-C_{ij}$. The change to the neuron's output activity is simply the sum of these, times a constant η. Once this network converges we have only to take the dot product with the vector of targets (equation 1), which is easily achieved via a second layer of weights whose values are set to their respective target outputs (Figure 1).

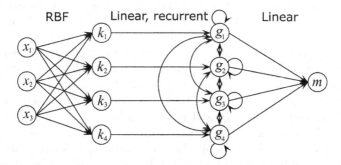

Fig. 1. A network architecture that implements Gaussian process regression. It converges on the mean m of the predicted output distribution, given input $\mathbf{x}$. Connections from $\mathbf{k}$ to $\mathbf{g}$ have weights of 1, recurrent connections have weights $-C_{ij}$, and those from $\mathbf{g}$ to the output m have weights $\mathbf{t}$. In this case the input is a 3-dimensional vector and inference is carried out on the basis of 4 input-output pairs

The rate of convergence depends on the choices for hyperparameters, as shown in Figure 2 for a representative range of outcomes. θ_2 plays a crucial role, as it effectively determines the expected number of datapoints involved in each prediction. If θ_2 is small then the new input is unlikely to be close to any previous data and therefore $\mathbf{k} \approx 0$, or it may be close to just one previous input, in which case only one element of $\mathbf{k}$ is significantly non-zero. Larger values of θ_2 make both $\mathbf{k}$ and $\mathbf{C}$ less sparse, and intuitively one can see that this will require more iterations to take account of the corresponding interrelationships.

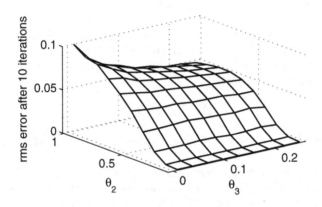

Fig. 2. The rms error between g and $\mathbf{k}^T\mathbf{C}^{-1}$ after 10 iterations of the dynamics. We used 100 data points chosen at random from within a 10-dimensional hypercube. θ_1 was fixed at 2.0 and the convergence rate for various values of θ_2 and θ_3 explored. Each vertex is an average over 100 independent runs. The rate parameter η was set to the value derived in the Appendix

The various connections in the system need to be set to particular values in order for this procedure to work. Firstly, the RBF units must each be centered on a unique input pattern. We don't address exactly how this might be implemented here, but one can imagine a constructive process in which a novel input pattern $\mathbf{x}_{n+1}$ triggers the recruitment of a new cell whose output is, and remains, maximal for that pattern. By thinking of the network in this constructive manner it is also clear how the other connections might be set: another new cell g_{n+1} is similarly recruited, and receives input from $\mathbf{x}_{n+1}$ with a synaptic weight of one. Its weights both to and from any other g cell, say g_i, need to be $-Cov(\mathbf{x}_i, \mathbf{x}_{n+1})$, which is simply the value taken by k_i for the current input. Indeed this is locally available as the instantaneous[1] value of g_i, amounting to a form of (anti) Hebbian learning. Finally the synaptic weight from g_{n+1} to the "output" must be set to t_{n+1}, which we may assume is the output cell's current value. In this way a network is both constructed and "learned" by local mechanisms as input-output pairs are presented to it.

The variance of the prediction is given by the expression $\mathbf{k}^T\mathbf{C}^{-1}\mathbf{k}$. Part of this ($\mathbf{k}^T\mathbf{C}^{-1}$) has already been calculated by the network which determines the

---

[1] *i.e.* the value g_i takes, prior to being perturbed by the recurrent neural dynamics

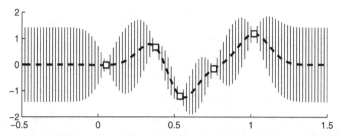

Fig. 3. A 1-dimensional example for illustrative purposes. There are 5 data points (squares). Predictions were then made by running the dynamics for 100 iterations, for a range of inputs. The dashed line is the mean and vertical bars indicate one standard deviation of the uncertainty, calculated as described in the text

mean, so we can reuse the previous calculation and essentially get the variance for (almost) no added cost. All that remains is to find the dot product of the **g** vector with **k**. Initially this seems like a trivial problem, but from a biological perspective it poses some difficulty. A possible mechanism is suggested by the process known as *shunting inhibition*, proposed as a possible mechanism for neurons to divide numbers [1] in which the output of one neuron inhibits the transmission of charge between two other neurons. As the elements of **k** are between 0 and 1, computing $\mathbf{k}^T\mathbf{C}^{-1}\mathbf{k}$ can be considered to be scaling the elements of $\mathbf{k}^T\mathbf{C}^{-1}$ by the elements of **k**, a task to which shunting inhibition seems ideally suited. Against this, some precise wiring is now required, as the ith **k** neuron must gate the effect of the ith **g** neuron on the output.

3.1 Faster Predictions over Time

The inference mechanism described here is very fast to learn (one-shot Hebbian), but is slow in making predictions due to the iterative process by which it arrives at the solution. However, we can use the iterative algorithm to generate "targets" with which to learn a second, single layer forward-feed network which runs in parallel with the Gaussian process mechanism and attempts to learn weights corresponding to $\mathbf{C}^{-1}$. Given **k** this secondary network can then directly compute $\mathbf{k}^T\mathbf{C}^{-1}$ in a single pass (see Figure 4). One can think of the inversion network as an oracle, which generates training data for the direct network given the raw inputs. We have shown experimentally and analytically [5] that this process converges exponentially quickly to the correct solution.

4   Discussion

A multi-layer perceptron neural network has Gaussian process behaviour when the number of hidden neurons tends to infinity, provided weight decay is employed [9]. We have argued that the converse is also true in the sense that the calculations required to calculate the expected output can be carried out by a

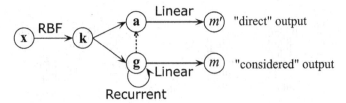

Fig. 4. Schematic representation of a parallel network that produces fast predictions and is trained on targets provided by the slower iterative process. The output of the **k** neuron is used as an input to the neurons labeled **a** on the "direct" path. They use the target of the **g** neurons (shown by the dotted line) to adjust their weights. Another possibility (not investigated further here) would be to learn a direct linear mapping from **k** to m'

simple neural network. In effect an infinite number of hidden units in a feed-forward architecture can be replaced by a merely finite number, together with recurrent connections and the ability to accumulate activity over time.

Recovery from intermittent errors can be shown to be exponentially fast [5]. This leads to the appealing property that accuracy improves exponentially with time: early results are rough, later results become exact.

However there are some difficulties with our proposal. Calculating the correct variance is considerably more problematic than finding the mean. While shunting inhibition is a potential mechanism for achieving this, it does require some rather precise neural wiring. Similarly, we have avoided dealing with the setting of hyperparameters Θ. While there are several possible avenues that might be pursued [5] they all appear to involve further additions to the architecture described here.

There is an interesting relationship between the algorithm presented here and a neural architecture suggested for faithful recoding of sensory input data by the visual cortex[14], [15]. Essentially the Daugman algorithm minimizes the difference between sensory input and internal template-based models by step-wise gradient descent. The dynamics are similar to those we describe except that there is feedback from the equivalent of the **g** layer (the internal model) *back* to the **k** layer (the sensory input), rather than recurrent connections within **g**. Perfoming this simplistic gradient descent on $Q = -\frac{1}{2}(\mathbf{g} - \mathbf{Ck})^T(\mathbf{g} - \mathbf{Ck})$ is dimensionally inconsistent [6]. Fortunately, this is not a fatal problem and can be remedied by premultiplying Q by its curvature, which is simply $\mathbf{C}^{-1}$ [5]. This leads to the remarkable conclusion that our algorithm is actually a covariant form of the biologically inspired algorithm proposed by Daugman.

References

1. Dayan, P., and Abbott, L. *Theoretical Neuroscience.* Massachusetts Institute of Technology, 2001, p. 189.
2. Gibbs, M. N. *Bayesian Gaussian Processes for Regression and Classification.* PhD thesis, University of Cambridge, 1997.

3. Hebb, D. O. *The Organisation of Behaviour*. Wiley, New York, 1949.
4. J.Y. Lettvin, H.R. Maturana, W. M., and Pitts, W. *The Mind: Biological Approaches to its Functions*. Interscience Publishers, 1968, ch. 7, pp. 233–258.
5. Lilley, M. Gaussian processes as neural networks. Honours thesis, Victoria University of Wellington, 2004. Available from
   `http://www.mcs.vuw.ac.nz/people/Marcus-Frean`
6. MacKay, D. *Information Theory, Inference, and Learning Algorithms*. University Press, 2003, ch. 34.
7. MacKay, D. J. Gaussian processes - a replacement for supervised neural networks? Lecture notes for a tutorial at NIPS 1997.
   `http://www.inference.phy.cam.ac.uk/mackay/gpB.pdf`
8. McIntosh, H. V. *Linear Cellular Automata*. Universidad Autonoma de Puebla, 1987, ch. 9.4.
9. Neal, R. Priors for infinite networks. Tech. rep., University of Toronto, 1994.
10. Petersen, K. The matrix cookbook. Technical University of Denmark, 2004.
    `http://2302.dk/uni/matrixcookbook.html`
11. Weisstein, E. W. Eigen decomposition theorem.
    `http://mathworld.wolfram.com/EigenDecompositionTheorem.html`.
12. Weisstein, E. W. Positive definite matrix.
    `http://mathworld.wolfram.com/PositiveDefiniteMatrix.html`.
13. Williams, C. K. I., and Rasmussen, C. E. Gaussian processes for regression. *Advances in Neural Information Processing Systems 8* (1996), 514–520.
14. Daugman, J. Complete Discrete 2-D Gabor Transforms by Neural Networks for Image Analysis and Compression. *IEEE Trans. ASSP*, vol.36 no. 7 (1988), pp. 1169-1179
15. Pece, A.E.C. Redundancy reduction of a Gabor representation: a possible computational role for feedback from primary visual cortex to lateral geniculate nucleus, *Unpublished manuscript*, 1993.

Appendix

Here we prove that our algorithm is correct using infinite series, which clarifies the conditions under which the inversion converges, and leads to a technique to force otherwise non-convergent matrices to converge. We start by assuming the value of $\mathbf{g}$ at time zero is $\mathbf{0}$. Then, at time t, $\mathbf{g}_t = \mathbf{g}_{t-1} + \mathbf{k}^T - \mathbf{C}\mathbf{g}_{t-1}$ which is $\mathbf{g}_{t-1}(\mathbf{I} - \mathbf{C}) + \mathbf{k}^T$. The closed form for $\mathbf{g}$ at time t is then

$$\mathbf{g}(t) = \mathbf{k}^T \sum_{i=0}^{t-1} (\mathbf{I} - \mathbf{C})^i .$$

Multiplying both sides by $(\mathbf{I} - \mathbf{C})$, subtracting from $\mathbf{g}(t)$, and right-multipling by $\mathbf{C}^{-1}$ yields

$$\mathbf{g}(t) = \mathbf{k}^T \left(\mathbf{I} - (\mathbf{I} - \mathbf{C})^t \right) \mathbf{C}^{-1} \qquad (4)$$

Taking the limit as $t \to \infty$ gives $\mathbf{g}(t) = \mathbf{k}^T \mathbf{C}^{-1}$, as required. In order for $\mathbf{g}(t)$ to converge, we must assume that $\lim_{n\to\infty} (\mathbf{I} - \mathbf{C})^n = 0$. Making use of the eigendecomposition theorem [11] we can rewrite $\mathbf{I} - \mathbf{C}$ in terms of the matrix D which has the eigenvalues of $\mathbf{I} - \mathbf{C}$ along its diagonal so that $\mathbf{I} - \mathbf{C} = P^{-1}DP$, and since $(P^{-1}DP)^n = P^{-1}D^n P$ all that remains is to show that

$$\lim_{n \to \infty} P^{-1}D^n P \tag{5}$$

is defined and finite. Because D is diagonal, $[D^n]_{ij} = [D]_{ij}^n$ and so we conclude that if for all eigenvalues λ_i of $\mathbf{I} - \mathbf{C}$, $|\lambda_i| < 1$ then this is simply the zero matrix, which is defined, and finite. Otherwise, the limit is infinite, and therefore the algorithm fails. In general, $|\lambda_i| \not< 1$, but we can force the condition by introducing a new parameter, η, as follows. If $\mathbf{g}_t = \mathbf{g}_{t-1} + \eta \mathbf{k}^T - \eta \mathbf{C} \mathbf{g}_{t-1}$ then by a similar process to which equation 4 was derived, we have

$$\mathbf{g}(t) = \eta \mathbf{k}^T \left(\mathbf{I} - (\mathbf{I} - \eta \mathbf{C})^t \right) (\eta \mathbf{C})^{-1} \tag{6}$$

If we choose η such that the eigenvalues of $\mathbf{I} - \eta \mathbf{C}$ are of magnitude less than one, then equation 5 will converge, and ultimately equation 6 will converge also. It is an identity that the eigenvalues λ of $\mathbf{I} + \alpha M$ are $1 + \alpha \lambda$ [10], and the eigenvalues of a positive definite matrix are all positive or zero [12], therefore by letting α be $-\frac{1}{\max \lambda}$, we guarantee that all eigenvalues of $\mathbf{I} - \mathbf{C}$ are of magnitude equal to or less than one. Imposing the condition that θ_3 is non-zero effectively prevents the matrix from being ill-conditioned. The largest eigenvalue of $\mathbf{C}$ is strictly less than the maximal row sum (for a symmetric matrix) [8], which in turn is bounded by $N(\theta_1 + \theta_3)$, for a matrix having N columns.

$$\eta_{estimate} = |N(\theta_1 + \theta_3) + 1|^{-1} \tag{7}$$

Equation 7 gives a tractable way to approximate an appropriate value of η. Empirical evidence suggest that using the estimate described in equation 7 indeed has similar performance to using the inverse of the largest eigenvalue of $\mathbf{I} - \mathbf{C}$, which appears to be optimal.

A Dynamic Merge-or-Split Learning Algorithm on Gaussian Mixture for Automated Model Selection*

Jinwen Ma and Qicai He

Department of Information Science, School of Mathematical
Sciences and LMAM, Peking University, Beijing, 100871, China
jwma@math.pku.edu.cn

Abstract. Gaussian mixture modelling is a powerful tool for data analysis. However, the selection of number of Gaussians in the mixture, i.e., the mixture model or scale selection, remains a difficult problem. In this paper, we propose a new kind of dynamic merge-or-split learning (DMOSL) algorithm on Gaussian mixture such that the number of Gaussians can be determined automatically with a dynamic merge-or-split operation among estimated Gaussians from the EM algorithm. It is demonstrated by the simulation experiments that the DMOSL algorithm can automatically determine the number of Gaussians in a sample data set, and also lead to a good estimation of the parameters in the original mixture. Moreover, the DMOSL algorithm is applied to the classification of Iris data.

1 Introduction

Many problems in data analysis, especially in clustering analysis and classification, can be solved through Gaussian mixture model [1]. Actually, several statistical methods have been proposed for Gaussian mixture modelling (e.g., the EM algorithm [2] and k-means algorithm [3]). But it is usually assumed that the number k of Gaussians in the mixture is given in advance. However, in many cases, this key information is not available and the selection of an appropriate number of Gaussians must be made with the parameter estimation, which is a rather difficult task [4].

The traditional approach to this task is to choose a best k^* via some selection criterion, such as the Akaike's information criterion [5] or its extensions. However, these methods incur a large computational cost since we need to repeat the entire parameter estimation process independently at a number of different values of k. Moreover, all these criteria have their limitations and often lead to a wrong result.

Recently, a new kind of automated model selection approach has been developed using the idea that an appropriate number of Gaussians can be automatically allocated during the parameter learning, with the mixing proportions of

---

* This work was supported by the Natural Science Foundation of China for Project 60471054

M. Gallagher, J. Hogan, and F. Maire (Eds.): IDEAL 2005, LNCS 3578, pp. 203–210, 2005.
© Springer-Verlag Berlin Heidelberg 2005

the extra Gaussians attenuating to zero. From the Bayesian Ying-Yang (BYY) harmony learning theory, the gradient-type harmony learning algorithms [6]-[7] have been proposed via the maximization of a harmony function on the architecture of the BYY system for Gaussian mixture. The simulation experiments showed that these algorithms can make model selection automatically with parameter estimation on Gaussian mixture. Moreover, from the point of view of penalizing the Shannon entropy of the mixing proportions on maximum likelihood estimation (MLE), an entropy penalized MLE iterative algorithm was also proposed to make model selection automatically with parameter estimation on Gaussian mixture [8]. However, an obvious drawback of this approach is that the initial value of k cannot be smaller than the number of actual Gaussians in the sample data. Although we can always select k to be large enough, the algorithms may lead to a wrong result when the initial value of k is much larger than the number of actual Gaussians in the sample data.

On the other hand, the EM algorithm is an efficient algorithm for Gaussian mixture modelling when the number of actual Gaussians is given in advance. But it often suffers from local convergence. In order to overcome this problem, a split-and-merge operation was introduced in the EM algorithm so that the EM algorithm can probably escape a local solution [9]-[10]. In these revised EM algorithms, the split and merge operations on the estimated Gaussians are forced to come together in each phase. Moreover, a greedy EM algorithm was also proposed to search the number of actual Gaussians in the sample data by increasing k step by step from $k = 1$ [11].

In the current paper, we further propose a dynamic merge-or-split learning (DMOSL) algorithm for Gaussian mixture modelling such that the merge and split operations can be dynamically and independently conducted on the estimated Gaussians in each phase of the learning process. In this way, the number of actual Gaussians in the sample data can be automatically detected no matter when the initial value of k is larger or smaller than the number of actual Gaussians in the sample data. It is demonstrated by the simulation experiments that the DMOSL algorithm can automatically determine the number of actual Gaussians in a data set, with a good estimation of the parameters in the actual mixture. Moreover, the DMOSL algorithm is applied to the classification of Iris data.

2   The DMOSL Algorithm

Given a sample data set from an original mixture with k^* Gaussians and a initial number k, we can use the (conventional) EM algorithm to get k estimated Gaussians with the associated parameters. If $k > k^*$, some estimated Gaussians cannot match the actual Gaussins and should be merged into one Gaussian. On the other hand, if $k < k^*$, some estimated Gaussians also cannot match the actual Gaussians and should be split into two or more Gaussians. The main idea of the DMOSL algorithm is to construct a merge criterion and a split criterion for the estimated Gaussians so that the merge-or-split operation can be added to the EM algorithm dynamically and independently. According to this idea, we now propose the DMOSL algorithm in the following subsections.

2.1   Gaussian Mixture Model

We begin to introduce the Gaussian mixture model as follows:

$$P(x|\Theta) = \sum_{i=1}^{k} \alpha_i P(x|m_i, \Sigma_i), \qquad \alpha_i \geq 0, \quad \sum_{i=1}^{K} \alpha_i = 1, \tag{1}$$

where

$$P(x|m_i, \Sigma_i) = \frac{1}{(2\pi)^{\frac{d}{2}} |\Sigma_i|^{\frac{1}{2}}} e^{-\frac{1}{2}(x-m_i)^T \Sigma_i^{-1}(x-m_i)} \tag{2}$$

and where k is the number of Gaussians or components in the mixture, x denotes a sample vector and d is the dimensionality of x. The parameter vector Θ consists of the mixing proportions α_i, the mean vectors m_i, and the covariance matrices $\Sigma_i = (\sigma_{pq}^{(i)})_{d \times d}$ which are assumed positive definite.

For a sample data set $\mathcal{S} = \{x_t\}_{t=1}^{N}$ from the Gaussian mixture, we define the posteriori probability of a sample x_t over the j-Gaussian or component as follows.

$$P(j|x_t; \Theta) = \frac{\alpha_j P(x_t|m_j, \Sigma_j)}{P(x_t|\Theta)} = \frac{\alpha_j P(x_t|m_j, \Sigma_j)}{\sum_{i=1}^{k} \alpha_i P(x_t|m_i, \Sigma_i)}. \tag{3}$$

According to these posteriori probabilities, we can divide the sample points into k clusters corresponding to the k Gaussians in the mixture by

$$G[j] = \{x_t : P(j|x_t; \Theta) = \max_{i=1,\cdots,k} P(i|x_t; \Theta)\}. \tag{4}$$

2.2   The Merge and Split Criteria

We further introduce the merge and split criteria on the estimated Gaussians after the EM algorithm has converged. Actually, via the estimated parameters, we can obtain the clusters $G[j]$. For the merge or split operation, we first check whether the sample points in two or more neighboring clusters are subject to a Gaussian distribution. If they are, we think the corresponding estimated Gaussians should be merged. Furthermore, we check whether the sample points in each remaining $G[j]$ (excluding these ones to be merged) are subject to a Gaussian distribution. If they are not, the estimated Gaussian should be split.

Specifically, we give the merge and split criteria as follows.

Merge Criterion: For the i−th and j−th estimated Gaussians, we introduce the following merge degree:

$$J_{merge}(i, j; \Theta) = \frac{P_i(\Theta)^T P_j(\Theta)}{\|P_i(\Theta)\|\|P_j(\Theta)\|} \tag{5}$$

where $P_l(\Theta)$ is an N-dimensional vector consisting of posterior probabilities of the sample points over the l−th Gaussian, and $\|\cdot\|$ denotes the Euclidean vector norm. Clearly, when the two estimated Gaussians should be merged together, $P_i(\Theta)$ and $P_j(\Theta)$ should be similar at a ceratin degree so that $J_{merge}(i, j; \Theta)$ will be high. According to this merge degree and a threshold value $\alpha > 0$, we have the merge criterion: if $J_{merge}(i, j; \Theta) \geq \delta$, these two Gaussians will be merged together, otherwise, they will not.

In the simulation experiments, we found that J_{merge} has a relationship with N. So, by experience, we set $\delta = 0.004N^{1/2}$ in the following experiments. Moreover, we also found in the simulation experiments that if the two estimated Gaussians should not be merged, J_{merge} becomes very small (in general, $J_{merge}(i, j; \Theta) < 10^{-3}$). Therefore, the merge degree is reasonable.

Split Criterion: We use the Srivastav method [10] to check the normality for the sample points in each remaining cluster. In fact, via the singular value decomposition, the Srivastav method turns the test of multivariate normality into the test for a number of independent normal variables. For the test of univariate normality, we implement the Kolmogorov-Smirnov test. For the j−th estimated Gaussian (remaining from the merge criterion), according to the Srivastav method, if the sample points in $G[j]$ are not subject to a normal distribution, it will be split into two Gaussians; otherwise, there will be no need for the split on this estimated Gaussian.

2.3   The Procedure of the DMOSL Algorithm

With the above preparations, we can now present the procedure of the DMOSL algorithm. Structurally, the DMOSL algorithm consists of a number of phases. At the beginning phase, we set k as the best possible estimation of the number of actual Gaussians in the sample data. With this initial k, the EM algorithm is conducted to get the estimated Gaussians. Then, the DMOSL algorithm turns into the second phase. In this or the sequential phase, according to the obtained Gaussians or clusters, we check whether the merge or split operation is needed. If a merge or split operation is needed, we can use the mathematical method proposed in [10] to put the two estimated Gaussians into one or split one estimated Gaussian into two, with the parameters being modified. Starting from the obtained and modified parameters in the new Gaussian mixture setting, the EM algorithm is further conducted to the new estimated Gaussians for the following phase. In this way, the model selection will be made dynamically and automatically during the learning phases via the merge and split operations. Finally, the DMOSL algorithm will be halted when there is no need for the merge or split operation on the estimated Gaussians.

For the fast convergence, we also add a component eliminating mechanism to the DMOSL algorithm on the mixing proportions obtained from the EM algorithm. That is, if $\alpha_j < 0.01$, the j−th Gaussian will be eliminated directly. Clearly, this component eliminating operation can be considered as an additional merge operation.

Concretely, the procedure of the DMOSL algorithm is given as follows.

Step 1 Initialization: set the initial value of k, $t = 0$, and the initial parameters Θ^0 in the Gaussian mixture.

Step 2 At phase t, we perform the EM algorithm starting from the parameters obtained from the last phase after the merge and split operations if $t > 0$ or from the initial parameters if $t = 0$. After the EM algorithm has converged, we get Θ^t at the t-th phase. According to Θ^t, we can get the estimated Gaussians and the corresponding clusters $G[j]$. If there is no need for the merge or split operation on the estimated Gaussians, the DMOSL algorithm is halted. Otherwise, we go to the next step.

Step 3 Merge operation: we compute $J_{merge}(i, j; \Theta^t)$ for $i, j = 1, \cdots, k$ and $i \neq j$. and sort them in a descend order. If these exists any $J_{merge}(i, j; \Theta^t)$ that is no less than δ, i.e., $J_{merge}(i, j; \Theta^t) \geq \delta$, we merge these two Gaussians into a new Gaussian i'. The parameters of this new Gaussian are computed as follows.

$$\alpha_{i'} = \alpha_i + \alpha_j; \tag{6}$$
$$m_{i'} = (\alpha_i m_i + \alpha_j m_j)/\alpha_{i'}; \tag{7}$$
$$\Sigma_{i'} = (\alpha_i \Sigma_i + \alpha_j \Sigma_j + \alpha_i m_i m_i^T + \alpha_j m_j m_j^T - \alpha_{i'} m_{i'} m_{i'}^T)/\alpha_{i'}. \tag{8}$$

It can be found in the experiments that sometimes $\Sigma_{i'}$ may not be positive. In this special case, we can use the covariance matrix of the sample data in $G[i]$ and $G[j]$ instead. If one estimated Gaussian can be merged into two or more estimated Gaussians, we merge the two estimated Gaussians with the highest merge degree. When a merge operation is implemented, k is automatically decreased by one, i.e., $k = k - 1$.

Step 4 Split operation: after the merge operation, there are certain estimated Gaussians remained. For each remaining estimated Gaussian, we check whether it should be split according to the split criterion. If it should be, say the i-th Gaussian, we split it into two Gaussians i' and j' as follows.

From the covariance matrix Σ_j, we have its singular value decomposition $\Sigma_j = USV^T$, where S is a diagonal matrix with nonnegative diagonal elements in a descent order, U and V are two (standard) orthogonal matrices. Then, we further set $A = U\sqrt{S}$ (refer to [10] for the derivation), and get the first column A_1 of A. Finally, we have the parameters for the two split Gaussians as follows.

$$\alpha_{i'} = \alpha_i * \gamma, \alpha_{j'} = \alpha_i * (1 - \gamma); \tag{9}$$
$$m_{i'} = m_i - (\alpha_{j'}/\alpha_{i'})^{1/2}\mu A_1; \tag{10}$$
$$m_{j'} = m_i + (\alpha_{i'}/\alpha_{j'})^{1/2}\mu A_1; \tag{11}$$
$$\Sigma_{i'} = (\alpha_{j'}/\alpha_{i'})\Sigma_i + ((\beta - \beta\mu^2 - 1)(\alpha_i/\alpha_{i'}) + 1)A_1 A_1^T; \tag{12}$$
$$\Sigma_{j'} = (\alpha_{i'}/\alpha_{j'})\Sigma_i + ((\beta\mu^2 - \beta - \mu^2)(\alpha_i/\alpha_{j'}) + 1)A_1 A_1^T, \tag{13}$$

where γ, μ, β are all equal to 0.5.

When a split operation is implemented, k is automatically increased by one, i.e., $k = k + 1$.

Step 5 We let $t = t + 1$ and return to Step 2.

We finally give some remarks on the DMOSL algorithm. (1). The split criterion or operation is based on the test of the normality on the sample points in the resulted clusters $G[j]$. Actually, only when the number of the sample points from each actual Gaussian is large enough and the actual Gaussians are separated in a certain degree, this normality test can be reasonable and lead to a correct result. Hence, the DMOSL algorithm can be only suitable for the sample data set in which the actual Gaussians have a large number of sample points and are separated in a certain degree. (2). The split criterion is based on the statistical test and the merge criterion is based on the merge degrees between two estimated Gaussians through a threshold value selected by experience. Theoretically, there exists a small probability of the error on the DMOSL algorithm. (3). In Step 4, for consideration of robustness, we can add a checking step on the two split Gaussians to make sure whether this split operation is really necessary. If the two split Gaussians i' and j' on the data set $G[i]$ should be merged under the merge criterion on these two Gaussians only, we abandon the split operation. Otherwise, we keep the split operation. However, it is found in the experiments that this checking step is hardly active.

3   Experimental Results

In this section, several simulation experiments are carried out to demonstrate the DMOSL algorithm for automated model selection as well as parameter estimation on seven data sets from Gaussian mixtures. Moreover, we apply the DMOSL algorithm to the classification of Iris data.

3.1   Simulation Experiments

We conducted several experiments on seven sets of samples drawn from a mixture of four or three bivariate Gaussians densities (i.e., $n = 2$). As shown in Fig. 1, each data set of samples is generated at different degree of overlap among the clusters (Gaussians) and with equal or unequal mixing proportions of the clusters in the mixture.

Using k^* to denote the number of actual Gaussians in the sample data or the original mixture, we implemented the DMOSL algorithm on these seven data sets with different initial values such as $k < k^*$, $k = k^*$ and $k > k^*$. The other parameters were initialized randomly within certain intervals.

Typically, we give the experimental results of the DMOSL algorithm on the sample data set (d) in which $k^* = 4$. For $k = k^* = 4$, the DMOSL algorithm was halted immediately with no merge or split operation and the result is shown in Fig. 2. In this and the following figures, T represents the number of merge and split operations in each phase, k is the initial number of Gaussians, k' is the changing number of estimated Gaussians in each phase of the algorithm. For $k = 1$, the DMOSL algorithm first split one Gaussian into two Gaussians and then split two into four, see Fig.3 for $k' = 2$. On the other hand, when $k = 8$, the 8 estimated Guassians merged into 4 Gaussian only in one phase, and we show the results in Fig.4 for $k' = 8$. From these figures, we can observe that, through the dynamic merge or split operations, the DMOSL algorithm can make model selection automatically on the sample data set and at the same time lead to a good estimation of the parameters in the original mixture.

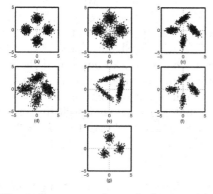

Fig. 1. Seven sets of sample data used in the experiments

Fig. 2. $k^* = 4, k = 4, k' = 4, T = 0$ (stopped)

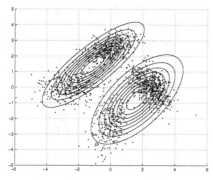

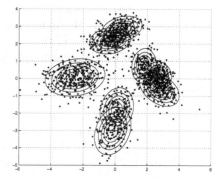

Fig. 3. $k^* = 4, k = 1, k' = 2, T = 2$ (2 split operations)

Fig. 4. $k^* = 4, k = 8, k' = 8, T = 4$ (4 merge operations)

The further experiments of the DMOSL algorithm on the other sample sets had been also made successfully for the automated model selection and parameter estimation in the similar cases. Since the DMOSL algorithm can escape the local solution with the merge or split operation, it outperforms the conventional EM algorithm. It also outperforms the split-and-merge EM algorithms given in [9]-[10] since it has the ability of automated model selection. As compared with the automated model selection algorithms in [6]-[8],[11], the DMOSL algorithm has no limitation for the initial value of k and converges more quickly in the general case.

3.2   Experiments on Classification of Iris Data

We further apply the DMOSL algorithm to the classification of the Iris data[1] which is a typical real dataset for testing the classification algorithm. The Iris data set consists of 150 4-dimension data from three classes: Iris Versicolor, Iris

---

[1] Retrieved from http://www.ics.uci.edu/ mlearn/MLRepository.html

Virginca and Iris Setosa. Each class contains 50 samples. We implemented the DMOSL algorithm on the Iris data with $k = 1 - 8$. When $k = 1 - 4$, the DMOSL algorithm can detect the three classes correctly, with the classification accuracy over 96.65%. However, when $k = 5 - 8$, the DMOSL algorithm always leads to 4 or 5 Gaussians in which three major Gaussians can be located the actual classes approximately, while one or two abundant small Gaussians cannot be eliminated. The reason may be that the number of samples in the Iris data is not large enough and each class cannot match a Gauussian well so that some small Gaussians cannot be eliminated when k is much larger than $k^* = 3$.

4   Conclusions

We have investigated the automated model selection and the parameter estimation on Gaussian mixture modelling via a dynamic merge-or-split learning (DMOSL) algorithm. The DMOSL algorithm is constructed with a merge or split operation on the estimated Gaussians from the EM algorithm. It is demonstrated by the simulation experiments that the DMOSL algorithm can automatically determine the number of actual Gaussians in the sample data, also with a good estimation of the parameters in the original mixture. The DMOSL algorithm can be also successfully applied to the classification of Iris data.

References

1. G. Mclachlan, D. Peel, *Finite Mixture Models*, New York: Wiley, 2000.
2. R. A. Render and H. F. Walker, "Mixture densities, maximum likelihood and the EM algorithm," *SIAM Review*, 26(2): 195-239, 1984.
3. A. K. Jain and R. C. Dubes, *Algorithm for Clustering Data*, Englewood Cliffs, N. J.: Prentice Hall, 1988.
4. J. A. Hartigan, "Distribution problems in clustering," *Classification and clustering*, J. Van Ryzin Eds., pp: 45-72, New York: Academic Press, 1977.
5. H. Akaike, "A New Look at the Statistical Model Identification," *IEEE Trans. on Automatic Control,* AC-19: 716-723, 1974.
6. J. Ma, T. Wang and L. Xu, "A gradient BYY harmony learning rule on Gaussian mixture with automated model selection," *Neurocomputing*, 56: 481-487, 2004.
7. J. Ma, B. Gao, Y. Wang, and Q. Cheng, "Two further gradient BYY learning rules for Gaussian mixture with automated model selection," *Lecture Notes in Computer Science*, 3177: 690-695, 2004.
8. J. Ma, T. Wang, "Entropy penalized automated model selection on Gaussian mixture," *International Journal of Pattern Recognition and Artificial Intelligence*, 18(8): 1501-1512, 2004.
9. N. Ueda, R. Nakano, Y. Z. Ghahramani, and G. E. Hiton, "SMEM algorithm for mixture models," *Neural Computation*, 12(10): 2109-2128, 2000.
10. Z. Zhang, C. Chen, J. Sun, and K. L. Chan, "EM Algorithm for learning Gaussian mixture models with split-and-merge operation," *Pattern Recognition*, 36(9): 1973-1983, 2003.
11. N. Vlassis and A. Likas, "A Greedy EM Algorithm for Gaussian Mixture Learning," *Neural Processing Letters*, 15: 77-87, 2002.
12. M. S. Srivastava, *Methods of Multivariate Statistics*, New York: Wiley-Interscience, 2002.

Bayesian Radial Basis Function Neural Network

Zheng Rong Yang

Department of Computer Science, University of Exeter, Exeter EX4 4QF, UK
z.r.yang@ex.ac.uk
http://www.dcs.ex.ac.uk/~zryang

Abstract. Bayesian radial basis function neural network is presented to explore the weight structure in radial-basis function neural networks for discriminant analysis. The work is motivated by the empirical experiments where the weights often follow certain probability density functions in protein sequence analysis using the bio-basis function neural network, an extension to radial basis function neural networks. An expectation-maximization learning algorithm is proposed for the estimation of the weights of the proposed Bayesian radial-basis function neural network and the simulation results show that the proposed novel radial basis function neural network performed the best among various algorithms.

1 Introduction

Radial basis function neural networks (RBFNNs) [1], [2] as a kind of powerful learning algorithms have been applied to many areas with success. For instance, in the application to biology, RBFNNs were used to classify the narcosis mechanism of aquatic toxicity for organic compounds [3]. Based on five molecular descriptors derived from the structures of the substituted aromatic acids, the dielectric constant of mixed solvents and the energy of the highest occupied molecular orbital of the methanol and ethanol, the electrophoretic mobility of 26 substituted aromatic acids in two different aqueous–alcoholic (ethanol and methanol) solvents in capillary zone electrophoresis were predicted using RBFNNs [4]. The theoretical analysis of RBFNNs structures and algorithms includes the orthogonal least square algorithm [5], the approximation capability analysis [5], [6], the design of RBFNN structure using fuzzy clustering method [7], the error-bound estimation [8], the optimization of RBFNN structure using kernel orthonormalization method or combined supervised and unsupervised learning method [9] and the use of Fisher ratio for the selection of RBFNN centers [10]. Evolutionary computation algorithms have also been used to optimize RBFNN structures, for instance, for variable selection [11] and for model selection [12].

A successful construction of a RBFNN classifier depends on three factors, the selection of a proper basis function, the selection of proper centers and the selection of a proper weight structure. Except for many studies for the first two issues [9], [13], [14], [15], [16], researchers have also concerned with the third issue. Weight decay is a method for this issue, where an additive cost term was added on the error function to penalize the weights with large values (hence small probabilities) based on the assumption that the weights follow a single Gaussian [17], [18], [19]. The relevance vector machine [20], on the other hand, assumes that each weight follows a single Gaussian. Through a learning process, the centers (vectors) with very small variances of the weights will be discarded. The algorithm finally selects the most contributing centers (vectors) for a model. In terms of the optimization of a classifier's structure, this method has shown its advantages over the support vector machines. In pattern recognition, if a subset of centers plays a similar, but mutually independent role in recognizing an object or discriminating an object, it is no doubt that their strength (parameterized using numerical values) should be similar. For instance, a support vector machine model can be defined as

$$\text{sign}(\sum_{\mathbf{x}_i \in C_1} \alpha_i f(\mathbf{x}, \mathbf{x}_i) - \sum_{\mathbf{x}_k \in C_2} \alpha_k f(\mathbf{x}, \mathbf{x}_k)) \tag{1}$$

where $\mathbf{x}_i$ and $\mathbf{x}_k$ are two centers of two classes (C_1 and C_2) respectively, α_i and α_k are two positive constants (weights). If we re-write this equation, we can have $\text{sign}(\sum \alpha_i f(\mathbf{x}, \mathbf{x}_i))$, where $\alpha_i < 0$ is $\mathbf{x}_i \in C_2$ while $\alpha_i > 0$ is $\mathbf{x}_i \in C_1$. It can be seen that the weights are learnt to follow two distributions, i.e., negative and positive ones.

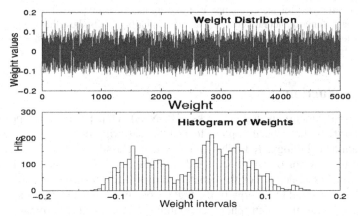

Fig. 1. The weight distribution for a discriminant analysis using the bio-basis function neural network for the prediction of O-linkage sites in glycoproteins. The upper part shows the weight values, where the horizontal axis indicates the number of the weights of 50 Monte-Carlo simulations and the vertical one the values of the weights. The lower part shows the histogram of the weights. The horizontal axis is the weight values and the vertical one the hits. Reproduced from Yang and Chou [21] with permission

This has also been observed in our earlier empirical experiments on protein sequence classification using a bio-basis function neural network, an extension to radial basis function neural networks [14], [15], [16]. In the experiment, it has been found that the weights demonstrated two Gaussian distributions for a discriminant analysis task [21]. Fig. 1 demonstrates the distribution of the weights. Further empirical experiments on more protein sequence data demonstrated the same phenomenon. This work is then investigating a novel RBFNN algorithm to place a weight structure as a prior in a learning process.

2 Bayesian Radial Basis Function Neural Network

Suppose there are K centers, for a D-dimensional input vector $\mathbf{x}$, identifying its class membership using a RBFNN classifier is as follows

$$y = \sum_{k=1}^{K} w_k \phi(\mathbf{x}, \mathbf{c}_k) = t - e \tag{2}$$

where t is the target, y the prediction, w_k the kth weight, $\mathbf{c}_k$ the kth center, e the error and $\phi(\circ,\circ)$ the radial-basis function which is defined as

$$\phi(\mathbf{x}, \mathbf{c}_k) = \exp(-\beta L_\pi(\mathbf{x}, \mathbf{c}_k)). \tag{3}$$

$L_\pi(\circ,\circ)$ is the dissimilarity measure using the Euclidean distance ($\pi = 2$) and β the smooth parameter (0.1 in this study). If $\mathbf{x}$ and $\mathbf{c}_k$ are similar, $\phi(\mathbf{x}, \mathbf{c}_k)$ gives a large value, otherwise a small value. After the mapping using K centers, an input space is mapped to a feature space, $\Re^D \mapsto \Re^K$, where $\Re$ means real numbers and each vector in $\Re^D$ is mapped to a specific point denoted as a feature vector $\boldsymbol{\varphi} = (\phi(\mathbf{x}, \mathbf{c}_1), \phi(\mathbf{x}, \mathbf{c}_2), \cdots, \phi(\mathbf{x}, \mathbf{c}_K))^T$ in the feature space $\Re^K$. Suppose there are M training vectors, the prediction of the class membership for the mth training vector $\mathbf{x}_m$ is then

$$y_m = \sum_{k=1}^{K} w_k \phi(\mathbf{x}_m, \mathbf{c}_k) = t_m - e_m . \tag{4}$$

We use α and β to denote negative and positive classes, respectively. From this, the feature matrix can be expressed as $\mathbf{F} = \mathbf{F}_\alpha \bigcup \mathbf{F}_\beta$

$$
\mathbf{F}_\alpha = \begin{pmatrix}
\phi(\mathbf{x}_1, \mathbf{c}_1) & \phi(\mathbf{x}_1, \mathbf{c}_2) & \cdots & \phi(\mathbf{x}_1, \mathbf{c}_{K_\alpha}) \\
\phi(\mathbf{x}_2, \mathbf{c}_1) & \phi(\mathbf{x}_2, \mathbf{c}_2) & \cdots & \phi(\mathbf{x}_2, \mathbf{c}_{K_\alpha}) \\
\vdots & \vdots & \vdots & \vdots \\
\phi(\mathbf{x}_M, \mathbf{c}_1) & \phi(\mathbf{x}_M, \mathbf{c}_2) & \cdots & \phi(\mathbf{x}_M, \mathbf{c}_{K_\alpha})
\end{pmatrix}
$$

$$
\mathbf{F}_\beta = \begin{pmatrix}
\phi(\mathbf{x}_1, \mathbf{c}_1) & \phi(\mathbf{x}_1, \mathbf{c}_2) & \cdots & \phi(\mathbf{x}_1, \mathbf{c}_{K_\beta}) \\
\phi(\mathbf{x}_2, \mathbf{c}_1) & \phi(\mathbf{x}_2, \mathbf{c}_2) & \cdots & \phi(\mathbf{x}_2, \mathbf{c}_{K_\beta}) \\
\vdots & \vdots & \vdots & \vdots \\
\phi(\mathbf{x}_M, \mathbf{c}_1) & \phi(\mathbf{x}_M, \mathbf{c}_2) & \cdots & \phi(\mathbf{x}_M, \mathbf{c}_{K_\beta})
\end{pmatrix} .
\tag{5}
$$

Note that K_α and K_β are the number of the centers of negative and positive classes, respectively. Suppose ϑ is a set of hyper parameters for network parameters (weights) and the errors, a Bayes formula of the posterior probability is as follows

$$p(\mathbf{w}, \vartheta | \mathbf{y}) = \frac{p(\mathbf{y} | \mathbf{w}, \vartheta) p(\mathbf{w}, \vartheta)}{p(\mathbf{y})} \tag{6}$$

where, $p(\mathbf{w}, \vartheta | \mathbf{y})$ is the posterior, $p(\mathbf{y} | \mathbf{w}, \vartheta)$ the likelihood and $p(\mathbf{y})$ the normalization factor and $p(\mathbf{w}, \vartheta) = p(\mathbf{w} | \vartheta) p(\vartheta)$. As $p(\mathbf{w} | \vartheta)$ is the likelihood of the weights depending on the hyper-parameters and $p(\vartheta)$ the *a priori* probability of the hyper-parameters, Eq. (6) can be further re-written as

$$p(\mathbf{w}, \vartheta | \mathbf{y}) \propto p(\mathbf{y} | \mathbf{w}, \vartheta) p(\mathbf{w}, \vartheta) = p(\mathbf{y} | \mathbf{w}, \vartheta) p(\mathbf{w} | \vartheta) p(\vartheta) . \tag{7}$$

We assume that the weights of the centers of the negative class follow one Gaussian $w_{\alpha i} \sim G(u_\alpha, \sigma_\alpha^2 = 1/\gamma_\alpha)$, the ones of the positive class the other Gaussian $w_{\beta i} \sim G(u_\beta, \sigma_\beta^2 = 1/\gamma_\beta)$ and the error a Gaussian as well $e_m \sim G(0, \sigma_e^2 = 1/\gamma_e)$. Note that u_α, u_β, γ_α, γ_β and γ_e are the hyper-parameters and they are denoted as $\vartheta = \{u_\alpha, u_\beta, \gamma_\alpha, \gamma_\beta, \gamma_e\}$ with $\vartheta_\alpha = \{u_\alpha, \gamma_\alpha\}$, $\vartheta_\beta = \{u_\beta, \gamma_\beta\}$, and $\vartheta_e = \{\gamma_e\}$. We also assume that each hyper-parameter follows a uniform distribution. The negative logarithm of the posteriori probability of a RBFNN classifier with two Gaussian distributions of the weights is as follows

$$L = -\ln[p(\mathbf{y} \mid \mathbf{w}, \vartheta)p(\mathbf{w}_\alpha \mid \vartheta_\alpha)p(\mathbf{w}_\beta \mid \vartheta_\beta)p(\vartheta_\alpha)p(\vartheta_\beta)p(\vartheta_e)]$$

$$= \frac{1}{2}[\gamma_e \|\mathbf{e}\|^2 + \gamma_\alpha \|\mathbf{w}_\alpha - \mathbf{u}_\alpha\|^2 + \gamma_\beta \|\mathbf{w}_\beta - \mathbf{u}_\beta\|^2 \qquad (8)$$

$$- M \ln \gamma_e - K_\alpha \ln \gamma_\alpha - K_\beta \ln \gamma_\beta + C]$$

where $\mathbf{w}_\alpha$ is the weight vector of the centers of negative class, $\mathbf{w}_\beta$ the one of positive class, $\mathbf{u}_\alpha = u_\alpha \mathbf{i}_{K_\alpha}$, $\mathbf{u}_\beta = u_\beta \mathbf{i}_{K_\beta}$ and $\mathbf{i}_r = (1,1,...,1)^T_{\underbrace{\quad}_{r}}$. Let the partial derivative of L with respect to the parameters be zero leads to

$$\gamma_e = \frac{M}{\|\mathbf{e}\|^2} \ , \ \gamma_\tau = \frac{K_\tau}{\|\mathbf{w}_\tau - \mathbf{u}_\tau\|^2}, \ u_\tau = \frac{\gamma_\tau}{1 + K_\tau \gamma_\tau} \mathbf{w}_\tau^T \mathbf{i}_{K_\tau} \qquad (9)$$

and

$$(\gamma_e \mathbf{F}^T \mathbf{F} + \gamma_\tau \mathbf{I})\mathbf{w} = \gamma_e \mathbf{F}^T \mathbf{t} + \gamma_\tau \mathbf{I} \mathbf{u} . \qquad (10)$$

Note that τ represents either α or β. Besides, $\gamma_\tau \mathbf{I}$ is defined as follows, the first α diagonal elements are assigned value of γ_α and the last β diagonal elements are assigned value of γ_β

$$\gamma_\tau \mathbf{I} = \begin{pmatrix} \gamma_\alpha & 0 & \cdots & 0 & 0 & 0 & \cdots & 0 \\ 0 & \gamma_\alpha & \cdots & 0 & 0 & 0 & \cdots & 0 \\ \vdots & \vdots & \vdots & \vdots & \vdots & \vdots & \vdots & \vdots \\ 0 & 0 & \cdots & \gamma_\alpha & 0 & 0 & \cdots & 0 \\ 0 & 0 & \cdots & 0 & \gamma_\beta & 0 & \cdots & 0 \\ 0 & 0 & \cdots & 0 & 0 & \gamma_\beta & \cdots & 0 \\ \vdots & \vdots & \vdots & \vdots & \vdots & \vdots & \vdots & \vdots \\ 0 & 0 & \cdots & 0 & 0 & 0 & \cdots & \gamma_\beta \end{pmatrix} . \qquad (11)$$

Suppose $\widetilde{\mathbf{F}} = \gamma_e \mathbf{F}^T \mathbf{F} + \gamma_\tau \mathbf{I}$ and $\upsilon = \gamma_e \mathbf{F}^T \mathbf{t} + \gamma_\tau \mathbf{I} \mathbf{u}$, the solution to the system is then

$$\mathbf{w} = \widetilde{\mathbf{F}}^{-1} \upsilon . \qquad (12)$$

The learning of the parameters including hyper-parameters can be implemented using an expectation-maximization (EM) algorithm. Each parameter is assigned a random value at the beginning. In the cth learning cycle of the E-step, hype-parameters are estimated as follows (note that we use the superscript to denote the cycle index for the hyper-parameters and the subscript to denote the parameters)

$$\gamma_e^{c+1} = \frac{M}{\| \mathbf{e}^c \|^2}$$

$$\gamma_\tau^{c+1} = \frac{K_\tau}{\| \mathbf{w}_\tau^c - \mathbf{u}_\tau^c \|^2} \tag{13}$$

$$u_\tau^{c+1} = \frac{\gamma_\tau^{c+1}}{1 + K_\tau \gamma_\tau^{c+1}} \mathbf{w}_\tau^c \mathbf{i} K_\tau$$

where ϑ^c is the newly estimated value for ϑ at cth learning cycle. In the cth cycle of the M-step, network parameters are estimated as follows

$$\widetilde{\mathbf{F}}_{c+1} = \gamma_e^{c+1} \mathbf{F}_{c+1}^T \mathbf{F}_{c+1} + \gamma_\tau^{c+1} \mathbf{I}$$

$$\upsilon_c = \gamma_e^{c+1} \mathbf{F}_{c+1}^T \mathbf{t} + \gamma_\tau^{c+1} \mathbf{I} \mathbf{u}_\tau^{c+1} \tag{14}$$

$$\mathbf{w}_{c+1} = \widetilde{\mathbf{F}}_{c+1}^{-1} \upsilon_{c+1}$$

The stop criterion can be defined as

$$\| \mathbf{e} \|^2 < \varepsilon . \tag{15}$$

The alternative is to measure if the system has approached the steady state where the system parameters do not change too much for a certain period T, i.e.,

$$\sum_{c=1}^T \left\| \mathbf{u}_\tau^{c+1} \bmod T - \mathbf{u}_\tau^c \right\| < \delta , \tag{16}$$

where ε and δ are two small positive values. In case simulation may take long time, the limit of learning cycles is 100.

3   Simulation Results

Support vector machines (SVM) was used for the comparison with the Bayesian radia-basis function neural network (bRBF). SVM[light] [22] was used to conduct simulations with SVM, where the "C" value was set to 100 and "g" value was set to 0.1 (the same as that used in equation (13)). The value of ε in bRBF is 0.1. Ten-fold cross-validation is used. The models will be assessed using the confusion matrix.

The first data set was collected from [23]. There are 224 UK private construction companies within a period from 1990 to 1995. Of 224 companies, half were bankrupted and half were still surviving till 1995. Each company has eight financial ratios. The previous study was using robust heteroscadestic probibilistic neural net (rhPNN) [23] to construct a prediction model. From Table 1, we can see that bRBF outperformed the others. No cross-validation result was reported in [23].

The second data set was collected from the UCI Machine Learning Repository (http://www.ics.uci.edu/~mlearn/MLRepository.html). Linear perceptron (LP), nonlinear perceptron (NP), nearest neighbors (NN), decision trees (C4.5), and backprop (BP) were applied to the data. All these simulations were based on the following

Table 1. The 10-fold cross-validation simulation results on the construction data set

	TNf	TPf	Total	Min-max(total)
rhPNN[a]	89.83%	72.90%	81.37%	n.a.
SVM	88.67 ± 9.26%	97.22 ± 4.38%	93.10 ± 4.88%	85-100%
bRBF	94.86 ± 5.44%	98.17 ± 3.76%	96.60 ± 3.03%	92-100%

[a] Results from [23].

data organization: first 100 "good" and the first 100 "bad" were used to construct a model and the later 123 "good" and 24 "bad" instances were used for testing. No cross-validation was used. Because of this bias, accuracy on "good" instances was much higher than for "bad" instances in the earlier studies as indicated in the data archive. Shown in Table 2 were the simulation results. It can be seen that bRBF performed the best. No cross-validation results were reported in http://www.ics.uci.edu/~mlearn /MLRepository.html and [24].

Fig. 2 showed the changes of the mean values of two Gaussians of the weights in learning for the first data set and 10 cross-validation models. All the weights converged to two centers within about 10 simulation cycles using different data and different initialization values.

Table 2. The 10-fold cross-validation simulation results on the ionosphere data set

	TNf	TPf	Total	Min-max(total)
LP[b]	n.a.	n.a.	90.7%[a]	n.a.
NP[b]	n.a.	n.a.	92.0%[a]	n.a.
NNs[b]	n.a.	n.a.	92.1%[a]	n.a.
C4.5[b]	n.a.	n.a.	94.0%[a]	n.a.
BP[b]	n.a.	n.a.	96.0%[a]	n.a.
RBF[c]	n.a.	n.a.	91.5%[a]	n.a.
MLP[c]	n.a.	n.a.	95.5%[a]	n.a.
SVM	84.24 ± 9.26%	93.55 ± 5.16%	90.11 ± 5.18%	81-100%
bRBF	91.86 ± 5.16%	96.05 ± 4.42%	94.32 ± 3.19%	89-100%

[a] Only one model was available
[b] Recorded in http://www.ics.uci.edu/~mlearn/MLRepository.html
[c] Obtained from [24]

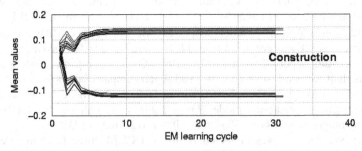

Fig. 2. The mean values through simulation. The horizontal axis is the iteration times during learning and the vertical axis the mean values of the weights. It can be seen that the mean values of the weights of two classes converged less than 10 iterations

The third data (pima) was collected from the UCI Machine Learning Repository (http://www.ics.uci.edu/~mlearn/MLRepository.html) as well. Shown in Table 3 were the simulation results. It can be seen that bRBF is comparable with SVM.

Table 3. The 10-fold cross-validation simulation results on the construction data set

	TNf	TPf	Total	Min-max(total)
RBF	82.10±6.15%	59.68±11.17%	74.72±3.27%	67-78%
SVM	78.34±6.15%	72.41±9.07%	76.48±3.34%	70-82%
bRBF	80.32±6.43%	69.45±9.29%	**76.96±3.07%**	72-81%

4 Discussion

It should be noted that Bayesian method has been intensively used in radial basis function neural networks. However, they all addressed different aspects in training a radial basis function neural networks. For instance, Bayesian method was used for determining the variable dimension in [25], one Gaussian was used for radial basis function neural networks in [26].

The feature matrix used in bRBF for discriminant analysis can be expressed as

$$\mathbf{F} = \begin{bmatrix} \mathbf{F}_{nn} & \mathbf{F}_{np} \\ \mathbf{F}_{pn} & \mathbf{F}_{pp} \end{bmatrix} \tag{17}$$

where $\mathbf{F}_{nn}$ and $\mathbf{F}_{np}$ are the maps of negative input vectors on the negative and positive bases respectively, $\mathbf{F}_{pn}$ and $\mathbf{F}_{pp}$ are the maps of positive input vectors on the negative and positive bases respectively. The response vectors can be expressed as

$$\begin{aligned} \mathbf{y}_n &= \mathbf{F}_{nn}\mathbf{w}_n + \mathbf{F}_{np}\mathbf{w}_p \\ \mathbf{y}_p &= \mathbf{F}_{pn}\mathbf{w}_n + \mathbf{F}_{pp}\mathbf{w}_p \end{aligned} \tag{18}$$

where $\mathbf{w}_n$ and $\mathbf{w}_p$ are the weights connecting the negative and positive bases respectively, $\mathbf{y}_n$ and $\mathbf{y}_p$ are the response vectors of negative and positive input vectors respectively. As the output values of all the bases will be positive with the maximum value as unity, it is assumed that $\mathbf{F}_{nn}$ and $\mathbf{F}_{pp}$ have a similar distribution denoted as $\mathbf{F}_1$ while $\mathbf{F}_{np}$ and $\mathbf{F}_{pn}$ have a similar distribution denoted as $\mathbf{F}_2$

$$\begin{aligned} \mathbf{y}_n &= \mathbf{F}_1\mathbf{w}_n + \mathbf{F}_2\mathbf{w}_p \\ \mathbf{y}_p &= \mathbf{F}_2\mathbf{w}_n + \mathbf{F}_1\mathbf{w}_p \end{aligned} \tag{19}$$

Note that it is assumed that $|\mathbf{y}_n| = |\mathbf{y}_p|$. For a classification problem, it is desired to maximise

$$\max(\mathbf{y}_p - \mathbf{y}_n)^{\mathrm{T}}(\mathbf{y}_p - \mathbf{y}_n) \tag{20}$$

or

$$\max((\mathbf{w}_p - \mathbf{w}_n)^{\mathrm{T}}\mathbf{Q}(\mathbf{w}_p - \mathbf{w}_n)) \tag{21}$$

where $\mathbf{Q} = (\mathbf{F}_1 - \mathbf{F}_2)^{\mathrm{T}} (\mathbf{F}_1 - \mathbf{F}_2)$ is a constant matrix. It can be seen that in order to maximise $(\mathbf{y}_p - \mathbf{y}_n)^{\mathrm{T}} (\mathbf{y}_p - \mathbf{y}_n)$, the distance between two weight vectors must be as large as possible.

5 Summary

This paper has presented a novel radial-basis function neural network for discriminant analysis. The basic idea behind it is the use of the Bayes learning method assuming that the weights follow two Gaussians. Through the experiment on two benchmark cases, it can be seen that the proposed Bayesian radial-basis function neural network outperformed support vector machines and others. The future work will study the theoretical aspect of this approach and extend the algorithm to allow the automatic selection of centers.

References

1. Bishop, C. Neural Networks for Pattern Recognition, Oxford Press (1995)
2. Moody, J., Darken, C.: Fast learning in networks of locally tuned units. Neural Computations, 1 (1989) 281-294
3. Yao, X., Panaye, A., Doucet, J., Chen, H., Zhang, R., Fan, B., Liu, M., Hu, Z.: Comparative classification study of toxicity mechanisms using support vector machines and radial basis function neural networks. Analytica Chimica Acta, (in press)
4. Liu, H., Zhang, R., Yao, X., Liu, M., Fan, B.: Prediction of electrophoretic mobility of substituted aromatic acids in different aqueous–alcoholic solvents by capillary zone electrophoresis based on support vector machine. Analytica Chimica Acta, 525 (2004) 31-41
5. Chen, T., Chen, H.: Approximation capability to functions of several variables, nonlinear functionals, and operators by radial basis function neural networks. IEEE Transactions on Neural Networks, 6 (1995) 904 – 910
6. Schilling, R., Carroll, J., Al-Ajlouni, A.: Approximation of nonlinear systems with radial basis function neural networks. IEEE Transactions on Neural Networks, 12 (2001) 1 – 15
7. Pedrycz, W.: Conditional fuzzy clustering in the design of radial basis function neural networks. IEEE Transactions on Neural Networks, 9 (1998) 601 – 612
8. Townsend, N., Tarassenko, L.: Estimations of error bounds for neural-network function approximators. IEEE Transactions on Neural Networks, 10 (1999) 217 – 230
9. Kaminski, K., Strumillo, P.: Kernel orthonormalization in radial basis function neural networks. IEEE Transactions on Neural Networks, 8 (1997) 1177 – 1183
10. Mao, K.Z.: RBF neural network center selection based on Fisher ratio class separability measure. IEEE Transactions on Neural Networks, 13 (2002) 1211 – 1217
11. Alexandridis, A., Patrinos, P., Sarimveis, H., Tsekouras, G.: A two-stage evolutionary algorithm for variable selection in the development of RBF neural network models. Chemometrics and Intelligent Laboratory Systems, 75 (2005) 149-162
12. Rivas, V., Merelo, J., Castillo, R., Arenas, M., Castellano, J.: Evolving RBF neural networks for time-series forecasting with EvRBF. Information Sciences, 165 (2004) 207-220
13. Chen, S., Cowan, C.F., Grant, P.M.: Orthogonal least squares learning algorithm for radial basis function networks. IEEE Transactions on Neural Networks, 1 (1991) 302-309
14. Thomson, R., Hodgman, C., Yang, Z.R., Doyle, A.K.: Characterising Proteolytic Cleavage Site Activity Using Bio-Basis Function Neural Network. Bioinformatics, 21 (2003) 1741-1747

15. Yang, Z.R., Thomson, R.: A novel neural network method in mining molecular sequence data. IEEE Trans. on Neural Networks, 16 (2005) 263- 274
16. Yang, Z.R.: Orthogonal kernel machine in prediction of functional sites in preteins. IEEE Trans on Systems, Man and Cybernetics, 35 (2005) 100-106
17. Bartlett, P.L.: For valid generalization, the size of the weights is more important than the size of the network. NIPS, 9 (1997) 134-140
18. Geman, S., Bienenstock, E., Doursat, R.: Neural Networks and the Bias/Variance Dilemma. Neural Computation, 4 (1992) 1-58
19. Weigend, A., Rumelhart, D.E., Huberman, B.A.: Generalization by weight-elimination with application to forecasting. NIPS, 3 (1991)
20. Tipping, M.E.: The relevance vector machine. NIPS, 12 (2000) 652-658
21. Yang, Z.R., Chou, K.C.: Bio-basis function neural networks for the prediction of the O-linkage sites in glyco-proteins. Bioinformatics, 20 (2004) 903-908
22. Vapnik, V.: The Nature of Statistical Learning Theory. Springer-Verlag, New York (1995)
23. Yang, Z.R., Chen, S., James, H.: Robust maximum likelihood training of probabilistic neural networks. Neural Networks, 11 (1998) 739-747
24. Sykacek, P.: On input selection with reversible jump Markov chain Monte Carlo sampling. NIPS, 12 (2000) 638-644
25. Holmes, C.C.H., Mallick, B.K.: Bayesian radial basis functions of variable dimension. Neural Computation, 10 (1998) 1217-1233
26. Andrieu, C., de Freitas, N., Doucet, A.: Robust full Bayesian learning for radial basis networks. Neural Computation, 13 (2001) 2359 - 2407

An Empirical Study of Hoeffding Racing
for Model Selection in *k*-Nearest Neighbor Classification

Flora Yu-Hui Yeh and Marcus Gallagher

School of Information Technology and Electrical Engineering
University of Queensland, 4072, Australia
{flora,marcusg}@itee.uq.edu.au

Abstract. Racing algorithms have recently been proposed as a general-purpose method for performing model selection in machine learning algorithms. In this paper, we present an empirical study of the Hoeffding racing algorithm for selecting the k parameter in a simple k-nearest neighbor classifier. Fifteen widely-used classification datasets from UCI are used and experiments conducted across different confidence levels for racing. The results reveal a significant amount of sensitivity of the k -nn classifier to its model parameter value. The Hoeffding racing algorithm also varies widely in its performance, in terms of the computational savings gained over an exhaustive evaluation. While in some cases the savings gained are quite small, the racing algorithm proved to be highly robust to the possibility of erroneously eliminating the optimal models. All results were strongly dependent on the datasets used.

1 Introduction

Model selection is an important task in the application of many machine learning methods. Racing algorithms [1, 2] take a computational approach to the model selection problem. Given a set of candidate models (i.e. machine learning algorithms with fully specified parameter values), together with a set of training data for a given problem, an exhaustive search over the model set would require each model to be trained and evaluated on the entire training set. Racing works by initially implementing all models in parallel. The algorithm repeatedly estimates the performance of each model, and eliminates poorly performing candidates from the evaluation process. Hence, racing aims to efficiently find a small number of models that perform well on the given learning problem, by a process of elimination. Racing methods are generally applicable to model selection problems in that they make few assumptions about the space of models. In addition, racing can be used to search a heterogeneous set of models, where it is not clear how to define a distance metric between points in the space. All that is required is the ability to evaluate the performance of a candidate model. However, only a few applications of racing algorithms have appeared in the literature to date [1-4].

In this paper, we present an empirical study of one particular racing algorithm (Hoeffding races) for selecting the k parameter in a simple k-nearest neighbor classifier. The aim of this study is to gain a better understanding of the behaviour of this racing algorithm on a relatively simple model selection problem, and to explore the relationship between these techniques and the datasets applied. In the following section, we briefly describe Hoeffding racing and its application to model selection in k-nearest neighbour classification. Section 3 describes our methodology and the details

M. Gallagher, J. Hogan, and F. Maire (Eds.): IDEAL 2005, LNCS 3578, pp. 220–227, 2005.

of our experiments. Section 4 presents the results of the experiments, and Section 5 summarizes and concludes the paper.

2 Hoeffding Races, Model Selection and Lazy Learning

2.1 Model Selection

There are a variety of different existing approaches to the model selection problem in machine learning [5]. In some cases, a model-specific approach may be available (e.g. if model selection is restricted to a single class of models), while for other situations a general search technique could be applied, depending on the parametric form the set of models to be considered. Racing algorithms represent a very general, search-based approach to model selection. Since racing only requires the ability to evaluate a given model on the learning task at hand, it is possible to apply racing to model selection across a set of instantiations of completely different classes of models. In this paper, we focus on Hoeffding races [1, 2], which makes a minimal assumption regarding the data used to generate statistics in evaluating the set of models used.

2.2 Hoeffding Racing

Consider a supervised learning (e.g. classification) problem where a data set of labeled examples is given. A classifier can be applied to this problem, and its performance evaluated, for example by partitioning the data into training and test sets, or by cross-validation over the data. Assume that N data points are available for testing. This yields an estimate of the true prediction error of the classifier, E_{true}. Consider an estimate of the prediction error after n points, E_{est}, where $n < N$. As n increases, E_{est} becomes closer to E_{true}. Assuming that test points are drawn independently, the Hoeffding bound states that the probability of E_{est} being more than ε away from E_{true} is

$$\Pr\left(\left|E_{true} - E_{est}\right| > \varepsilon\right) < 2e^{-2n\varepsilon^2 / B^2} \tag{1}$$

where B bounds the greatest possible error that a model can make. For classification problems, B is simply 1, as a misclassification has an error of 1. A confidence parameter, δ can be introduced and (1) can be rewritten as

$$\Pr\left(\left|E_{true} - E_{est}\right| > \varepsilon\right) < \delta \tag{2}$$

denoting that, with confidence 1-δ, E_{est} is within ε of E_{true}. The error bound ε can be expressed as a function of n, B and δ as

$$\varepsilon(n) = \sqrt{\frac{B^2 \log(2 / \delta)}{2n}} \tag{3}$$

Alternatively, (3) can be rearranged to give the number of points, n, needed to achieve accuracy, ε, with confidence, δ, as

$$n > \frac{B^2 \log(2 / \delta)}{2\varepsilon^2} \tag{4}$$

Hoeffding racing is applied to model selection as follows. Consider a set of classifiers $\{C_i\}$, $i=1,\ldots,p$, where each classifier (candidate model) is fully specified in terms of its model parameter values. In each iteration of the racing process, a data point is selected randomly without replacement from the original test set and added to the current test set of each classifier (which is initially empty). The classifiers use this new data to calculate a revised error estimate, E_{est}. The current error bound for each C_i is then calculated using (3). This process results in a set of error estimates for the classifiers, together with (upper and lower) error bounds (see Fig. 1).

Using this information, the racing algorithm may attempt to eliminate classifiers. A model will only be eliminated when its lower error bound is higher than the upper error bound of the best model at that iteration. For example, in Fig. 1, model C_3 is currently the best learning box.. Since the lower bounds of models C_4 and C_5 are higher than the upper bound of C_3, they can be eliminated in this iteration. This racing process will iterate repeatedly until only one of the learning box left or the accuracy, ε, or the confidence, δ, has reached the threshold. In another word, the ending state of the racing is either when there is only one model left in the racing or when all models left satisfy requirements we set for the racing. Classifiers with their current estimated errors within $2\varepsilon(n)$ range cannot be distinguished; hence, it is unlikely that many models will be eliminated in the first few iterations of racing. As n gets larger, the bound, ε gets smaller and bad models start to be eliminated. In practice, for computational efficiency, it is possible to only consider eliminating boxes periodically (rather than in every single iteration), since the error estimate is likely to vary slowly as n increases.

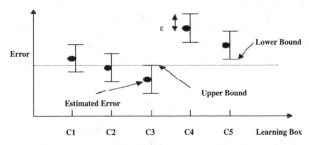

Fig. 1. Hoeffding racing learning boxes: estimated error and error bounds

The Hoeffding racing algorithm attempts to combine the strength of exhaustive search with the computational efficiency of descent methods. It assumes that all learning boxes are independent of each other. Also, the error of current iteration point does not affect the error of next iteration point at all. Hoeffding racing never does worse than brute force and it is not concerned with the models' structure and complexity.

This racing algorithm has better performance when there are some clear winners in the initial set of models, so the elimination begins early and proceeds quickly. Unlike descent methods, the racing algorithm guarantees the true best model will never be eliminated even though it cannot distinguish the best one out from other good ones left. The speed of racing can be accelerated by using "Bayesian" bound, which assumes the errors are normally distributed and gives a tighter bound than Hoeffding bound [2]. However, Bayesian racing is not considered in this paper.

2.3 Lazy Learning

Lazy learning (or memory-based learning) refers to a class of machine learning algorithms that make predictions based on computations over the stored training set, rather than, for example, fitting a model to the data via an iterative process [6]. Well known examples include k-nearest neighbor classifiers and locally weighted regression techniques. In lazy learners, very little work is needed to perform training and most of the computational expense comes when a prediction query is made.

The k-nearest neighbor (k-nn) classifier is a widely applied technique, due to its simplicity and its demonstrated good performance on a range of practical problems [7]. Given a test data point to be classified, k-nn returns the class (output) of the points with the most similar attributes (input). The similarity between examples and the queried case is typically measured by using the Euclidean or some other distance metric, depending on the type of the attributes. k-nn has a single adjustable model parameter, k, which represents the number of nearest neighbors selected to determine the class prediction. The predicted class output is obtained via a majority vote rule of all contributed example points. When the votes are equal (for an even value of k), the tie might be broken at random, or (as done in this paper) the closest neighbor's class is selected as the predicted class. Generally speaking, it is expected that as k gets larger, the stability against noisy data increases, but at the same time the locality advantage of k-nn is destroyed. However, the sensitivity of the performance of the algorithm will also be problem-dependent.

3 Experimental Methodology

In this research, we are interested in studying the behaviour of the Hoeffding racing algorithm for model selection in k-nn, on a large set of real-world benchmark classification problems. Experimental results will be dependent on the variable factors in the racing algorithm, classifier and dataset used. Nevertheless, we have attempted to consider an experimental scenario that is as simple as possible, and to explore a range of values for each factor.

For the k-nn algorithm, Euclidean distance is used throughout. Leave-one-out cross-validation (LOOCV) was used to evaluation the performance of each classifier. One advantage of using a lazy learner is that no retraining is required to carry out cross-validation; the training set and test point(s) used are simply exchanged appropriately. For each dataset, k-nn was applied exhaustively, i.e. for each possible value of k (in this case from k=1 up to k=N-1), the performance of the classifier E_{true} is calculated using LOOCV. This represents an exhaustive or brute force approach to the model selection problem for k-nn and is used to compare with the results of racing.

Hoeffding races was applied as an alternative to the above brute force approach. Complete LOOCV uses every point in the dataset for testing, while Hoeffding races sequentially through the data, attempting to eliminate candidate models. Maximum efficiency gain is obtained when as many candidate models as possible are eliminated as quickly as possible. The confidence parameter in Hoeffding races controls the likelihood that models will be eliminated. For low values of δ, models are eliminated on the basis of minimal statistical evidence. Hence, more models are eliminated frequently; however, this increases the chance that a good model will be eliminated erroneously. Alternatively, high confidence values minimize the risk of eliminating the best models, at a possible cost of eliminating less models overall (and reducing the efficiency gain over brute force). In the experiments reported below, Hoeffding racing was run with ☐=0.95, 0.9, 0.8, 0.6, 0.5, 0.2 and 0.05. Racing proceeds by randomly selecting points (without replacement) to test (and thereby update E_{est}). Therefore, the result of the algorithm depends on the sequence of test points processed and is a random variable. Hence, each racing experiment was repeated 5 times. The set of models considered for racing included $k=1,...,20$ for each dataset used. In addition, 10 further models were used for each dataset, selected with some consideration of the brute force results (see Section 4). Racing runs until the entire dataset has been evaluated – models remaining at the end of the run must therefore satisfy the specified confidence/accuracy.

Fifteen commonly used benchmark datasets were selected from the UCI Machine Learning Repository [8] for these experiments. The characteristics of the datasets are summarized in Table 1. From Table 1, it is clear that a variety of real world classification datasets are included. Also, these datasets cover a wide range in number of instances, number of attributes and maximum class distribution. All datasets selected have either numerical or nominal numerical values. For datasets that have nominal class representation (iris, new-thyroid, soybean-small, balance-scale, vehicle, wdbc and yeast), the class representations are modified manually to appropriate numerical representations. The hayes-roth dataset tested has a randomly generated attribute called "hobby". We created a separate dataset called "hayes-rothMod" by deleting the "hobby" attribute from hayes-roth and included in the experiments to show how this random attribute affects the racing performance.

4 Results

Table 1 also summarizes the results for k-nn on all the selected datasets. In terms of the lowest LOOCV error obtained, it is evident that k-nn shows a variety of different performances on the different datasets. Interestingly, the optimal value(s) for k also varies widely across the datasets. For some datasets, $k=1$ proves to be optimal, while in other cases, vary large values of of k perform best. Fig 2 shows the complete error profiles for all k values, across all datasets used.

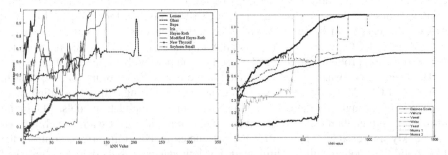

Fig. 2. LOOCV error with respect to different k values in k –nn

Table 1. Summary of the dataset characteristics and results for exhaustive k-nn. Shown are the k values that have lowest E_{true} (multiple values indicate multiple optimal values of k), the E_{true} for the best value(s) of k, and the error difference between the best and worst performing k

Dataset	#Class	#Attrs	#Pts	Max. Class Distrib	Best k value	Lowest Average Error	Error Difference
Iris	3	4	150	33.33%	19-21	0.020	0.980
NT	3	5	215	69.77%	1	0.051	0.251
Glass	6	9	214	35.51%	1	0.266	0.664
Bupa	2	6	345	57.97%	9, 32	0.304	0.116
SS	4	35	47	36.17%	3	0.000	0.638
M1	2	6	432	50.00%	5,-7, 9	0.000	1.000
M2	2	6	432	67.13%	1	0.278	0.120
HR	3	4	132	38.63%	1, 2	0.424	0.576
HRMod	3	3	132	38.63%	66-70	0.341	0.659
BS	3	4	625	46.08%	10	0.094	0.906
Lenses	3	4	24	62.50%	4	0.625	0.375
Vehicle	4	18	846	25.37%	3	0.337	0.663
Vowel	11	10	990	9.09%	1	0.097	0.236
Wdbc	2	30	569	62.74%	38-569	0.627	0.053
Yeast	10	8	1484	31.20%	21, 29	0.402	0.079

The complexities of these profiles show that the performance of k-nn can be highly sensitive to the value of k. In many cases, the curve does not flatten out as k increases. Our expectation, based on intuition about how k-nn works, was that curves would typically increase (and to an extent it is clear that low k values tend to work better in general) and flatten out to some asymptotic value as k approached the size of the training set. Evidently, using a local search or trial-and-error approach to perform model selection in k-nn is likely to yield suboptimal results. As mentioned above, in addition to racing models from k=1,...,20, we selected 10 further values of k by selecting values which were at a variety of different error values, to try and provide variation in the models used in racing.

The results of the racing experiments are shown in Fig. 3, in terms of the percentage saving in computation compared to running 30 models exhaustively (i.e. for the entire LOOCV calculation over the dataset) and the number of models eliminated by the end of the racing run. Note that, as model are eliminated dynamically at various points during the race, the percentage saving and the total number of boxes eliminated at the end of the trails do not describe the same information. All values are averaged over the 5 repeated trials of each racing run. As the confidence value decreases, the number of models eliminated (and hence the % saving) generally tends to increase. This is in line with the aim of the confidence parameter; nevertheless, due to the random selection of data points in racing, occasionally this saving decreases. In addition, lower confidence values generally results in models being eliminated earlier in the racing run, which results in a bigger saving in computation time.

The performance of racing in terms of the computational savings gained was variable and overall perhaps lower than expected. For 90% confidence, racing only produced a saving of greater than 50% on two of the datasets. On the other hand, racing proved to be very conservative in terms of which models were eliminated. It was not until the confidence was set to 5% that any racing run eliminated any of the best performing k values for any datasets, and then this happened only occasionally (twice for

"Glass" and "Bupa" and once for "HayesRoth" and "Yeast"). The distribution-free assumption behind the Hoeffding bound results in a conservative confidence estimate, and our results suggest that this is true even with lower confidence values that have been previously considered.

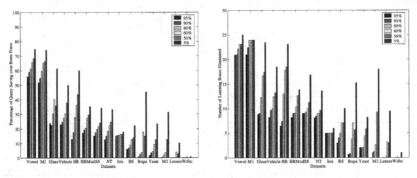

Fig. 3. Racing results for each dataset over different confidence levels: average percentage of computation time saving compared to exhaustive evaluation of 30 models and average number of learning models eliminated over each racing run

5   Conclusion

This paper has presented an empirical study of the performance of the Hoeffding racing algorithm for model selection in the simple k-nn classifier, on a suite of UCI datasets. The results reveal surprising variability in the performance of k-nn with respect to the value of k, and highlight the danger in relying on trial-and-error approaches to parameter tuning. The results of applying Hoeffding races to the k-nn model selection problem show that this racing algorithm is sometimes able to provide significant computation benefits compared with an exhaustive evaluation; however, performance depends strongly on the dataset in question. In addition, on these datasets the racing algorithm was more likely to provide less computational saving that to incorrectly eliminate the best models from consideration. Although it is not possible to directly compare our results with those in [1, 2] (where different datasets were considered), the results in this paper indicate that racing is sometimes less effective than might have been previously thought.

We have only considered Hoeffding racing in this paper. Alternative racing criteria (e.g. Bayesian races [2]) provide tighter bounds as a result of making stronger assumptions about the distribution over the evaluation error. It would be interesting to conduct experiments comparing a variety of racing criteria to examine their sensitivity to different datasets.

Acknowledgement

This research was funded by the Australian Research Council Centre of Complex Systems scholarship.

References

1. O. Maron and A. W. Moore. Hoeffding Races: Accelerating Model Selection Search for Classification and Function Approximation, in Advances in Neural Information Processing System, J.D. Cowan, Tesauro, G. Alspector, J., Editor. 1994, Morgan Kaufmann.
2. O. Maron and A. W. Moore. The Racing Algorithm: Model Selection for Lazy Learners, in Artificial Intelligence Review. 1997. p. 193-225.
3. M. Birattari, T. Stuetzle, L. Paquete and K. Varrentrapp, A Racing Algorithm for Configuring Metaheuristics, in Genetic and Evolutionary Computation Conference 2002. 2002, Morgan Kaufmann Publishers: New York, USA. p. 11-18.
4. B. Yuan and M. Gallagher. Statistical Racing Techniques for Improved Empirical Evaluation of Evolutionary Algorithms, in Parallel Problem Solving from Nature VIII, X. Yao, E. Burke, J. A. Lozano, J. Smith, J. J. Merelo-Guervos, J. A. Bullinaria, J. Rowe, P. Tino, A. Kaban, H-P. schwefel, Editor. 2004, Springer: Birmingham, UK. p. 172-181.
5. T. Hastie, R. Tibshirani and J.Friedman. The Elements of Statistical Learning: Data Mining, Infererence and Prediction, in Springer series in statistics. 2001, Springer: New York, USA.
6. C. G. Atkeson, A.W. Moore and S. Schaal. Locally Weighted Learning. Artificial Intelligence Review. Vol. 10. 1996.
7. T. M. Mitchell. Machine Learning. 1997. New York, USA: The McGraw-Hill Companies, Inc.
8. S. Hittich, C. L. Blake and C. J. Merz, UCI Repository of Machine Learning Databases. 1998: University of California Irvine, USA.
   http://www.ics.uci.edu/~mlearn/MLRepository.html

Designing an Optimal Network
Using the Cross-Entropy Method

Sho Nariai[1], Kin-Ping Hui[2], and Dirk P. Kroese[1]

[1] Department of Mathematics, University of Queensland, Brisbane 4072, Australia
[2] IN Division, DSTO, Edinburgh 5111, Australia

Abstract. Consider a network of unreliable links, each of which comes with a certain price and reliability. Given a fixed budget, which links should be bought in order to maximize the system's reliability? We introduce a Cross-Entropy approach to this problem, which can deal effectively with the noise and constraints in this difficult combinatorial optimization problem. Numerical results demonstrate the effectiveness of the proposed technique.

1 Introduction

One of the most basic and useful approaches to network reliability analysis is to represent the network as an undirected graph with unreliable links. Often, the reliability of the network is defined as the probability that certain nodes in the graph are connected by functioning links.

This paper is concerned with network *planning*, where the objective is to maximize the network's reliability subject to a fixed budget. More precisely, given a fixed amount of money, the question is which links should be purchased, in order to maximize the reliability of the purchased network. Each link has a pre-specified price and reliability. This Network Planning Problem (NPP) is difficult to solve, not only because it is a constrained integer programming problem, which complexity grows exponentially in the number of links, but also because for large networks the value of the objective function – that is, the network reliability – becomes difficult or impractical to evaluate [1, 2].

We show that the *Cross-Entropy* (CE) method provides an effective way to solve the NPP. The CE method is a new method for discrete and continuous optimization. It consists of two steps which are iterated:

1. generate random states in the search space according to some specified random mechanism, and
2. update the parameters of this mechanism in order to obtain better scoring states in the next iteration. This last step involves minimizing the distance between two distributions, using the Kullback-Leibler or Cross-Entropy distance; hence the name.

A tutorial introduction can be found in [3], which is also available from the CE homepage http://www.cemethod.org. A comprehensive treatment can be found in [4].

M. Gallagher, J. Hogan, and F. Maire (Eds.): IDEAL 2005, LNCS 3578, pp. 228–233, 2005.

The rest of the paper is organized as follows. In Section 2 we formulate the network planning in mathematical terms. In Section 3 we present the CE approach to the problem. In Section 4 we consider a *noisy* version of the CE method [5, 6], where the network reliability is estimated (rather than evaluated) using *graph evolution* techniques [7–9]. We conclude with a numerical experiment in Section 5 that illustrates the effectiveness of our approach.

2 Problem Description

Consider a network represented as an undirected graph $\mathcal{G}(\mathcal{V}, \mathcal{E})$, with set $\mathcal{V}$ of nodes (vertices), and set $\mathcal{E}$ of links (edges). Suppose the number of links is $|\mathcal{E}| = m$. Without loss of generality we may label the links $1, \ldots, m$. Let $\mathcal{K} \subseteq \mathcal{V}$ be a set of *terminal* nodes. With each of the links is associated a *cost* c_e and *reliability* p_e. The objective is to buy those links that optimize the reliability of the network – defined as the probability that the terminal nodes are connected by functioning links – subject to a total budget $C_{\max}$. Let $\boldsymbol{c} = (c_1, \ldots, c_m)$ denote vector of link costs, and $\boldsymbol{p} = (p_1, \ldots, p_m)$ the vector of link reliabilities.

We introduce the following notation. For each link e let x_e be such that $x_e = 1$ if link e is purchased, and 0 otherwise. We call the vector $\boldsymbol{x} = (x_1, \ldots, x_m)$ the *purchase vector* and $\boldsymbol{x}^*$ the *optimal purchase vector*. Similarly, to identify the operational links, we define for each link e the link *state* by $y_e = 1$ if link e is bought and is functioning, and 0 otherwise. The vector $\boldsymbol{y} = (y_1, \ldots, y_m)$ is called the *state vector*. For each purchase vector $\boldsymbol{x}$ let $\varphi_{\boldsymbol{x}}$ be the *structure function* of the purchased system. This function assigns to each state vector $\boldsymbol{y}$ the state of the system (working = terminal nodes are connected = 1, or failed = 0). Next, consider the situation with *random* states, where each purchased link e works with probability p_e. Let Y_e be random state of link e, and let $\boldsymbol{Y}$ be the corresponding random state vector. Note that for each link e that is *not* bought, the state Y_e is per definition equal to 0. The reliability of the network determined by $\boldsymbol{x}$ is given by

$$r(\boldsymbol{x}) = \mathbb{E}[\varphi_{\boldsymbol{x}}(\boldsymbol{Y})] = \sum_{\boldsymbol{y}} \varphi_{\boldsymbol{x}}(\boldsymbol{y}) \Pr\{\boldsymbol{Y} = \boldsymbol{y}\} . \tag{1}$$

We assume from now on that the links fail independently, that is, $\boldsymbol{Y}$ is a vector of independent Bernoulli random variables, with success probability p_e for each purchased link e and 0 otherwise. Defining $\boldsymbol{p_x} = (x_1 p_1, \ldots, x_m p_m)$, we write $\boldsymbol{Y} \sim \mathrm{Ber}(\boldsymbol{p_x})$. Our main purpose is to determine

$$\max_{\boldsymbol{x}} r(\boldsymbol{x}) , \quad \text{subject to} \quad \sum_{e \in \mathcal{E}} x_e c_e \leq C_{\max} . \tag{2}$$

Let $r^* := r(\boldsymbol{x}^*)$ denote the optimal reliability of the network.

3 The CE Method

In order to apply the CE method to the optimization problem (2), we need to specify (a) a random mechanism to generate random purchase vectors that satisfy the constraints, and (b) the updating rule for the parameters in that random mechanism.

A simple and efficient method to generate the random purchase vectors is as follows: First, generate a "uniform" random permutation $\pi = (e_1, e_2, \ldots, e_m)$ of edges. Then, in the order of the permutation π, flip a coin with success probability a_{e_i} to decide whether to purchase link e_i. If successful and if there is enough money available to purchase link e_i, set $X_{e_i} = 1$, that is, link e_i is purchased; otherwise set $X_{e_i} = 0$. The algorithm is summarized next.

Algorithm 1 (Generation Algorithm)

1. *Generate a uniform random permutation $\pi = (e_1, \ldots, e_m)$. Set $k = 1$.*
2. *Calculate $C = c_{e_k} + \sum_{i=1}^{k-1} X_{e_i} c_{e_i}$.*
3. *If $C \leq C_{\max}$, draw $X_{e_k} \sim \mathsf{Ber}(a_{e_k})$. Otherwise set $X_{e_k} = 0$.*
4. *If $k = m$, then stop; otherwise set $k = k + 1$ and reiterate from step 2.*

The usual CE procedure [4] proceeds by constructing a sequence of reference vectors $\{a_t, t \geq 0\}$ (i.e., purchase probability vectors), such that $\{a_t, t \geq 0\}$ converges to the degenerate (i.e., binary) probability vector $a^* = x^*$. The sequence of reference vectors is obtained via a two-step procedure, involving an auxiliary sequence of reliability levels $\{\gamma_t, t \geq 0\}$ that tend to the optimal reliability $\gamma^* = r^*$ at the same time as the a_t tend to a^*. At each iteration t, for a given a_{t-1}, γ_t is the $(1 - \rho)$-quantile of performances (reliabilities). Typically ρ is chosen between 0.01 and 0.1. An estimator $\widehat{\gamma}_t$ of γ_t is the corresponding $(1 - \rho)$-sample quantile. That is, generate a random sample $X_1, \ldots, X_N$ using the generation algorithm above; compute the performances $r(X_i)$, $i = 1, \ldots, N$ and let $\widehat{\gamma}_t = r_{(\lceil (1-\rho)N \rceil)}$, where $r_{(1)} \leq \cdots \leq r_{(N)}$ are the order statistics of the performances. The reference vector is updated via CE minimization, which (see [4]) reduces to the following: For a given fixed a_{t-1} and γ_t, let the j-th component of a_t be $a_{t,j} = \mathbb{E}_{a_{t-1}}[X_j \mid r(X) \geq \gamma_t]$. An estimator $\widehat{a}_t$ of a_t is computed via

$$\widehat{a}_{t,j} = \frac{\sum_{i=1}^N I_{\{r(X_i) \geq \widehat{\gamma}_t\}} X_{ij}}{\sum_{i=1}^N I_{\{r(X_i) \geq \widehat{\gamma}_t\}}}, \quad j = 1, \ldots, m, \tag{3}$$

where we use the *same* random sample $X_1, \ldots, X_N$ and where X_{ij} is the j-th coordinate of X_i.

The main CE algorithm for optimizing (2) using the above generation algorithm is thus summarized as follows.

Algorithm 2 (Main CE Algorithm)

1. *Initialize $\widehat{a}_0$. Set $t=1$ (iteration counter).*
2. *Generate a random sample $X_1, \ldots, X_N$ using Algorithm 1, with $a = \widehat{a}_{t-1}$. Compute the $(1 - \rho)$-sample quantile of performances $\widehat{\gamma}_t$.*
3. *Use the **same** sample to update $\widehat{a}_t$, using (3).*
4. *If some stopping criterion is met then stop; otherwise set $t = t + 1$ and reiterate from step 2.*

4 Noisy Optimization

As mentioned in the introduction, for networks involving a large number of links the exact evaluation of the network reliability is in general not feasible, and simulation becomes a viable option. In this section we show how the CE method can be easily modified to tackle *noisy* NPPs.

In order to adapt Algorithm 2, we again, at iteration t, generate a random sample $X_1, \ldots, X_N$ according the $\mathrm{Ber}(\widehat{a}_{t-1})$ distribution. However, the corresponding performances (network reliabilities) are now not computed exactly, but estimated by means of Monte Carlo simulations. An efficient approach to network reliability estimation is to use *Network Evolution* [7]. This works also well for highly reliable networks. The idea is as follows: Consider a network with structure function φ and reliability r as defined in (1). Assume for simplicity that all the links are bought, that is $x = (1, 1, \ldots, 1)$. Now, observe a *dynamic* version of the network $\mathcal{G}(V, E)$ which starts with all links failed and in which all links are being independently repaired; each link e has an exponential repair time with repair rate $\lambda(e) = -\log(1 - p_e)$. The state of e at time t is denoted by $Y_e(t)$ and, similar to before, the states of all the links is given by the vector $Y(t)$. Then, $(Y(t))$ is a Markov process with state space $\{0, 1\}^m$. Let Π denote the *order* in which the links become operational. Note that the probability of link e being operational at time $t = 1$ is p_e. It follows that the network reliability at time $t = 1$ is the same as in (1). Hence, by conditioning on Π we have

$$r = \mathbb{E}[\varphi(Y(1))] = \sum_{\pi} \Pr\{\Pi = \pi\} \Pr\{\varphi(Y(1)) = 1 \mid \Pi = \pi\}, \qquad (4)$$

The crucial point is that from the theory of Markov processes it is possible to *calculate* the probability $G(\pi) = \Pr\{\varphi(Y(t)) = 0 \mid \Pi = \pi\}$ in terms of convolutions of exponential distribution functions. Hence, we can estimate r by first drawing a random sample $\Pi_1, \ldots, \Pi_N$, each distributed according to Π, and then estimating r as

$$\widehat{r} = \frac{1}{K} \sum_{i=1}^{K} G(\Pi_i). \qquad (5)$$

5 Numerical Experiment

To illustrate the effectiveness of the proposed CE approach, consider the 6-node fully-connected graph with 3 terminal nodes given in Figure 1. The links costs and reliabilities are given in Table 1. Note that the direct links between the terminal nodes have infinite costs. We have deliberately excluded such links to make the problem more difficult to solve. The total budget is set to $C_{\max} = 3000$.

Note that for a typical purchase vector x the network reliability $r(x)$ will be high, since all links are quite reliable. Consequently, to obtain an accurate estimate of the network reliability, or better, the network unreliability $\overline{r}(x) = 1 - r(x)$, via conventional Monte Carlo methods, would require a large simulation effort. The optimal purchase vector for this problem – which was computed by

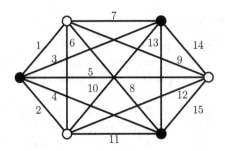

Fig. 1. Network with 3 terminal nodes, denoted by black vertices

Table 1. Link costs and reliabilities

i	c_i	p_i	i	c_i	p_i	i	c_i	p_i
1	382	0.990	6	380	0.998	11	397	0.990
2	392	0.991	7	390	0.997	12	380	0.991
3	∞	0.992	8	395	0.996	13	∞	0.993
4	∞	0.993	9	396	0.995	14	399	0.992
5	320	0.994	10	381	0.999	15	392	0.994

brute force – is equal to $\boldsymbol{x}^* = (1,1,0,0,1,0,1,1,0,1,0,0,0,0,1)$ which yields a minimum network unreliability of $\bar{r}^* = 7.9762 \times 10^{-5}$.

We used the following parameters for our algorithm: the sample size in Step 2 of the CE algorithm $N = 300$; the sample size in (5) $K = 100$; the initial purchase probability $\hat{\boldsymbol{a}}_0 = (0.5, \ldots, 0.5)$; the rarity parameter $\rho = 0.1$. The algorithm stops when $\max(\min(\hat{\boldsymbol{a}}_t, 1 - \hat{\boldsymbol{a}}_t)) \le \beta = 0.02$, that is, when all elements of $\hat{\boldsymbol{a}}_t$ are less than β, away from either 0 or 1. Let T denote the final iteration counter. We round $\hat{\boldsymbol{a}}_T$ to the nearest binary vector and take this as our solution $\hat{\boldsymbol{a}}^*$ to the problem. As a final step we estimate the optimal system reliability via (5) using a larger sample size of $K = 1000$.

Table 2 displays a typical evolution of the CE method. Here, t denotes the iteration counter, $\hat{\gamma}_t$ the $1 - \rho$ quantile of the estimated unreliabilities, and $\hat{\boldsymbol{a}}_t$ the

Table 2. A typical evolution of the CE algorithm with $N = 300$, $K = 100$ $\rho = 0.1$, and $\beta = 0.02$

t	$\hat{\gamma}_t$	$\hat{\boldsymbol{a}}_t$
0		0.50 0.50 0.50 0.50 0.50 0.50 0.50 0.50 0.50 0.50 0.50 0.50 0.50 0.50 0.50
1	4.0e-03	0.66 0.69 0.15 0.15 0.62 0.48 0.59 0.64 0.38 0.62 0.52 0.38 0.15 0.41 0.62
2	2.6e-04	0.69 0.63 0.05 0.05 0.72 0.21 0.88 0.71 0.33 0.75 0.58 0.26 0.05 0.38 0.77
3	1.4e-04	0.67 0.75 0.01 0.01 0.78 0.11 0.89 0.89 0.12 0.76 0.57 0.22 0.01 0.44 0.77
4	1.0e-04	0.76 0.76 0.00 0.00 0.89 0.03 0.97 0.90 0.06 0.83 0.43 0.11 0.00 0.41 0.84
5	8.1e-05	0.79 0.88 0.00 0.00 0.97 0.01 0.99 0.97 0.02 0.90 0.15 0.03 0.00 0.33 0.95
6	6.7e-05	0.94 0.96 0.00 0.00 0.97 0.00 1.00 0.99 0.01 0.97 0.07 0.01 0.00 0.10 0.99
7	6.3e-05	0.98 0.99 0.00 0.00 0.99 0.00 1.00 1.00 0.00 0.99 0.02 0.00 0.00 0.03 1.00
8	5.8e-05	0.99 1.00 0.00 0.00 1.00 0.00 1.00 1.00 0.00 1.00 0.01 0.00 0.00 0.01 1.00

purchase probability vector, at iteration t. The important thing to notice is that $\hat{a}_t$ quickly converges to the optimal degenerate vector $a^* = x^*$. The estimated network unreliability was found to be 8.496×10^{-5} with relative error of 0.0682. The simulation time was 154 seconds on a 3.0GHz computer using a Matlab implementation.

In repeated experiments, the proposed CE algorithm performed effectively and reliably in solving the noisy NPP, which constantly obtained the optimal purchase vector. Moreover, the algorithm only required on average 9 iterations with a CPU time of 180 seconds.

Acknowledgement

This research was supported by the Australian Research Council, grant number DP0558957.

References

1. Colbourn, C.J.: The Combinatorics of Network Reliability. Oxford University Press (1987)
2. Provan, J.S., Ball, M.O.: The complexity of counting cuts and of computing the probability that a graph is connected. SIAM Journal of Computing **12** (1982) 777–787
3. de Boer, P.T., Kroese, D.P., Mannor, S., Rubinstein, R.Y.: A tutorial on the cross-entropy method. Annals of Operations Research **134** (2005) 19 – 67
4. Rubinstein, R.Y., Kroese, D.P.: The Cross-Entropy Method: A unified approach to Combinatorial Optimization, Monte Carlo Simulation and Machine Learning. Springer Verlag, New York (2004)
5. Alon, G., Kroese, D.P., Raviv, T., Rubinstein, R.Y.: Application of the buffer allocation problem in simulation-based environment. Annals of Operations Research **134** (2005) 137 – 151
6. Chepuri, K., Homem de Mello, T.: Solving the vehicle routing problem with stochastic demands using the cross-entropy method. Annals of Operations Research **134** (2005) 153 – 181
7. Elperin, T., Gertsbakh, I.B., Lomonosov, M.: Estimation of network reliability using graph evolution models. IEEE Transactions on Reliability **40** (1991) 572–581
8. Hui, K.P., Bean, N., Kraetzl, M., Kroese, D.P.: The tree cut and merge algorithm for estimation of network reliability. Probability in the Engineering and Informational Sciences **17** (2003) 24–45
9. Hui, K.P., Bean, N., Kraetzl, M., Kroese, D.P.: Network reliability estimation using the tree cut and merge algorithm with importance sampling. Proceedings. Fourth International Workshop on Design of Reliable Communication Networks (2003) 254–262

Generating Predicate Rules
from Neural Networks

Richi Nayak

Centre for Information Innovation Technology,
Queensland University of Technology, Brisbane Qld 4001, Australia

Abstract. Artificial neural networks play an important role for pattern
recognition tasks. However, due to poor comprehensibility of the learned
network, and the inability to represent explanation structures, they are
not considered sufficient for the general representation of knowledge. This
paper details a methodology that represents the knowledge of a trained
network in the form of restricted first-order logic rules, and subsequently
allows user interaction by interfacing with a knowledge based reasoner.

1 Introduction

Artificial neural networks (ANN) are a powerful general purpose tool applied to
classification, prediction and clustering tasks. A recognised drawback of neural
networks is an absence of the capability to explain the decision process in a
comprehensive form. This can be overcome by reformation of numerical weights
representing network into the symbolic description known as *Rule extraction*.
Previous researchers have successfully extract the learned knowledge in a propositional attribute-value language [1]. While this is sufficient for some applications,
but for many applications the sheer number of propositional rules often makes
their comprehension difficult.

A means to generate fewer general rules that are equivalent of many more
simple rules in propositional ground form is necessary. A further reason to use a
predicate, rather than a propositional calculus, is the greater expressiveness of
the former. Predicate rules allow learning of general rules as well as learning of
internal relationships among variables.

This paper presents an approach which extracts rules from a trained ANN
using a propositional rule-extraction method. It further enhances the expressiveness of generated rules with the introduction of universally quantified variables,
terms, and predicates, creating a knowledge base equivalent to the network.

2 The Methodology

Given a set of *positive training examples* E^+, a set of *negative examples* E^- and
a hypothesis in the form of the *trained neural network ANN*, the task is to find
the *set of rules consisting of n-ary predicates and quantified variables KR* such
that: $ANN \cup KR \models e_i^+, \forall e_i^+ \in E^+$ and $ANN \cup KR \not\models e_i^-, \forall e_i^- \in E^-$.

M. Gallagher, J. Hogan, and F. Maire (Eds.): IDEAL 2005, LNCS 3578, pp. 234–241, 2005.

The methodology includes four phases:(1) Select and train an ANN until it reaches the minimum training and validation error; (2) Start pruning the ANN to remove redundant links and nodes, and retrain; (3) Generate the representation consisting of a type-hierarchy, facts and predicate rules; and (4) Interface the generated knowledge base with a knowledge base (KB) reasoner to provide user interface.

2.1 Phase 1: ANN Training and Phase 2: Pruning

A feedforward neural networks is trained for the given problem. When the ANN learning process completes, a pruning algorithm is applied to remove redundant nodes and links in the trained ANNs. The remaining nodes and links are trained for a few epochs to adjust the weights.

2.2 Phase 3: Rule Extraction

The next task is interpretation of the knowledge embedded in trained ANNs as symbolic rules. Following is the discussion of generalisation inference rules required to implicate specific to general relationship in this phase [5]:

1. **θ-subsumption:** *A clause C θ-subsumes ($\preceq$) a clause D, if there exists a substitution θ such that $C\theta \subseteq D$. C is known as the least general generalisation (lgg) of D, and D is specialisation of C if $C \preceq D$ and, for every other E such that $E\theta \subseteq D$, it is also the case that $E\theta \subseteq C$ [6].* The definition is extendible to calculate the least general generalisation of a set of clauses. The clause C is the lgg of a set of clauses S if C is the generalisation of each clause in S, and also a least general generalisation.
2. **Turning constants into variables:** If a number of descriptions with different constants are observed for a predicate or a formula, these observations are generalised into a generic predicate or formula. E.g., if a unary predicate (p) holds for various constants $a, b, ..l$ then the predicate p can be generalised to hold every value of a variable V with V being either of $a, b, ..l$.
3. **Counting arguments:** Constructive generalisation rules generate inductive assertions during learning that use descriptors, originally not present in the given examples. The CQ *count quantified variables* rule generates descriptors $\#V\_cond$, representing the number of V_i that satisfy some condition *cond*, if a concept descriptor is in the form of $\exists V_1, V_2, .., V_l \cdot p(V_1, V_2, .., V_k)$. The CA *count arguments of a predicate* rule generates new descriptors $\#V\_cond$, by measuring the number of arguments in the predicate that satisfy some condition *cond*, if the descriptor is a predicate with several arguments, $p(V_1, V_2, ..)$ [5].
4. **Term-rewriting:** This reformulation rule transforms compound terms in elementary terms. Let p be an n-ary predicate, whose first argument is a compound term consisting of t_1 and t_2, and the $n - 1$ arguments are represented by a list A. The rules to perform such transformation are:
$p(t_1 \vee t_2, A) \leftrightarrow p(t_1, A) \vee p(t_2, A)$
$p(t_1 \wedge t_2, A) \leftrightarrow p(t_1, A) \wedge p(t_2, A)$

The generalisation algorithm. The method of mapping predicate rules from propositional expressions, summarised in Figure 1, is an automatic bottom-up processing utilising Plotkin's lgg concept [6]. This is defined as the task of finding a generalised rule set represented in the subset language of first-order logic such that $KR^+ \models C_1^+ \vee ... \vee C_n^+$ and $KR^- \models C_1^- \vee ... \vee C_n^-$, where KR^+ and KR^- are knowledge representations that cover all positive (C_i^+) and negative (C_i^-) conjunctive expressions respectively.

---

1. Search for a DNF expression equivalent to the neural network.
2. Generate a single-depth type-hierarchy by input-space mapping,
   with attributes as concepts, and values as sub-concepts.
3. Perform a symbol mapping for predicates to convert each conjunctive
   expression into a ground fact (such as $Nodename\#_1\_\#_2$, $hidden1\_1$
   or $output1\_2$, or simply $p\_1, p\_2, .., p\_n$).
4. Utilise the fact definitions to create specific clauses (clauses with constants,
   $C_1, C_2, .., C_n$).
5. **For** all specific clauses do
   5.1 Search for any two compatible clauses C_1 and C_2.
       Let $C_1 \equiv \{l_1, .., l_k\}$ and $C_2 \equiv \{m_1, .., m_k\}$
       where each l_i, m_i has same predicate and sign.
   5.2 **If** such a pair C_1 and C_2 exists do
       5.2.1 Determine a set of selections, $S(C_1, C_2) := \{(l_1, m_1), .., (l_k, m_k)\}$
       5.2.2 Compute a new word symbol to hold the two k-ary predicates
             $word_1 := Temp(l_1, .., l_k)$, $word_2 := Temp(m_1, .., m_k)$
       5.2.3 let $\theta_1 := \emptyset$, $\theta_2 := \emptyset$, $q_1 := word_1$ and $q_2 := word_2$
       5.2.4 **While** $q_1 \neq q_2$ do
             • Search arguments of q_1 and q_2
             • find $t_1 \in q_1$ and $t_2 \in q_2$ such that t_1 and t_2 are occurring at the
               same position in q_1 and q_2 and $t_1 \neq t_2$ or one of them is a
               variable.
             • Replace t_1 and t_2 with a new variable X whenever they occur
               in the same position of q_1 and q_2.
             • Let $\theta_1 := \theta_1 \cup \{t_1/X\}$, $\theta_2 := \theta_2 \cup \{t_2/X\}$
       5.2.5 A rule with predicates and variables is generated
             $(word_1 = q_1\sigma_1, word_2 = q_2\sigma_2)$
6. **Return** the knowledge representation consisting of rules in the subset
   language of first order logic, facts and a type-hierarchy.

Fig. 1. The process to generate the formalism of predicate rules

In this representation, definitions of predicates and terms are same as those in first-order logic except that terms are *function free*. The explicit negation of predicates is allowed in describing the goal concepts to avoid 'negation-by-failure'. A fact is an instantiated/ground predicate if all its predicate variables are constant. There is a single-depth type-hierarchy corresponding to input space of an ANN, in which attributes are concepts, and their values are sub-concepts.

During the process of converting conjunctive expressions into ground facts: (1) If a conjunctive expression contains only one value per attribute, it results in one fact; (2) If a conjunctive expression contains more that one value for an attribute, it results in multiple fact by transforming the expression according to *'term-rewriting rule of generalisation'*. Minimisation procedures such as *(1) deletion of duplicated instances of facts, (2) replacing specific facts by more general ones and (3) deleting redundant entities in compatible facts-same predicate symbol and sign*, are applied to remove the redundant facts or entities in facts. The fact definitions are utilised to express specific rules. These specific rules are now expressed as clauses (disjunction of literals) by applying the logical equivalence law, $P \Rightarrow Q \equiv \neg P \vee Q$.

Plotkin's *'θ-subsumption rule of generalisation'* [6] is utilised to compute the mapping of literals of specific clauses to general clauses. To compute the generalisation of two clauses, literals must represent each possible mapping between the two clauses. The mapping is done by forming a set of pairs of compatible literals (*i.e.* same predicate symbol and sign) from the two clauses (in the same way as is done for Plotkin's concept of *selection* [6,8]). The set of selections of two clauses $C_1 = \{l_1, .., l_k\}$ and $C_2 = \{m_1, .., m_k\}$ is defined as: $S(C_1, C_2) := \{(l_i, m_j) | \forall l_i \in C_1 \wedge m_j \in C_2 \wedge compatible\}$. For computing the least general generalisation (lgg) of two clauses, the lgg of two literals requires to be computed first, and then the lgg of two terms (function free). The lgg of two clauses C_1 and C_2 is defined as:

$$lgg(C_1, C_2) = lgg(S(C_1, C_2)) = lgg(Temp(l_1, .., l_k), Temp(m_1, .., m_k))$$
$$lgg(l_1, m_1) = p(lgg(t_1, s_1), .., (t_n, s_n))$$

A substitution $\theta = \{X/t_1, X/t_2\}$ uniquely maps two terms to a variable X in compatible predicates by replacing all occurrences of t_1 and t_2 with the variable X, whenever they occur together in the same position. This ensures that θ is the proper substitution of t_1 and t_2. The size of the set of selections of two clauses C_1, C_2 can be at most $i \times j$, where i is the number of literals in C_1 and j is the number of literals in C_2. In general the resulting lgg of two clauses contains a maximum of $i \times j$ literals, many of which may be redundant and can be reduced by applying Plotkin's equivalence property.

The lgg of two incompatible literals is undefined [6]. If there is a rule (with constants) left alone in the original set that does not have a pair with which to generalise this rule, is not reduced and just mapped in the appropriate format.

An example. We use a simple example of Monk1 (consisting of six attributes and 432 patterns) to illustrate the rule generalisation process. The decision rule for membership of the target class (*i.e.* a monk) is: (1) *Head_shape = Body_shape*, or (2) *Jacket_color = red*. After training and pruning of an ANN over this problem, the input space is: *Head_shape* $\in$ {*round, square, octagon*}, *Body_shape* $\in$ {*round, square, octagon*}, and *Jacket_color* $\in$ {*red, not-red*}. A rule-extraction algorithm is applied to extract the knowledge of the ANN in propositional rules form. The DNF (disjunctive normal form) expression representing the *output node having high output* is:

1. (Head_shape = round ∧ Body_shape = round) ∨
2. (Head_shape = square ∧ Body_shape = square) ∨
3. (Head_shape = octagon ∧ Body_shape = octagon) ∨
4. (Jacket_color = red) ∨

The extracted DNF expression indicating the *low output* for the output node is:

5. (Head_shape = round ∧ Body_shape = square) ∨
6. (Head_shape = round ∧ Body_shape = octagon) ∨
7. (Head_shape = square ∧ Body_shape = round) ∨
8. (Head_shape = square ∧ Body_shape = octagon) ∨
9. (Head_shape = octagon ∧ Body_shape = round) ∨
10. (Head_shape = octagon ∧ Body_shape = square).

Each conjunctive expression is expressed as a ground fact. The first three expressions having the same arguments are mapped to the same predicate symbol: *monk1(round, round)*, *monk1(square, square)*, and *monk1(octagon,octagon)*. The fourth expression is inferred as *monk2(red)*. Likewise expressions 5 to 10 indicating a different category (low output) are mapped to a new predicate symbol *monk3* with their corresponding values.

A concept definition -*monk(Head_shape, Body_shape, Jacket_color)* or *monk (X, Y, Z)*- for the output node (the consequent of rules) is formed by collecting dependencies among attributes (associated within facts). The specific inference rules including the ground facts are:

1. monk(round, round, Z) ⇐ monk1(round, round)
2. monk(square, square, Z) ⇐ monk1(square, square)
3. monk(octagon,octagon, Z) ⇐ monk1(octagon,octagon)
4. monk(X, Y, red) ⇐ monk2(red)
5. ¬monk(round, square, Z) ⇐ monk3(round, square)
6. ¬monk(round, octagon, Z) ⇐ monk3(round, octagon)
7. ¬monk(square, round, Z) ⇐ monk3(square, round)
8. ¬monk(square, octagon, Z) ⇐ monk3(square, octagon)
9. ¬monk(octagon, round, Z) ⇐ monk3(octagon, round)
10. ¬monk(octagon, square, Z) ⇒ monk3(octagon, square)

The algorithm discussed in Figure 1 iterates over the rules to find two compatible rules. Let us take the compatible rules 5 to 10 to show the process of finding a lgg rule. On applying the logical equivalence law, $P \Rightarrow Q \equiv \neg P \vee Q$, the rules 5 & 6 are transformed into:

1. ¬monk3(round, square) ∨ ¬monk(round, square, Z)
2. ¬monk1(round,octagon) ∨ ¬monk(round,octagon, Z)

A new word symbol *Temp* is utilised to form two k-ary predicates to hold the set of selections generated from rules 5 and 6. Considering two choices for each antecedent, the set of selections of two rules contains a maximum of 2^n literals. These two clauses have two selections with consequent predicate.

1. Temp(¬monk3(round,square),¬monk(round,square,Z))
2. Temp(¬monk3(round,octagon),¬monk(round,octagon,Z))

The θ-subsumption proceeds with the following steps:

1. Temp(¬monk3(round,Y),¬monk(round,Y,Z))
2. Temp(¬monk3(round,Y),¬monk(round,Y,Z))

resulting in the inference rule:

- ¬monk(round,Y,Z) ⇐ monk3(round,Y) with θ = [Y/square] or [Y/octagon]

This lgg rule is further θ-subsumpted with the rest of the compatible rules 7,8,9,10, resulting in the following rule: ∀ **X,Y,Z** ¬**monk(X,Y,Z)** ⇐ **monk3 (X,Y)**

The algorithm also finds an inference rule out of three *compatible rules* 1, 2 & 3: ∀ **X,Z monk(X,X,Z)** ⇐ **monk1(X,X)**

For rule 4, the algorithm does not find any other compatible rule. This rule will therefore be: ∀ **X,Y,Z monk(X,Y,Z)** ⇐ **(Z == red)**

It can be observed that these generated rules are able to capture the true learning objective of the Monk1 problem domain *i.e.* the higher order proposition that *(Head_shape = Body_shape)* (rule 1 & 2) rather than yielding each propositional rule such as *Head_shape = round and Body_shape= round* etc.

2.3   Phase 4: User Interaction

The generated knowledge base is interfaced with a KB reasoner that allows user interaction and enables greater explanatory capability. The inference process is activated when the internal knowledge base is operationally loaded and consultation begins. For example, if the query *monk(square, square, not-red)* is posed, the KB system initiates and executes the appropriate rules and returns the answer *true* with the explanation:

- monk(square,square,not-red) ⇐ monk1(square, square)

3   Evaluation

The methodology is successfully tested on a number of synthetic data sets such as Monks, Mushroom, Voting, Moral reasoner, Cleveland heart and Breast cancer from UCI machine learning repository and real-world data sets such as remote sensing and Queensland Railway crossing safety. The results are compared with symbolic propositional learner C5 and symbolic predicate learner FOIL [7].

Tables 1 and 2 report the relative overall performance of predicate rulesets utilising different algorithms. The average performance is determined by separately measuring the performance on each data set, and then calculating the average performance across all data sets, for each rule set. Several neural network learning techniques such as cascade correlation (CC), BpTower (BT) and constrained error back propagation (CEBP) are utilised to build networks. This is to show the the applicability of predicate (or restricted first-order) rule-extraction to a variety of ANN architectures. The included results are after the application of pruning algorithm (P) to reduce the input space. The proposed rule extraction techniques *LAP* [4] and *RulVI* [3] are applied on the cascade and BpTower ANNs. The *Rulex* [2] technique is applied to extract rules from the trained CEBPNs.

Table 1 shows that the accuracy of the generated predicate rules very much depends on the rule-extraction algorithm that has been employed to extract the propositional expressions from the trained ANN. The expressiveness of the extracted propositional expressions is enhanced by introducing variables and predicates in rules without the loss of accuracy or of fidelity to the ANN solution.

Table 1. The relative average predictive accuracy of predicate rules over 10 data sets

Predicate rules using		Accuracy (%) Training	Accuracy (%) Testing	Fidelity (%) to the network
LAP	PCC	98.28	95.05	99.04
	PBT	98.21	95.15	98.88
RuleVI	PCC	97.65	89.57	98.27
	PBT	97.59	84.71	96.87
Rulex CEBPN		96.41	89.51	93.23
C4.5		96.99	94.05	
Foil		97.1	83.98	

Table 2. The relative average comprehensibility of predicate rules over 10 data sets

		No of Conjunctive expressions	No of Predicate rules
LAP	PCC	64	28
	PBT	63	21
RuleVI	PCC	39	18
	PBT	48	24
Rulex CEBPN		4.6	4
C4.5		10	
Foil			8

If the relevance of a particular input attribute depends on the values of other input attributes, then the generalisation algorithm is capable of showing that relationship in terms of variables (as in Monk1). Otherwise the generalisation algorithm simply translates the propositional rules into predicate form without significantly reducing the number of rules.

The generalization accuracy (when moving from training to test data) of FOIL is worse than our system. The generalization accuracy even becomes worse when the data has noise. Our method performed (in terms of accuracy and comprehensibility) better than symbolic learners when small amount of data (less than 100 patterns) is available for training. When a large number of data is available for training, symbolic learners performed better. Our system preformed better than FOIL when the distribution of patterns among classes is uneven.

The algorithmic complexity of this methodology depends upon the core algorithms used in different phases. The generalisation algorithm used in phase 3 requires $O(l \times m^2)$, where l is the number of clauses according to the DNF expression equivalent to the trained ANN and m is the total number of attributes in the problem domain. However, application of the pruning algorithm in phase 2 significantly reduces the total number of attributes.

4   Conclusion

We presented a methodology which comprehensively understands the decision process of an ANN, and provides explanations to the user by interfacing the network's output with a KB reasoner. The powerful advantage of ANNs, the ability to learn and generalise, is exploited to extract knowledge from a set of examples. Even though ANNs are only capable of encoding simple propositional data, with the addition of the inductive generalisation step, the knowledge represented by the trained ANN is transformed into a representation consisting of rules with predicates, facts and a type-hierarchy. The qualitative knowledge representation ideas of symbolic systems are combined with the distributed computational advantages of connectionist models.

The logic required in representing the network is restricted to pattern matching for the unification of predicate arguments and does not contain functions. Despite this fact, the predicate formalism is appropriate for real-life problems as shown in experiments. The benefit in using such a logic to represent networks is that (1) knowledge can be interactively queried leading to an identification of newly acquired concepts, (2) an equivalent symbolic interpretation is derived describing the overall behaviour, and (3) a fewer number of rules are relatively easier to understand.

References

1. R. Andrews, J. Diederich, and A. Tickle. A survey and critique of techniques for extracting rules from trained artificial neural networks. *Knowledge Based Systems*, 8:373–389, 1995.
2. R. Andrews and S. Geva. Rule extraction from a constrained error back propagation mlp. In *Proc. of 5th Australian Conference on Neural Networks, Brisbane, Australia*, pages 9–12, 1994.
3. R. Hayward, C. Ho-Stuart, and J. Diederich. Neural networks as oracles for rule extraction. In *Connectionist System for Knowledge Representation and Deduction*, pages 105–116. Queensland University of Technology, Australia, 1997.
4. R. Hayward, A. Tickle, and J. Diederich. Extracting rules for grammar recognition from cascade-2 networks. In *Connectionist, Statistical and Symbolic Approaches to Learning for Natural Language Proc.*, pages 48–60. Springer-Verlag, Berlin, 1996.
5. R. S. Michalski and R. L. Chilausky. Knowledge acquisition by encoding expert rules versus computer induction from examples-a case study involving soya-bean pathology. *International Journal of Man-Machine Studies*, 12:63–87, 1980.
6. D. G. Plotkin. A further note on inductive generalisation. In B. Meltzer and D. Michie, editors, *Machine Intelligence 6*, volume 6, pages 101–124. Edinburgh University Press, 1971.
7. J. R. Quinlan. Learning logical definitions from relations. *Machine Learning*, 5(3):239–266, 1990.
8. S. Wrobel. Inductive logic programming. In G. Brewka, editor, *Principles of Knowledge Representation*. CSLI Publications and FoLLI, 1996.

Improving Ensembles
with Classificational Cellular Automata

Petra Povalej, Mitja Lenič, and Peter Kokol

Faculty of Electrical Engineering and Computer Science University of Maribor,
Smetanova ulica 17,2000 Maribor, Slovenia
{Petra.Povalej,Mitja.Lenic,Kokol}@uni-mb.si
http://lsd.uni-mb.si

Abstract. In real world there are many examples where synergetic cooperation of multiple entities performs better than just single one. The same fundamental idea can be found in ensemble learning methods that have the ability to improve classification accuracy. Each classifier has specific view on the problem domain and can produce different classification for the same observed sample. Therefore many methods for combining classifiers into ensembles have been already developed. Most of them use simple majority voting or weighted voting of classifiers to combine the single classifier votes. In this paper we present a new approach for combining classifiers into an ensemble with Classificational Cellular Automata (CCA), which exploit the cellular automata self-organizational abilities. We empirically show that CCA improves the classification accuracy of three popular ensemble methods: Bagging, Boosting and MultiBoosting. The presented results also show important advantages of CCA, such as: problem independency, robustness to noise and no need for the user input.

1 Introduction

In recent years there has been a growing interest in the area of combining classifiers into ensembles also known as committees or multiple classifier systems. The intuitive concept of ensemble learning methods is that no single classifier can claim to be uniformly superior to any other, and that the integration of several single approaches will enhance the performance of final classification [1]. Hence, using the classification capabilities of multiple classifiers, where each classifier may make different and perhaps complementary errors, tend to yield an improved performance over single classifiers. Some ensemble learning approaches are actively trying to perturb some aspects of the training set, such as training samples, attributes or classes, in order to ensure classifier diversity. One of the most popular perturbation approaches are Bootstrap Aggregation (Bagging) and Boosting.

Bagging firstly introduced by Breimen [2] in 1996 manipulates the training samples and forms replicate training sets. The final classification is based on a majority vote. Boosting introduced by Freund and Schapire in 1996 [3] combines classifiers with weighted voting and is more complex since the distribution of training samples in training set is adaptively changed according to the performance of sequentially constructed classifiers.

In general ensemble learning approaches can be divided into three groups: (1) ensemble learning approaches that combine different independent classifiers (such as:

M. Gallagher, J. Hogan, and F. Maire (Eds.): IDEAL 2005, LNCS 3578, pp. 242–249, 2005.

Bayesian Voting, Majority Voting, etc.), (2) ensemble learning approaches which construct a set of classifiers on the basis of one base classifier with perturbation of training set (such as: Bagging, Boosting, Windowing, etc.) and (3) a combination of (1) and (2). A detailed empirical study is presented in [4].

When studying the groups (1) and (2) we came across some drawbacks. The most essential deficiency in (1) is their restriction with predefined way of combining classifiers induced on the basis of different predefined methods of machine-learning. On the contrary, the ensemble learning approaches that are based on improving one base classifier (2), use only one method for constructing all classifiers in ensemble. Therefore a problem of selecting the appropriate method for solving a specific task arises.

As an example of an ensemble learning approach which combines (1) and (2) we presented Classificational Cellular Automata (CCA) in [5]. The basic idea of CCA is to combine different classifiers induced on the basis of various machine-learning methods into an ensemble in a non-predefined way. After several iterations of applying adequate transaction rules only the set of classifiers, which contribute most to the final classification, is preserved. Consequently the problem of choosing appropriate machine learning method or a combination of them is automatically solved. The idea of using cellular automata as a model for ensemble learning is presented in section 3.

In this paper we focus on CCAs ability to improve the classification accuracy of ensemble learning methods. The experiments using Bagging, Boosting and Multi-Boost ensemble learning methods on 9 randomly chosen databases from UCI repository are presented in section 4. The paper concludes with some final remarks.

2   The Basics of Cellular Automata

The concept of CA was firstly proposed in early 1960's by J. Von Neumann [6] and Stan Ulam. From those early years until now, the CA have attracted many researchers from all science domains – physical and social. The reason for the popularity of CA is their simplicity and enormous potential of modeling behavior of complex systems.

CA can be viewed as a simple model of a spatially extended decentralized system made up of a number of individual components (cells). Each individual cell is in a specific state which changes through the time depending on the state of neighborhood cells and according to the transaction rules. In spite of their simplicity, when iterated several times, the dynamics of CA is potentially very rich, and ranges from attracting stable configurations to spatio-temporal chaotic features and pseudo-random generation abilities. Those abilities enable the diversity that can possibly overcome local optima by solving engineering problems. Moreover, from the computational viewpoint, they are universal, could say, as powerful as Turing machines and, thus, classical Von Neumann architectures.

These structural and dynamical features make them very powerful: fast CA-based algorithms are developed to solve engineering problems in cryptography and microelectronics for instance, and theoretical CA-based models are built in ecology, biology, physics and image-processing. On the other hand, these powerful features make CA difficult to analyze – almost all long-term behavioral properties of dynamical systems, and cellular automata in particular, are unpredictable. However, in this paper the aim is not to analyze the process of CA rather to use it for superior classification tasks.

3 Classificational Cellular Automata

In this section we will introduce the basic structure, learning algorithm and initial parameters of CCA.

CCA is presented as a classifier. Generally, learning a classifier is based on samples from a training set. Every training instance is completely described by a set of attributes (instance properties) and class (decision).

CCA is initially defined as a 2D lattice of cells. Each cell can contain a classifier and according to it's classification of an input instance the cell can be in one of the k states, where k is the number of possible classes plus the state "can not classify". The last state has especially important role when such classifier is used, which is not defined on a whole learning set, i.e. when using *if-then* rule. Therefore, from the classification point of view in the learning process the outcome of each cell can be: (1) the same as the training instance's class, (2) different from the training instance's class or (3) "cannot classify". However, a cell with unknown classification for current training instance should be treated differently as misclassification.

Beside the cell's classification ability, the neighborhood plays a very important role in the self-organization ability of a CCA. Transaction rules depend on the specific neighborhood state to calculate a new cell's state and have to be defined in such a way to enforce self-organization of CCA, which consequently should lead to generalization process.

In general we want to group classifiers that support similar hypothesis and have therefore similar classification on training instances. Therefore even if instance is wrongly classified, the neighborhood can support a cell by preventing the elimination of its classifier from automata. With that transaction rule we encourage a creation of decision centers for a specific class and in this way we can overcome the problem of noisy training instances.

As for all ensemble learning approaches it is clear that if all classifiers are identical or even similar, there can be no advantage in combining their decisions, therefore some difference among base classifiers is a necessary condition for improvement. The diversity of classifiers in CCA cells is ensured by using different machine-learning methods for classifier induction. However, there is only limited number of machine-learning methods, which can present a problem for large CCA. But most of the methods have some tuning parameters that affect classification and therefore, with changing those parameters, a lot of different classifiers can be obtained. Another possibility for obtaining several different classifiers is by changing expected probability distributions of input instances, which may also result in different classifiers, even by using the same machine learning method with the same parameters. Still another approach is the feature reduction/selection. That technique is recommended when a lot of features are presented.

3.1 Learning Algorithm

Once the diversity of induced classifiers is ensured by the means discussed above, the classifiers are placed into a pool. For each classifier the basics statistic information such as confidence and support is preserved. In the process of filling CCA for each cell a classifier is randomly chosen from the pool. After filling a CCA the following learning algorithm is applied:

```
Input: learning set with N learning samples
Number of iterations: t=1,2,…T
For t=1,2…T:
    - choose a learning sample I
    - each cell in automaton classifies the learning sample I
    - change cells energy according to the transaction rules
    - a cell with energy bellow zero does not survive
    - probabilistically fill the empty cells with classifiers from
      the pool
```

Beside its classifier information, each cell contains also statistical information about its successfulness in a form of cell's energy. Transaction rules can increase or decrease the energy level dependent on the successfulness of classification and the state of the cell's neighbors. Each neighborhood cell influences the energy of the current cell dependent on its *score* (Eq. 1).

$$score = support \bullet conficence \bullet distance ; \tag{1}$$

where *distance* is the Euclidian distance from the neighborhood cell to the current cell.

The sum of *scores* of all neighborhood cells that equally classified the learning sample as the current cell (*eqScore*) is used in transaction rules to calculate the cells new energy (*e*). Similarly, the sum of *scores* of all neighborhood cells which can not classify the learning sample (*noClassScore*) is calculated and used in the following transaction rules:

- If a cell has the same classification as the sample class:
  (a) if *noClassScore*>0 than increase energy of the cell using the equation (Eq. 2).

$$e = e + \left(100 - \frac{eqScore \bullet 100}{noClassScore} \right) \tag{2}$$

  (b) if all neighbourhood cells classified the learning sample (*noClassScore=0*) than increase cell's energy according to (Eq. 3).

$$e = e + 400 \tag{3}$$

- If a cell classification differs from the learning sample class:
  (a) if *noClassScore*>0 than decrease energy of the cell using (Eq. 4).

$$e = e - \left(100 - \frac{eqScore \bullet 100}{noClassScore} \right) \tag{4}$$

  (b) if *noClassScore=0* than decrease cell's energy using (Eq. 5).

$$\tag{5}$$

- If a cell cannot classify learning sample then slightly decrease energy state of the cell (Eq. 6).

$$e = e - 10 \tag{6}$$

Through all iterations all cells use one point of energy (to live). If energy drops below zero the cell is terminated (blank cell). A new cell can be created dependent on learning algorithm parameters with its initial energy state and a classifier used from pool of classifiers or newly generated classifier. Of course if cell is too different from the neighborhood it will ultimately die out and the classifier will be returned to the pool.

The learning of a CCA is done incrementally by supplying samples from the learning set. Transaction rules are executed first on the whole CCA with a single sample and then continued with the next until the whole problem is learned by using all samples – that is a similar technique than used in neural networks [Towel *et al.*, 1993].

Transaction rules do not directly imply learning, but the iteration of those rules creates the self-organizing ability. However, this ability depends on classifiers used in CCAs cells, and its geometry. Stopping criteria can be determined by defining fixed number of iterations or by monitoring accuracy.

3.2 Inference Algorithm

Inference algorithm differs from learning algorithm, because it does not use self-organization.

```
Input: a sample for classification
Number of iterations: t=1,2,…V
For t=1,2…V
    – each cell in automaton classifies the sample
    – change cells energy according to the transaction rules
    – each cell with energy bellow zero does not survive
Classify the sample according to the weighted voting of the survived
cells
Output: class of the input sample
```

The simplest way to produce single classification would be to use the majority voting of cells in CCA. However some votes can be very weak from the transaction rule point of view. Therefore the transaction rules which consider only the neighborhood majority vote as a sample class are used in order to eliminate all weak cells. After several iterations of transaction rules only cells with strong structural support survive. The final class on an input sample is determined by weighted voting where the energy state of each survived cell is considered as a weight.

4   Experiments and Results

In order to compare CCA with other ensemble methods we used Weka 3 – Data Mining Open Source written in Java [7]. The following three well known ensemble methods implemented in Weka were used on a collection of 9 randomly chosen datasets from UCI Machine Learning Repository [8]:

- Bagging [2],
- AdaBoostM1 – a method of boosting by using AdaBoost algorithm [3],
- MultiBoostAB – a method that combines AdaBoost with wagging [9].

As a basic classifier a C4.5 decision tree [10] was used in all ensemble methods listed above.

The direct comparison between CCA and other methods for combining classifiers into an ensemble listed above was made using classifiers induced by each ensemble method as a source for filling CCA. In fact all classifiers were put in the pool of classifiers and then used in the process of initialization and learning of CCA.

CCA was initialized with the following parameters: size: 10x10 matrix (bounded into torus), neighborhood radius $r=5$ and stopping criteria: number of iterations $t=1000$.

Through all iterations all cells use one point of energy (to live). If the energy level of a cell drops below zero the cell is terminated. In the experiments presented in this section we used the same evaluation criteria as presented in [5].

4.1 Empirical Evaluation

In the first experiment Bagging was used for creating an ensemble of 50 classifiers. All classifiers from the ensemble were introduced in the pool and then used as a source of diverse classifiers for CCA (Bagged CCA). The results gained on 9 randomly chosen UCI databases are presented in Table 1. If the accuracy and class accuracy on learning set is compared, we can see that there is no essential deviation. However, when an accuracy of classifying unseen test cases is considered an observation can be made that Bagged CCA had better or at least equal performance as Bagging in all cases. Since in both methods the same base classifiers, we can conclude, that improvement of classification accuracy results only from organization and transaction rules of CCA.

Table 1. Comparison between Bagging and CCA with bagged classifiers

Data	Bagging				Bagged CCA			
	Learn set		Test set		Learn set		Test set	
	Δ	▫	Δ	▫	Δ	▫	Δ	▫
australian	94,35	94,30	86,52	86,78	95,00	94,91	87,39	87,32
breast	98,71	98,86	96,99	97,45	98,71	98,86	96,99	97,45
cleve	95,05	95,06	77,23	76,52	96,54	96,52	84,16	83,12
diabetes	95,31	94,36	73,83	69,94	93,75	92,27	75,00	72,80
glass	94,37	95,47	69,44	66,13	95,07	95,81	70,83	72,08
golf	100,00	100,00	100,00	100,00	100,00	100,00	100,00	100,00
heart	96,11	95,83	84,44	84,41	95,00	94,71	88,89	88,61
iris	100,00	100,00	92,00	92,00	100,00	100,00	92,00	92,00
pima	96,48	95,84	78,13	74,41	94,73	94,46	78,52	76,90
Average	**96,71**	**96,63**	**84,29**	**83,07**	**96,53**	**96,39**	**85,97**	**85,59**

Δ accuracy   ▫ average class accuracy

Additional experiment was made in order to compare CCA with one of the most successful methods for combining classifiers into an ensemble – AdaBoostM1. 50 individual classifiers induced with AdaBoost M1 method were used a source classifiers for CCA (AdaBoostM1 CCA). As expected AdaBoostM1 ensemble method boosted the classification accuracy on learning set to 100% in all cases which can not be affirmed for CCA that used the same classifiers (Table 2). Despite of that a closer look shows that the accuracy and average class accuracy on the learning set has not decreased more than 3,98% in the worst case when using CCA. On the other hand, the accuracy and average class accuracy of classifying unseen test samples has increased in all cases except in two (where CCA obtained the same result as AdaBoostM1) when using CCA. Thereafter an observation can be made that a consequence of a slight decrement in learning accuracy is probably less overfitting and consequently better results on test set. Accordingly the same conclusion can be made as in previous experiment – the improvement in classification accuracy is a direct consequence of using CCA as a method for combining classifiers into an ensemble.

Table 2. CCA using classifiers induced with AdaBoostM1 compared to AdaBoostM1

Data	AdaBoostM1				AdaBoostM1 CCA			
	Learn set		Test set		Learn set		Test set	
	Δ	▫	Δ	▫	Δ	▫	Δ	▫
australian	100,00	100,00	86,96	86,59	99,78	99,77	88,70	88,77
breast	100,00	100,00	97,00	97,87	99,36	99,49	99,00	97,87
cleve	100,00	100,00	77,23	77,57	96,04	96,02	85,15	85,49
diabetes	100,00	100,00	71,48	68,17	100,00	100,00	75,39	72,26
glass	100,00	100,00	81,94	72,46	100,00	100,00	81,94	79,11
golf	100,00	100,00	100,00	100,00	100,00	100,00	100,00	100,00
heart	100,00	100,00	84,44	84,41	98,33	98,27	90,00	90,28
iris	100,00	100,00	92,00	92,00	100,00	100,00	92,00	92,00
pima	100,00	100,00	75,39	71,76	97,66	97,11	79,69	76,20
Average	**100,00**	**100,00**	**85,16**	**83,43**	**99,02**	**98,96**	**87,98**	**86,89**

Δ accuracy   ▫ average class accuracy

The last experiment was made with MultiBoostAB ensemble learning method. 50 individual classifiers induced with MultiBoostAB were used as source of classifiers for CCA (MultiBoostAB CCA) (Table 3). Likewise AdaBoostM1 ensemble method the MultiBoostAB reached 100% classification accuracy on learning set in all cases. MutiBoostAB CCA made a classification error only on two databases when classifying learning samples. However, the results on test sets are much more interesting. The MultiBoostAB CCA performed better (in 7 cases out of 9) or at least as good as MultiBoostAB (in 2 cases) according to accuracy and average class accuracy of classifying unseen test samples. The presented results show additional example of CCAs ability to improve classification accuracy of ensembles.

Table 3. CCA using classifiers induced with MultiBoostAB compared to MultiBoostAB

Data	MultiBoostAB				MultiBoostAB CCA			
	Learn set		Test set		Learn set		Test set	
	Δ	▫	Δ	▫	Δ	▫	Δ	▫
australian	100,00	100,00	86,96	86,59	99,35	99,33	88,26	88,59
breast	100,00	100,00	97,00	97,87	100,00	100,00	97,00	97,87
cleve	100,00	100,00	77,23	77,57	98,52	98,51	83,17	84,94
diabetes	100,00	100,00	71,48	68,17	100,00	100,00	75,39	72,09
glass	100,00	100,00	81,94	72,46	100,00	100,00	86,11	83,33
golf	100,00	100,00	100,00	100,00	100,00	100,00	100,00	100,00
heart	100,00	100,00	84,44	84,41	100,00	100,00	87,78	88,01
iris	100,00	100,00	92,00	92,00	100,00	100,00	94,00	94,23
pima	100,00	100,00	75,39	71,76	100,00	100,00	78,52	75,02
Average	**100,00**	**100,00**	**85,16**	**83,43**	**99,76**	**99,76**	**87,80**	**87,12**

Δ accuracy   ▫ average class accuracy

5   Discussion and Conclusion

In this paper we presented a new approach to combine diverse classifiers an ensemble using the model of cellular automata. We empirically proved CCAs ability to improve the classification accuracy compared to Bagging, Boosting and MultiBoost ensemble learning methods on 9 randomly chosen databases from UCI repository by using the same base classifiers as compared methods and different combination technique.

We can conclude that improvement of classification accuracy results only from organization ability and transaction rules of CCA.

However, CCA approach has also some drawbacks. From computation point of view CCA approach uses additional power to apply transaction rules, which can be expensive in the learning process, but its self-organizing feature can result in better classification, that can also mean less costs. But additional advantages of the resulting self-organizing structure of cells in CCA is the problem independency, robustness to noise and no need for the additional user input. The important research direction in the future are to analyze the resulting self-organized structure, impact of transaction rules on classification accuracy, introduction other social aspect for cells survival.

References

1. Wolpert, D., Macready, W.: No Free Lunch Theorems for optimization. IEEE Transactions on Evolutionary Computation 1(1), (1997) 67-82
2. Breiman, L.: Bagging Predictors. Machine Learning. Vol. 24, No. 2, (1996) 123-140 [http://citeseer.ist.psu.edu/breiman96bagging.html]
3. Freund, Y., Schapire, R.E.: Experiments with a new boosting algorithm, In: Proceedings Thirteenth International Conference on Machine Learning, Morgan Kaufman, San Francisco, (1996) 148-156
4. Dietterich, T., G.: Ensemble Methods in Machine Learning, In: J. Kittler and F. Roli (Ed.) First International Workshop on Multiple Classifier Systems, Lecture Notes in Computer Science (2000) 1-15, New York: Springer Verlag.
5. Kokol, P., Povalej, P., Lenič, M., Štiglic, G.: Building classifier cellular automata, In: Slot, P. M.A. (Ed.), Chopard, B. (Ed.). 6th international conference on cellular automata for research and industry, ACRI 2004, Amsterdam, The Netherlands, October 25-27, 2004: (Lecture notes in computer science, 3305), Springer Verlag, (2004) 823-830
6. Neumann J.: Theory of Self-Reproducing Automata, Burks, A. W. (Ed.), Univ. of Illinois Press, Urbana and London (1966)
7. Witten, H. I., Frank, E.: Data Mining: Practical machine learning tools with Java implementations, Morgan Kaufmann, San Francisco (2000)
8. Blake, C., L., Merz, C., J.: UCI Repository of machine learning databases, Irvine, CA: University of California, Department of Information and Computer Science. [http://www.ics.uci.edu/~mlearn/MLRepository.html].
9. Webb, G.: MultiBoosting: A Technique for Combining Boosting and Wagging, Machine Learning, 40(2) (2000) 159-196
10. Quinlan, R.: C4.5: Programs for Machine Learning, Morgan Kaufmann Publishers, San Mateo, CA (1993).

A Gradient BYY Harmony Learning Algorithm on Mixture of Experts for Curve Detection[*]

Zhiwu Lu, Qiansheng Cheng, and Jinwen Ma[**]

Department of Information Science, School of Mathematical Sciences
and LMAM, Peking University, Beijing, 100871, China
jwma@math.pku.edu.cn

Abstract. Curve detection is a basic problem in image processing and has been extensively studied in the literature. However, it remains a difficult problem. In this paper, we study this problem from the Bayesian Ying-Yang (BYY) learning theory via the harmony learning principle on a BYY system with the mixture of experts (ME). A gradient BYY harmony learning algorithm is proposed to detect curves (straight lines or circles) from a binary image. It is demonstrated by the simulation and image experiments that this gradient algorithm can not only detect curves against noise, but also automatically determine the number of straight lines or circles during parameter learning.

1 Introduction

Detecting curves (straight line, circle, ellipse, etc.) is one of the basic problems in image processing and computer vision. In the traditional pattern recognition literature, there are two kinds of studies on this problem. The first kind of studies use the generate-and-test paradigm to sequentially generate hypothetical model positions in the data and test the positions (e.g., [1]). However, this kind of methods are sensitive to noise in the data. The second kind of studies are Hough Transform (HT) variations (e.g.,[2]). They are less sensitive to noise, but their implementations for complex problems suffer from large time and space requirements and from the detection of false positives, although the Random Hough Transform (RHT) [3] and the constrained Hough Transform [4] were proposed to improve these problems. In the field of neural networks, there have also been some proposed learning algorithms that can detect curves in an image (e.g., [5]-[6]).

Proposed in 1995 [7] and systematically developed in past years [8]-[9], Bayesian Ying-Yang (BYY) harmony learning acts as a general statistical learning framework not only for understanding several existing major learning approaches but also for tackling the learning problem with a new learning mechanism that makes model selection automatically during parameter learning [10].

[*] This work was supported by the Natural Science Foundation of China for Projects 60471054 and 40035010
[**] The corresponding author

M. Gallagher, J. Hogan, and F. Maire (Eds.): IDEAL 2005, LNCS 3578, pp. 250–257, 2005.

Specifically, the BYY harmony learning has been already applied to detecting the best number k^* of straight lines via a selection criterion $J(k)$ on the mixture of experts (ME) in [8]. However, the process of evaluating the criterion incurs a large computational cost since we need to repeat the entire parameter learning process at a number of different values of k.

In this paper, we implement the BYY harmony learning on an architecture of the BYY system with the ME via a gradient harmony learning algorithm so that the curve detection can be made automatically during parameter learning on the data from a binary image, which is demonstrated by the simulation and image experiments for both straight lines and circles.

2   Gradient Harmony Learning Algorithm

A BYY system describes each observation $x \in \mathcal{X} \subset R^n$ and its corresponding inner representation $y \in \mathcal{Y} \subset R^m$ via the two types of Bayesian decomposition of the joint density $p(x, y) = p(x)p(y|x)$ and $q(x, y) = q(x|y)q(y)$, being called Yang machine and Ying machine, respectively. Given a data set of x, the aim of learning on a BYY system is to specify all the aspects of $p(y|x), p(x), q(x|y), q(y)$ with a harmony learning principle implemented by maximizing the harmony functional:

$$H(p||q) = \int p(y|x)p(x)ln[q(x|y)q(y)]dxdy - lnz_q, \tag{1}$$

where z_q is a regularization term. The details are referred to [8]-[9].

The BYY system and harmony learning can also be applied to supervised leaning tasks of mapping $x \rightarrow y$ based on a given data set $\{x_t, y_t\}_{t=1}^N$, when a model variable $l = 1, \cdots, k$ is introduced [9]. In this case, x denotes the input patters, l denotes the inner representation of x, and y denotes the output. Likewise, we take into account another Ying-Yang pair:

$$p(x, y, l) = p(l \mid x, y)p(y \mid x)p(x), \qquad q(x, y, l) = q(y \mid x, l)q(x, l), \tag{2}$$

$$q(x, l) = \begin{cases} q(x \mid l)q(l), & \text{for a Ying-dominated system;} \\ p(l \mid x)p(x), & \text{for a Yang-dominated system.} \end{cases} \tag{3}$$

Here, we only consider the Ying-dominated system and specify the BYY system with the following architecture:

$$p(l \mid x, y) = \sum_j P(j \mid x, y)\delta(j - l), \qquad p(y|x) = \begin{cases} \delta(y - y_t), x = x_t \\ \text{not care, otherwise} \end{cases},$$

$$p(x) = \frac{1}{N}\sum_{t=1}^N \delta(x - x_t), \qquad q(l) = \sum_j \alpha_j \delta(j - l),$$

$$\sum_{l=1}^k \alpha_l = 1, \alpha_l \geq 0, \qquad P(l \mid x, y) = q(y \mid x, l)q(x \mid l)\alpha_l / \sum_{j=1}^k q(y \mid x, j)q(x \mid j)\alpha_j,$$

where $\delta(x)$ is the δ-function. Then, we get the following alternative ME model for mapping $x \longrightarrow y$ implied in the BYY system:

$$q(y \mid x) = \sum_l q(y \mid x, l)P(l \mid x), \qquad P(l \mid x) = q(x \mid l)\alpha_l / \sum_{j=1}^{k} q(x \mid j)\alpha_j. \qquad (4)$$

Letting the output of expert l be $f_l(x, \theta_l)$, we have the following expected regression equation:

$$E(y \mid x) = \int y q(y \mid x)dy = \sum_l f_l(x, \theta_l)P(l \mid x). \qquad (5)$$

That is, $E(y \mid x)$ is a sum of the experts weighted by the gate functions $P(l \mid x)$, respectively.

We now ignore the normalization term (i.e., set $z_q = 1$), substitute these components into Eq.(1), and have

$$H(p\|q) = \frac{1}{N} \sum_{t=1}^{N} \sum_{l=1}^{k} \frac{q(y_t \mid x_t, l)q(x_t \mid l)\alpha_l}{\sum_{j=1}^{k} q(y_t \mid x_t, j)q(x_t \mid j)\alpha_j} \ln(q(y_t \mid x_t, l)q(x_t \mid l)\alpha_l), \qquad (6)$$

where

$$q(y \mid x, l) = \frac{1}{\sqrt{2\pi}\tau_l} e^{-\frac{(y - w_l^T x - b_l)^2}{2\tau_l^2}}, \qquad q(x \mid l) = \frac{1}{(2\pi)^{\frac{n}{2}}\sigma_l^n} e^{-\frac{\|x - m_l\|^2}{2\sigma_l^2}},$$

$$\sigma_l = e^{d_l}, \tau_l = e^{r_l}, \quad \alpha_l = e^{\beta_l} / \sum_{j=1}^{k} e^{\beta_j}.$$

By the derivatives of $H(p\|q)$ with respect to the parameters w_l, b_l, r_l, m_l, d_l and β_l, respectively, we have the following gradient learning algorithm:

$$\Delta w_l = \frac{\eta}{N} \sum_{t=1}^{N} U(l \mid x_t, y_t) \frac{(y_t - w_l^T x_t - b_l)}{e^{2r_l}} x_t, \qquad (7)$$

$$\Delta b_l = \frac{\eta}{N} \sum_{t=1}^{N} U(l \mid x_t, y_t) \frac{(y_t - w_l^T x_t - b_l)}{e^{2r_l}}, \qquad (8)$$

$$\Delta r_l = \frac{\eta}{N} \sum_{t=1}^{N} U(l \mid x_t, y_t) \frac{(y_t - w_l^T x_t - b_l)^2 - e^{2r_l}}{e^{2r_l}}, \qquad (9)$$

$$\Delta m_l = \frac{\eta}{N} \sum_{t=1}^{N} U(l \mid x_t, y_t) \frac{(x_t - m_l)}{e^{2d_l}}, \qquad (10)$$

$$\Delta d_l = \frac{\eta}{N} \sum_{t=1}^{N} U(l \mid x_t, y_t) \frac{(x_t - m_l)^2 - ne^{2d_l}}{e^{2d_l}}, \qquad (11)$$

$$\Delta \beta_l = \frac{\eta}{N} \sum_{t=1}^{N} \sum_{j=1}^{k} U(j \mid x_t, y_t)(\delta_{jl} - \alpha_l), \qquad (12)$$

where

$$U(l \mid x_t, y_t) = P(l \mid x_t, y_t)(1 + \sum_{j=1}^{k}(\delta_{jl} - P(j \mid x_t, y_t))\ln(q(y_t \mid x_t, j)q(x_t \mid j)\alpha_j),$$

δ_{jl} is the Kronecker function, and η is the learning rate which is usually a small positive constant.

The above gradient BYY harmony learning algorithm is designed for straight line detection. Here, a set of black points $\{x_t\}_{t=1}^{N}$ ($x_t = [x_{1t}, x_{2t}]^T$) are collected from a binary image with each point being denoted by its coordinates $[x_1, x_2]$. Suppose that $w_l^T x + b_l = 0, l = 1, \cdots, k$ are the parametric equations of all the straight lines to be detected in the image. For each point x, if $w_l^T x + b_l = 0$, we let $L(x) = l$. Then, the mapping between x and y implemented by the BYY system is just $y = w_{L(x)}^T x + b_{L(x)}$. For each point in $\{x_t\}_{t=1}^{N}$, it is supposed to be on some straight line (at most disturbed by some noise) and we always set $y_t = 0$. We train the ME model implied in the BYY system on the sample set $\{x_t, y_t\}_{t=1}^{N}$ via this gradient BYY harmony learning algorithm and lead to the result that each expert will finally fit a straight line $w_l^T x + b_l = 0$ with the mixing proportion α_l representing the proportion of the number of points on this straight line over N, i.e., the number of all the black points in the image.

As for circle detection, we can use $f_l(x, \theta_l) = (x - c_l)^T(x - c_l) - R_l^2, R_l = e^{bl}$ instead of $f_l = w_l x + b_l$ in the above model and derivations for the output of each expert in the ME model. Hence, the gradient BYY harmony learning algorithm is modified by replacing the first three learning rules Eqs (7)-(9) with the following ones:

$$\Delta c_l = -2\frac{\eta}{N}\sum_{t=1}^{N} U(l \mid x_t, y_t)\frac{(y_t - (x_t - c_l)^T(x_t - c_l) + R_l^2)}{e^{2r_l}}(x_t - c_l), \qquad (13)$$

$$\Delta b_l = -2\frac{\eta}{N}\sum_{t=1}^{N} U(l \mid x_t, y_t)\frac{(y_t - (x_t - c_l)^T(x_t - c_l) + R_l^2)}{e^{2r_l}}e^{2b_l}, \qquad (14)$$

$$\Delta r_l = \frac{\eta}{N}\sum_{t=1}^{N} U(l \mid x_t, y_t)\frac{(y_t - (x_t - c_l)^T(x_t - c_l) + R_l^2)^2 - e^{2r_l}}{e^{2r_l}}. \qquad (15)$$

3   Experimental Results

In this section, several experiments are carried out for both straight line and circle detection with the gradient BYY harmony learning algorithm. On the one hand, we make some simulation experiments to demonstrate that the algorithm can detect the straight lines or the circles automatically. On the other hand, we apply the algorithm to the strip line detection and the container recognition.

3.1   Automated Detection on the Straight Lines and Circles

Using k^* to denote the true number of curves in the original image, we implemented the gradient algorithm on data sets from binary images always with

$k \geq k^*$ and $\eta =$0.1. Here, k is the number of experts in the ME model. Moreover, the other parameters were initialized randomly within certain intervals. In all the experiments, the learning was stopped when $|\Delta H| < 10^{-6}$.

During the BYY harmony learning process, some mixing proportions of the experts can be reduced to a very small number. In this case, $(-\ln \alpha_l)$ will become very large. However, as shown in the mathematical expressions of the gradient algorithm, it is always regulated by α_l so that $\alpha_l \ln \alpha_l$ will tend to zero. Therefore, the gradient algorithm will always converge to a reasonable solution and cannot diverge to infinity.

The experimental results on the straight line and circle detections are given in Fig.1 (a), (b), respectively, with the parameters listed in Table 1, 2, respectively. From Fig.1(a) and Table 1, we find that the four straight lines in the binary image are successfully detected, with the mixing proportions of the other four straight lines reduced below 0.001, i.e., these straight lines are extra and should be discarded. That is, the correct number of straight lines have been detected from the image. Likewise, from Fig.1(b) and Table 2, we find that the two circles are successfully detected, while the mixing proportions of the other two extra circles become less than 0.001.

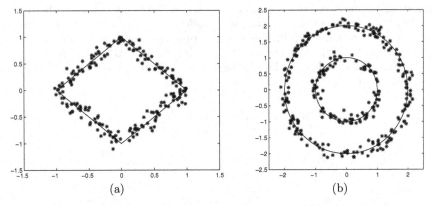

(a)   (b)

Fig. 1. The experiments results of model selection by the gradient BYY harmony learning algorithm. (a). The straight line detection; (b). The circle detection

In the above experiments, since we generally don't know the number of curves(straight lines or circles) in an image, we can overestimate it with k. In this way, k is larger than the number k^* of curves in the image. However, since the BYY harmony learning makes the ME model as simple as possible, the gradient BYY harmony learning algorithm will automatically detect the k^* curves by forcing the mixing proportions of $k - k^*$ experts to be zero or a very small number, i.e., discarding these ones from the image.

The further experiments on the other binary images had been also made successfully for the straight line and circle detection in the similar cases. Especially, as for circle detection, when the two circles are intersectant or separate, the gradient algorithm will converge faster to a reasonable solution. Hence, we can

Table 1. The empirical result of the straight line detection on the data set from Figure 1(a), with k=8 and k*=4

l	α_l	$w_{1l}x_1 + w_{2l}x_2 + b_l = 0$
1	0.0008	$1.2070x_1 - 0.7370x_2 - 0.2235 = 0$
2	0.0007	$-1.0329x_1 + 0.9660x_2 - 0.0455 = 0$
3	0.2319	$-0.9778x_1 - 1.0217x_2 - 0.9814 = 0$
4	0.0009	$-0.8693x_1 + 1.1155x_2 - 0.2002 = 0$
5	0.2369	$1.0181x_1 - 0.9816x_2 + 1.0813 = 0$
6	0.2542	$-0.9597x_1 - 1.0387x_2 + 1.0772 = 0$
7	0.2737	$1.0114x_1 - 0.9885x_2 - 1.0370 = 0$
8	0.0008	$-0.7057x_1 + 1.2256x_2 - 0.2659 = 0$

Table 2. The empirical result of the circle detection on the data set from Fig.1 (b), with k=4 and k*=2

l	α_l	$(x_1 - c_{1l})^2 + (x_2 - c_{2l})^2 = R_l^2$
1	0.3413	$(x_1 - 0.0125)^2 + (x_2 + 0.0097)^2 = 0.9688^2$
2	0.0005	$(x_1 - 0.3559)^2 + (x_2 + 0.5241)^2 = 3.8218^2$
3	0.0005	$(x_1 + 0.1751)^2 + (x_2 + 0.0323)^2 = 14.4621^2$
4	0.6577	$(x_1 - 0.0142)^2 + (x_2 + 0.0016)^2 = 2.1882^2$

conclude that the gradient BYY harmony learning algorithm can automatically determine the number of curves in the image. In addition, it can be observed that this kind of curve detection is noise resistant.

3.2 Strip Line Detection

We further applied the gradient BYY harmony learning algorithm to the strip line detection and make a comparison with the HT method. As shown in Fig. 2(a), the original image contains a thick letter W and we need to identify each thick, linear pattern from it. The algorithm was implemented to solved this strip line detection problem with $k = 8$. As shown in Fig. 2(b), it detects the four strip lines correctly, with the four extra lines being canceled automatically.

As compared with the results of the HT method on this image which are shown in Fig. 2(c)&(d) for processing with and without the preprocessing of edge detection, respectively, the gradient BYY harmony learning algorithm performs much better, since the main skeleton of the original image is not outlined by the HT method.

3.3 Container Recognition

Automated container recognition system is very useful for customs or logistic management. In fact, the gradient BYY harmony learning algorithm can be applied to assisting to construct such a system. Container recognition is usually based on the captured container number located at the back of the container. Specifically, the container shown in Fig.3(a), can be recognized by the numbers "A123456" ,"B456123" and "654321C". The recognition process consists of

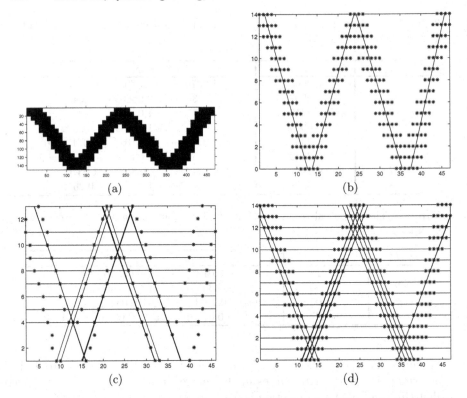

Fig. 2. The experiments results on the strip line detection. (a). The original image; (b). The result of the strip line detection by the gradient BYY harmony learning algorithm; (c). The strip line detection by the HT method with the preprocessing of edge detection; (d). The strip line detection by the HT method without the preprocessing of edge detection

two steps. The first step is to locate and extract each rectangular area in the raw image that contains a series of numbers, while the second step is to actually recognize these numbers via some image processing and pattern recognition techniques.

For the first step, we implemented the gradient BYY harmony learning algorithm to roughly locate the container numbers via detecting the three strip lines through the three series of the numbers, respectively. As shown in Fig.3(b), these three strip lines can locate the series of numbers very well. Based on the detected strip lines, we can extract the rectangular areas of the numbers from the raw image. Finally, the numbers can be subsequently recognized via some image processing and pattern recognition techniques.

4   Conclusions

We have investigated the curve detection problem from the BYY harmony learning system and theory. The straight line and circle detections from a binary im-

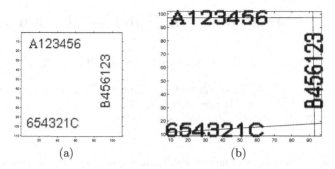

Fig. 3. The experiments results on container recognition. (a). The original image; (b). The result of the gradient BYY harmony learning algorithm

age have been converted to a supervised learning task on the mixture of experts implied in a BYY system. In help of a gradient learning algorithm derived, a number of experiments have demonstrated that the number of straight lines or circles can be correctly detected automatically during parameter learning with a good estimation of each curve against noise.

References

1. M. A. Fisher and R. C. Bolles, "Random sample consensus: a paradigm for model fitting with applications to image analysis and automated cartography," *Communications of the ACM*, 24: 381-396, 1981.
2. D. Ballard, "Generalizing the Hough transform to detect arbitrary shapes," *Pattern Recognition*, 13(2): 111-122, 1981.
3. L. Xu, E. Oja, and P. Kultanen, "A new curve detection method: randomized Hough transform (RHT)," *Pattern Recognition Letter*, 11: 331-338, 1990.
4. C. F. Olson, "Constrained Hough transform for curve detection," *Computer Vision and Image Understanding*, 73(3): 329-345, 1999.
5. L. Xu, A. Krzyak, and E. Oja, "Rival penalized competitive learning for clustering analysis, RBF net, and curve detection," *IEEE Trans. on Neural Networks*, 4(4): 636-649, 1993.
6. Z. Y. Liu, K. C. Chiu, and L. Xu, "Strip line detection and thinning by RPCL-based local PCA," *Pattern Recognition Letters*, 24: 2335-2344, 2003.
7. L. Xu, "Ying-Yang machine: a Bayesian-Kullback scheme for unified learnings and new results on vector quantization," *Proc. 1995 Int. Conf. on Neural Information Processing (ICONIP'95)*, 30 October-3 November 1995, vol.2, pp. 977-988.
8. L. Xu, "RBF nets, mixture experts, and Bayesian Ying-Yang learning," *Neurocomputing,* 19: 223-257, 1998.
9. L. Xu, "BYY harmony learning, structural RPCL, and topological self-organzing on mixture modes," *Neural Networks*, 15: 1231-1237, 2002.
10. J. Ma, T. Wang, and L. Xu, "A gradient BYY harmony learning rule on Gaussian mixture with automated model selection," *Neurocomputing*, 56: 481-487, 2004.

A Novel Anomaly Detection Using Small Training Sets

Qingbo Yin, Liran Shen, Rubo Zhang, and Xueyao Li

College Of Computer Science & Technology, Harbin Engineering University,
Harbin 150001, P.R. China
yinqingbo@hrbeu.edu.cn, yinq2003@eyou.com

Abstract. Anomaly detection is an essential component of the protection mechanism against novel attacks. Traditional methods need very large volume of purely training dataset, which is expensive to classify it manually. A new method for anomaly intrusion detection is proposed based on supervised clustering and Markov chain model, which is designed to train from a small set of normal data. After short system call sequences are clustered, Markov chain is used to learn the relationship among these clusters and classify the normal or abnormal. The observed behavior of the system is analyzed to infer the probability that the Markov chain of the norm profile supports the observed behavior. Markov information source entropy and condition entropy are used to select parameters. The experiments have showed that the method is effective to detect anomalistic behaviors, and enjoys better generalization ability when a small number of training dataset is used only.

1 Introduction

There are two general approaches to intrusion detection: misuse detection and anomaly detection. Misuse detection via signature verification compares a user's activities with the known signatures of attackers. While misuse detection is useful for finding known intrusion types, it cannot detect novel attacks. Anomaly detection identifies activities that deviate from established statistical patterns for users, systems or networks. In spite of their capability of detecting unknown attacks, anomaly detection systems suffer from high false alarm rate when normal user profiles and system or network behavior vary widely.

Traditional anomaly detection approaches build models of normal data and detect deviation from the normal model in observed data [1]. These methods need large numbers of purely normal data from which they train their model. In practice, it is impossible that large number of purely normal data readily available were achieved. But, it is sure that a small number of purely train dataset can be obtained. To solve this difficulty, we need a technique that enjoys the better generalization ability when a small number of train dataset are used only.

Since many intrusions are composed of a series of related computer actions, the temporal profile of action sequence is important to detect intrusions [2]. In the past, we dealt with short system call sequences as features. But the relative location between the features wasn't used. So the capability of the past methods is limited when we only use the limited data to train. Now, we can look upon the traces of system call as consecutive logic actions. If we consider the short system call sequence is a computer action, an action space (or feature space) is made up of the actions. When the action space is partitioned into subspaces or clusters, the relationship of clusters from

M. Gallagher, J. Hogan, and F. Maire (Eds.): IDEAL 2005, LNCS 3578, pp. 258–263, 2005.

the transition of short system call sequences will be found. So we can use a little training data to achieve a concise model.

In this paper, a new method based on supervised clustering and Markov chain model (SCMC) is proposed to learn program behavior. After the short system call sequences are clustered, Markov chain (MC) is used to learn the relationship of the clusters from the transition of short system call sequences and classify the normal or abnormal. The observed behavior of the system is analyzed to infer the probability that the Markov chain of the norm profile supports the observed behavior. Markov information source entropy (MISE) and condition entropy (CE) are used to select parameters. The experiments show this method is effective and efficient.

2 Anomaly Detection Method

2.1 Notations

Let Σ denote the set of system call. A trace is simply a sequence of system call generated by a process. A trace over Σ is a finite sequence of system call. The set of finite traces over Σ is denoted by $\Sigma*$, and the set of traces of length n is denoted by Σ_n. Let O_{tr} denote the set of the training traces, $O_{tr} \subseteq \Sigma*$; O_{te} denote the set of the testing traces. Given a trace $\alpha \in \Sigma*$, $|\alpha|$ denotes the length of the trace; α_i and $\alpha[i]$ denote the prefix consisting of the first i system call and the i th system call respectively.

2.2 Feature Extractions and Clustering

A sliding window $w(k)$ of size k is used to run across the sample $\alpha \in O_{tr}$, and move one symbol at one time:

$$x_i = \alpha(k+i) \cdot w(k) \tag{1}$$

The way in which the set of training vector $X = \{x_i, i = 1,2,\cdots\}$ can be clustered into a set of clusters $Y = \{y_i, i = 1,\cdots,m\}$, is the following:

Step 1. Initialization: arbitrarily   choose m vector   out   of   training   set $X = \{x_i, i = 1,2,\cdots\}$ as the initial cluster center of the clustering space.

Step 2. Nearest-neighbor search: for each train vector, find the correct cluster in the current $Y = \{y_i, i = 1,\cdots,m\}$, which is closest in term of Euclidean distance, and assign that vector to the corresponding cluster.

Step 3. Centroid update: update the each cluster center c_j to get the best set of centroids.

$$c_j = \frac{1}{|y_j|} \sum_{x_i \in y_j} (x_i), j = 1,\cdots,m \tag{2}$$

Step 4.Iterate step 2 and 3 until the average distortion E falls below a present threshold, $\varepsilon = 0.0001$.

$$E = \sum_{j=1}^{m} \sum_{x_i \in y_j} d(x_i, c_j) \tag{3}$$

2.3   Constructing Markov Chains Model of the Clusters

Define $Y = \{y_i, i=1, \cdots; m\}$, as the state space S_{MC} of MC, $S_{MC} \subseteq R^k$. The transition probability matrix P and the initial probability distribution π of a stationary MC can be learned from the observations of the system state in the past. In the paper, the frequencies of the states transition are used to approximate the transition probabilities. Provided with the observations of the system state X_0, $X_1, X_2, \ldots, X_{n-1}$ at time $t = 0, \cdots, n-1$, the transition probability matrix can be calculated by the following procedure.

$$p_{ij} = \frac{N_{ij}}{N_{i\cdot}}, \ i \neq 0, j \neq 0 \text{ and } \sum_{j \neq 0} p_{ij} = 1 \tag{4}$$

Where N_{ij} is the number of observation pairs X_t and X_{t+1} with X_t in state i and X_{t+1} in state j; N_i is the number of observation pairs X_t and X_{t+1} with X_t in state i and X_{t+1} in any one of the states.

By observation, it can be found out that the initial state is fixed if only the size k is selected correctly. Then the initial probability distribution is defined as $\pi = [1, 0, \cdots, 0]$.

2.4   Anomaly Detection

Anomaly detection matches current behavior against the normal behavior models and calculates the probability, which it is generated out of each model. The probability that the l consecutive states before time t occurs in the context of the stationary MC is computed as follows:

Step 1.Extracting k system calls as vector x_i, and cluster as the state of MC.

$$S_i = \arg \min_{1 \leq j \leq m} d(x_i, y_j) \tag{5}$$

Step 2.Calculating the probability of l consecutive states $P_t(S_{t-l+1}, \cdots, S_t)$.

$$P_t(S_{t-l+1}, \cdots, S_t) = \pi_{S_{t-l+1}} \prod_{i=t-l+1}^{l} p_{S_{i-1}S_i} \tag{6}$$

A sequence of states from intrusive activities is expected to receive a low probability of support from the Markov model of the norm profile.

3 Parameter Determination

The correct selection of parameter k and l is a key problem in this method. Entropy was used to describe the characteristics of a data set and justify the performance of the models. So the k order MISE H_{k+1} is used to measure the appropriate k.

$$H_{k+1} = -\sum_{i=1}^{m}\sum_{j=1}^{m} p(s_i)p(s_j|s_i)\log(s_j|s_i) \tag{7}$$

CE can be used as a criterion of regularity of sequential dependencies [3]. Then it is used to estimate the l as follows:

$$\Delta H = \frac{H(s_{l+1}/s_1\cdots s_l) - H(s_l/s_1\cdots s_{l-1})}{H(s_l/s_1\cdots s_{l-1})} \tag{8}$$

If ΔH is smaller than a given threshold ξ, then the shorter l is better.

4 Experiments

The system call dataset used in experiments have been obtained from the University of New Mexico. The 10% of normal data was used for training, and the remaining 90% of normal data as well as the intrusion data for testing.

For performance evaluation and comparing with other methods, three measures were defined, namely, true positive rate (TPR), False positive rate (FPR) and Sub-False positive rate (SFPR):

$$TPR = \frac{\text{number of intrusive testing traces detected as intrusive}}{\text{number of intrusive traces in testing set}}$$

$$FPR = \frac{\text{number of normal testing traces as intrusive}}{\text{number of normal trasces in testing set}}$$

$$SFPR = \frac{\text{number of normal sub-sequences as intrusive}}{\text{number of normal sub-sequences in testing set}}$$

Fig. 1 shows the correct smallest value of k is 5 because MISE varies very small after it. From fig 2, it can be found that there are some key points such as 4, 8, 10 that are suitable to the value of l.

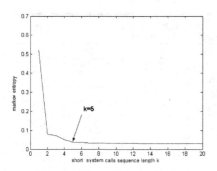

Fig. 1. MISE of training data

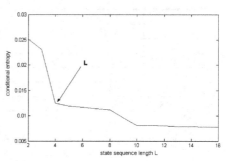

Fig. 2. Conditional entropy of the state sequence

From Table 1, it is found out that when $m = 128$, the best performance can be obtained if $k = 5$ and $l = 6$.

Table 1. The result when $k = 5$ and $l = 6$

	m=64	m=128	m=256
TPR	100%	100%	100%
FPR	171/3000	21/3000	93/3000

From fig 3, when TPR=100, FPR and SFPR have the same trend that is monotony decreasing if the number of train sequences is over 80. So we can prefer that when the number of train sequences add up to 80, the method proposed in this paper have taken enough training data.

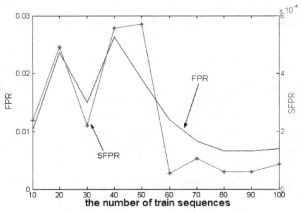

Fig. 3. The relationship of FPR and SFPR and the number of train sequences

In Table 2, the experiments results of SCMC are compared with those of S. Mukkamala[4][5], Warrender and Forrest[1], Yao[6], Shah[7], Yeung[8], Hu[9] and others. The method proposed in this paper enjoys better generalization ability when a small number of training dataset is used.

Table 2. Comparing with other methods

	Training set		Testing set		TPR	FPR
	Normal	Abnormal	Normal	Abnormal		
Stide	805	—	4468	2002	96.9%	—
t-Stide	805	—	4468	2002	96.9%	—
RIPPER	805	—	4468	2002	95.3%	—
HMM	805	—	4468	2002	96.9%	—
CTBIDS	162	—	251	38	97.37%	3.9%
SVM /RSVM	300	28	5285	22	100%	14.2% /3%
Fuzzy Clustering	80%		20%		100%	46.5%
SCMC	80	0	3000	1000	100%	0.67%

5 Conclusion

A novel method for anomaly intrusion detection is proposed based on supervised clustering and Markov chain model. After the short system call sequences are clustered, Markov chain is used to learn the relationship among these clusters and classify the normal or abnormal. Markov information source entropy and condition entropy are used to select parameters. The relative locations of the short system call sequences are analyzed. So when a small number of training dataset is used only, SCMC enjoys better generalization ability. The experiments show this method is effective and efficient.

Acknowledgment

This work reported in this paper has been supported in part by the Basic Research Fund Project (HEUF04084) of Harbin Engineering University.

References

1. Warrender. C, Forrest. S and Pearlmutter. B.: Detecting Intrusion Using System Calls: Alternative Data Models. IEEE Symposium on Security and Privacy, May (1999)
2. Lane, T. and Brodley, C. E.: Temporal sequence learning and data reduction for anomaly detection. ACM Transactions on Information and System Security, vol. 2, (1999) 295-331
3. Lee W, Dong X.: Information-Theoretic measures for anomaly detection. Proceedings of the 2001 IEEE Symposium on Security and Privacy. Oakland, CA (2001) 130-143
4. S. Mukkamala, G. Janowski, A. H. Sung. Intrusion Detection Using Neural Networks and Support Vector Machines. Proceedings of IEEE IJCNN, (2002) 1702-1707
5. S. Mukkamala, G. I. Janoski, and A. H. Sung. Intrusion Detection Using Support Vector Machines. Proceedings of the High Performance Computing Symposium - HPC 2002, San Diego, April (2002) 178-183
6. Yao Lihong, Zi Xiaocao, Huang Hao, Mao Bing, Xie Li. Research of system call based intrusion detection. ACTA ELECTRONICA SINICA, Vol.31. (2003) 1134-1137
7. Hiren Shah, Jeffrey Undercoffer, Dr. Anupam Joshi.: Fuzzy Clustering for Intrusion Detection. Proceedings of the 12th IEEE International Conference on Fuzzy Systems, April 2003
8. Dit-Yan Yeung, Yuxin Ding.: Host-based intrusion detection using dynamic and static behavioral models. Pattern Recognition, Vol.36 (2003) 229-243
9. Wenjie Hu, Yihua Liao, and V. Rao Vemuri.: Robust Support Vector Machines for Anamoly Detection in Computer Security. International Conference on Machine Learning, Los Angeles, CA, July (2003)

Induction of Linear Decision Trees with Real-Coded Genetic Algorithms and k-D Trees

Sai-cheong Ng and Kwong-sak Leung

The Chinese University of Hong Kong
nelson@alumni.cuhk.net, ksleung@cse.cuhk.edu.hk

Abstract. Although genetic algorithm-based decision tree algorithms are applied successfully in various classification tasks, their execution times are quite long on large datasets. A novel decision tree algorithm, called Real-Coded Genetic Algorithm-based Linear Decision Tree Algorithm with k-D Trees (RCGA-based LDT with kDT), is proposed. In the proposed algorithm, a k-D tree is built when a new node of a linear decision tree is created. The use of k-D trees speeds up the construction of linear decision trees without sacrificing the quality of the constructed decision trees.

1   Introduction

Decision trees are tree structures which classify an input sample into one of its possible categories. At each non-leaf node, the associated decision function is used to select the appropriate child node. In univariate decision trees, the decision function depends on only one of the input attributes. CART [2] and C4.5 [12] are example univariate decision tree algorithms. In linear decision trees, the decision function is a linear combination of input attributes, which is equivalent to a half-plane in the attribute space. CART-LC [2], OC1 [11], LMDT [3] and Ltree [6] are example linear decision tree algorithms.

Genetic algorithms (GAs) were introduced by Holland [9]. GAs are stochastic optimization algorithms inspired by the principles of natural selection and genetics. A population of chromosomes is maintained. Each chromosome is either a binary string or a vector of real numbers. It represents a candidate solution to a problem. A fitness function is used to evaluate the quality of the solution represented by each chromosome. Offspring chromosomes are generated using selection, mutation and recombination operators.

A k-D tree [1] recursively subdivides a d-dimensional space into 2 subspaces. There are 2 children at each non-leaf node of a k-D tree. One of the attributes is used to divide a d-dimensional space at each non-leaf node.

In univariate decision tree algorithms, large decision trees with poor generalization may be constructed on datasets whose input attributes are correlated. Linear decision tree algorithms are usually more suitable for these datasets. The problem of finding the optimal linear decision tree is an NP-complete problem [7]. In BTGA [5] and OC1-GA [4], GAs are applied to find the optimal half-plane

M. Gallagher, J. Hogan, and F. Maire (Eds.): IDEAL 2005, LNCS 3578, pp. 264–271, 2005.

at each internal node. Although these GA-based linear decision tree algorithms have better scalability to the dimensionality of a dataset [4], their execution times are quite long on a large dataset. A novel decision tree algorithm, called Genetic Algorithm-based Linear Decision Tree Algorithm with k-D Trees (RCGA-based LDT with kDT), is proposed. In the proposed algorithm, GAs are employed to search for the optimal half-plane at each internal node. The proposed algorithm is a real-coded genetic algorithm (RCGA), using a vector of real numbers to represent a half-plane because the search space is multidimensional and continuous. k-D trees can be applied to speed up the construction of linear decision trees without sacrificing the quality of the constructed decision trees.

The rest of the paper is organized as follows. In section 2, the algorithm to build a linear decision tree is discussed. In section 3, we describe how to find the optimal half-plane at each internal node using GAs. In section 4, we discuss how to build a linear decision tree with the aid of k-D trees. In section 5, the performance of RCGA-based LDT with kDT was evaluated and compared. A conclusion is given in the last section.

2   Induction of Linear Decision Trees

Before a linear decision tree is constructed, a set of input samples is divided into two disjoint subsets, called training set and testing set. The training set is applied to construct a decision tree. A constructed decision tree should minimize the number of misclassifications on the testing set, instead of the training set. The following shows the algorithm of the procedure `createLDT()`. The procedure `createLDT()` outlines the steps to create a new node and its descendants of an RCGA-based LDT with kDT. To construct an RCGA-based LDT with kDT, the procedure `createLDT()` accepts the training set as the parameter.

- PROCEDURE `createLDT`
- INPUT A set S_h of training samples
- OUTPUT A new node N_h

1. IF the training samples in the set S_h belong to one single class or the depth of the node N_h from the root is greater than or equal to d_0, THEN N_h is declared as a leaf node and go to step 6.
2. Construct a k-D tree using the set S_h.
3. Find the optimal half-plane $\sum_{i=1}^{d} w'_i x_i > w'_0$, where w'_i, $i = 1, 2..., d$, is the coefficient of x_i and w'_0 is the constant term, using GAs such that the impurity reduction is maximized after dividing the set S_h into 2 disjoint subsets R'_h and L'_h.
4. IF the impurity reduction is less than g_0, THEN N_h is declared as a leaf node and go to step 6.
5. Invoke `createLDT(`R'_h`)` and `createLDT(`L'_h`)`, and skip step 6.
6. Determine the class label associated with the node N_h.

3 Evolving the Optimal Half-Plane Using Genetic Algorithms

The following outlines the steps to evolve the optimal half-plane using a GA after a new node N_h of a linear decision tree is created:

1. Initialize a population P of L chromosomes.
2. Evaluate the fitness values of all chromosomes in P.
3. Let T be the number of generations, τ be the current generation number.
4. FOR $\tau = 1$ TO T
   (a) Let $\mathbf{w_{best}}$ be the best chromosome in P.
   (b) Select L chromosomes from P (with replacement) using the roulette wheel selection method. The selected chromosomes are replicated to the mating pool M.
   (c) The mating pool M undergoes arithmetical crossover [8] and another population M' is generated.
   (d) The population M' undergoes mutation (see Section 3.3) and another population M'' is generated.
   (e) Evaluate the fitness values of all chromosomes in M''.
   (f) Let $\mathbf{w_{worst}}$ be the worst chromosome in M''.
   (g) Set $P = M'' \setminus \{\mathbf{w_{worst}}\} \cup \{\mathbf{w_{best}}\}$.
5. The chromosome $\mathbf{w_{best}}$ is chosen to divide the set S_h of training samples arriving at the node N_h into two disjoint subsets.

An elitist strategy is employed to ensure the best chromosome in the current generation is preserved in the next generation.

3.1 Population Initialization

Each chromosome is a $(d+1)$-dimensional vector of real numbers. A chromosome $\mathbf{w} = (w_0, w_1, w_2..., w_d)$ represents the following half-plane:

$$w_1 x_1 + w_2 x_2 + ... + w_d x_d > w_0 \quad \text{such that} \quad w_1^2 + w_2^2 + ... + w_d^2 = 1 \quad (1)$$

where w_i, $i = 1, 2..., d$, is the coefficient of x_i and w_0 is a real constant. Each candidate half-plane is a perpendicular bisector between a pair of randomly selected training samples of two different classes.

3.2 Fitness Evaluation

The fitness value of each chromosome equals the impurity reduction when the corresponding half-plane is applied to divide a set of training samples into two disjoint subsets. In this paper, the impurity of a set of samples is measured by entropy. Suppose S is the set of training samples arriving at a node of a decision tree. The entropy of the set S is defined as:

$$E(S) = -p_1 \log_2 p_1 - p_2 \log_2 p_2 - ... - p_C \log_2 p_C \quad (2)$$

where C is the number of classes and p_i, $i = 1, 2..., C$, is the ratio of the number of training samples of the set S for class i to that of the set S. Suppose S_R is the set of training samples arriving at node N_h such that (1) is satisfied, the fitness value of the corresponding chromosome is given by:

$$E(S) - \frac{|S_R|}{|S|} \times E(S_R) - \frac{|S \setminus S_R|}{|S|} \times E(S \setminus S_R) \tag{3}$$

The details of finding the number of training samples of the set S_R for each class will be described in section 4.

3.3   Mutation

When a chromosome $\mathbf{w} = (w_0, w_1, w_2..., w_d)$ representing the half-plane in (1) undergoes mutation, the value of w_i, $i = 0, 1, 2..., d$, is modified with a fixed probability p_m. When the value of w_i, $i = 1, 2..., d$, is mutated, it is set to zero or modified by Gaussian mutation [10]. When the value of w_0 is mutated, it is modified by Gaussian mutation.

4   Induction of Linear Decision Trees Using k-D Trees

In this paper, k-D trees are applied to speed up the induction of a linear decision tree. After a new node N_h of a linear decision tree is created, a k-D tree is constructed before the optimal half-plane is found. Each node of a k-D tree store the statistics of a subset of training samples. Suppose the node N_Q of a k-D tree stores the statistics of the set $S_Q \subseteq S_h$ of training samples. Here are the characteristics of the node N_Q:

- The extreme values (the maximum and the minimum values) of each input attribute of the set S_Q is stored.
- The number of training samples of the set S_Q for each class is stored.
- If N_Q is the root node of a k-D tree, the statistics of the set S_h are stored. Otherwise N_Q has two child nodes, each of which stores the statistics of one of the two disjoint subsets of the set S_Q.
- The set S_Q is not necessarily homogeneous.

In subsection 3.2, the fitness value of the chromosome representing the half-plane in (1) depends on the number of training samples satisfying (1) for each class. Intuitively, the number of training samples satisfying (1) for each class can be evaluated by considering whether each training sample lies on the positive side of the half-plane. Alternatively, a k-D tree can be constructed so that it is necessary to consider a subset of training samples only. At each node of a k-D tree, the extreme values of each input attribute of a subset of training samples are stored. The smallest hyperrectangle containing this subset can be determined using the extreme values of each input attribute. If the whole hyperrectangle lies on the positive side (or the negative side) of the half-plane, all the training samples inside the hyperrectangle must also lie on the positive side (or the negative side) of the half-plane. The computational time can be greatly reduced if the hyperrectangle contains a sufficient number of training samples.

The following shows the algorithm of the procedure `createKDT()`, which outlines the steps of creating a new node (and the descendants) of a k-D tree. The procedure `createKDT(`$S_h, 0$`)` is invoked to construct a k-D tree.

- PROCEDURE `createKDT`
- INPUTS
  - A set of training samples $S_Q = \{\mathbf{x}_Q^{(1)}, \mathbf{x}_Q^{(2)}..., \mathbf{x}_Q^{(|S_Q|)}\}$, where $\mathbf{x}_Q^{(i)} = (x_{Q,1}^{(i)}, x_{Q,2}^{(i)}..., x_{Q,d}^{(i)}, c_Q^{(i)})^T$, $i = 1, 2..., |S_Q|$, $x_{Q,1}^{(i)}, x_{Q,2}^{(i)}..., x_{Q,d}^{(i)}$, are the input attributes and $c_Q^{(i)}$ is the class label of the sample $\mathbf{x}_Q^{(i)}$.
  - An integer $k' \in \{1..., d\}$.
- OUTPUT A pointer to a new node N_Q of a k-D tree.

1. Initialize the vector $\mathbf{y}_Q = (y_{Q,1}, y_{Q,2}..., y_{Q,d})$, where $y_{Q,i}$, $i = 1, 2..., d$, is the minimum value of the ith input attribute of the set S_Q of training samples.
2. Initialize the vector $\mathbf{z}_Q = (z_{Q,1}, z_{Q,2}..., z_{Q,d})$, where $z_{Q,i}$, $i = 1, 2..., d$, is the maximum value of the ith input attribute of the set S_Q of training samples.
3. IF $|S_Q| < n_Q$ OR $\mathbf{y}_Q = \mathbf{z}_Q$, THEN N_Q is declared as a leaf node and return the pointer to N_Q.
4. Set $k = k' + 1$ such that the kth input attribute is used to partition the set S_Q into 2 disjoint subsets.
5. WHILE $y_{Q,k} = z_{Q,k}$
   Set $k = ((k + 1) \bmod d) + 1$.
6. Set $\gamma = \frac{1}{|S_Q|} \sum_{j=1}^{|S_Q|} x_{Q,k}^{(j)}$
7. Set $X_{Q,L} = X_{Q,R} = \phi$
8. FOR $i = 1$ TO $|S_Q|$ DO
   IF $x_{Q,k}^{(i)} \leq \gamma$, THEN Set $X_{Q,L} = X_{Q,L} \cup \{\mathbf{x}_Q^{(i)}\}$
   ELSE Set $X_{Q,R} = X_{Q,R} \cup \{\mathbf{x}_Q^{(i)}\}$
9. Set $\Gamma_{Q,L} = $ `createKDT(`$X_{Q,L}, k$`)` and $\Gamma_{Q,R} = $ `createKDT(`$X_{Q,R}, k$`)`, where $\Gamma_{Q,L}$ and $\Gamma_{Q,R}$ are pointers to the child nodes of N_Q.

The following shows the algorithm of the procedure `processKDT()`, which outlines the steps to evaluate the number of training samples satisfying the half-plane in (1) for each class.

- PROCEDURE `processKDT`
- INPUTS
  1. A node N_Q of a k-D tree.
  2. A set of training samples $S_Q = \{\mathbf{x}_Q^{(1)}, \mathbf{x}_Q^{(2)}..., \mathbf{x}_Q^{(|S_Q|)}\}$, where $\mathbf{x}_Q^{(i)} = (x_{Q,1}^{(i)}, x_{Q,2}^{(i)}..., x_{Q,d}^{(i)}, c_Q^{(i)})^T$, $i = 1, 2..., |S_Q|$, $x_{Q,1}^{(i)}, x_{Q,2}^{(i)}..., x_{Q,d}^{(i)}$ are the input attributes and $c_Q^{(i)}$ is the class label of the sample $\mathbf{x}_Q^{(i)}$.
  3. A $(d+1)$-dimensional vector $\mathbf{w} = (w_0, w_1, ..., w_d)^T$ which represents the half-plane in (1).

- INPUT/OUTPUT
  A C-dimensional vector $\mathbf{r_h} = (r_{h,1}, r_{h,2}..., r_{h,C})$, where $r_{h,i}$, $i = 1, 2..., C$, is the number of training samples for class i arriving at a node of a decision tree such that (1) is satisfied and C is the number of possible classes.

1. If the node N_Q is the root node of a k-D tree, set $r_{h,i} = 0$, $i = 1, 2..., C$.
2. IF $|S_Q| \leq 2$, THEN
   (a) FOR $i = 1$ TO $|S_Q|$ DO
       IF $\sum_{j=1}^{d} w_j x_{Q,j}^{(i)} > w_0$, THEN set $r_{h,c_Q^{(i)}} = r_{h,c_Q^{(i)}} + 1$.
   (b) Return.
3. Initialize the set $S_{Q,i}$, $i = 1, 2, ..., C$, of training samples for class i in the set S_Q.
4. Define $y_{Q,i}$ and $z_{Q,i}$, $i = 1, 2..., d$ as the minimum and the maximum values of the ith input attribute of the set S_Q respectively.
5. Initialize the hyperrectangle $H_Q = [y_{Q,1}, z_{Q,1}] \times [y_{Q,2}, z_{Q,2}] \times ... \times [y_{Q,d}, z_{Q,d}]$.
6. IF H_Q lies on the positive side of the half-plane in (1) (i.e. $\sum_{j=1}^{d}[y_{Q,j}(|w_j| + w_j) + z_{Q,j}(|w_j| - w_j)] > 2w_0$), THEN set $r_{h,i} = r_{h,i} + |S_{Q,i}|$, $i = 1, 2, ..., C$
   ELSE IF the half-plane in (1) cuts the hyperrectangle H_Q (i.e. $\sum_{j=1}^{d}[y_{Q,j}(|w_j| - w_j) + z_{Q,j}(|w_j| + w_j)] > 2w_0$), THEN
   IF the node N_Q is a non-leaf node, THEN
   (a) Let $X_{Q,L}$ and $X_{Q,R}$ be the sets of training samples arriving at the left and the right child nodes of the node N_Q respectively.
   (b) Let $\Gamma_{Q,L}$ and $\Gamma_{Q,R}$ be the pointers to the child nodes of the node N_Q.
   (c) Invoke the procedure processKDT$(\Gamma_{Q,L}, X_{Q,L}, \mathbf{w}, \mathbf{r_h})$ and the procedure processKDT$(\Gamma_{Q,R}, X_{Q,R}, \mathbf{w}, \mathbf{r_h})$.
   ELSE FOR $i = 1$ TO $|S_Q|$ DO
   IF $\sum_{j=1}^{d} w_j x_{Q,j}^{(i)} > w_0$, THEN set $r_{h,c_Q^{(i)}} = r_{h,c_Q^{(i)}} + 1$.

5   Performance Evaluation

In this section, the performance of the proposed algorithm is evaluated in terms of validation accuracy and execution time. A variant of the proposed algorithm, called RCGA-based LDT, is also included for performance comparison in this section. RCGA-based LDT is very similar to RCGA-based LDT with kDT, except that no k-D tree is applied to facilitate the construction of linear decision trees. Four datasets were chosen for performance comparison. All the experiments were executed on an Intel P4 2.4GHz machine under Linux platform.

The first dataset, called ADS1, is an artificial dataset with 1000 samples. ADS1 is a three-class problem. Two straight lines are used to separate the samples into three classes. Each sample is a two-dimensional vector (x_1, x_2), where $x_1, x_2 \in [0, 1000]$. If a sample satisfies (4), it is labeled as class 1. If a sample violates (4) but satisfies (5), it is labeled as class 2. If a sample satisfies neither (4) nor (5), it is labeled as class 3.

$$-0.1x_1 + 0.9x_2 > 400 \tag{4}$$
$$0.2x_1 - 0.8x_2 < 350 \tag{5}$$

ADS2 and ADS3, are artificial datasets with 10,000 and 100,000 samples respectively. The class boundaries of ADS2 and ADS3 are identical to that of ADS1.

A real life dataset, called SPOT, is a satellite image taken by SPOT satellite. 88,992 pixels of the satellite image are labeled with one of the twelve possible classes. Each labeled pixel has five numeric input attributes, including the intensities of four spectral bands and the height above the sea level.

The validation accuracy of RCGA-based LDT with kDT is compared with that of various decision tree algorithms, including C4.5, OC1, Ltree, OC1-GA, OC1-ES [4], BTGA and RCGA-based LDT. The number of generations and the population size for OC1-GA, BTGA, RCGA-based LDT and RCGA-based LDT with kDT are 500 and 20 respectively. The parameters for each decision tree algorithm (except number of generations and population size, if applicable) are adjusted so as to maximize its validation accuracy.

Table 1. Comparison of Validation Accuracies (%) of Various Decision Tree Algorithms

Algorithm	ADS1	ADS2	ADS3	SPOT
C4.5	96.4 ± 0.7	98.74 ± 0.12	99.632 ± 0.018	89.17 ± 0.09
OC1	98.1 ± 0.6	99.59 ± 0.13	99.750 ± 0.013	88.47 ± 0.13
Ltree	98.3 ± 0.3	98.76 ± 0.25	99.131 ± 0.079	89.16 ± 0.07
OC1-GA	98.4 ± 0.6	99.31 ± 0.13	99.680 ± 0.017	88.80 ± 0.09
OC1-ES	98.6 ± 0.5	99.60 ± 0.13	99.710 ± 0.026	88.75 ± 0.09
BTGA	99.3 ± 0.3	99.81 ± 0.06	99.900 ± 0.026	87.61 ± 0.64
RCGA-based LDT	99.4 ± 0.3	99.88 ± 0.03	99.924 ± 0.004	89.43 ± 0.14
RCGA-based LDT with kDT	99.4 ± 0.3	99.88 ± 0.03	99.924 ± 0.004	89.43 ± 0.14

Table 1 shows the average and the standard deviation of the validation accuracies of various decision tree algorithms on ADS1, ADS2, ADS3 and SPOT when 2-fold cross-validation is applied over 10 runs. According to the one-sided t-tests, RCGA-based LDT and RCGA-based LDT with kDT outperform the others on all the datasets in terms of validation accuracy at 95% confidence interval.

Since RCGA-based LDT and RCGA-based LDT with kDT outperform the others in terms of validation accuracy, their execution times were compared. Table 2 shows their execution times on ADS1, ADS2, ADS3 and SPOT when 2-fold cross-validation is applied over 10 runs.

RCGA-based LDT with kDT run faster than RCGA-based LDT on all the datasets. The execution times on the artificial datasets show that the speed-up of RCGA-based LDT with kDT with respect to RCGA-based LDT increases as the size of a dataset increases.

6   Conclusion

In this paper, a novel decision tree algorithm, where a k-D tree is constructed before searching for the optimal linear decision function at each internal node

Table 2. Comparison of Execution Times (in seconds) of RCGA-based LDT and RCGA-based LDT with kDT

Dataset	RCGA-based LDT	RCGA-based LDT with kDT
ADS1	2.43 ± 0.02	0.57 ± 0.01
ADS2	23.43 ± 0.16	2.39 ± 0.18
ADS3	246.8 ± 0.8	11.47 ± 0.13
SPOT	1903.3 ± 32.4	760.7 ± 5.9

of a decision tree, is introduced. The proposed algorithm constructs a better linear decision tree when compared with other linear decision tree algorithms. The proposed algorithm uses k-D trees to speed up the construction of linear decision trees without sacrificing the quality of the constructed decision trees.

References

1. Bentley, J. L.: Multidimensional Binary Search Trees Used for Associative Searching. Communications of the ACM **18(9)** (1975) 509–517
2. Breiman, L., Friedman, J. H., Olshen, R. A., Stone, C.J.: Classification and Regression Trees. Wadsworth International Group (1984)
3. Brodley, C. E., Utgoff, P. E.: Multivariate Decision Trees. **UM-CS-1992-083** (1992)
4. Cantú-Paz, E., Kamath, C.,: Inducing Oblique Decision Trees with Evolutionary Algorithms. IEEE Transactions on Evolutionary Computation **7(1)** (2003) 54–68
5. Chai, B. B., Huang T., Zhuang, X., Zhao, Y., Sklansky, J.: Piecewise Linear Classifiers using Binary Tree Structure and Genetic Algorithm. Pattern Recognition **29(11)** (1996) 1905–1917
6. Gama, J.: Oblique Linear Tree. Lecture Notes in Computer Science **1280** (1997) 187–198
7. Heath, D., Kasif, S., Salzberg, S.: Induction of Oblique Decision Trees. Proceedings of the 13th International Joint Conference on Artificial Intelligence (1993) 1002-1007
8. Herrera, F., Lozano, M., Verdegay, J. L.: Tackling Real-Coded Genetic Algorithms: Operators and Tools for Behavioural Analysis. Artificial Intelligence Review **12(4)** (1998) 265–319
9. Holland, J. H.: Adaption in Natural and Artificial Systems. MIT Press (1975)
10. Michalewicz, Z.: Genetic Algorithms + Data Structures = Evolution Programs. New York: Springer-Verlag (1996)
11. Murthy, S. K., Kasif, S., Salzberg, S.: A System for Induction of Oblique Decision Trees. Journal of Artificial Intelligence Research **2** (1994) 1–32
12. Quinlan, J. R.: C4.5: Programs for Machine Learning. Morgan Kaufmann (1993)

Intelligent Predictive Control
of a 6-Dof Robotic Manipulator
with Reliability Based Performance Improvement

Ahmet Akbas

Marmara University, Vocational School of Technical Sciences, 34722 Istanbul, Turkey
ahmetakbas@marmara.edu.tr

Abstract. A six-degree of freedom (dof) robotic manipulator from Stanford family is controlled with an intelligent control system designed by using Elman network and generalized predictive control (GPC) algorithm. Three of Elman networks are trained by using GPC based data. They are used in parallel form to improve the reliability of the system by error minimization. At the end of parallel implementation, the results of networks are evaluated by using torque equations to select the network with best result. Simulation based test results showed that the proposed controller improves the performance of the system.

1 Introduction

The overall complexity of robot control problems, and ideal of a truly general robotic system, have led to much discussion on the use of artificial neural networks (ANN) to learn the characteristics of the robot system, rather than having to specify explicit robot system models. On the other hand, in process control applications the controller makes explicit use of ANN based process model to determine the k-steps ahead of the process outputs [1]. As a result, ANN based nonlinear predictive control has taken great deal of interest in recent years.

Many papers have been presented on this subject [2][3][4]. Gupta and Sinha [5] have presented an intelligent control system using PD controller and ANN. They have found the algorithm successful. Additionally, Koker [6][7] has developed an intelligent predictive controller for a 3-joint robotic manipulator by using conventional backpropagation algorithm.

Koker has mentioned in his studies that, robotic manipulators can be controlled by learning; however, it is also difficult to imagine a useful non-repetitive task that involves making random motions spanning the entire control space of the mechanical system. Gupta et. al. have also stated a similar result. This results an intelligent robot concept, which is trained to carry out certain class of operations rather than all virtually possible applications.

These points have also been observed in this study and a different approach has been designed to control a 6-dof robotic manipulator from Stanford family. Three of Elman networks, which have profound impact on the learning capability and performance of the network, have been trained by using GPC based data. They are used in parallel form to improve the reliability of the system by error minimization approach so that at the end of parallel implementation the results of networks can be evaluated by using torque equations in order to select the network with best result.

M. Gallagher, J. Hogan, and F. Maire (Eds.): IDEAL 2005, LNCS 3578, pp. 272–279, 2005.
© Springer-Verlag Berlin Heidelberg 2005

2 GPC Controller Design for Stanford Robot

Basically, GPC is the algorithm predicting $y(t)$ output throughout finite horizon and, control signals string $u(t)$ computed using the minimization of a quadratic perform-ance criterion [8][9]. The discrete time CARIMA model given below is used to design the controller:

$$A(z^{-1})y(t) = B(z^{-1})u(t-1) + e(t) \tag{1}$$

To make calculations with GPC, it is necessary to have predictors throughout the chosen horizon $(t+1,\ t+N_2)$. N_2 is known as maximum prediction horizon. The prediction for j step later may be given as follows:

$$y(t+j) = G_j \Delta u(t+j-1) + F_j y(t) + E_j \zeta(t+j)$$
$$[I] = E_j(z^{-1})A(z^{-1})\Delta + z^{-j}F_j(z^{-1}) \tag{2}$$
$$E_j(z^{-1})B(z^{-1}) = G_j(z^{-1})$$

Here $[I]$ is the definition matrix in the appropriate dimension. To express the predictions in more closed forms, the vectors below may be defined as

$$\hat{y} = [y(t+1)^r, \dots, y(t+N_2)^r]^T$$
$$\tilde{u} = [\Delta u(t)^r, \dots, \Delta u(t+N_2-1)^r]^T \tag{3}$$
$$f = [f(t+1)^r, \dots, f(t+N_2)^r]^T$$

Here $f(t+j)$ is the component which is composed of the known signals of $y(t+j)$ at an instant t. For instance;

$$f(t+1) = \left[G_1(z^{-1}) - g_{10}\Delta u(t) + F_1 y(t) \right] \tag{4}$$

Here $G_i(z) = g_{i0} + g_{i1}^{-1} + \dots$. Then, the predictions may be shown in closed form as

$$\hat{y} = G\tilde{u} + f \quad , \quad G = \begin{bmatrix} G_i & 0 & 0 & . & 0 \\ G_i & G_i & & . & . & 0 \\ . & & . & . & . \\ G_{i_1} & . & & . & . & 0 \\ G_{i_1} & G_{i_2}-1 & . & . & G_i \end{bmatrix} \tag{5}$$

The performance index of GPC is given as

$$J = \sum_{j=1}^{N_2}\left\{ [y(t+j) - w(t+j)]^T [y(t+j) - w(t+j)] \right\} + \sum_{j=1}^{N_2} \Delta u(t+j-1)\Lambda(j)\Delta u(t+j-1) \tag{6}$$

Here $\Lambda(j)$ is the weight vector in control increases and w is the reference trajectory. Using the eq. (5), the control law that minimizes the eq. (6) may be obtained as

$$\Delta u(t) = [I\,0\,0\dots0](G\,G^T + \Lambda)^{-1}G^T(w - f) \quad , \quad \Lambda = diag[\Lambda(1), \Lambda(2), \dots, \Lambda(N_2)]^T \tag{7}$$

In this study, to design a predictive controller, the trajectory that is to be followed is decided as joint speeds in the form of discrete points by using $v^d(t)$ vector. The problem is solved using Carima model given in eq. (1) for the motion of joints. A_j $(j=1,\dots,n_a)$ and B_j $(j=1,\dots,n_b)$ are the matrixes, which contain 36 (6x6) unknown, but will be predicted elements. The output value is selected as joint speed vector which can be expressed as $v(t) = [v_1(t), v_2(t), v_3(t), v_4(t), v_5(t), v_6(t)]^T$. In the Carima model used in simulation studies, the valu of n_a and n_b selected as "1" ($n_a=1$, $n_b=1$) to model the manipulator with the minimum number of elements:

$$v(t) = -A_1\, v(t-1) + B_0\, u(t-1) + B_1\, u(t-2) + e(t) \qquad (8)$$

Here, $u(t)=[u_1(t), u_2(t), u_3(t), u_4(t), u_5(t), u_6(t)]^T$ shows the torques applied to the joints. Error vector is shown as $e(t)=[e_1(t), e_2(t), e_3(t), e_4(t), e_5(t), e_6(t)]^T$. Eq. (8) can be written in the following form where, Q is the parameter matrix (6x18) that will be predicted:

$$v(t) = Q\phi(t-1) + e(t) \quad , \quad \phi(t-1) = \left[u(t-1)^T, u(t-2)^T, v(t-1)^T\right]^T \qquad (9)$$

The parameter prediction process is done using the recursive least squares (RLS) algorithm [11]. The target function that will be minimized is arranged as given below:

$$J(\Delta u) = \sum_{j=1}^{N_2}\left\{\left[v(t+j)-v^d(t+j)\right]^T\left[v(t+j)-v^d(t+j)\right]\right\} + \sum_{j=1}^{N_u}\Delta u(t+j-1)\,\Lambda(j)\,\Delta u(t+j-1) \qquad (10)$$

Here, $v^d(t+j) = [v_1^d(t+j),\ldots, v_6^d(t+j)]^T$ is the speed reference vector of joints. $\Delta u(t)$ is obtained as eq. (7) by minimizing the eq. (10). v^d will be used instead of w in eq. (7).

3   The Structure of Stanford Robot

A 6-joint Stanford robot model used in the simulation is shown in Fig. 1. The dynamics of a robot arm can be expressed by the following general set of equations [12]:

$$\sum_j d_{kj}(q)\ddot{q}_j + \sum_{i,j} c_{ijk}(q)\,\dot{q}_i\dot{q}_j + f_k(q) = \tau_k \quad ; \quad i,j,k = 1,\ldots,n \qquad (11)$$

Here q_j is jth generalized coordinate, q is generalized coordinate vector, τ_k is kth generalized force, n is the number of joints, d_{kj} is inertial coefficients, c_{ijk} is centrifugal Coriolis coefficient and f_k is loading item due to gravity.

In order to compute the reference positions, the cubic trajectory algorithm is used:

$$\theta_i(t) = \theta_{i0} + \frac{3}{t_f^2}(\theta_{if} - \theta_{i0})t^2 - \frac{2}{t_f^3}(\theta_{if} - \theta_{i0})t^3 \quad , \quad i = 1,\ldots,n \qquad (12)$$

Here t_f is total simulation time, θ_{if} is the final result of angular position for ith joint, θ_{i0} is the starting position of ith joint, t is time and n is the number of joints. By the derivation of eq. (12) the speed equation is obtained as follows:

$$\dot{\theta}_i(t) = 2\left(\frac{3}{t_f^2}(\theta_{if} - \theta_{i0})t\right) + 3\left(\frac{2}{t_f^2}(\theta_{if} - \theta_{i0})t^2\right) \quad , \quad i = 1,\ldots, n \qquad (13)$$

In addition to these, the third link can be expressed in metric form because of its structure. In simulations, it is carried out by using a linear function. These equations related to dynamics and kinematics of the robot are included by the simulation software [6].

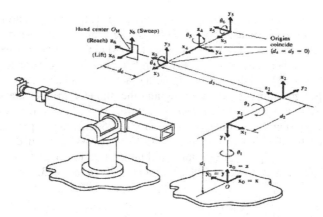

Fig. 1. Stanford robotic manipulator [13]

4 Controller Design by Using Elman Networks

In this stage, it is aimed to present the design of ANN, which is working on-line to produce applied torque values for each joint of 6-dof Stanford robot. Elman network shown in Fig.2 is used to model GPC algorithm. The data prepared during the implementation of traditional GPC algorithm are used to train Elman network, which has 24 inputs and 6 outputs. To obtain the torque values (u) at time "t" as an output, the torque values at time (t-1), (t-2), speed (v) and reference speed (v^d) values at time (t-1) are used in input stage as 24 input elements.

To design a controller which is generalized for the whole area of working volume of the robot is a very time consuming study due to the training difficulty. Therefore, training process is implemented on some areas in the working volume of the robotic manipulator. For this aim, the manipulator is controlled by implementation of conventional GPC for different trajectories selected uniformly. At the same time, payload variations between 0 to 5000 grams are taken into consideration to generate the training data set.

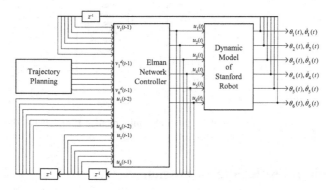

Fig. 2. The block diagram of Elman network used to model GPC algorithm

10000 input and output vector sets are generated using robot control simulation software for each of Elman networks. 8000 of these are used as learning set, and others are used in the test. The ANN toolbox of the Matlab program is used in the off-line training of Elman networks. Conventional back propagation error-learning algorithm, which uses a threshold with a sigmoidal activation function and gradient descent-learning algorithm is used. Learning and the momentum rates are selected optimally by Matlab program. The numbers of neurons in the hidden layers are selected experimentally during the training and these are 60, 75 and 120, respectively for each network. After the off-line training, three of Elman networks are coded with obtained synaptic weights in Delphi. An example of obtained torque curves together with one of the trained Elman network and GPC controller is given in Fig. 3.

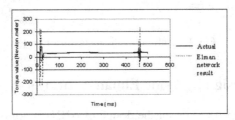

Fig. 3. Obtained torque curves by trained Elman network and GPC (actual) controllers

To obtain the designed intelligent controller three of Elman networks are used in parallel form to produce on-line control vector as shown in Fig. 4. For this aim, obtained torque values from each Elman network are given as an input to the dynamic model of robotic manipulator. Error vector is computed by using the difference between reference and obtained speed and position values. Then, the results are evaluated to select the network with the best result. In the end, the torque vector is assigned as the torque vector related to the network, which generates the best result.

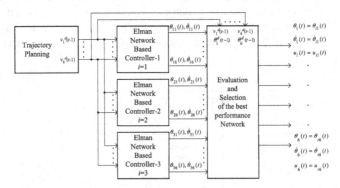

Fig. 4. Block diagram of the parallely-implemented Elman networks

5   Simulation Results and Discussion

Stanford robotic manipulator, which has 6 joints, has been used in the simulations. Some scenarios have been generated related to working volume of the robot and experienced by using the designed ANN controller. The sampling period is selected as 0.001 s., and totally 500 steps are included in a simulation. An example of the obtained results corresponding to the GPC, unique Elman network, and parallel Elman networks implementation is given in Fig. 5, Fig. 6 and Fig. 7, respectively.

In these simulations, it has been observed that the GPC algorithm has been taken by the control system a few iterations later. So, the error is too much at the starting points in speed curves. The same error has also been observed in ANN controller results, as seen in Fig. 6. However, the obtained error by paralelly-implemented networks is much less than the errors obtained in the case of unique ANN. These error signals seen in Fig. 6 have been removed due to the parallel usage of networks, as seen in Fig. 7. The speed and position errors are given in Table 1. The speed error is calculated as the sum of the square of speed errors for each joint in Table 1.

Table 1. Position and speed errors for each joint using GPC and parallel implementation

Joint Nr	Position Errors (rad.)		Speed Errors (rad/sec.)	
	GPC	Elman Controller	GPC	Elman Controller
1	0.0018291	0.004191	0.156272	0.078865
2	0.0004332	0.007867	0.075681	0.041987
3	0.01923 m.	0.011322 m.	0.316854 m/sec	0.128287 m/sec
4	0.0007865	0.000735	0.725471	0.331154
5	0.0053281	0.004258	0.127254	0.071256
6	0.0098275	0.000982	0.147356	0.088112

The reliability based approach provides advantages in two ways: from the view point of selecting the best results among three networks and from the view point of unlearned data in test set. 24 unlearned data for the first network, 30 unlearned data for the second network and 26 unlearned data for the third network have been observed in the test process of each network.

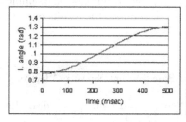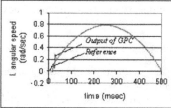

Fig. 5. The results of the GPC controller for joint 1; position and speed curves

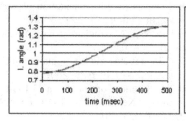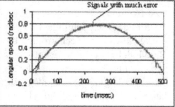

Fig. 6. The results of unique Elman network controller for joint 1; position and speed curves

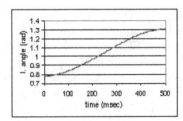 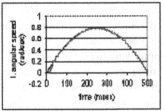

Fig. 7. The results of the parallel implementation for joint 1; position and speed curves

Furthermore, the designed parallel neural network controller has been implemented 5 times faster than the traditional GPC controller in the simulations and this means the designed controller has reduced the process time substantially.

6 Conclusions

Three separate Elman network controllers based on parallel usage of ANNs have been designed and implemented for a 6-dof Stanford robot. The aim is to reduce the error in the system using parallel structure. The performance of the designed controller, used instead of GPC, has been proved to be successful. Normally, ANNs work with an acceptable error. In this system, the output of each Elman network controller was evaluated with a feedback to select the best result among the results of three networks. By this way, the errors in noisy output in sampling periods were reduced.

On the other hand, GPC algorithm has highly mathematical computations where as ANNs have the capability of fast and on-line working features. Therefore, modeling GPC by ANNs can have an important role in real time systems by reducing the process time. In addition, parallel implementation of ANNs makes the system more reliable. In the future studies, the developed control algorithm can be examined with a real robot to observe its real time accuracy and to compare the results of simulations.

References

1. Kasparian, V., Batur, C.: Model Reference Based Neural Network Adaptive Controller. ISA Transactions 37, (1998), 21-39
2. Huang, D., Cauwenberghe, V.A.R.: Neural Network Based Multiple Feedback Long Range Predictive Control. Neurocomputing 18 (1998), 127-139
3. Donat, S., Bhat, N., Mc Avoy, T.J.: Neural Net Based Model Predictive Control. Int. J. of Control 54 (6) (1991), 1453-1468
4. Rensen, P.H.S., Rgaard, M.N., Ravn, O., Poulsen, N.K.: Implementation of Neural Network Based Nonlinear Predictive Control. Neurocomputing 28 (1999), 37-51
5. Gupta, P., Sinha, N.K.: Intelligent Control of Robotic Manipulators: Experimental Study Using Neural Networks. Mechatronics 10 (2000), 289-305
6. Koker, R.: Model Based Intelligent Control of 3-Joint Robotic Manipulator with Machine Vision System. Phd Thesis, Science Institute of Sakarya University (2002)
7. Koker, R., Ferikoglu, A.: Model Based Intelligent Control of a 3-Joint Robotic manipulator: A Simulation Study Using Artificial Neural Networks. Lecture Notes in Computer Science, Vol. 3280, Springer-Verlag (2004), 31-40
8. Koker, R., Oz, C., Kazan, R.: Vision Based Robot Control Using Generalized Predictive Control. Intern. Conf. on Electrics and Electronics Eng. ELECO'01, Bursa, (2001)

9. Ozsoy, C., Kazan, R.: Self-tuning Predictive Controllers For Robotic Manipulators. 2. Project Workshop on Cim and Robotics Applications, Regional UNDP/UNIDO Project, Belgrad, (1991), 99-115

10. Koker, R., Ekiz, H., Boz, A.F.: Design and Implementation of a Vision Based Control System Towards Moving Object Capture For a 3-Joint Robot. 11th Mediterranean Conf. on Control and Automation, Rhodes, Greece, (2003), 55

11. Borinson, U.: Self-tuning Regulators for a Class of Multivariable Systems. Automatica, Vol. 15, (1979), 209-215

12. Acosta, L., Marichal, G.N., Moreno, L., Rodrigo, J.J., Hamilton, A., Mendez, J.A.: A Robotic System Based On Neural Network Controllers. Artificial Intelligence in Engineering 13 (1999), 393-398

13. Fu, K.S., Gonzalez, R.C., Lee, C.S.G.: Robotics: Control, Sensing, Vision and Intelligence. Mcgraw-Hill Book Company, (1987), 38

Sequential Search for Decremental Edition[*]

José A. Olvera-López, J. Ariel Carrasco-Ochoa, and José Fco. Martínez-Trinidad

Computer Science Department, National Institute of Astrophysics, Optics and Electronics
Luis Enrique Erro No. 1 Sta María Tonanzintla, Puebla, CP: 72840, Mexico
{aolvera,ariel,fmartine}@inaoep.mx

Abstract. The edition process is an important task in supervised classification because it helps to reduce the size of the training sample. On the other hand, Instance-Based classifiers store all the training set indiscriminately, which in almost all times, contains useless or harmful objects, for the classification process. Therefore it is important to delete unnecessary objects to increase both classification speed and accuracy. In this paper, we propose an edition method based on sequential search and we present an empirical comparison between it and some other decremental edition methods.

Introduction

Instance based classifiers work on a training set T that is a set of objects previously assessed and labeled. In practical situations, it is common that some training sets contain objects with a null or even negative contribution for classification accuracy; therefore, it is convenient to consider only useful objects to obtain higher accuracy. The edition or object selection is defined as the process of choosing objects from the training set which contribute to improve the classification accuracy. The goal of edition methods is to find a training sample S which contains fewer objects than the original training set T and such that the classification accuracy using S would be higher than using T.

When a subset S from T is searched, we can proceed in three directions [1]: *incremental, decremental and batch*.

Incremental. An incremental search begins with the empty set S and in each step adds objects that fulfill the selection criteria.

Decremental. This search begins with $S=T$ and removes from S objects that do not fulfill the selection criteria.

Batch. This search involves deciding if each object fulfills the removal criteria before removing any of them. Then all those that fulfill the criteria are removed at once, that is, this strategy does not remove one object at each step, this strategy removes sets of objects.

In this paper, we propose an edition method based on sequential search and present an empirical comparison between it and some other decremental edition methods.

---

[*] This work was financially supported by CONACyT (Mexico) through the project J38707-A.

M. Gallagher, J. Hogan, and F. Maire (Eds.): IDEAL 2005, LNCS 3578, pp. 280–285, 2005.

Decremental Edition Methods

In this section, some previous works related to edition in the decremental direction are reviewed. Gates [2] proposed the *Reduced Nearest Neighbor Rule (RNN)*. This method starts with $S=T$ and removes objects from S if such removal does not cause that any other object in T would be misclassified by the remaining objects in S.

Wilson [3] introduced an edition method called *Edited Nearest Neighbor Algorithm (ENN)*, this method removes from S objects that do not agree with the majority of their nearest neighbors. Wilson suggests a small and odd value for k, the *ENN* method uses $k=3$.

RENN is a modification to *ENN; RENN* applies *ENN* repeatedly until each object in S has the same class that the majority of its k nearest neighbors.

Wilson and Martínez [1] introduced the *DROP1,...,DROP5* methods (*Decremental Reduction Optimization Procedure*). The *DROP1* method is identical to *RNN*, with the exception that classification accuracy is verified on S instead of T. This method is based on the rule: *remove an object P if at least as many of its associates in S would be classified correctly without P*. In this rule, an associate is an object such that P is one of its nearest neighbors. The *DROP1* method is depicted in figure 1.

DROP1(Training set T): Object set S

    Let $S=T$

    For each object P in S:

        Find the k nearest neighbors of P in S

        Calculate its list of associates

    For each object P in S:

        Let *with* = # of associates of P classified correctly with P as a neighbor.

        Let *without* = # of associates of P classified correctly without P.

        If (*without - with*) ≥ 0

            Remove P from S

            For each associate A of P

                Remove P from A's list of nearest neighbors

                Find a new nearest neighbor for A.

                Move A to its new nearest neighbor's list of associates

            For each neighbor N of P

                Remove P from N's lists of associates

        Endif

    Return S

Fig. 1. *DROP1* Method

DROP2 method considers the effect in T of removing an object in S, that is, *DROP2* removes the object P if its associates in T would be classified correctly without P.

DROP3 uses a noise-filtering step before applying *DROP2*; the noise filter used is similar to *ENN*.

DROP4 differs from *DROP3* in the filtering criterion since it is different to *ENN*. In this case, an object is removed only if it is misclassified by its k nearest neighbors and it does not hurt the classification of other objects.

DROP5 is similar to *DROP2* but *DROP5* starts with objects that are nearest to their nearest enemy, that is, nearest neighbors with different output class.

In this paper, we propose an edition method based on backward sequential search, which is called *BSE (Backward Sequential Edition)*.The *BSE* method starts from the original training sample *T* and finds a subset *S*. At each step, *BSE* removes the object with the smallest contribution for the subset quality, in terms of the accuracy of a classifier, which is calculated by the *Classifier()* function. If there is more than one object with the smallest contribution, only the last is eliminated. *BSE* is depicted in figure 2.

BSE(Training set *T*): Object set *S*
    Let *S=T*
    BestEval = *Classifier(S)*
    Repeat
        WorstP = *null*
        For each object *P* in *S*
        S' = *S* – *{P}*
        If *Classifier(S')* $\geq$ *BestEval* then
                WorstP = *P*
                BestEval = *Classifier(S')*
        If *WorstP* $\neq$ *null* then
           S = *S* – { *WorstP*}
    Until *WorstP* == *null* or *S* == $\varnothing$
    Return *S*

Fig. 2. *BSE* method

Comparative Analysis

This section presents a comparative analysis between *BSE* and other decremental edition methods.

We begin analyzing *ENN*. This method removes noisy objects, that is, objects with an output class different from their nearest neighbors majority class. Notice that this method only considers as bad objects such objects that are misclassified by their nearest neighbors. However, it is possible that although the bad objects had been deleted, some well-classified objects be harmful for the classification process. That is, such objects are not useful even though they have been filtered as good objects. In this point, there is a difference with *BSE* because the last one analyzes all objects, including objects, which are classified correctly.

The complexity of *ENN* method is O(*NF*) where *N* is the total number of objects in the sample and *F* is the number of features.

Since *RENN* applies *ENN* repeatedly, *RENN* has the same problem that *ENN*, i.e., it is possible that although the bad-classified objects had been deleted, some well-classified objects be harmful for the classification process. That is, such objects are not useful even though they have been filtered as good objects.

RENN applies *ENN* at most *N* times, and the complexity of *ENN* method is O(*NF*). So the complexity of *RENN* method is O(N^2F).

The methods *DROP1-DROP5* remove noisy objects using the concept of associates of each object. *DROP1* cleans directly the sample and in *DROP2-DROP5* the selection of the resultant sample is made more carefully because, before applying the method, they use a noise filter and after they verify the classification accuracy. The accuracy is checked using the associates in the original training set.

The complexity of *DROP* methods at each step is $O(NF)$ because the associates lists are computed at the beginning, so, when an object is removed, the associates list is modified for each object in the training set.

The difference between *BSE* and these methods is the number of considered objects for verifying if an object must be removed. Also, *BSE* verifies the removal effect in all the training set, on the other hand, *DROP* methods only verify in the list of associates.

The complexity of *BSE* is $O(N^4F)$, since that, in each step the complexity for analyzing the removal effect of one object in the training set is $O(N^2F)$. In addition, this must be done for each object, in order to decide which are the objects with the smallest contribution to the classification accuracy. So the process for eliminating one object is $O(N^3F)$ and at most *N-1* objects could be removed.

Experimental Results

In [1], the *DROP1-DROP5* methods were compared against *ENN*, *RENN*, and other decremental edition methods. Wilson and Martínez reported that the *DROP3* method had better behavior, so in our experimentation we compared *DROP1-DROP5* against *BSE*. They were tested on 11 datasets taken from the Machine Learning Database Repository at the University of California, Irvine [4]. For all the tests, the same training and testing sets, the same classifier *k-NN* with *k=3*, the same distance function, and the same computer, were used. We have used *k-NN* with *k=3* because this value was used for comparing the DROP methods in [1].

The distance function for the experiments was the heterogeneous distance function *HVDM* [1], which is defined as:

$$HVDM(x,y) = \sqrt{\sum_{a=1}^{F} d_a^{\ 2}(x_a, y_a)} \qquad (1)$$

where $d_a(x,y)$ is the distance for the feature *a* and it is defined as:

$$d_a(x,y) = \begin{cases} 1 & \text{if } x \text{ or } y \text{ is unknown} \\ vdm_a(x,y) & \text{if } a \text{ is nominal} \\ \dfrac{|x-y|}{4\sigma_a} & \text{if } a \text{ is numeric} \end{cases} \qquad (2)$$

where σ_a is the standard deviation of the values occurring for feature *a* and $vdm_a(x,y)$ is defined as:

$$vdm_a(x,y) = \sum_{c=1}^{C} \left(\frac{N_{a,x,c}}{N_{a,x}} - \frac{N_{a,y,c}}{N_{a,y}} \right)^2 \qquad (3)$$

Where $N_{a,x}$ is the number of times that the feature a had value x in the training set; $N_{a,x,c}$ is the number of times that the feature a had value x in the class c; and C is the number of classes.

Table 1. Accuracy and retention percentage for: k-NN with 100% of the data, $DROP1$-$DROP5$ and BSE

Dataset	k-NN	%	DROP n										BSE	%
			1	%	2	%	3	%	4	%	5	%		
Breast Cancer(WI)	96.28	100	93.13	2.85	96.28	5.80	95.42	3.26	95.99	3.70	95.56	4.18	98.71	2.09
Iris	94.67	100	89.33	9.56	94.67	16.96	95.33	15.33	94.67	15.26	94.00	12.44	99.33	6.14
Glass	71.90	100	66.84	23.21	65.89	31.05	66.28	24.35	67.77	29.39	62.16	25.91	89.67	13.18
Ionosphere	84.60	100	87.73	7.72	89.16	11.90	86.87	7.15	86.31	10.60	86.87	9.50	92.86	3.60
Promoters	93.36	100	89.64	6.50	87.36	17.09	90.27	16.46	90.45	16.98	85.91	10.38	100	16.25
Tae	51.08	100	55.75	30.54	53.67	33.56	49.75	26.27	53.71	31.71	52.42	32.01	90.12	10.88
Wine	95.00	100	94.97	10.36	95.52	14.80	94.41	15.04	94.41	15.04	93.86	10.55	100	4.62
Liver(Bupa)	65.22	100	57.98	31.53	64.08	39.26	67.82	26.83	66.41	33.11	63.46	30.59	96.52	12.69
Zoo	93.33	100	87.78	16.79	86.67	20.37	90.00	20.37	91.11	21.36	95.56	18.77	97.77	10.86
New Thyroid	95.39	100	85.56	8.32	90.78	14.88	93.98	9.77	93.51	10.39	94.46	8.84	97.70	3.61
Voting	95.63	100	94.94	3.27	95.18	7.23	95.86	4.65	96.09	5.06	95.86	7.41	97.46	3.49
Average	85.13	100	82.15	13.70	83.57	19.35	84.18	15.41	84.58	17.51	83.65	15.51	96.38	7.95

In each experiment, 10 fold cross validation was used. The dataset was divided into 10 partitions and each edition algorithm was applied to T which is built with 9 of the 10 partitions (90% of the data) and the left partition (10% of the data) was the testing set. Each partition was used as testing set, so 10 tests were made with each dataset. In the table 1, the average results for each experiment are shown.

In Table 1, the results obtained with k-NN considering 100% of the data, $DROPs$, and BSE, are shown. For each method, there are two columns, the left one is the average classification accuracy and the right one (%) shows the percentage of the original training set that was retained by the edition method.

Based on the results showed in Table 1, we can see that $DROP1$ had a lower average number of retained objects, among the DROP methods, but in many cases, its average accuracy was lower than average accuracy of $DROP2$-$DROP5$. On the other hand, $DROP4$ had better average accuracy than the other $DROPs$.

Results obtained by BSE are good because it obtained high classification accuracy and low retention percentages. The average accuracy of BSE was higher than such obtained with $DROP1$-$DROP5$ and than using k-NN with 100% of the data.

Conclusions

In supervised classification, the training set quality is very important because it is the basis of the training process. But in practical cases there could be irrelevant objects, which could be harmful objects for classifying, so it is necessary editing the training sample to obtain higher, equal or similar classification accuracy than that one obtained with the original training set, but with less objects. Therefore, the search time is reduced and the classification speed is increased for Instance-Based classifiers.

A characteristic of BSE method is that it can use any classifier; it does not depend of the k-NN rule or any other particular classifier.

From the obtained results, we can conclude that BSE reduces significantly the number of objects and increases the classification accuracy. Of course, these are only preliminary results and it is necessary to make more experiments and to compare against other edition methods. However, *BSE* method seems to be a good option for solving edition problems.

The complexity of the *BSE* method is higher than the complexity of *DROP1-DROP5* because at each step, *BSE* checks the accuracy obtained when each object in the training subset is removed.

Even though *BSE* is of high complexity, the edition process is made only once. Anyway, it is important, as future work, to propose strategies or heuristics for reducing the execution time of this method.

References

1. Wilson, D. Randall and Tony R. Martínez. Reduction Techniques for Instance-Based Learning Algorithms. *Machine Learning*, vol 38. pp. 257-286, 2000.
2. Gates, G. W. The Reduced Nearest Neighbor Rule. *IEEE Transactions on Information Theory*, vol. 18(3), pp. 431-433. 1972.
3. Wilson, Dennis L. Asymptotic Properties of Nearest Neighbor Rules Using Edited Data. *IEEE Transactions on Systems, Man, and Cybernetics*, vol. 2(3), pp. 408-421. 1972.
4. Blake, C., Keogh, E., Merz, C.J.: UCI repository of machine learning databases [http://www.ics.uci.edu/~mlearn/MLRepository.html], Department of Information and Computer Science, University of California, Irvine, CA. 1998

Bearing Similarity Measures
for Self-organizing Feature Maps

Narongdech Keeratipranon and Frederic Maire

Faculty of Information Technology
Queensland University of Technology
Box 2434, Brisbane Q 4001, Australia
n.keeratipranon@student.qut.edu.au, f.maire@qut.edu.au

Abstract. The neural representation of space in rats has inspired many navigation systems for robots. In particular, *Self-Organizing (Feature) Maps* (SOM) are often used to give a sense of location to robots by mapping sensor information to a low-dimensional grid. For example, a robot equipped with a panoramic camera can build a 2D SOM from vectors of landmark bearings. If there are four landmarks in the robot's environment, then the 2D SOM is embedded in a 2D manifold lying in a 4D space. In general, the set of observable sensor vectors form a low-dimensional Riemannian manifold in a high-dimensional space. In a landmark bearing sensor space, the manifold can have a large curvature in some regions (when the robot is near a landmark for example), making the Eulidian distance a very poor approximation of the Riemannian metric. In this paper, we present and compare three methods for measuring the similarity between vectors of landmark bearings. We also discuss a method to equip SOM with a good approximation of the Riemannian metric. Although we illustrate the techniques with a landmark bearing problem, our approach is applicable to other types of data sets.

1 Introduction

The ability to navigate in an unknown environment is an essential requirement for autonomous mobile robots. Conventional *Simultaneous Localization and Mapping* (SLAM) involves fusing observations of landmarks with dead-reckoning information in order to track the location of the robot and build a map of the environment [1]. *Self Organizing (Feature) Maps* (SOM) are capable of representing a robot's environment. Sensor readings collected at different locations throughout the environment make up the training set of the SOM. After training, self-localization is based on the association of the the neurons of the SOM with locations in the environment [2,3]. Robustness to noise in the sensors can be achieved with probabilistic methods such as Extended Kalman Filters [4–7] or Particle Filters [8–10].

Navigation systems based on range sensors such as radar, GPS, laser or ultrasonic sensors are significantly more expensive than navigation systems relying only on vision [11–13]. An omni-directional vision sensor is composed of a digital

M. Gallagher, J. Hogan, and F. Maire (Eds.): IDEAL 2005, LNCS 3578, pp. 286–293, 2005.

camera aiming at a catadioptric mirror. Although it is not straightforward to obtain distance estimations from omni-directional images due to the shape of the mirror, the bearings of landmarks relative to the robot are reasonably accurate and easy to derive from omni-directional images [14–16].

The Euclidean metric is the default distance used in most neural network toolboxes. Unfortunately, using this distance to train a SOM on a data-set of landmark bearing vectors collected at different locations uniformly distributed throughout the environment does not produce a grid of neurons whose associated positions in the environment are evenly distributed.

This is not very suprising as the Euclidian distance gives the same importance to all the components of the sensor vectors (here landmark bearings). It is intuitively clear that is not the right thing to do. The further a landmark is from the robot the larger the importance of its bearing becomes, as the bearing of a near landmark changes more wildly than the bearing of a far landmark when the robot is in motion. Therefore, we should give a relatively large weight to a far landmark and a relatively small weight to a near landmark. But, what values should these weights take? How to determine them in practice? In this paper, we provide answers to those questions.

Section 2 relates three landmark bearing vector metrics to probabilistic classifiers. In the same section, we present numerical experiments comparing these metrics. Section 3 outlines a method for estimating the intrincic metric of a Riemannian manifold of sensor inputs. Section 4 concludes this paper.

2   Similarity Measures for Bearing Vectors

In this section, we present three different methods to assess the similarity between two vectors of landmark bearings. The movitation of this project was to give a robot a sense of location and distance by building a SOM. The input vectors of the SOM are vectors of landmark bearings. Figure 1 illustrates the environment of the robot. In this example, the robot roves in a room equipped with 3 landmarks. The robot collects training sets by performing random walks. For a 2×3 rectangular grid SOM, we could expect that the neurons of a trained SOM would be uniformely distributed. That is, the neurons should end up at the centres of the rectangular cells of Figure 1. Experiments with real and simulated robots show that the SOM fails to spread uniformly (with respect to the ground) if the Euclidian distance is used in sensor space.

To better understand the causes of the failure of the SOM to spread uniformly, we have investigated the shapes of the cells induced by bearing vector prototypes corresponding to regularly spaced observations on the ground. Observations were collected throughout the environment of Figure 2. The ground is partitioned into $15 = 3 \times 5$ equal size grid cells. The average direction to each landmark in each cell are represented by the arrows at the centres of the cells. The length of an arrow represents the importance of the pointed landmark. The computation of this importance value is explained later in the paper.

The $15 = 3 \times 5$ mean vectors of landmark bearings in the different cells play the role of SOM neurons. The corresponding Voronoi diagram computed with

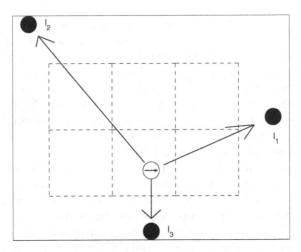

Fig. 1. A toy model of a robot environment

the Euclidian distance on the bearing vectors is shown in Figure 3. We observe that with the Euclidian distance a large proportion of points get assigned to an incorrect cell centre. In this context, the localization problem can indeed be cast as a classification problem. Given a new bearing vector x, determining the cell in which the observation was made reduces to computing the probabilities $P(i|x)$ that the obervation has been made in the different rectangular cells i of Figure 2.

A Naive Bayes classifier provides a principled way to assign weights to the different landmarks. Recall that a Naive Bayes classifier simply makes the assumption that the different features $x_1, \ldots, x_4$ of the input vector are conditionally independent with respect to class i. That is, $P(x_1, \ldots, x_4|i) = P(x_1|i) \times \ldots \times P(x_4|i)$. With this class conditioned independence hypothesis, the most likely cell i is determined by computing $\arg_i \max P(x_1|i) \times \ldots \times P(x_4|i)$. Let μ_{ji} be the mean value of x_j observed in cell i, and let σ_{ji} be the standard deviation of x_j (the bearing of landmark j) observed in cell i. Then, we have

$$P(x_j|i) = \frac{1}{\sqrt{2\pi}\sigma_{ji}} e^{-\frac{(x_j - \mu_{ji})^2}{2\sigma_{ji}^2}}$$

For the classification task, we compute the Naive Bayes pseudo-distance between the input vector x and μ_i the bearing vector prototype of cell i;

$$-\log(\prod_j P(x_j|i)) = \sum_j \frac{(x_j - \mu_{ji})^2}{2\sigma_{ji}^2} + \theta_i \tag{1}$$

where $\theta_i = \sum_j \log(\sqrt{2\pi}\sigma_{ji})$.

For this pseudo-distance, the weight of the bearing of a landmark j is determined by the standard deviation of the sample collected in the cell. The right hand side of Equation 1 is in agreement with our intuition that the further a

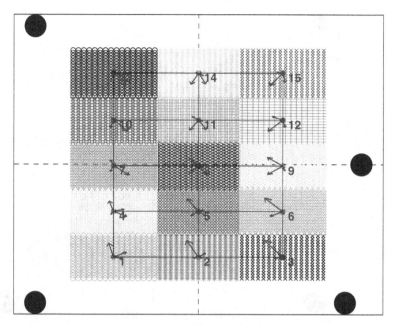

Fig. 2. An environment partitioned into $15 = 3 \times 5$ equal size grid cells. The four large dots are the landmarks

landmark j is, the more significant the difference $(x_j - \mu_{ji})^2$ becomes. Indeed the further the landmark is, the larger $\frac{1}{2\sigma_{ji}^2}$ is.

Figure 4 shows the Voronoi diagram induced by Naive Bayes pseudo-distance on landmark bearing vectors is more in agreement with the Euclidian distance on the ground (compare Figures 3 and 4).

Further improvement in the accuracy of the localization can be obtained by estimating the covariance matrices of the sensor vector random variable in the different cells of Figure 2. Let C_i denote the covariance matrix of the n-dimensional bearing vectors collected in cell i. The general multivariate Gaussian density function for a sensor vector x observed in cell i is given by

$$P(x|i) = \frac{1}{(2\pi)^{\frac{n}{2}}|C_i|^{\frac{1}{2}}} e^{-\frac{1}{2}(x-\mu_i)^T C_i^{-1}(x-\mu_i)} \tag{2}$$

The Mahalanobis distance is obtained by taking the negative logarithm of Equation 2. The Mahalanobis distance has been successfully used for a wide range of pattern recognition and data mining problems. It has been also extended to mixed data [17]. In robotics, the Mahalanobis distance has proved useful for the data association problem [18,19]. In previous work, the covariance matrix was used differently. It was used to model the noisy sensors. That is, given the Cartesian coordinates of the robot and the landmarks, measuments are repeated (without moving the robot) to estimate the noise in the sensors. Our approach is fundamentally different. The covariance matrix of the bearing vectors collected in

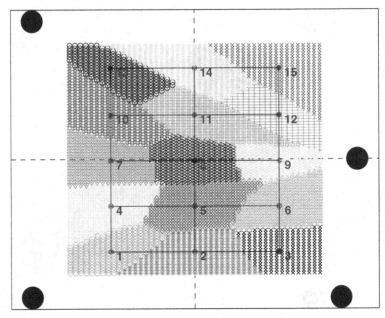

Fig. 3. Voronoi diagram compruted with the Euclidian distance on the bearing vectors. The induced partition is quite different from the ideal partition of Figure 1. In particular, observation vectors corresponding to points close to the centre of cell 1 are incorrectly assigned to cell 2

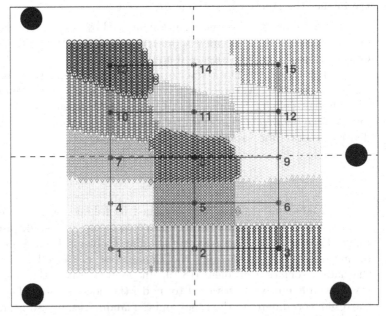

Fig. 4. Voronoi diagram computed with the *Naive Bayes classifier* weighted distance on the bearing vectors. About 250 observations per cell were made for the evaluation of the statistical parameters of the Gaussian distributions

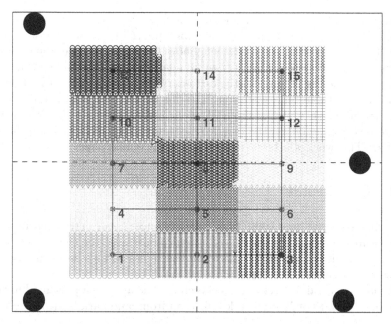

Fig. 5. The best classification is achieved with the Mahalanobis distance

a given cell i provides us with some information on the geometry of the manifold around this point in sensor space.

Figure 5 shows the classification results when using the Mahalanobis distance. Our experimental results (in simulation) show that the Euclidean distance achieves a classification accuracy of 92.17% percents, whereas the Naive Bayes distances achieves a classification accuracy of 97.14% percents. However, the best results are achieved with the Mahalanobis distance which reaches an accuracy of 99.32%.

3 Strategy for Approximating the Riemannian Manifold

It is desirable to automatically build the partition of Figure 2. Unfortunately, a training set of observations does not allow us to directly compute the covariance matrices (assuming we have only access to bearing information). Moreover, we already saw that using a standard SOM training algorithm is not an option (failure to spread the neurons evenly with respect to the ground). A possible strategy is to consider the weighted complete graph G whose vertices are the bearing vectors of a training set T and whose edge-weigths are the Euclidian distance between the bearing vectors. Unfortunately, methods that build an auxiliary graph based on the k-nearest neighbors (like [20]) fail to build a proper grid for manifolds that have significantly different curvatures in orthogonal directions (the k nearest neighbors will be along the same direction). To address this problem, we build a graph G_θ obtained from G by removing all edges whose weights are larger than θ, (or equivalently setting the weights of those edges to ∞). We then compute a grid-like subgraph H of G_θ by imposing constraints on the relative positions of the neighbors. Preliminary experiments have shown that it is possible to compute H by simulating annealing using a fitness function based on the discrepancy of the degrees of the vertices of H (the desired degree is 4). A suitable representation of H for this search is as a union of a set of cycles of length 4 of G_θ. From H, we can then estimate the distance between two bearing vectors on the manifold by computing the length of a shortest path in H. This work will be presented in a forthcoming paper.

4 Conclusion

In this paper, we have highligthed the differences between three natural similarity measures for bearing vectors. We have demonstrated the clear superiority of the Mahalanobis distance for localization based on bearings problems. We have also sketched a method for approximating the distance on the Riemannian manifold defined by a training set of sensor vectors. The approach presented in this paper is generic and not limited to localization from landmark bearing problems.

References

1. Costa, A., Kantor, G., Choset, H.: Bearing-only landmark initialization with unknown data association. In: Proceedings of the 2004 IEEE International Conference on Robotics and Automation. Volume 2. (2004) 1764 – 1770
2. Nehmzow, U.: Map Building Through Self-Organisation for Robot Navigation. 1812 edn. Lecture Notes in Computer Science. Springer-Verlag (2000)
3. Gerecke, U., Sharkey, N.E., Sharkey, A.J.C.: Common evidence vectors for self-organized ensemble localization. Neurocomputing **55** (2003) 499–519
4. Smith, R., Self, M., Cheeseman, P.: Estimating uncertain spatial relationships in robotics. Automous robot vehicles (1990) 167–193
5. Dissanayake, G., Clark, S., Newman, P., Durrant-Whyte, H., Csorba, M.: Estimating uncertain spatial relationships in robotics. IEEE Transactions on Robotics and Automation **17** (2001) 229 – 241
6. Negenborn, R.: Robot Localization and Kalman Filters. PhD thesis, UTRECHT UNIVERSITY (2003)
7. Bailey, T.: Constrained initialisation for bearing-only slam. In: Robotics and Automation IEEE International Conference. Volume 2. (2003) 1966–1971 vol.2
8. Montemerlo, M., Thrun, S.: Fastslam 2.0: An improved particle filtering algorithm for simultaneous localization and mapping that provably converges. In: Proceedings of the International Joint Conference on Artifiical Intelligence. (2003)
9. Thrun, S.: Particle filters in robotics. In: Proceedings of the 17th Annual Conference on Uncertainty in AI (UAI). (2002)
10. Fox, D.: Adapting the sample size in particle filters through kld-sampling. The International Journal of Robotics Research **22** (2003) 985–1003
11. Borenstein, J., Everett, H.R., Feng, L.: Navigating mobile robots: systems and techniques. Wellesley, Massachusetts: A K. Peters (1996)

12. Garcia-Alegre, M., Garcia-Perez, A.R.L., Martinez, L., Guinea, R., Pozo-Ruz, D.: An autonomous robot in agriculture tasks. In: 3ECPA-3 European Conf. On Precision Agriculture, France. (2001) 25–30

13. Hanek, R., Schmitt, T.: Vision-based localization and data fusion in a system of cooperating mobile robots. In: Proceedings of Intelligent Robots and Systems. (2000)

14. Rizzi, A., Cassinis, R.: robot self-localization system based on omni-directional color images. In: Robotics and Autonomous Systems 34. (2001) 23–38

15. Yagi, Y., Fujimura, M., Yashida, M.: Route representation for mobile robot navigation by omnidirectional route panorama transformation. In: Proceeding of the IEEE International Conference on Robotics and Automation, Leuven, Belgium. (1998)

16. Delahoche, L., Pegard, C., Marhic, B., Vasseur, P.: A navigation system based on an omni-directional vision sensor. In: Int. Conf. on Intelligent Robotics and Systems. (1997) 718–724

17. de Leon, A.R., Carriere, K.C.: A generalized mahalanobis distance for mixed data. Journal of Multivariate Analysis **92** (2005) 174–185

18. Wang, C.C.: Simultaneous Localization, Mapping and Moving Object Tracking. PhD thesis, Robotics Institute, Carnegie Mellon University, Pittsburgh, PA (2004)

19. Lisien, B., Morales, D., Silver, D., Kantor, G., Rekleitis, I., Choset, H.: Hierarchical simultaneous localization and mapping. In: Intelligent Robots and Systems. Volume 1. (2003) 448–453

20. Saul, L.K., Roweis, S.T.: Think globally, fit locally: Unsupervised learning of low dimensional manifolds. Journal of Machine Learning Research **4** (2003) 119–155

Efficient Spatial Clustering Algorithm Using Binary Tree

Mohsin Ali, Xue Li, and Zhao Yang Dong

School of Information Technology and Electrical Engineering
The University of Queensland, Brisbane QLD 4072, Australia
{mohsin,xueli,zdong}@itee.uq.edu.au

Abstract. In this paper we present an efficient k-Means clustering algorithm for two dimensional data. The proposed algorithm re-organizes dataset into a form of nested binary tree*. Data items are compared at each node with only two nearest means with respect to each dimension and assigned to the one that has the closer mean. The main intuition of our research is as follows: We build the nested binary tree. Then we scan the data in raster order by in-order traversal of the tree. Lastly we compare data item at each node to the only two nearest means to assign the value to the intendant cluster. In this way we are able to save the computational cost significantly by reducing the number of comparisons with means and also by the least use to Euclidian distance formula. Our results showed that our method can perform clustering operation much faster than the classical ones.

1 Introduction

Efficient and effective data mining have numerous requirements. There are many issues involved in data mining including data mining methodology, user interaction, performance and scalability, and processing of very large and heterogeneous data bases. Among these issues the performance and scalability factors are the most important ones [1]. In this paper we focus on the performance and scalability issues in data mining. The huge size of many databases, the wide distribution of data and the computational complexity of some data mining methods are factors motivating the development of efficient algorithms in the field of data mining.

There are many techniques used in data mining and clustering is one them. It is a process of grouping of objects into meaningful subsets. This process has many applications in data mining and knowledge discovery, machine learning, vector quantization pattern recognition [14], pattern classification [9, 14]. Due to the increase in large amount of data obtained from high resolution images, GIS, X-Ray, environmental assessment and planning are the applications require efficient algorithms for getting the useful patterns from them. Many algorithms have been proposed previously. The k-Means method has been shown to be effective in producing good clustering results [2]. However it is computationally very expensive for large datasets [2]. The classical k-Means clustering method requires time complexity $O(nkt)$, where n is the number of data items, k is the number of required clusters and t is the number of iteration per-

---

* We construct the nested binary tree in this way that first we construct a binary tree with respect to the values of first dimension and then we construct a binary tree at each node of this tree with respect to values of second dimension for multiple occurrences of the values of first dimension in all data items

M. Gallagher, J. Hogan, and F. Maire (Eds.): IDEAL 2005, LNCS 3578, pp. 294–301, 2005.

formed to cluster that data items. K-Mediods [7] also works in the same way as k-Means. The only difference between k-Means and k-Mediods is the selection criteria of defining the mean value. In k-Means the average of the cluster is treated as the mean for next iteration while in k-Mediods the actual data item closest to mean is treated as centre of the cluster. The time complexity of k-Mediods is $O(k(n-k)^2)$. CLARA [1, 7] is the enhanced form of k-Mediods with time complexity equal to $O(ks^2 + k(n-k))$, where S is size of sample, n is number of data items and k is number of required clusters. It was developed based on k-Mediods to work for large data-bases. CLARANS [7] was developed to enhance the efficiency of CLARA with time complexity $O(n^2)$.

AGNES, DIANA and BIRCH [1,7] algorithms are classified as hierarchical algorithms. BIRCH uses CF-Tree. DBSCAN uses R* Tree, STING [7] uses Quad Tree, DENCLUE uses B+ Tree. These last three are classified as Grid Based clustering algorithms. These algorithms are evolution of each other but the purpose of all these algorithms is to provide the better quality of results or to improve the performance of the existing ones. K-Mean and k-Mediods are the most basic algorithms in this category. The other algorithms are enhanced forms of k-Mediods either to give better results or increase efficiency; therefore they are also dependent on these basic methods.

In order to further enhance the efficiency of the algorithm, we propose an efficient algorithm for implementation of the k-Means method. In our algorithm we selected Binary Tree. B-Tree [5, 12] and R-Tree [12, 13] are also used in indexing the large data but they have some limitations in insertion and updating when the node needs to split or to delete [12], while Binary Tree does not have same problems. B-Tree and R-Tree contain the indexes of data in the leaf nodes and used to deal with large data, but their leaf nodes contain the chunks of data like the memory pages and in those chunks the search may be linear. The purpose of this research is to gain efficiency, by building updating and traversing the Binary Trees. This method provides the same results as classical k-Means algorithm but, with better performance. This method is also very scalable especially with the increase in number of required clusters, because its performance does not reduce with increase the number of required clusters. If we analyse all the previously proposed algorithms, we observe that they all deal with k means of the clusters at same time and try to find the closest mean to assign the data item to the relevant cluster. In our proposed algorithm, we deal with only two means at any one time for each dimension and find the closer mean rather than closest mean, so that the performance of our algorithm remains almost constant regardless of the number of clusters.

The rest of the paper is organized as follows. In Section 2, we review the k-Means, and analyse the time complexity of k-Means algorithm in detail before we present the new algorithm in Section 3. Experiments and performance evaluation is described in Section 4 and we conclude our paper in Section 5.

2 K-Means Clustering

K-Means clustering is a partitioning algorithm. It attempts to break the dataset into k clusters such that the partition optimizes on a given criteria. This is an iterative clustering algorithm in which items are moved among the set of clusters until the desired set is reached [1, 2]. The cluster mean of $m_i = \{m_1, m_2, m_3, \ldots m_k\}$ is defined as means of k number of desired clusters and

$$m_i = \frac{1}{n}\sum_{j=1}^{n} t_{ij}$$

Where m_i is the mean of cluster i and n is the number of items in that cluster i. The k-Means algorithm takes the input parameter, k and partitioned the set of items into k clusters so that the similarity between the items in the resulting cluster is high while the similarity between the items of different clusters is low [1]. Assuming that there are n data items in a dataset to be clustered in k different sets and d is the dimension of data items; the computational cost of classical k-Means algorithm per iteration is decomposed into following three parts [2]:

- The time required for the first *for* loop is O(nk).
- The time required for calculating centroids of the next loop is O(n).
- The time required for calculating the error function is O(n).

The number of distance calculation which are O(k) per iteration. The number of comparisons involved to find the closest mean of the cluster to assign the data item is O($k-1$) for simple linear search method. These figures are given with the assumption that the data is single dimensional. Despite of the efficiency, k-Means are very sensitive to the presence of noise and outliers [6, 10].

3 A New Clustering Algorithm – Advanced K-Clustering Algorithm

Our new approach works on the idea of traversing the two dimensional data in raster scan order and compare the data items row wise to only closest means. We use the Euclidian Distance formula least possible. In this way we can save the computational cost by least use of distance calculations and comparing the distance to only closer means. Main idea behind our approach is shown in Figure 1. We construct a nested binary tree from the data set through binary insertion operation [3, 4, 5]. The nested binary tree is constructed in such a way that each node has two left pointers and two

```
INPUT       Data = {d₁, d₂, d₃…dₙ} /*data items set */
            k              /*number of desired clusters */
OUTPUT      k              /*set of desired clusters*/
BEGIN
      Call Function Construct_Tree ( Data )
      /* Through binary tree insertion operation [3]  */
      Assign initial values for means m₁, m₂, m₃,.. mₖ and
         Arrange them in order with respect to each dimension
      /* One sorted list for each dimension */
      Assign the initial values to Xₗₒwₑᵣ, Xₕᵢgₕₑᵣ, Yₗₒwₑᵣ and Yₕᵢgₕₑᵣ
      REPEAT
            Call Function Cluster (Root_Node )
               /* given in Figure 2 /
            Calculate new means of clusters
      UNTIL     (convergence criteria is meet)
END
```

Fig. 1. Proposed k-Means Algorithm Using Nested Binary Tree

right pointers for each dimension. Initially we construct the binary tree with respect to one dimension (lets suppose Y-dimension) values of the data items. Then we construct another binary tree at each node for the X-dimension values for all data items having Y-dimension value similar to Y-dimension value at that node. So, by in-order traversing of such a tree, we can process all data items in raster scan order.

For the next step we assign the initial values to all means of the required number of clusters and form two ordered lists with respect to each dimension. We start our clustering procedure as given in Figure 2 by in-order traversal [3, 4] [left sub-tree w.r.t. Y → (left sub-tree w.r.t. X → node → right sub-tree w.r.t. X) → right sub-tree w.r.t. Y] of the nested binary tree. First of all we pick the two initial means from each sorted list and assign those values to X_{Lower}, X_{Higher}, Y_{Lower} and Y_{Higher} respectively and then we perform clustering procedure as follows.

First of all we find the closest mean with respect to X-dimension. If X-dimension value of the data item at that node is closer to the X_{lower} then we select X_{lower} as the nearest else we assign X_{Higher} to X_{lower} and pick another value from the ordered list of means with respect to X-dimension. And repeat the process until we reach at the end. In this case we choose X_{Higher} as the closest mean value with respect to X-dimension. Similarly we perform the same process to select the closest mean with respect to Y-dimension. After selecting the nearest means with respect to both dimensions, we check if both values represent the same mean value then we assign the data item to the cluster having that mean value. In other case we find the closer mean among both means by using the Euclidian Distance formula and assign the data item to the cluster having closer mean value. At the end of traversing one row, we initialize the variables X_{lower} and X_{Higher}. At the end of iteration we calculate the new means and bring them in order. This process continues until some convergence criteria are meet.

Here we observe that we are not computing the distance of data items with all means. Instead of this we are comparing the distance for only two means for each dimension regardless of the number of clusters, As the number of clusters are very less than the number of data items so ordering of means in each iteration does not effect the over all performance. This process definitely decreases our computation time. This difference between two algorithms is more visible by increasing the number of clusters. All these factors make the proposed algorithm more efficient than the classical k-Means Algorithm.

As we deal with only two means with respect to each dimension so we only need to allocate memory for required clusters, while in classical method we need to allocate memory for k clusters and in worse case the size of each cluster can be nearly equal to the size of dataset. We can also save this memory allocation by using the pointers of the data items. So in this way our method is also efficient in terms of memory usage.

4 Performance Evaluation

We perform these experiments on two dimensional data on a 2.8 GHz Pentium 4 machine with 512 MB physical memory and 40 GB hard drive, running on Microsoft XP operating system. Both algorithms were implemented in Visual C++ Win32 console application. By running both programs developed for both algorithms we performed two experiments to compute the performance. We used the two dimensional numeric data representing the coordinates of the points.

```
Function Cluster (Node *node)
BEGIN
    IF node->left_Y_Pointer NOT NULL
        Call Function Cluster (node->left_Y_Pointer )
        Initialize X_Lower and X_Higher
    END_IF
    IF node->left_X_Pointer NOT NULL
        Call Function Cluster ( node->left_X_Pointer )
    END_IF
    Define near_XPoint and near_YPoint as Point
    WHILE TRUE
        IF data item at node is closer to X_Lower
            Assign X_Lower to near_XPoint
            Break
        ELSE
            IF X_Higher is the last Item is the means list sorted wrt X Di-
            mension
                Assign X_Higher to near_XP
                Break
            ELSE
                Assign the value of X_Higher to X_Lower
                Assign next higher order mean value to X_Higher
            END_IF
        END_IF
    END_WHILE
    WHILE TRUE
        IF data item at node is closer to Y_Lower
            Assign Y_Lower to Near_YPoint
            Break
        ELSE
            IF Y_Higher is the last Item is the means list sorted wrt Y Di-
            mension
                Assign Y_Higher to near_YP
                Break
            ELSE
                Assign the value of Y_Higher to Y_Lower
                Assign next higher order mean value to Y_Higher
            END_IF
        END_IF
    END_WHILE
    IF near_XP is equal to near_YP
        Assign the data item to the cluster having mean near_XP
        /* near_XP and near_YP are same Points*/
    ELSE
        Find the closer Point to the data item at the node between
            near_XP and near_YP
        IF the data item at the node is closer to near_XP
            Assign the Data Item to the cluster having mean near_XP
        ELSE
            Assign the Data Item to the cluster having mean near_YP
        END_IF
    END_IF
    IF node->right_X_Pointer NOT NULL
        Call Function Cluster ( node->right_X_Pointer )
    END_IF
    IF node->right_Y_Pointer NOT NULL
        Initialize X_Lower and X_Higher
        Call Function Cluster (node->left_Y_Pointer )
    END_IF
END
```

Fig. 2. Proposed k-Means Algorithm Using Binary Tree

In the first experiment we computed the time required to cluster the data into 15 clusters. In this experiment we changed the size of dataset consists of data points ranging from 1,000 to 15,000 keeping the number of required clusters constant. We computed each result three times and got their average value. If we observe the graph shown in the Figure 3, the results show that our proposed algorithm performs clustering much faster than the classical-k-Means clustering.

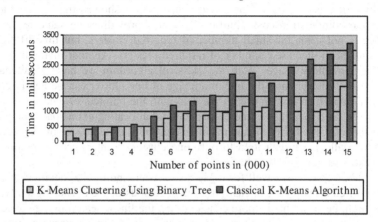

Fig. 3. Performance Evaluation -Graph between sizes of dataset in thousands verses time to perform clustering with 15 numbers of required clusters

In our second experiment we kept the size of data constant at 10,000 data points and we changed the number of required clusters to evaluate the performance. These results are shown in Figure 4. These results show that classical k-Means method is good for small number of clusters, which gives even better results as compare to our proposed algorithm. But with the increase in the number of required clusters its performance decreases. While using the binary tree method we can get much better performance with higher number of required clusters.

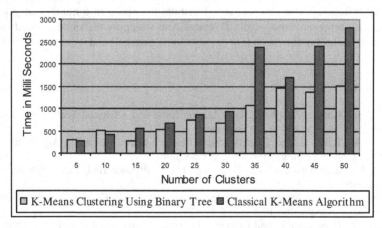

Fig. 4. Performance Evaluation - Graph between numbers of clusters verses time to perform clustering with 10,000 data items

Our both tests prove that the new proposed algorithm is able to provide the same results with much faster way as compared to the classical k-Means algorithms.

5 Conclusion

In this paper, we presented an efficient algorithm for performing the k-Means clustering on two dimensional data. Our experimental results showed that our method can decrease the computation cost significantly whilst providing the same results. This difference is not clear for small number of required clusters, but this difference is more visible with increased number of required clusters. Another main advantage is the efficient memory usage. With the classical algorithm we have to allocate the memory for all clusters and the maximum size of one cluster can be nearly equal to the size of dataset. In this algorithm we deal with the pointers of data items at node which can be used to assign to the cluster without allocating extra space for that data item. As the total number of data items in all clusters is equal to size of data set and in one time we allocate a data item to only one cluster, pointers are recommended to save the extra memory for the clusters.

This method also works well for k-Mediods. After finding the mean value of each cluster in efficient way we can easily find the Mediods of the cluster by applying the binary search, because this is more efficient than the linear search in the cluster data. By doing so we can easily enhanced the efficiency of other algorithms which are based on k-Mediods like CLARA and CLARANS

In this paper we simulated our work on two dimensional data and we can also implement this algorithm successfully for higher dimensional data through the same method. Now lets say if $a = (x_1, x_2, x_3, ... x_i)$ and $b = (y_1, y_2, y_3, ... y_i)$, then the Euclidian distance between a and b can be defined as $d(a,b) = \sqrt{(x_1 - y_1)^2 + (x_2 - y_2)^2 + ... (x_i - y_i)^2}$.

This formula shows that we have to calculate the square of the difference for each dimension value, which consumes much computing cycle. We have tried to least use of this formula in order to save computing time.

We can run this algorithm in distributed environment for large amount of data to get better efficiency. For this, we can distribute the space in a number of grid cells and each cell represents the small 2D space. And we apply the same method on each cell by only including the mean that belongs to its own cell and its nearest neighbours.

References

1. Han J, and Kamber M, (2001). Data Mining Basic and Advanced Technigues. San Francisco, Calif, Morgan Kaufmann Publishers.
2. Alsabti K., Ranka S. and Singh V, An Efficient k-Means Clustering Algorithm, (1998): 11th International Parallel Processing Symposium
3. Wirth N., Algorithms and Data Structures, (1986) Prentice Hall, Inc., Englewood cliffs, New Jersey.
4. Weiss M. A., Data Structures and Algorithm Analysis, (1992) The Benjamin/Cummings Publishing Company, Inc. Redwood City, CA
5. Aho A. V., Hopcroft J. E. and Ullman J. D., Data structures and algorithms (1983), Reading, Mass. London ; Sydney : Addison-Wesley
6. Karyapis G., Han E.H. and Kumar V., CHAMELEON: A Hierarchical Clustering Algorithm Using Dynamic Modeling 1999, IEEE Computer, Special Issue on Data Analysis and Mining.

7. Han, J.; Kamber, M.; and Tung, A. 2001. Spatial Clustering Methods in Data Mining: A Survey. In Miller, H., and Han, J., eds., Geographic Data Mining and Knowledge Discovery. Taylor and Francis. 21

8. Halkidi M., Batistakis Y. and Vazirgiannis M., Cluster Validity Methods: Part 1, ACM SIGMOD Record, Volume 31, Issue 2 (June 2002)

9. Kanungo T., David M. M, Nathan S. N. and Piatko C. D., A Local Search Approximation Algorithm for k-Means Clustering, ACM Press, New York, NY, USA, 2002

10. Kanungo T., Mount D. M., Netanyahu N., Piatko C., Silverman R., and Wu A. Y., An efficient k-means clustering algorithm: analysis and implementation *IEEE Trans.* Pattern Analysis and Machine Intelligence, 24 (2002), 881-892.

11. Estivill-Castro V. and Fast J. Y., Robust General Purpose clustering algorithms, Data Mining and knowledge discovery, 8, 127-150, 2004, Kluwer Academic Publishers, Manufactured in the Netherlands. (Pacific Rim International Conference on Artificial Intelligence)

12. Volker Grade and Oliver, Multidimensional Access Methods, ACM Computing Surveys, Vol. 30, No. 2, June 1998.

13. Antonin Guttman, R-Trees: Adynamic Index Structure for Spatial Searching, SIGMOD Conference 1984: Boston, Massachusetts ACM

14. Karen L. Oehler and Robert M. Gray, "Combining Image Compression and Classification Using Vector Quantization" IEEE TRANSACTIONS ON PATTERN ANALYSIS AND MACHINE INTELLIGENCE, VOL. 17, NO. 5, MAY 1995

Cluster Analysis of High-Dimensional Data: A Case Study

Richard Bean[1] and Geoff McLachlan[1,2]

[1] ARC Centre in Bioinformatics, Institute for Molecular Bioscience, UQ
[2] Department of Mathematics, University of Queensland (UQ)

Abstract. Normal mixture models are often used to cluster continuous data. However, conventional approaches for fitting these models will have problems in producing nonsingular estimates of the component-covariance matrices when the dimension of the observations is large relative to the number of observations. In this case, methods such as principal components analysis (PCA) and the mixture of factor analyzers model can be adopted to avoid these estimation problems. We examine these approaches applied to the Cabernet wine data set of Ashenfelter (1999), considering the clustering of both the wines and the judges, and comparing our results with another analysis. The mixture of factor analyzers model proves particularly effective in clustering the wines, accurately classifying many of the wines by location.

1 Introduction

In recent times much attention has been given in the scientific literature to the use of normal mixture models as a device for the clustering of continuous data; see, for example, McLachlan and Peel (2000b). With this approach, the observed data $y_1, \ldots y_n$, are assumed to have come from the normal mixture distribution,

$$f(\boldsymbol{y}; \boldsymbol{\Psi}) = \sum_{i=1}^{g} \pi_i \phi(\boldsymbol{y}; \boldsymbol{\mu}_i, \boldsymbol{\Sigma}_i),\tag{1}$$

where $\phi(\boldsymbol{y}; \boldsymbol{\mu}, \boldsymbol{\Sigma})$ denotes the p-variate normal density function with mean $\boldsymbol{\mu}$ and covariance matrix $\boldsymbol{\Sigma}$. Here the vector $\boldsymbol{\Psi}$ of unknown parameters consists of the mixing proportions π_i, the elements of the component means $\boldsymbol{\mu}_i$, and the distinct elements of the component-covariance matrix $\boldsymbol{\Sigma}_i$. The normal mixture model (1) can be fitted iteratively to an observed random sample $y_1, \ldots, y_n$ by maximum likelihood (ML) via the expectation-maximization (EM) algorithm of Dempster et al., (1977); see also McLachlan and Krishnan (1997). Frequently, in practice, the clusters in the data are essentially elliptical, so that it is reasonable to consider fitting mixtures of elliptically symmetric component densities. Within this class of component densities, the multivariate normal density is a convenient choice given its computational tractability.

Under (1), the posterior probability that an observation with feature vector y_j belongs to the ith component of the mixture is given by

$$\tau_i(\boldsymbol{y}_j) = \pi_i \phi(\boldsymbol{y}; \boldsymbol{\mu}_i, \boldsymbol{\Sigma}_i) / f(\boldsymbol{y}_j; \boldsymbol{\Psi})\tag{2}$$

M. Gallagher, J. Hogan, and F. Maire (Eds.): IDEAL 2005, LNCS 3578, pp. 302–310, 2005.

for $i = 1, \ldots, g$. The mixture approach gives a probabilistic clustering in terms of these estimated posterior probabilities of component membership. An outright partitioning of the observations into g nonoverlapping clusters $C_1, \ldots, C_g$ is effected by assigning each observation to the component to which it has the highest estimated posterior probability of belonging. Thus the ith cluster C_i contains those observations assigned to the ith component.

The g-component normal mixture model (1) with unrestricted component-covariance matrices is a highly parameterized model with $\frac{1}{2}p(p+1)$ parameters for each component-covariance matrix $\boldsymbol{\Sigma}_i (i = 1, \ldots, g)$. In order for a non-singular estimate of a component-covariance matrix to be obtained, effectively $(p + 1)$ observations need to be assigned to that component. Hence problems arise in the fitting of normal mixtures with unrestricted component-covariance matrices, especially if p is large relative to the number of observations n. In microarray experiments, for example, p can be several thousand while n may be no greater than 100 or so. This represents an extreme case; there can be problems for p as small as, say, 20 if n is not relatively large. Hence in practice, there is a need for methods that can handle the analysis of high-dimensional data.

Banfield and Raftery (1993) introduced a parameterization of the component-covariance matrix $\boldsymbol{\Sigma}_i$ based on a variant of the standard spectral decomposition of $\boldsymbol{\Sigma}_i (i = 1, \ldots, g)$. A common approach to reducing the the number of dimensions is to perform a principal component analysis (PCA). But projections of the feature data $\boldsymbol{y}_j$ onto the first few principal axes are not always useful in portraying the group structure; see McLachlan and Peel (2000a, Page 239). This point was also stressed by Chang (1983), who showed in the case of two groups that the principal component of the feature vector that provides the best separation between groups in terms of Mahalanobis distance is not necessarily the first component.

Another approach for reducing the number of unknown parameters in the forms for the component-covariance matrices is to adopt the mixture of factor analyzers model, as considered in McLachlan and Peel (2000a, 2000b). In this paper, we present an example to demonstrate further the differences between using principal components and mixtures of factor analyzers to cluster high-dimensional data. The example concerns the Cabernet wine data set of Ashenfelter (1999). In this data set, 32 judges ranked 46 wines from nine different countries on a scale of 1 to 46. All the information about the wines is known, but the judges refused to be identified.

2 Mixtures of Factor Analyzers

Factor analysis is commonly used for explaining data, in particular, correlations between variables in multivariate observations. It can be used also for dimensionality reduction, although the method of PCA is more widely used in this role. However, the effectiveness of these two statistical techniques is limited by their global linearity. A global nonlinear approach can be obtained by postulating a finite mixture of linear submodels (factor analyzers) for the distribution of the full observation vector $\boldsymbol{Y}_j$. That is, with the mixture of factor analyzers model, we can provide a local dimensionality reduction method by assuming that the distribution of the observation Y_j can be modelled by (1), where

$$\Sigma_i = B_i B_i^T + D_i \quad (i = 1, \ldots, g), \tag{3}$$

where B_i is a $p \times q$ matrix of factor loadings and D_i is a diagonal matrix ($i = 1, \ldots, g$). The parameter vector Ψ now consists of the elements of the μ_i, the B_i, and the D_i, along with the mixing proportions π_i ($i = 1, \ldots, g - 1$), on putting $\pi_g = 1 - \sum_{i=1}^{g-1} \pi_i$. Unlike the PCA model, the factor analysis model (3) enjoys a powerful invariance property: changes in the scales of the feature variables in y_j, appear only as scale changes in the appropriate rows of the matrix B_i of factor loadings.

We can represent an original data point y_j in q-dimensional space by plotting the estimated conditional expectation of each factor given y_j and its component membership, that is, the (estimated) posterior mean of the factor U_{ij} ($i = 1, \ldots, g; \ j = 1, \ldots, n$), where U_{ij} is the latent factor corresponding to the jth observation in the ith component (see Section 8.7.4 in McLachlan and Peel, 2000b).

It can be seen that the mixture of factor analyzers model provides a way of controlling the number of parameters through the reduced model (3) for the component-covariance matrices. It thus provides a model intermediate between the independent and unrestricted models. The adequacy of the fit of a mixture of factor analyzers with q factors can be tested using the likelihood ratio statistic, as regularity conditions hold for tests on the value of q for a fixed number of components g. The model can be fitted by using the alternating expectation–conditional maximization (AECM) algorithm, whereby the single M-step of the EM algorithm is replaced by a number of computationally simpler conditional maximization (CM) steps and where the specification of the complete data is allowed to be different on each CM-step.

If the number of factors q is chosen sufficiently small relative to the number of observations n, then there will be no singularity problems in fitting a mixture of factor analyzers for equal component-covariance matrices. For unrestricted component-covariance matrices, there may still be some problems if the clusters are small in size; in which case, they can be avoided by specifying the diagonal matrices D_i to be the same.

3   Clustering of Wines

The list of wines is given in Table 1, with the numbering of the wine in the first column and the ranking of the wine in the final column. In the scatter plots, the wine numbers are prefixed by a two letter ISO country code, or by CA or WA when the wine is from California or Washington.

For these data there is interest in two clustering problems: the clustering of the wines on the basis of the (judges') scores and the clustering of the judges on the basis of their scores for the wines. We consider first the former problem, by fitting a mixture of $g = 2$ factor analyzers with $q = 2$ factors to the $n = 46$ wines on the basis of the $p = 32$ scores of the judges.

Table 1. List of wines with ranking in final column

1	Quilced Creek Cab. Sauv. '95	21
2	Chateau Latour '95	43
3	l'Ermita, Palacios (Priorat) '95	36
4	Chateau Ceval-Blanc '95	29
5	Ornellaia '94	39
6	Harlan Napa Valley Cab. Sauv. '94	11
7	Gallo Northern Sonoma Cab. Sauv. '94	14
8	Mitchelton Victoria Print Shiraz '95	24
9	Quintessa of Rutherford '95	33
10	Grans Muralles, Torres '96	20
11	Chateau Kefraya Comte de M Cuvee '96	10
12	Dalla Valle Napa Valley Maya '94	6
13	Grace Family Vineyard Napa Valley Cab. Sauv. '94	18
14	Henry Lagarde Lujan de Cuyo Syrah '95	45
15	Dave Nichol Stag's Leap Hillside Reserve Cab. Sauv.'91	37
16	Chateau Pichon-Longueville, Comtesse de Lalande5	28
17	Ridge Vineyards Monte Bello Red Table Wine '95	17
18	Plaisir de Merle Paarl Cab. Sauv.'95	41
19	Stag's Leap Wine Cellars Napa Valley Cab. Sauv.,Cask 23 '95	4
20	Arietta Napa Valley Red Table Wine '96	9
21	Sassicaia '94	34
22	Caymus Vineyard Napa Valley Cab. Sauv. '95	5
23	Chateau Lefite '95	40
24	Chateau Le Pin '95	NR
25	Longridge Hawkes Bay Merlot '95	46
26	Plumpjack Napa Valley Cab. Sauv. '95	13
27	Clark-Clauden Napa Valley Cab. Sauv. '95	1
28	Staglin Napa Valley Cab. Sauv., reserve '95	12
29	Chateau Margaux '95	23
30	Araugo napa Valley Cab. Sauv., Eisele Vineyard '94	3
31	Brant family Vineyard Napa Valley Cab. Sauv. '95	22
32	Chateau Los Boldos Cab. Sauv. Vieille Vignes '97	32
33	Beringer Napa Valley Cab. Sauv., Bancroft Vineyard '94	2
34	Cogin Napa Valley Cab. Sauv., Herb Lamb Vineyard '94	27
35	Penfold's Cab. Sauv., Bin 707 '90	25
36	Ridge Vineyards Geyersville Red Table Wine '95	16
37	Screaming Eagle Napa Valley Cab. Sauv. '95	8
38	Martinelli Jackass Hill Zinfandel '94	35
39	Chateau Petrus '95	26
40	De Lille Cellars Chaleur Estate Red Table Wine '94	19
41	Turley Napa Valley Zinfandel, Aida Vineyard '95	42
42	Chateau hout-Bion '95	31
43	Lionetti Cab. Sauv. '95	7
44	Forman Winery Napa Valley Cab. Sauv. '94	15
45	Tarapaca Maipo Valey Zavala Red Table Wine '96	30
46	Chateau Mouton-Rothschild '95	38
47	Veramonte Primus Casablanca Valley Merlot '96	44

A test of the value of the number of components g corresponding to the number of clusters in the data can be based on the likelihood ratio statistic λ. However, regularity conditions do not hold for $-2\log\lambda$ to have its usual (asymptotic) null distribution of chi-squared with degrees of freedom d equal to the difference between the number of parameters under the null and alternative hypotheses. Thus we adopted a resampling approach (McLachlan, 1987). On the basis of $B = 19$ replications of $-2\log\lambda$, we rejected the null hypothesis $H_0 : g = 1$ versus of the alternative $H_1 : g = 2$ at the 5% level. The null hypothesis of a single normal component was rejected also using the Bayesian information criterion (BIC) since it was found that

$$-2\log\lambda > d\log(n) \tag{4}$$

The case of unequal unrestricted component-covariance matrices was considered but rejected on the basis of BIC in favour of a common covariance matrix for the components. In the latter case, we can fit a mixture of two $p = 32$ dimensional normal components to the $n = 46$ wines, but we decided to work with a mixture of factor analyzers to keep the number of parameters down to a reasonable level compared to n. With the fitting of a mixture of $g = 2$ factor analyzers and $q = 2$ factors and equal component-covariance matrices, the wines fall into two clear groups. To illustrate the separation between the two clusters we plot the first canonical variate of the 46 wines in Figure 1. As there are only two groups, the canonical space is one-dimensional.

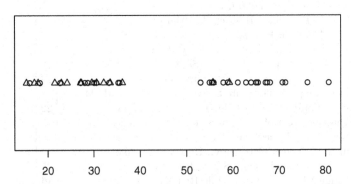

Fig. 1. First canonical variate of the 46 wines. Napa Valley wines are represented by triangles and other wines by circles

The choice of $q = 2$ factors was taken after the test of this value versus $q = 3$ was not significant according to the likelihood ratio statistic with null distribution taken to be chi-squared with 60 degrees of freedom. Although regularity conditions do not hold for the likelihood ratio test on the number of components g, they do for the number factors q for a given g. More specifically, for the test of the null hypothesis that $H_0 : q = q_0$ versus the alternative $H_1 : q = q_0 + 1$, the likelihood ratio statistic $-2\log\lambda$ under H_0 is asymptotically chi-squared with $d = g(p - q_0)$ degrees of freedom.

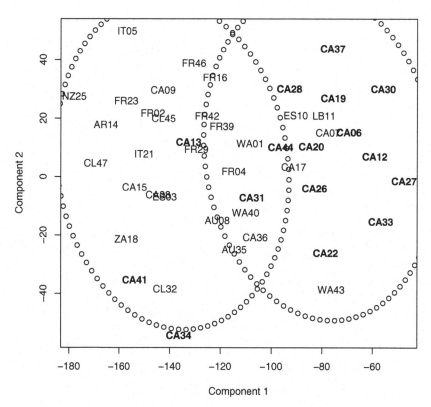

Fig. 2. Plot of the first two principal components of a PCA on the 46 wines. Here CA indicates California, WA indicates Washington, and any other two letter code is an ISO country code. The ellipses indicate the two groups given by fitting a mixture of two normals with equal covariance matrices to the PCs. Napa Valley wines are in bold

It is of interest to compare the clustering obtained using mixtures of $g = 2$ factor analyzers ($q = 2$ factors) with that obtained using a mixture of two normals fitted to the first two PCs. To this end, we display in Figure 2 a scatter plot of the first two PCs with the wine labels and implied clustering obtained fitting a mixture of two bivariate normals to these PCs. For comparative purposes, we give the clustering obtained by mixtures of factor analyzers in the space of the first two PCs in Figure 3. The larger cluster obtained using mixtures of factor analyzers contains 14 of the 16 Napa Valley wines from California, while the smaller cluster obtained using mixtures of normals fitted to the first two PCs contains 12 of the 16 Napa Valley wines.

4   Cluster Analysis of Judge Scores

Young (2005) indicated that "there are three judges (16, 26, 31) that march to the beat of a different drummer." These atypical judges were detected with the PowerMV program of Liu et al. (2005) using an R/G plot of the outer product of the right and left eigenvectors.

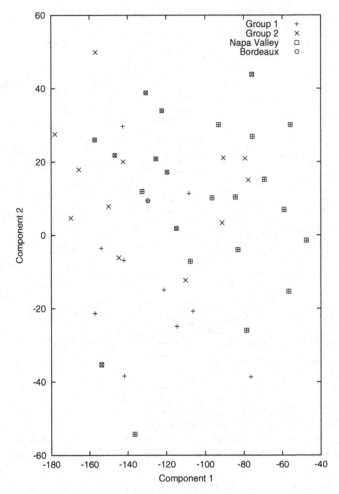

Fig. 3. Clusters obtained by mixtures of factor analyzers together with Napa Valley and Bordeaux wines

A plot of the estimated posterior means of the (unobservable) factors from fitting a single factor analysis model with $q = 2$ factors also suggests that these judges (plus judge 15) are quite distinct from the others in their scores. The plot is given in Figure 4.

It is of interest to consider the clustering of the 32 judges on the basis of their scores for 46 wines. For this clustering problem, we now have $n = 32$ and $p = 46$. Using equal covariance matrices and fitting $g = 2$ factor analyzers with $q = 2$ resulted in two clusters each of size 16, placing judges 16 and 26 in one cluster and judge 31 in the other.

A resampling approach with $B = 19$ replications, as above, showed that the test of $g = 1$ versus $g = 2$ groups was significant at the 5% level.

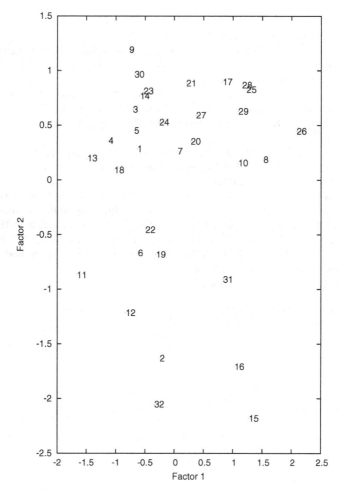

Fig. 4. Plot of the estimated posterior means of the $q = 2$ factors following a single-component factor analysis of the judge scores in the wine data set

References

Ashenfelter, O. (1999). California Versus All Challengers: The 1999 Cabernet Challenge. http://www.liquidasset.com/report20.html

Banfield, J.D. and Raftery, A.E. (1993). Model-based Gaussian and non-Gaussian clustering. *Biometrics* **49**, 803–821.

Chang, W.C. (1983). On using principal components before separating a mixture of two multivariate normal distributions. *Applied Statistics* **32**, 267–275.

Dempster, A.P., Laird, N.M., and Rubin, D.B. (1977). Maximum likelihood from incomplete data via the EM algorithm (with discussion). *Journal of the Royal Statistical Society B* **39**, 1–38.

Healy, M.J.R. (1986). Matrices for Statisticans. Clarendon: Oxford.

Liu, J., Feng, J., and Young, S.S. (2005). PowerMV v0.61.
   http://www.niss.org/PowerMV/

Liu, L., Hawkins, D.M., Ghosh, S., and Young, S.S. (2003). Robust singular value decomposition analysis of microarray data. *Proceedings of the National Academy of Sciences USA* **100**, 13167–13172.

McLachlan, G.J. (1987). On bootstrapping the likelihood ratio test statistic for the number of components in a normal mixture. *Applied Statistics* **36**, 318–324.

McLachlan, G.J. and Krishnan, T. (1997). *The EM Algorithm and Extensions*. New York: Wiley.

McLachlan, G.J. and Peel, D. (2000a). Mixtures of factor analyzers. In *Proceedings of the Seventeenth International Conference on Machine Learning*, P. Langley (Ed.). San Francisco: Morgan Kaufmann.

McLachlan, G.J. and Peel, D. (2000b). *Finite Mixture Models*. New York: Wiley.

McLachlan, G.J., Peel, D., and Bean, R.W. (2003). Modelling high-dimen-sional data by mixtures of factor analyzers. Comput. Statist. Data Anal. **41**, 379–388.

Troyanskaya, O., Cantor, M., Sherlock, G., Brown, P., Hastie, T., Tibshirani, R., Bostein, D. and Altman, R.B. (2001) Missing value estimation methods for DNA microarrays. *Bioinformatics* **17**, 520–525.

Young, S. (2005). Private communication.

Universal Clustering with Family of Power Loss Functions in Probabilistic Space*

Vladimir Nikulin

Computer Science Laboratory, Australian National University,
Canberra, ACT 0200, Australia
vladimir.nikulin@anu.edu.au

Abstract. We propose universal clustering in line with the concepts of universal estimation. In order to illustrate the model of universal clustering we consider family of power loss functions in probabilistic space which is marginally linked to the Kullback-Leibler divergence. The model proved to be effective in application to the synthetic data. Also, we consider large web-traffic dataset. The aim of the experiment is to explain and understand the way people interact with web sites.

1 Introduction

Clustering algorithms group empirical data according to the given criteria into several clusters with relatively stable and uniform statistical characteristics.

In this paper we consider prototype-based or distance-based clustering model. The corresponding solution may be effectively approximated using k-means algorithm within *Clustering-Minimization* (*CM*) framework [1]. This algorithm includes 2 main steps. Initially, we have to choose k *prototypes*. The corresponding empirical clusters will be defined in accordance to the criteria of nearest prototype measured by the distance Φ. Respectively, we will generate initial k clusters (Clustering step). As a second Minimization step we will recompute *centroids* or cluster centers using data strictly from the corresponding clusters. Then, we can repeat Clustering step using new prototypes obtained from the Minimization step as a centroids. Above algorithm has monotonical descending property. As a direct consequence, it will reach local minimum in a finite number of steps.

Recently, the Divisive Information-Theoretic Feature Clustering algorithm in probabilistic space $\mathcal{P}^m$ was proposed by [2]. It provides an attractive approach based on the Kullback-Leibler (*KL*) divergence. As it is outlined in [3], the probabilistic model can be extremely useful in many applications including information retrieval and filtering, natural language processing, machine learning from text and in related areas.

According to [4] and [5], in practice, however, an exact form of a loss function is difficult to specify. Hence, it is important to study a domination criterion simultaneously under a class of loss functions. Respectively, we introduce the

---

* This work was supported by the grants of the Australian Research Council

M. Gallagher, J. Hogan, and F. Maire (Eds.): IDEAL 2005, LNCS 3578, pp. 311–318, 2005.

family of power loss function in probabilistic space with KL-divergence as a marginal limit. As it is demonstrated in the Sect. 4, universal clustering may be effectively used in application to such important problem as determination of the number k of significant clusters in the sample. For example, [6] proposed G-means algorithm which is based on the *Gaussian* fit of the data within particular cluster. Usually [7], attempts to estimate the number of Gaussian clusters lead to a very high value of k. Most simple criteria such as *AIC* (*Akaike Information Criterion* [8]) and *BIC* (*Bayesian Information Criterion* [9], [10]) either overestimate or underestimate the number of clusters which severely limits their practical usability.

2   Prototype-Based Approach

Suppose that $\mathbf{X} := \{x_1, \ldots, x_n\}$ is a sample of i.i.d. observations drawn from probability space $(\mathcal{X}, \mathcal{A}, \mathbb{P})$ where probability measure $\mathbb{P}$ is assumed to be unknown.

We denote by $\mathcal{Q} \in \mathcal{X}^k$ a codebook as a set of *prototypes* $q(c)$ indexed by the code $c = 1..k$ where k is a *clustering size*.

Following [11] we estimate actual distortion error

$$\Re^{(k)}[\mathcal{Q}, \Phi] := \mathbf{E}\, \Phi(x \| \mathcal{Q})$$

by the empirical error

$$\Re^{(k)}_{\text{emp}}[\mathcal{Q}, \Phi] := \frac{1}{n} \sum_{t=1}^{n} \Phi(x_t \| \mathcal{Q}) \tag{1}$$

where $\Phi(x \| \mathcal{Q}) := \Phi(x, q(f(x)))$, $\Phi(\cdot, \cdot)$ is a loss function, and

$$f(x) := \underset{c \in \{1..k\}}{\operatorname{argmin}} \Phi(x, q(c)). \tag{2}$$

Above rule will split the given sample $\mathbf{X}$ into k empirical clusters: $\mathbf{X}_c := \{x_t : f(x_t) = c\}$, $\mathbf{X} = \cup_{c=1}^{k} \mathbf{X}_c$, $\mathbf{X}_i \cap \mathbf{X}_c = \emptyset, i \neq c$.

The algorithms within CM-framework have a heuristic nature. Respectively, their performance depends essentially on the selection of initial settings if number of clusters is bigger than one. Bhatia [12] proposed an adaptive technique that grows clusters without regard to initial selection of cluster representation or *cluster seeds*. As such, the technique can identify k clusters in an input data set by merging existing clusters and by creating new ones while keeping the number of clusters constant.

3   Probabilistic Framework

We work in a probabilistic setting where data-objects are probabilistically characterized by attributes or classes. We denote by $\mathcal{P}^m$ the m-dimensional probability simplex or probabilistic space of all m-dimensional probability vectors, and assume that the probabilities

$$p_{it} = P(i|x_t), p(x_t) = \{p_{1t}, \cdots, p_{mt}\}, \sum_{i=1}^{m} p_{it} = 1, t = 1..n,$$

represent relations between observations x_t and attributes $i = 1..m, m \geq 2$. Accordingly, we define the clustering model $(\mathcal{P}^m, KL)$ with *Kullback-Leibler* divergence:

$$KL(\mathbf{v}, \mathbf{u}) := \sum_{i=1}^{m} v_i \cdot \log \frac{v_i}{u_i} = \langle \mathbf{v}, \log \frac{\mathbf{v}}{\mathbf{u}} \rangle, \quad \mathbf{v}, \mathbf{u} \in \mathcal{P}^m. \tag{3}$$

3.1   Power Loss Functions in Probabilistic Space

Monograph [13], pp. 56-57, introduced an important class of f-divergences which we formulate using slightly different notations:

$$D_f(\mathbf{v}, \mathbf{u}) := \sum_{i=1}^{m} v_i f\left(\frac{u_i}{v_i}\right)$$

where f is a convex function and $f(1) = 0$.

Important examples of smooth f-divergences are given by the α-divergence $D^{(\alpha)} := D_{f^{(\alpha)}}$ for a real number α, which is defined by

$$f^{(\alpha)}(t) = \begin{cases} 1 - \sqrt{t^{1+\alpha}} & \text{if} \quad |\alpha| \neq 1; \\ t \log t & \text{if} \quad \alpha = 1; \\ -\log t & \text{if} \quad \alpha = -1 \end{cases} \tag{4}$$

where second and third lines correspond to $KL(\mathbf{u}, \mathbf{v})$ and $KL(\mathbf{v}, \mathbf{u})$, respectively. The most important here first line corresponds to

$$D^{(\alpha)}(\mathbf{v}, \mathbf{u}) = 1 - \sum_{i=1}^{m} \sqrt{v_i^{1-\alpha} u_i^{1+\alpha}}. \tag{5}$$

However, there are two problems associated with above definition: first, divergence (5) is not marginally linked to the second or third lines in (4); second, divergence (5) may be negative if $\alpha < -1$ or $\alpha > 1$ (at the same time $D^{(\alpha)}(\mathbf{v}, \mathbf{v}) = 0 \ \forall \mathbf{v} \in \mathcal{P}^m, \forall \alpha \in R$).

In order to overcome above problems we consider 2 families of loss functions

$$L\Phi_\gamma(\mathbf{v}, \mathbf{u}) := \sum_{i=1}^{m} v_i^{1+\gamma} u_i^{-\gamma} - 1, \quad 0 < \gamma < \infty; \tag{6}$$

$$R\Phi_\gamma(\mathbf{v}, \mathbf{u}) := 1 - \sum_{i=1}^{m} v_i^{1-\gamma} u_i^{\gamma}, \quad 0 < \gamma < 1. \tag{7}$$

Proposition 1. *The loss functions (6) and (7) are non-negative and equal to 0 if and only if $\mathbf{v} \equiv \mathbf{u}$.*

Above statement may be proved using the method of mathematical induction.

Based on the above Proposition, we can define a new family of loss functions as an average of (6) and (7)

$$\Phi_\gamma(\mathbf{v}, \mathbf{u}) := \frac{1}{2}\left(L\Phi_\gamma(\mathbf{v}, \mathbf{u}) + R\Phi_\gamma(\mathbf{v}, \mathbf{u})\right), \ 0 < \gamma < 1. \tag{8}$$

Note, that the KL-divergence may be regarded as a marginal limit in relation to the family of loss functions (8):

$$\lim_{\gamma \to 0} \frac{\Phi_\gamma(\mathbf{v}, \mathbf{u})}{\gamma} = KL(\mathbf{v}, \mathbf{u}).$$

Minimizing $\sum_{x_t \in \mathbf{X}_c} \Phi_\gamma(p(x_t), q) = \sum_{i=1}^{m}\left(A_{ic}(\gamma)q_i^{-\gamma} - A_{ic}(-\gamma)q_i^{\gamma}\right), A_{ic}(\gamma) = \sum_{x_t \in \mathbf{X}_c} p_{it}^{1+\gamma}$, as a function of $q \in \mathcal{P}^m$ we formulate iterative algorithm for the computation of centroids in the sense of the loss function (8) with fixed value of the parameter $\gamma > 0$

$$q_i(c, j+1) \propto \sqrt[1+\gamma]{A_{ic}(\gamma) + A_{ic}(-\gamma)q_i^{2\gamma}(c, j)} \tag{9}$$

where j is a sequential number of iteration, initial values of centroids may be computed using k-means for the loss function (6):

$$q_i(c, 1) \propto \sqrt[1+\gamma]{A_{ic}(\gamma)}, \ 0 \le \gamma < \infty,$$

where $q(c, j) = \{q_1(c, j), \cdots, q_m(c, j)\}, c = 1..k$, are vectors of centroids.

Remark 1. According to [5], it seems rather natural to investigate the situation where the estimator is the same for every loss from a certain set of loss functions under consideration. Comparing clustering results for different input parameters γ we can make an assessment of the stability of clustering: the smaller fluctuation of the centroids indicates the higher quality of clustering.

3.2   Extension to the Euclidean Space

Similar to the Sect. 3.1 we can define universal clustering in $\mathbb{R}^m$ with the following family of exponential loss functions: $\Phi_\gamma(\mathbf{v}, \mathbf{u}) := \varphi_\gamma(\mathbf{v} - \mathbf{u})$ where $\mathbf{v}, \mathbf{u} \in \mathbb{R}^m$, and $\gamma \in \mathbb{R}_+^m$ is m-dimensional regulation parameter,

$$\varphi_\gamma(\mathbf{v}) := \sum_{i=1}^{m} \cosh(\gamma_i \cdot v_i) - m, \tag{10}$$

and corresponding centroids:

$$q_i^{(\gamma)}(c) = \frac{1}{2\gamma_i} \log \frac{\sum_{x_t \in \mathbf{X}_c} e^{\gamma_i x_{ti}}}{\sum_{x_t \in \mathbf{X}_c} e^{-\gamma_i x_{ti}}} \tag{11}$$

where components (11) represent a unique k-means solution for the loss function (10).

Remark 2. In accordance with an essential property
$\lim_{\gamma \to 0} \frac{1}{\gamma^2}(\cosh(\gamma \cdot v) - 1) = v^2$ the family of loss functions (10) is marginally linked to the classical Euclidean metric.

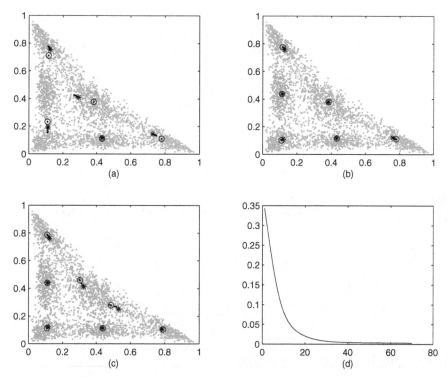

Fig. 1. Probabilistic 3D-synthetic data, $n = 3000$ with 6 clusters; random selection of the cluster seeds; centroids were re-computed using CM algorithm with loss function (8), $\gamma = 0.09 + 0.13 \cdot (i - 1), i = 1..8$; symbol $\odot$ marks centroids which correspond to $\gamma = 0.09$; $*$ marks centroids which correspond to $\gamma = 1.0$, other centroids are marked by bold black dots $\cdot$; (a): **k=5**; (b): **k=6**; (c): **k=7**; (d): behavior of the distance between consecutive codebooks in (9) which was computed as a sum of absolute differences between corresponding components

4   Experiments

The sample of the $3D$-probabilistic data was generated using the following procedure.

As a first step, the cluster code c was drawn randomly according to the probabilities p, see Table 1, using standard uniform random variable. Then, we used the multinomial logit model in order to generate coordinates of the $3D$-probability data: $v_i \propto \exp\{b_{ci} + e_c r\}, \sum_{i=1}^{3} v_i = 1$, where r is a standard normal random variable.

By definition, the family of power loss functions (8) is marginally linked to the KL-divergence if $\gamma \to 0$. By the increase of γ we will increase the power of diversification. Respectively, any centroid, which corresponds to a non significant empirical cluster will move around. On the other hand, centroids of the "strong" empirical clusters will be stable. Table 2 demonstrates correct selection of the number of clusters $k = 6$.

Table 1. Simulation coefficients for the 3D-synthetic data, see Figure 1

Cluster	Coefficients				Probabilities
c	b_1	b_2	b_3	e	p
1	1	-1	-1	0.5	0.15
2	-1	1	-1	0.5	0.15
3	-1	-1	1	0.5	0.15
4	-0.4	-0.4	-0.8	0.4	0.25
5	-0.4	-1.9	-0.4	0.3	0.15
6	-1.9	-0.4	-0.4	0.3	0.15

Table 2. 3D-probabilistic synthetic data: determination of the clustering size k where D is defined in (12), used parameters: $\gamma_0 = 0.002, \delta = 0.01, \tau = 20, C = 1000$

k:	3	4	5	6	7	8	9
D:	0.6478	0.0263	0.0045	**0.0011**	0.8535	0.9264	2.7150

k:	10	11	12	13	14	15	16
D:	0.8041	1.9056	0.1474	0.3063	0.9377	5.0651	12.1121

Algorithm 1. (Universal Clustering)

1: Order number of clusters k, and select randomly initial codebook with k probability vectors which will be used for all $\tau \geq 2$ runs of the CM algorithm in the next step.
2: Run CM-algorithm using loss function (8) with $\gamma = \gamma_0 + (j-1) \cdot \delta, j = 1..\tau$, where $0 < \gamma_0 < 1$ and $0 < \delta \leq \frac{1-\gamma_0}{\tau-1}$. As an outcome we obtain a set of $k \cdot \tau$ probability vectors $\{\tilde{q}(j,c), j = 1..\tau, c = 1..k\}$.
3: Compute maximum distance between first and other codebooks

$$D := C \cdot \max_{c=1..k} \max_{j=2..\tau} KL(\tilde{q}(1,c), \tilde{q}(j,c)) \tag{12}$$

where $C > 0$ is a constant.

The second experiment was conducted using a large Web navigation **msnbc** dataset. This dataset comes from Internet Information Server **msn.com** for the entire day of *September, 28, 1999* [14]. The dataset [15] includes $n = 989818$ sequences of events with lengths ranging from 1 to 12000.

Each sequence in the dataset corresponds to page views of a user during that twenty-four hour period. Each event in the sequence corresponds to a user's request for a page. In total, there are 4698794 events.

The page categories were developed prior to investigation. There are $m = 17$ particular web categories. The number of pages per category ranges from 10 to 5000.

Analysis of the **msnbc** data had revealed the following general properties: 1) users have tendency to stay within particular category; 2) transitions from one category to another are relatively rare.

Respectively, we considered an ultimate simplification of the model by ignoring 1) dependencies between subsequent events and 2) length of the sequence of events for any particular user. As a result, we reduced the given variable-length data to the fixed length data where any user is represented by the m-dimensional probability vector of the frequencies of m categories.

The aim of this experiment is to explain and understand the way people interact with web sites, explore human behavior within internet environment. Briefly, we observed that the table of centroids in the case of $k = 8$ demonstrates clearly user's preferences. Detailed numerical and graphical illustrations may be found in [1].

Also, the paper [1] introduced clustering regularisation based on the balanced complex of two conditions: 1) significance of any particular cluster; 2) difference between any 2 clusters. Subject to some input regulation parameters the corresponding system detected the interval $34 \leq k \leq 47$ as the most likely range for the number of significant clusters in **msnbc**. Another solution for the same task may be found using principles of universal clustering.

A Pentium 4, 2.8GHz, 512MB RAM, computer was used for the computations. The overall complexity of a CM cycle is $O(k \cdot n \cdot m)$. The computer conducted computations according to the special program written in C. The computation time for one CM cycle in the case of 51 clusters was 110 seconds.

5   Concluding Remarks

The proposed in the paper universal clustering represents a promising direction. We can make an assessment of quality of clustering using set of codebooks as a function of regulation parameter. The quality function may be computed as a decreasing function of the fluctuation of codebooks.

Besides, it will be important to consider the following cyclic procedure: 1) create a new cluster (forward move) where a new prototype may be defined as a function of existing prototypes so that the corresponding cluster will split existing clusters with bigger number of elements and smaller uniformity; 2) make an assessment of any particular cluster as a component within the complex of $k + 1$ clusters; 3) remove the cluster which is the most insignificant (backward move). Comparing previous and current codebooks we will test stability of the existing clustering configuration. Go to the first step if convergence test is not fulfilled, alternatively, stop the algorithm.

Acknowledgment

We are grateful to anonymous referees for the helpful comments and suggestions. For example, one of the referees had drawn our attention to the very relevant monograph [13].

References

1. Nikulin, V., Smola, A.: Parametric model-based clustering. In Dasarathy, B., ed.: Data Mining, Intrusion Detection, Information Assurance, and Data Network Security, 28-29 March 2005, Orlando, Florida, USA. Volume 5812., SPIE (2005) 190–201
2. Dhillon, I., Mallela, S., Kumar, R.: Divisive information-theoretic feature clustering algorithm for text classification. Journal of Machine Learning Research **3** (2003) 1265–1287
3. Cohn, D., Hofmann, T.: The missing link - a probabilistic model of document content and hypertext connectivity. In: 13th Conference on Neural Information Processing Systems. (2001)
4. Hwang, J.T.: Universal domination and stochastic domination: Estimation simultaneously under a broad class of loss functions. The Annals of Statistics **13** (1985) 295–314
5. Rukhin, A.: Universal Bayes estimators. The Annals of Statistics **6** (1978) 1345–1351
6. Hamerly, G., Elkan, C.: Learning the k in k-means. In: 16th Conference on Neural Information Processing Systems. (2003)
7. Zhong, S., Ghosh, J.: A unified framework for model-based clustering. Journal of Machine Learning Research **4** (2003) 1001–1037
8. Akaike, H.: On the likelihood of a time series model. The Statistician **27** (1978) 217–235
9. Schwarz, G.: Estimating the dimension of a model. The Annals of Statistics **6** (1978) 461–464
10. Fraley, C., Raftery, A.: How Many Clusters? Which Clustering Method? Answers via Model-based Cluster Analysis. The Computer Journal **41** (1998) 578–588
11. Pollard, D.: Strong consistency of k-means clustering. The Annals of Statistics **10** (1981) 135–140
12. Bhatia, S.: Adaptive k-means clustering. FLAIRS (2004) 695–699
13. Amari, S., Nagaoka, H.: Methods of Information Geometry. Oxford University Press (1993)
14. Cadez, I., Heckerman, D., Meek, C., Smyth, P., White, S.: Model-based clustering and visualization of navigation patterns on a web site. Data Mining and Knowledge Discovery **7** (2003) 399–424
15. Msnbc: msnbc.com anonymous web data. In: UCI Knowledge Discovery in Databases Archive: http://kdd.ics.uci.edu/summary.data.type.html. (1999)

Circular SOM for Temporal Characterisation of Modelled Gene Expressions

Carla S. Möller-Levet and Hujun Yin

School of Electrical and Electronic Engineering, The University of Manchester, Manchester M60 1QD, UK
c.moller-levet@postgrad.manchester.ac.uk
h.yin@manchester.ac.uk

Abstract. A circular Self-Organising Map (SOM) based on a temporal metric has been proposed for clustering and characterising gene expressions. Expression profiles are first modelled with Radial Basis Functions. The co-expression coefficient, defined as the uncentred correlation of the differentiation of the models, is combined in a circular SOM for grouping and ordering the modelled expressions based on their temporal properties. In the proposed method the topology has been extended to temporal and cyclic ordering of the expressions. An example and a test on a microarray dataset are presented to demonstrate the advantages of the proposed method.

1 Introduction

The DNA microarray has become a useful high throughput experiment for the study of genomics in molecular biology. With the DNA Microarray experiment it is possible to gather mRNA expression levels for thousands of genes at the same time [1]. The information obtained can be studied and analysed to identify the genetic changes associated with diseases, drug treatments, stress response and stages in cellular processes among others.

The absolute intensity of gene expression is often not important. Instead, the relative change of intensity characterised by the shape of the expression profile is regarded as characteristic and informative. Modelling the profiles can provide more generalised and smoothed characterisation of gene expressions, while reducing noise and overcoming uneven sampling problems [2]. Rather than directly comparing the profiles, the models can be differentiated to capture the shape characteristics. An appropriate metric for measuring the similarities of the expression profiles is critical to the success of further analysis such as clustering. To evaluate the similarity of the gene expressions based on their shapes and the distribution of time points, a shape similarity metric was introduced in [3] and further generalised and defined in [4].

Based on this shape metric, in this paper we propose a circular SOM for clustering gene expression profiles in order to extract temporal relationships among clusters. The SOM is an unsupervised learning algorithm, which uses a finite grid of nodes to map and relate the input data [5]. Each node has an

M. Gallagher, J. Hogan, and F. Maire (Eds.): IDEAL 2005, LNCS 3578, pp. 319–326, 2005.

associated weight vector which, after learning, will come to represent a number of original input vectors. In the learning process, the nodes that are topographically close to the winner in the grid up to a certain geometric neighbourhood, will be activated to learn from the same input. Therefore, on the trained map similar data points are likely to be projected to nearby nodes. The map can be used to show the spatial relationships amongst data with respect to the nodes, hence, different grid structure can reveal different relationships. We identified that the circular structure can provide temporal characters of sequential data, such as time orders and periodicity, when an appropriate temporal metric is used. SOMs have been used for clustering, including gene expressions, predominately based on rectangular grid and Euclidean distance [6]. Time characteristics cannot be naturally represented by rectangular grid and Euclidian distance.

2   SOM for Temporal Sequences

Several attempts have been made to include the order of temporal sequences in the SOM [7]. Temporal sequence processing involves the modelling of temporal relations and recognition of patterns among data items that are vectors of a time series.

A common approach is to visualise the trajectories on SOMs. Succeeding best matches can be connected through paths called trajectories which are then visualised on the map. The idea is to keep track of the best matches as a function of time by describing the trajectory that the sequence elements follow in the topographic map. Other methods are based on the adaptation of the learning algorithm, as is the case of the hypermap architecture [8]. The idea is to recognise a pattern that occurs in the context of other patterns in sequential phases. The context around the pattern is first used to select a subset of nodes in the network, from which the best-matching node is then identified on the basis of the pattern part.

Other typical approaches are based on modifications of the learning topology by introducing recurrent connections, e.g. Temporal Kohonen Maps (TKM) [9] or Recurrent SOM (RSOM) [10, 11], or by using several hierarchical layers of SOMs, e.g. [12]. In TKM the participation of earlier input vectors in each unit is represented by using a recursive difference equation which defines the current unit activity as a function of the previous activations and the current input vector. In the RSOM, which is a modification of the TKM, the scalar node activities of the TKM are replaced by difference vectors defined as a recursive difference equation of the new input, the previous difference vectors, and the weight vectors of the units. One potential problem with the recurrent models is stability.

In the case of temporal gene expression clustering, the data items presented to the map are not a spatial vector, but a sequence with time order in itself. They are time-series corresponding to the expression levels over time of a particular gene. Therefore, if a common 2-D SOM is used, the trained map can then be used to mark the trajectories of the expressions of the genes for comparison. In [13], a self-organising latent lattice is proposed to identify pairs of genes with similar co-expressions. The co-expression of a pair of genes x and y is represented by a vector whose elements are the difference of present expression levels $x(t)$ and $y(t)$, and differences of slopes at present t, past $t-1$ and future $t+1$. All possible combinations of genes and their resulting sequence of vectors are selected to find out meaningful pairs of correlated genes. The vectors are mapped to the lattice and the patterns of trajectories of different pairs are compared. Similar trajectory patterns on the lattice may imply similar co-regulation patterns. There can be as many as millions possible pairs to examine and only pair-wise relations rather than group relations or clusters are revealed.

We approach the temporal extension of the SOM from another aspect, i.e. the similarity metric. If the similarity metric considers temporal properties, then the neurons in the resultant map will exhibit temporal relationships. As time is one dimension, 1-D SOM is more appropriate. In addition, a circular, i.e. closed 1-D SOM, can further detect cyclic temporal characteristics.

3   Modelling with Radial Basis Functions

Radial basis functions have a single hidden layer, where the nodes are Gaussian kernels, and a linear output layer. The radial basis function has the form:

$$f(x) = \sum_{i=1}^{n_r} w_i \phi(\|c_i - x\|) + b \qquad (1)$$

where x is the input vector, $\phi(\cdot)$ is a Gaussian function kernel, $\|\cdot\|$ denotes the Euclidean norm, w_i are the weights of the second layer, c_i is the vector of the centre of the ith kernel, and n_r is the total number of kernels.

The modelling of gene expressions time-series with RBFs using the orthogonal least squares (OLS) method was introduced in [2]. The OLS learning algorithm [14] allows the selection of the centres in a rational procedure. Each selected centre maximises the increment to the explained variance of the desired output. This method considers all kernels to have an equal width, however, this is inadequate when time sampling points are not evenly distributed, which commonly occurs in microarray gene expressions. In order to improve the approximation, the OLS learning algorithm is complemented with a heuristic search for the optimal width for each of the candidate centres [2].

4   Co-expression Coefficient

In [3] the advantages of using the derivatives of modelled profiles for the comparison of shapes are illustrated. In [4], the co-expression coefficient is defined as the correlation coefficient of the first order differentiations of the modelled profiles. However, the correlation coefficient does not consider vertical shifts which, in the case of positive and negative derivatives, are important to identify. If the uncentred correlation coefficient is used instead, the mean is not subtracted and the sign of the derivative is preserved. Therefore, the co-expression coefficient, ce, can be generalised as:

$$ce(x,y) = \frac{\int x'y'dt}{\sqrt{\int x'^2 dt \int y'^2 dt}}, \tag{2}$$

where x' and y' are first order time-differentiations of modelled gene expressions $x(t)$ and $y(t)$, respectively. It can be easily shown that the metric satisfies, $-1 \leq ce(x_\alpha, x_\beta) \leq 1, \forall_{\alpha\beta}$ and $ce(x_\alpha, x_\alpha) = 1, \forall_\alpha$.

5   Circular SOM

In order to use the SOM based on the co-expression coefficient, the dot-product SOM is adopted and trained with norm one normalised data. When the dot-product is defined as the similarity metric between the input data and the weights, the learning equations should be modified accordingly by selecting the maximum of the dot-product as the winner node and by normalising the new weights at each step.

Figure 1 (a) shows the structure of the circular SOM. The proposed co-expression coefficient varies from -1 to 1 corresponding to negative and positive similarities. In the resulting circle, the nodes opposite to each other (e.g. nodes 1 and 5) contain the most dissimilar profiles, and the nodes on two sides of a particular node will exhibit opposite trend in similarity (in this case it is time shift, leading or lagging). Figure 1 (b) presents the clustering results on artificial temporal dataset generated from $y = sin(x - a\pi/8) + \delta$, where $a = 0, 2, 4, 6, 8, 10, 12, 14$, respectively, $0 \leq x \leq 2\pi$ and δ is Gaussian noise with zero mean and the standard deviation 0.5. The circular SOM is able to cluster the artificial profiles according to the different time/phase properties. Furthermore, it automatically orders the profiles according to their temporal characteristics, such that smaller phase shifts are closer on the SOM than larger phase shifts, and opposite temporal patterns are found in opposite extremes. In the case

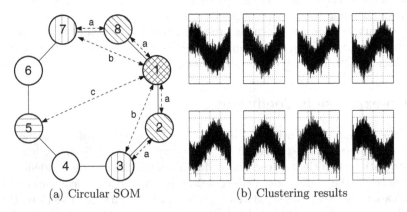

(a) Circular SOM   (b) Clustering results

Fig. 1. (a) Circular SOM (b) Clustering results of the artificial temporal dataset

of unknown number of clusters, the Bayesian information criterion (BIC) [15] can be used to validate or detect the underlying number of groups. This is particularly appropriate as the SOM is approximating Gaussian mixtures [16].

5.1 Yeast Cell Cycle Dataset

The temporal expression of the yeast culture synchronised by α factor arrest in [17] is used to illustrate the proposed method. Eight hundred cell-cycle-regulated genes of the Yeast *Saccharomayces cerevisiae* were identified by microarray hybridisation. The yeast cells were sampled every 7 minutes for 119 minutes, producing 18 sampling points. Among the 800 genes 511 have no missing values and are available[1]. In [17], the genes are grouped based on their periodicity and classified according to different cell cycle phases, M/G1, G1, S, G2 and M. As benchmark data, we used the 71 genes which have being identified as cell-cycle-regulated by traditional biological methods and are available from this dataset.

The two datasets (511 and 71 genes) are modelled using RBFs and the modelled profiles were differentiated. The BIC is used to validate the number of clusters, however, when using circular SOM, the number of clusters has a low impact in the performance of the algorithm. Each node presents the smaller distance only to its two neighbouring nodes in a chain ordered fashion, this implies that characteristic traits are split or merged with larger or fewer number of clusters without changing the order or relation between them.

A five-node circular SOM has been verified for the 71 genes dataset. In the case of the 511 genes dataset, the BIC value does not show a significant change after eight clusters, therefore, circular SOM of eight nodes is used to cluster this dataset. Figure 2 presents the resulting SOMs and prototype profiles of the

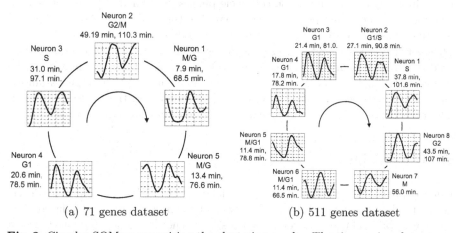

(a) 71 genes dataset   (b) 511 genes dataset

Fig. 2. Circular SOMs summarising the clustering results. The time series plots correspond to the cluster mean expressions and the times correspond to the cluster mean peak times

---

[1] The dataset is available from http://cellcycle-www.stanford.edu

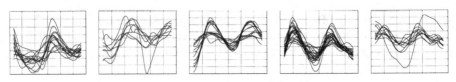

Fig. 3. Clustering results of modelled profiles for the 71 genes dataset

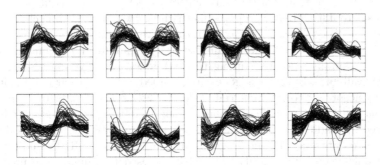

Fig. 4. Clustering results of modelled profiles for the 511 genes dataset

clusters. It can be easily seen that topology exists in the profiles. The topological order here refers to the time shift. It demonstrates that the proposed method is able to group profiles based on their temporal characteristics and can automatically order the groups based on their periodical properties. Figures 3 and 4 plot all the expression profiles clustered to these five or eight groups. In each plot the horizontal axis denotes time [mins] and the vertical axis denotes expression level (log_2 ratio). Tables 1(A) and 2 present the distribution of the genes in each cluster among the cell cycle phases. Similar to [3], the genes were classified based on their peak times compared to the peak times described in [17] for each phase. In both datasets, the genes in each cluster belong mainly to one phase or the two adjacent phases. The genes identified as cell-cycle-regulated by traditional biological methods can be used to evaluate the performance of the proposed technique. Table 1 (B) shows the distribution of these genes among the cell cycle phases identified by biological methods, over the clusters obtained. The tables show high relevance between clustered and predefined phase groups.

6   Conclusions

Gene expression time-series can be modelled with RBFs to obtain smoother, generalised expressions which can be (evenly) resampled and differentiated. The co-expression coefficient is defined as cosine of the first order derivative of the modelled profiles to quantify shape information. In this paper we have incorporated the co-expression coefficients into a circular SOM for clustering temporal, cyclic gene expressions. It is shown that it is able to include automatically temporal characteristics of cyclic data in the clustering. The results indicate that

Table 1. Clustering results of the 71 genes dataset versus five cell cycle phases defined in [17] (A) and identified by traditional biological methods (B)

Cluster	A					B				
	M/G1	G1	S	G2	M	M/G1	G1	S	S/G2	G2/M
I(15)	13	1	0	0	1	11	2	0	0	2
II(8)	0	0	0	4	4	0	0	0	4	4
III(14)	0	1	13	0	0	0	6	6	2	0
IV(23)	0	26	0	0	0	1	22	0	0	0
V(11)	5	6	0	0	0	1	8	0	0	2

Table 2. Clustering results of the 511 genes dataset versus five cell cycle phases defined in [17]

Cluster	M/G1	G1	S	G2	M
I(47)	0	0	27	20	0
II(57)	1	31	22	3	3
III(72)	0	69	3	0	0
IV(81)	7	73	0	1	0
V(51)	33	15	3	0	0
VI(58)	42	6	1	0	8
VII(61)	14	1	2	12	32
VIII(85)	1	3	1	73	7

the proposed method is a useful technique for gene expression and general time series temporal characterisation.

Acknowledgments

This research was supported in part by grants from an Overseas Research Studentship (ORS) award by Universities U.K. and Consejo Nacional de Ciencia y Tecnologia (CONACYT).

References

1. D. Duggan, M. Bittner, Y. Chen, P. Meltzer, and J. Trent, "Expresssion profiling using cDNA microarrays," *Nature*, vol. 21, pp. 10–14, 1999.
2. C. S. Möller-Levet, H. Yin, K.-H. Cho, and O. Wolkenhauer, "Modelling gene expression time-series with radial basis function neural networks," in *Proc. of the International Joint Conference on Neural Networks*, vol. II, Budapest, Hungary, 2004, pp. 1191–1196.
3. C. S. Möller-Levet and H. Yin, "Modelling and clustering of gene expressions using RBFs and a shape similarity metric," in *Proc. of The Fifth International Conference on Intellingent Data Engineering and Automated Learning*, ser. Lecture Notes in Computer Sciences, A. R. Yang, R. Everson, and H. Yin, Eds., vol. 3177. Germany: Springer-Verlag, August 2004, pp. 1–10.

4. C. S. Möller-Levet and H. Yin, "Modeling and analysis of gene expressions based on coexpressions," *International Journal of Neural Systems*, 2005 (submitted).
5. T. Kohonen, "The self-organizing map," *Proc. IEEE*, vol. 78, no. 9, pp. 1464–1480, 1990.
6. S. Tavazoie, J. D. Hughes, M. J. Campbell, R. J. Cho, and G. M. Church, "Systematic determination of genetic network architecture," *Nature Genetics*, vol. 22, pp. 281–285, 1999.
7. G. Guimaraes and F. Moura-Pires, "An essay in classifying Self-Organizing Maps for temporal sequence processing," in *Advances in Self-Organising Maps*, N. Allison, H. Yin, L. Allison, and J. Slack, Eds., 2001, pp. 259–260.
8. T. Kohonen, "The hypermap architecture," in *Artificial Neural Networks*, T. Kohonen, K. Mkisara, O. Simula, and J. Kangas, Eds., vol. 2. The Netherlands: Elsevier Science Publishers, 1991.
9. G. J. Chappel and J. G. Taylor, "The temporal Kohonen map," *Neural Networks*, vol. 6, pp. 441–445, 1993.
10. M. Varsta, J. D. R. Millan, and J. Heinkkonen, "A recurrent Self-Organizing Map for temporal sequence processing," in *Proc. of the 7th Int. Conf. Artificial Neural Networks*, ser. Lecture Notes in Computer Science, W. Gerstner, A. Germond, M. Hasler, and J. D. Nicoud, Eds., vol. 1327. Germany: Springer-Verlag, October 1997, pp. 421–426.
11. T. Koskela, M. Varsta, J. Heikkonen, and K. Kaski, "Temporal sequence processing using recurrent SOM," in *Second Int. Conf. on Knowldege-Based Intelligent Engineering Systems*, vol. 1, April 1998, pp. 290–297.
12. C. Kemke and A. Wichert, "Hierarchical Self-Organizing Feature Map for speech recognition," in *Proc. of the World Congress on Neural Networks*, vol. 3, Hillsdale, NY, USA, 1993, pp. 45–47.
13. B.-T. Zhang, J. Yang, and S. W. Chi, "Self-Organizing latent lattice models for temporal gene expression profiling," *Machine Learning*, vol. 52, pp. 67–89, 2003.
14. S. Chen, C. F. N. Cowan, and P. M. Grant, "Orthogonal least squares learning algorithm for radial basis function networks," *IEEE Transactions on Neural Networks*, vol. 2, no. 2, pp. 302–309, March 1991.
15. G. Schwarz, "Estimating the dimension of a model," *The Annals of Statistics*, vol. 6, no. 2, pp. 461–464, 1978.
16. H. Yin and N. M. Allison, "A Bayesian self-oganising map for Gaussian mixture," *IEE Proc.- Vision, Image and Signal Processing*, vol. 148, no. 4, pp. 234–240, 2001.
17. P. T. Spellman, G. Sherlock, M. Q. Zhang, V. R. Iyer, K. Anders, M. B. Eisen, P. O. Brown, D. Botstein, and B. Futcher, "Comprehensive identification of cell cycle-regulated genes of yeast *Saccharamyces cerevisiae* by microarray hybridization," *Molecular Biology of the Cell*, vol. 9, pp. 3273–3297, 1998.

Recursive Self-organizing Map
as a Contractive Iterative Function System

Peter Tiňo[1], Igor Farkaš[2], and Jort van Mourik[3]

[1] School Of Computer Science, University Of Birmingham
Birmingham B15 2TT, UK
[2] Faculty of Mathematics, Physics and Informatics, Comenius University
Mlynská dolina, 842 48 Bratislava, Slovak Republic
[3] Neural Computing Research Group
Aston University
Aston Triangle, Birmingham B4 7ET, UK

Abstract. Recently, there has been a considerable research activity in extending topographic maps of vectorial data to more general data structures, such as sequences or trees. However, the representational capabilities and internal representations of the models are not well understood. We rigorously analyze a generalization of the Self-Organizing Map (SOM) for processing sequential data, Recursive SOM (RecSOM [1]), as a non-autonomous dynamical system consisting of a set of fixed input maps. We show that contractive fixed input maps are likely to produce Markovian organizations of receptive fields on the RecSOM map. We derive bounds on parameter β (weighting the importance of importing past information when processing sequences) under which contractiveness of the fixed input maps is guaranteed.

1 Introduction

Several modifications of the self-organizing map (SOM) [2] to sequences and/or tree structures have been proposed in the literature. For comprehensive reviews, see [3, 4]. Modified versions of SOM that have enjoyed a great deal of interest equip SOM with *additional feed-back connections* that allow for natural processing of recursive data types. Typical examples of such models are Temporal Kohonen Map [5], recurrent SOM [6], feedback SOM [7], recursive SOM [1], merge SOM [8] and SOM for structured data [9]. However, the representational capabilities and internal representations of the models are not well understood [3, 10, 11].

In this paper we concentrate on the Recursive SOM (RecSOM) [1], because RecSOM transcends the simple local recurrence of leaky integrators of earlier models and it has been demonstrated that it can represent much richer dynamical behavior [11]. We propose to study the RecSOM model as a non-autonomous dynamical system with internal dynamics driven by a stream of external inputs. It is argued that contractive fixed input maps are likely to produce Markovian organizations of receptive fields on the RecSOM map.

M. Gallagher, J. Hogan, and F. Maire (Eds.): IDEAL 2005, LNCS 3578, pp. 327–334, 2005.
© Springer-Verlag Berlin Heidelberg 2005

2 Recursive Self-organizing Map (RecSOM)

In the RecSOM model [1], Each neuron $i \in \{1, 2, ..., N\}$ in the map has two weight vectors associated with it:

- $\mathbf{w}_i \in \mathbb{R}^n$ – linked with an n-dimensional input $\mathbf{s}(t)$ feeding the network at time t
- $\mathbf{c}_i \in \mathbb{R}^N$ – linked with the context

$$\mathbf{y}(t-1) = (y_1(t-1), y_2(t-1), ..., y_N(t-1))$$

containing map activations $y_i(t-1)$ from the previous time step.

The output of a unit i at time t is computed as $y_i(t) = \exp(-d_i(t))$, where[1]

$$d_i(t) = \alpha \cdot \|\mathbf{s}(t) - \mathbf{w}_i\|^2 + \beta \cdot \|\mathbf{y}(t-1) - \mathbf{c}_i\|^2. \tag{1}$$

In eq. (1), $\alpha > 0$ and $\beta > 0$ are model parameters that respectively influence the effect of the input and the context upon neuron's profile. Both weight vectors can be updated using the same form of learning rule [1]:

$$\Delta\mathbf{w}_i = \gamma \cdot h_{ik} \cdot (\mathbf{s}(t) - \mathbf{w}_i), \tag{2}$$
$$\Delta\mathbf{c}_i = \gamma \cdot h_{ik} \cdot (\mathbf{y}(t-1) - \mathbf{c}_i), \tag{3}$$

where k is an index of the best matching unit at time t, $k = \mathrm{argmin}_{i \in \{1,2,...,N\}} d_i(t)$, and $0 < \gamma < 1$ is the learning rate. Neighborhood function h_{ik} is a Gaussian (of width σ) on the distance $d(i, k)$ of units i and k in the map:

$$h_{ik} = e^{-\frac{d(i,k)^2}{\sigma^2}}. \tag{4}$$

The 'neighborhood width' σ decreases in time to allow for forming topographic representation of input sequences.

3 Contractive Fixed-Input Dynamics in RecSOM

Under a fixed input vector $\mathbf{s} \in \mathbb{R}^n$, the time evolution of (1) becomes

$$d_i(t+1) = \alpha \cdot \|\mathbf{s} - \mathbf{w}_i\|^2 + \beta \cdot \left\| \left(e^{-d_1(t)}, e^{-d_2(t)}, ..., e^{-d_N(t)} \right) - \mathbf{c}_i \right\|^2. \tag{5}$$

After applying a one-to-one coordinate transformation $y_i = e^{-d_i}$, eq. (5) reads

$$y_i(t+1) = e^{-\alpha\|\mathbf{s}-\mathbf{w}_i\|^2} \cdot e^{-\beta\|\mathbf{y}(t)-\mathbf{c}_i\|^2}, \tag{6}$$

or, in the vector form:

$$\mathbf{y}(t+1) = \mathbf{F}_\mathbf{s}(\mathbf{y}(t)). \tag{7}$$

---

[1] $\|\cdot\|$ denotes the Euclidean norm

Given a fixed input $\mathbf{s}$, we aim to study the conditions under which the map $\mathbf{F_s}$ becomes a contraction. Then, by the Banach Fixed Point theorem, the autonomous RecSOM dynamics $\mathbf{y}(t+1) = \mathbf{F_s}(\mathbf{y}(t))$ will be dominated by a unique attractive fixed point $\mathbf{y_s} = \mathbf{F_s}(\mathbf{y_s})$.

A mapping $\mathbf{F} : \mathbb{R}^N \to \mathbb{R}^N$ is said to be a contraction with contraction coefficient $\rho \in [0, 1)$, if for any $\mathbf{y}, \mathbf{y}' \in \mathbb{R}^N$,

$$\|\mathbf{F}(\mathbf{y}) - \mathbf{F}(\mathbf{y}')\| \leq \rho \cdot \|\mathbf{y} - \mathbf{y}'\|. \tag{8}$$

$\mathbf{F}$ is a contraction if there exists $\rho \in [0, 1)$ so that $\mathbf{F}$ is a contraction with contraction coefficient ρ.

We denote the Gaussian kernel of inverse variance $\eta > 0$, acting on $\mathbb{R}^N$, by $G_\eta(\cdot, \cdot)$, i.e. for any $\mathbf{u}, \mathbf{v} \in \mathbb{R}^N$,

$$G_\eta(\mathbf{u}, \mathbf{v}) = e^{-\eta \|\mathbf{u} - \mathbf{v}\|^2}. \tag{9}$$

Denote by $\mathbf{G}_\alpha(\mathbf{s})$ the collection of activations coming from the feed-forward part of RecSOM,

$$\mathbf{G}_\alpha(\mathbf{s}) = (G_\alpha(\mathbf{s}, \mathbf{w}_1), G_\alpha(\mathbf{s}, \mathbf{w}_2), ..., G_\alpha(\mathbf{s}, \mathbf{w}_N)). \tag{10}$$

Then we have the following theorem:

Theorem 1. *Consider an input* $\mathbf{s} \in \mathbb{R}^M$. *If for some* $\rho \in [0, 1)$,

$$\beta \leq \rho^2 \frac{e}{2} \|\mathbf{G}_\alpha(\mathbf{s})\|^{-2}, \tag{11}$$

then the mapping $\mathbf{F_s}$ *(7) is a contraction with contraction coefficient* ρ.

Sketch of the proof: The proof is rather lengthy and complicated. Due to space limitations, we refer the reader to [12]. The proof follows the worst case analysis of the distances $\|\mathbf{F_s}(\mathbf{y}) - \mathbf{F_s}(\mathbf{y}')\|$ between the $\mathbf{F_s}$-images of $\mathbf{y}, \mathbf{y}'$, under the constraint $\|\mathbf{y} - \mathbf{y}'\| = \delta$:

$$D_\beta(\delta) = \sup_{\mathbf{y}, \mathbf{y}'; \|\mathbf{y} - \mathbf{y}'\| = \delta} \|\mathbf{F_s}(\mathbf{y}) - \mathbf{F_s}(\mathbf{y}')\|.$$

The analysis is quite challenging, because $D_\beta(\delta)$ can be expressed only implicitly. Nevertheless, one can prove that, for a given $\beta > 0$, the function $D_\beta : \mathbb{R}^+ \to (0, 1)$ has the following properties:

1. $\lim_{\delta \to 0+} D_\beta(\delta) = 0$,
2. D_β is a continuous monotonically increasing concave function of δ.
3. $\lim_{\delta \to 0+} \frac{dD_\beta(\delta)}{d\delta} = \sqrt{\frac{2\beta}{e}}$.

Therefore, we have the following upper bound:

$$D_\beta(\delta) \leq \delta \sqrt{\frac{2\beta}{e}}. \tag{12}$$

Writing (6) as

$$y_i(t+1) = G_\alpha(\mathbf{s}, \mathbf{w}_i) \cdot G_\beta(\mathbf{y}, \mathbf{c}_i),$$

we get that if

$$\delta^2 \frac{2\beta}{e} \sum_{i=1}^{N} G_{2\alpha}(\mathbf{s}, \mathbf{w}_i) \le \rho^2 \, \delta^2, \tag{13}$$

then $\mathbf{F_s}$ will be a contraction with contraction coefficient ρ. Inequality (13) is equivalent to

$$\frac{2\beta}{e} \|\mathbf{G}_\alpha(\mathbf{s})\|^2 \le \rho^2. \tag{14}$$

$$Q.E.D.$$

Corollary 1. *Consider a RecSOM fed by a fixed input* $\mathbf{s}$. *Define*

$$\Upsilon(\mathbf{s}) = \frac{e}{2} \|\mathbf{G}_\alpha(\mathbf{s})\|^{-2}. \tag{15}$$

Then, if $\beta < \Upsilon(\mathbf{s})$, $\mathbf{F_s}$ *is a contractive mapping.*

4   Experiments

We illustrate our results on natural language data used to demonstrate RecSOM in [1]. The data is a corpus of written English, the novel "Brave New World" by Aldous Huxley. In the corpus we removed punctuation symbols, upper-case letters were switched to lower-case and the space between words was transformed into a symbol '-'. The complete data set (after filtering) comprised 356606 symbols. Letters of the Roman alphabet were binary-encoded using 5 bits and presented to the network one at a time. RecSOM with $20 \times 20 = 400$ neurons was trained for two epochs using the following parameter settings: $\alpha = 3$, $\beta = 0.7$, $\gamma = 0.1$ and $\sigma : 10 \to 0.5$. Radius σ reached its final value at the end of the first epoch and then remained constant to allow for fine-tuning of the weights.

We constructed a map of the neurons' receptive fields (RFs) (shown in figure 1). Following [1], RF of a neuron is defined as the common suffix of all sequences for which that neuron becomes the best-matching unit. Note that the RF map contains regions in which RFs are topographically ordered with respect to the most recent symbols.

Let us consider, how the character of the RecSOM fixed-input dynamics (7) for each individual input symbol $s \in \mathcal{A}$ (coded as n-dimensional input vector $\mathbf{s} \in \mathbb{R}^n$) shapes the overall organization of the map. In order to investigate the fixed-input dynamics (7), we initialized context activations $\mathbf{y}(0)$ in 10,000 different positions within the state space $(0, 1]^N$. For each initial condition $\mathbf{y}(0)$, we checked asymptotic dynamics of the fixed input maps $\mathbf{F}_s$ by monitoring L_2-norm of the activation differences $(\mathbf{y}(t) - \mathbf{y}(t-1))$ and recording the limit set (after 1000 iterations).

Figure 2 illustrates asymptotic regimes of the fixed-input RecSOM dynamics (7) in terms of map activity differences between consecutive time steps. We observed a variety of behaviors. For some symbols, the activity differences converge to zero (attractive fixed points); for other symbols, the differences level at

n–	n–	h–	ad–	d–	he–	he–	a–	ag	.	in	ig	.	–th	–th	–th	th	ti
an–	u–	–	l–	nd–	e–	re–	–a–	ao	an	ain	in	.	l	t–h	th	.	.
y–	l–	g–	ng–	ed–	f–	–to–	o–		en	un	–in	ai	–al	h	wh		ty
ot–	at–	p–	–a–	n–	on–	m–	o–		–an	n	rn	ul	ll	e–i	e–h	gh	x	y
to	t–	es–	as–	er–	er–	mo	o	–to		–on	ion		ol	e–m	m	.	ey
t–	ut–	s–	is–	or–	ero	t–o	o	lo	ho	on	on	oo	.	om	um	im	am	ai	ry
ts	tw	ts–	r–	r–	ro	wo	io	e–o	–o	e–n	on		–m	t–m	si	ai	ri
e–s	he–w	–w	t–w	no	so	tio	–o	ng–o	–o	–n	–l	–h	e–l	di	ei	ni	ui
he–s	e–w	w	nw	ong	no	ak	k	–k	––	–o	.	–l	–h	–i	t–l	–wi	–hi	–ll	–thl
ns	rs	ing	ng	nf	e–k	l	e–c	–s		–g	–m	–y	–l	–l	i	ll	hi
s	us	uc	e–g	g	if	e–f	e–b	–c	–s	–w	–w	–e	.	–a	–a	n–a	ia	la	ha
is	c	nc	f	of	–f	–f	–b		–u	–u	–d	d–a	t–a	na	da	.	–ha
as	ac	ic	ib	b	.	oc	–v	.	–p	g–t	–t	–d	–e	–q	e–a	a	wa	era	ra
ac		ir	e–r	.	os			–r	–p	–t	s–t		.	ow	sa	ore	re
ar	ar	hr	r	tr	or	op	ov	–v	t–t	d–t	–t	ot	od	.	u	se	we	ere	pe
es	er	her	z	p	e–p	p	av		d–t	n–t	e–t	ot		ou	au	–se	be	ue	me
es	.	her	ter	ap	.	mp	v	st	rt	–st	tt	ut	out	lu	tu	e	e–e	ce	–he
ew		ev	.	q	ea	.	.	at	t	o–t	ent	ont	ind	d	dd	de	te	e	he
the–	e–	e–		em	ec	.		at	–at	ht	–it	nt	–and	rd	e–d	ne	–the	the
he–	e–	eo	.	.	ee	ed	ed	ad	it	it	id	ond	nd	and	ud	ld	le	–the	he

Fig. 1. Receptive fields of RecSOM trained on English text. Dots denote units with empty RFs

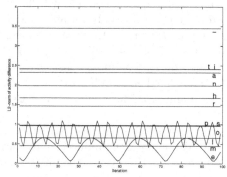

Fig. 2. Fixed-input asymptotic dynamics of RecSOM after training on English text. Plotted are L_2 norms of the differences of map activities between the successive iterations. Labels denote the associated input symbols (for clarity, not all labels are shown)

nonzero values (periodic attractors of period two, e.g. symbols 'i', 't', 'a', '-'). Fixed input RecSOM dynamics for symbols 'o' and 'e' follows a complicated a-periodic trajectory.

For each input symbol s, the autonomous dynamics $\mathbf{y}(t) = \mathbf{F}_s(\mathbf{y}(t-1))$ induces a dynamics of the winner units on the map:

$$i_s(t) = \underset{i \in \{1,2,...,N\}}{\mathrm{argmax}} \; y_i(t) \qquad (16)$$

The dynamics (16) is illustrated in figure 3[2].

---

[2] For each of the 10,000 initial conditions $\mathbf{y}(0)$, we first let the system (7) settle down by preiterating it for 1000 iterations and then mark the map position of the winner units $i_s(t)$ for further 100 iterations

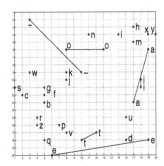

Fig. 3. Dynamics of the winning units on the RecSOM map induced by the fixed-input dynamics. The map was trained on a corpus of written English ("Brave New World" by Aldous Huxley)

When the fixed-input dynamics for $s \in \mathcal{A}$ is dominated by a unique attractive fixed point $\mathbf{y}_s$, the induced dynamics on the map, (16), settles down in neuron i_s, corresponding to the mode of $\mathbf{y}_s$, $i_s = \mathrm{argmax}_{i \in \{1,2,...,N\}} y_{s,i}$. The neuron i_s will be most responsive to input subsequences ending with long blocks of symbols s. Receptive fields of neurons on the map will be organized with respect to closeness of neurons to the fixed input winner i_s. Assuming a unimodal character of the fixed point $\mathbf{y}_s$, as soon the symbol s is seen, the mode of the activation profile $\mathbf{y}$ will drift towards the neuron i_s. The more consecutive symbols s we see, the more dominant the attractive fixed point of $\mathbf{F}_s$ becomes and the closer the winner position is to i_s. In this manner, a Markovian suffix-based RF organization is created.

As evident in figure 3, for symbols s with dynamics $\mathbf{y}(t) = \mathbf{F}_s(\mathbf{y}(t-1))$ dominated by a single fixed point $\mathbf{y}_s$, the induced dynamics on the map settles down in the mode position of $\mathbf{y}_s$. However, some autonomous dynamics $\mathbf{y}(t) = \mathbf{F}_s(\mathbf{y}(t-1))$ of period two (e.g. $s \in \{n, h, r, p, s\}$) induce a trivial dynamics on the map driven to a single point (grid position). In those cases, the points $\mathbf{y}^1, \mathbf{y}^2$ on the periodic orbit ($\mathbf{y}^1 = \mathbf{F}_s(\mathbf{y}^2)$, $\mathbf{y}^2 = \mathbf{F}_s(\mathbf{y}^1)$) lie within the representation region (Voronoi compartment) of the same neuron. Interestingly enough, the complicated dynamics of $\mathbf{F}_o$ and $\mathbf{F}_e$ translates into aperiodic oscillations between just two grid positions. Still, the suffix based organization of RFs in figure 1 is shaped by the underlying collection of the fixed input dynamics of $\mathbf{F}_s$ (illustrated in figure 3 through the induced dynamics on the map).

Theoretical upper bounds on β (eq. (15)) are shown in figure 4. Whenever for an input symbol s the bound $\Upsilon(s)$ is above $\beta = 0.7$ (dashed horizontal line) used to train RecSOM (e.g. symbols 'j', 'q', 'x'), we can be certain that the fixed input dynamics given by the map $\mathbf{F}_s$ will be dominated by an attractive fixed point. For symbols s with $\Upsilon(s) < \beta$, there is a possibility of a more complicated dynamics driven by $\mathbf{F}_s$. Indeed, the theoretical bounds $\Upsilon(s)$ for all symbols s with asymptotic fixed-input dynamics that goes beyond a single stable sink are below $\beta = 0.7$. Obviously, $\Upsilon(s) < \beta$ does not necessarily imply more complicated fixed input dynamics on symbol s.

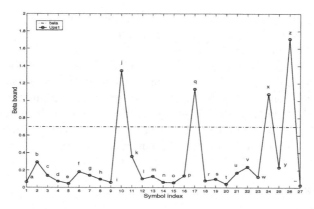

Fig. 4. Theoretical bounds on β for RecSOM trained on the English text

5   Discussion

Assume that for each input symbol $s \in \mathcal{A}$, the fixed-input RecSOM mapping $\mathbf{F}_s$ (7) is a contraction with contraction coefficient ρ_s. Set $\rho_{max} = \max_{s \in \mathcal{A}} \rho_s$. For a sequence $s_{1:n} = s_1...s_{n-2}s_{n-1}s_n$ over $\mathcal{A}$ and $\mathbf{y} \in (0,1]^N$, define

$$\mathbf{F}_{s_{1:n}}(\mathbf{y}) = \mathbf{F}_{s_n}(\mathbf{F}_{s_{n-1}}(...(\mathbf{F}_{s_2}(\mathbf{F}_{s_1}(\mathbf{y})))...))$$
$$= (\mathbf{F}_{s_n} \circ \mathbf{F}_{s_{n-1}} \circ ... \circ \mathbf{F}_{s_2} \circ \mathbf{F}_{s_1})(\mathbf{y}). \tag{17}$$

Then, if two prefixes $s_{1:p}$ and $s_{1:r}$ of a sequence $s_1...s_{p-2}s_{p-1}s_p...s_{r-2}s_{r-1}s_r...$ share a common suffix of length L, we have

$$\|\mathbf{F}_{s_{1:p}}(\mathbf{y}) - \mathbf{F}_{s_{1:r}}(\mathbf{y})\| \le \rho_{max}^L \sqrt{N}, \tag{18}$$

where $\sqrt{N}$ is the diameter of the RecSOM state space $(0,1]^N$.

For sufficiently large L, the two activations $\mathbf{y}^1 = \mathbf{F}_{s_{1:p}}(\mathbf{y})$ and $\mathbf{y}^2 = \mathbf{F}_{s_{1:r}}(\mathbf{y})$ will be close enough to have the same location of the mode[3],

$$i_* = \operatorname*{argmax}_{i \in \{1,2,...,N\}} y_i^1 = \operatorname*{argmax}_{i \in \{1,2,...,N\}} y_i^2,$$

and the two subsequences $s_{1:p}$ and $s_{1:r}$ yield the same best matching unit i_* on the map, *irrespective of the position of the subsequences in the input stream.* All that matters is that the prefixes share a sufficiently long common suffix. We say that such an *organization of RFs on the map has a Markovian flavour,* because it is shaped solely by the suffix structure of the processed subsequences, and it does not depend on the temporal context in which they occur in the input stream. Obviously, one can imagine situations where **(1)** locations of the modes of $\mathbf{y}^1$ and $\mathbf{y}^2$ will be distinct, despite a small distance between $\mathbf{y}^1$ and $\mathbf{y}^2$, or where **(2)** the modes of $\mathbf{y}^1$ and $\mathbf{y}^2$ coincide, while their distance is quite

---

[3]   Or at least mode locations on neighboring grid points of the map

large. This is the price to be paid for discontinuity of the best-matching-unit operation. However, in our extensive experimental studies, we have registered only a negligible number of such cases.

We suggest the theory of non-autonomous dynamical systems as a possible framework for studying representations of temporal structures in SOMs endowed with recursive processing mechanism. Contractive fixed input maps are likely to produce Markovian organizations of receptive fields on the RecSOM map. Periodic or aperiodic dynamics of $\mathbf{F}_s$ can result in a 'broken topography' of RFs and embody a potentially unbounded memory structure.

References

1. Voegtlin, T.: Recursive self-organizing maps. Neural Networks **15** (2002) 979–992
2. Kohonen, T.: Self–organizing formation of topologically correct feature maps. Biological Cybernetics **43** (1982) 59–69
3. de A. Barreto, G., Araújo, A., Kremer, S.: A taxanomy of spatiotemporal connectionist networks revisited: The unsupervised case. Neural Computation **15** (2003) 1255–1320
4. Hammer, B., Micheli, A., Strickert, M., Sperduti, A.: A general framework for unsupervised processing of structured data. Neurocomputing **57** (2004) 3–35
5. Chappell, G., Taylor, J.: The temporal kohonen map. Neural Networks **6** (1993) 441–445
6. Koskela, T., znd J. Heikkonen, M.V., Kaski, K.: Recurrent SOM with local linear models in time series prediction. In: 6th European Symposium on Artificial Neural Networks. (1998) 167–172
7. Horio, K., Yamakawa, T.: Feedback self-organizing map and its application to spatio-temporal pattern classification. International Journal of Computational Intelligence and Applications **1** (2001) 1–18
8. Strickert, M., Hammer, B.: Neural gas for sequences. In: Proceedings of the Workshop on Self-Organizing Maps (WSOM'03). (2003) 53–57
9. Hagenbuchner, M., Sperduti, A., Tsoi, A.: Self-organizing map for adaptive processing of structured data. IEEE Transactions on Neural Networks **14** (2003) 491–505
10. Schulz, R., Reggia, J.: Temporally asymmetric learning supports sequence processing in multi-winner self-organizing maps. Neural Computation **16** (2004) 535–561
11. Hammer, B., Micheli, A., Sperduti, A., Strickert, M.: Recursive self-organizing network models. Neural Networks **17** (2004) 1061–1085
12. Tiňo, P., Farkaš, I., van Mourik, J.: Topographic organization of receptive fields in recursive self-organizing map. Technical Report CSRP-05-06, University of Birmingham, School of Computer Science, http://www.cs.bham.ac.uk/~pxt/PAPERS/tino.tr05.pdf (2005)

Differential Priors for Elastic Nets

Miguel Á. Carreira-Perpiñán[1], Peter Dayan[2], and Geoffrey J. Goodhill[3]

[1] Dept. of Computer Science & Electrical Eng., OGI, Oregon Health & Science University
miguel@cse.ogi.edu
[2] Gatsby Computational Neuroscience Unit
dayan@gatsby.ucl.ac.uk
[3] Queensland Brain Institute and Dept. of Mathematics, University of Queensland
goodhill@uq.edu.au

Abstract. The elastic net and related algorithms, such as generative topographic mapping, are key methods for discretized dimension-reduction problems. At their heart are priors that specify the expected topological and geometric properties of the maps. However, up to now, only a very small subset of possible priors has been considered. Here we study a much more general family originating from discrete, high-order derivative operators. We show theoretically that the form of the discrete approximation to the derivative used has a crucial influence on the resulting map. Using a new and more powerful iterative elastic net algorithm, we confirm these results empirically, and illustrate how different priors affect the form of simulated ocular dominance columns.

1 Introduction

The elastic net was originally introduced as a continuous optimisation method for the traveling salesman problem (TSP) [1]. The basic idea is to represent a tour in continuous city space by a collection of linked centroids (the elastic net) that optimizes a trade-off between matching the given cities and keeping the sum of squared link lengths small. This trade-off is biased towards short nets at first and is slowly reversed until only the matching term matters – a deterministic annealing algorithm. From a dimension reduction perspective [2], the elastic net is a probabilistic model (Gaussian mixture) with a specific type of prior (the sum of squared link lengths) that models a high-dimensional city space in terms of a low-dimensional, discretized space. It is thus related to latent-variable models such as the generative topographic mapping [3], and can be seen as a probabilistic self-organising map (SOM) [4]. The elastic net has also been applied to modeling ocular dominance and orientation maps [5, 6], by interpreting the net centroids as the preferred stimuli of points in a discretized primary visual cortex and using the training set of "cities" as a sample of the continuous stimulus space. Biologically, the learning rule can be interpreted in terms of Hebbian learning and the prior in terms of an intracortical connectivity function. In this context, Dayan [7] suggested the use of more general quadratic forms for the intracortical connectivity prior. Here we define the generalized probabilistic model and analyse by theory and simulations the effect of different discrete priors on the structure of the resulting cortical maps.

M. Gallagher, J. Hogan, and F. Maire (Eds.): IDEAL 2005, LNCS 3578, pp. 335–342, 2005.

2   The Generalized Elastic Net

Given a collection of centroids $\{\mathbf{y}_m\}_{m=1}^M \subset \mathbb{R}^D$ and a scale parameter $\sigma \in \mathbb{R}^+$, consider a Gaussian-mixture density $p(\mathbf{x}) = \sum_{m=1}^M \frac{1}{M} p(\mathbf{x}|m)$ with $\mathbf{x}|m \sim \mathcal{N}(\mathbf{y}_m, \sigma^2 \mathbf{I}_D)$. Expressing the centroids as a $D \times M$ matrix $\mathbf{Y} = (\mathbf{y}_1, \ldots, \mathbf{y}_M)$, define a smoothing, or neighborhood-preserving, prior on the centroids $p(\mathbf{Y}; \beta) \propto \exp\left(-\frac{\beta}{2} \operatorname{tr}\left(\mathbf{Y}^T \mathbf{Y} \mathbf{S}\right)\right)$ where β is a regularisation hyperparameter and $\mathbf{S}$ is a (semi)positive definite $M \times M$ matrix. This prior can also be seen as a Gaussian process prior, with matrix $\mathbf{S}$ the inverse of the Gaussian process covariance matrix. Without the prior, the centroids could be permuted at will with no change in the model, since the variable m is just an index. The prior can be used to convey the topological (dimension and shape) and geometric (e.g. curvature) structure of a manifold implicitly defined by the centroids – i.e., as if the centroids resulted from discretizing a continuous latent variable model with a uniform density in a latent space of dimension L (the "cortex"), a nonparametric mapping from latent to data space (defined by the centroids $\mathbf{Y}$) and an isotropic Gaussian noise model in data space of dimension D (the "stimuli space") [8].

Given a training set expressed as a $D \times N$ matrix $\mathbf{X} = (\mathbf{x}_1, \ldots, \mathbf{x}_N)$, we are interested in deterministic annealing algorithms that minimize the energy function

$$E(\mathbf{Y}, \sigma) = -\sigma \sum_{n=1}^N \log \sum_{m=1}^M e^{-\frac{1}{2} \left\| \frac{\mathbf{x}_n - \mathbf{y}_m}{\sigma} \right\|^2} + \frac{\beta}{2} \operatorname{tr}\left(\mathbf{Y}^T \mathbf{Y} \mathbf{S}\right) \tag{1}$$

over $\mathbf{Y}$ for fixed σ, starting with a large σ and tracking the minimum to a small value of σ. E is derived from the log posterior of the full model. We call the first term the *fitness term*, arising from the Gaussian mixture $p(\mathbf{X}|\mathbf{Y}, \sigma)$, and the second term the *tension term*, arising from the prior $p(\mathbf{Y})$. The multiplication of the fitness term by σ downweights the fitness term with respect to the tension term as σ decreases. We do this because (1) one can find good solutions to combinatorial optimisation problems such as the TSP (which require $\sigma \to 0$); and (2) if considered as a dynamical system for a continuous latent space, the evolution of the net as a function of σ and the iteration index models the temporal evolution of cortical maps [5, 6]. We also investigate the behavior of the model for a larger range of β values than has previously been possible, thanks to the new algorithm we introduce in Sect. 5.

To apply the elastic net to practical problems such as the TSP or cortical map modeling, $\mathbf{S}$ should incorporate some knowledge of the problem being modeled. $\mathbf{S}$ specifies the expected topological and geometric structure of the solutions. Here, we fix the topology, i.e., the neighborhood relationship in the net, to be one or two dimensions, with open or periodic boundary conditions, and focus on the way that $\mathbf{S}$ represents priors on curvature. The prior has a crucial impact on the final solutions. For instance, in the application of the elastic net to ocular dominance, it helps determine the (empirically testable) width of the ocular dominance stripes. The next section studies this in an idealized, continuum limit; Sect. 4 considers the unexpectedly dramatic effect of discretization; Sect. 5 presents the new elastic net algorithm which allows us to study a much wider range of conditions; and Sect. 6 uses this algorithm to verify and extend our theoretical results. In Sect. 3–4 we assume an $M \times 1$ vector $\mathbf{y} \stackrel{\text{def}}{=} \mathbf{Y}^T$, since the tension term separates in a sum of D terms, one per dimension in $\mathbb{R}^D$ (stimulus space).

3   Regularisation of a Continuous Elastic Net

In a 1D continuous setting for which $\mathbf{y} = (y_m)$ becomes a real function of a real variable $y = y(t)$, consider a tension term of the smoothness functional type:

$$\frac{\beta}{2} \int_{-\infty}^{\infty} (\mathcal{D}y(t))^2 \, dt = \frac{\beta}{2} \int_{-\infty}^{\infty} ((s * y)(t))^2 \, dt. \tag{2}$$

$\mathcal{D}$ is a differential operator and s a kernel, e.g. for the pth-order derivative $\mathcal{D}_p = \frac{d^p}{dt^p}$ and $s = \frac{d^p \delta}{dt^p}$ where δ is the delta function. Such operators characterize the metric properties of y, such as its curvature. Note that a basis of the nullspace of $\mathcal{D}_p$ is $\{1, t, \ldots, t^{p-1}\}$. When the fitness term is also quadratic, such as $\int (y - g)^2 \, dt$ for fixed g, regularisation problems like this can be approached from the point of view of function approximation in a Hilbert space – e.g. of the functions y having derivatives up to order p that are square-integrable, i.e., with seminorm $\int \|\cdot\|^2$. This is the case for spline regression. In our case, the fitness term is not quadratic but results from Gaussian-mixture density estimation; however, we can still gain insight in the Fourier domain. By applying Parseval's theorem to the continuous tension term (2) with pth-order derivative $\mathcal{D}_p$ and calling $\hat{y}$ the Fourier transform of y, we can see that the tension energy is the same in both domains:

$$\frac{\beta}{2} \int_{-\infty}^{\infty} \left(\frac{d^p y}{dt^p} \right)^2 dt = \frac{\beta}{2} \int_{-\infty}^{\infty} |(i 2 \pi k)^p \hat{y}(k)|^2 \, dk = \frac{\beta}{2} \int_{-\infty}^{\infty} (2 \pi k)^{2p} |\hat{y}(k)|^2 \, dk$$

since the Fourier transform of $\frac{d^p y}{dt^p}$ is $(i 2 \pi k)^p \hat{y}(k)$. This means that $\mathcal{D}_p$ is acting as a high-pass filter whose cutoff frequency increases monotonically with p; see Fig. 1(A). Therefore, high-frequency functions will incur a high penalty and the minima of the energy will likely have low frequencies – subject to the effect of the fitness term.

Regularization is therefore straightforward in the continuous case. How this extends to the discrete case is the topic of the rest of the paper.

4   Discrete Nets: Construction of S, Analysis of the Tension Term

We consider $\mathbf{S} = \mathbf{D}^T \mathbf{D}$ where $\mathbf{D}$ is obtained from a translationally invariant (convolution) filter that we represent via a *stencil*. The stencil approximates a derivative via a finite-difference scheme, so $\mathbf{S}$ has a zero eigenvalue associated with the eigenvector of ones. This implies that $\mathbf{S}$ will not be positive definite so the prior will be improper, and that the tension term will be invariant to rigid motions of the net (note the fitness term is invariant to permutations of $\mathbf{Y}$ but not to rigid motions of it). We thus have a differential prior $\mathrm{tr}\left(\mathbf{Y}^T \mathbf{YS} \right) = \|\mathbf{DY}^T\|^2$ in terms of the Frobenius norm.

In 1D, we write a stencil as $\varsigma = (\ldots, \varsigma_{-2}, \varsigma_{-1}, \varsigma_0, \varsigma_1, \varsigma_2, \ldots)$, so that the rows of the $\mathbf{D}$ matrix result from successively shifting ς and padding with zeros at the ends. We have $\mathbf{D}^T \mathbf{y} = \varsigma * \mathbf{y}$. If M is large and ς has only a few nonzero coefficients, $\mathbf{D}$ will be sparse. For example, for $M = 7$ and periodic boundary conditions (b.c.):

$$\varsigma = (a\,b\,c\,d\,e) \qquad \mathbf{D} = \begin{pmatrix} c & d & e & 0 & 0 & a & b \\ b & c & d & e & 0 & 0 & a \\ a & b & c & d & e & 0 & 0 \\ 0 & a & b & c & d & e & 0 \\ 0 & 0 & a & b & c & d & e \\ e & 0 & 0 & a & b & c & d \\ d & e & 0 & 0 & a & b & c \end{pmatrix} \qquad \mathbf{y} = \begin{pmatrix} y_1 \\ \vdots \\ y_7 \end{pmatrix}.$$

With periodic b.c., $\mathbf{D}$ is a *circulant* matrix. When other types of b.c. are used, e.g. for nets with non-rectangular shapes or holes, $\mathbf{D}$ will be in general a *quasi-Toeplitz* matrix ($d_{mn} = d_{n-m}$ except at a few elements). In elastic nets of two or more dimensions, $\mathbf{D}$ is circulant or quasi-Toeplitz by blocks. The original elastic net model [1, 2, 5] is obtained by using a stencil $(0, -1, 1)$; in 1D the tension term simplifies to the sum of squared lengths $\frac{\beta}{2} \sum_m \|\mathbf{y}_{m+1} - \mathbf{y}_m\|^2$.

Compared with the continuous case, the discrete case has an extra degree of freedom since the pth derivative can be represented by many different stencils differing in truncation error. If the goal is accuracy at a reasonable computation cost (as in the numerical solution of PDEs), then one seeks stencils having few nonzero coefficients and high-order truncation error. For example, both $(0, -1, 1)$ (forward-difference) and $(-\frac{1}{2}, 0, \frac{1}{2})$ (central-difference) approximate the first derivative, but with linear and quadratic error, respectively, so the latter is preferred. Surprisingly, in the elastic net (where accuracy is not the goal) it turns out that stencils of the same order can result in nets of completely different characteristics. In particular, the highest frequency components can fail to be penalized, giving rise to a "sawtooth" solution (Fig. 3), which is physically unreasonable. Here, we give a characterisation of discrete differential stencils. The basic idea is that we can understand the tension term in terms of the eigenspace of $\mathbf{S}$, and that the latter coincides for periodic b.c. with the Fourier spectrum of the stencil, i.e., the eigenvectors are (co)sinewaves in a bounded, discrete frequency interval.

For periodic b.c., $\mathbf{D}$ and $\mathbf{S}$ are circulant. The mathematical analysis of 1D nets is straightforward; we state the main results without proof (full details appear in [9]). Many of them carry over to the L-dimensional case. Assume the net has M centroids (where M is even, for simplicity).

The eigenvectors of $\mathbf{S}$ are discrete plane waves $v_{mn} = \cos\left(2\pi \frac{m}{M} n\right)$ and $w_{mn} = \sin\left(2\pi \frac{m}{M} n\right)$. Unlike the continuous case, the discrete frequency m is upper bounded by $\frac{M}{2}$. This highest frequency corresponds to a sawtooth wave $(1, -1, 1, -1, \ldots, 1, -1)^T$, which plays a significant role with certain stencils. $\mathbf{S}$ has $\frac{M}{2}$ distinct eigenvalues ν_m (since $\nu_m = \nu_{M-m}$ for $m = 1, \ldots, M - 1$) which are real nonnegative. The power spectrum of the stencil ς is equal to the eigenspectrum of $\mathbf{S}$, i.e., $|\hat{\varsigma}_\kappa|^2 = \nu_\kappa$ where $\hat{\varsigma}_\kappa = \sum_{m=0}^{M-1} \varsigma_m e^{-i2\pi \frac{\kappa}{M} m}$ is the discrete Fourier transform of ς. $\nu_0 = 0$ is associated with the constant eigenvector $\mathbf{v}_0 = (1, \ldots, 1)^T$; and $\nu_{\frac{M}{2}}$ is associated with the sawtooth eigenvector $\mathbf{v}_{\frac{M}{2}} = (1, -1, 1, -1, \ldots, 1, -1)^T$.

By decomposing the net in the eigenvector basis of $\mathbf{S}$ as a superposition of plane waves, it becomes clear that frequency m contributes a tension-term penalty proportional to ν_m. Thus, given a stencil, its power spectrum gives the penalty for each frequency of the net. The constant eigenvector of ones is the sampled version of a constant net and incurs zero penalty since $\nu_0 = 0$ for a differential operator. However, since the rest of eigenvalues are nonzero in general, eigenvectors of the form $v_{mn} = n^m$ for fixed $m \in \mathbb{Z}^+$, corresponding to a monomial t^m, are not nullified by $\mathbf{D}$ in the circulant case (but they can be nullified in the nonperiodic b.c. case).

A stencil ς has zero power at the sawtooth frequency iff $\sum_{m \text{ even}} \varsigma_m = \sum_{m \text{ odd}} \varsigma_m = 0$. We call *sawtooth stencil* a stencil satisfying this condition. The convolution of any stencil with a sawtooth stencil is also sawtooth. For sawtooth stencils, the highest frequency incurs no penalty in the tension term, just as the zero-frequency wave (the constant net) does – unlike the continuous case, where a wave of frequency m has an average penalty proportional to m^{2p}.

Applying p times a first-order stencil ς results in a pth-order stencil with matrix $\mathbf{S}^p$. The family of ς consists of all such stencils for $p \geq 1$. We give specific results for two families that are particularly important; see Fig. 1(B,C).

Forward-difference family. This is defined by the first-order forward-difference stencil $\varsigma = (0, -1, 1)$. The pth-order derivative stencil has eigenvalues $\nu_m = \left(2 \sin \left(\pi \frac{m}{M}\right)\right)^{2p}$. The stencils are not sawtooth. The first four stencils are:

p	Finite difference scheme	Error term	Stencil
1	$y'_m \approx \frac{y_{m+1}-y_m}{h}$	$-y''(\xi)\frac{h}{2}$	$(0,\underline{1},1)$
2	$y''_m \approx \frac{y_{m+2}-2y_{m+1}+y_m}{h^2}$	$-y'''(\xi)h$	$(0,0,1,\underline{2},1)$
3	$y'''_m \approx \frac{y_{m+3}-3y_{m+2}+3y_{m+1}-y_m}{h^3}$	$-y^{iv}(\xi)\frac{3h}{2}$	$(0,0,0,\underline{1},3,\underline{3},1)$
4	$y^{iv}_m \approx \frac{y_{m+4}-4y_{m+3}+6y_{m+2}-4y_{m+1}+y_m}{h^4}$	$-y^v(\xi)2h$	$(0,0,0,0,1,\underline{4},6,\underline{4},1)$

Figure 1(B) shows that the forward-difference family forms a progression with p similar to that of the continuous case where the curves slope up more slowly for larger p. Even though the nullspace is strictly that of the constant wave, since the only null eigenvalue is ν_0, as p increases there are ever more near-zero eigenvalues for the low frequencies. Thus, in this family low frequencies are practically not penalized for high p.

Central-difference family. This is defined by the first-order central-difference stencil $\varsigma = \left(-\frac{1}{2}, 0, \frac{1}{2}\right)$. The pth-order derivative stencil has eigenvalues $\nu_m = \sin^{2p}\left(2\pi \frac{m}{M}\right)$. All stencils are sawtooth. The stencil of order p can be obtained from the forward-difference stencil of order p by intercalating 0 every two components and dividing by 2^p. Fig. 1(C) shows that this family also has a progression with decreasing slopes at low frequencies, but since every one of its stencils is a sawtooth stencil, both the low and high frequencies are not penalized. As M grows, more frequencies are allowed and the net approaches the continuum limit. However, for the central-difference family the sawtooth frequency remains unpenalized.

5   Annealing Algorithms for Parameter Estimation

Existing algorithms for optimizing the elastic net energy function include gradient descent [1] and matrix iteration methods (Gauss-Seidel in [5]). However, for large β, the step size required for convergence of gradient descent becomes very small, and the matrix iteration methods may occasionally diverge. We therefore developed a new, more powerful, iteration scheme. For constant σ, we look for stationary points:

$$\frac{\partial E}{\partial \mathbf{Y}} = -\frac{1}{\sigma}(\mathbf{XW} - \mathbf{YG}) + \beta \mathbf{Y}\left(\frac{\mathbf{S}+\mathbf{S}^T}{2}\right) = 0 \quad \Longrightarrow \quad \mathbf{YA} = \mathbf{XW} \quad (3)$$

with weight matrix $\mathbf{W} = (w_{nm})$ and invertible diagonal matrix $\mathbf{G} = \mathrm{diag}\,(g_m)$

$$w_{nm} \stackrel{\text{def}}{=} \frac{e^{-\frac{1}{2}\left\|\frac{\mathbf{x}_n-\mathbf{y}_m}{\sigma}\right\|^2}}{\sum_{m'=1}^{M} e^{-\frac{1}{2}\left\|\frac{\mathbf{x}_n-\mathbf{y}_{m'}}{\sigma}\right\|^2}} \qquad g_m \stackrel{\text{def}}{=} \sum_{n=1}^{N} w_{nm} \qquad \mathbf{A} \stackrel{\text{def}}{=} \mathbf{G} + \sigma\beta\left(\frac{\mathbf{S}+\mathbf{S}^T}{2}\right).$$

The weight w_{nm} is also the responsibility $p(m|\mathbf{x}_n)$ of centroid $\boldsymbol{\mu}_m$ for generating point $\mathbf{x}_n$, and so g_m is the total responsibility of centroid $\boldsymbol{\mu}_m$. The matrix $\mathbf{XW}$ is then a list of average centroids. Since $\mathbf{S}$ will typically be sparse (with a banded or block-banded structure), we can solve the system $\mathbf{YA} = \mathbf{XW}$ efficiently and robustly without inverting $\mathbf{A}$ by computing (with prior reordering if desired) the Cholesky factorisation $\mathbf{A} = \mathbf{LL}^T$, where $\mathbf{L}$ is lower triangular with nonnegative diagonal elements. $\mathbf{Y}$ is then obtained by solving two triangular systems by Gaussian elimination.

The Cholesky factorisation [10] is stable for symmetric semipositive definite matrices and terminates in $\mathcal{O}(\frac{1}{3}M^3)$ for dense $\mathbf{A}$ but much faster for sparse $\mathbf{A}$, since $\mathbf{L}$ preserves the banded structure. Naturally, since $\mathbf{W}$ and $\mathbf{G}$ depend on $\mathbf{Y}$, the method should be iterated. The algorithm can be seen as an EM algorithm, so it converges with linear order. Thus, although compared with conventional gradient descent, it requires slightly more computation time per step (which is always dominated by the computation of $\mathbf{W}$), it generally requires fewer iterations to converge. This and its reliability render it preferable.

6 Simulation Results for Cortical Map Modeling

In cortical map modeling [5, 6], the nets first develop uniform retinotopy, and then at a bifurcation of the energy, ocular dominance (OD) and orientation (OR) maps emerge. There, the maps are waves of a specific frequency κ^* for a range of β values. This frequency κ^* results from a trade-off between the fitness term pushing for high frequencies and the tension term penalizing frequency m proportionally to $\beta\nu_m$. The analysis of the tension term alone indicates that the frequency κ^* should decrease with β and increase with the stencil order p, given the progression of the eigenvalue curves towards passing higher frequencies with increasing p. This is confirmed by our simulations (Fig. 2; only OD is shown). In [11], we show that these differential priors correspond to Mexican-hat lateral interactions with p oscillations (excitatory vs inhibitory); and that for $p > 1$ the geometric relations between the OD and OR maps (e.g. intersection angles) do not match those of the biological maps that have been observed so far.

The elastic nets resulting from the central-difference family very often contain saw-tooth patterns. Such sawtooth patterns may take all the net or part of it, and can appear superimposed on a lower-frequency wave for some values of σ (see Fig. 3). One can also understand why this happens by noting that the tension term decouples in two, one for the even centroids and the other for the odd centroids. Other well-known stencils are also sawtooth, for example in 2D the quadratic-error Laplacian $\nabla^2_\times = \frac{1}{2}\begin{pmatrix} 1 & 0 & 1 \\ 0 & -4 & 0 \\ 1 & 0 & 1 \end{pmatrix}$.

7 Discussion

The behavior of the generalized elastic net is determined by the joint effect of the fitness and tension terms of its energy function. Our separate analysis of the tension term provides insight into the structure of the minima of the energy and makes explicit the discrepancies between the continuous and the discrete formulations of the net. This analysis paves the way for further work in the generalized elastic net, such as the study

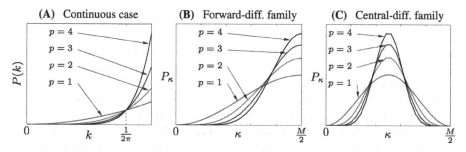

Fig. 1. 1D power spectrum associated with the derivative of order p of a continuous function, $P(k) = (2\pi k)^{2p}$, $k \in \mathbb{R}^+$; and for discrete nets with stencils (normalized by total power) from the forward- and central-difference families, $P_\kappa \overset{\text{def}}{=} |\hat{\varsigma}_\kappa|^2$, $\kappa = 0, \ldots, M/2$

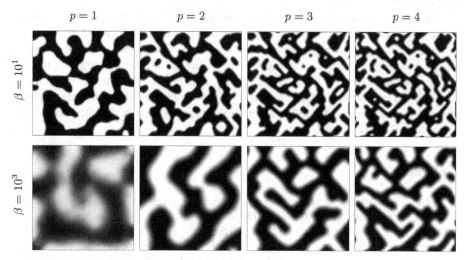

Fig. 2. Selected subset of ocular dominance map simulations with a 2D net with the forward-difference family and open b.c. Except for p and β, all other parameters and the initial conditions are the same. The stripes are narrower for low β and high p

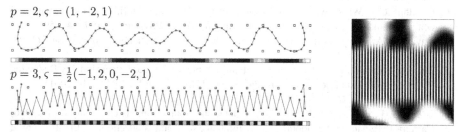

Fig. 3. Sawtooth stencils. *Left*: 1D nets in a stimulus space of (retinotopy, ocular dominance), open b.c., with a non-sawtooth stencil above and a sawtooth one below. *Right*: 2D sawteeth in ocular dominance with 3rd-order stencil $\varsigma = \frac{1}{2}(-1, 2, 0, -2, 1)$; cf. Fig. 2

of other stencil types, nonperiodic b.c., and the analysis of bifurcations from the Hessian of E and the character of the emergent nets. It also applies to other problems for which a discretized version of a quadratic smoothness regularizer is used, e.g. in computer vision, image processing or inverse problems. The model can also be used for unsupervised learning. We can extract MAP estimates for both Y and σ (perhaps with a prior on σ) with an EM algorithm, again based on Cholesky factorization; or perform Bayesian inference on β to attain good generalisation to unseen data (e.g. [12]).

Can differential priors be used with the SOM and GTM? This is tricky for the SOM, since it is not defined through an objective function. However, it may be possible to introduce them in the learning rule (similarly to momentum terms). Since GTM defines a continuous mapping, differential priors can, in principle, be used exactly. However, this is practically cumbersome, so that they may be more conveniently approximated by discrete stencils as here.

Difference schemes have been used extensively in the numerical solution of differential equations [13]. In this context, the concerns regarding the choice of difference scheme are: accuracy (whether the truncation error is of high order, which will mean a faster convergence), stability (whether the approximate solution converges to the true one as the step size tends to zero) and sparsity (whether the scheme has few nonzero coefficients, for computational efficiency). In our context of differential priors with a discrete net, accuracy and stability are not so relevant, while whether the stencil is for instance sawtooth is crucial.

References

1. Durbin, R., Willshaw, D.: An analogue approach to the traveling salesman problem using an elastic net method. Nature **326** (1987) 689–691
2. Durbin, R., Szeliski, R., Yuille, A.: An analysis of the elastic net approach to the traveling salesman problem. Neural Computation **1** (1989) 348–358
3. Bishop, C.M., Svensén, M., Williams, C.K.I.: GTM: The generative topographic mapping. Neural Computation **10** (1998) 215–234
4. Kohonen, T.K.: Self-Organizing Maps. Springer-Verlag (1995)
5. Durbin, R., Mitchison, G.: A dimension reduction framework for understanding cortical maps. Nature **343** (1990) 644–647
6. Goodhill, G.J., Willshaw, D.J.: Application of the elastic net algorithm to the formation of ocular dominance stripes. Network: Computation in Neural Systems **1** (1990) 41–59
7. Dayan, P.: Arbitrary elastic topologies and ocular dominance. Neural Computation **5** (1993) 392–401
8. Carreira-Perpiñán, M.Á.: Continuous Latent Variable Models for Dimensionality Reduction and Sequential Data Reconstruction. PhD thesis, University of Sheffield, UK (2001)
9. Carreira-Perpiñán, M.Á., Goodhill, G.J.: Generalized elastic nets. In revision (2005)
10. Golub, G.H., van Loan, C.F.: Matrix Computations. Johns Hopkins University Press (1996)
11. Carreira-Perpiñán, M.Á., Goodhill, G.J.: Influence of lateral connections on the structure of cortical maps. J. Neurophysiol. **92** (2004) 2947–2959
12. Utsugi, A.: Hyperparameter selection for self-organizing maps. Neural Computation **9** (1997) 623–635
13. Samarskiĭ, A.A.: The Theory of Difference Schemes. Marcel Dekker (2001)

Graphics Hardware Implementation of the Parameter-Less Self-organising Map

Alexander Campbell[1], Erik Berglund[2], and Alexander Streit[1]

[1] Faculty of IT
Queensland University of Technology
GPO Box 2434, Brisbane QLD 4001, Australia
`ab.campbell@qut.edu.au`
[2] Information Technology and Electrical Engineering
University of Queensland
St. Lucia, QLD. 4072, Australia

Abstract. This paper presents a highly parallel implementation of a new type of Self-Organising Map (SOM) using graphics hardware. The Parameter-Less SOM smoothly adapts to new data while preserving the mapping formed by previous data. It is therefore in principle highly suited for interactive use, however for large data sets the computational requirements are prohibitive. This paper will present an implementation on commodity graphics hardware which uses two forms of parallelism to significantly reduce this barrier. The performance is analysed experimentally and algorithmically. An advantage to using graphics hardware is that visualisation is essentially "free", thus increasing its suitability for interactive exploration of large data sets.

1 Introduction

One of the consequences of the explosion of data collection size and dimensionality is the need for unsupervised approaches to analysis and, in particular, dimensionality reduction. The Self-Organising Map (SOM) is an unsupervised learning technique capable of mapping a high dimensional input space to a lower (generally two-dimensional) output space such that the topology of the input space is preserved in the output space. This allows intuitive exploration of the data in an easily comprehensible 2D map that preserves neighbourhood relations.

For large, high dimensional data sets, or for applications where interactive use of the SOM is required, training times become an issue. This has led to the development of specific hardware implementations such as [1]. However, in order to find widespread application as, for example, an interactive web search tool, custom hardware solutions are obviously infeasible.

Driven primarily by the games industry the speed and programmability of commodity graphics hardware have been developing apace - performance increases outstripping Moore's Law by approximately a factor of 3:1[2]. Over the last few years the graphics processing unit (GPU) has not surprisingly been gaining interest as an inexpensive high performance platform for non-graphics centric computation. General Purpose computation on Graphics Processing Units

M. Gallagher, J. Hogan, and F. Maire (Eds.): IDEAL 2005, LNCS 3578, pp. 343–350, 2005.

(GPGPU) is a burgeoning field. GPU is suited particularly to implementations which exploit the parallelism of the graphics rendering pipeline, and which match the single instruction multiple data (SIMD) format at some point in their execution.

A recent development, the Parameter-Less Self-Organising Map (PLSOM) [3, 4], markedly decreases the number of iterations required to get a stable and ordered map. It also has two features which make it highly suited to interactive use: *plasticity preservation* and *memory*. These mean that it handles well being retrained with new data which may be greater than the range of the previously used data (plasticity) or smaller than the range of previous data (memory).

These factors made it an ideal candidate for an efficient parallel implementation, which we present here. We seek to demonstrate the suitability of the PLSOM for parallelisation and graphics hardware implementation, and a significant theoretical and actual performance superiority of this implementation. We have not provided a reference implementation of the standard SOM - for the reasons already given our focus is on the *PLSOM* - however we do discuss briefly how they relate.

We start with the theoretical basis of the Parameter-Less SOM in Section 2, then provide an introduction to using graphics hardware for general purpose computation in Section 3. Section 4 contains the fusion of these elements in terms of implementation and algorithmic complexity. Experimental setup for performance testing and empirical results are presented in Section 5. We conclude by commenting briefly on the potential for sophisticated visualisation and interactive use.

2   The Parameter-Less SOM

The Self-Organising Map [5, 6] is an algorithm for mapping (generally) low-dimensional manifolds in (generally) high-dimensional input spaces. The SOM achieves this through unsupervised training, but one of the major problems have been selecting and tuning annealing schemes, since it must be done empirically in the absence of a firm theoretical basis. There is no need for a learning rate annealing scheme or neighbourhood size annealing schemes with the Parameter-Less SOM. The PLSOM, which is similar to the SOM in structure but differs in adaption algorithm, consists of an array of nodes, N. The nodes are arranged in a grid in output space so that one can calculate the distance between two given nodes. During training, an input in the form of a k-dimensional vector $\mathbf{x}$ is presented to the PLSOM. The winning node at timestep t, $c(t)$, is the node with an associated weight which most closely resembles the input, $c(t)$ is selected using Equation 1.

$$c(t) = \arg\min_i(||\mathbf{x}(t) - \mathbf{w}_i(t)||) \tag{1}$$

where $\mathbf{w}_i(t)$ is the weight vector associated with node i at timestep t. Then the weights are updated using Equations 4-5. The basic idea is to move the weight nodes associated with nodes close to c towards the input $\mathbf{x}$. How much to move the weight vector of a given node i depends on the distance from i to c (in output space) and the neighbourhood function. The scaling of the neighbourhood function (the neighbourhood size) determines how a node which is far away from c is affected. A small neighbourhood size means relatively few nodes, close to c, are affected while a large neighbourhood function will lead to updates on more nodes further away from c. The weight update is scaled by a variable ϵ which is calculated according to Equations 2 and 3.

$$\epsilon(t) = \frac{||\mathbf{w}_c(t) - \mathbf{x}(t)||}{\rho(t)} \tag{2}$$

where $\rho(t)$ ensures that $\epsilon(t) \leq 1$.

$$\rho(t) = \max(||\mathbf{x}(t) - \mathbf{w}_c(t)||, \rho(t-1)),$$
$$\rho(0) = ||\mathbf{x}(0) - \mathbf{w}_c(0)|| \tag{3}$$

ϵ is used to scale the weight update in two ways; directly, as part of Equation 4 and indirectly as part of Equation 5.

$$\Delta\mathbf{w}_i(t) = \epsilon(t)h_{c,i}(t)[\mathbf{x}(t) - \mathbf{w}_i(t)] \tag{4}$$

where $\Delta\mathbf{w}_i(t)$ is the change in the weight associated with node i at timestep t and $h_{c,i}$ is the neighbourhood function given in Equation 5.

$$h_{c,i}(t) = e^{\frac{-d(i,c)^2}{\Theta(\epsilon(t))^2}} \tag{5}$$

where e is the Euler number, $d(i,c)$ is the Euclidean distance from node i to node c in output space and $\Theta(\epsilon(t))$ is given by Equation 6.

$$\Theta(\epsilon(t)) = \beta \ln(1 + \epsilon(t)(e-1)) \tag{6}$$

where β is a scaling constant related to the size of the network. For a n-by-m node network one would usually select β according to Equation 7:

$$\beta = \frac{m+n}{2} \tag{7}$$

The PLSOM achieves faster ordering, is independent of input space distribution, eases application and has a firmer theoretical basis.

3   Programmable Graphics Hardware

Commodity graphics hardware is designed primarily for real time approximation of lighting for 3D scenes. In the quest for more realistic approximations, recent graphics hardware has allowed programming of the graphics operations directly using programs that are referred to as *shaders*.

   Through the careful construction of graphics commands, we can adapt the hardware to perform calculations, much like a co-processor. The graphics hardware expects polygons that are defined by their edge vertices. Each polygon is transformed into fragments, which are multi-valued cells. We will refer to the collection of fragments as streams, in keeping with parallel computation terminology. Each fragment is processed by a *fragment shader*, also referred to as a kernel. As part of the hardware process, fragments are written to the framebuffer as pixels, ready for display to the user.

Control over the execution of the process remains with the CPU, since the CPU must instigate any instance of the stream operations. This is achieved by *rendering* a quadrilateral, which passes four vertices that bound the stream output, causing an instance of the kernel to be invoked for each element within the output stream. In our implementation we re-use the contents of the frame buffer as input, which under the architecture of the GPU means passing it to the fragment program as a texture.

The architecture of the graphics hardware is SIMD both as a vector processor and as a stream processor. As a vector processor each instruction can operate on up to four components of a vector simultaneously. As a stream processor the same program, or kernel, is executed for every element in the stream concurrently.

4   GPU Implementation of the PLSOM

There are two strategies to parallelising the self-organising map - vectorisation and partitioning [7] - and these essentially correspond to the two SIMD characteristics just mentioned. Vectorisation is the use of a vector-processor to operate on the (k-dimensional) components of each input in parallel. Partitioning of the map is done to allocate different processors to different sections; on which they can execute identical kernels. So by using graphics hardware we are well positioned to take advantage of both these optimisations. It should be possible to extend the algorithm given below to a standard SOM with very little modification: the only real difference is that way that the neighbourhood is chosen.

4.1   Self-organising Map Kernels

We focus on a single weight update for the whole map, that is to say a single value of t for Equations 1-6. This computation maps itself well to the stream paradigm and requires three separate kernels which we denote *computeDist<>*, *findMin<>* and *updateWeights<>*.

If we extract $d_i = ||\mathbf{x}(t) - \mathbf{w}_i(t)||$ from Equation 1 and formulate it as a single operation for the whole map, we have the distance vector $\mathbf{d} = ||\mathbf{x}(t) - \mathbf{w}(t)||$, and *computeDist*$< \mathbf{x}, \mathbf{w} >$ becomes our first kernel. The weight update is also easily treated as a stream operation using kernel *updateWeights*$< \mathbf{w}, c, \epsilon >$. Provided $c(t)$ is available for Equation 4 this approach should lead to significant speedup. Therefore our main focus is to construct a kernel which can be used to find $\arg \min_i(\mathbf{d})$ in an efficient manner.

Finding the maximum or minimum value of a set in parallel, and with only localised knowledge of state, can be achieved by iterating many local finds on ever smaller sets. This divide-and-conquer style of operation is termed a *reduction*

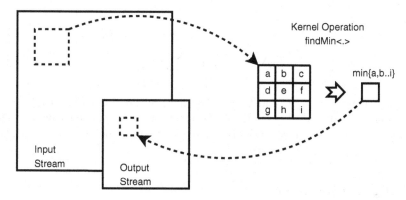

Fig. 1. Reduction Kernels

operation in the GPGPU literature. There are a number of implementation issues to be considered. With each iteration of the kernel operation we modify the coordinates of the quad we render to reduce the bounds of the stream each time. Eventually we are left with a one pixel buffer which is our desired value. Each time the kernel executes, the stream output is copied from its destination into a texture ready for input to the next stream operation. The kernel itself is relatively simple: it gathers a small number of values from the input texture and outputs the minimum value.

Given that our initial set size is N, we only require $q = \lceil log_\eta N \rceil$ iterations, where η is the size of the local sub-sets (and therefore the reduction factor). We term this operation $findMin < \mathbf{d}_j >$, where $\mathbf{d}_j$ represents the vector of values in the input stream at iteration j, $j = 1 \ldots q$, ie $\mathbf{d}_1 = \mathbf{d}$ and $|\mathbf{d}_q| = 1$. The nature of this reduction process is expressed in Figure 1.

4.2   Algorithm Analysis

Using these three stream operations leads to a concise algorithm:

1: $\mathbf{d} \leftarrow computeDist < \mathbf{x}, \mathbf{w} >$
2: $q \leftarrow ceil(log_\eta N)$
3: **for all** $j \leftarrow 1, 2, \ldots, q$ **do**
4:     $\mathbf{d}_{j+1} \leftarrow findMin < \mathbf{d}_j >$
5: **end for**
6: $c \leftarrow \mathbf{d}_q$
7: $updateWeights < \mathbf{w}, c, \epsilon >$

Assuming a number of processors equal to the number of nodes in the map, we have two standard stream operations - $computeDist<>$ and $updateWeights<>$ - with constant order time complexity, plus $\lceil log_\eta N \rceil$ iterations of $findMin<>$, which is essentially η compare instructions. This would result in a time complexity $T = \eta \lceil log_\eta N \rceil$ which is $O(logN)$.

However, in reality we have a limited number of processors, these being the twelve parallel pixel shader pipelines on our GeForce 6800 graphics card. With

P processors our time complexity is

$$T(N) = k\left\lceil\frac{N}{P}\right\rceil + \sum_{i=0}^{q-1}\eta\left\lceil\frac{\eta^i}{P}\right\rceil \tag{8}$$

where k is the number of (constant order) instructions in *computeDist* and *updateWeights* combined. This is $O(N/P)$ which demonstrates clearly the extent to which *partitioning* parallelism is exploited. Until some point $N >> P$, we should see roughly $logN$ growth.

4.3 Higher Dimensions

Our treatment so far has ignored the issue of what happens when we have greater than four dimensions. Arbitrary dimensions can be modelled using a 3D texture, with 4 dimensions to each z coordinate. The winning node is now found using a 2-step reduction. First the dimension distance is reduced to a scalar for each node, then the 2D coordinate and scalar distance are reduced as above. In our 3D texture, the x,y dimension are the 2D SOM grid, the z dimension is all the dimensions of that node. The graphics hardware's two SIMD characteristics are both utilised heavily in this situation indicating that similar performance advantages can be expected. Future work will explore this avenue.

5 Training Speed on Various Platforms

In order to give an estimation of the benefit of using programmable graphics hardware for PLSOM training we implemented the same training algorithm on 3 different platforms. In addition to a basic CPU implementation on a desktop and a GPU implementation using an NVIDIA graphics card on that same machine, we also tested a semi-parallelised implementation on a supercomputer.

- Target machine 1: A Coretech desktop with a 3.0 GHz Pentium 4 CPU and 1G RAM. Compiler: MSVC running in debug configuration with no optimisations. Operating system: Windows XP.
  Graphics Hardware: Albatron GeForce 6800 with 12 parallel pipelines.
- Target machine 2: The Queensland Parallel Supercomputing Foundation (QPSF) SGI Altix (64 bit) 3700 Bx2 supercomputer with 64 Intel Itanium 2 (1500Mhz) processors (although we only used 6 for our test) and 121 GB RAM. Compiler: icpc, the Intel parallelising C++ compiler. Optimisation level 3, parallelisation enabled. Operating system: 64-bit GNU/Linux.

For the test we trained an m-by-m node network with 2-dimensional input. The map is presented with 1000 inputs that are randomly generated, uniformly distributed in the unit square. The inputs are presented sequentially. The test program was written in C++ for the two non-GPU versions, a combination of C++ and Cg for the graphics implementation, and the code was functionally

Table 1. Execution Times 1000 Map Updates (Seconds)

number of nodes	Desktop computer	Super computer	Graphics card
729	3.93	0.24	1.67
4096	22.03	0.59	1.71
6561	36.37	1.18	1.72
16384	88.42	2.95	1.72
59049	317.80	11.51	3.32
236196	1278.04	69.26	6.65
531441	-	157.13	14.51
1048576	-	291.67	31.43

identical. Table 1 shows the execution times for 1000 map updates on these platforms.

Figure 2 shows the execution time growth rates of the PLSOM on the supercomputer and the GPU. This observed data indicates an time complexity of $O(N)$) for the GPU and the supercomputer after a critical point, however prior to this the GPU exhibits $logN$ growth as suggested in section 4.2. The parallelism of the graphics card is unable to overcome certain hardware-specific overheads until a certain point, however it is never slower than the desktop implementation in our experiments and it quickly overtakes the supercomputer performance. At

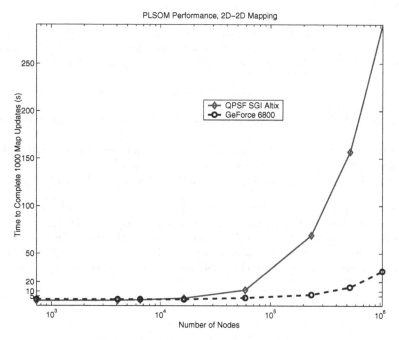

Fig. 2. Execution time growth rates

a map size of $1024 * 1024$ nodes we can see a 90% performance improvement of the GPU over the supercomputer.

This performance superiority cannot be *directly* translated to high dimensional data sets, however as we mentioned in section 4.3 both forms of parallelism would be heavily used in such an implementation and we plan to look at this in future work.

6   Discussion and Conclusion

In this paper we have described an implementation of the Parameter-Less Self Organising Map on commodity graphics hardware and provided an empirical performance analysis. As noted by [7] a desirable application of high speed training and re-training of the self-organising map is interactive analysis of web search results. Given this, inexpensive commodity graphics hardware is an ideal way to provide the computational power required, especially given that while the GPU is busy, the CPU is free for other tasks. Additionally, the visualisation capabilities of graphics hardware are 'on-tap' during the computational process - the execution times for the graphics card included displaying the weight matrix to the screen every ten iterations. This combination of superior visualisation power and what is essentially a tool for visualising higher-dimensional spaces seems synergetic.

References

1. Porrmann, M., Kalte, H., Witkowski, U., Niemann, J.C., Rückert, U.: A dynamically reconfigurable hardware accelerator for self-organizing feature maps. In: SCI 2001 (5th World Multi-Conference on Systemics, Cybernetics and Informatics). (2001) 242–247
2. NVIDIA Corporation: Cg toolkit user's manual: A developer's guide to programmable graphics. (2004)
3. Berglund, E., Sitte, J.: The parameter-less som algorithm. In: ANZIIS 2003. (2003) 159–164
4. Berglund, E., Sitte, J.: The parameter-less self-organizing map algorithm. (ITEE transactions on Neural Networks, accepted. In revisions)
5. Kohonen, T.: The self-organizing map. Proceedings of the IEEE **78** (1990) 1464–1480
6. Ritter, H., Martinetz, T., Schulten, K.: Neural Computation and Self-Organizing Maps - An Introduction. Addison-Wesley publishing company (1992)
7. Rauber, A., Tomsich, P., Merkl, D.: A parallel implementation of the self-organizing map exploiting cache effects: Making the som fit for interactive high-performance data analysis. In: IJCNN 2000 (International Joint Conference on Neural Networks). (2000) 24–27

Weighted SOM-Face: Selecting Local Features for Recognition from Individual Face Image

Xiaoyang Tan[1,2,3], Jun Liu[1], Songcan Chen[1,3], and Fuyan Zhang[2]

[1] Department of Computer Science and Engineering
Nanjing University of Aeronautics & Astronautics, Nanjing 210016, China
{x.tan,s.chen}@nuaa.edu.cn
[2] National Laboratory for Novel Software Technology
Nanjing University, Nanjing 210093, China
fyzhang@nju.edu.cn
[3] Shanghai Key Laboratory of Intelligent Information Processing
Fudan University, Shanghai 200433, China

Abstract. In human face recognition, different facial regions have different degrees of importance, and exploiting such information would hopefully improve the accuracy of the recognition system. A novel method is therefore proposed in this paper to automatically select the facial regions that are important for recognition. Unlike most of previous attempts, the selection is based on the facial appearance of individual subjects, rather than the appearance of all subjects. Hence the recognition process is class-specific. Experiments on the FERET face database show that the proposed methods can automatically and correctly identify those supposed important local features for recognition and thus are much beneficial to improve the recognition accuracy of the recognition system even under the condition of only one single training sample per person.

1 Introduction

Face recognition has been an active research area of computer vision and pattern recognition for decades [1]. Recently, great attention has been paid to the recognition methods using local features of face images due to its robust performance against such variation as noise, occlusion and expression [1-7].

An interesting question that then should be answered in this context is: which portions of a face image are really important for recognition? Empirically, such local regions are eyes, mouth and nose et al. Several authors have tried to manually identify such significant regions with different masks [2, 3]. For example, Brunelli and Poggio [2] used four masks respectively to extract the regions of eyes, mouth and the whole face for recognition, and their experimental results confirmed the discriminating power of such local facial features. Later, Pentland et al. [3] extended Brunelli and Poggio's work by projecting each local feature onto its corresponding eigenspace and using the obtained eigenfeatures for recognition. Both the above works need the involvement of great human endeavor, which is not desired in real applications. Moreover, defining in advance the same regions for all the classes seems to be inconsistent with our intuition that each class should have its own class-specific features, which are really meaningful to the recognition.

Recently, several researchers have also used disrciminant analysis for separating useful from useless facial variation [5,12,13], however, those approaches require a

M. Gallagher, J. Hogan, and F. Maire (Eds.): IDEAL 2005, LNCS 3578, pp. 351–358, 2005.

number of training samples per class in general, while it is not uncommon in practice that there is only one training image per person available to the system (such scenarios including law enforcement, passport or identification card verification, and so on). This suggests additional research needed in this direction. Several works have been developed to attack the *one training sample per person* problem from different respects, including synthesizing virtual samples [6,7], probabilistic matching[7], localizing the single training image [4,5] and neural network method[4].

The self-organizing maps (SOM, [8]) is an artificial neural networks model that implements a characteristic nonlinear projection from the high-dimensional space of signal data into a low-dimensional array of neurons in an orderly and discretely fashion. In the classification of data with a large number of classes such as face recognition, it is very difficult to obtain the hard class boundaries, while the properties of topological preservation and *one to many* mapping supported by SOM are especially useful in such situation.

In this paper, a novel method of automatically selecting some important local features from a single training face image for recognition is proposed. The method is based on a SOM-based face representation model called "SOM-face", which will be briefly reviewed in section 2. We described the proposed method in section 3 and the classification method in section 4. The experiments are reported in section 5. Finally, conclusions are drawn in section 6.

2   The SOM-Face

The essence of SOM-face [4] is to express each face image as a function of local information presented in the image. This is achieved by dividing the face image I into M different local sub-blocks $R_i\big|_{i=1}^M$ at first, each of which potentially preserves some structure information of the image.

Then, a self-organizing map (SOM) neural network is trained using all the obtained sub-blocks from all the available training images. After the SOM map has been trained, each sub-block R_i from the same face image I can be mapped to its corresponding Best Matching Units (BMUs) by a nearest neighbor strategy, whose location in the 2D SOM topological space is denoted as a location vector $l_i = \{x_i, y_i\}$. We can group all the location vectors from the same face as a set, i.e., $I = \{l_i\}_{i=1}^M = \{x_i, y_i\}_{i=1}^M$, which is called the face's "SOM-face" representation. Note that such a representation is both compact and robust: on one hand, the possible faults like noise in the original face image can be eliminated in the process of SOM training, on the other hand, the "SOM-face" representation is different from other SOM-based VQ methods in that only the location vector of each sub-block will be as prototype for later recognition purpose, while the weight vector is not used here.

Moreover, in the SOM-face, the information contained in the face is distributed in an orderly way and represented by several neurons instead of only one neuron or vector, so the common features of different classes can be easily identified. This merit is extremely useful for the work in this paper.

Fig.1 shows an example of an original image, its projection ("SOM-face") and the reconstructed image with the corresponding weight vectors.

a) Original face   b) SOM-face   c) Reconstructed face

Fig. 1. Example of an original face image, its projection and the reconstructed image

3   Identifying Important Local Features Adaptively

In human face recognition, different facial regions have different degrees of importance. Hopefully, exploiting such information would improve the accuracy of the
recognition system [7]. However, many local face recognition approaches do not
consider that, thus a test image can be easily misclassified. Here we present a novel
method able to extract such important information from the SOM-face representation
of a face image automatically.

In the proposed method, each neuron in SOM topological space is regarded as a
code word denoting some local area of the original face image. So, each original face
image can be described by a specializing subset of those code words, and all the face
images share the same dictionary which is actually all the neurons existing in the
SOM topological space. This novel interpretation of the SOM output neurons make it
feasible for us to analyze the degrees of importance of different local areas by computing the weights of corresponding neurons.

Consider a face image I that has been partitioned into M non-overlapping sub-
blocks as described in Section 2. To measure the degree of significance of each sub-
block in I, we present all the sub-blocks of I to the trained SOM network once again,
counting for each activated neuron the number of sub-blocks that are attracted. Formally, let the number of sub-blocks of I attracted by the j-th neuron be tf_j, then tf_j can
be regarded as some measure of the expressive power of the neuron for I: the more
sub-blocks it attracts, the stronger the expressive power it has. However, most expressive features may not be the most discriminating features, and the distribution of
the neurons in the whole face space should also be considered.

Let the number of different classes attracted by the j-th neuron be n_j, which is considered here as an indicator of the distribution of the sub-blocks in SOM topological
space. Big n_j values indicate much overlap between the distributions for different
classes and hence low discriminability, whereas small n_j values indicate little overlap
and hence high discriminability.

Combining both the above factors (i.e. tf_j and n_j), we can evaluate the importance
of a neuron to a given face. And the importance of each sub-block to a given face can
therefore be calculated indirectly by evaluating the significance of its corresponding
neuron (in other words, BMU). Formally, let the corresponding neuron of the i-th
sub-block of face I be j, then the sub-block's degree of importance w_i can be evaluated as follows [9]:

$$w_i = tf_j * \log(C/n_j + 1)$$ (1)

where C is the total number of classes to be recognized.

4 Recognition Based on Weighted SOM-Face

Now we describe a soft-kNN-based classification method (called weighted SOM-face) used to give a label to a testing face. The soft-kNN decision strategy is used here to reduce kNN's sensitivity to noise and to exploit the SOM's topological pres-ervation property. Note that the selection of important local facial features becomes a natural derivation of the algorithm, just by setting the weights of unimportant features to zero.

Formally, suppose that the probe face is divided into M sub-blocks, denoted as $I_{probe} = \{R_1, R_2, ..., R_M\}$, where R_r is the r-th sub-block, whose BMU's locations in the 2D SOM topological space is $l_r = \{x_r, y_r\}$. Then we denote the set of k nearest neighbors of l_r as $N_k(l_r) = \{l_{r,1}, l_{r,2}, ..., l_{r,k}\}$, where each element $l_{r,i}\big|_{i=1}^k$ is a prototype vector of the r-th sub-block from one of the C classes.

The confidence value $C_{r,i}$ describing the probability for the r-th sub-block's mem-bership in the C_i can be evaluated based on their pairwise distance in the SOM topo-logical space, as follows:

$$c_{r,i} = f(d(l_r, l_{r,i})) \tag{2}$$

where $d(,)$ is the function to compute Euclidean distance, and $f(.)$ is a real-valued monotonous decreasing function, satisfying the condition $f(0)=1$. In this paper, the $f(.)$ function adopted is as follows:

$$f(d) = \frac{\log(\tau(d)+1)}{\log(d+1)} \quad d > 0 \tag{3}$$

where $\tau(d) = \min\{d(l_r, l_{r,i}), j = 1, ..., k\}$, that is, the minimum pairwise distance be-tween r-th block and its k nearest neighbors in the SOM topological space.

Finally, a weighted linearly-summed voting scheme (Eq.4) is employed to assign the final label of the test image as the class with the maximum total confidence value. The weight (importance) w_i of each neuron obtained in Section 3 is of course incor-porated into the calculation, as follows:

$$label = \arg\max_j (\sum_{i=1}^M w_i c_{r,j}) \quad j = 1, 2, ..., C \tag{4}$$

where w_i is subject to the condition: $\sum_{i=1}^M w_i = 1$.

5 Experiments

The experimental face database used in this work comprises 400 gray-level frontal view face images from 200 persons, with the size of 256×384. There are 71 females and 129 males. Each person has two images (**fa** and **fb**) with different facial expres-sions. The **fa** images are used as gallery for training while the **fb** images as probes for testing. All the images are randomly selected from the FERET face database [11]. Some samples of the database are shown in Fig.2. Before the recognition process, the raw images were normalized and cropped to a size of 60×60 pixels.

In the localizing phase, the training images are partitioned into non-overlapping sub-block with size of 3×3. Then a single SOM map with the size of 88×16 using the sub-blocks obtained from partitioning all images is trained. The training process is divided into two phases as recommended by Kohonen [4], that is, an ordering phase and a fine-adjustment phase. 1000 updates are performed in the first phase, while 2000 times in the second one. The initial weights of all neurons are set to the greatest eigenvectors of the training data, and the learning parameter and the neighborhood widths of the neurons converge exponentially to 1 with the time of training.

Fig. 2. Some raw images in the FERET database

The analysis described in Section 3 indicates that the performance of the recognition system may be improved by exploiting the discriminating information contained in different local features. In order to verify this hypothesis, we first perform experiments to compare the performance of the proposed methods with that of some other approaches dealing with face recognition with one training image per person, such as eigenface [2], Enhanced $(PC)^2A$ algorithm($E(PC)^2A$,[8]) and Matrix Fisher Linear Discriminant Analysis (MatFLDA, [5]).

The comparison result is tabulated in Table.1, which reveals that when the top 1 match rate is concerned, the weighted SOM-face method achieves the best performance among the compared approaches. This result indicates that the weights of different sub-blocks are indeed informative for face recognition.

Table 1. Comparison of recognition accuracies (%) for different approaches

Method	Accuracy
Standard Eigenface	83.0
$E(PC)^2A$[6]	85.5
MatFLDA[5]	86.5
Regular SOM-face	87.5
Weighted SOM-face	**89.5**

To further study the behavior of the weighted methods, another set of experiments are conducted to compare the performance of the weighted and non-weighted SOM-face methods, concerning different k value used in the soft kNN decision. The results are shown in Fig.3, with eigenface as the benchmark.

It can be observed from Fig.3 that the weighted strategy outperforms the non-weighted SOM-face on the whole. In particular, when $k=1$, the top1 match rate of the weighted strategy is only 77.0%. However, with the increase of k-value, the matching rate rises as well. In particular, when k gradually increases to 50 (i.e. about half of the image database size), the weighted method began to perform better than its non-weighted counterpart, and since then, a large performance margin between the two methods can be observed. This again reveals the usefulness of the weight information to the recognition system.

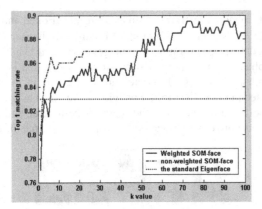

Fig. 3. Top 1 match rate as a function of k-value with different methods

Now we shall visualize the important local features selected by the weighted method to help us interpret the obtained results. Fig.4 shows some images and its corresponding important local features. The brighter the color of a sub-block, the higher degree of importance it has.

The images of Fig.4 reveal that the selected important local features contain in most case the regions of the face supposed important for classification: eyes, mouth, nose and hair, while the cheek is *not* considered important. These results are in accord with the observations reported by other researchers [2,3]. In addition, the figure shows that the important local areas of different classes are also different. This confirms our intuition that the local areas important to face recognition should be class-specific. This motivates us to further study on this issue to fully exploit the potential discriminative power of the local facial features.

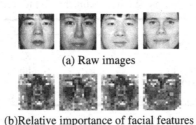

(a) Raw images

(b)Relative importance of facial features

Fig. 4. Some images and the distribution of important local features weighted by the proposed method

Finally, it is worthy to take some discusses about the size of sub-blocks. The choice of sub-block size reflects the balance between generalization and specialization. Specialization means the unique properties of the given face image (not necessarily of the individual himself), while generalization means generic properties that are less sensitive to the minor changes of a given image, such as noise, illumination, etc. Generally, as the sub-block gets smaller, the degree of generalization grows higher, at the same time the degree of specialization becomes lower. In this sense, to improve the robustness of the system, a smaller sub-block size may be desired, nevertheless, it is nonsense if too small size is used because each face consists of the same set of gray-value pixels in some view. More experimental details please refer to [4].It is also worthy to note that in this implementation, only the appearance-type feature (i.e., the grey values of each pix in a sub-block) is used, while other more complex invariant feature such as Gabor wavelet can be readily used. However, in that case, the size of sub-block should be relatively large to make the feature extraction possible. This will be the focus of our future research.

6   Conclusions

In this paper, a feature weighting strategy is proposed to calculate the importance of different local facial features from individual face image, based on simple statistics computed from its classification distributions on SOM surfaces. In light of the ideas from the automatic text analysis field, the proposed method assigns higher weights to local features which are both expressive and discriminative to the face image. Experiments on FERET database show that the proposed method can automatically identify those supposed important local features as eyes, mouth, nose and hair for recognition and furthermore, exploiting such information is much beneficial to improve the recognition accuracy of the recognition system even under the condition of only one single training sample per person.

Acknowledgement

This work was partially supported by the Jiangsu Science Foundation Key Project (BK2004001). Portions of the research in this paper use the FERET database of facial images collected under the FERET program.

References

1. Zhao, W., Chellappa, R., Phillips, P. J., and Rosenfeld, A., "Face Recognition: A Literature Survey, "ACM Computing Survey, 2003, 35(4): 399-458
2. Brunelli R. and Poggio T. Face recognition: features versus templates. IEEE TPAMI, 1993,15(10): 1042-1062
3. Pentland A., Moghaddam B., and Starner T. View-based and modular eigenspaces for face recognition. In: Proc. of the IEEE Inter. Conf. CVPR, Seattle, WA, 1994, 84-91
4. Tan, X.Y., Chen, S.C., Zhou, Z.-H., and Zhang, F.. Recognizing partially occluded, expression variant faces from single training image per person with SOM and soft kNN ensemble. IEEE Transactions on Neural Networks, in press
5. Chen, S. C., Liu, J., and Zhou, Z.-H. Making FLDA applicable to face recognition with one sample per person. Patt. Recog., 2004, 37(7): 1553-1555
6. Chen, S. C., Zhang, D. Q., and Zhou, Z.-H., Enhanced (PC)2A for face recognition with one training image per person. Patt. Recog. Lett., 2004, 25:1173-1181
7. Martinez, A.M., Recognizing imprecisely localized, partially occluded, and expression variant faces from a single sample per class. IEEE TPAMI, 2002, 25(6): 748-763
8. Kohonen T. Self-Organizing Map, 2nd edition, Berlin: Springer-Verlag, 1997
9. Grossman D. A. and Frieder O. Information Retrieval: Algorithms and Heuristics, Boston, MA: Kluwer, 1998.

10. Singh, S., Singh, M. and Markou, M., " Feature Selection for face Recognition based on Data Partitioning", Proc. 15th Int. Conf. Patt. Recog., ICPR'02, 11-15 August, 2002
11. Phillips P. J., Wechsler H., et al. The FERET database and evaluation procedure for face recognition algorithms. Image and Vision Computing, 1998, 16(5): 295-306
12. Moghaddam, B., Pentland, A., 1997. Probabilistic visual learning for object representation. IEEE Trans. on Pattern Analysis and Machine Intelligence 19(7), 696-710.
13. Belhumeur P., Hespanha J., and Kriegman, D. Eigenfaces vs. fisherfaces: recognition using class specific linear projection. IEEE TPAMI, 1997, 19(7): 711-720.

SOM-Based Novelty Detection Using Novel Data

Hyoung-joo Lee and Sungzoon Cho*

Dept. of Industrial Engineering, Seoul National University,
San 56-1, Shillim-dong, Kwanak-gu, 151-742, Seoul, Korea
{impatton,zoon}@snu.ac.kr

Abstract. Novelty detection involves identifying novel patterns. They are not usually available during training. Even if they are, the data quantity imbalance leads to a low classification accuracy when a supervised learning scheme is employed. Thus, an unsupervised learning scheme is often employed ignoring those few novel patterns. In this paper, we propose two ways to make use of the few available novel patterns. First, a scheme to determine local thresholds for the Self Organizing Map boundary is proposed. Second, a modification of the Learning Vector Quantization learning rule is proposed so that allows one to keep codebook vectors as far from novel patterns as possible. Experimental results are quite promising.

1 Introduction

In a typical binary classification problem, a model is trained with two classes of data and discriminates a new input pattern as either one of the two classes. However, in practice, there are situations where patterns from one class are too rare or difficult to obtain. For example, it is practically impossible to obtain patterns such as counterfeits in currency validation problems, let alone to construct a classifier based on them. In these cases, therefore, the novelty detection framework [1] is employed where a model learns characteristics of normal patterns in a given training dataset and detects novel patterns that are much different from the normal ones. In a geometric sense, the model generates closed boundaries around the normal patterns [2].

Various methods have been proposed for novelty detection tasks [3]-[5]. Most of them utilize only normal data during training, since they do not assume that novel data exist in their training processes, with a few exceptions [6]-[9]. But, in many cases, there exist, if few, novel patterns in the training data. Although they are not sufficient to train a binary classifier, they can help determine the boundaries around the normal class. It is experimentally shown that one can achieve a higher classification performance by utilizing information on novel data during training [6], [7], [9].

In novelty detection, generalization is to characterize patterns from the normal class while specialization is to exclude patterns from all other classes [10]. A

---

* The corresponding author

M. Gallagher, J. Hogan, and F. Maire (Eds.): IDEAL 2005, LNCS 3578, pp. 359–366, 2005.
© Springer-Verlag Berlin Heidelberg 2005

balance between the two concepts is critical to classification performance. Even though novelty detectors are able to generalize from normal data, most of them cannot specialize from data, but from a particular internal bias, since they ignore novel data. In this sense, using novel data during training helps a novelty detector specialize also from data.

In this paper, two approaches are proposed, which can be applied to situations where a few novel patterns exist in the training data. The first approach is a self-organizing map (SOM-L) concerned with determining local thresholds, i.e. one for each "cluster". The second one is a one-class learning vector quantization (LVQ) which utilizes the novel data to update its codebooks lest they should lie within boundaries surrounding the normal class. Just as the SOM-L, the one-class LVQ (OneLVQ) determines its thresholds based on both classes of data. Eventually, it is expected that the two methods generate more accurate and tighter boundaries than other methods trained with the normal class only.

The proposed approaches, the SOM-L and the OneLVQ, are described in the next Section. In Section 3, they are applied to an artificial and real-world datasets, and compared with other novelty detectors. In Section 4, conclusions and future research directions are discussed.

2   Proposed Approaches

2.1   Self-organizing Maps for Novelty Detection

Suppose a training dataset $\mathbf{X} = \{(\mathbf{x}_i, y_i)|i = 1, 2, \ldots, N\}$ is given, where $\mathbf{x}_i \in \mathbb{R}^d$ is an input pattern and $y_i \in \{+1, -1\}$ is its class label. The normal (or target) and the novel (or outlier) classes are denoted as $\mathbf{T} = \{\mathbf{x}_i|y_i = +1\}$ and $\mathbf{O} = \{\mathbf{x}_i|y_i = -1\}$, respectively. In general, the number of normal patterns is much greater than that of novel ones, i.e. $|\mathbf{T}| \gg |\mathbf{O}|$. For a conventional SOM [11], only the normal patterns are used. A SOM generates a set of codebooks $\mathbf{W} = \{\mathbf{w}_k|k = 1, 2, \ldots, K\}$, $K \ll N$, to describe the normal data.

After updating the codebooks, the codebook vector $\mathbf{m}(\mathbf{x})$ of an input pattern $\mathbf{x}$ and the Voronoi region $\mathbf{S}_k$ of each codebook $\mathbf{w}_k$ are defined as follows,

$$\mathbf{m}(\mathbf{x}) = \mathbf{w}_k \iff \mathbf{x} \in \mathbf{S}_k, \quad \text{if } \|\mathbf{w}_k - \mathbf{x}\|^2 < \|\mathbf{w}_l - \mathbf{x}\|^2, \forall l \neq k. \quad (1)$$

Given a test pattern $\mathbf{z}$, one will reject it as novel if the Euclidean distance (or quantization error) $e(\mathbf{z})$ between $\mathbf{z}$ and $\mathbf{m}(\mathbf{z})$ is greater than some threshold, or accept it as normal otherwise. A conventional SOM employs one "global" threshold, so let us denote it as a SOM-G. Usually, only one threshold is defined for all the codebooks to separate normal and novel, no matter which codebook is closest to $\mathbf{z}$. The threshold is determined according to the pre-determined fraction, θ, of the normal patterns to be rejected. That is,

$$e(\mathbf{z}) = \|\mathbf{z} - \mathbf{m}(\mathbf{z})\|^2 \leq r^2, \quad (2)$$

where $\frac{\sum_{\mathbf{x}_i \in \mathbf{T}} I\{e(\mathbf{x}_i) > r^2\}}{N} = \theta$ and $I\{\cdot\}$ is an indicator function.

2.2   Determination of Local Thresholds for a SOM

While some codebooks lie in dense lumps of input patterns, others lie in regions where patterns are sparsely scattered. If a single global threshold is applied for all the codebooks as in (2), some codebooks may be responsible for too large regions or too many normal patterns may be located outside of the boundaries. For that reason, it is desirable to set different thresholds for different codebooks.

In this subsection, a method for setting thresholds are presented, which resembles the support vector data description (SVDD) [9]. When the codebook update is finished, each training pattern belongs to the corresponding Voronoi region $\mathbf{S}_k$, which also has the codebook vector $\mathbf{w}_k$. For each Voronoi region, a hypersphere with a center at $\mathbf{w}_k$ and a minimal radius is obtained, so that it surrounds as many normal patterns and as few novel patterns as possible. Thus, an "optimization" problem can be considered as follows,

$$\min \quad \bar{E}(r_k) = r_k^2 + C_1 \sum_{y_i=+1} \epsilon_i + C_2 \sum_{y_i=-1} \xi_i, \tag{3}$$

$$\text{subject to} \quad \|\mathbf{x}_i - \mathbf{m}(\mathbf{x}_i)\|^2 \leq r_k^2 + \epsilon_i, \quad \forall \mathbf{x}_i \in \mathbf{T}_k,$$
$$\|\mathbf{x}_i - \mathbf{m}(\mathbf{x}_i)\|^2 \geq r_k^2 - \xi_i, \quad \forall \mathbf{x}_i \in \mathbf{O}_k,$$
$$\epsilon_i, \xi_i \geq 0, \forall i, \tag{4}$$

where $\mathbf{T}_k = \mathbf{T} \cap \mathbf{S}_k$ and $\mathbf{O}_k = \mathbf{O} \cap \mathbf{S}_k$. On one hand, a hypersphere with a large radius can surround many normal patterns, but may increase the possibility of false acceptance. On the other hand, a hypersphere with a small radius can exclude many novel patterns, but may reject more normal patterns than desired. Therefore, two positive constants, C_1 and C_2 are introduced to control the trade-off between the radius r_k and the errors, ϵ_i and ξ_i. The solution r_k^* of (3) can be found by an exhaustive search with $|\mathbf{T}_k|$ computations. Ultimately, a small threshold is found for a codebook in a dense region, a large threshold for one in a sparse region.

$$(r_k^*)^2 = e(\mathbf{x}_u), \quad \text{where } u = \underset{\mathbf{x}_i \in \mathbf{T}_k}{\operatorname{argmin}} \, \bar{E}\Big(e(\mathbf{x}_i)\Big). \tag{5}$$

For each codebook, the optimal threshold can be found independently. A test pattern $\mathbf{z}$ is classified as normal ($\mathbf{z} \in \mathbf{T}$) if satisfying (6), or as novel ($\mathbf{z} \in \mathbf{O}$) otherwise.

$$\|\mathbf{z} - \mathbf{w}_q\|^2 \leq (r_q^*)^2. \tag{6}$$

For a SOM-L, a conventional SOM is trained, but local thresholds such as (6) are used to classify a new test pattern.

It should be mentioned that local thresholds can be determined in other ways, among which the most well-known is by adopting a mixture model to generate a probability density function. To apply this sort of approach, however, one should be able to estimate the density of the novel class or explicitly assume it to follow some distribution as discussed in [8]. That is not only difficult, but also too risky, since we focus on a situation where only a handful of novel data exist. So we have adopted the proposed method that does not make a distributional assumption on the novel class.

2.3   Modified LVQ Learning Rule

The OneLVQ is based on the LVQ learning rule. For the original LVQ, the codebooks represent all of the classes and a pattern is classified as a class to which the nearest codebook belongs. However, unlike the original LVQ, the OneLVQ assigns the codebooks to only one class, i.e. the normal class, an attribute from which the name, one-class LVQ, came.

When novel patterns are included in the training data, a modified error function can be defined as

$$E = \int y \|\mathbf{x} - \mathbf{m}(\mathbf{x})\|^2 d\mathbf{x}d\mathbf{y} \cong \frac{1}{N} \sum_i y_i \|\mathbf{x}_i - \mathbf{m}(\mathbf{x}_i)\|^2$$

$$= \frac{1}{N} \sum_k \left[\sum_{\mathbf{x}_i \in \mathbf{T}_k} \|\mathbf{x}_i - \mathbf{m}(\mathbf{x}_i)\|^2 - \sum_{\mathbf{x}_i \in \mathbf{O}_k} \|\mathbf{x}_i - \mathbf{m}(\mathbf{x}_i)\|^2 \right]. \qquad (7)$$

Minimizing this error forces the codebooks to be located as close to the normal patterns and as far away from the novel patterns as possible, leading to a different learning rule from that of the original LVQ. Given an input pattern $\mathbf{x}$,

$$\mathbf{w}_k \leftarrow \begin{cases} \mathbf{w}_k & \text{if } \mathbf{x} \notin \mathbf{S}_k \\ \mathbf{w}_k + \eta(\mathbf{x} - \mathbf{w}_k) & \text{if } \mathbf{x} \in \mathbf{T}_k \\ \mathbf{w}_k - \eta(\mathbf{x} - \mathbf{w}_k) & \text{if } \mathbf{x} \in \mathbf{O}_k \end{cases}. \qquad (8)$$

According to this rule, if $\mathbf{x}$ does not belong to the Voronoi region $\mathbf{S}_k$ that $\mathbf{w}_k$ represents, $\mathbf{w}_k$ remains unchanged. If $\mathbf{x}$ does belong to $\mathbf{S}_k$, $\mathbf{w}_k$ moves toward $\mathbf{x}$ if $\mathbf{x}$ is normal, or moves away from $\mathbf{x}$ otherwise. That is, the normal patterns pull their codebook vectors while the novel patterns push away their codebooks. The codebook update in (8) is iterated until the error function does not improve or the maximum number of iteration is reached.

A OneLVQ is initialized by a conventional SOM and trained by the learning rule in (8). For classification, like the SOM-L, local thresholds (6) are used.

3   Experimental Results

3.1   Artificial Dataset

In order to demonstrate the novelty detection capabilities of the SOM-L and the OneLVQ, an experiment is conducted on a simple two-dimensional artificial dataset. A horseshoe-shaped dataset is learned by three novelty detectors, the SOM-G, the SOM-L, and the OneLVQ. Their decision boundaries are shown in Fig.1. The "true" boundaries of the normal and the novel regions are represented

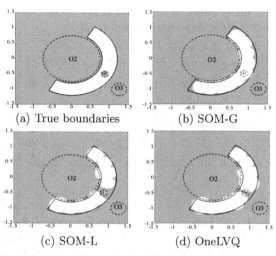

(a) True boundaries   (b) SOM-G

(c) SOM-L   (d) OneLVQ

Fig. 1. Decision boundaries by three novelty detectors on the horseshoe-shaped data

by the solid curves and the broken curves, respectively. An important assumption in a novelty detection problem is that novel patterns may appear in regions other than the regions where novel data exist in the training set. Novel data are given in the training set at O1 and they may also appear at O2 and O3 despite not being in the training set. Each model classifies the lighter area as normal, and the darker area as novel. The parameters are experimentally set. The SOM-G correctly classifies O2 and O3 outside of the normal region as novel, but misclassifies O1 in the normal region as novel. The SOM-L correctly classifies O1, but fails to recognize a large part of the normal region. On the other hand, the OneLVQ correctly classifies all of O1, O2, and O3, indicating that it is more productive to utilize the novel data during training than to ignore them.

3.2 Rätsch's Benchmark Datasets

Another set of experiments were conducted on six benchmark datasets, Banana, Breast Cancer, Diabetes, German, Heart, and Titanic, all of which were reported in [12] and available at http://ida.first.fraunhofer.de/~raetsch/. Each dataset consists of 100 splits of training and test sets, of which 30 splits are used in this experiment. Since all of the datasets are for binary classification problems, they were transformed into the novelty detection context. At first, for each split of each dataset, the common class of the two was assigned as the normal class, and the rare class as the novel class. Then a number of novel data were randomly sampled so that the number of the novel data should be 10% of that of the normal data in the training dataset.

As a classification performance criterion, the area under receiver operating characteristic (AUROC) was used. This value was calculated from an ROC curve that plots true rejection rates (TRR) over false rejection rates (FRR) from 1 to 50%. The experimental results are shown in Table 1, where the AUROC values

Table 1. Average AUROC values on six benchmark datasets (%). * indicates a statistically significant difference with a significance level of 5%

Dataset	Input Dim	Gauss	Parzen	SOM-G	AANN	OneSVM	SVDD	SOM-L	OneLVQ
Banana	2	16.25	**42.73***	41.06	39.00	39.87	40.44	40.93	41.85
Breast-cancer	9	24.11	24.92	26.83	25.89	22.22	23.34	27.17	**27.86**
Diabetes	8	25.23	27.36	27.27	25.30	23.91	25.84	27.40	**28.47***
German	20	19.90	21.45	22.48	20.31	18.70	19.65	23.90	**24.83***
Heart	13	31.69	31.11	33.36	26.86	23.68	30.77	33.38	**35.09***
Titanic	3	28.43	28.11	28.45	28.01	27.62	27.89	28.55	**28.75**

of eight novelty detectors over 30 splits are listed by their mean values. The OneLVQ provides the highest AUROC values for most datasets and for Diabetes, German, and Heart datasets, its AUROC values are significantly higher than other methods with a significance level of 5%. The SOM-L came second to the OneLVQ in most cases. This difference seems due to the way that the codebooks are updated, since it is the only difference between the two methods. On the other hand, the fact that the SOM-L, on the whole, was better than the SOM-G allows us to conclude that employing local thresholds rather than a global one is effective. The one-class support vector machine (OneSVM) and the SVDD resulted in AUROC values comparable to that of the Gaussian density estimator (Gauss), indicating that the solutions found by the two support vector-based methods were basically hyperellipsoids. The Parzen density estimator (Parzen) was the best for Banana dataset, which is two-dimensional, but not much better than the Gaussian method for other datasets. The auto-associative neural network (AANN) exhibited poor performances.

3.3 Keystroke Pattern Datasets

As real-world problems, we applied novelty detectors to a set of keystroke pattern datasets. The objective is to characterize a user's password-typing patterns and to detect potential impostors' password-typing patterns so that a computer system can be protected against intrusions. 21 users typed their own passwords generating the normal class of data, and to simulate potential intrusion attempts, 15 "impostors" typed the 21 users' passwords. In all, 21 datasets were constructed for 21 users. For each user's password, 76 to 388 normal patterns were collected for training and 75 for test and 75 novel patterns were also collected. For a more detailed description of these datasets, see [13]. In these experiments, 50 normal patterns and 5 novel patterns were sampled for training. The 75 normal patterns for test and the rest of 70 novel patterns consisted of the test set. Ten different training and test sets were randomly sampled for each password to reduce a sampling bias. The dimensionality of each dataset was reduced to about a half via principal component analysis with 80% of variance retained.

In Table 2, false rejection rates (FRR) and false acceptance rates (FAR) of seven novelty detectors for the 21 passwords are listed by their mean values.

Table 2. Average FRR and FAR values for 21 password datasets (%)

Password	Parzen		SOM-G		AANN		OneSVM		SVDD		SOM-L		OneLVQ	
	FRR	FAR	FRR	FAR	FRR	FAR	FRR	FAR	FRR	FAR	FRR	FAR	FRR	FAR
90200jdg	99.07	0.57	51.73	6.29	86.80	1.14	23.07	8.57	18.00	10.00	28.67	7.29	31.47	7.29
ahrfus	88.00	89.87	0.00	19.07	0.14	68.00	0.00	11.47	0.29	10.13	0.71	7.47	2.14	8.00	2.29
anehwksu	92.67	0.00	24.13	5.14	68.67	1.86	15.73	7.29	14.80	8.14	11.20	12.43	12.93	8.29
autumnman	100	0.00	16.40	0.00	43.20	0.00	18.93	0.00	14.67	0.00	7.60	0.00	6.80	0.00
beaupowe	48.13	0.00	12.67	3.00	25.33	8.29	9.20	19.29	9.07	12.57	3.47	13.57	6.67	12.14
c.s.93/ksy	98.67	0.00	16.53	0.00	63.07	0.00	15.47	0.00	11.87	0.00	7.60	0.00	8.13	0.00
dhfpql.	85.73	0.29	18.27	8.00	70.40	2.00	13.20	9.14	13.73	8.57	10.13	13.29	9.73	12.71
dirdhfmw	97.60	0.14	18.93	5.86	45.60	5.43	12.27	9.57	11.87	8.71	5.07	13.86	6.27	11.71
dlfjs wp	98.40	0.00	24.27	1.14	64.27	0.57	22.27	1.00	19.07	1.57	12.67	2.86	12.00	1.71
dltjdgml	94.00	0.00	8.67	0.00	57.20	0.00	4.93	0.14	3.33	0.71	2.80	0.14	2.67	0.00
drizzle	89.87	0.00	23.33	2.71	39.87	2.14	14.80	2.86	13.47	3.57	9.07	9.29	7.87	9.29
dusru427	82.00	0.00	12.93	0.00	33.60	0.00	15.87	0.14	15.07	0.00	4.67	0.14	4.93	0.00
i love 3	94.93	0.00	10.40	9.71	49.47	4.71	7.20	11.43	6.00	12.14	5.20	14.14	6.27	12.00
love wjd	99.47	0.00	30.67	3.71	64.53	1.43	28.80	6.57	27.07	8.43	21.07	8.43	14.67	10.00
loveis.	82.53	0.00	16.53	0.29	58.93	0.43	13.47	0.43	13.20	0.86	8.53	6.14	9.07	1.14
manseiii	80.27	0.00	14.53	2.43	48.67	1.29	13.20	5.43	12.27	6.00	10.53	5.00	7.33	4.29
rhkdwo	76.40	0.43	30.80	3.14	76.93	0.43	18.40	9.14	17.07	9.43	13.20	10.14	12.67	6.14
rla sua	79.73	0.00	13.07	2.57	57.20	0.14	8.40	3.71	7.20	2.29	5.20	10.14	6.40	4.71
tjddmswjd	99.73	0.00	16.93	3.71	51.07	3.57	16.40	2.71	15.20	3.71	7.60	9.14	11.07	4.86
tmdwnsl1	87.73	0.00	28.40	0.71	58.13	0.43	15.73	2.86	14.80	3.14	11.33	5.14	9.87	5.29
yuhwa1kk	96.00	0.00	12.00	0.00	47.07	0.00	11.60	0.00	8.00	0.00	5.73	0.00	4.80	0.00
Average	89.18	0.07	20.01	2.79	56.10	1.61	14.78	4.79	13.14	4.78	9.47	6.82	9.51	5.42

The parameters were set using five-fold cross validation. Compared to the SOM-G, the OneSVM, and the SVDD, the OneLVQ, on average, provides markedly lower FRRs and slightly higher FARs. Compared to the SOM-L, the OneLVQ has approximately equal FRRs but slightly lower FARs. The Parzen and the AANN rejected almost all patterns regardless of their classes. For the Parzen method, it is well-known that density estimation is difficult when applied to a high-dimensional dataset with a small number of patterns. The AANN could not avoid overfitting, since it had to estimate too many weights for the given number of data. The OneLVQ exhibits good applicability to practical domains, performing well with only 55 training data.

It should be stressed that among the novelty detectors, only the OneLVQ and the SVDD utilize the novel data during training. Aside from that property, the former is equivalent to the two SOM-based approaches and, to some extent, the latter to the OneSVM. Considering that the OneLVQ and the SVDD, on average, outperformed at least slightly their counterparts, it can be said that utilizing information on the novel class improves novety detection performance.

4   Conclusions and Discussion

This paper focuses on how to utilize, if they exist, the novel data and presents two novelty detection methods, the SOM-L and the OneLVQ. We have proposed the procedure for the two models to determine thresholds for which the trade-off between FRR and FAR is considered. For the OneLVQ, the error function and the learning rule of the original LVQ were modified to utilize information on the novel class as well as the normal class.

The experiment on a simple artificial dataset showed that the OneLVQ can resolve serious problems which may arise when considering only the normal data. When applied to the six benchmark datasets and the keystroke pattern datasets, both of the proposed methods show their competence as novelty detectors. Especially the OneLVQ performs better than other widely-used novelty detectors.

A few points and future directions have to be addressed. First, it is difficult to determine the parameters, K and (C_1, C_2), all of which play pivotal roles in training. To the best of our knowledge, they can be determined empirically by techniques such as cross-validation. When one class has an insufficient number of data, however, this may not be the best way. Note that the number of codebooks should be chosen as to minimize the classification error, rather than to maximize the goodness-of-fit to the data, since the ultimate goal is to detect novel patterns correctly. Second, a more efficient initialization procedure is desired. Third, it demands an investigation on how many novel patterns are needed for a OneLVQ to be productive. Finally, it can be pointed out that despite being named from the SOM, the SOM-G and SOM-L have little to do with the original purpose of the SOM. Instead, they keep and use only the codebooks from the SOM.

References

1. Bishop, C.: Novelty Detection and Neural Network Validation. In Proceedings of IEE Conference on Vision and Image Signal Processing (1994) 217-222
2. Schölkopf, B., Platt, J.C., Shawe-Taylor, J., Smola, A.J., Williamson, R.C.: Estimating the Support of a High-dimensional Distribution. Neural Computation 13 (2001) 1443-1471
3. Markou, M., Singh, S.: Novelty Detection: A Review - Part 1: Statistical Approaches. Signal Processing 83 (2003) 2481-2497
4. Markou, M., Singh, S.: Novelty Detection: A Review - Part 2: Neural Network Based Approaches. Signal Processing 83 (2003) 2499-2521
5. Marsland, S.: Novelty Detection in Learning Systems. Neural Computing Surveys 3 (2003) 157-195
6. Gori, M., Lastrucci, L., Soda, G.: Autoassociator-based Models for Speaker Verification. Pattern Recognition Letters 17 (1995) 241-250
7. Frosini, A., Gori, M., Priami, P.: A neural Network-based Model for Paper Currency Recognition and Verification. IEEE Transactions on Neural Networks 7(6) (1996) 1482-1490
8. Lauer, M.: A Mixture Approach to Novelty Detection Using Training Data with Outliers. In: De Raedt, L., Flach, P. (eds): Proceedings of the 12th European Conference on Machine Learning, Springer, Freiburg (2001) 300-311
9. Tax, D.M.J., Duin, R.P.W.: Support Vector Data Description. Machine Learning 54 (2004) 45-66
10. Japkowicz, N.: Supervised versus Unsupervised Binary-learning by Feed-forward Neural Networks. Machine Learning 42(1-2) (2001) 97-122
11. Kohonen, T.: Self Organizing Maps. Springer, Berlin (2001)
12. Rätsch, G., Onoda, T., Müller, K.R.: Soft Margins for AdaBoost. Machine Learning 42(3) (2001) 287-320
13. Yu, E., Cho, S.: Keystroke Dynamics Identity Verification - Its Problems and Practical Solutions. Computer and Security 23(5) (2004) 428-440

Multi-level Document Classifications
with Self-organising Maps

Huilin Ye

School of Electrical Engineering and Computer Science
The University of Newcastle, Callaghan, NSW 2308, Australia
Huilin.Ye@newcastle.edu.au

Abstract. The Self-Organising Map (SOM) is widely used to classify document collections. Such classifications are usually coarse-grained and cannot accommodate accurate document retrieval. A document classification scheme based on Multi-level Nested Self-Organising Map (MNSOM) is proposed to solve the problem. An MNSOM consists of a top map and a set of nested maps organised at different levels. The clusters on the top map of an MNSOM are at a relatively general level achieving retrieval recall, and the nested maps further elaborate the clusters into more specific groups, thus enhancing retrieval precision. The MNSOM was tested by a software document collection. The experimental results reveal that the MNSOM significantly improved the retrieval performance in comparison with the single SOM based classification.

1 Introduction

The Self-Organising Map (SOM) [1-2] is a general unsupervised neural network and has been extensively used in text classification [3-7]. Such classifications are usually coarse-grained and can be used for large volume information analysis, but cannot accommodate accurate document retrieval. The performance of a retrieval system is usually measured by *recall* and *precision*. Recall is the proportion of relevant material retrieved, measuring how well a system retrieves *all* the relevant documents; and precision is the proportion of retrieved material that is relevant, measuring how well the system retrieves *only* the relevant documents. Recall and precision tend to be related inversely. When a search is broadened to achieve better recall, precision tends to go down. Conversely, when the scope of a search is restricted to improve precision, recall tends to deteriorate. Current SOM based applications is capable of achieving the desired recall but failed in precision. Orwig et al. [8] reported a poor result for precision when they used SOM to classify electronic meeting output. Therefore, how to improve precision without excessive compromise of recall is crucial for the SOM based information retrieval systems.

We propose to use a sophisticated neural network architecture, called Multi-level Nested Self-Organising Map (MNSOM), to address the above problem. Based on the MNSOM, the classification will be done in multi-levels and the accuracy of the classification will be enhanced gradually from the top level to the lowest level to fine-grained classifications. The coarse-grained classification at the top level is used to maintain a high level of recall and the precision will be improved by the fine-grained classifications. It is expected the retrieval performance can be significantly improved in such a multi-level classification based retrieval system in comparison with the

M. Gallagher, J. Hogan, and F. Maire (Eds.): IDEAL 2005, LNCS 3578, pp. 367–374, 2005.

single SOM based systems. The proposed approach has been tested by a software document collection containing the first section of UNIX user manual pages. Results obtained from a retrieval experiment reveal that MNSOM significantly enhanced retrieval precision without excessively sacrificing recall. MNSOM has also been compared with Guru and achieved a better level of precision at the same level of recall. Guru is a software document retrieval system considered capable of achieving a better-than-average retrieval performance [9].

The remainder of this paper is organised as follows. Section 2 will present the architecture and the procedure of how to construct an MNSOM. Section 3 will report the experimental result. Section 4 will conclude the paper.

2   Architecture and Construction of MNSOM

When classifying a document collection using the SOM, each document in the collection can be represented by a feature vector that can be generated based on Salton's vector space model [10]. The SOM has a learning rule that enables it to learn without any supervision. During the training, the feature vectors representing the document collection will be repeatedly sent to the SOM for learning. When the learning converges the documents will be projected to the map and be ordered in a natural way [2].

Instead of using one single map in the standard SOM, an MNSOM consists of a top map (TM) and a number of nested maps (NM). These nested maps are organised into different levels. The TM is set at level 0 and the NMs derived from the TM are at level 1. Each NM at level 1 can also give rise to further NMs which are at level 2, and so on. A two-level MNSOM is shown in Fig. 1 (only one example of the NMs at level 1 is illustrated). The TM corresponds to a standard single map. An NM at level 1 is a map containing the documents located within a certain sub-area of the TM. Since such a sub-area on a TM will correspond to a nested map, the sub-area on the TM is called *nested area* (*N-area*) for the NM.

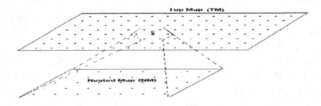

Fig. 1. A 2-level MNSOM

The number of documents located within an N-area is generally small in comparison with the total number of documents in the whole collection. Thus, the number of features associated with this sub-collection is much fewer than those associated with the whole collection. As a result, the sub-collection can be represented by a set of feature vectors with a much lower dimension. These feature vectors will be used to train an NM. The low dimension of the input feature vectors enables the NM to further discriminate the documents in the sub-collection. On completion of the training, a more accurate classification of the sub-collection on the map will be established.

When the same query is mapped onto the NM, it is expected that a higher level of precision will be achieved in comparison with the result obtained from the TM.

An N-area on a TM can be defined by two parameters, a *seed node*, the centroid of the N-area, determining the location of the N-area on the TM and a geometric distance, called *nested distance, dn*, prescribing the range of the N-area. All the neighbouring nodes that have a geometric distance to the seed node less than or equal to *dn* will form an N-area, where the geometric distance, in general, means that the steps from one node to another on the map. For example, the N-area shown in Fig. 1 is centred by its seed node *c* with a *dn=1*.

When a retrieval query is issued, it will be converted into a feature vector and mapped onto a node, whose reference vector has the highest similarity to the query feature vector, of the TM. This node is called the winning node. For the query, most retrieval target documents should reside on the winning node or its neighbouring nodes. The size of the neighbourhood will be determined by a defined geometric distance cutoff (dc) for the retrieval. Thus, ideally, for any given query mapped on the TM there should be an N-area that is centred at the winning node and includes its neighbourhood. Every node on a TM may become a winning node when different queries are mapped onto the TM. Therefore, each node on a TM may be a seed node based on which an N-area can be identified.

N-areas identified in this way are generally overlapping. This overlap is necessary to meet the requirement of a desired level of recall being achieved for all queries on the corresponding NMs. If N-areas identified on a TM are not overlapping, some clusters formed cross borders of the N-areas may be split into more N-areas. As a result, the documents located in such a split cluster may be assigned to different NMs. However, for a given query, the retrieval candidates are retrieved from only one corresponding NM. If the retrieval targets for the query are located in such a split cluster, recall may be deteriorated because part of the cluster is lost in the NM.

The overlapping should be as small as possible. It is not practicable to have too many N-areas as the number of identified N-areas will influence the efficiency of the construction of the NMs. The larger the number of N-areas, the more the NMs need to be constructed. The following strategies are used to identify N-areas:

- Reduce the number of NMs: Instead of constructing an NM for each node on a TM, nodes located within a certain area of a TM may share an NM.
- Set an appropriate size for the identified N-areas: The identified N-areas should be large enough to achieve a high recall, but should not be too large to maintain the accuracy of the classification on the corresponding NMs.

To identify a set of N-areas, first the TM must be divided into a number of disjoined areas, called *shared area (S-area)*. The nodes located in each S-area will share an N-area. Similar to an N-area, an S-area is also determined by a seed node and a sharing distance, *ds*. All the nodes on a map having a geometric distance to the seed node less than or equal to *ds* determine an S-area. The selection of the seed nodes on a TM is not very strict but following conditions should be satisfied:

- The generated S-areas must cover the whole TM and are not overlapping.
- There is a seed node in each S-area which has an equal geometric distance to the other nodes located in the S-area.
- Each S-area includes a balanced number of nodes except the S-areas located on the border of a TM.

The seed nodes identified for the S-areas are also the seed nodes for the N-areas. The next step is to set the nested distance to determine the range of the N-areas. When a query is mapped onto any node in an S-area, the retrieval targets for the query should be located within the corresponding N-area. The retrieval targets for a query will be selected by a distance cutoff. Documents located on the winning node and its neighbouring nodes with a geometric distance to the winning node less than, or equal to, the cutoff will be selected for the query. To enlarge an S-area to an N-area that can include all the retrieval targets for any node in the S-area, the nested distance must be at least equal to the sharing distance plus the distance cutoff, predefined for the retrieval. This will guarantee that possible retrieval candidates for all queries mapped onto the S-area are included in the corresponding NM.

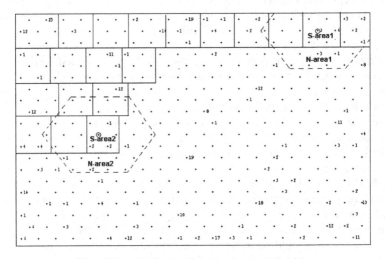

Fig. 2. The TM for the Unix document collection

A software document collection containing all the manual pages in the first section of the Unix User Manual was used to construct an MNSOM. The generated TM is shown in Fig. 2. The numbers shown on the figure indicate how many documents are allocated at the corresponding nodes. Part of the identified S-areas with a sharing distance $ds=1$, divided by solid lines, have been shown in Fig. 2. A distance cutoff is set to 2. Thus, the nested distance for the N-areas is 3 $(dn=ds+dc=3)$. Two examples of the N-areas, N-area1 and N-area2, are plotted in dotted lines in Fig. 2.

3 Retrieval Experiment

The constructed MNSOM presented in the preceding section is chosen for an retrieval experiment. The major focus of this experiment is to measure the retrieval effectiveness quantitatively by recall and precision. First, the retrieval effectiveness of the MNSOM will be compared with a single SOM based retrieval. And then the MNSOM will be compared with Guru [9], which is a representative of current information retrieval based methods in software document storage and retrieval.

The hypotheses to be tested in this experiment are:

- The MNSOM-based retrieval performance is significantly improved in comparison with the single SOM based retrieval performance.
- The MNSOM is capable of achieving a more effective retrieval performance in comparison with Guru.

An MNSOM was trained based on the collection containing more than 440 Unix command manual pages. The top map has been shown in Fig. 2. It is impossible to list the names of all the documents in Fig. 2 because of the large number of documents and the limited space of the map. Instead, numbers shown in Fig. 2 is used to indicate how many documents are allocated at each node on the map. A number of NMs have also been generated but cannot be presented here due to the limited space of the paper.

As specified earlier, for a given query, the retrieved documents in a map are determined by a distance cutoff, i.e. documents located at the winning node and its neighbouring nodes with a distance less than, or equal to, the cutoff would be selected. The same distance cutoff will be used for the single SOM based retrieval and the MNSOM based retrieval. The cutoff was set to 1 in this experiment. The retrieval performance for a single SOM can be measured by the retrieval results obtained directly from the TM. Queries will be mapped onto the TM only and the retrieval candidates will be selected from the TM based on the distance cutoff. For the MNSOM based retrieval, queries will be first mapped to the TM. Based on the winning node found on the TM, the corresponding NMs for the queries can be determined. And then the queries will be mapped onto the NM to find the finally matched documents based on the same distance cutoff.

Guru is an information retrieval system for the storage and retrieval of software documents developed by Maarek et al. [11]. In Guru, software components are automatically indexed from natural language documentation by using an indexing scheme based on the notions of lexical affinities and quantity of information. Indexed documents are organised in the library into a browsing hierarchy by using clustering techniques. Guru was tested on the same document collection (first section of the Unix manual pages) and we used the same set of queries (18 queries) as used in Guru for this experiment. The validity of the test collection, queries and their relevance judgements was defended in [12].

The retrieval results based on the 18 queries for the single SOM, the MNSOM, and Guru are compared in Table 1. The average recall achieved by the single SOM is 0.926 and the average precision is 0.209. In comparison with the average recall of 0.866 and precision of 0.743 achieved by MNSOM, precision has been improved by 355% at the expense of 6.4% compromise of the recall. It is obvious that the first hypothesis has been satisfied, i.e. the MNSOM-based retrieval performance is significantly improved in comparison with the single SOM based retrieval performance.

Guru was considered a better-than-average retrieval system and its retrieval performance was believed to be more than satisfactory [9]. The average precision and recall achieved by Guru is 0.637 and 0.828. In comparison, MNSOM improved the recall by 4.59% and the precision by 16.60 % respectively. It was observed that the MNSOM-based retrieval is capable of achieving a more effective retrieval performance in comparison with Guru, which satisfied the second hypothesis.

Table 1. Retrieval results comparison

| Query | Single SOM | | MNSOM | | Guru | |
No.	Recall	Precision	Recall	Precision	Recall	Precision
1	1	0.25	0.75	1	1	1
2	1	0.187	1	1	1	0.75
3	1	0.25	0.75	1	0.75	0.6
4	1	0.187	1	1	1	0.6
5	0	0	0	0	1	1
6	1	0.2	1	0.5	0	0
7	1	0.111	1	1	1	0.5
8	1	0.056	1	0.5	1	0.25
9	1	0.056	1	0.5	1	0.25
10	1	0.111	1	1	1	1
11	1	0.111	1	1	1	1
12	0.83	0.5	0.667	1	0.33	1
13	0.83	0.5	0.667	1	0.33	1
14	1	0.33	0.75	1	0.5	1
15	1	0.5	1	0.5	1	0.2
16	1	0.09	1	0.667	1	0.5
17	1	0.25	1	0.5	1	0.5
18	1	0.07	1	0.2	1	0.33
Mean	0.926	0.209	0.866	0.743	0.828	0.637

The problem of summarising information retrieval data has always been a hurdle ever since the beginning of the subject. The distributions of recall and precision obtained from the experiment are far from bell-shaped so that the mean is not a particularly good "average" indicator [13]. In addition to presenting the values of mean, figures of *cumulative frequency distribution* of recall and precision are also presented to show the variation in recall and precision.

Let $\{Z(Q_1), Z(Q_2), ..., Z(Q_i), ..., Z(Q_n)\}$ be a set of retrieval results, where Z denotes any arbitrary measure, $\{Q_1, Q_2, ..., Q_i, ..., Q_n\}$ is a set of test queries, then the cumulative frequency distribution function $F(z)$ is a function of z which equals the proportion of $Z(Q_i)$ which are less than or equal to z. The cumulative frequency distributions of recall and precision for single SOM, the MNSOM, and Guru are shown in Fig. 3, where recall and precision are such that the larger their values the more effective the retrieval, then the lower the curve the better [13].

Looking at the recall cumulative distribution for SOM and MNSOM, the curve of SOM is a bit lower than the curve of MNSOM. The difference between the values of the median for both SOM and MNSOM is less than 10%. While turning to look at the precision, the curve of MNSOM is much lower than that of SOM and the values of median have a very large difference (0.12 in comparison with 0.7). In comparison with a single SOM, MNSOM achieves a significant improvement on precision without excessive compromise of recall.

Looking at the recall cumulative distribution for MNSOM and Guru, the two curves are very close. The values of median for both Guru and MNSOM differ very little. Roughly speaking, the performance of recall can be considered at the same level. While turning to look at the precision, the curve of MNSOM is always lower than that of Guru and the values of median have a relatively large difference (0.54 in comparison with 0.7). It is concluded that MNSOM achieves better precision than Guru while the same level recall is maintained.

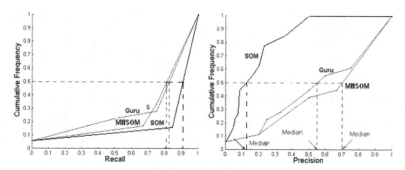

Fig. 3. Cumulative frequency distribution of recall & precision

It is also observed from the figure that the retrieval performance of the single SOM is much worse than that of Guru. Consequently a single SOM based classification is not good for document retrieval.

4   Conclusions

In this paper, the multi-level document classification scheme based on the MNSOM is discussed. The architecture of the MNSOM and the procedure of constructing a MNSOM are presented. A document collection can be classified onto an MNSOM consisting of a TM and a set of NMs organised in different levels. The problem of inaccurate clustering occurred in previous SOM-based applications is isolated on the TM and these inaccurate clusters can be fine-grained on the NMs. As a result, a much higher level of precision can be achieved on the NMs without compromising recall.

Experimental results were compared and discussed. The results reveal that the MNSOM significantly improved the retrieval performance in comparison with the single SOM based classification. Retrieval precision has been improved by 355% at the expense of only 6.4% compromise of the recall. The retrieval performance of MNSOM has also been compared with Guru. Guru's retrieval performance was believed to be more than satisfactory and better than the average information retrieval systems [9]. The comparison results show that the MNSOM is capable of achieving a more effective retrieval performance in comparison with Guru. The improvement for recall and precision are 4.59% and 16.60 % respectively.

References

1. Kohonen, T.: Self-Organisation and Associative Memory. Springer-Verlag, Berlin (1988)
2. Kohonen, T.: Self-Organising Maps. Spring-Verlag, Berlin (1997)
3. Honkela, T., Kaski, S., Lagus, K., Kohonen, T.: Newsgroup Exploration with WEBSOM Method and Browsing Interface. Technical Report, Report A32. Helsinki University of Technology, Helsinki (1996)
4. Kohonen, T., Self-Organisation of Very Large Document Collections: State of the Art. In Proc. of the 8th International Conference on Artificial Neural Networks. Springer, Skovde, Sweden (1998) 55-74
5. Chen, H., Houston, A., Sewell, R., Schatz, B.: Internet Browsing and Searching: User Evaluations of Category Map and Concept Space Techniques. J. American Society Info. Sci. 49 (1998) 582-603

6. Merkl, D.: Text Classification with Self-Organising Maps: Some Lessons Learned. Neurocomputting 21 (1998) 61-77
7. Lin, X., Soergel, D., Marchionini, G.: A Self-Organising Semantic Map for Information Retrieval. In Proc. of the 14th Annual International ACM/SIGIR Conference on Research and Development in Information Retrieval. Chicago, IL (1991) 262-269
8. Orwig, R., Chen, H., Nunamaker, J.: A Graphical, Self-Organising Approach to Classifying Electronic Meeting Output. J. American Society Info. Sci. 48 (1997) 157-170
9. Maarek, Y.: Using Structural Information for Managing Very Large Software Systems. Computer Science Department, PhD thesis. Technion, Israel Institute of Technology (1989)
10. Salton, G., Wong, A., Yang, C.: A Vector Space Model for Automatic Indexing. Comm ACM 18 (1975) 613-620
11. Maarek, Y., Berry, D., Kaiser, G.: An Information Retrieval Approach for Automatically Construction of Software Libraries. IEEE Trans. Softw. Eng. 17 (1991) 800-813
12. Maarek, Y.: Software Library Construction from an IR Perspective. SIGIR Forum 25 (1991) 8-18
13. Rijsbergen, C.: Information Retrieval. Butterworths: London (1980)

Predictive Vaccinology: Optimisation of Predictions Using Support Vector Machine Classifiers

Ivana Bozic[1,2], Guang Lan Zhang[2,3], and Vladimir Brusic[2,4]

[1] Faculty of Mathematics, University of Belgrade, Belgrade, Serbia
bozic@eunet.yu
[2] Institute for Infocomm Research, 21 Heng Mui Keng Terrace, Singapore 119613
{guanglan,vladimir}@i2r.a-star.edu.sg
[3] School of Computer Engineering, Nanyang Technological University,
Nanyang Avenue, Singapore 639798
[4] School of Land and Food Sciences and the Institute for Molecular Bioscience,
University of Queensland, Brisbane, Australia

Abstract. Promiscuous human leukocyte antigen (HLA) binding peptides are ideal targets for vaccine development. Existing computational models for prediction of promiscuous peptides used hidden Markov models and artificial neural networks as prediction algorithms. We report a system based on support vector machines that outperforms previously published methods. Preliminary testing showed that it can predict peptides binding to HLA-A2 and -A3 supertype molecules with excellent accuracy, even for molecules where no binding data are currently available.

1 Introduction

Computational predictions of peptides (short sequences of amino acids) that bind human leukocyte antigens (HLA) molecules of the immune system are essential for designing vaccines and immunotherapies against cancer, infectious disease and auto-immunity [1]. There are more than 1800 different HLA molecules characterised to date, and many of them have unique peptide binding preferences. A HLA supertype is a group of HLA molecules that share similar molecular structure and also have similar binding preferences – they bind largely overlapping sets of peptides [2]. Some dozen class I HLA supertypes have been described, of which four major supertypes (HLA-A2, -A3, -B7, and -B44) are present in approximately 90% of the human population [2]. Prediction of peptide binding to a single HLA molecule is less relevant for the design of vaccines applicable to a large proportion of human population. However, predictions of promiscuous peptides, i.e. those that bind multiple HLA molecules within a supertype, are important in the development of vaccines that are relevant to a broader population. Identification of peptides that bind HLA molecules is a combinatorial problem. Therefore high accuracy of such predictions is of great importance, because it makes identification of vaccine targets more cost- and time-effective.

A large number of prediction methods have been used for identification of HLA binding peptides. They include [reviewed in 3] binding motifs, quantitative matrices, decision trees, artificial neural networks, hidden Markov models, and molecular modeling. In addition, it was reported that models using support vector machines (SVM) perform better than other prediction methods when applied to a single HLA molecule [4,5]. Predictions of peptide binding to multiple HLA molecules of a supertype were

M. Gallagher, J. Hogan, and F. Maire (Eds.): IDEAL 2005, LNCS 3578, pp. 375–381, 2005.

performed using hidden Markov models (HMM) [6] and artificial neural networks (ANN) [7]. These reports also showed that accurate predictions promiscuous peptides within a supertype can be performed for HLA variants for which no experimental data are available. The accuracy of predictions of peptide binding to multiple HLA variants within A2 and A3 supertypes was measured by the area under the receiver operating characteristic curve (A_{ROC}) [8]. The reported values were $0.85 < A_{ROC} < 0.90$ for A2. We developed SVM models for prediction of peptide binding to molecules of HLA-A2 and -A3 supertypes and compared their prediction power to the corresponding ANN and HMM models. SVM models use a machine learning technique that implements *structural risk minimization principle*, which minimizes the upper bound on the expected generalization error thus giving high generalization ability [9]. SVMs exhibit great resistance to over-fitting. In addition, training of SVMs is a convex programming problem – it always finds a global solution, in contrast to training of ANNs, where many local minima usually exist.

2   Data Preprocessing

Nine amino acids long (9-mer) peptide data were collected from MHCPEP database [10], published articles, and a set of HLA non-binding peptides (V. Brusic unpublished data). Our datasets contain peptides with experimentally verified binding affinities (binder or non-binder) for fifteen variants of HLA-A2 and eight variants of HLA-A3 supertype. Data used for training represents the interaction (contact amino acids) between a 9-mer peptide and a HLA molecule. A peptide/HLA interaction is represented as a virtual peptide comprising nine peptide residues plus HLA residues that come in contact with the peptide. Only those contact residues that vary across the molecules belonging to one supertype were considered for the analysis. There are 19 non-conserved residues across A2 supertype and 14 non-conserved contact residues across A3 supertype molecules. The representation for each non-conserved residue is longer since it is a binary vector whose length equals the number of different residues observed at each contact position and only one position can take value 1. A virtual peptide for A2 supertype comprises 58 amino acids and for A3 62 amino acids. Detailed explanation of the data representation is given in [6,7,11]. If A is a set of 20 amino-acids, a virtual peptide is defined as $(a_1, a_2,...,a_l)$, $a_j \in A$, $j \in \{1, ..., l\}$, $l = 58$ for A2 and $l = 62$ for A3 supertype. The HLA protein sequences used in the processing of virtual peptides were extracted from HLA Sequences Data release 2.4.0 in the IMGT/HLA Sequence Database (http://www.anthonynolan.org.uk/HIG/). This representation enables binding peptide predictions for different molecules of the entire supertype.

3   Description of the Method

3.1   Support Vector Machines

Let X be a training set of virtual peptides and Y be a set of their experimentally determined binding affinities. Each member of X can have one of the two possible binding affinities (1 if it is a binder, -1 if it is not); $X = \{\mathbf{x}_1,..., \mathbf{x}_m\}$, $\mathbf{x}_j \in \mathbf{R}^n$ and $Y =$

$\{y_1,...,y_m\}$, $y_j \in \{-1,1\}$, $j \in \{1,...,m\}$. We seek to find a classification function $f : \mathbf{R}^n \rightarrow \mathbf{R}$ with the property: $f(\mathbf{x}) > 0 \Leftrightarrow y = 1$ and $f(\mathbf{x}) < 0 \Leftrightarrow y = -1$, which would accurately predict the classes of unseen data points. The value

$$\rho := \min_{1 \leq j \leq m} f(\mathbf{x}_j) \cdot y_j \tag{1}$$

is called the *margin* and stands for "the worst" classification over the whole training set. Training examples that lie right on the margin are called *support vectors*.

If the training data are linearly separable, we seek to find a linear function $f(\mathbf{x})$ that has the maximum margin. This is equivalent to constructing a maximum-margin hyperplane that separates the two classes (binders and non-binders) in n-dimensional space of our training data. In the case of linearly non-separable data, the idea is to map the training data into a higher-dimension feature space F (Hilbert space) via a non-linear map $\Phi : \mathbf{R}^n \rightarrow F$, dim $F > n$, and construct a separating maximum-margin hyperplane there. This mapping is simplified by introducing a *kernel function* k:

$$k(\mathbf{x}, \mathbf{x}') = (\Phi(\mathbf{x}), \Phi(\mathbf{x}')) . \tag{2}$$

Because real-life data are usually non-separable (even in the feature space) due to noise, we allow some misclassified training examples. This is enabled by introduction of a new parameter C, which is a trade-off between the margin and the training error.

Constructing a maximum-margin hyperplane is a constrained convex optimization problem. Thus, solving the SVM problem is equivalent to finding a solution (see [12]) to the Karush-Kuhn-Tucker (KKT) conditions, and, equivalently, the Wolfe dual problem:

Find α_j which maximize $W(\alpha)$,

$$W(\alpha) = \sum_{j=1}^{m} \alpha_j - \frac{1}{2} \sum_{j,s=1}^{m} \alpha_j \alpha_s y_j y_s k(\mathbf{x}_j, \mathbf{x}_s) ,$$

$$0 \leq \alpha_j \leq C, \quad \sum_{j=1}^{m} \alpha_j y_j = 0. \tag{3}$$

This is a linearly constrained convex quadratic program, which is solved numerically.

The decision function is

$$f(\mathbf{x}) = \sum_{j=1}^{m} y_j \alpha_j k(\mathbf{x}, \mathbf{x}_j) + b . \tag{4}$$

α_i are the solutions of the corresponding quadratic program and b is easily found using the KKT complementarity condition [12]. Commonly used kernels include linear, Gaussian and polynomial.

3.2 Implementation

We used the SVMlight package with a quadratic programming tool for solving small intermediate quadratic programming problems, based on the method of Hildreth and D'Espo [13]. Prior to training, every peptide from our dataset was transformed into a virtual peptide. This data were then transformed into a format compatible with the package used, and every virtual peptide $(a_1,a_2,...,a_l)$ was translated into a set of $n = 20 \times l$ indicators (bits). Each amino acid of a virtual peptide is represented by 20 indicators. In the complete sequence of indicators, l indicators are set to 1, representing specific residues that are present at a given position, and the other $20 \times (l-1)$ indicators are set to 0. In our case, $\mathbf{x}_j = (i_1,i_2,...,i_n)$, $i_s \in \{0,1\}$, $s \in \{1,...,n\}$, $j \in \{1,...,m\}$ represents a virtual peptide. The values $y_j = \pm 1$ indicate whether a peptide binds (1) or does not bind (-1) to a HLA molecule.

Blind testing was performed for assessing the performance of SVM for prediction of promiscuous peptides. To test the predictive accuracy of peptide binding to each of the HLA-A2 and -A3 variants, we used all peptides (binders and non-binders) related to this variant as the testing data and used all peptides related to other variants from the same supertype as training data. For example, the training set of HLA-A*0201 contained all peptides related to all HLA-A2 molecules except for HLA-A*0201. Testing of peptide binding to each HLA variant was performed without inclusion of experimental data for this particular HLA variant in the training set. Testing results, therefore, are likely to represent an underestimate of the actual performance since the final model contains available data for all HLA variants. We performed blind testing on five HLA-A2 and seven HLA-A3 molecules, for which sufficient data were available for valid testing (Table 1). Other variants of HLA-A2 and -A3 molecules were excluded from testing, since there was insufficient data for generating adequate test sets.

Throughout blind testing, we examined three kernels (linear, Gaussian and polynomial) and various combinations of the SVM parameters (trade-off c, σ for Gaussian and d for polynomial kernel). We trained 50 different SVM models for each supertype, with c varying from 0.01 to 20, d from 1 to 10 and σ from 0.001 to 1. Models with the best prediction performance (highest average A_{ROC}) were Gaussian kernel with σ=0.1, c=0.5 for HLA-A2 and Gaussian kernel with σ=0.1 and c=2 for HLA-A3.

Table 1. Blind testing: number of peptides in training and test sets for A2 and A3 supertype. Each training data set contained peptides related to other [*]14 HLA-A2 or [**]7 HLA-A3 molecule variants

HLA-A2 molecule	[*]Training data		Test data		HLA-A3 molecule	[**]Training data		Test data	
	Binders	Non-binders	Binders	Non-binders		Binders	Non-binders	Binders	Non-binders
*0201	224	378	440	1999	*0301	573	1447	107	89
*0202	619	2361	45	25	*0302	534	1277	146	259
*0204	641	2162	23	224	*1101	538	1313	142	223
*0205	648	2346	16	40	*1102	538	1325	142	211
*0206	621	2349	43	37	*3101	636	1482	44	54
					*3301	645	1474	35	62
					*6801	621	898	59	638

4   Experimental Results

A_{ROC} values of the SVM models that showed the best prediction performance are shown in Table 2 along with the corresponding values for optimized HMM [6] and ANN [7] predictions. The average SVM prediction accuracy is excellent for both A2 (A_{ROC}=0.89) and A3 supertype predictions (A_{ROC}=0.92). SVMs performed marginally better than HMM and ANN prediction methods on A2 supertype molecules, and significantly better on A3 supertype molecules ($p < 0.05$, Student's t-test).

Table 2. A_{ROC} values for blind testing of A2 and A3 models; comparison with HMM and ANN

HLA-A2 molecule	SVM	HMM	ANN	HLA-A3 molecule	SVM	ANN	HMM
*0201	0.90	0.93	0.87	*0301	0.93	0.89	0.94
*0202	0.81	0.73	0.76	*0302	0.86	0.84	0.86
*0204	0.93	0.92	0.88	*1101	0.96	0.91	0.91
*0205	0.97	0.94	0.93	*1102	0.96	0.86	0.86
*0206	0.85	0.88	0.91	*3101	0.87	0.69	0.66
				*3301	0.92	0.63	0.58
				*6801	0.98	0.96	0.95
Average	**0.89**	**0.88**	**0.87**	**Average**	**0.93**	**0.83**	**0.82**
Std.dev.	0.063	0.087	0.066	Std.dev.	0.044	0.144	0.120

Comparison of predictive performances of all three kernels is shown in Table 3. For both A2 and A3 supertypes, the prediction models with Gaussian kernel demostrated the best overall performance. A_{ROC} values for models with polynomial kernel are very close to those of Gaussian kernels. Models using linear kernel had the lowest average A_{ROC} on predictions for both supertypes.

Table 3. Performance comparison of SVMs with linear, polynomial and Gaussian kernels on a) HLA-A2 and b) HLA-A3. The tables show A_{ROC} values for blind testing. The values where all three kernels performed similarly are shown in bold

a)

HLA-A2 molecule	Kernel		
	Linear	Gaussian	Polynomial
A*0201	**0.92**	**0.90**	**0.92**
A*0202	0.73	0.81	0.76
A*0204	**0.90**	**0.93**	**0.92**
A*0205	0.93	0.97	0.97
A*0206	**0.83**	**0.85**	**0.85**
Average	**0.86**	**0.89**	**0.88**

b)

HLA-A3 molecule	Kernel		
	Linear	Gaussian	Polynomial
A*0301	**0.91**	**0.93**	**0.92**
A*0302	**0.84**	**0.86**	**0.86**
A*1101	**0.94**	**0.96**	**0.93**
A*1102	0.89	0.96	0.91
A*3101	0.82	0.87	0.90
A*3301	0.81	0.92	0.96
A*6801	**0.99**	**0.98**	**0.98**
Average	**0.89**	**0.93**	**0.92**

5 Discussion and Conclusion

Gaussian kernel performed best on both HLA-A2 and -A3 supertype predictions, while the linear kernel had the lowest average A_{ROC}. This is in contrast to report [4] where the linear kernel showed the best performance. However, the model in [4] was trained only for a single HLA molecule (A*0201) and their training dataset contained smaller number of peptides (total of 203). It is possible that linear kernel performs well on small datasets, because there may not be sufficient data for fine-tuning of the boundary. Selection of an optimal kernel for prediction of HLA binding peptides is dependant on the training data (both the data set and the natural properties of the studied HLA molecule). In the report [5] each of the three kernels (linear, Gaussian and polynomial) was determined as optimal for some of the HLA molecules. In this study we report that although Gaussian kernel had the highest average A_{ROC}, all three kernels have comparable performances for prediction of peptide binding to molecules belonging to a HLA supertype. Possible improvement may be achieved by combining predictions by SVMs that use different kernels. For example, improved HLA-A3 predictions can be achieved by combining Gaussian (e.g. A*0301, 0302, 1101, 1102) and polynomial (e.g. A*3101, 3301, 6801) kernels. Further experimental data are needed for validation of this hypothesis. Although linear kernel performed best in some cases (e.g. A*0201 and 6801), the improvement relative to other kernels is miniscule.

SVM showed significantly better performance than HMM and ANN on A3 supertype molecules, but the same conclusion could not be drawn for A2 supertype. This is probably due to the imbalance of the A2 training data with data for A*0201 being significantly larger than any other A2 set. It was reported that SVM often do not have the highest accuracy on imbalanced datasets [14], and dataset for A2 supertype is imbalanced in two ways: binders/non-binders ratio is close to 1:4, and peptides related to A*0201 constitute 6/7; peptides related to all other variants constitute only 1/7 of the data set. We have developed SVM models for prediction of peptides that bind molecules belonging to HLA-A2 and -A3 supertypes. Predictions were of excellent overall accuracy for both models. In comparison to other methods for prediction of promiscuous peptides, HMM and ANN, SVM slightly outperform HMM and ANN on unbalanced data sets (A2), but significantly outperform them on balanced data sets (A3).

Acknowledgements

This project has been funded in part (ZG and VB) with the USA Federal funds from the NIAID, NIH, Department of Health and Human Services, under Grant No. 5 U19 AI56541 and Contract No. HHSN266200400085C.

References

1. Brusic,V., August,J.T.: The changing field of vaccine development in the genomics era. Pharmacogenomics 5 (2004) 597-600
2. Sidney, J. et al: Practical, biochemical and evolutionary implications of the discovery of HLA class I supermotifs. Immunol. Today 17 (1996) 261-266
3. Brusic,V., Bajic,V.B., Petrovsky,N.: Computational methods for prediction of T-cell epitopes-a framework for modelling, testing, and applications. Methods 34 (2004) 436-443
4. Zhao,Y. et al.: Application of support vector machines for T-cell epitopes prediction. Bioinformatics 19 (2003) 1978-1984
5. Donnes,P. and Elofsson,A.: Prediction of MHC class I binding peptides, using SVMHC. BMC Bioinformatics 3 (2002) 25

6. Brusic,V. *et al.*: Prediction of promiscuous peptides that bind HLA class I molecules, Immunol. Cell Biol. 80 (2002) 280-285
7. Zhang,G.L. *et al.*: Neural models for predicting viral vaccine targets. J. Bioinform. Comp. Biol. (In press)
8. Swets,J.: Measuring the accuracy of diagnostic systems. Science 240 (1988) 1285-1293
9. Vapnik,V.N.: The Nature of Statistical Learning Theory. Springer, Berlin (1995)
10. Brusic,V. *et al.*: MHCPEP, a database of MHC-binding peptides: update 1997. Nucleic Acids Res. 26 (1998) 368-371
11. Chelvanayagam,G.: A roadmap for HLA-A, HLA-B and HLA-C peptide binding specificities. Immunogenetics 45 (1996) 15-26
12. Burges,C.J.C.: A Tutorial on Support Vector Machines for Pattern Recognition. Data Mining and Knowledge Discovery 2 (1998) 121-167
13. Joachims,T.: Making Large-Scale SVM Learning Practical. Advances in Kernel Methods – Support Vector Learning. MIT Press, Cambridge (1999)
14. Wu,G. Chang,E.Y.: Adaptive feature-space conformal transformation for imbalanced-data learning. Proceedings of the 20th ICML, Washington DC (2003) 816-823

Evolving Neural Networks for the Classification of Malignancy Associated Changes

Jennifer Hallinan

Institute for Molecular Bioscience and School of ITEE,
The University of Queensland, Brisbane, Australia, 4072
j.hallinan@imb.uq.edu.au

Abstract. Malignancy Associated Changes are subtle changes to the nuclear texture of visually normal cells in the vicinity of a cancerous or precancerous lesion. We describe a classifier for the detection of MACs in digital images of cervical cells using artificial neural networks evolved in conjunction with an image texture feature subset. ROC curve analysis is used to compare the classification accuracy of the evolved classifier with that of standard linear discriminant analysis over the full range of classification thresholds as well as at selected optimal operating points. The nonlinear classifier does not significantly outperform the linear one, but it generalizes more readily to unseen data, and its stochastic nature provides insights into the information content of the data.

1 Introduction

Cancer arises from mutations causing genetic instability in the nuclei of cells [1]. Cancer cells are visibly abnormal under the microscope, having scanty cytoplasm and large, dark, misshapen nuclei. As far back as the beginning of the twentieth century it was suggested that apparently normal cells in the vicinity of a tumor could exhibit less obvious nuclear abnormalities [2], but the subtlety of such changes made their detection by eye in stained slides too slow and imprecise to be of use.

The theory of Malignancy Associated Changes (MACs) was first formalized by Nieburgs, et al. in 1959 [3]. Briefly, the most common theory about the origins of MACs is that malignant cells produce some sort of "field effect", probably chemical in nature, which affects the organization of DNA in the nuclei of otherwise apparently normal cells in the patient. Due to the subtle nature of these changes, and the amount of variability present in any population of cells, they are hard to detect by eye, and little progress was made in MAC detection until the advent of relatively powerful, reasonably-priced computer and camera hardware and software in the last decade or so. There are currently several groups working on the detection and characterization of MACs.

MACs have been identified in many different tissues, including blood, buccal cells, sputum, cervix, thyroid, breast and colon. Of these, cervical cells can be obtained in a (relatively) non-invasive manner, and are routinely collected for the purpose of cervical cancer screening via the Papanicolaou (Pap) smear. Developers of automated Pap smear screening systems face a daunting task in reliably distinguishing cancer cells from the cell clumps and other debris that are common on Pap smears; the ability to reliably identify MACs in free-lying, visually normal cells would significantly boost the power of automated screeners.

M. Gallagher, J. Hogan, and F. Maire (Eds.): IDEAL 2005, LNCS 3578, pp. 382–389, 2005.

In studies to develop image analysis-based MAC detectors (e.g. [4],[5]) images of visually normal cells from patients of known diagnosis (cancerous/pre-cancerous condition or normal) are digitally captured. A variety of features such as nuclear area, optical density, shape and texture features are then calculated from the images, and linear discriminant analysis is used to classify individual cells as either "normal" or "abnormal". Patients are then classified on the basis of the proportion of their cells which were classified as "abnormal". The cutoff proportion is an arbitrary decision made by individual research groups.

The problem with the traditional approach is that the data is inherently noisy. Visually normal cells from "normal" (i.e. cancer-free) patients may come from individuals with undiagnosed or pre-clinical malignancies. Further, not all cells from "abnormal" patients will, in fact, be abnormal. The proportion of MAC-affected cells from an abnormal patient is not known *a priori*, and probably varies with the stage of the cancer, its rate of progression, and possibly other factors. Still more noise is introduced into the classification procedure by the existence of two more-or-less arbitrary cutoff values - the value of the discriminant score at which individual cells are classified as "normal" or "abnormal", and the proportion of "abnormal" cells used to classify a patient as "normal" or "abnormal". Furthermore, biological systems are inherently noisy in themselves, and cervical cells may show textural changes related to factors such as hormonal exposure, inflammation and other external factors, in addition to the changes caused by MACs.

Several of the early MACs papers reported accuracies of close to 100%. In a review of the literature the sensitivity of the classifiers reported from the computerized studies ranges from 63% to 95%, with an average of 78.2%. Closer examination of the outstandingly good results, however, reveal that many of them are test-on-train results derived from small data sets, and as such are unlikely to be representative of the results which could be achieved in a clinical setting. Large-scale studies reporting test results on unseen data all appear to produce an overall accuracy of around 80%, although different classifiers perform better or worse at different points on the Receiver Operating Characteristic (ROC) curve, which provides an overall, threshold-independent view of the performance of a classifier.

2 Methods

2.1 Image Analysis

The data set used for this study was generously provided in the form of digital cell images by the British Columbia Cancer Agency (BCCA), which has a long-standing interest in MACs (e.g. [6]). Images of the nuclei of visually normal thionin-SO_2 stained intermediate cervical cells were collected in the BCCRA laboratory using an Oncometrics Cyto-Savant™ computerized cytometry system [7]. Cells were selected for inclusion in the data set based on nuclear area and optical density, as well as diagnosis, in order to ensure that only visually normal cells were included. The resulting data set consists of a training set comprising 94 normal slides (18,480 cells) and 218 abnormal slides (62,524 cells), and a separate test set of 91 normal slides (38,429 cells) and 212 abnormal slides (125,558 cells).

A total of 90 features were extracted from the digital images, including those identified in the literature as useful for the detection of MACs and nuclear texture features under investigation within our research group. Full details are in [8]. For each slide the mean and standard deviation of each feature was calculated, yielding a total of 186 features.

Because the different raw features have values ranging from the order of 10^{-6} to 10^6, the features were rescaled to lie between 0 and 1, to avoid the effects of the larger features "swamping" those of the smaller features and possible numerical errors caused by a large range in values. This was done for each data subset using the maximum and minimum values for each feature, x, as observed in that data set.

2.2 Classifier Evolution

We used an artificial neural network (ANN) classifier, on the premise that if the features do not interact in a linear way higher-order interactions would be missed by a linear classifier. In accord with standard ANN practice, a three-layer feedforward net was used for this algorithm, with a sigmoid activation function on the hidden and output units, evolvable weights on the hidden and output units and an evolvable bias weight on the hidden nodes.

The feature subsets and network weights were selected using a simple genetic algorithm (Genetic Algorithm/Neural Network, or GA/NN). Each net was encoded as a single binary string, with each eight bits coding for a single integer in the range 0 – 255. Eight bits was chosen as the length for the feature representation because there are 184 features in the data set, and eight bits can encode numbers from 0 to 255. The integers representing weights were also coded in eight bits so that feature "genes" and weight "genes" would be subject to the same chances of mutation and crossover (Figure 1).

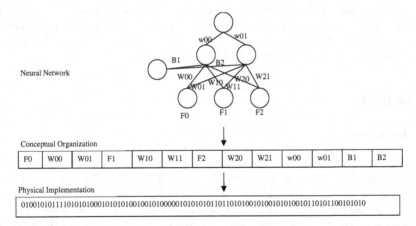

Fig. 1. Organization of a chromosome coding for a simple three-layer neural network. In this figure *F0 ... F2* are features, Ws are weights

The objective function for the GA attempts to minimize the mean squared error of the net over the training data. That is, for each fitness assessment, a single chromosome is decoded into its neural net "phenotype". Each member of the training set is presented to the net, and the output and squared error are calculated. The errors are summed over the whole training set and divided by the number of training exemplars to give the Mean Squared Error (MSE). The fitness of an individual chromosome is then (1 − MSE), and the GA attempts to maximize this. Roulette wheel selection was used, with elitism. The selection of parameter values for the GA started with the values recommended by Mitchell [9]. The methodology used can be summarized as follows:

1. One parameter was selected and several runs were made with values of the parameter at, above and below those suggested in [9];
2. The parameter setting which produced the highest maximum fitness at convergence of the GA was selected and used from then on;
3. Another parameter was selected, and the process iterated until all parameters were decided.

The final parameterization chosen was: Population size 50; Crossover rate 0.6; Mutation rate 0.01; Elite proportion 0.1; Input features 6; Hidden units 3.

2.3 ROC Curve Analysis

The ratio of true positive to false positive classifications varies for every classifier depending upon the classification threshold used. In order to compare classifiers, a Receiver Operating Characteristic (ROC) curve can be constructed, to allow evaluation of classifier performance over the full range of classification thresholds at which they may operate.

A ROC curve is constructed by first classifying the data set of interest. Our algorithm produces a single scalar number as output. The true positive and false positive rates will depend upon the classification threshold chosen; to plot a ROC curve this threshold is varied over all possible output values and the true positive proportion is plotted against the false positive proportion for each threshold [10]. The resulting curve will follow the diagonal from 0,0 to 1,1 if the classifier has no power (area under the curve (AUC) is 0.5), and will hug the top left corner of the plot for a perfect classifier (AUC is 1.0). Most classifiers produce ROC curves intermediate to these extremes.

The area under the ROC curve is commonly used as a measure of the overall performance of the classifier. In order to compare classifiers, it is necessary to estimate the standard error of the area under the curve, SE(AUC). To do this, we used the standard error of the Wilcoxon statistic, SE(W) [11].

3 Results

Generalizability is the ability of a trained classifier to perform well upon unseen data. The generalizability of the GA/NN classifiers and a standard stepwise linear discriminant analysis (SLDA) is depicted in Figure 1. For each classifier the AUC achieved on the training data is plotted against the AUC on unseen test data. If the point lies on the diagonal it indicates perfect generalizability, while a point below the diagonal implies some degree of overfitting of the classifier to the training data. The point representing the performance of the SLDA is marked; the numbers indicate which run of the GA/NN each point represents.

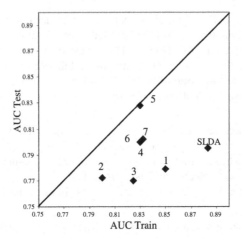

Fig. 2. AUC for classifiers tested on the training against that for the same classifier tested on the test set

It is clear from this figure that the SLDA classifier has the poorest generalization performance of any of the classifiers examined.

Because of the stochastic nature of genetic algorithms, the classifier must be evolved and run repeatedly in order to get a picture of the overall performance of the classifier. Figure 3 shows the ROC curves for seven runs of the algorithm, plus the SLDA, which only needs to be run once, as it is a deterministic algorithm. Other runs were performed with similar results, but are not shown in Figure 3, for the sake of clarity. The line for the SLDA is marked X and that for the best of the GA/NN runs (run 12) is indicated with a Y.

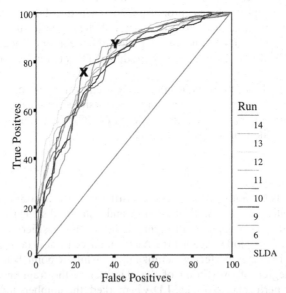

Fig. 3. ROC curves for runs of the GA/NN and SLDA algorithms

None of the test-on-test curves are significantly different from each other at the 95% level. The average AUC of all the GA/NN runs is 0.830, while that of the SLDA is 0.882.

The performance of all the classifiers at the closest point to the top left corner of the graph is compared, in terms of the measures often used to assess clinical classifiers [12], in Table 1.

Table 1. Performance of classifiers at the optimum point as determined by ROC curve analysis. Figures in brackets are the standard deviations of the GA/NN runs

Run	Sensitivity	Specificity	Accuracy
SLDA	0.77	0.76	0.77
GA/NN	0.80 (0.06)	0.68 (0.06)	0.76 (0.03)

4 Discussion

The strongest aspect of the GA/NN algorithm is its generalization performance. All of the evolved classifiers generalized better than the SLDA, with the best-performing classifier also being the best generalizer. Generalization ability is important to a classifier, since its use implies a belief that the performance observed on the training data is similar to that on the test data, a belief which is very often unjustified.

When it comes to classification sensitivity, previous studies fall in the range 63% to 95%, with an average of 78.2%. The SLDA described for this data set performs at about this level, with 77% sensitivity. The GA/NN, with a sensitivity of 80%, is not outstandingly better than that which has previously been achieved.

A very interesting point is the apparent existence of multiple equivalent subsets of features. The curves in Figure 2 are all very similar, but incorporate very different sets of features. In total, the eight runs (the SLDA and the seven GA/NN runs) selected 41 features, of which two occurred three times, five occurred twice, and the remainder were selected once each. The overlap between the feature sets is minimal, and yet the performance of the resulting classifiers is very similar.

When selecting features from a large feature set the question of correlations between features arises. Correlations may explain to some extent why several feature subsets appear to perform equivalently. A single run of the GA or the SLDA should not select correlated features, since the addition of a feature which to a subset containing highly correlated features is unlikely to add to the discriminatory power of the classifier. However, two runs may initially select different but correlated features which essentially play the same role in each subset. The pattern of relationships between features in this dataset is probably more complex than simple pairwise correlations. Features tend to come from one of several different classes – grey level coocurrence matrix features, features calculated from the distribution of optical density, and so on. Features within a single class are likely to be correlated to some extent, and a different pattern of correlation probably exists between feature classes.

It appears to be possible that many of the features used in these experiments are discriminatory to about the same extent, and that there are no higher-order interactions between them. In such a case, one would expect to find many equivalent subsets of features, as observed. The use of a neural network classifier would reinforce this pattern of results, since the neural network will weight input features according to their usefulness, and hence may be able to "even out" the effects of minor variations in discriminating power amongst the features used.

There is a second possible explanation for the existence of multiple subgroups of features with very similar discriminatory power. This dataset comprises cells from individuals with cancerous or precancerous cervical lesions. Many such lesions spontaneously regress, and it has been suggested that MACs may be associated only with progressive lesions [13],[14]. If this was the case, not all "abnormal" slides would exhibit MACs, and 100% accuracy against a cytological gold standard would be impossible for any classifier.

We conclude that the use of a nonlinear classification algorithm incorporating feature selection improves the generalizability of MACs classification, although it does not improve the accuracy of classification of MACs. The fact that the stochastic algorithm selected multiple equivalent but minimally overlapping subsets of features suggests that the information content of the dataset is limited by noise, and a classification accuracy of around 80% may be the maximum achievable, as reported in earlier work.

References

1. Grimm, D.: Disease backs cancer origin theory. Science (2004) 5695:389
2. Gruner, O. C.: Study of the changes met with the leukocytes in certain cases of malignant disease. British Journal of Surgery (1916) 3:506 - 522
3. Nieburgs, H. E., Zak, R. G., Allen, D. C., Reisman, H., Clardy, T.: Systemic cellular changes in material from human and animal tissues in the presence of tumours. Transactions of the 7th Annual Meeting of the International Society for Cytology (1959) 137 - 144
4. Bibbo, M., Bartels, P. H., Sychra, J. J., Weid, G. L.: Chromatin appearance in intermediate cells from patients with uterine cancer. Acta Cytologica (1981) 25:23 - 28.
5. Susnik, B., Worth, A., LeRiche, J., Palcic, B.: Malignancy-associated changes in the breast: changes in chromatin distribution in epithelial cells in normal-appearing tissue adjacent to carcinoma. Analytical and Quantitative Cytology and Histology (1995) 17:62 - 68
6. Palcic, B. & MacAulay, C.: 'Malignancy associated changes: Can they be employed clinically?', in Compendium on the Computerized Cytology and Histology Laboratory, ed G. L. Wied, P. H. Bartels, D. L. Rosenthal & U. Schenk, Tutorials of Cytology, Chicago (1994)
7. Garner, D., Harrison, A., MacAulay, C. & Palcic, B. 1994, 'Cyto-Savant and its use in automated screening of cervical smears' in Compendium on the Computerized Cytology and Histology Laboratory, ed G. L. Wied, P. H., Bartels, D. L., Rosenthal & U. Schenck, Tutorials of Cytology (1994)
8. Hallinan, J.: Detection of Malignancy Associated Changes in cervical cells using statistical and evolutionary computation techniques. Unpublished PhD Thesis, The University of Queensland (2000)
9. Mitchell, M.: An Introduction to Genetic Algorithms, MIT Press, Cambridge, Massachusetts (1996)
10. van Erkel, A. R. & Pattynama, P. M.: Receiver operating characteristsic (ROC) analysis: Basic principles and applications in radiology. European Journal of Radiology 27: 88 - 94 (1998)
11. Hanley, J. A. & McNeil, B. J.: The meaning and use of the area under a receiver operating characteristic (ROC) curve. Radiology 143: 29 - 36 (1982)
12. Bradley, A. P.: The use of the area under the ROC curve in the evaluation of machine learning algorithms. Pattern Recognition (1997) 30:1145 - 1159.

13. Palcic, B., Susnik, B., Garner, D., Olivotto, I.: Quantitative evaluation of malignant potential of early breast cancer using high resolution image cytometry. Journal of Cellular Biochemistry (1993) Suppl. 17G:107 - 113
14. Payne, P. W., Sebo, T. J., Doudkine, A., Garner, D., MacAulay, C., Lam, S., LeRiche, J. C., Palcic, B.: Sputum screening by quantitative microscopy: A reexamination of a portion of the National Cancer Institute Cooperative early lung study. Mayo Clinic Proceedings (1997) 72:697 - 704

Matching Peptide Sequences with Mass Spectra

K.W. Lau[1], B. Stapley[2], S. Hubbard[2], and H. Yin[1]

[1] School of Electrical and Electronic Engineering
[2] School of Life Sciences
The University of Manchester, PO Box 88, Manchester, M60 1QD, UK

Abstract. We study a method of mapping both mass spectra and sequences to feature vectors and the correlation between them. The method of calculating the feature vector from mass spectra is presented, together with a method for representing sequences. A correlation metric comparing both representations is studied. It shows strong correlation between two representation for the same peptides. It also demostrates that the effect of correlation is increased by using the longer sequences induced from the theoretical mass spectra. The method provides a promising step towards de novo sequencing.

1 Introduction

One of the most challenging problems in proteomics is to map mass spectra to corrsponding peptide sequences. We try to identify the mapping by extracting features from both mass spectra and the corrsponding sequences. We further use the features to find the maximum likelihood between the mass spectra and the corrsponding sequences.

The classic approaches identify the sequences from the mass spectra. This approach has been studied by many researchers such as Mascot [1, 2], SEQUEST [3, 4]. In the case of Mascot, a probability-based scoring system is used to match database sequences to the search data. The scoring system calculates the likelihood between the experimental mass spectrum and the theoretical mass spectrum. SEQUEST uses a filter to select the first 500 sequences from the database, and then compares the experimental spectral peaks with the theoretical mass spectrum using the cross-correlation.

Another approach to determine the sequences from the mass spectra is known as de novo peptide sequencing. The most distinguish feature of de novo sequencing is that it searches for a sequence without recourse of the database. This feature is most useful when the sequence is not contained in the database. De novo sequencing was first proposed by Dancik et. al. [5]. A dynamical programming approach has been investigated by Chen et. al. [6] and Bafna et. al. [7].

The mapping between the sequences and the mass spectra is investigated in this paper. In Section 2 we review the method of generating the theoretical mass spectrum from a given sequence. In Section 3 we present the feature vector which extracts feature from both sequences and mass spectra. The result is shown in Section 4 and in Section 5 we review the method of measuring the distance of binary vectors. In Section 6 conclusions are given.

M. Gallagher, J. Hogan, and F. Maire (Eds.): IDEAL 2005, LNCS 3578, pp. 390–397, 2005.

2   Theoretical Mass Spectrum

Proteins and their component peptides are linear molecules, consisting of repeating units with an identical backbone, $-NH - CH(R) - C\emptyset-$, but differing in the nature of the side chain, R. Every side chain corresponds to one of 20 different, naturally occurring amino acids. The protein retains an unreacted amino group NH_3^+ at one end, known as the N-terminus, and an unreacted carboxyl group $C\emptyset\emptyset^-$, known as the C-terminus at the other end. The repeated unit is joined by combining the amino group and carboxyl group, i.e. $NH_3^+ + C\emptyset\emptyset^- \longrightarrow C\emptyset - NH + H_2\emptyset$.

Fragmentation in the mass spectrometer results in cleavage of different bonds, most usefully at the $C\emptyset - NH$ bond generating a series of ions of increasing mass. The mass difference between consecutive pairs reveals the identities of the consecutive amino acids. The exception occurs when the mass of the amino acids are identical, such as isoleucine and leucine. In practice, cleavage also occurs at many of the other bonds generating complicated spectra dominated by several ion series [8, 9]. The mobile proton model has been developed and refined by many researchers as a means to understand how peptides fragment in the gas phase. This has been recently reviewed and used to explain the formation of these various peptide ion series [10, 11]. In a recent work, this model has been expanded to classify $5,500$ mass spectra into different categories dependent on the number of charges on the parent peptide ion of each mass spectra and the putative location and mobility of the proton [12]. If the proton is located at the N-terminus, the cleavage leads to fragments of type a_n and b_n ions. The masses of the a_n, b_n can be described by [13],

$$N_n = \sum_{i=1}^{n} aa_i + N + o, \qquad (1)$$

where N_n is $\{a_n, b_n\}$, aa_i the mass of the ith amino acid from the N-terminus, N is the mass of the N-terminus and o is the mass offest of the series. If the proton is retained on the C-terminus, the cleavage leads to fragments of type y_n ions. The masses of the y_n can be described by Equation (2).

$$y_n = \sum_{i=1}^{n} aa_i + C + o, \qquad (2)$$

where aa the mass of an amino acid from the C-terminus, C is the mass of the C-terminus and o is the mass offest of the series. The primary structure of the ions series are shown in Figure 1.

3   Feature Extraction of Sequences and Mass Spectra

A sequence is represented as a 19×19 dimensional matrix of 2-mers substrings starting from the second amino acid of both ends of the sequence [14]. For the sequence ADDRESS, a 2-mers substrings matrix is shown in Table 1.

Fig. 1. The molecular formula of the a, b, y ion series

Table 1. Numerical representation of the sequence ADDRESS

	A	R	N	D	C	Q	E	G	H	I	K	M	F	P	S	T	W	Y	V
A	0	0	0	1	0	0	0	0	0	0	0	0	0	0	0	0	0	0	0
R	0	0	0	1	0	0	1	0	0	0	0	0	0	0	0	0	0	0	0
N	0	0	0	0	0	0	0	0	0	0	0	0	0	0	0	0	0	0	0
D	1	1	0	1	0	0	0	0	0	0	0	0	0	0	0	0	0	0	0
C	0	0	0	0	0	0	0	0	0	0	0	0	0	0	0	0	0	0	0
Q	0	0	0	0	0	0	0	0	0	0	0	0	0	0	0	0	0	0	0
E	0	1	0	0	0	0	0	0	0	0	0	0	0	0	1	0	0	0	0
G	0	0	0	0	0	0	0	0	0	0	0	0	0	0	0	0	0	0	0
H	0	0	0	0	0	0	0	0	0	0	0	0	0	0	0	0	0	0	0
I	0	0	0	0	0	0	0	0	0	0	0	0	0	0	0	0	0	0	0
K	0	0	0	0	0	0	0	0	0	0	0	0	0	0	0	0	0	0	0
M	0	0	0	0	0	0	0	0	0	0	0	0	0	0	0	0	0	0	0
F	0	0	0	0	0	0	0	0	0	0	0	0	0	0	0	0	0	0	0
P	0	0	0	0	0	0	0	0	0	0	0	0	0	0	0	0	0	0	0
S	0	0	0	0	0	0	1	0	0	0	0	0	0	0	1	0	0	0	0
T	0	0	0	0	0	0	0	0	0	0	0	0	0	0	0	0	0	0	0
W	0	0	0	0	0	0	0	0	0	0	0	0	0	0	0	0	0	0	0
Y	0	0	0	0	0	0	0	0	0	0	0	0	0	0	0	0	0	0	0
V	0	0	0	0	0	0	0	0	0	0	0	0	0	0	0	0	0	0	0

A mass spectrum can be viewed as multiple sequences with various lengths. In order to find all the sequences from the mass spectrum, a graph is constructed as follows: each node represents an amino acid resulting from the distance between the ith peak and the jth peak and the node is denoted as (i, j). Each edge connects two nodes together labelled as $(i, j), (j, k)$. The root node (j, k) of each sequence is found by checking whether the node (i, j), for $i < j$, exists. Once the root node is found, all the sequences beginning to the root node can be found by a traversal tree algorithm. For examples, for a sequence ADDRESS, the sequence has b and y ions as shown in 2, then a graph is created as shown in Table 2 and the corresponding sequences are DDRES and SERDD, respectively. All of the sequences induced from a mass spectrum are represented as a 19×19 dimensional matrix of 2-mers substrings. The result of the induced sequences DDRES and SERDD are shown in Table 3.

Table 2. A graph of peaks representing mass spectrum of ADDRESS

peak no	1	2	3	4	5	6	7	8	9	10	11	12	13
1	0	0	D	0	0	0	0	0	0	0	0	0	0
2	0	0	0	S	0	0	0	0	0	0	0	0	0
3	0	0	0	0	0	D	0	0	0	0	0	0	0
4	0	0	0	0	0	0	E	0	0	0	0	0	0
5	0	0	0	0	0	0	0	0	0	0	0	0	0
6	0	0	0	0	0	0	0	R	0	0	0	0	0
7	0	0	0	0	0	0	0	0	R	0	0	0	0
8	0	0	0	0	0	0	0	0	0	E	0	0	0
9	0	0	0	0	0	0	0	0	0	0	D	0	0
10	0	0	0	0	0	0	0	0	0	0	0	S	0
11	0	0	0	0	0	0	0	0	0	0	0	0	D
12	0	0	0	0	0	0	0	0	0	0	0	0	0
13	0	0	0	0	0	0	0	0	0	0	0	0	0

Table 3. Numerical representation of ADDRESS from the b and y ions

	A	R	N	D	C	Q	E	G	H	I	K	M	F	P	S	T	W	Y	V
A	0	0	0	0	0	0	0	0	0	0	0	0	0	0	0	0	0	0	0
R	0	0	0	1	0	0	1	0	0	0	0	0	0	0	0	0	0	0	0
N	0	0	0	0	0	0	0	0	0	0	0	0	0	0	0	0	0	0	0
D	0	1	0	1	0	0	0	0	0	0	0	0	0	0	0	0	0	0	0
C	0	0	0	0	0	0	0	0	0	0	0	0	0	0	0	0	0	0	0
Q	0	0	0	0	0	0	0	0	0	0	0	0	0	0	0	0	0	0	0
E	0	1	0	0	0	0	0	0	0	0	0	0	0	0	1	0	0	0	0
G	0	0	0	0	0	0	0	0	0	0	0	0	0	0	0	0	0	0	0
H	0	0	0	0	0	0	0	0	0	0	0	0	0	0	0	0	0	0	0
I	0	0	0	0	0	0	0	0	0	0	0	0	0	0	0	0	0	0	0
K	0	0	0	0	0	0	0	0	0	0	0	0	0	0	0	0	0	0	0
M	0	0	0	0	0	0	0	0	0	0	0	0	0	0	0	0	0	0	0
F	0	0	0	0	0	0	0	0	0	0	0	0	0	0	0	0	0	0	0
P	0	0	0	0	0	0	0	0	0	0	0	0	0	0	0	0	0	0	0
S	0	0	0	0	0	0	1	0	0	0	0	0	0	0	0	0	0	0	0
T	0	0	0	0	0	0	0	0	0	0	0	0	0	0	0	0	0	0	0
W	0	0	0	0	0	0	0	0	0	0	0	0	0	0	0	0	0	0	0
Y	0	0	0	0	0	0	0	0	0	0	0	0	0	0	0	0	0	0	0
V	0	0	0	0	0	0	0	0	0	0	0	0	0	0	0	0	0	0	0

The traversal tree algorithm can be described as follows: Let f denote the forward traveling from the parent node to child node, b denote the backward traveling from the child node to parent node and c denote the cross traveling from one node to another node at the same level. A path contains all connected nodes from the root node to the current node. If the current state is f, the algorithm travels from the current node to another node by $\{f, c, b\}$ respectively.

If the current state is b, the algorithm travels from the current node to another node by $\{c, b\}$ respectively. If the current state is c, the algorithm travels from the current node to another node by $\{f, c, b\}$ respectively. The traversal tree algorithm is summarized in Figure 3. When the algorithm fails to travel from the current node forward to another node, the sequence is read from the path. The algorithm is terminated when the root node reaches from any child node.

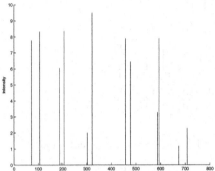

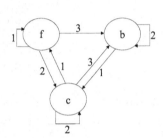

Fig. 2. The theoretical mass spectrum of the sequence ADDRESS using b and y series plus one noisy peak, the intensity of the peaks are chosen randomly

Fig. 3. The state diagram for the traversal tree algorithm, $1, 2, 3$ show the travelling priority from one state to another state

4   Correlation Metric for Feature Vectors

In order to measure the correlation of 19×19 dimensional binary matrix, the matrix is reorganized as a 361×1 binary vector. The contingency table is defined 4. The entities of the contingency table is define as

$$M_{00}^{xy} = \sum_{i=1}^{N} I(x_i = 0, y_i = 0) \tag{3}$$

$$M_{10}^{xy} = \sum_{i=1}^{N} I(x_i = 1, y_i = 0) \tag{4}$$

$$M_{01}^{xy} = \sum_{i=1}^{N} I(x_i = 0, y_i = 1) \tag{5}$$

$$M_{11}^{xy} = \sum_{i=1}^{N} I(x_i = 1, y_i = 1) \tag{6}$$

$$M_0^y = M_{00}^{xy} + M_{10}^{xy} \tag{7}$$

$$M_1^y = M_{01}^{xy} + M_{11}^{xy} \tag{8}$$

$$M_0^x = M_{00}^{xy} + M_{01}^{xy} \tag{9}$$

$$M_0^y = M_{10}^{xy} + M_{11}^{xy} \tag{10}$$

$$M = M_{00}^{xy} + M_{10}^{xy} + M_{01}^{xy} + M_{11}^{xy} \tag{11}$$

A correlation metric to measure the similarity between two representations can be defined as Equation (12) with different values of δ and λ [15] as shown in Table 5.

$$d = \frac{M_{11}^{xy} + \delta M_{00}^{xy}}{M_{11}^{xy} + \delta M_{00}^{xy} + \lambda(M_{10}^{xy} + M_{01}^{xy})} \tag{12}$$

Table 4. The contingency table

	$x = 0$	$x = 1$	
$y = 0$	M_{00}^{xy}	M_{10}^{xy}	M_0^y
$y = 1$	M_{01}^{xy}	M_{11}^{xy}	M_1^y
	M_0^x	M_0^y	

Table 5. Correlation functions of feature vectors

name	δ	λ
Jaccard	0	1
Tanimoto	1	2
Simple Matching	1	1
Dice	0	0.5

5   Result

The mass spectra were downloaded from the Open Proteomics Database [16]. A in-house database is created to store and query the data. The database contains all of the spectrum from three different files 021112.EcoliSol37.1.sequest.zip, 4-23-03.sequest.zip and 6-04-03-YPD-test.sequest.zip corresponding to different mass spectrum from three species known as Escherichia coli, Mycobacterium smegmatis and Saccharomyces cerevisiae respectively. 1000 unique sequences with length smaller than 12 amino acids are selected from the in-house database.

The sequences are used to generate the a, b and y series theoretical mass spectra, and then both sequences and theoretical mass spectra are feature extracted to 361-dimensional feature vectors using the procedures described in Section 3. Figure 4 shows the histogram of the various correlations for theoretical mass spectra and sequences. It can be seen that the correlation tends to 1 indicating strong correlation or matching between two representations. Figure 5 is similar to Figure 4 but using only the longest induced sequences from the theoretical mass spectra. It can be seen that the number of sequences greater than the upper margin is higher than that using all of the induced sequences theoretical mass spectra.

6   Conclusion

In this paper, a method of representing both sequences and mass spectra is presented. The calculation of the representation of sequences are straight forward and the traversal tree algorithm is used to calculate the representation of the mass spectra. The result shows strong correlations between sequences and the corresponding mass spectra. In addition, such a correlation is increased with long sequences induced from the theoretical mass spectra.

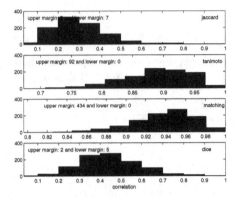

Fig. 4. The correlation between feature vector from a, b and y ion series and the feature vector from all of the induced sequences

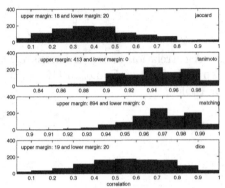

Fig. 5. The correlation between feature vector from a, b and y ion series and the feature vector from using the longest induced sequences

Acknowledgment

This research is funded by a grant from the UK BBSRC (EGM 17685).

References

1. Perkins, D.N., Pappin, D.J.C., Creasy, D.M., Cottrell, J.S.: Probability-based protein identification by searching sequence databases using mass spectrometry data. Electrophoresis **20** (1999) 3551–3567.
2. Creasy, D.M., Cottrell, J.S.: Error tolerant searching of uninterpreted tandem mass spectrometry data. Proteomics **2** (2002) 1426–1434.
3. Eng, J.K., McCormack, A.L., Yates, J.R., III: An approach to correlate tandem mass spectral data of peptides with amino acid sequences in a protein database. J. Am. Soc. Mass Spectrom. **5** (1994) 976–989.
4. Yates, J.R., III, Eng, J.K., Clauser, K.R., Burlingame, A.L.: Search of Sequence Databases with Uninterpreted High-Energy Collision-Induced Dissociation Spectra of Peptides. J. Am. Soc. Mass Spectrom. **7** (1996) 1089–1098.
5. Dancik, V., Addona, T.A., Clauser, K.R., Vath J.E., Pevzner P.A.: De novo peptide sequencing via tandem mass spectrometry. J. Comp. Biol. **6** (1999) 327–342.
6. Chen, T., Kao, M.Y., Tepel, M., Rush, J., Church G.M.: A dynamic programming approach to de novo peptide sequencing via tandem mass spectrometry. J. Comp. Biol. **8** (2001) 325–337.
7. Bafna, V., Edwards, N.: On de novo interpretation of tandem mass spectra for peptide identification. Annual Conference on Research in Computational Molecular Biology, Proceedings of the seventh annual international conference on Computational molecular biology (2003) 9–18.
8. Johnson, R.S., Martin, S.A., Biemann, K., Stults, J.T., Throck, W.J.: Novel fragmentation process of peptides by collision-induced decomposition in a tandem mass spectrometer: differentiation of leucine and isoleucine. Anal. Chem. **59** (1987) 2621–2625.

9. Biemann, K.: Contributions of mass spectrometry of peptide and protein structure. Biomed. Env. Mass Spectrom. **16** (1988) 99–111.

10. Burlet, O., Yang, C.Y., Gaskell, S.J.: Influence of cysteine to cysteic acid oxidation on the collision-activated decomposition of protonated peptides: evidence for intraionic interactions. J. Am. Soc. Mass Spectrom. **3** (1992) 337–344.

11. Summerfield, S.G., Cox, K.A., Gaskell, S.J.: The Promotion of d-type Ions During the Low Energy Collision-Induced Dissociation of Some Cysteic Acid-Containing Peptides. J. Am. Soc. Mass Spectrom. **8** (1997) 25–31.

12. Kapp, E.A, Schütz, F., Reid, G.E., Simpson, R.J.: Mining a tandem mass spectrometry database to determine the trends and global factors influencing peptide fragmentation. Anal. Chem. **75** (2003) 6251–6264.

13. Bartels, C.: Fast algorithm for peptide sequencing by mass spectroscopy. Biomed. Env. Mass Spectrom. **19** (1990) 363–368.

14. Leslie, C., Eskin, E., Noble, W.S.: The spectrum kernel: a string kernel for SVM protein classification. Proceedings of the Pacific Symposium on Biocomputing. (2002) 564–5752.

15. Lee L.: Measures of Distributional Similarity. 37th Annual Meeting of the ACL. (1999) 25–32.

16. Prince, J.T., Carlson, M.W., Wang, R., Lu, P. Marcotte, E.M.: The need for a public proteomics repository. Nature Biotech. **22** (2004) 471–472.

Extraction by Example: Induction of Structural Rules for the Analysis of Molecular Sequence Data from Heterogeneous Sources

Olivo Miotto[1,2,3], Tin Wee Tan[2], and Vladimir Brusic[2,3]

[1] Institute of Systems Science, National University of Singapore,
25 Heng Mui Keng Terrace, Singapore 119615
olivo@iss.nus.edu.sg
[2] Department of Biochemistry, Faculty of Medicine, National University of Singapore,
10 Medical Drive, Singapore 117597
tinwee@bic.nus.edu.sg
[3] Institute for Infocomm Research, Singapore,
21 Heng Mui Keng Terrace, Singapore 119613
vladimir@i2r.a-star.edu.sg

Abstract. Biological research requires information from multiple data sources that use a variety of database-specific formats. Manual gathering of information is time consuming and error-prone, making automated data aggregation a compelling option for large studies. We describe a method for extracting information from diverse sources that involves structural rules specified *by example*. We developed a system for aggregation of biological knowledge (ABK) and used it to conduct an epidemiological study of dengue virus (DENV) sequences. Additional information on geographical origin and isolation date is critical for understanding evolutionary relationships, but this data is inconsistently structured in database entries. Using three public databases, we found that structural rules can be used successfully even when applied on inconsistently structured data that is distributed across multiple fields. High reusability, combined with the ability to integrate analysis tools, make this method suitable for a wide variety of large-scale studies involving viral sequences.

1 Introduction

Biological research increasingly relies on computational analysis of molecular data available in molecular sequence and structure databases. Additional information, such as functional properties, detailed description of biological systems, and description of experimental settings is available in literature databases. A large number of public repositories of biological information are available [1], including thousands of molecular databases, millions of scientific articles, and tens of millions of web pages. The databases range from extensive generic sequence databases, such as NCBI GenBank [2], to smaller specialized repositories that provide richer annotations for smaller sets of biological sequence data. To make use of both the breadth of coverage of large general purpose databases, and the depth of detail offered by specialized database, information from one source is often combined with complementary data

M. Gallagher, J. Hogan, and F. Maire (Eds.): IDEAL 2005, LNCS 3578, pp. 398–405, 2005.

from other sources. Most public sources provide access through Web interfaces, but their query and retrieval mechanisms vary. Currently, there is no consensus on standards for structuring and encoding biological sequence information [3]. The resulting heterogeneity combined with the enormous volume of data, large number of data sources, and presence of errors and discrepancies in databases [4] make automated information extraction a daunting task. This situation is further complicated by the weak computational background of most users of biological data sources. For an average user, who requires a certain level of control of their data, the most practical option currently is to search databases interactively using Web forms, manually extract relevant data from returned results, and use spreadsheets to perform their analyses. This approach limits both the number of records that a researcher can process and the range of sources that can be used, making it unsuitable for large-scale studies of thousands of sequences. The information retrieved using manual processing becomes decoupled from its original source, limiting both the extent of incremental analysis and reuse of the same analysis method with new data.

Several strategies for integrating biological information have been proposed. *Federated databases* [5] require cooperation between participating databases, an impractical requirement since biological data sources are managed by different organizations. *Data warehouses* [6] are databases constructed and maintained from data retrieved from various sources. They can be built to suit specific needs, and managed independently of public data sources. *Mediators* [7] translate user queries, submit them to multiple sources by means of components known as *wrappers*, and reformat the returned results into the desired form. Mediators offer flexible on-demand integration, but lower performance than data warehouses. All of these strategies require backend implementations, such as SRS [8], Kleisli [9], EnsMart [10] and BioWare [11], among others. Biological researchers increasingly require frequent access to rapidly changing data, but do not possess the computational expertise needed to support these requirements. Therefore, there is a need for simple and reusable software for building database system and deploying analysis tools by means of intuitive user interfaces. Unfortunately, current solutions require significant computational skills and infrastructure, and therefore do not fulfill the needs of many biological researchers. We developed a tool for aggregation of biological knowledge (ABK) that bridges this gap.

The ABK system is a software tool for aggregating data from multiple sources, which brings the power of both mediators and data warehousing to the user's desktop. It allows end users to specify queries, search diverse databases (molecular, literature, etc.), retrieve relevant results, extract desired data from the results, and apply analysis tools. It provides simple end-user mechanisms for specifying rules for extracting the desired data from the results. ABK automatically identifies and highlights discrepancies and errors in data through a simple spreadsheet-like user interface. The analysis tools within ABK are integrated as plug-in modules. We applied ABK to a phylogenetic and epidemiological analysis of viral sequences, which required sequences to be accompanied by corresponding geographical and historical data. This information is difficult to extract because it is encoded inconsistently within data structures across diverse databases. This report focuses on Dengue Virus (DENV) sequences, but the approach is applicable to epidemiological studies of other viruses and can be extended to other organisms.

2 XML Structural Rules for Information Extraction

Biological researchers visit databases using Web interfaces, and understand the database schema intuitively, from the information presented in tables contained in HTML pages. Once the information of interest is located in one page (e.g. database record) the process can be repeated with other records from the same source. Researchers can therefore formulate *structural rules* for the extraction of targeted information because that information is presented in a structured form. ABK presents data from a remote source in its native form (without restructuring) and allows the user to express structural rules from the inspection of small number of records – extraction by example.

The Extensible Markup Language (XML) [12] has several features which make it particularly suitable as encoding mechanism in ABK. An XML document is structured and consists of a hierarchy of elements which can represent a wide variety of schemas. XML is thus capable of structuring records from any database. The document structure is self-descriptive, since structural tags are encoded within the document. The tagging removes the need for *a priori* knowledge of the schema for defining structural rules. Furthermore, XML has a syntax (XPath [13]) for expressing structural rules.

The ABK system retrieves and processes records in their native form as XML documents. Some of the larger public databases (such as GenBank and UniProt [14]) provide output in the specific (to individual databases) XML formats which can be handled directly by the system. This is not the case for many smaller databases, which may require conversion from their native representation to a suitable XML format.

3 ABK System Architecture and Operation

The ABK system comprises four basic building subsystems (Figure 1): a *mediator framework* which provides connectivity for searching remote databases; a *rule-based extractor and resolver* which extracts the information from search results, according to rules specified by the user; a *recordset manager* which manages locally the information; and *plug-in tools* which analyze and manipulate stored information.

The **mediator framework** supports an extensible set of wrappers (database clients) for search and retrieval. Generic user-specified queries are translated into data source-specific queries, and submitted by the wrappers to the remote data sources. In contrast with other mediator-based systems, ABK do not attempt to restructure the result data into a common schema, but rather keeps the results as XML documents, preserving their native structure. Documents retrieved by the mediator framework are stored locally by the **recordset manager**, which constructs collections of local records. The local records field structure is defined by the user through a graphical spreadsheet-like user interface. Frequently, documents from various sources describe the same entity (for instance, the protein product of DNA sequence records in GenBank is often described by records in both UniProt and NCBI Protein [2] databases). If specified by the user, ABK will populate local records with data from multiple source documents.

To create a new field in a local record set, users need to specify one or more structural rules. The rule is formulated *by example*: the user is presented with a structured view of the corresponding XML document (see Fig. 2), and the rule is captured as an

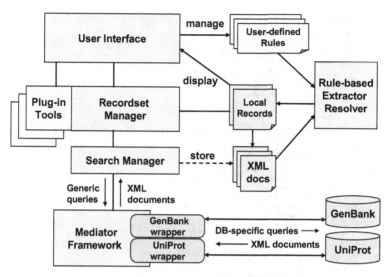

Fig. 1. Architecture of the ABK system

XPath expression, optionally containing simple constraints (see "XML Path" in Figure 2). These rules are listed in order of priority by the user, and are subsequently automatically applied by the **rule-based extractor and resolver.** Any given rule is defined for XML documents originating from the same source. The resolver identifies conflicts among the field values extracted from different documents. It also identifies conflicts among values extracted from the same document using different rules. Such conflicts are highlighted by text in red font colour (see Fig. 3). This alerts user to check and, if necessary, reconcile the value after manual inspection, or reject the record altogether.

The **plug-in tools** are analysis tools that can be applied to the whole dataset, or to a subset of records. They are useful for connecting to external systems, and are generally application-specific.

4 Experimental Results

We used the ABK software to perform an epidemiological study of DENV sequences, involving the construction of phylogenetic trees to show the evolutionary relationship between different viral strains. DENV is present in four different serotypes (DENV-1, -2, -3, and -4). The DENV genome encodes twelve proteins, which need to be studied individually for establishing evolutionary relation between virus strains [15]. Dating of sequence isolates is important for determination of the mutation rates, while information on the country of origin of each sequence helps understanding of the geographical spread of the virus.

We used ABK to gather all DENV-1 sequence records from three different public databases: 385 protein sequences from the NCBI Protein database, 362 from UniProt, and 491 nucleotide sequences from GenBank. Based on cross-references, equivalent records from different databases were merged, producing a dataset of 502 unique

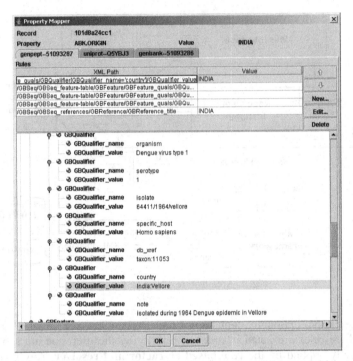

Fig. 2. Screenshot of the ABK Record viewer – representative protein record in a tree format. This allows the user specification of the extraction rules. The rules are represented as paths corresponding to the fields in the tree structure that contain target information, in this case geographic location. In this example, five separate rules were specified, two of which returned consistent results. Although the record structure is specific to the originating database, the XML labels make it understandable to biologists

records. DNA and protein sequences were extracted from each data source with a single rule per source, while strain identifiers required two rules for GenBank records.

Extracting geographical information was considerably more challenging, due to inconsistent encoding within the databases. In GenBank records, for example, country information was found in six separate fields: *country* (279 records), *isolation source* (19), *strain* (19), *isolate* (7) *reference title* (221) and *definition* (90). Six different rules were thus required, in conjunction with a basic text filter, to identify the country name. Using these rules, the country of origin was automatically identified for 441 records (88% of all unique sequences), with no false positives. Most of the 40 conflicts highlighted could not be resolved by manual inspection. Of the 60 records that were not classified, 31 had no discernible indicator of geographic origin, 21 identified entities that were not countries (e.g. Hawaii), 5 used alternative names (e.g. Burma, Surinam), and 4 contained misspellings. We estimate that more sophisticated text filtering algorithms would have improved the performance by additional 2%.

Retrieval of the date information required 5 rules for each of GenBank and NCBI Protein. The year of isolation was automatically identified for 321 records (64%),

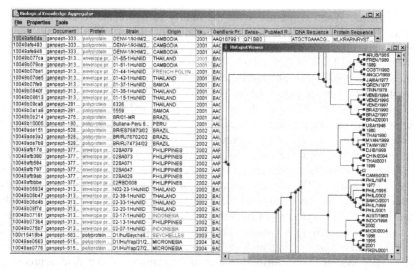

Fig. 3. Screenshot of the ABK system main widow (left), containing a recordset of DENV-1 sequences, and of the phylogenetic tool (right), showing a fragment of a maximum-likelihood tree computed from Envelope (E) Protein sequences derived from this dataset. Each table row represents a local record, referencing up to 3 different data sources. The system highlights conflicts by displaying them in red. Resolved conflicts are displayed in green

with 13 highlighted conflicts. Besides paucity of information, there are other reasons why performance is worse than for geographical data: dates may be encoded as two-digit numbers, embedded among other characters as part of a strain identifier, among others.

Following data extraction and cleaning, specialized plug-in tools were used for the analysis of the resulting data set. Since the sequences mostly represented fragments of protein or nucleotide sequences, the ABK-aligner tool aligned each sequence against a reference genome, and cleaved them into constituent proteins. The ABK-aligner tool automatically created twelve datasets, each containing all available nucleotide and peptide sequences for a given protein, plus their geographical and date information. An additional tool performed multiple alignments of DNA sequences, constructing phylogenetic trees to determine DENV evolutionary relationships (see Fig. 3).

A notable strength of the ABK system is the direct reusability of the initial setup. Capitalizing on the DENV-1 work, the preparation of datasets for the remaining three DENV serotypes, including verification of geographical data, genomic alignment and protein cleavage, was possible in a matter of hours, for a total of 4,969 sequences. The tools developed for DENV are reusable for other Flavivirus species such as Yellow Fever Virus (YFV) and West Nile Virus (WNV), and will require minimum modification for other types of RNA viruses.

5 Discussion and Future Work

We have shown that, following the inspection of records, to the ABK system allowed the expression by example of structural rules that reconcile data dispersed across multiple fields. When combined with the ability to aggregate results from records retrieved from diverse sources and to automatically identify conflicts, our approach offers a very effective addition to existing data warehousing techniques. ABK requires a minimal level of technological involvement by biological researchers. Currently, structural rules are captured by simple XPath expressions. The intuitiveness of the tool will be further enhanced by simplified mechanism for capturing the rules (through selection of fields and relationships by point-and-click mechanism).

After the initial setup effort, the analysis process was rapid, with manual inspection required for only 12% of the records. The cleavage of the sequences, and subsequent creation of separate recordsets for each protein, showed the potential of ABK for large-scale analysis: phylogenetic studies often focus on one particular region of the genome, while ABK extracts fragments of interest from any of the 12 sets of sequences. Such analysis would be time-consuming for a manual approach. We have shown that he ABK system can be valuable in studies that compare viral proteins, across a range of different viruses. The ABK system significantly speeds up data collection, data pre-processing, and application of the analysis tools.

The ABK system helps furthering our understanding of the data sources, their structure, and the quality of the retrieved data. Data inconsistencies, a plague of data warehousing systems, are easily analyzed and corrected since they are automatically highlighted. We have observed that the rules for extracting information do not apply uniformly: an initial study of sequences of Influenza A H5N1 Virus shows a different strategy for encoding date and country information in these records, possibly driven by stronger interest in the epidemiology of influenza virus. Our approach offers the necessary flexibility for addressing such changing needs, because it allows for rapid definition of structural rules.

Future work will also focus on improving the analysis capabilities of the ABK platform, and extending its connectivity to a wider range of data sources, including smaller databases that do not provide XML output. Interestingly, our extraction by rule method can be directly applied to Web pages encoded in XML-compliant HTML (XHTML), which may facilitate the integration of existing Web pages into the analysis process.

References

1. Galperin,M.Y.: The Molecular Biology Database Collection: 2005 update. Nucleic Acids Res. 33 (2005) D5-24
2. Benson,D.A. *et al.*: GenBank. Nucleic Acids Res. 33 (2005) D34-38
3. Brazma,A.: On the importance of standardisation in life sciences. Bioinformatics. 17 (2001). 113-114
4. Karp,P.D., Paley,S., Zhu,J.: Database verification studies of SWISS-PROT and GenBank. Bioinformatics. 17 (2001) 526-532
5. Heimbigner, D., McLeod, D.: A Federated Architecture for Information Management. ACM Transactions on Information Systems. 3 (1985) 253-278
6. Widom,J.: Research Problems in Data Warehousing. Proc. of the Int. Conf. on Information and Knowledge Management (CIKM '95) (1995) 25-30.Baltimore USA.
7. Wiederhold,G.: Mediators in the Architecture of Future Information Systems. IEEE Computer, 25 (1992) 38-49
8. Zdobnov,E.M. *et al.*: The EBI SRS server- new features. Bioinformatics 18 (2002) 1149-1150

9. Chung,S.Y., Wong,L.: Kleisli: a new tool for data integration in biology. Trends Biotechnol. 17 (1999) 351-355
10. Kasprzyk,A. *et al.*: EnsMart: a generic system for fast and flexible access to biological data. Genome Res. 14 (2004) 160-169
11. Koh,J.L.Y. *et al.*: BioWare: A framework for bioinformatics data retrieval, annotation and publishing. ACM SIGIR Workshop on Search and Discovery in Bioinformatics (SIGIRBIO) (2004). Sheffield, UK
12. Yergeau,F. *et al.*: Extensible Markup Language (XML) 1.0 (Third Edition). (2004) http://www.w3.org/TR/2004/REC-xml-20040204/
13. Clark,J., DeRose,S.: XML Path Language (XPath) Version 1.0. (1999) http://www.w3c.org/TR/xpath
14. Bairoch,A. *et al.*: The Universal Protein Resource (UniProt). Nucleic Acids Res. 33 (2005) D154-159
15. dos Santos,C.N. *et al.*: Genome analysis of dengue type-1 virus isolated between 1990 and 2001 in Brazil reveals a remarkable conservation of the structural proteins but amino acid differences in the non-structural proteins. Virus Res. 90 (2002) 197-205

A Multi-population χ^2 Test Approach to Informative Gene Selection[*]

Jun Luo and Jinwen Ma[**]

Department of Information Science
School of Mathematical Sciences and LMAM
Peking University, Beijing, 100871, China
jwma@math.pku.edu.cn

Abstract. This paper proposes a multi-population χ^2 test method for informative gene selection of a tumor from microarray data based on the statistical multi-population χ^2 test with the sample data being grouped evenly. To test the effectiveness of the multi-population χ^2 test method, we use the support vector machine (SVM) to construct a tumor diagnosis system (i.e., a binary classifier) based on the identified informative genes on the colon and leukemia data. It is shown by the experiments that the constructed diagnosis system with the multi-population χ^2 test method can 100% correctness rate of diagnosis on colon dataset and 97.1% correctness rate of diagnosis on leukemia dataset, respectively.

1 Introduction

With the rapid development of DNA microarray technology, we can now get the expression levels of thousands of genes via one single experiment. Certainly, these gene expression profiles or simply called microarray data provide important and detailed evidences to health state of human tissues for tumor analysis and diagnosis. Mathematically, the microarray data corresponding to a tumor can be represented by a matrix $A = (a_{ij})n \times m$, where the i−th row represents the i−th gene, the j−th column represents the j−th sample, and the element a_{ij} represents the expression level of the i−th gene in the j−th sample. Many microarray data sets are now available on the web.

In tumor diagnosis, each sample can be identified as "tumorous" or "normal", and it is expected to construct a binary classifier as a diagnosis system to classify them as correctly as possible. Clearly, this is just a problem of supervised binary classification. However, as there are always thousands of genes in a microarray chip, the microarray data are generally complete, but may be redundant since some irrelevant genes can be involved. The existence of irrelevant genes not only increases the computational complexity, but also impairs the efficiency of the diagnosis system with the noise. In order to achieve a higher diagnosis accuracy,

---

[*] This work was supported by the Natural Science Foundation of China for Project 60471054

[**] The corresponding author

M. Gallagher, J. Hogan, and F. Maire (Eds.): IDEAL 2005, LNCS 3578, pp. 406–413, 2005.

we should first select the informative or related genes that are discriminative between the tumor and normal or two kinds of tumor phenotypes. Meanwhile, the informative genes provide clues to medical or biological studies.

The problem of informative gene selection or discovery has been studied extensively in the past several years. In 1999, Golub et al. [1] proposed a kind of discrimination measurement or criterion on the genes via a simple statistic similar to t statistic. In their experiments, 50 most informative genes were selected and used to construct the tumor classifier with a good result on the leukemia data set. Later on, some other ranking criteria were proposed sequentially, such as F statistic method [2], mutual information scoring method [3], Markov blanket method [4], etc.. Moreover, the experiments carried out by Brown et al. [5], Dudoit[6], Furey et al. [7] and Guyon et al. [8] have shown that the support vector machine (SVM) [9] is one optimal choice for constructing the classifier or tumor diagnosis system on a microarray data set.

However, there exist two serious problems in former methods. On the one hand, these methods require a user-specified threshold on the number of informative genes. That is, they select the top k genes as the informative ones. However, it is often difficult for a user to specify such a parameter. Certainly, we can use the SVM to test the best number for k, but the testing process incurs a large computational cost. On the other hand, some methods use the t-statistic or its variations as the selection criteria. The t-statistic requires that the data follows the normal (or Gaussian) distribution. However, the assumption of normal distribution often does not hold in gene expression data [10]. In order to solve these problems, Deng et al. [10] proposed a rank sum test method that utilizes a significance level to select informative genes through the rank sum test (as a typical non-parametric statistical method) with the quality guarantee in statistics. It was shown by the experiments that the rank sum test method considerably improves the performance of tumor diagnosis on the colon and leukemia data.

In this paper, we further propose a non-parametric statistical test method, called the multi-population χ^2 test method, to select informative genes from a microarray data. It is based on the statistical multi-population χ^2 test with the sample data being grouped evenly. It is shown by the experiments that the constructed diagnosis system with the multi-population χ^2 test method can 100% correctness rate of diagnosis on colon dataset and 97.1% correctness rate of diagnosis on leukemia dataset, respectively.

2   Multi-population χ^2 Test Method and Tumor Diagnosis System via SVM

We begin to introduce the multi-population χ^2 test [11]. Suppose that there are k populations, denoted by $X_1, \cdots, X_k$, with their cumulative distribution functions denoted by $F_1(x), \cdots, F_k(x)$, respectively. From each population, we have collected a number of samples and the whole samples from these k populations, denoted by the sample set A, are divided into r exclusive groups or subsets $A_1, \cdots, A_r$ such that $A = \bigcup_{i=1}^{r} A_i$, $A_i \subset A$, $A_i \cap A_j = \emptyset (i \neq j)$. Our aim is to test the hypothesis $H0 : F_1(x) = \cdots = F_k(x)$, i.e., the identity of the distributions of these k populations.

In order to do so, we define the number n_{ij} as the number of samples from the i–th population in the j–th group, with $n_{i.} = \sum_{j=1}^{r} n_{ij}$, $n_{.j} = \sum_{i=1}^{k} n_{ij}$ and $n = \sum_{j=1}^{k} n_{.j} = \sum_{i=1}^{k} n_{i.}$. We then calculate the statistic χ_n^2 by

$$\chi_n^2 = \sum_{i=1}^{k} \sum_{j=1}^{r} \frac{(n_{ij} - n_{i.}\widehat{p}_j)^2}{n_{i.}\widehat{p}_j} \tag{1}$$

where $\widehat{p}_j = \frac{n_{.j}}{n}(j = 1, 2, \cdots, r)$. In fact, it has been proved in statistics[11] that the distribution of χ_n^2 approximates $\chi^2((k-1)(n-1))$ as $n \to \infty$. So, we can use this statistic to test the hypothesis of identical distributions of the k populations via a given significance level α. That is, according to α, we get the rejection field $(\chi_\alpha^2((r-1)(k-1)), +\infty)$ or the threshold value $\chi_\alpha^2((r-1)(k-1))$. If $\chi_n^2 > \chi_\alpha^2((r-1)(k-1))$, we reject the hypothesis $H0$; otherwise, we accept it. Clearly, the multi-population χ^2 test is non-parametric.

We now consider how to utilize the multi-population χ^2 test for informative gene selection. From the perspective of statistics, the distribution of expression level of one informative gene for a tumor should be quite different between the normal and tumorous samples. That is, this difference can be checked or proved by a statistical hypothesis test method. In this way, we can apply the multi-population χ^2 test to informative gene selection on the microarray data collected from both tumorous and normal tissues. In this case, the number of populations is just 2. Correspondingly, the hypothesis becomes $H0 : F_1(x) = F_2(x)$, where $F_1(x)$ and $F_2(x)$ represent the cumulative distribution functions of expression level on the normal and tumorous samples, respectively. However, there exists one problem: how are these samples (or sample values at one gene) divided into groups (or subsets as described above)? It is clear that the number of groups should be neither too large nor too small. In fact, a small number of groups makes the division too rough, with certain differences being obscured, whereas a large number of groups makes the division too precise, with an exaggerated interference from noise. Therefore, the number of groups should be proper to the total number of samples, which will be further discussed in the following experiments. On the other hand, the number of samples in each group should also be neither too large nor too small. One particular idea is that, we can divide the samples evenly so that each group approximately has the same number of samples, which will be detailed in the following experiments. After the samples are divided into a number of groups, we can use the multi-population χ^2 test to select the informative genes only if the hypotheses on these genes are rejected.

To test the effectiveness of the multi-population χ^2 test method for informative gene selection, we build a tumor diagnosis system (i.e., a binary classifier) using the support vector machine (SVM). It has been derived from the optimal classification problem in the sample space with a finite number of samples under the statistical learning theory. Actually, there are many softwares of SVM available on the web and we will use the version OSU SVM 3.0 in the toolbox of MATLAB (It can be downloaded from http://eewww.eng.ohio-state.edu/~maj/osu svm). Three types of kernel functions are used for comparison in our experiments: (1). Linear kernel function (no kernel); (2). RBF kernel function $K(x, xi) = exp\{-\frac{|x-xi|}{\sigma^2}\}$; and (3). 3-order Polynomial kernel function $K(x, xi) = [(x \cdot xi) + 1]^3$.

3   Experimental Results and Comparisons

3.1   The Experimental Results on the Colon and Leukemia Datasets

In our experiments, we use the multi-population χ^2 test method to select the informative genes for both the colon and leukemia data sets, and then apply the SVM to constructing a tumor diagnosis system with the identified informative genes on the colon and leukemia data sets. Before the experiments, we normalize each microarray data set column by column with zero mean and unit variance, which can eliminate some possible noises in the data set.

A. The Experimental Results on the Colon Data Set

The colon cancer data set[1] contains the expression profiles of 2000 genes from 22 normal tissues and 40 tumorous tissues. In most of our experiments, we use the training set (22 normal and 22 tumorous) and the test set (18 tumorous) provided by the web site. The parameters in the SVM are set as u_PolySVC($\star,\star$,3,0.001) for the 3-order polynomial kernel function, and u_ RbfSVC($\star,\star$,0.01,100) for the RBF kernel function.

To utilize the multi-population χ^2 test method, we now group the samples evenly. On each gene, we first put the 22 normal and 40 tumorous expression values together. Suppose that we expect each group to contain 9 sample values. Then, we select six real numbers according to which the whole real region R can be divided into 7 intervals. By adjusting these six numbers properly, we can divide the 62 sample values into seven groups that contain 9, 9, 9, 9, 9, 9, and 8, respectively. In this way, the 62 sample values at each gene are grouped evenly, with each group containing almost 9 sample values.

From Table 1, we can find that the SVM with the multi-population χ^2 test method can lead to a very good classification accuracy on the colon data set when the significance level is 0.001 or 0.01 and the number of sample values per group is properly selected. From the perspective of kernel functions, the 3-order polynomial function performs best with the two 100% classification accuracies (at $\alpha = 0.001$), which outperform the SVM on the original colon data set. Actually, the classification accuracies of the SVM with the three kernel functions on the original colon data set are 94.4%, 94.4%, 94.4%, respectively.

In order to illustrate the potential relation between the number of sample values per group and the classification effectiveness, we provide the average classification accuracies over the three kernel functions and the number of sample values per group under the significance level 0.001 in Table 2.

---

[1] retrieved from
http://microarray.princeton.edu/oncology/affydata/index.html

Table 1. The result on the colon data set

Kernel Functions	#	$\alpha = 0.1$	$\alpha = 0.05$	$\alpha = 0.01$	$\alpha = 0.001$
	8	88.9% / 408	88.9% / 265	94.4% / 95	94.4% / 21
Linear	9	88.9% / 415	88.9% / 254	94.4% / 93	94.4% / 19
	10	88.9% / 409	88.9% / 276	94.4% / 87	94.4% / 29
	8	94.4% / 408	94.4% / 265	94.4% / 95	94.4% / 21
RBF	9	94.4% / 415	94.4% / 254	94.4% / 93	94.4% / 19
	10	94.4% / 409	94.4% / 276	94.4% / 87	94.4% / 29
	8	88.9% / 408	94.4% / 265	88.9% / 95	100% / 21
3-order	9	94.4% / 415	94.4% / 254	94.4% / 93	100% / 19
Polynomial	10	88.9% / 409	94.4% / 276	94.4% / 87	94.4% / 29

In this and the following tables, the symbol # represents the number of sample values per group. The two numbers on the sides of "/" represent the classification accuracy on the test set or the diagnosis accuracy, and the number of informative genes, respectively. α is the significance level for the multi-population χ^2 test.

Table 2. The relation between the classification accuracy and the number of sample vaules per group

#	6	7	8	9	10	12
Accuracy	87.0%	94.4%	96.3%	96.3%	94.4%	94.4%

From Table 2, we can find that the multi-population χ^2 test method reaches the optimum result when there are 8 or 9 sample values per group. Moreover, from the stability of classification accuracy, it performs better at 9 sample values per group, which is further shown by other experiments on a plenty of data sets constructed by randomly selecting 44 samples from the colon data set as a new training set and leaving the other 18 as a new test set.

B. The Experimental Results on the Leukemia Data Set

The leukemia cancer data set[2] consists of expression profiles of 7129 genes from 47 acute lymphoblastic leukemia (ALL) and 25 acute myeloid leukemia (AML) samples. Specifically, the training set contains 38 samples (27 ALL and 11 AML), while the test set contains 34 samples (20 ALL, 14 AML). Actually, the training and test sets are provided at the web site. The parameters in the SVM are selected as above.

From Table 3, we can find that the classification accuracy of the multi-population χ^2 test method on the leukemia data set is good and stable, compared to that on the original leukemia data set with 94.1%, 85.7% and 97.1% to three kernel functions respectively. Also, the number of related genes is reduced to a low level. We further apply our method to a plenty of data sets constructed using the same method on colon data set, and find that on some data sets, our method can reach the optimal average accuracy 100% over three kernel functions. Our

---

[2] retrieved from http://www-genome.wi.mit.edu/cgi-bin/cancer/datasets.cgi

Table 3. The result on the leukemia data set

Kernel Functions	#	$\alpha = 0.1$	$\alpha = 0.05$	$\alpha = 0.01$	$\alpha = 0.001$
	8	97.1% / 1733	97.1% / 1039	97.1% / 557	97.1% / 260
Linear	9	97.1% / 1948	97.1% / 1356	97.1% / 619	97.1% / 274
	10	97.1% / 1807	97.1% / 1320	97.1% / 605	97.1% / 257
	8	97.1% / 1733	97.1% / 1039	97.1% / 557	97.1% / 260
RBF	9	97.1% / 1948	97.1% / 1356	97.1% / 619	97.1% / 274
	10	97.1% / 1807	97.1% / 1320	97.1% / 605	97.1% / 257
	8	94.1% / 1733	97.1% / 1039	97.1% / 557	97.1% / 260
3-order	9	97.1% / 1948	97.1% / 1356	97.1% / 619	97.1% / 274
Polynomial	10	97.1% / 1807	97.1% / 1320	97.1% / 605	97.1% / 257

experiment results also show that the multi-population χ^2 test method performs best when the number of sample values per group is 9.

C. Further Discussions and Remarks

According to the experimental results, we give some further discussions and remarks on the multi-population χ^2 test method as follows.

(1). In general, we can select 0.01 as the best choice of the significance level for the multi-population χ^2 test method. The slight difference between the optimal significance levels on the colon and leukemia data sets may be owing to the characteristics of the distributions of the two data sets. However, the multi-population χ^2 test method is rather good on both the colon and leukemia data set at 0.01 significance level.

(2). As to the number of sample values per group, it should be determined through the experiments. However, we can set it 9 as an initial value and make some adjustments based on the experiment results.

(3). The principle of grouping the samples evenly is demonstrated to be effective in our experiments. However, it does not mean that this is just the optimal one. Actually, the optimal division of the sample values for the multi-population χ^2 test method should be theoretically studied in the future.

(4). By the experiments, we can find that the performance of the the multi-population χ^2 test method is sensitive to the number of sample values per group as well as the significance level α. However, it is interesting that when we chart the diagram with the number of sample values per group as x-coordinate and the number of identified informative genes as y-coordinate, we can discover that the optimum number "9" of samples per group is located near the so-called "plateau" of the polygonal line, which is shown in Fig. 1. If it can be proved theoretically, we will have a good method to get the best number of the sample values per group in the general case.

(5). Our experiments indicate that the classification accuracy of our method is related to which samples are used for training and for testing. It is possible to select proper training set to construct our diagnosis system.

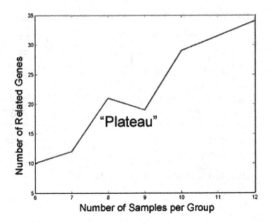

Fig. 1. The plateau for the best number of sample values per group

3.2   Comparisons with the Rank Sum Test Method

We now compare the multi-population χ^2 test method with the rank sum test method [10] on these two data sets. Obviously, these two test methods are both non-parametric, getting rid of the normality assumption on the microarray data. We implemented the rank sum test to select the informative genes on each data set and obtained the classification result through the SVMs with the same three kernel functions. The comparison results are listed in Table 4. Since we use the test set provided in the website, our results of the rank sum test method are different from those in [10].

Table 4. Comparison result between the multi-population χ^2 test method and the rank sum test method

Data set	α	0.1	0.05	0.01	0.001	0.0001
Colon	χ^2	92.6%	92.6%	94.4%	96.3%	100%
cancer	rank sums	92.6%	92.6%	92.6%	94.4%	96.3%
	χ^2	97.1%	97.1%	97.1%	97.1%	96.1%
Leukaemia	rank sums	96.1%	97.1%	97.1%	97.1%	97.1%

For the multi-population χ^2 test method, we use the experimental result with 9 sample values per group.

From Table 4, we can find that the multi-population χ^2 test method out-performs the rank sum test method on both the diagnostic accuracy and the stability on results. However, since the multi-population χ^2 test method needs to group the samples evenly on each gene, its computational cost is higher than that of the rank sum test method. Nevertheless, this does not impair its efficiency in practice.

4 Conclusions

We have investigated the informative gene selection problem on a microarray data set via the multi-population χ^2 test. When the sample data are grouped evenly, the multi-population χ^2 test can be applied to selecting the informative genes of a tumor. The evenly grouping method on the sample data is suggested and demonstrated. By the experiments on real data sets utilizing the SVM for tumor classification or diagnosis, we show that this multi-population χ^2 test method is efficient and even better than the rank sum test method. However, there are still circumstances where the diagnostic accuracy under the selected informative genes is not satisfactory. This may be due to an unreasonable grouping on the sample data. However, in general, the multi-population χ^2 test method can reach excellent results, even without any diagnostic error when the parameters are set properly.

References

1. T. R. Golub, D. K. Slonim, P.Tamayo, et al., "Molecular classification of cancer: class discovery and class prediction by gene expression monitoring," *Science*, 286: 531-537, 1999.
2. C. Ding, "Analysis of gene expression profiles: class discovery and leaf ordering," *Proceedings of the 6th Annual International Conference on Computational Molecular Biology (RECOMB'02)*, Washington, D. C., USA, April 18-21, 2002, pp: 601-680.
3. A. Ben-Dor, N. Friedman, and Z. Yakhini, "Scoring Genes for Relevance," *Agilent Technical Report*, no. AGL-2000-13, 2000.
4. E. P. Xing, M¿ I. Jordan, and R. M. Karp, "Feature selection for high-dimensional genomic microarray data," *Proceedings of the 18th International Conference of Machine Learning (ICML'01)*, Massachusetts, USA, June 28-July 1, 2001, pp: 601-608.
5. BrownM. P. S. Brown, W. N. Grundy, D. Lin, N. Cristianini, et al., "Knowledge-based analysis of microarray gene expression data by using support vector machines," *Proc. Nat'l Acad Sci*, 97(1): 262-267, 2000.
6. D. S. Dudoit, J. Fridyand, and T. P. Speed, "Comparison of discrimination methods for the classification of tumor using gene expression data," *Univ. of California, Dept. of Statistics, Tech Report*, no.576, 2000.
7. T. Furey, N. Cristianini, N. Duffy, et al., "Support vector machine classification and validation of cancer tissue samples using microarray expression data," *Bioinformatics*, 16(10): 909-914, 2000.
8. Guyon I. Guyon, J. Weston, S. Barnhill, V. Vapnik, "Gene selection for cancer classification using support vector machine," *Machine Learning*, 46(1/3): 389-422, 2002.
9. V. Vapnik, *Statistical Learning Theory*, New Your: Wiley, 1998.
10. L. Deng, J. Ma, and J. Pei, "Rank sum method for related gene selection and its application to tumor diagnosis," *Chinese Science Bulletin,* 49(15): 1652-1657, 2004.
11. M. Hollander and D. A. Wolfe, *Nonparametric statistical method*, New York: Wiley, 1999.

Gene Selection of DNA Microarray Data Based on Regularization Networks

Xin Zhou[1,2] and Kezhi Mao[2]

[1] Bioinformatics Research Centre,
Nanyang Technological University, Nanyang avenue, Singapore 639798
zhouxin@pmail.ntu.edu.sg
[2] School of Electrical & Electronic Engineering,
Nanyang Technological University, Nanyang avenue, Singapore 639798
ekzmao@ntu.edu.sg

Abstract. Normally the microarray data contain a large number of genes (usually more than 1000) and a relatively small number of samples (usually fewer than 100). This makes the discriminant analysis of DNA microarray data hard to handle. Selecting important genes to the discriminant problem is hence of much practically significance in microarray data analysis. If put in the context of pattern classification, gene selection can be casted as a feature selection problem. Feature selection approaches are broadly grouped into filter and wrapper methods. The wrapper method outperforms the filter method in general. However the accuracy of wrapper methods is coupled with intensive computations. In present study, we proposed a wrapper-based gene selection algorithm by employing the Regularization Network as the classifier. Compared with classical wrapper method, the computational costs in our gene selection algorithm is significantly reduced, because the evaluation criterion we used does not demand repeated trainings in the leave-one-out procedure.

1 Introduction

With recently developed technologies, such as DNA Microarray, researchers are able to simultaneously measure the expression level of a large number of genes in a single experiment. This provides the power of creating a comprehensive overview of the gene regulation network. Nevertheless, these studies produce a gigantic amount of data, which present challenges of extracting useful information from them. One of the properties of microarray data is that each sample is presented by a large number of genes (features), usually more than 1,000. Many of these genes are irrelevant, insignificant or redundant to the discriminant problem at hand. As a consequence, the identification of informative genes to a specific discriminant problem, such as presence of cancer, is of fundamental and practical importance. So the selected marker genes can be found of great value in further investigation of the disease and the gene function, and in further clinical diagnosis and prognosis. From the viewpoint of machine learning, for a typical microarray dataset, the number of training samples is relatively

M. Gallagher, J. Hogan, and F. Maire (Eds.): IDEAL 2005, LNCS 3578, pp. 414–421, 2005.

small (normally fewer than 100) when compared with the high dimensionality. In such a sparse space, it is quite easy to find a decision function that perfectly separates the training data. However, such a classifier might perform poorly on the unseen test data. In other words, gene selection, as the technique to reduce the high dimensionality, may help us find a discriminant classifier with better generalization performance.

The problem of approximating a multivariate function from sparse data is ill-posed and a classical way to solve it is regularization theory [4]. The general regularization theory leads to the following regularization problem, known as the Tikhonov regularization:

$$\min_{f \in \mathcal{H}} \frac{1}{l} \sum_{i=1}^{l} V(y_i, f(\mathbf{x}_i)) + \lambda \|f\|_K^2. \tag{1}$$

where $V(\cdot, \cdot)$ is a loss function, $\|f\|_K^2$ is a norm in a Reproducing Kernel Hilbert Space $\mathcal{H}$ defined by the positive definite function K, l is the number of training samples (the l pairs $\{\mathbf{x}_i, y_i\}$), and $\lambda(> 0)$ is a fixed regularization parameter. Support Vector Machines and Regularization Network [4] correspond to the minimization of Eq. (1) for different choices of loss function V. Choosing V to be the hinge loss function, $V(y_i, f(\mathbf{x}_i)) = (1 - y_i f(\mathbf{x}_i))_+$, where $(x)_+ = \max(0, x)$, leads to Support Vector Machines, while choosing V as squared loss function, $V(y_i, f(\mathbf{x}_i)) = (y_i - f(\mathbf{x}_i))^2$, leads to Regularization Networks.

As a classifier, the SVM is well performed with high dimensional data. However considering the intensive computational costs on training SVMs, it might not be suitable for gene selection in high dimensional gene expression data. In present study, Regularization networks, instead of SVMs, are employed for classification of microarray data, and to perform a gene selection algorithm based on the leave-one-out procedure. The advantage of Regularization Network is that the decision function can be obtained by solving a linear system of equations, which is much easier than the quadratic programming in the SVM.

The paper is organized as follows. The Regularization Networks (RN) is first briefly introduced, a new gene selection algorithm based on the leave-one-out cross validation of Regularization Networks is then proposed. The performance of our algorithm is finally tested with two benchmark microarray datasets, i.e. the colon cancer dataset [1], and the leukaemia dataset [5].

2   Methods

2.1   Regularization Networks

Consider l training data pairs: $\{\mathbf{x}_i, y_i\}$, $i = 1, \ldots, l$, where $\mathbf{x}_i$ is an n-dimensional vector representing the i'th sample, and y_i is the class label of $\mathbf{x}_i$, which is either +1 or -1. The framework of Regularization Network can be formulates as a variational problem of finding the function f that minimizes the functional

$$\min_{f \in \mathcal{H}} \frac{1}{l} \sum_{i=1}^{l} (y_i - f(\mathbf{x}_i))^2 + \lambda \|f\|_K^2. \tag{2}$$

According to the Representer Theorem [9], under rather general conditions the solution to the above regularization problem has the form

$$f(\mathbf{x}) = \sum_{i=1}^{l} c_i K(\mathbf{x}, \mathbf{x}_i). \tag{3}$$

Substituting Eq. (3) into the regularization functional (2), we can rewrite the problem as

$$\min_{\mathbf{c} \in \mathbf{R}^l} \frac{1}{l}(\mathbf{y} - K\mathbf{c})^T(\mathbf{y} - K\mathbf{c}) + \lambda \mathbf{c}^T K \mathbf{c}. \tag{4}$$

where $\mathbf{c}$ and $\mathbf{y}$ are defined as $\mathbf{c} = [c_1, c_2, \ldots, c_l]^T$ and $\mathbf{y} = [y_1, y_2, \ldots, y_l]^T$ respectively, and here the symbol K refers to either the positive definite (kernel) function K or the l-by-l matrix K defined by $K_{ij} = K(\mathbf{x}_i, \mathbf{x}_j)$. Note that the functional is differentiable, after taking the derivative with respect to $\mathbf{c}$, the optimal $\mathbf{c}$ can be found by solving the following linear system of equations:

$$(K + \lambda l I)\mathbf{c} = \mathbf{y}, \tag{5}$$

where I is the identity matrix. Because the symmetric matrix $K + \lambda l I$ is strictly positive definite and thus invertible, the solution f of the regularization problem (2) can be expressed as

$$f(\mathbf{x}) = \mathbf{K}^T(\mathbf{x})(K + \lambda l I)^{-1}\mathbf{y}, \tag{6}$$

where $\mathbf{K}(\mathbf{x})$ is the vector of functions such that $(\mathbf{K}(\mathbf{x}))_i = K(\mathbf{x}, \mathbf{x}_i)$.

2.2   Wrapper-Based Gene Selection Algorithm

If put in the context of pattern classification, gene selection can be solved as a feature selection problem. Feature selection approaches can be broadly grouped into filter and wrapper methods. The filter method evaluates feature subset based on intrinsic properties of data, which are related to the performance of the classifier but are not the direct function of the performance. In contrast the wrapper method evaluates the feature subset based on the performance of the classifier directly. Normally for better generalization, the leave-one-out cross validation result is often used to guide the selection procedure in the wrapper method.

It is proved that the leave-one-out procedure gives an almost unbiased estimate of the probability of test error [8]. But to obtain the leave-one-out error of each training data for a particular gene set, it requires repeated training of classifiers in the leave-one-out procedure, which makes the procedure a burdensome task. Several bounds on the expectation of SVMs from the leave-one-out estimator were introduced to reduce the high computational complexity in the leave-one-out procedure. But in practice the bounds proposed are quite loose, which makes the estimate of the leave-one-out cross validation inaccurate. To alleviate these problems, Regularization Networks, instead of SVMs, are employed to perform a wrapper-like gene selection in our present work. One amazing property of Regularization Networks, as we describe below, is that the leave-one-out cross validation of each training samples can be exactly computed without repeated training for the leave-one-out procedure.

For Regularization Networks, the following equation holds in the leave-one-out procedure:

$$y_p f^p(\mathbf{x}_p) = \frac{y_p(\mathbf{G}\mathbf{y})_p - G_{pp}}{1 - G_{pp}}, \tag{7}$$

where G is denoted as $G = K[K + \lambda(l-1)I]^{-1}$, G_{pp} is the pth item in the pth row of matrix G, $(\mathbf{G}\mathbf{y})_p$ is pth item in the vector $\mathbf{G}\mathbf{y}$, and f^p is the decision function given by the Regularization Network after the sample $\mathbf{x}_p$ has been removed. For the proof of Eq. (7), please refer to the extended paper in our website (http://www.ntu.edu.sg/home5/pg02776030/RN/RN.pdf).

The Eq. (7) illuminates that the computation of cross validation results only demands matrix G, without involving any repeated trainings of the l classifiers in the leave-one-out procedure. $f^p(\mathbf{x}_p)$ is the validation result for the sample $\mathbf{x}_p$ in the leave-one-out procedure. If $y_p f^p(\mathbf{x}_p)$ is negative the sample $\mathbf{x}_p$ is considered as an leave-one-out error, and if $y_p f^p(\mathbf{x}_p)$ is positive $\mathbf{x}_p$ is correctly classified in the leave-one-out procedure.

If we define $p(y|\mathbf{x})$ to be the probability that class label of $\mathbf{x}$ is y, Lin[7] proved that the solution of RN $f(\mathbf{x})$ is convergent to $2p(y = 1|\mathbf{x}) - 1$ when $\lambda \to 0$. So in the present study, we employed the following function to estimate the probability that a specific sample $\mathbf{x}_p$ is correctly classified in the leave-one-out procedure,

$$h(y_p f^p(\mathbf{x}_p)) = (\frac{y_p f^p(\mathbf{x}_p) + 1}{2})_{[0,1]}, \quad \text{where} \quad (x)_{[0,1]} = \begin{cases} 1 \text{ if } x > 1 \\ x \text{ if } 1 \geq x \geq 0 \\ 0 \text{ if } x < 0 \end{cases} \tag{8}$$

Combining all the estimates for training data together, we proposed the following evaluation criterion for gene selection:

$$\mathbf{M} = \sum_{p=1}^{l} (\frac{y_p f^p(\mathbf{x}_p) + 1}{2})_{[0,1]} \tag{9}$$

where $y_p f^p(\mathbf{x}_p)$ is computed by using Eq. (7). The criterion M gives an estimate on the generalization performance. The feature (gene) subset which maximizes the criterion M is preferred. In the present study, the criterion M was combined with the sequential forward selection (SFS) to form a gene selection algorithm. The SFS algorithm is a simple greedy heuristic search algorithm. The pseudo code of the sequential forward gene selection algorithm can be summarized as follows:

The gene selection algorithm combining the RN criterion M with SFS

```
(1) Initialize S to an empty set;
    /* S is the set of selected genes */
```

```
(2) Initialize C to the full gene set;
       /* C is the set of candidate genes for selection */
(3) For i = 1 to m    /* m genes are expected to be selected */
       p = number of genes in set C;
       For j=1 to p
           /* evaluate the goodness of each gene in set C
             together with all genes in set S */
           Take gene j from set C and temporarily put into set S;
           Calculate the criterion M using all genes in set S;
       End
       Select the gene with the maximal M;
       Put the selected gene into set S;
    End
```

The gene selection algorithm can be considered as a modification of classical wrapper method, in which the 0-1 function to compute the classification error is replaced by the function h in Eq. (8).

3   Results

In this section we reported the performance of the proposed gene selection algorithm on two publicly available microarray datasets: colon cancer [1], leukaemia [5]. For the colon cancer dataset, gene expression levels of 40 tumor and 22 normal colon tissues for 6500 human genes are measured using the Affymetrix oligonucleotide microarrays. The leukaemia dataset contains gene expression levels of 72 patients with either acute lymphoblastic leukaemia (ALL, 47 cases) or acute myeloid leukaemia (AML, 25 cases) for 7129 human genes.

Each of these datasets was pre-processed using the procedure described in [3]. After thresholding, filtering and log-transforming, the microarray data was standardized to zero mean and unit standard variance across genes. Because the dimensionality (number of genes) of microarray data is very huge, and most of the genes are irrelevant to the discriminant task, we employed a pre-selection procedure to reduce the searching space and computational time. The top 1000 genes were selected based on Fisher's ratio, $f = \dfrac{(\mu_1 - \mu_2)^2}{\sigma_1^2 + \sigma_2^2}$. All the simulations and comparisons in this paper are based on the pre-processed and pre-selected data.

We assessed the performance of our gene selection algorithm using external .632+ bootstrap. For details of external .632+ bootstrap, please refer to [2]. In this paper we employed balanced bootstrap samples, with K=200 replicates. We compared the performance with three other gene selection algorithms, including Weighting factor, Mahalanobis measure, and SVM RFE [6]. The weighting factor $(a = \dfrac{|\mu_1 - \mu_2|}{\sigma_1 + \sigma_2})$ is commonly used in the literature of microarray data analysis [5]. The Mahalanobis class separability measure is a well-known feature subset evaluation criterion in the literature of pattern recognition. In this work, the Mahalanobis class separability measure was combined with SFS algorithm for gene selection. SVM RFE is often considered as one of the best gene selection algorithm in the literature. The Regularization Network was used as the classifier to estimate the error rates of different gene selection algorithms. We chose RN instead of SVM for classification, because the RN received better performance in the experiments. The kernel used in RN was $K(\mathbf{x}_1, \mathbf{x}_2) = \mathbf{x}_1^T \mathbf{x}_2 + 1$, and the regularization parameter $\lambda = 0.5$ for all experiments. The comparison results were shown in Fig. 1 and Fig. 2. Obviously, the performance of our gene selection algorithm is quite well. Note that only 1, 2, 4, 8, 16, 32 genes are selected in SVM RFE due to its selection mechanism. By performing our gene selection algorithm on the entire dataset we selected 15 most important genes for classification. They were shown in Tab. (1).

Table 1. The top 15 selected genes for the colon cancer dataset and leukaemia dataset. The genes and ESTs without indicating the source are all from Homo sapiens

	colon cancer		leukaemia	
No.	Access No.	Gene Name	Access No.	Gene Name
1	R87126	MYH, nonmuscle [Gallus gallus]	M84526	Adipsin
2	X12671	HNRNPA1	M27878	ZFP84
3	Z50753	UGN	M92287	Cyclin D3
4	T61661	Inorganic Pyrophosphatase [Bos taurus]	X95735	Zyxin
5	R62549	Putative serine/threonine-protein kinase B0464.5 [Caenorhabditis elegans]	J05213	IBSP
6	D31885	ARL6IP	U05237	FALZ
7	H20709	Myosin light chain alkali	M23161	MCFD2
8	T58861	60s ribosomal protein L30E [Kluyveromyces lactis]	L16896	HKR3
9	K03474	MIS	M30625	DRD2
10	J03210	MMP2	D42041	GANAB
11	M76378	CRP	L11573	Surfactant protein B
12	X75208	EPHB3	M31951	PRF1
13	R88740	ATP synthase coupling factor 6	X03663	CSF1R
14	T57882	MYH, nonmuscle type A	D55643	Spleen PABL
15	R10066	Prohibitin	HG982-HT982	Pre-T/Nk-Cell-Associated Protein

4 Conclusion

In the present study, we have proposed a wrapper-based gene selection algorithm based on Regularization Networks. The strength of the algorithm we proposed is that it provides gene subset leading to accurate classification result owing to its evaluation criterion M derived from the leave-one-out procedure. On the other hand, unlike the classical wrapper method, the computation of the criterion M would not involve repeated trainings in the leave-one-out procedure, which make the gene selection algorithm computational attractive. The effectiveness of wrapper-based RN selection algorithm has been tested on two bench-

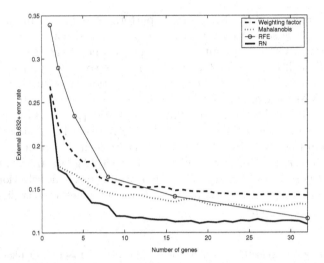

Fig. 1. The external B.632+ error for the colon cancer dataset, shown as the number of selected genes. The four curves are obtained from four gene selection algorithms: Weighting factor, Mahalanobis measure, SVM RFE and wrapper-based RN selection we proposed. The RN selection we proposed results in better performance than others

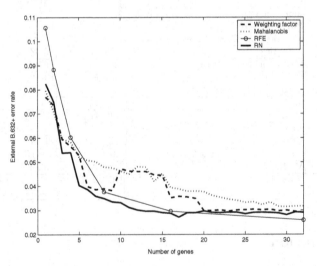

Fig. 2. The external B.632+ error for the leukaemia dataset, shown as the number of selected genes. The four curves are obtained from four gene selection algorithms: Weighting factor, Mahalanobis measure, SVM RFE and wrapper-based RN selection we proposed. The RN selection we proposed is slightly inferior to SVM RFE, but it outperforms others

mark microarray datasets. For more details, please refer to the extended paper (http://www.ntu.edu.sg/home5/pg02776030/RN/RN.pdf).

References

1. Alon, U., Barkai, N., Notterman, D., Gish, K., Ybarra, S., Mack, D. and Levine, A.: Broad patterns of gene expression revealed by clustering analysis of tumor and normal colon tissues probed by oligonucleotide arrays. PNAS. **96(12)** (1999) 6745-6750

2. Ambroise, C. and McLachlan, G. J.: Selection bias in gene extraction on the basis of microarray gene-expression data. PNAS. **99(10)** 2002 6562-6566

3. Dudoit, S., Fridlyand, J. and Speed, T. P.: Comparison of discrimination methods for the classification of tumors using gene expression data. Journal of the American Statistical Association. **97(457)** (2002) 77-87

4. Evgeniou, T., Pontil, M. and Poggio, T.: Regularization networks and support vector machines. Advanced In Computational Mathematics. **13(1)** (2000), 1-50

5. Golub, T., Slonim, D., Tamayo, P., Huard, C., Gaasenbeek, M., Mesirov, J., Coller, H., Loh, M., Downing, J., Caligiuri, M., Bloomfield, C. and Lander, E.: Molecular classification of cancer: class discovery and class prediction by gene expression monitoring. Science. **286** (1999) 531-537

6. Guyon, I., Weston, J., Barnhill, S. and Vapnik., V.: Gene selection for cancer classification using support vector machines. Machine Learning. **46** (2002) 389-422

7. Lin, Y.: Support vector machines and the bayes rule in classification. Data Mining and Knowledge Discovery. **6** (2002) 259-275

8. Luntz, A. and Brailovsky, V.: On estimation of characters obtained in statistical procedure of recognition(in russian). Technicheskaya Kibernatica. **3** (1969)

9. Scholkopf, B., Herbrich, R. and Smola, A. J.: A generalized representer theorem. In Proceedings of the 14th Annual Conference on Computational Learning Theory and 5th European Conference on Computational Learning Theory. Springer-Verlag. (2001) 416-426

Application of Mixture Models to Detect Differentially Expressed Genes

Liat Ben-Tovim Jones[1], Richard Bean[1], Geoff McLachlan[1,2,3], and Justin Zhu[1]

[1] ARC Centre in Bioinformatics, Institute for Molecular Bioscience, UQ
[2] Department of Mathematics, University of Queensland (UQ)
[3] ARC Special Research Centre for Functional and Applied Genomics, UQ

Abstract. An important and common problem in microarray experiments is the detection of genes that are differentially expressed in a given number of classes. As this problem concerns the selection of significant genes from a large pool of candidate genes, it needs to be carried out within the framework of multiple hypothesis testing. In this paper, we focus on the use of mixture models to handle the multiplicity issue. With this approach, a measure of the local FDR (false discovery rate) is provided for each gene. An attractive feature of the mixture model approach is that it provides a framework for the estimation of the prior probability that a gene is not differentially expressed, and this probability can subsequently be used in forming a decision rule. The rule can also be formed to take the false negative rate into account. We apply this approach to a well-known publicly available data set on breast cancer, and discuss our findings with reference to other approaches.

1 Introduction

DNA microarrays allow the simultaneous measurement of the expression levels of tens of thousands of genes for a single biological sample; see, for example, McLachlan et al. (2004). A major objective in these experiments is to find genes that are differentially expressed in a given number of classes. In cancer studies, the classes may correspond to normal versus tumour tissues, or to different subtypes of a particular cancer. Comparing gene expression profiles across these classes gives insight into the roles of these genes, and is important in making new biological discoveries. Yet now a real goal for microarrays is to establish their use as tools in medicine. This requires the identification of subsets of genes (marker genes) potentially useful in cancer diagnosis and prognosis.

In the early days of microarray technology, a simple fold change test with an arbitrary cut-off value was used to determine differentially expressed genes. This method is now known to be unreliable as it does not take into account the statistical variability. In order to determine statistical significance, a test such as the t-test, can be performed for each gene. However, when many hypotheses are tested the probability of a type I error (false positive) occurring increases sharply with the number of hypotheses. This multiplicity poses a considerable

M. Gallagher, J. Hogan, and F. Maire (Eds.): IDEAL 2005, LNCS 3578, pp. 422–431, 2005.

problem in microarray data, where there are many thousands of gene expression values.

Recently, a number of sophisticated statistical methods have been proposed, including several nonparametric methods. Tusher et al. (2001), in their significance analysis method (SAM), proposed a refinement on the standard Student's t-statistic. Because of the large number of genes in microarray experiments, there will always be some genes with a very small sum of squares across replicates, so that their (absolute) t-values will be very large whether or not their averages are large. The modified t-statistic of Tusher et al. (2001) avoids this problem. Pan et al. (2003) also considered a nonparametric approach in their mixture model method (MMM). These methods are reviewed in Pan (2002).

In this paper, we initially present the statistical problem and show how a prediction rule based on a two-component mixture model can be applied. In particular, we show how the mixture model approach can handle the multiplicity issue. It provides a measure of the local FDR (false discovery rate), but can be used in the spirit of the q-value. In the latter case, an upper bound, c_o, can be obtained on the posterior probability of nondifferential expression, to ensure that the FDR is bounded at some desired level α.

We finally apply this method to real data, in the well-known breast cancer study of Hedenfalk et al. (2001), with the aim of identifying new genes which are differentially expressed between BRCA1 and BRCA2 tumours. We compare our findings with those of Storey and Tibshirani (2003), and of Broët et al. (2004), who also analysed this data set using different approaches.

2   Two-Component Mixture Model Framework

2.1   Definition of Model

We focus on a decision-theoretic approach to the problem of finding genes that are differentially expressed. We use a prediction rule approach based on a two-component mixture model as formulated in Lee et al. (2000) and Efron et al. (2001). We let G denote the population of genes under consideration. It can be decomposed into G_0 and G_1, where G_0 is the population of genes that are not differentially expressed, and G_1 is the complement of G_0; that is, G_1 contains the genes that are differentially expressed.

We let the random variable Z_{ij} be defined to be one or zero according as the jth gene belongs to G_i or not $(i = 0, 1; j = 1, \ldots, N)$. We define H_j to be zero or one according as to whether the null hypothesis of no differential expression does or does not hold for the jth gene. Thus Z_{1j} is zero or one according as to whether H_j is zero or one.

The prior probability that the jth gene belongs to G_0 is assumed to be π_0 for all j. That is, $\pi_0 = \mathrm{pr}\{H_j = 0\}$ and $\pi_1 = \mathrm{pr}\{H_j = 1\}$. Assuming that the test statistics W_j all have the same distribution in G_i, we let $f_i(w_j)$ denote the density of W_j in G_i $(i = 1, 2)$. The unconditional density $f(w_j)$ of W_j is given by the two-component mixture model

$$f(w_j) = \pi_0 \, f_0(w_j) + \pi_1 \, f_1(w_j). \tag{1}$$

Using Bayes Theorem, the posterior probability that the jth gene is not differentially expressed (that is, belongs to G_0) is given by

$$\tau_0(w_j) = \pi_0 f_0(w_j)/f(w_j) \quad (j = 1, \ldots, N). \tag{2}$$

In this framework, the gene-specific posterior probabilities $\tau_0(w_j)$ provide the basis for optimal statistical inference about differential expression.

2.2 Bayes Decision Rule

Let e_{01} and e_{10} denote the two errors when a rule is used to assign a gene to either G_0 or G_1, where e_{ij} is the probability that a gene from G_i is assigned to G_j $(i, j = 0, 1)$. That is, e_{01} is the probability of a false positive and e_{10} is the probability of a false negative. Then the risk is given by

$$\text{Risk} = (1 - c)\pi_0 e_{01} + c\pi_1 e_{10}, \tag{3}$$

where $(1 - c)$ is the cost of a false positive. As the risk depends only on the ratio of the costs of misallocation, they have been scaled to add to one without loss of generality.

The Bayes rule, which is the rule that minimizes the risk (3), assigns a gene to G_1 if

$$\tau_0(w_j) \leq c; \tag{4}$$

otherwise, the jth gene is assigned to G_0. In the case of equal costs of misallocation ($c = 0.5$), the cutoff point for the posterior probability $\tau_0(w_j)$ in (4) reduces to 0.5.

2.3 The FDR and FNR

When many hypotheses are tested, the probability that a type I error (false positive) is made increases rapidly with the number of hypotheses. The Bonferroni method is perhaps the best known method for dealing with this problem. It controls the family-wise error rate (FWER), which is the probability that at least one false positive error will be made. Control of the FWER is useful for situations where the aim is to identify a small number of genes that are truly differentially expressed. However, in the case of exploratory type microarray analyses, approaches to control the FWER are too strict and will lead to missed findings. Here it is more appropriate to emphasize the proportion of false positives among the identified differentially expressed genes. The false discovery rate (FDR), introduced by Benjamini and Hochberg (1995), is essentially the expectation of this proportion and is widely used for microarray analyses. Similarly, the false nondiscovery rate (FNR) can be defined as the expected proportion of false negatives among the genes identified as not differentially expressed (Genovese and Wasserman 2002).

2.4   Estimated FDR

In practice, we do not know π_0 nor the density $f(w_j)$, and perhaps not $f_0(w_j)$. In some instances, the latter may be known as we may have chosen our test statistic so that its null distribution is known (or known to a good approximation). For example, we shall work with the oneway analysis of variance F-statistic, which can be so transformed that its null distribution is approximately the standard normal.

Alternatively, null replications of the test statistic might be created, for example, by the bootstrap or permutation methods. We shall estimate the population density $f(w)$ by maximum likelihood after its formulation using a mixture model. But it can be estimated also nonparametrically by its empirical distribution based on the observed test statistics w_j.

If $\hat{\pi}_0$, $\hat{f}_0(w_j)$, and $\hat{f}(w_j)$ denote estimates of π_0, $f_0(w_j)$, and $f(w_j)$, respectively, the gene-specific summaries of differential expression can be expressed in terms of the estimated posterior probabilities $\hat{\tau}_0(w_j)$, where

$$\hat{\tau}_0(w_j) = \hat{\pi}_0 \hat{f}_0(w_j)/\hat{f}(w_j) \quad (j = 1, \ldots, N) \tag{5}$$

is the estimated posterior probability that the jth gene is not differentially expressed. An optimal ranking of the genes can therefore be obtained by ranking the genes according to the $\hat{\tau}_0(w_j)$ ranked from smallest to largest. A short list of genes can be obtained by including all genes with $\hat{\tau}_0(w_j)$ less than some threshold c_o or by taking the top N_o genes in the ranked list.

Suppose that we select all genes with

$$\hat{\tau}_0(w_j) \leq c_o. \tag{6}$$

Then an estimate of the FDR rate is given by

$$\widehat{\mathrm{FDR}} = \sum_{j=1}^{N} \hat{\tau}_0(w_j) \, I_{[0,c_o]}(\hat{\tau}_0(w_j))/N_r, \tag{7}$$

where

$$N_r = \sum_{j=1}^{N} I_{[0,c_o]}(\hat{\tau}_0(w_j)) \tag{8}$$

is the number of the selected genes in the list. Here $I_A(w))$ is the indicator function that is one if w belongs to the interval A and is zero otherwise.

Thus we can find a data-dependent $c_o \leq 1$ as large as possible such that $\widehat{\mathrm{FDR}} \leq \alpha$. This assumes that there will be some genes with $\hat{\tau}_0(w_j) \leq \alpha$, which will be true in the typical situation in practice. This bound is approximate due to the use of estimates in forming the posterior probabilities of nondifferential expression and so it depends on the fit of the densities $f_0(w_j)$ and $f(w_j)$.

2.5   Bayes Risk in Terms of Estimated FDR and FNR

The Bayes prediction rule minimizes the risk of an allocation defined by (3). We can estimate the error of a false positive e_{01} and the error of a false negative e_{10} by

$$\hat{e}_{01} = \sum_{j=1}^{N} \hat{\tau}_0(w_j)\hat{z}_{1j} / \sum_{j=1}^{N} \hat{\tau}_0(w_j) \tag{9}$$

and

$$\hat{e}_{10} = \sum_{j=1}^{N} \hat{\tau}_1(w_j)\hat{z}_{0j} / \sum_{j=1}^{N} \hat{\tau}_1(w_j) \tag{10}$$

respectively, where $\hat{z}_{0j}$ is taken to be zero or one according as to whether $\hat{\tau}_0(w_j)$ is less than or greater than c in (4), and $\hat{z}_{1j} = 1 - \hat{z}_{0j}$. Also, we can estimate the prior probability π_0 as

$$\hat{\pi}_0 = \sum_{j=1}^{N} \hat{\tau}_0(w_j)/N. \tag{11}$$

On substituting these estimates (9) to (11) into the right-hand side of (3), the estimated risk can be written as

$$\widehat{\text{Risk}} = (1 - c)\hat{\omega}\widehat{\text{FDR}} + c(1 - \hat{\omega})\widehat{\text{FNR}}, \tag{12}$$

where

$$\widehat{\text{FDR}} = \sum_{j=1}^{N} \hat{\tau}_0(w_j)\hat{z}_{1j} / \sum_{j=1}^{N} \hat{z}_{1j} \tag{13}$$

and

$$\widehat{\text{FNR}} = \sum_{j=1}^{N} \hat{\tau}_1(w_j)\hat{z}_{0j} / \sum_{j=1}^{N} \hat{z}_{0j} \tag{14}$$

are estimates of the FDR and FNR respectively, and where

$$\hat{\omega} = \sum_{j=1}^{N} \hat{z}_{1j}/N$$
$$= N_r/N \tag{15}$$

is an estimate of the probability that a gene is selected.

Thus unlike the tests or rules that are designed to control just the FDR, the Bayes rule approach in its selection of the genes can be viewed as controlling a linear combination of the FDR and FNR. The balance between the FDR and the FNR is controlled by the threshold c.

3   Estimation of Posterior Probabilities

3.1   Mixture Model Approach

We choose our test statistic W_j so that it has a normal distribution under the null hypothesis H_j that the jth gene is not differentially expressed. For example, if F_j denotes the usual test statistic in a one-way analysis of variance of M observations from g classes, then we follow Broët et al. (2002) and transform the F_j statistic as

$$W_j = \frac{\left(1 - \frac{2}{9(M-g)}\right) F_j^{\frac{1}{3}} - \left(1 - \frac{2}{9(g-1)}\right)}{\sqrt{\frac{2}{9(M-g)} F_j^{\frac{2}{3}} + \frac{2}{9(g-1)}}} \tag{16}$$

The distribution of the transformed statistic W_j is approximately a standard normal under the null hypothesis that the jth gene is not differentially expressed (that is, given its membership of population G_0). As noted in Broët et al. (2002), it is remarkably accurate for $(M - g) \geq 10$.

With this transformation, we can take the null density $f_0(w_j)$ to be the standard normal density (which has mean zero and unit variance). In order to estimate the mixing proportion π_0 and the mixture density $f(w_j)$, we postulate it to have the h-component normal mixture form

$$f(w_j) = \sum_{i=0}^{h-1} \pi_i \phi(w_j; \mu_i, \sigma_i 2), \tag{17}$$

where we specify $\mu_0 = 0$ and $\sigma_i 2 = 1$. In (17), $\phi(w_j; \mu_i, \sigma_i 2)$ denotes the normal density with mean μ_i and unit variance $\sigma_i 2$. We suggest starting with $h = 2$, adding more components if considered necessary as judged using the Bayesian Information Criterion (BIC).

3.2   Use of P-Values

An an alternative to working with the test statistic W_j, we could follow the approach of Allison et al. (2002) and use the associated P-value p_j. We can find these P-values using permutation methods whereby we permute the class labels. Using just the B permutations of the class labels for the gene-specific statistic W_j, the P-value for $W_j = w_j$ is assessed as

$$p_j = \frac{\#\{b : w_{0j}^{(b)} \geq w_j\}}{B}, \tag{18}$$

where $w_{0j}^{(b)}$ is the null version of w_j after the bth permutation of the class labels.

3.3   Link with FDR

Suppose that $\tau_0(w)$ is monotonic (decreasing in w). Then the rule (6) for declaring the jth gene to be differentially expressed is equivalent to

$$w \geq w_o, \qquad (19)$$

where w_o is the value of w such that $\tau_0(w_o) = c_o$. The associated FDR, actually the positive FDR (Storey 2004), is given by

$$\pi_0 \frac{1 - F_0(w_o)}{1 - F(w_o)}. \qquad (20)$$

Using (17), the positive FDR can be approximated using the fully parametric estimate for $F(w_o)$,

$$\hat{F}(w_o) = \pi_0 \Phi(w_o) + \sum_{i=1}^{h-1} \hat{\pi}_i \Phi\left(\frac{w_o - \hat{\mu}_i}{\hat{\sigma}_i}\right) \qquad (21)$$

in the right-hand side of (21).

Alternatively, we could choose w_o, and hence c_o, so that (20) is equal to α. It thus also has an interpretation in terms of the q-value of Storey (2004). For if all genes with $\tau_0(w) \leq c_o$ are declared to be differentially expressed, then the FDR will be bounded above by α; see Efron et al. (2001).

Concerning the link of this approach with the tail-area methodology of Benjamini and Hochberg (1995), suppose that the right-hand side of (20) is monotonic (decreasing) in w_0. Then as shown explicitly in Wit and McClure (2004), if we set π_0 equal to one and estimate $F(w_0)$ by its empirical distribution in the right-hand side of (20), the consequent rule is equivalent to the Benjamini-Hochberg procedure.

4   Application to Hedenfalk Breast Cancer Data

We analyze the publicly available cDNA microarray data set of Hedenfalk et al. (2001). They studied the gene expression profiles of tumours from women with hereditary BRCA1- ($n_1 = 7$) and BRCA2-mutation positive cancer ($n_2 = 8$), here referred to as BRCA1 and BRCA2, as well as sporadic cases of breast cancer.

Hedenfalk et al. initially considered genes which could differentiate between the three types of breast cancer (BRCA1, BRCA2 and sporadic). They computed a modified F-statistic and used it to assign a P-value to each gene. A threshold of $\alpha = 0.001$ was selected to find 51 genes from a total of $N = 3,226$ that show differential gene expression. One of the main goals of the study was to identify the genes differentially expressed between the BRCA1 and BRCA2 cancers. They used a combination of three methods (modified t-test, weighted gene analysis and mutual-information scoring), and identified 176 significant genes.

Here we consider the gene expression data from the BRCA1 and BRCA2 tumours only. We use a subset of 3,170 genes, having eliminated genes with one or more measurements greater than 20, which was several interquartile ranges away from the interquartile range of all the data (as in Storey and Tibshirani 2003). We applied our decision-theoretic approach to this data set. In Table 1, we report the estimated values of the FDR, calculated using (13), for various levels of the threshold c_o.

Table 1. Estimated FDR for various levels of c_o

c_o	N_r	$\widehat{\text{FDR}}$
0.5	1702	0.29
0.4	1235	0.23
0.3	850	0.18
0.2	483	0.12
0.1	175	0.06

It can be seen that if we were to declare the jth gene to be differentially expressed if $\tau_0(w_j) \leq 0.1$, then 175 genes would be selected as being significant, with an estimated FDR equal to 0.06. The prior probability of a gene not being differentially expressed (π_0) was estimated to be 0.465. We found that the above estimates, based on the semi-parametric version (13), were the same (to the second decimal place) as those calculated using the fully parametric estimate given in (20).

Of these 175 significant genes, 137 are over-expressed in BRCA1 tumours relative to BRCA2. Hedenfalk et al. (2001), and also Storey and Tibshirani (2003) in their further analysis of this data set, found too that a large block of genes are over-expressed in BRCA1. In particular, these included genes involved in DNA repair and cell death, such as MSH2 (DNA repair) and PDCD5 (induction of apoptosis), also identified by us. In their study, Storey and Tibshirani (2003) identified 160 genes to be significant for differential expression between BRCA1 and BRCA2 by thresholding genes with q-values less than or equal to $\alpha = 0.05$ (an arbitrary cut-off value). Here the q-value of a particular gene is the expected proportion of false positives incurred when calling that gene significant, so that 8 of their 160 genes were expected to be false positives.

On comparing our 175 genes with the 160 identified by Storey and Tibshirani (2003), we found that there were 140 genes in common. Of the 35 excluded genes, 12 were included in the Hedenfalk set of 176. The functional classes (where known) of the remaining 23 genes are shown in Table 2, and interestingly include several genes involved in cell death as well as cell cycle control.

Broët et al. (2004) recently also applied a mixture model appproach to identify differentially expressed genes in this data set. However, they implemented a Bayesian approach, in contrast to the frequentist approach as applied here. They obtained a slightly different estimate for π_0 of 0.52, hence rejecting 52 %

Table 2. Functional classes for uniquely identified genes

Functional Class	Gene Identifier
Cell death	ITPK1, NALP1, GADD34
Cell cycle	MAPK6
Transcription	GATA3, TLE1, HDAC2, GTF2B
Cell-to-cell signalling	ANXA1
Cell growth/adhesion/motility	COL5A1, ACTB1
Protein synthesis	EIF2S2
Protein modification	PRKACA, CSTB
Metabolism	OXCT1, POX1

of the genes as not differentially expressed, as opposed to our value of 46.5 %. In their approach, they did not constrain the variance of the first component to be one because it presents computational problems implementing the Bayesian solution via MCMC methods. However, using the frequentist approach, we were able to fix the variance to be one.

In conclusion, we feel that a mixture model-based approach towards finding differentially expressed genes in microarray data can provide useful information beyond that of other methods. In particular, genes which score as most significant using standard methods for multiple hypothesis testing may not necessarily be of most biological relevance (see Broët et al. 2004). Genes with more subtle changes in their expression levels, indicating that they are more tightly regulated, may be of more importance in the biology of tumour formation.

References

Allison, D.B., Gadbury, G.L., Heo, M., Fernandez, J.R., Lee, C.-K., Prolla, T.A., and Weindruch, R. (2002). A mixture model approach for the analysis of microarray gene expression data. *Computational Statistics and Data Analysis* **39**, 1–20.

Benjamini, Y. and Hochberg, Y. (1995). Controlling the False Discovery Rate: A Practical and Powerful Approach to Multiple Testing. *Journal of the Royal Statistical Society* **B** 57, 289–300

Broët, P., Richardson, S., and Radvanyi, F. (2002). Bayesian hierarchical model for identifying changes in gene expression from microarray experiments. *Journal of Computational Biology* **9**, 671–683.

Broët, P., Lewin, A. Richardson, S., Dalmasso, C. and Magdelenat, H. (2004). A mixture model-based strategy for selecting sets of genes in multiclass response microarray experiments. *Bioinformatics* **20**, 2562–2571.

Efron, B., Tibshirani, R., Storey, J.D., and Tusher, V. (2001). Empirical Bayes analysis of a microarray experiment. *Journal of the American Statistical Association* **96**, 1151–1160.

Efron, B. and Tibshirani, R. (2002). Empirical Bayes methods and false discovery rates for microarrays. *Genetic Epidemiology* **23**, 70-86.

Genovese, C.R. and Wasserman, L. (2002). Operating Characteristics and Extensions of the False Discovery Rate Procedure. *Journal of the Royal Statistical Society B* **64**, 499–517

Hedenfalk, I., Duggan, D., Chen, Y.D., Radmacher, M., Bittner, M., Simon, R., Meltzer, P., Gusterson, B., Esteller, M., Kallioniemi, O.P., et al. (2001) Gene-expression profiles in hereditary breast cancer. *The New England Journal of Medicine* **344**, 539–548.

Lee, M.-L.T., Kuo, F.C., Whitmore, G.A., and Sklar, J. (2000). Importance of replication in microarray gene expression studies: statistical methods and evidence from repetitive cDNA hybridizations. *Proceedings of the National Academy of Sciences USA* **97**, 9834–9838.

McLachlan, G.J., Do, KA, and Ambroise C. (2004). *Analyzing Microarray Gene Expression Data*. New York: Wiley.

Pan, W. (2002). A comparative review of statistical methods for discovering differentially expressed genes in replicated microarray experiments. *Bioinformatics* **18**, 546–554.

Pan, W., Lin, J. and Le, C.T. (2003). A mixture model approach to detecting differentially expressed genes with microarray data. *Functional and Integrative Genomics* **3**, 117–124.

Storey, J.D. and Tibshirani, R. (2003). Statistical significance for genome-wide studies. *Proceedings of the National Academy of Sciences USA* **100**, 9440–9445.

Storey, J. (2004). The positive false discovery rate: a Bayesian interpretation and the q-value. *Annals of Statistics* **31**, 2013–2035.

Tusher, V.G., Tibshirani, R. and Chu, G. (2001). Significance analysis of microarrays applied to the ionizing radiation response. *Proceedings of the National Academy of Sciences USA* **98**, 5116–5121.

Wit, E. and McClure, J. (2004). *Statistics for Microarrays: Design, Analysis and Inference*. Chichester: Wiley.

A Comparative Study
of Two Novel Predictor Set Scoring Methods

Chia Huey Ooi and Madhu Chetty

School of Computing and Information Technology, Monash University,
Churchill, VIC 3842, Australia
{chia.huey.ooi,madhu.chetty}@infotech.monash.edu.au

Abstract. Due to the large number of genes measured in a typical microarray
dataset, feature selection plays an essential role in tumor classification. In turn,
relevance and redundancy are key components in determining the optimal predictor set. However, a third component – the relative weights given to the first
two also assumes an equal, if not greater importance in feature selection. Based
on this third component, we developed two novel feature selection methods capable of producing high, unbiased classification accuracy in multiclass microarray dataset. In an in-depth analysis comparing the two methods, the optimal
values of the relative weights are also estimated.

Keywords: Feature selection, microarray, tumor classification, redundancy

1 Introduction

Relevance and redundancy, or the embodiment thereof, are two essential criteria in
determining the set of features giving the most optimal classification accuracy. The
fact can be summarized in this axiom:

A good predictor set should contain features highly correlated with the target class
distinction, and yet uncorrelated with each other [1].

The attribute referred to in the first part of this statement is summarized by the
term *relevance*. The second part of the statement points to the measure of *redundancy*,
which considers relationships between pairs of genes.

Previous studies [1, 2] have established their filter-based feature selection method
on the basis of relevance and redundancy having equal role in the formation of a good
predictor set. Unfortunately, few have explored the possibility of varying the weights
of importance assigned to relevance and redundancy in feature selection. An example
is a study [3] which utilized a power factor for the purpose of weighting relevance and
redundancy. However, due to its use of a relevance measure that was inapplicable to
true multiclass problems, the study was limited to binary classification.

This paper presents two novel feature selection methods. The first method is based
on minimal redundancy, whereas the second method is rooted in maximizing a derivative anti-measure of redundancy, *antiredundancy*. Both incorporate the concept of
adjustable relative importance of relevance vs. redundancy in selecting the members
of a predictor set. With these two methods, the effect of the importance placed upon
redundancy vs. relevance on the efficacy of the predictor set can be analyzed in the
context of multiclass and complex microarray datasets. A new analysis technique for
evaluating the performance of each method has also been developed in this study.

M. Gallagher, J. Hogan, and F. Maire (Eds.): IDEAL 2005, LNCS 3578, pp. 432–439, 2005.

2 Scoring Methods

The original training data set upon which feature selection is to be implemented, T, consists of N genes and M samples. Sample j is represented by a vector $\mathbf{x}_j$ containing the expression of the N genes, $[x_{1j}, \ldots, x_{Nj}]^{\mathrm{T}}$ and a parameter, y_j representing the class the sample belongs to. A target class vector, $\mathbf{y}$, is defined as $[y_1, \ldots, y_M]$ where $y_j \in [1, K]$ in a dataset of K classes, From the total of N genes, the objective of the feature selection method is to form the subset of genes, called the predictor set S, which would give the optimal estimate of classification accuracy.

In the minimal-redundancy-based method, the score defined to measure the goodness of predictor set S is given as follows.

$$W_{R,S} = \frac{(V_S)^\rho}{(R_S)^{1-\rho}} \tag{1}$$

where $\rho \in (0, 1]$ defines the balance between the importance placed on relevance and redundancy. An approach similar to this method but limited to $\rho = 0.5$ (equal weights for relevance and redundancy) has been introduced in a previous study [2].

V_S denotes the measure of relevance for S and is computed by averaging the BSS/WSS (between-group sum of squares/within-group sum of squares) ratio of the members of S.

$$V_S = \frac{1}{|S|} \sum_{i \in S} F(i) \tag{2}$$

For gene i, $F(i)$ is the BSS/WSS ratio [4] given below.

$$F(i) = \frac{\sum_{j=1}^{M} \sum_{k=1}^{K} I(y_j = k)(\bar{x}_{ik} - \bar{x}_{i\bullet})^2}{\sum_{j=1}^{M} \sum_{k=1}^{K} I(y_j = k)(x_{ij} - \bar{x}_{ik})^2} \tag{3}$$

In equation (3), $I(.)$ is an indicator function returning 1 if the condition inside the parentheses is true, otherwise it returns 0. $\bar{x}_{i\bullet}$ is the average of the expression of gene i across all training samples, while $\bar{x}_{ik}$ is the average of the expression of gene i across training samples belonging to class k.

R_S represents the measure of redundancy for S.

$$R_S = \frac{1}{|S|^2} \sum_{i,j \in S} |R(i,j)| \tag{4}$$

$R(i, j)$ is the Pearson product moment correlation coefficient between members i and j of S.

In the maximal-antiredundancy-based method, we maximize a new measure which is the opposite of redundancy. This is the antiredundancy measure for S, U_S.

$$U_S = \frac{1}{|S|^2} \sum_{i,j \in S} 1 - |R(i,j)| \tag{5}$$

Since with this method, both relevance, V_S and antiredundancy, U_S are to be maximized, the maximal-antiredundancy score for S is the weighted product of both.

$$W_{A,S} = (V_S)^\alpha \cdot (U_S)^{1-\alpha} \tag{6}$$

where $\alpha \in (0, 1]$ defines the balance between the importance placed on relevance and antiredundancy. In this method, α plays a role similar to that of ρ in the minimal-redundancy-based method.

For each of the predictor set scoring methods, the optimal predictor set of sizes $P = 2,3,...,500$ are determined. The search method employed is the linear incremental search. The feature with the highest $F(i)$ is picked as the first member of S. For the subsequent members, we select the feature which enables S to achieve the highest score of $W_{R,S}$ or $W_{A,S}$. This technique, requiring only a complexity of the order $O(NP)$, has been applied in previous feature selection studies [2, 5].

2.1 Analyzing the Resulting Predictor Sets

Predictor sets are obtained from both methods using only the training set, thus ensuring minimal bias in the resulting accuracy upon the test set [6]. Each predictor set is used to train a classifier, which is then applied on the test set. In this study we employ the SVM-based multi-classifier, DAGSVM, which uses substantially less training time compared to either the standard algorithm or Max Wins [7].

Accuracy and Class Balance. From the classification of the samples in the test set, two important parameters can be identified for each predictor set: overall accuracy and class balance of accuracy. Balance among class accuracies, or 'class balance', is determined by the difference between the accuracies among samples of the class with the best class accuracy and among samples of the class with worst class accuracy.

t-test to Determine Equal Means. The Student's t-test is conducted by calculating, for each feature of the dataset, the probability that two groups of samples are likely to have come from the same two underlying populations that have the same mean. The first group being the training samples belonging to class k ($k = 1, 2, ..., K$), the second group consists of all samples of the training set. Hence each feature will have K such probabilities – one for each class. The t-test probability for feature i and class k is written as $t_{i,k}$. Lower $t_{i,k}$ implies stronger relevance to the target class vector of class k vs. all other classes for feature i. This is based on the assumption that for features with strong relevance to the said target class vector, the mean among training samples belonging to a particular class should be significantly different from the mean among all training samples.

In the t-test analysis, the number of the members of a predictor set S with $t_{i,k} < 0.0001$ is recorded for each class k. This number is denoted as $T_{k,S}$. The mean and the standard deviation of $T_{k,S}$ across the K classes, μ_T and σ_T respectively are then computed. The score Φ_S indicating the 'significance content' of S is given below.

$$\Phi_S = \frac{\left(\dfrac{\mu_T}{|S|}\right)}{\left(\dfrac{\sigma_T}{|S|}\right) + \theta} \tag{7}$$

θ is an arbitrary user-determined constant to avoid division by 0 in case of near-zero values of σ_T. In this study, θ is set to 0.01. High Φ_S implies that S contains large number of features with high t-test associated significance (>99.99%) for each of the K

classes (as represented by relatively large μ_T/S), while at the same time maintaining a balance of such features between classes (as characterized by relatively small σ_T/S).

3 Results

The redundancy-based and antiredundancy-based methods were tested on a 14-class microarray dataset of multiple primary tumor types ("Global Cancer Map", or GCM) [8]. 198 tumor samples of the GCM dataset were split into a training set of 144 samples and a test set of 54 samples. To enable comparisons, the exact split of training and test sets employed in the original studies on the dataset [8, 9] was maintained. Data pre-processing was implemented as recommended in [4]. In the experiments, several values were considered: 0.1, 0.2, ..., 0.9, 1.0 for ρ and α in the minimal-redundancy-based and the maximal-antiredundancy-based methods respectively.

3.1 Test Set Accuracy

The term 'optimal predictor set' refers to the predictor set with the highest accuracy among all other predictor sets (of different sizes) found using a particular method and a particular value of α or ρ. Among the optimal predictor sets obtained for each values of ρ from the $W_{R,S}$ method (Figure 1), $\rho = 0.8$ produces the highest accuracy of 83.3% using 197 genes. The $W_{A,S}$ method fares better, however, its best accuracy being 85.2% from the $\alpha = 0.9$ predictor set, which uses 381 genes. However, if one were to consider the trade-off between accuracy and predictor set size, then the optimal point would probably lie at $\rho = 0.7$ for the $W_{R,S}$ method (79.6%, 83 genes) and $\alpha = 0.4$ for the $W_{A,S}$ method (83.3%, 85 genes).

The $W_{R,S}$ method tends to produce large optimal predictor sets (>200 genes) for most values of ρ used except in the narrow range of $\rho \in [0.7,0.8]$. For the $W_{A,S}$ method, the size of the optimal predictor sets is relatively small (<200 genes) in the central region of the α domain ($\alpha \in [0.2,0.5]$). However, between $\alpha = 0.3$ and $\alpha = 0.8$, the optimal predictor set size increases steadily from 75 to 420 genes.

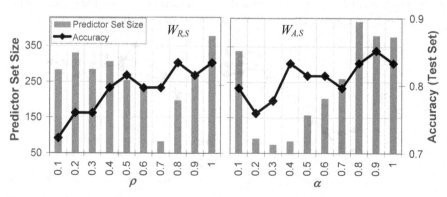

Fig. 1. Accuracy from optimal predictor sets and corresponding size vs. ρ (left) and α (right)

3.2 Balance of Class Accuracies

For each value of α or ρ, the average of the class balance among predictor sets of various sizes $P = 2,3,...,P_{max}$ is compared to the class balance of the optimal predictor set. Two different values of P_{max} are used: 150 and 500. The class balance from the optimal predictor sets and the average values are plotted against α or ρ (Figure 2).

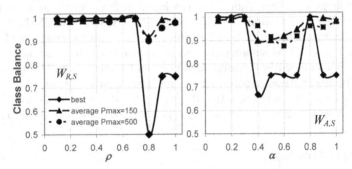

Fig. 2. Class balance vs. ρ (left) and α (right)

For the $W_{R,S}$ method, the optimal predictor set derived from $\rho = 0.8$ has the best class balance, with the smallest difference between the best and worst class accuracies (0.5). For the $W_{A,S}$ method, the optimal predictor set derived from $\alpha = 0.4$ has the best class balance, the difference between the best and worst class accuracies being 0.67. The trend shown by the plots of the average class balance from predictor sets of various sizes (at both $P_{max} = 500$ and $P_{max} = 150$) also concurs with the trend of class balance among the optimal predictor sets, with the exception of $\alpha = 0.8$ for the $W_{A,S}$ method.

3.3 Significance Content Analysis

For each value of α or ρ, the average of the score Φ_S among predictor sets of various sizes $P = 2,3,...,P_{max}$ is compared to the score Φ_S of the optimal predictor set. Two different values of P_{max} are used: 150 and 500. The scores Φ_S from the optimal predictor sets and the average scores are plotted against α or ρ (Figure 3).

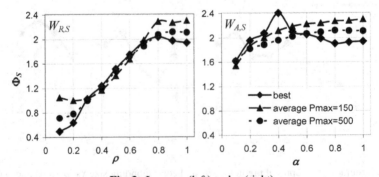

Fig. 3. Φ_S vs. ρ (left) and α (right)

Among optimal predictor sets obtained in the $W_{R,S}$ method, the optimal predictor set derived using $\rho = 0.8$ scores the highest in terms of Φ_S (Figure 3). For the $W_{A,S}$ method, the optimal predictor set obtained using the α value of 0.4 gives the highest Φ_S among optimal predictor sets derived from various values of α.

Both plots of Φ_S from the optimal predictor sets and the averaged Φ_S demonstrate that the Φ_S score is generally higher for predictor sets found using the $W_{A,S}$ method than the ones from the $W_{R,S}$ method, especially in the lower range of α or ρ. Moreover, the peaks in performance as measured using Φ_S are located in the same region along the ρ or α domain for the $W_{R,S}$ and the $W_{A,S}$ methods respectively as the performance peaks identified using accuracy and class balance analyses.

3.4 Results from Different Training and Test Sets Splits

The experiments with both $W_{R,S}$ and $W_{A,S}$ methods were repeated using 10 different splits of the training and test sets (while still maintaining the 144:54 ratio between the two sets). Due to computational limitations, P_{max} is set at 150. The value of α or ρ at which the best accuracy occurs is *smaller* when using multiple splits than the value of α or ρ at which the best accuracy occurs when using the original single split (Figure 4). This is true for both $W_{R,S}$ and $W_{A,S}$ methods.

The results reaffirm that unequal weights for relevance and antiredundancy are vital for optimal classification of multiclass datasets in case of the $W_{A,S}$ method. For this method, the bias towards stronger emphasis on antiredundancy is very pronounced since better accuracy is achieved at α values below 0.5, especially $\alpha = 0.2$. Above $\alpha = 0.2$, accuracy then drops steadily as α increases. In case of the $W_{R,S}$ method, with the peak accuracy occurring around $\rho = 0.5$, the bias towards relevance is not as distinct as the bias towards antiredundancy shown in case of the $W_{A,S}$ method.

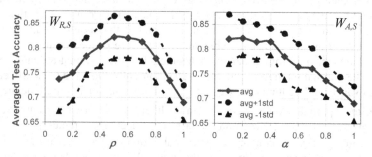

Fig. 4. Plot of test set accuracies averaged over 10 different splits of training and test sets

4 Discussion

Judging by the 3 criteria (accuracy, class balance and significance content) used in evaluating predictor set performance, we can conclude that

- The $W_{R,S}$ method works best with values of ρ at 0.5 or higher
- The $W_{A,S}$ method gives optimal performance at values of α below 0.5.

The $W_{A,S}$ method is able to produce smaller optimal predictor sets at equal accuracy rate compared to the $W_{R,S}$ method. Furthermore, among the optimal predictor sets, difference between the best and worst class accuracies stays low (<0.8) for most values of α in the $W_{A,S}$ method, whereas similar class balance is only achieved in the much narrower range of $\rho \in [0.8,1]$ for the $W_{R,S}$ method (Figure 2).

The t-test significance content analysis enables us to judge each method's ability to

- pick as many features likely to differentiate each class from all other classes, and
- preserve as balanced collection of such features for each class as possible,

without resorting to the need for defining a One-vs.-All (OVA)-based measure of relevance, a step which magnifies the order of complexity by a factor of K. The aforementioned ability might contribute to the usefulness of a method in forming a good predictor set. This is supported by the observations that the values of ρ or α at which the Φ_S score is highest (Figure 3) are close to the values of ρ or α with which the best accuracy-and-predictor-set-size tradeoff and class balance are obtained.

To our knowledge, the accuracy rate reported in this study is not only the highest ever achieved for the GCM dataset using un-aggregated classifiers, but is also obtained using smaller predictor sets. In previous studies [8, 9], a 78% test set accuracy has been reported for the same dataset but using all 16000 features of the original dataset. A more recent study [10] has managed a comparable accuracy of 81.5% with 84 genes using the highly complex SANN. However, the focus of the SANN study is mainly on the merits of the SANN as a classifier rather than on feature selection itself: The members of the predictor set used in that study were obtained from the list of top significant genes made available in the original study of the GCM dataset [10].

5 Conclusion

The importance of the relative weights given to relevance and (anti)redundancy in feature selection has been established in this study. The results show that optimal predictor sets are not necessarily found using methods that assigned equal weights to relevance and (anti)redundancy. Depending on the type of method used, the relative weights might be far from equal to each other. For the minimal-redundancy-based method, the optimal relative weight has been empirically shown to be nearly equal for both relevance and redundancy ($\rho \approx 0.5$). For the maximal-antiredundancy-based method, the optimal relative weight is more likely to be larger for antiredundancy than relevance ($\alpha < 0.5$). Based on the criteria of accuracy, predictor set size, class balance and significance content, the maximal-antiredundancy-based method gives a better overall performance compared to the minimal-redundancy-based method.

References

1. Hall, M.A., Smith, L.A.: Practical feature subset selection for machine learning. In: McDonald, C. (ed.): Proc. of the 21stAustralasian Computer Science Conference. Springer, Singapore (1998) 181–191
2. Ding, C., Peng, H.: Minimum Redundancy Feature Selection from Microarray Gene Expression Data. In: Proc. 2nd IEEE Computational Systems Bioinformatics Conference. IEEE Computer Society (2003) 523–529

3. Knijnenburg, T.A.: Selecting relevant and non-redundant features in microarray classification applications. M.Sc. Thesis. Faculty of Electrical Engineering, Mathematics, and Computer Science (EEMCS) of the Delft University of Technology.
http://ict.ewi.tudelft.nl/pub/marcel/Knij05b.pdf (2004)
4. Dudoit, S., Fridlyand, J., Speed, T.: Comparison of discrimination methods for the classification of tumors using gene expression data. JASA 97 (2002) 77–87
5. Yu, L., Liu, H.: Efficiently Handling Feature Redundancy in High-Dimensional Data. In: Domingos, P., Faloutsos, C., Senator, T., Kargupta, H., Getoor, L. (eds.): Proc. of the 9th ACM SIGKDD International Conference on Knowledge Discovery and Data Mining. ACM Press, New York (2003) 685–690
6. Ambroise, C., McLachlan, G. J.: Selection bias in gene extraction on the basis of microarray gene-expression data. Proc. Natl. Acad. Sci. 99 (2002) 6562–6566
7. Platt, J.C., Cristianini, N., Shawe-Taylor, J.: Large Margin DAGs for Multiclass Classification. Advances in Neural Information Processing Systems (NIPS) 12 (2000) 547–553
8. Ramaswamy, S., Tamayo, P., Rifkin, R., Mukherjee, S., Yeang, C.H., Angelo, M., Ladd, C., Reich, M., Latulippe, E., Mesirov, J.P., Poggio, T., Gerald, W., Loda, M., Lander, E.S., Golub, T.R.: Multi-class cancer diagnosis using tumor gene expression signatures. Proc. Natl. Acad. Sci. 98 (2001) 15149–15154
9. Rifkin, R., Mukherjee, S., Tamayo, P., Ramaswamy, S., Yeang, C.H., Angelo, M., Reich, M., Poggio, T., Lander, E.S., Golub, T.R., Mesirov, J.P.: An Analytical Method for Multi-class Molecular Cancer Classification. SIAM Review 45 No. 4 (2003) 706–723
10. Linder, R., Dew, D., Sudhoff, H., Theegarten D., Remberger, K., Poppl, S.J., Wagner, M.: The "Subsequent Artificial Neural Network" (SANN) Approach Might Bring More Classificatory Power To ANN-based DNA Microarray Analyses. Bioinformatics Advance Access. Published on July 29, 2004. Bioinformatics, doi:10.1093/bioinformatics/bth441

Deriving Matrix of Peptide-MHC Interactions in Diabetic Mouse by Genetic Algorithm

Menaka Rajapakse[1,2], Lonce Wyse[1], Bertil Schmidt[2], and Vladimir Brusic[1,3]

[1] Institute for Infocomm Research, 21 Heng Mui Keng Terrace, Singapore 119613
{menaka,lonce,vladimir}@i2r.a-star.edu.sg
[2] School of Computer Engineering, Nanyang Technological University,
Block N4, Nanyang Avenue, Singapore 639798
asbschmidt@ntu.edu.sg
[3] School of Land and Food Sciences and the Institute for Molecular Bioscience,
University of Queensland, Brisbane QLD 4072, Australia

Abstract. Finding motifs that can elucidate rules that govern peptide binding to medically important receptors is important for screening targets for drugs and vaccines. This paper focuses on elucidation of peptide binding to I-A^{g7} molecule of the non-obese diabetic (NOD) mouse - an animal model for insulin-dependent diabetes mellitus (IDDM). A number of proposed motifs that describe peptide binding to I-A^{g7} have been proposed. These motifs results from independent experimental studies carried out on small data sets. Testing with multiple data sets showed that each of the motifs at best describes only a subset of the solution space, and these motifs therefore lack generalization ability. This study focuses on seeking a motif with higher generalization ability so that it can predict binders in all A^{g7} data sets with high accuracy. A binding score matrix representing peptide binding motif to A^{g7} was derived using genetic algorithm (GA). The evolved score matrix significantly outperformed previously reported motifs.

1 Introduction

An I-A^{g7} motif shown in Fig. 1 describes commonly observed amino acid residues find in peptides that bind major histocompatibility complex (MHC) molecule of the non-obese diabetic (NOD) mouse (Rammensee I-A^{g7} motif) [1]. These residues, which contribute significantly to peptide binding, are called primary anchor residues and the positions they occur are called anchor positions. Anchor positions may be occupied by so called preferred residues which are tolerated, but alone contribute little to peptide binding strength. I-A^{g7} is critical for the development of insulin-dependent diabetes mellitus (IDDM) in NOD mice [2-10]. To understand the molecular basis of development of IDDM in NOD mice it is important to understand peptide binding properties to I-A^{g7}. I-A^{g7} binds peptides that are 9-30 amino acids long. Peptide binding to I-Ag7 is mediated through a binding core that is 9 amino acids long. For example, a well-known I-A^{g7} binding peptide EEIAQVATISANGDKDIGNI (mouse HSP protein 166-185) binds to I-A^{g7} via residues 171V, 174I, 176A, and 179D [4]. Of these positions, three (171V, 176A, and 179D) correspond to the primary anchors and 174I corresponds to a preferred residue in the Rammensee motif. When associated with appropriate metrics, a binding motif can be used for prediction

M. Gallagher, J. Hogan, and F. Maire (Eds.): IDEAL 2005, LNCS 3578, pp. 440–447, 2005.

of peptides that bind I-A^{g7}. For example, weights of primary anchors can be set to 4 and of preferred residues to 2. The score for mouse HSP peptide 166-185 will be 14 (4+2+4+4 for 171V, 174I, 176A, and 179D). High scoring peptides are thus predicted as I-A^{g7} binders. A widely used extension of the binding motif scoring scheme is a quantitative matrix that contain 9×20 coefficients. Nine rows represent positions and 20 columns represent each of the 20 amino acids, while matrix cells contain weights for each amino acid at a given position. The score for the prediction is calculated by summing or multiplying the coefficients. Examples of binding matrices are given in [8,9]. To our best knowledge, a quantitative matrix for I-A^{g7} has not been reported to date.

				Position					
	1	**2**	**3**	**4**	**5**	**6**	**7**	**8**	**9**
Primary anchors	K,H, S,A, V			L		V,A			D,S, E
Preferred residues	R,T			I,V, M		T			

Fig. 1. Peptide binding motif for the I-A^{g7} molecule – see the main text for the description

Some high-affinity binders to I-A^{g7} such as mouse GAD (247-261) peptide NMYAMLIERYKMEPE [7] do not correspond well to the Rammensee motif – the best 9-mer window in this peptide has one primary anchor (250A) and one preferred residue (253I). This indicates that any one binding motif is likely to be an imperfect approximation of rules that describe peptide binding to I-A^{g7}. Indeed, we found seven different I-A^{g7} motifs derived from largely unrelated experimental data sets. These include reported motifs Reizis [4], Harrison [5], Gregori [7], Latek [6], Rammensee [1], Reich [2], and Amor [3]. These seven motifs are mutually inconsistent and some are completely different. Each motif describes amino acids at primary and secondary anchor positions, as well as "forbidden" amino acids at specific positions. We interpreted these as well-tolerated, weakly-tolerated, and non-tolerated amino acids. We adopted the following metrics: well-tolerated residues have weight 4, weakly-tolerated 2, and non-tolerated amino acids -4. Anchor positions were assigned weights – primary anchor positions have weight 4 and secondary anchor positions weight 2. The primary and secondary anchor positions were defined according to the motif descriptions by the authors. The binding motifs and the scoring scheme can be accessed at <research.i2r.a-star.edu.sg/Ag7motifs>. In this work we seek to: a) compare the predictive ability of the seven reported motifs, b) combine existing data and develop a method for the derivation of a unified motif that describes well all available data, and c) compare several data-driven methods for the identification of the unified motif. The I-A^{g7} 7-related data were extracted from multiple data sets shown in Table 1. We adopted a quantitative matrix as a model for the unified I-A^{g7} motif. Three well-known methods were employed in the search for the best I-A^{g7} quantitative matrix: Multiple EM for Motif Elicitation (MEME) [14], Gibbs sampling [see 9], and genetic algorithm [see 15]. Here we report the unified motif for I-A^{g7}, and the comparative analysis of the motifs used in this study.

Table 1. I-A^{g7} related peptide data sets

Data set	Non binders	Binders	Reference
Reizis	21	33	[4]
Harrison	19	157	[5]
Gregori	31	109	[7]
Latek	8	37	[6]
Corper	35	13	[10]
MHCPEP	-	176	[11]
Yu	16	10	[12]
Stratmann	3	118	[13]
Brusic	37	-	[unpublished]

2   Characterization of Motif Using a Binding Score Matrix

In this section we give a formal definition of the target model as a quantitative matrix. A k-mer motif in an amino acid sequence is usually characterized by a binding score matrix $\mathbf{Q} = \{q_{ia}\}_{kx20}$ where q_{ia} denotes the *binding affinity* of the site i of the motif, when it occupies by the amino-acid $a \in \Sigma$; Σ denotes the set of 20 amino-acid residues. The cumulative binding score for a k-mer not only indicates the likelihood of the presence of a particular motif but also determines the likelihood that a sequence containing the motif binds to another sequence. Therefore, the binding score matrix can be viewed as a quantification of a real biological functioning or binding of the motif to other peptides as described in [13]. Given a binding score matrix $\mathbf{Q}$ of size $k \times 20$ we define the *binding score, s* for a k–mer motif in a sequence of length n as:

$$s = \max_{j \in \{1,\ldots,n-k+1\}} s_j \tag{1}$$

$$s_j = \sum_{i=0}^{k-1} \sum_{a \in \Sigma} q_{ia} \cdot \delta_{ij} \quad \text{with} \quad \delta_{ij} = \begin{cases} 1 & \text{if } x_{j+i} = a \\ 0 & \text{otherwise} \end{cases} \tag{2}$$

We define m^* as the k-mer of sequence x at position j, i.e. $m^* = (x_j,\ldots,x_{j+k-1})$, where

$$j = \arg\max_{j \in \{1,\ldots,n-k+1\}} s_j \tag{3}$$

3   Description of the Method

Let the number of training data sets extracted be d, and the number of motifs inferred from different experiments be Ψ. We can then express the available prior information as $\mathbf{D} = \{(D_i, m_l): i=1,2,\ldots.d, l=1,2,.., \Psi \}$ where m_l is the consensus motifs found in the experiments. Let $D_i = \{(\mathbf{x}_{ij}, b_{ij}): j = 1, 2,\ldots, n_i \}$ where $\mathbf{x}_{ij}$ is the jth sequence in the ith dataset and $b_{ij} \in \{0, 1\}$ indicates whether the sequence $\mathbf{x}_{ij}$ is a binder (when equal to one), or a non-binder (when equal to zero). The collated dataset is then given by $\Gamma = \{\mathbf{x}_{ij}: i=1,2,\ldots..d; j=1,2,\ldots n_i\}$ where n_i is the number of sequences in i^{th} dataset. With these information extracted from the experimentally validated motifs we seek a motif $\mathbf{m}^*$ that best describes the consensus segment in all the sequences in Γ.

3.1 Training and Test Data Sets

The training and test data sets in the experiments are given in Table 1. These data sets consist of short peptides ranging from 9-30 amino acids per sequence. Except for the Stratmann data set, all other data sets were used in the training. The Stratmann test set contains only 118 binders and three non binders. Because of the small number of experimentally determined non-binders, we extended the number of non-binders in this set to 1000 by generating random peptides. The generation of random peptides involved adding correct proportions of amino acids to each peptide so that the gener-ated peptide mimics real protein peptides [16]. Of 1000 random peptides generated, at most five percent are presumed to be binders. This percentage was estimated based on the analysis of I-A^{g7} binding data given in [10].

3.2 Multiple EM for Motif Elicitation (MEME)

MEME is a tool for discovering motifs in protein or DNA sequences in an unsuper-vised manner [14]. All I-A^{g7} binders were converted to *fasta* format and submitted to the public domain MEME analysis tool [17] and three motifs were requested. The position scoring matrices retrieved were assessed for predictive accuracy.

3.3 Gibbs Sampling

Another tool, Gibbs sampling is also used in the analysis. Gibbs sampling is less susceptible to becoming trapped in a local minima. Details about the Gibbs Motif Sampler can be found in [18, 19]. Input data for the Gibbs sampling are the same as for MEME. A single motif was retrieved. A scoring scheme was formulated based on the mutual information contain in each position and assessed for predictive accuracy.

3.4 Genetic Algorithm

Genetic algorithms work with a fixed number of individuals as its population each representing a particular solution. Let the population at time or iteration t of evolution be Q(t). During a single iteration, each chromosome is evaluated against the goodness of the solution by using a fitness function, f.

Binary String Representation: The binding strengths of elements of binding score matrix, q_{ia}, $\{i=1,....k, a \in \Sigma\}$ for each a sequence have been empirically determined and quantitatively expressed in the data sets. Each individual (binding score matrix) in the population is represented by a binary string. A binding score matrix of size k x n, where k represents motif length and n represents number of residues has kn ele-ments.

Fitness Computation: The definition of the fitness function is crucial. The fitness function, in our case, is expected to yield a unified consensus motif for the training set. The dataset of each experiment in the literature gives the information whether the particular sequence is a binder or non-binder. Using this information, the numbers of true positives (TP) and true negatives (TN) determined by solutions in the population could be computed. A highly probable candidate solution must produce lower binding score when tested on a non-binding peptide than on a binding peptide. By incorporating the TPs and TNs resulting from the evaluation and taking into account binding scores for binders and non-binders, we defined a fitness function f on a putative motif, m, representing a binding score matrix Q is defined as:

$$f(Q) = \frac{\sum\limits_{i=1}^{d} \sum\limits_{j=1}^{n_i} s(x_{ij} : m)(1-b_{ij})}{TP + \eta * TN} \qquad (4)$$

The GA finds a score matrix that minimizes the above fitness value. An empirically obtained constant, η is used to minimize the number of possible false positives that can arise from the solution matrix with respect to the non binders.

Construction of Template Score Matrices (Seeds) for Initial Population: In our analysis, seven template scoring matrices were constructed as seeds for the initial population. These template scores are based on the knowledge inferred from the literature. A scoring scheme was enforced on the template formation of scoring matrices by assigning a score of 0 that are non tolerant at a specific site. The highest score of 80 was assigned if the site is in a critical position and the amino acid at that position is categorized as a well tolerant. A base score of 10 was assigned for all the other positions that have no significant contribution. The seeding for the rest of the population was carried out with a super-uniform random generator which yields a population representing all schemata up to a certain defining length (limited by the population size) with large global correlations [see 20].

4   Experimental Results

The motifs generated from MEME, Gibbs sampling and the best GA-derived scoring matrix for the cumulative data set are shown below. Using these motifs and scoring matrices we measured the predictive performance on the Stratmann data set combined with randomly generated non-binders (Tables 3 and 4). The performance was measured by the area under the receiver operating characteristics (AROC) curve and estimates of cut-off points between sensitivity and specificity plots (SE=SP). These metrics indicate the generalization ability of each method across different data sets.

MEME Motifs: Motif1: MKRHGLDNY *Motif2:* AE(Y)Y(Q)LI(K)N(T)VMD *Motif3:*CAKKIVSDG. Multi-level motif derived from the Gibbs Sampling: *Gibbs Motif:* N(MP)K(V)A(RI)T(H)G(A)E(FL)D(Q)N(YL)K(YV). The amino-acid inside the bracket indicates a possible substitution for the amino-acid to its immediate left.

The predictive performance was measured by A_{ROC} values and generalization ability by estimating the cut-off points between sensitivity and specificity plots for previously unseen data (Stratman A^{g7} binders, plus randomly generated non-binders). The GA based scoring matrix outperformed the next best method by some 10% on Stratmann data set. Most of the motifs showed marginal predictive accuracy $(0.8 > A_{ROC} > 0.7)$. As expected, majority of the motifs performed well on the data sets they were derived from, but less so on the independent data sets. While Gibbs sampling produced marginal results, the performance of MEME on these data sets was unremarkable.

Table 2. The final scoring matrix derived by GA

Pos	A	C	D	E	F	G	H	I	K	L	M	N	P	Q	R	S	T	V	W	Y
P1	56	69	61	76	31	2	29	77	69	65	62	66	21	34	66	39	78	17	65	69
P2	28	28	10	26	34	15	10	33	8	35	2	2	31	21	0	35	13	22	10	31
P3	17	40	20	11	22	21	4	44	5	0	7	28	36	24	33	47	40	21	0	47
P4	1	75	0	3	18	5	45	1	6	84	4	47	22	17	95	9	54	93	94	3
P5	24	23	15	24	12	2	32	39	17	38	0	4	36	12	40	41	2	41	29	40
P6	53	63	78	0	68	10	118	44	11	41	58	117	58	57	112	38	17	93	58	35
P7	0	44	45	13	24	44	58	13	25	63	34	6	0	28	49	59	0	62	58	62
P8	39	5	58	11	4	48	0	46	39	13	54	2	50	52	7	2	57	0	57	21
P9	126	124	12	80	41	91	50	110	20	61	11	30	120	43	106	90	86	8	3	74

Table 3. Table 3. The A_{ROC} values from predictions using each motif across all the data sets. $A_{ROC}>0.9$ correspond to excellent, $0.8<A_{ROC}<0.9$ to good, $0.7<A_{ROC}<0.8$ to marginal prediction accuracy. $A_{ROC}=0.5$ corresponds to random guessing, and $0.5<A_{ROC}<0.7$ to poor predictions

	A_{ROC} values							
Motif for	INDIVIDUAL DATA SETS							
predictions	Reizis	Harrison	Gregori	Latek	Corper	MHCPEP	Yu	Stratman
Reizis	**0.95**	0.68	0.74	0.95	0.50	0.59	0.48	0.67
Harrison	0.75	**0.88**	0.69	0.64	0.53	0.72	0.33	0.79
Gregori	0.64	0.68	0.71	0.73	0.40	0.64	0.61	0.79
Latek	0.66	0.72	**0.80**	**0.95**	0.64	0.52	0.75	0.75
Rammense	0.49	0.64	0.76	0.82	0.60	0.48	0.43	0.77
Reich	0.55	0.64	0.69	0.58	0.56	0.47	0.50	0.73
Amor	0.69	0.54	0.66	0.70	0.56	0.66	0.40	0.78
MEME1	0.61	0.58	0.49	0.60	0.43	0.55	0.36	0.49
Gibbs	0.33	0.79	0.77	0.81	0.39	0.64	0.58	0.82
GA	0.76	0.86	0.76	**0.96**	**0.79**	**0.83**	**0.94**	**0.88**

Table 4. Cutoff points (SE=SP) for predictions using each motif across all the data sets

	Cut-off points SE=SP							
Motif for	INDIVIDUAL DATA SETS							
predictions	Reizis	Harrison	Gregori	Latek	Corper	MHCPEP	Yu	Stratman
Reizis	**0.87**	0.79	0.69	0.89	0.50	0.57	0.56	0.74
Harrison	0.64	**0.84**	0.65	0.58	0.50	0.68	0.40	0.73
Gregori	0.58	0.62	0.62	0.65	0.42	0.63	0.58	0.74
Latek	0.66	0.68	**0.73**	**0.92**	0.60	0.50	0.65	0.72
Rammense	0.52	0.58	0.70	0.77	0.52	0.46	0.51	0.70
Reich	0.54	0.60	0.62	0.57	0.56	0.48	0.50	0.67
Amor	0.62	0.54	0.62	0.66	0.55	0.60	0.42	0.71
MEME1	0.48	0.55	0.68	0.47	0.63	0.50	0.47	0.47
Gibbs	0.32	0.68	0.71	0.66	0.37	0.58	0.56	0.71
GA	0.72	0.80	0.72	0.92	**0.64**	**0.75**	**0.90**	**0.83**

5   Discussion and Conclusions

We have devised a scoring matrix representing a consensus motif with higher generalization ability than other proposed motifs derived for I-A^{g7} data sets found in the literature. Motifs described in the literature for I-A^{g7} data were tested on an independent data set (Stratmann data set together with 1000 randomly generated non-binders) for the estimation of the prediction accuracy of the evolved matrix. Random non-binders were generated using approximated amino acid compositions. The GA matrix performed well across all data sets, and showed higher generalization ability than the other proposed motifs. The ability of the GA to search a larger solution space in a context independent manner may have eliminated biases in the data sets such as fewer training data, an unequal number of binders and non-binders in the data sets, thereby providing a better solution in finding a consensus motif for difficult and unbalanced data sets.

References

1. Rammensee, H. *et al.*: SYFPEITHI:database for MHC ligands and peptide motifs. Immunogenetics 50 (1999) 213-219
2. Reich,E.P. *et al.*: Self peptides isolated from MHC glycoproteins of non-obese diabetic mice. J. Immunology 152 (1994) 2279-2288
3. Amor,S. *et al.*: Encephalitogenic epitopes of myelin basic protein, proteolipid proteing, and myelin oligodendrocyte glycoprotein for experimental allergic en-cephalomyelitis induction in Biozzi AB/H(H-2A^{g7}) mice share an amino acid motif. J. Immunology 156 (1996) 3000-3008
4. Reizis,B., *et al.*: Molecular characterization of the diabetes mouse MHC class-II protein, I-A^{g7}. Int. Immunology 9 (1997) 43-51
5. Harrison,L.C. *et al.*: A peptide binding motif for I- A^{g7}, the class II major jistocompatibility complex (MHC) molecule of NOD and Biozzi AB/H mice. J. Exp. Med. 185 (1997) 1013-1021
6. Latek,R.R. *et al.*: Structural basis of peptide binding and presentation by the type I diabetes-associated MHC class II molecule of NOD mice. Immunity 12 (2000) 699-710
7. Gregori,S. *et al.*: The motif for peptide binding to the insulin-dependent diabetes mellitus-associated class II MHC molecule I-A^{g7} validated by phage display library. Int. Immunology 12(4) (2000) 493-503
8. Brusic,V. *et al.*: Application of genetic search in derivation of matrix models of peptide binding to MHC molecules. Proc. Int. Conf. Intell. Syst. Mol. Biol. 5 (1997) 75-83
9. Nielsen,M, *et al.* Improved prediction of MHC class I and class II epitopes using a novel Gibbs sampling approach. Bioinformatics 20 (2004) 1388-1397.
10. Corper,A.L. *et al.*: A structural framework for deciphering the link between I-A^{g7} and autoimmune diabetes. Science 288 (2000) 505-511
11. Brusic,V., Rudy,G., Harrison,L.C. MHCPEP, a database of MHC-binding peptides: update 1997. Nucleic Acids Res. 26 (1998) 368-371
12. Yu,B. *et al.*: Binding of conserved islet peptides by human and murine MHC class II molecules associated with susceptibility to type I diabetes. J. Immunology 30(9) 2497-506
13. Stratman,T. *et al.*: The I-A^{g7} MHC class II molecule linked to murine diabetes in a promiscuous peptide binder. J. Immunology 165 (2000) 3214-3225
14. Bailey,T.L., Elkan,C. The value of prior knowledge in discovering motifs with MEME. Proc Int Conf Intell Syst Mol Biol. 3 (1995) 21-29
15. Brusic V, Schonbach C, Takiguchi M, Ciesielski V, Harrison LC. Application of genetic search in derivation of matrix models of peptide binding to MHC molecules. Proc Int Conf Intell Syst Mol Biol. 5 (1997) 75-83
16. Pe'er I. *et al.* Proteomic Signatures:Amino Acid and Oligopeptide Compositions Differentiate Among Phyla. Proteins 54 (2004) 20-40

17. http://meme.scdc.edu/meme/website/meme.html
18. Neuwald, A. F. *et al*.: Gibbs motif sampling: detection of bacterial outer membrane protein repeats. Protein Science 4 (1995) 1618-32
19. Lawrence,C.E *et al*.: (1993) Detecting Subtle Sequence Signals: A Gibbs Sampling Strategy for Multiple Alignment. Science 262 (1993) 208-214
20. Schraudolph,N., Grefenstette J.: A User's Guide to GAucsd 1.4, Technical Report, University of California, San Diego, (1992) CS 92-249

SVM Based Prediction
of Bacterial Transcription Start Sites

James Gordon and Michael Towsey

Centre for Information Technology and Innovation, Faculty of Information Technology,
Queensland University of Technology, GPO Box 2434, Brisbane QLD 4001, Australia
{jj.gordon,m.towsey}@qut.edu.au

Abstract. Identifying bacterial promoters is the key to understanding gene expression. Promoters lie in tightly constrained positions relative to the transcription start site (TSS). Knowing the TSS position, one can predict promoter positions to within a few base pairs, and vice versa. As a route to promoter identification, we formally address the problem of TSS prediction, drawing on the RegulonDB database of known (mapped) *Escherichia coli* TSS locations. The accepted method of finding promoters (and therefore TSSs) is to use position weight matrices (PWMs). We use an alternative approach based on support vector machines (SVMs). In particular, we quantify performance of several SVM models versus a PWM approach, using area under the detection-error tradeoff (DET) curve as a performance metric. SVM models are shown to outperform the PWM at TSS prediction, and to substantially reduce numbers of false positives, which are the bane of this problem.

1 Introduction

Bacterial promoters are sections of DNA lying upstream of a gene transcription start site (TSS), which regulate transcription via selective binding by an RNA Polymerase (RNAP) / sigma factor complex [1]. They are difficult to find because they lie at an unknown distance upstream of the gene start codon, and their associated DNA is weakly conserved. Importantly, they consist of two binding sites (hexamers) which lie in a well-defined window upstream of the TSS. Knowing the TSS location, one can predict promoter locations to within a few base pairs (bp), and vice versa.

As a route to identifying promoters, this paper uses support vector machines (SVMs) [2] to predict TSS locations. We consider TSSs for the class of *Escherichia coli* sigma-70 promoters. Sigma-70 promoters are bound by the *E. coli* sigma-70 transcription factor, and are located around the -10 and -35 positions with respect to the TSS. The RegulonDB database contains approximately 700 mapped sigma-70 TSS locations [3].

The accepted method of finding promoters is to use a position weight matrix (PWM) to search for matches to known promoter hexamers [4]. This approach utilizes only information contained in the two hexamers and the intervening gap length. Based on information theoretic reasoning, it is known that the mapped hexamers (and gap length) are insufficiently conserved to identify all expected promoters in the background genome [5].

In addition to the promoter hexamers, a TSS is surrounded by a number of other regulatory binding sites. These include binding sites for proteins such as activators and repressors, that enhance or repress the level of transcription initiation. Through

M. Gallagher, J. Hogan, and F. Maire (Eds.): IDEAL 2005, LNCS 3578, pp. 448–453, 2005.

the use of machine learning techniques – in our case, SVMs – one might hope to exploit this expanded set of patterns in order to achieve better TSS and promoter prediction. We use the term 'TSS prediction' to refer to this more general approach to TSS and promoter identification.

TSS prediction has an analogue in the problem of translation initiation site (TIS) prediction, the goal of which is to find gene start codons. Recent improvements at TIS prediction have been achieved with a multi-stage approach [6,7]. The problem of sigma-70 TSS / promoter prediction is acknowledged to be a difficult one. It is possible that multi-stage approaches to this problem will likewise improve on results achieved to date. We view the SVM models described in this paper as possible first-stage algorithms, that could be used for identifying likely promoter regions. Future research could involve pairing these models with appropriate second-stage algorithms to achieve higher levels of accuracy.

2 Data

This paper utilized TSS locations derived from the RegulonDB database [3], and sequences extracted from the *E. coli* K12 genome (www.genome.wisc.edu). Two parallel data sets were constructed. The first data set, used to train and test different SVM models, consisted of 450 positive sequences (each containing a single mapped TSS) and 450 negative sequences (not containing known TSSs). The positive sequences extended from –150 to +50 bases relative to each TSS[1].

Negative sequences were derived from parts of the genome that did not contain a known TSS and were all 200 bases long. They contained a reference position at the 151 position corresponding to the TSS in positive sequences. We derived three sets of negative sequences for the first data set: sequences from (a) coding regions (CDRs), (b) non-coding regions between divergent genes (DNCRs), and (c) non-coding regions between convergent genes (CNCRs). In each case, candidate negative regions were generated from the whole genome and randomly shuffled before selecting 450 examples. Because there were relatively few candidate CNCRs, some CNCR regions were permitted to overlap by 100 bp. Due to the positional nature of the SVM models employed here, this was not expected to influence our results.

Note that because of their location between divergently transcribed genes, DNCRs are inherently likely to contain (unmapped) promoters and TSSs. Like coding regions, CNCRs are inherently less likely to contain promoters and TSSs.

A second data set was used to test the SVM models on a biologically realistic task and to compare their performance with that of a standard PWM. It consisted of 450 sequences extending 750 bp upstream of gene start codons. Hereafter we refer to these as *gene upstream regions* (USRs). Each USR contained a single known TSS (the same TSS as in the corresponding positive SVM training sequence). Of the 450 USRs, only nine consisted entirely of non-coding DNA. The remainder overlapped coding regions to varying degrees. We used only 450 of the 676 known sigma-70 TSSs available in the RegulonDB database [3] to ensure that all USRs were non-overlapping.

---

[1] According to biological convention, the TSS position is denoted by +1. The position immediately upstream is -1. There is no 0 position

3 SVM Approach

In an SVM approach, DNA sequences are represented as vectors in a feature space. The SVM is presented with positive and negative examples. From these it determines an optimal decision plane through the feature space separating positive and negative examples. In real problems one is unlikely to achieve complete separation. SVM performance is therefore measured by 'generalization error' – the percentage of unseen test examples that fall on the wrong side of the decision plane.

The data representation employed for this study was a variant of the string kernel proposed by Leslie et al [8]. Each sequence was represented by a vector of scaled counts of 5-mers occurring within the sequence. A single mismatch was allowed in each 5-mer. After collapsing each mismatch neighbourhood onto a single 5-mer, the number of possible 5-mers used to represent a sequence was $\{A,C,G,T\}^4 = 256$.

Our enhancement of the approach in [8] was to 'tag' each motif with its offset from the sequence's reference (151) position. For example, an occurrence of 5-mer ACCGT in positions [–5,+5] (relative to the reference position) was registered as an occurrence of the position-tagged motif ACCGT(0). The same 5-mer in positions [–15, –6] was registered as ACCGT(–10), and in [+6,+15] as ACCGT(+10). Employing a window of size 10 was intended to allow 'fuzziness' of up to 10 bp in identifying TSSs.

Position-tagging increased the SVM feature space dimension. In sequences extending from –150 to +50, the number of possible position tags is 21 (–150, –140, ..., –10, 0, +10, ..., +50). The total number of possible position-tagged motifs was therefore 21 x 256 = 5,376. These position-tagged motifs (i.e., features) were ranked according to their symmetric uncertainty as in [6], and the top 200 were retained in SVM vectors. Note that position-tagged motif counts were scaled by their symmetric uncertainty before insertion into SVM vectors. This was intended to increase the margin associated with significant motifs. All SVM vectors were then normalized to unit length. SVMs were generated using either SVM-Light [9] or the GPDT [10].

4 PWM Approach

PWMs were derived from USRs. The first step in PWM construction was to look for the best match to the *E. coli* sigma-70 promoter consensus hexamers TTGACA and TATAAT upstream of each TSS. The 5′ end of the best fit TATAAT-like motif was constrained to occur in the range [–19,–9] relative to the TSS. The gap between the TTGACA and TATAAT-like motifs was constrained to be in the range [14,20].

Each candidate motif pair within these parameter ranges was assigned a score, equal to the number of bases matching the consensus hexamers, plus some gap weightings to give preference to gaps in the centre of the [14,20] range. For each TSS, the motif pair with the highest score was selected as the best fit. Having identified best fit hexamers for every TSS, based on closeness to the consensus, a PWM was then constructed using the background nucleotide frequencies sampled from all USRs [4,5].

5 Method

A unique index from 1 to 450 was assigned to each USR, positive sequence, and negative sequence within each set (CDR, DNCR and CNCR). Note that USRs and positive sequences having the same index were neighbourhoods of the same TSS. Based on index, each of the datasets was then divided into 10 equal parts. Each of these 10 parts was successively held in reserve as a test set, while the remaining 90% of the data was used to train SVM models and generate a PWM. The resulting SVMs and PWM were then evaluated on the 10% of USRs held in reserve (i.e., 10-fold cross-validation). Results reported below represent average performance over the 10 test sets.

Evaluation of the PWM and SVMs involved applying the models to each of the 750 positions within each test USR. The PWMs and SVMs generated a score for each position. In the case of the SVMs, this score was the perpendicular distance from the decision plane of the [−150,+50] neighbourhood of the candidate position. In the case of PWMs, it was the highest PWM score that could be obtained from two upstream hexamers, the first with its 5′ end at −14 bp upstream of the candidate position, and the second lying at a gap of 14 − 20 bp upstream of the first. (Note that these parameters are consistent with those used to generate the SVMs and PWMs.)

Next a threshold T was defined. Within USRs, the TSS position itself and the five positions on either side of it were considered to be positives. These positions were scored as true positives (TP) if the SVM or PWM score exceeded T, and false negatives (FN) if it fell below T. All other positions in the USRs were considered to be negatives and were scored as false positives (FP) if the SVM or PWM score exceeded T, and true negatives (TN) if it fell below T.

By varying T over the range of scores, it is possible to construct detection-error tradeoff (DET) curves. These are plots of false negative rate (FNR) versus false positive rate (FPR), as shown in Figure 1. [FNR = FN / (FN + TP) and FPR = FP / (FP + TN).] Note that the area under a DET curve is a measure of the classifier's ability to correctly identify TSS positions. The smaller the area, the better the performance. DET area constitutes a rigorous and objective measure of performance, similar to the receiver operating characteristic (ROC) curves used in other areas of statistics.

6 Results and Conclusions

Figure 1 compares performance of three SVM models and the PWM at predicting TSSs in the USR sequences of dataset 2. Table 1 gives areas under the DET curves in Figure 1, and corresponding generalization errors on data set 1 (i.e., SVM test sequences). The most notable result is that the CDR and CNCR SVM models perform substantially better than the PWM on the biologically realistic promoter prediction task. This is true regardless of whether false negatives are scored in a window around the TSS (Table 1), or only at the TSS position itself (results not shown).

The relatively poor performance of the DNCR SVM model is unsurprising. The DNCRs we isolated are likely to contain (unmapped) TSSs and promoters and are therefore a poor source of negative sequences. By contrast, CNCRs are unlikely to contain promoters, but still have characteristics of non-coding regions, and thus are a useful source of negative sequences.

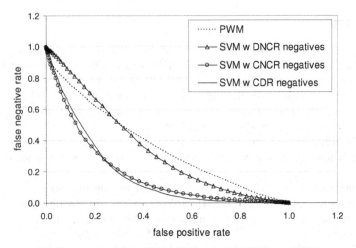

Fig. 1. Detection-Error Tradeoff Curves for PWM and SVMs

Table 1. Generalization errors, DET areas and optimum FP/TP ratios for four methods (standard deviations are derived from 10-fold cross validation)

Method	Gen. Error	DET Area	Optimum FP/TP Ratio
PWM	—	0.36 ± 0.01	155,000 / 300
SVM (DNCR negs)	25.1 ± 2.4%	0.35 ± 0.03	75,000 / 215
SVM (CNCR negs)	27.2 ± 4.3%	0.19 ± 0.03	71,000 / 320
SVM (CDR negs)	15.0 ± 3.8%	0.18 ± 0.02	58,000 / 310

An important conclusion from Table 1 is that SVM performance on the TSS classification task is not a reliable indicator of performance on a biologically realistic task. In particular, the CNCR SVM model performed poorly on the classification task but well on the more realistic TSS prediction task where false positives must be reduced. Papers often present promoter identification algorithms tested only on artificial classification tasks with equal numbers of positives and negatives. This is not a reliable indicator of performance in the less constrained biological setting.

The use of coding region negatives is often criticized because they have quite different statistics from non-coding TSS regions resulting in an artificially simple promoter classification task. However in our results, the CDR SVM model trained with CDR negatives performed well on both the classification task and the realistic TSS prediction task. In the compact bacterial genome, some promoters may extend into the upstream gene. In such cases the use of coding region negatives will be helpful.

In the laboratory setting, the biggest problem in using PWMs and other classifiers is the high rate of false positives. When the expected FP/TP ratio is on the order of 1000, in-silico detection of bacterial promoters does not offer the biologist meaningful guidance for laboratory testing. Therefore it is particularly important to identify what the expected optimum FP/TP ratio is for any method. Table 1 gives the FP/TP ratio for each of our four models in their optimum configuration (point on DET curve closest to origin). Note that we have both increased the rate of true positives and reduced the FP/TP ratio from 517 to 187. These results suggest that SVM models can outperform PWMs for a realistically constructed promoter prediction task. The goal of our future work will be to further reduce the false positive rate to levels that allow efficient laboratory investigation of in-silico predicted promoters.

Acknowledgements

The authors are grateful to colleagues J. Hogan, P. Timms and S. Mathews for their input to and review of this work. We also thank administrators of the RegulonDB database [3] for access to their data, and Joachims [9] and Serrafini et al [10] for access to the SVM Light and GPDT software packages.

References

1. Lewin,B.: Genes. Wiley (1985).
2. Vapnik,V.: The Nature of Statistical Learning Theory. Springer-Verlag (1995).
3. Salgado,H., Santos-Zavaleta,A., Gama-Castro,S., Millán-Zárate, D., Díaz-Peredo,E., Sánchez-Solano,F., Pérez-Rueda,E., Bonavides-Martínez,C., Collado-Vides,J.: RegulonDB (version 3.2): Transcriptional Regulation and Operon Organization in Escherichia coli K-12. Nucleic Acids. Res. 29: 72-74 (2001).
4. Stormo, G.: DNA Binding Sites: Representation and Discovery. Bioinformatics 16: 16-23 (2000).
5. Schneider,T.D., Stormo,G.D., Gold,L., Ehrenfeucht,A.: Information Content of Binding Sites on Nucleotide Sequences. J. Mol. Biol. vol. 188 pp. 415-431 (1986).
6. Liu, H., Wong,L.: Data Mining Tools for Biological Sequences. J. Bioinformatics and Computational Biology vol. 1 pp. 139 – 167 (2003).
7. Hatzigeorgiou, A.G.: Translation Initiation Start Prediction in Human cDNAs with High Accuracy. Bioinformatics 18 pp. 343 - 350 (2002).
8. Leslie,C.S., Eskin,E., Cohen,A., Weston, J., Noble, W.S.: Mismatch String Kernels for Discriminative Protein Classification. Bioinformatics vol. 20 pp. 467-476 (2004).
9. Joachims,T.: Making Large Scale SVM Learning Practical. Advances in Kernel Methods – Support Vector Learning, B. Scholkopf, C. Burges, A. Smola eds., MIT Press (1999).
10. Serrafini,T., Zanghirati,G., Zanni, L.: Parallel GPDT: A Parallel Gradient Projection-Based Decomposition Technique for Support Vector Machines, http://dm.unife.it/gpdt/ (2004).

Exploiting Sequence Dependencies
in the Prediction of Peroxisomal Proteins

Mark Wakabayashi[1,2], John Hawkins[2], Stefan Maetschke[2], and Mikael Bodén[2]

[1] ARC Centre for Complex Systems
[2] School of Information Technology and Electrical Engineering,
The University of Queensland, Australia
mikael@itee.uq.edu.au

Abstract. Prediction of peroxisomal matrix proteins generally depends on the presence of one of two distinct motifs at the end of the amino acid sequence. PTS1 peroxisomal proteins have a well conserved tripeptide at the C-terminal end. However, the preceding residues in the sequence arguably play a crucial role in targeting the protein to the peroxisome. Previous work in applying machine learning to the prediction of peroxisomal matrix proteins has failed to capitalize on the full extent of these dependencies. We benchmark a range of machine learning algorithms, and show that a classifier – based on the Support Vector Machine – produces more accurate results when dependencies between the conserved motif and the preceding section are exploited. We publish an updated and rigorously curated data set that results in increased prediction accuracy of most tested models.

1 Introduction

A cell requires that each of it many proteins are localized to the appropriate compartment or membrane. Of the smaller cellular compartments, the peroxisome is an organelle lined by a single membrane, lodging essential enzymes for a variety of specialized functions (e.g. lipid metabolism). All peroxisomal proteins are nuclear encoded, synthesized on free ribosomes in the cytosol, folded, and inserted into the organelle via at least two pathways. The import process is not fully understood but involves receptor proteins in the cytosol which recognize a signal of the newly synthesized protein and protein docking complexes at the surface of the peroxisome. Several diseases are caused by deficient peroxisomal import (e.g. Zellwegger's disease), making the peroxisomal import machinery a prime research target.

The vast majority of proteins localised to the peroxisomal matrix rely on a short motif on the C-terminal end of the sequence called the PTS1 signal. PTS1 is often described as the tripeptide SKL with some substitution flexibility. Even though this motif is highly conserved in most peroxisomal proteins, it is also present in many non-peroxisomal proteins. Statistical analysis of the PTS1 transport mechanism has indicated that the last twelve C-terminal residues of the protein sequence are the most significant determinants of PTS1 peroxisomal proteins [5, 6].

M. Gallagher, J. Hogan, and F. Maire (Eds.): IDEAL 2005, LNCS 3578, pp. 454–461, 2005.

The PeroxiP predictor [3] uses a three stage process to predict peroxisomal localisation via the PTS1 pathway. Stage one makes use of existing predictors to eliminate sequences that are targeted to other organelles or are predicted to have a membrane spanning region[1]. Secondly, a motif identification module examines the C-terminus of the sequence and rejects all sequences without an approved PTS1 motif. In the final stage a machine learning module predicts whether the PTS1 bearing protein is peroxisomal. For this last step, PeroxiP employs a neural network and a Support Vector Machine that are trained independently and operate in union. The sequence is predicted as peroxisomal if either model indicates so [3]. Importantly, the models in PeroxiP are distinctive in evaluating only the 9-mer of amino acids that precede the PTS1 motif, implying that the specific PTS1 motif had no further information to offer. However, independent statistical analysis demonstrated significant correlation between positions -1 and -2 of the PTS1 with positions between -3 and -6 of the 9-mer [6]. As previous work in machine learning has failed to capitalize on the full range of the PTS1 signal, we develop a new, extensive but non-redundant data set and explore a variety of machine learning techniques. We show that dependencies between the 9-mer and the elements of the PTS1 motif can be exploited.

2 Sequence Data

Data for training and testing classifiers is collected in accordance with the methodology employed in [3] but from release 45 of SWISS-PROT. In brief, all entries with a SUBCELLULAR LOCATION annotation in the comments field that included any of PEROXISOM, GLYOXYSOM, or GLYCOSOM using a case-insensitive search were initially considered as positives. Each protein was also required to identify a MICROBODY TARGETING SIGNAL in the feature table, indicating a PTS1 target signal, resulting in an initial set of 202 proteins. The initial set was then filtered manually but conservatively for proteins not likely to be targeted by a PTS1 and for membrane proteins. An initial set of 573 negatives was similarly created, requiring a C-terminal tripeptide identical to one of the initially identified positives, and a subcellular location not specified as peroxisomal, glyoxysomal or glycosomal. By consulting the literature for suspicious cases, a few records appeared to be erroneously annotated in SWISSPROT and shuffled between the positive and negative subsets. The resulting data set had 206 positives and 564 negatives. Given this overrepresentation of non-peroxisomal proteins and to increase the quality of the data set, the negative subset was cleaned of all proteins whose subcellular location was qualified as POTENTIAL, PROBABLE, or BY SIMILARITY leaving 348 proteins, a sufficient size given the smaller size of the positive subset.

Both steps of redundancy reduction employed in [3] were performed. Highly similar proteins were first removed such that each pair of proteins differed in at least two positions in the nine residues preceding the C-terminal tripeptide. The

---

[1] The localisation of peroxisomal membrane proteins is governed by a separate set of signals [4], often consisting partly of a membrane spanning region

final stage of redundancy reduction was performed using BLASTClust (clustering on basis of pairwise sequence alignments). In order to reproduce a data set of the same size as in [3] we found that a similarity threshold of 1.675 was required. The final sequence data set, henceforth called the 2005-set, consisted of 124 peroxisomal proteins and 214 non-peroxisomal proteins. To ensure fair comparisons we also created what we believe to be a close replica of the data set originally used in [3] consisting of 90 positives and 160 negatives, henceforth referred to as the 2003-set (based on SWISS-PROT release 39.27).

3   Simulations

We conducted two sets of exploratory simulations during the development of the PTS1 peroxisomal predictor. In the first set of simulations we benchmarked a range of machine learning models on both the replicated 2003-data set and our new 2005-data set.

In the second set of simulations we took the better of the machine learning models and explored the effect of using different input window sizes. This was done in the interests of producing an optimal window size for the final classifier.

3.1   Machine Learning Algorithms

For the benchmarking study we used the WEKA library [7] and deployed the following machine learning algorithms: a naive Bayes classifier, multilayer and single layer perceptrons, Support Vector Machines, a k-nearest neighbor classifier and the C4.5 decision tree algorithm. The algorithms were evaluated using the Matthews correlation coefficient (MCC)[2]. We tested a range of encodings of which an orthonormal encoding gave consistently better performance for all of the machine architectures, thus all results reported herein were generated with this encoding.

The outcome of benchmarking machine learning algorithms is summarised in Table 1. In agreement with [3] the polynomial support vector machine performed

Table 1. The average MCC (std) over all models (5-fold cross validation over 10 runs). NB – Naive Bayes, SLP – Single Layer Perceptron, SVM(P2) – Support Vector Machine with Polynomial Kernel Order 2, SVM(G) – Support Vector Machine with Gaussian Kernel (var=0.1), KNN(1) – K-nearest neighbours (k=1), C4.5 – Decision tree algorithm (rev. 8)

| Data set | Machine Learning Model | | | | | |
	NB	SLP	SVM(P2)	SVM(G)	KNN(1)	C4.5
2003	0.30 (0.12)	0.40 (0.13)	0.46 (0.12)	0.38 (0.12)	0.43 (0.12)	0.23 (0.12)
2005	0.27 (0.10)	0.40 (0.11)	0.59 (0.09)	0.47 (0.09)	0.53 (0.11)	0.28 (0.12)

[2] The MCC is defined as $(tp \cdot tn - fp \cdot fn)/\sqrt{(tp + fn)(tp + fp)(tn + fp)(tn + fn)}$, where tp is the number of true positives, tn is the number of true negatives, fp is the number of false positives and fn is the number of false negatives. Higher MCC is better (max is 1)

best. The Naive Bayes classifier achieved the lowest MCC, which we conclude is due to the non-negligible dependencies between sequence positions. Also the C4.5 decision tree algorithm seemed unable to identify these dependencies and was only slightly better than the Naive Bayes classifier. The k-nearest neighbor classifier performed surprisingly well (second best) with a k-value equals one, indicating that the class boundaries are not strongly overlapping, thus the noise level of the data is quite low. We tested a number of neural network architectures, single and multilayer perceptrons, varying the number of hidden neurons. Of these, the Single Layer Perceptron (i.e. no hidden neurons at all) performed best, although the 2 and 3 node MLPs were very close behind (results not shown). The highest MCC was achieved with a Support Vector Machine with a polynomial kernel of order two. The linear and the Gaussian kernels were inferior.

Table 2. The average MCC (std) for Support Vector Machines with a polynomial kernel of varying orders. 5-fold cross validation over ten runs

Dataset	SVM(P) - Polynomial Order				
	1	2	3	4	5
2003	0.30 (0.11)	0.46 (0.12)	0.47 (0.11)	0.34 (0.12)	0.24 (0.12)
2005	0.34 (0.10)	0.59 (0.09)	0.59 (0.08)	0.47 (0.10)	0.37 (0.10)

In Table 2 we see that the optimum MCC occurs with a polynomial kernel of order 2. We noted that the specificity of the models increased with the degree of the polynomial kernel (advancing from 0.834 for order 2 to 1.000 for order 5 and beyond) as the sensitivity went down. Thus, in an ensemble of predictors a higher order may be preferred (cf. [3]).

3.2   Range of Inputs

The developers of PeroxiP exclude the tripeptide from the input window because the sequences have already been filtered for PTS1 motifs. They further argue that including the tripeptide would cause the prediction to be dominated by the PTS1 motif neglecting the information contained in the adjacent 9-mer [3]. However, if there are dependencies in the structure of the motif and the preceding residues, then excluding the motif from the classifier – as is done in PeroxiP – may be hiding crucial information. Some co-dependencies between the physical characteristics of residues appearing inside and outside the PTS1 motif were recently put forward [6]. For instance, Neuberger *et al.* note that "Variations of the hydrophobicity level at position -1 can be compensated by positions -3 and -2" (*ibid.* p. 571) and the -3 residue is outside the tripeptide motif. Amery *et al.*, on the motif ASL in protein Q9UHK6 state that it is "active [as a PTS1] only when preceded by a lysine residue (or likely a positively charged amino acid)" [1] (p. 1758).

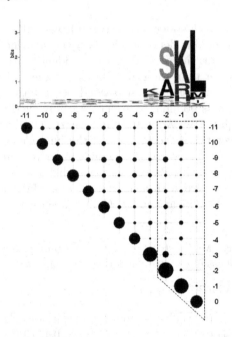

Fig. 1. A logo of the C-terminal 12-mer aligned with inter-residue dependencies

In order to obtain a deeper insight into the potential dependencies between the tripeptide and the 9-mer, we performed a probabilistic analysis of the maximal dependencies between locations within these last 12 residues.

The dependencies were extracted in the following manner: Given a set of aligned sequences $S = \{s_k | k \in 1..n\}$, where a sequence s_k is defined as a tuple $(r_{k1}, .., r_{ki}, .., r_{km})$ of residues, the dependencies D_{ij} between two positions i and j over all sequences in S are calculated as the maximum difference between the joint probability $P(r_{ki}, r_{kj})$ and the product of the independent probabilities $P(r_{ki})$ and $P(r_{kj})$:

$$D_{ij} = \max_{k \in 1..n} \left(P(r_{ki}, r_{kj}) - P(r_{ki})P(r_{kj}) \right) \qquad (1)$$

If two positions are statistically independent (or perfectly conserved) D_{ij} equals zero. Figure 1 displays the logo and $\log(D_{ij})$ [3] for the last 12 residues of the positive set.

The marked area reveals dependencies between residues in the c-terminal tripeptide and the adjacent 9-mer. Any predictor for peroxisomes which analyses the tripeptide and the 9-mer independently neglect these dependencies and is therefore expected to perform worse than a classifier which takes all 12 residues into account.

---

[3] A logarithmic scale was chosen to magnify smaller dependencies

In a final set of simulations we investigated the optimal window size for the classifier, both including and excluding the tripeptide. In all simulations excluding the tripeptide the classifier performed worse than those in which it was included, these results are summarised in Table 3.

Table 3. MCC (std) of the SVM with two different window sizes both including and excluding the C-terminal tripeptide. 5-fold cross validation over 50 runs

Window size	Tripeptide Included	Excluded
9	0.48 (0.03)	0.47 (0.04)
12	0.60 (0.03)	0.50 (0.04)

For the classifiers that included the tripeptide we ran a number of simulations for which the size of the window was varied between 1 and 20 residues. The accuracy of the models with different window sizes is shown in Fig. 2. In general, the classification accuracy increases up to a window of size 12, at which point the performance stabilises.

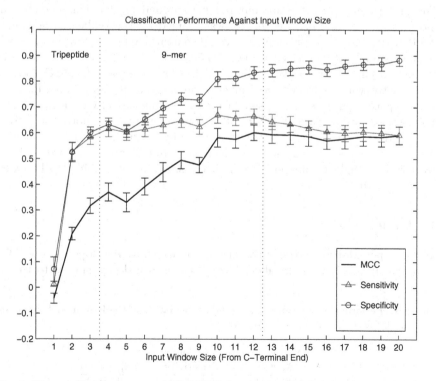

Fig. 2. The prediction accuracy of SVM(P2) for a range of different input window sizes relative to the C-terminus

3.3 Final Model

The overall structure of the model employs similar filtering steps as PeroxiP. Instead of TargetP, we use Protein Prowler – a subcellular localisation predictor with slightly better accuracy [2] – to disqualify sequences that are likely to be secreted. A motif filter rejects sequences with a C-terminal tripeptide not occurring amongst peroxisomal proteins in SWISS-PROT release 45, and an SVM analyses the sequence and classifies the protein as PTS1 targeted or not.

A scan by the Protein Prowler of the positive and negative sets (before re-dundancy reduction) showed only one protein, with a moderately high prediction as being secreted (0.82). The negative set, on the other hand, contained 100 proteins with scores above 0.82. 0.95 was chosen as a suitably high cutoff, including 74 proteins in the negative set.

Because no peroxisomal proteins are predicted to be secreted, the sensitivity did not decline by including this filter, however the filter increased specificity by an average of 0.034 (an increase of 3.9%) and the MCC by an average of 0.025 (an increase of 4%). Results were generated using 100 runs of five-fold cross-validation.

3.4 Results

The performance statistics for our full peroxisomal localisation predictor are shown in Table 4. When our model was trained on the replicated version of the PeroxiP data set it provided an overall comparable performance to PeroxiP. Emanuelsson *et al.* published values of 0.50, 0.78, and 0.64 for MCC, sensitivity and specificity respectively. Our model gives a comparable MCC, but has significantly worse sensitivity and much greater specificity than PeroxiP.

The performance increased significantly when our model was trained on the new data set, an increase of 29% in MCC. Interestingly, the reported sensitivity of PeroxiP still greatly exceeded that achieved by our final model. This suggests that a reasonable strategy for combined peroxisomal prediction would be to give greater weight to our positive predictions, and greater weight to PeroxiP's negative predictions.

4   Conclusion

In this paper we have outlined the process by which we developed a new PTS1 peroxisomal localisation classifier. The system uses a design similar to that of

Table 4. Performance measures and standard deviation of the final model (including filtering) 5-fold cross validation over 100 runs

Data set	Dataset performance comparison		
	MCC	Sensitivity	Specificity
2005	0.66 (0.03)	0.64 (0.03)	0.91 (0.02)
2003	0.51 (0.04)	0.52 (0.03)	0.82 (0.04)

the PeroxiP classifier, first filtering for other signaling peptides and then for known PTS1 motifs, finally using a classifier to predict peroxisomal proteins. Unlike PeroxiP, our model consists of a single SVM that processes a window of 12 residues from the C-terminal. In addition we have achieved three outcomes with this research.

Firstly, the development of a updated and highly curated data set for peroxisomal localisation via the PTS1 motif. The quality of this data set improved the accuracy of our final prediction system, measured as a 29% increase in MCC.

Secondly we argued and demonstrated that a PTS1 classifier should include the terminal tripeptide within the input window, even when input is prefiltered for known PTS1 motifs. The argument relied on existing analysis of the dependencies between the tripeptide and the 9-mer, as well as simulation based results showing that its inclusion improved overall prediction accuracy.

Finally, through a series of benchmarking studies we have established that a Support Vector Machine with a polynomial kernel of order two produces the best performance of all individual classifiers tested on the new data set. When trained on our replicated version of the PeroxiP data set, our predictor provided comparable performance to the PeroxiP model but with a simpler structure.

Acknowledgment

This work was supported by the Australian Research Council Centre for Complex Systems.

References

1. L. Amery, M. Fransen, K. De Nys, G. P. Mannaerts, and P. P. Van Veldhoven. Mitochondrial and peroxisomal targeting of 2-methylacyl-coa racemase in humans. *J. Lipid Res.*, 41(11):1752–1759, 2000.
2. M. Bodén and J. Hawkins. Prediction of subcellular localisation using sequence-biased recurrent networks. *Bioinformatics*, 2005. Accepted pending minor revision.
3. O. Emanuelsson, A. Elofsson, G. von Heijne, and S. Cristobal. In silico prediction of the peroxisomal proteome in fungi, plants and animals. *Journal of Molecular Biology*, 330(2):443–456, 2003.
4. J. M. Jones, J. C. Morrell, and S. J. Gould. Multiple distinct targeting signals in integral peroxisomal membrane proteins. *Journal of Cell Biology*, 153(6):1141–1150, 2001.
5. G. Lametschwandtner, C. Brocard, M. Fransen, P. Van Veldhoven, J. Berger, and A. Hartig. The difference in recognition of terminal tripeptides as peroxisomal targeting signal 1 between yeast and human is due to different affinities of their receptor pex5p to the cognate signal and to residues adjacent to it. *Journal of Biological Chemistry*, 273(50):33635–33643, 1998.
6. G. Neuberger, S. Maurer-Stroh, B. Eisenhaber, A. Hartig, and F. Eisenhaber. Motif refinement of the peroxisomal targeting signal 1 and evaluation of taxon-specific differences. *Journal of Molecular Biology*, 328(3):567–579, 2003.
7. I. H. Witten and E. Frank. *Data Mining: Practical machine learning tools with Java implementations*. Morgan Kaufmann, San Francisco, 2000.

Protein Fold Recognition Using Neural Networks and Support Vector Machines

Nan Jiang, Wendy Xinyu Wu, and Ian Mitchell

School of Computing Science, Middlesex University, London, NW4 4BA, UK
j.nan@mdx.ac.uk

Abstract. In this paper, a new fold recognition model with mixed environment-specific substitution mapping (called MESSM) is proposed with three key features: 1) a structurally-derived substitution score is generated using neural networks; 2) a mixed environment-specific substitution mapping is developed by combing the structural-derived substitution score with sequence profile from well-developed sequence substitution matrices; 3) a support vector machine is employed to measure the significance of the sequence-structure alignment. Tested on two benchmark problems, the MESSM model shows comparable performance to those more computational intensive, energy potential based fold recognition models. The results also demonstrate that the new fold recognition model with mixed substitution mapping has a better performance than the one with either structure or sequence profile only. The MESSM model presents a new way to develop an efficient tool for protein fold recognition.

1 Introduction

Fold recognition technique refers to recognizing structural similarity of proteins without significant sequence identity. One approach is to perform 3D-1D matching using protein alignment techniques. The accuracy of the approach relies on a substitution matrix that scores the proximity of the aligned amino acids. Some well-developed sequences substitution matrices [1] provide different symmetric matrices suited to align one sequence to another sequence at different evolutionary distances. They are essential for many structure prediction and database search techniques. However, some environment–specific substitution tables [2] take account of different structure environment to identify the optimal alignment between a probe protein sequence and the most suitable folds from a library of known structure. Many studies have been shown that by including structural information, the performance of fold recognition could be improved [2, 3].

Neural Networks (NNs) and Support Vector Machines (SVMs) are both machine learning methods [4, 5], which learn a pattern based on training data and predict on future data. They have been widely applied within the area of bioinformatics due to their astonishing performance. For example, Ding and Dubchak [6] employed ensembles of both NNs and SVMs in protein fold recognition. Each ensemble consisted of many two-class classifiers. Bologna and Appel [7] used a 131 dimensional feature vector and an ensemble of four-layer Discretized Interpretable Multi-layer Perceptrons (DIMLP), where each network learns all protein folds simultaneously.

M. Gallagher, J. Hogan, and F. Maire (Eds.): IDEAL 2005, LNCS 3578, pp. 462–469, 2005.

In this paper, a new fold recognition model with mixed environment-specific substitution mapping (namely MESSM) is proposed using NNs and SVMs. It consists of three main parts, as outlined in Figure 1. In the first step, unlike the environment-specific amino acid substitution tables that the structural environments are defined as groups, NNs are trained to extract more precisely structural information with a protein residue-level environmental description. The substitution probability of each pair of amino acids at any chosen structural environment can be generated and transformed into log-odds scores. A representative fold profile library is built on the substitution probabilities. We call this step as building fold profile library. According to consensus theory, the second step is to combine information from both the structurally-derived substitution score and sequence profile from traditional sequences substitution matrices (for example, BLOSUM30) to produce a mixed substitution mapping. The third step is to evaluate sequence-structure alignment by SVMs. We call this step as confidence evaluation. Thus, given a query sequence, it could be aligned with mixed profiles in the library using dynamic programming.

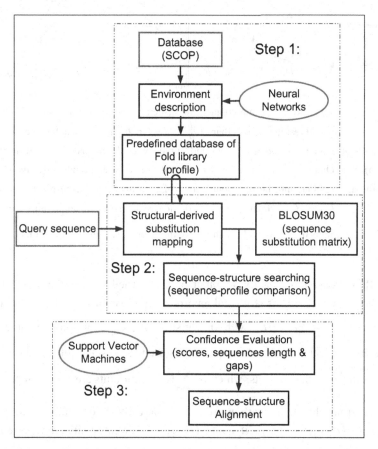

Fig. 1. A diagram of mixed substitution mapping for fold recognition. It includes three main steps. Step one is to build fold profile library, step two is to obtain mixed substitution mapping and step three is confidence evaluation

2 Methods and Materials

2.1 Building Fold Profile Library

Description of Structural Environments. The structural environment description in this research is on amino acid residue level and follows our previous work [8]. Each amino acid residue is described as main-chain and pseudo side-chain spheres. If the space between two amino acids is larger than one water molecule or a third residue, then they are regarded as neighbors and considered to have a contact. Thus, two kinds of contact are considered. They are side chain to side chain contact and side chain to main chain contact, as shown in Figure 2(a) and Figure 2(b).

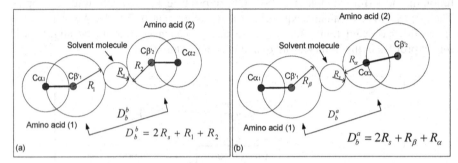

Fig. 2. (a). Side chain to Side chain contact: the distance between two pseudo side-chain centres of two amino acid residues is less than $D_b^b = 2R_s + R_1 + R_2$, which is the sum of side-chain radius of two amino acid residues (1 and 2) plus twice the radius of the solvent molecule (R_s). (b). Side chain to main chain contact: the distance between pseudo side-chain centre of one amino acid residue and the backbone centre of the other amino acid residue is less than $D_b^a = 2R_s + R_\beta + R_\alpha$, which is the sum of side-chain radius of one amino acid (1) plus the main chain radius of amino acid (2) and twice the radius (R_s) of the solvent molecule

Input Representation. Totally 45 input units are used to describe the features of amino acid residue with its structural environment. Given an amino acid a_i on protein sequence $S = a_1 a_2 \cdots a_n$ with known structure, C_{ij} represents the other amino acid a_j has contact with a_i. One input unit is used forl residue solvent ability, measured by sum of all the contacts, which is $\sum_j C_{ij}$. Four units are used to represent the distances from the alpha carbon to the alpha carbons of amino acid pairs of (a_{i-4}, a_i), (a_{i-2}, a_i), (a_{i+2}, a_i) and (a_{i+4}, a_i). Twenty units are represented the type of a_i, which is encoded by orthogonal encoding scheme. The left twenty input units are employed to encode the neighbor contacts of a_i [8].

The structure classification database of SCOP (v1.65) [9] is used to select training and testing data sets for NNs. 1150 pairs of non-redundant domains with lower than 40% sequences similarities are selected. 881 pairs are in the family level, 269 pairs in the superfamily level. All the protein pairs are aligned using structure alignment program-FLASH (**F**ast a**L**ignment **A**lgorithm for finding **S**tructural **H**omology of proteins) [10]. So, totally 190,603 residue pairs are used to train NNs, in which one-eighth are randomly selected for testing.

The NN Model. In this research, a fully connected three-layered NN is used to predict the probabilities of one amino acid residue with its environment being replaced by other amino acids. The NN has 45 input units, 30 hidden units and 20 output units. The input of 45 real numbers describes the amino acid type with its structural environment, as described above. The target 20 output of neural network is the substituted amino acid type, which is encoded by orthogonal encoding scheme. A back-propagation training algorithm is employed to minimize the mean difference between the predictions and the real amino acid types. An eight-fold cross-validation approach is used in the training with 10~20 times different initial weights and biases. The neural network with the best performance is chosen as the model to build substitution mapping.

Structurally-Derived Substitution Score and Fold Library. Our representative fold library is built on the basis of 3D-PSSM [3] but keep SCOP sequences only. For each sequence $S = a_1 a_2 \cdots a_n$ in the database of length n, where a_i is one of the 20 amino acids, a_i and its structural environment are encoded as input of the trained NN. $P(a_j \mid a_i, E)$, the probabilities of a_i replaced by each of the 20 amino acids a_j are generated from the outputs of NN. A log-odds score of the substitution is given by:

$$S(a_i, E \rightarrow a_j) = \ln(\frac{P(a_j \mid a_i, E)}{P(a_j)}) \tag{1}$$

where $P(a_j)$ is the occurrence of the residue a_j in the sequence. The higher the logarithm likelihood score is, the better residue a_i is replaced by a_j in the structural environment E. A profile matrix of $n \times 20$ is built for each sequence in the library.

2.2 Mixed Substitution Mapping

Following the consensus theory, a mixed substitution mapping is developed to combine the structurally-derived score generated from the trained NN and the sequences substitution matrix. Thus, for each alignment, if these two measurements agree, then positive consensus create a good alignment; if one gives a strong object, the alignment is in doubt even the second one shows a positive signal.

Suppose $S(x \mid y)$ represents the sequence substitution matrix BLOSUM30, and environment-specific substitution mapping given from the output of neural networks is $S(y, E \rightarrow x)$. The combined substitution mapping $M(x \mid y, E)$ is defined as:

$$M(x \mid y, E) = \mu S(y, E \rightarrow x) + (1 - \mu)S(x \mid y) \tag{2}$$

The parameter μ is a constant between zero and one. It is optimized using the Fischer's benchmark [11] in this research.

2.3 Confidence Evaluation

The classical approach to access alignment significance use Z-scores or p-values to recognize the best-fit templates [12], whereas GenTHREADER [13] and PROSPECT-I [14] introduce NNs to assign alignment significance. In Gen-THREADER model, a NN model is trained with the length of two protein domains, alignment length, the alignment score, and the scores of sequence-structure compatibility from pseudo energy function to predict the significance of the alignment.

Since SVMs have been demonstrated to have superior performance in various problems compared to NNs [6, 7], in our model, SVM is employed to evaluate the sequence-structure alignment. Therefore, given a sequence-structure alignment of two domains in SCOP, if the two domains are from the same family or superfamily, it is counted as positive samples (true), otherwise negative samples (false). Feature vectors are extracted from the outputs of sequence-structure alignment, which are alignment length, mixed profile length, query sequence length and alignment score. Totally 14533 pairs are randomly chosen from SCOP to train the SVM, in which one sixth pairs are used as test data.

The SVM still has a few adjustable parameters to be determined. SVM training includes the selection of the proper kernel function parameters and the regularization parameter C. Both linear and RBF kernel functions are investigated in this research. Polynomial kernel function is not selected due to its slow training. The predicted accuracy on test data reached 87.2% with the linear kernel function. However, the accuracy was improved to 90.7% using RBF kernel function. Thus, RBF kernel function is used with $\gamma = 5.0$ and $C=1000$ for alignment evaluation.

3   Experiment and Results

3.1   Optimization Parameter μ with Fischer's Benchmark

For the MESSM model proposed in this research, there is an adjustable parameter (μ) in the substitution score. The grid search method is adopted with Fischer's test sets [11] to optimize the parameter. A correct hit is counted if there are no incorrect folds having a better score than the expected match [13]. The optimization procedure is stopped when there is no more improvement on the maximum number of correct hit.

Fischer's 68 test sets [11] comprise a variety of structural types. The lengths of the proteins vary from 62 to 581 residues. Fischer's data sets have very low sequence similarity, but with highly similar folds, which are extremely suitable for testing fold recognition model. The highest success rate for our proposed MESSM model is 56/68 when μ =0.725. The result is the same as that of GenTHREADER [13] and SPARKS [15] (fold recognition model built on knowledge-based energy score combining with sequence-profile and secondary structure information).

3.2   Wallner's Benchmark for Fold-Recognition Sensitivity

The Wallner's benchmark [16] is built on a subset of SCOP (from class a to e) and contains 4972 proteins. There are 1543, 905, and 579 pairs of proteins in the same family, superfamily and fold respectively. The performance of MESSM is tested by checking whether or not the model can recognize the member of same family, super-family, or fold as the first rank or within the top five ranks. The identified pairs at different similarity level are shown as top ranks listed in Table 1.

Table 1. Performance of MESSM on Wallner's benchmark

Method	Family Only		Superfamily Only		Fold Only	
	Top 1	Top 5	Top 1	Top 5	Top 1	Top 5
MESSM	74.94%	76.37%	54.03%	64.86%	20.03%	35.92%

The sensitivity-specificity curves are drawn in Figure 3 and Figure 4. For comparison purpose, the results with sequence substitution matrix only (μ =0, called SSM) and structurally-derived substitution mapping only (μ =1, called ESM) are also computed. Figure 3 and Figure 4 demonstrate that with the structural information extracted by NN, the model ESM could obtain a better performance than the SSM with sequence substitution matrix. The new fold recognition model MESSM performs better than both ESM and SSM. At the family level, the MESSM model obtains a sensitivity of 72% at 99% specificity, whereas ESM achieves a sensitivity of 69% and SSM achieves a sensitivity of 63% at 99% specificity respectively. At superfamily level, the MESSM model obtains a sensitivity of 34% at 90% specificity. In contrast, ESM achieves a sensitivity of 27% and SSM achieves a sensitivity of 19% at 90% specificity respectively. Figure 4 shows that at fold level, MESSM achieves a sensitivity of 20%, whereas ESM achieves a sensitivity of 18% and SSM achieves a sensitivity of 14% at 90% specificity respectively. Our results are also compared with the best results of profile-profile method reported by Wallner et al. [16], which have a sensitivity of 72% at 99% specificity on family level and a sensitivity of 22% at 90% specificity on superfamily level. Though this is not a strict comparison due to the different confidence-evaluation method used by each model, it shows that our MESSM model performs well on protein fold recognition.

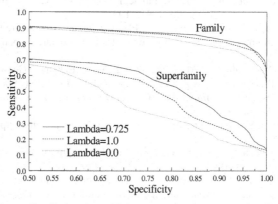

Fig. 3. Family and superfamily level specificity-sensitivity curves on the Wallner's benchmark

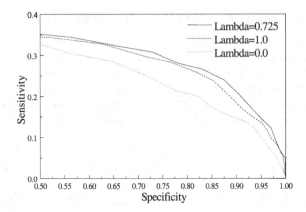

Fig. 4. Fold level specificity-sensitivity curves on the Wallner's benchmark

4 Conclusion

This paper proposed a new fold recognition model with mixed protein environment-specific amino acid substitution mapping using NNs and SVMs. With a residue level environmental description, NN is employed to generate structurally-derived substitution scores rather than the commonly used environment-specific amino acid substitution tables. SVM is used to evaluate the alignment significance for a query sequence. Tested on two benchmark problems, the model MESSM was found to lead to a good performance on protein fold recognition. In this work, residue-level environmental description is used to simulate structural information and is shown to be successful in improving performance on sensitivities compared with sequence substitution matrixes, but there might be a better approach to describe protein structural environment. More detailed environmental description at atom level might be one solution and might result in further improvement on the model.

References

1. Henikoff, S. and Henikoff. J. G.: Amino-acid substitution matrices from protein blocks. *Proc. Natl. Acad. Sci. U S A.*, 89(22): 10915-10919. (1992)
2. Shi, J., Blundell, T. L. and Mizuguchi, K.: FUGUE: sequence-structure homology recognition using environment-specific substitution tables and structure- dependent gap penalties. *J. Mol. Biol.*, 310:243-257. (2001)
3. Kelley, L. A., MacCallum, R. M. and Sternberg, M. J.: Enhanced Genome Annotation using Structural Profiles in the Program 3D-PSSM. *J. Mol. Biol.*, 299(2): 501-522. (2000)
4. Baldi, P. and Brunak, S: *Bioinformaics: The Machine Learning Approach,* MIT Press, Cambridge, MA. (2001)
5. Wang, L.P. (Ed.), *Support Vector Machines: Theory and Application.* Springer, Berlin Heidelberg New York (2005)
6. Ding, C. and Dubchak, I.: Multi-class protein fold recognition using support vector machines and neural networks. *Bioinformatics*, 17:349-358. (2001)
7. Bologna, G., Appel, R.D.: A comparison study on protein fold recognition. *Proceedings of the 9th International Conference on Neural Information Processing (ICONIP '02)* Vol.5 2492 – 2496. (2002)

8. Jiang, N., Wu, X. and Mitchell, I.: Protein threading with residue-environment matching by artificial neural networks. *Proceeding of the 2004 ACM Symposium on Applied Computing*, 209. (2004)

9. Lo Conte, L., Brenner, S. E., Hubbard, T. J. P. et al.: SCOP database in 2002: refinements accommodate structural genomics. *Nucl. Acids. Res.*, 30(1): 264-267. (2002)

10. Shih, E. S. C. and Hwang, M. J.: Protein structure comparison by probability-based matching of secondary structure elements. *Bioinformatics*, 19:735-741. (2003)

11. Fischer, D., Elofsson, A., Rice, D. W. et al.: Assessing the performance of fold recognition methods by means of a comprehensive benchmark. *Proceedings of the Pacific Symposium on Biocomputing*, 300-318. (1996)

12. Bryant, S.H. and Altschul, S.F.: Statistics of sequence-structure threading. *Current Opinions in Structural Biology*, 5, 236-244. (1995)

13. Jones, D. T.: GenTHREADER: An efficient and Reliable Protein Fold recognition Method for Genomic Sequences. *J. Mol. Biol.*, 287:797-815. (1999)

14. Xu, Y., Xu, D. and Olman, V.: A practical method for interpretation of threading scores: an application of neural networks. *Statistical Sinica Special Issue on Bioinformatics*, 12, 159-177. (2002)

15. Zhou, H. and Zhou, Y.: Single-body residue-level knowledge-based energy score combined with sequence-profile and secondary structure information for fold recognition. *Proteins*, 55:1005-1013. (2004)

16. Wallner, B. Fang, H. Ohlson, T. Frey-skott, J. and Elofsson, A.: Using evolutionary information for query and target improves fold recognition. *Proteins*, 54:342-350. (2004)

Support Tool for Multi-agent Development*

Hyunsang Youn, Sungwook Hwang, Heeyong Youn, and Eunseok Lee

School of Information and Communication Engineering Sungkyunkwan University
300 Chunchun Jangahn Suwon, 400-746, Korea
{Youn,eslee}@ece.skku.ac.kr
{hwangsw,wizehack}@selab.skku.ac.kr

Abstract. Recently, there is a massive use of the agent technology to develop the intelligent software and smart control module. In this paper, we propose a support tool for Multi-Agent Development, which enables the overall development time to be reduced. The proposed tool provides the general architecture constructed by components, interfaces, and functions of an agent an It also provides the extended Message Sequence Diagram for the communication of Multi-Agent. With the aid of proposed tool, developers who are inexperience in agent development can design and implement Multi-Agent rapidly.

1 Introduction

Recently, agent technology is increasingly being used for development intelligent software and smart control modules, such as those used to automate the process purchasing items in the M-Commerce domain [1]. IBM proposes the ABLE (Agent Building and Learning Environment) development tool for intelligent Agent for the field of Autonomic Computing [2]. JADE (Java Agent DEvelopment Framework) complies with the Agent Specification defined by FIPA as Java APIs [8].

Generally, an agent consists of three components. The first component handles communication with other agents, therefore deals with external operations. The second handles the internal operations of the agent such as inference, control, etc. Finally the agent also has an environmental interface for the purpose of interacting with the user or other software, with the exception of other agents. The internal operations of an agent are able to be designed using modeling language such as UML, however there is no suitable tool available to design the external operations involving other agents. Therefore, the implementation time is increased and developers need to have the extensive knowledge of the APIs involved and the good coding skills. In this paper, we propose a support tool for Agent development by assembling of the modularized code at design time. With this tool, the implementation time can be reduced and developers free to focus on the efficiency of the design and the customer's requirements.

This paper is organized as follows. Section 2 reviews related work. Section 3 presents the proposed approach. Section 4 evaluates our scheme. Section 5 concludes the paper and identifies future work.

---

* This work was supported by the Ubiquitous Autonomic Computing and Network Project, 21st Century Frontier R&D Program in Korea and the Brain Korea 21 Project in 2004. Dr. E. Lee is the corresponding author

M. Gallagher, J. Hogan, and F. Maire (Eds.): IDEAL 2005, LNCS 3578, pp. 470–477, 2005.

2 Related Works

UCM is a useful technique for building abstract designs describing scenarios [3]. UCM bridges the gap between the analysis of the user's requirements and the production of a detailed design. UCM operates at the abstract design stage and allows estimation of the performance including the latencies by transformation to the LQN (Layered Queuing Network) [4] [6]. However, UML tends to be most useful in presenting the details of the software design. And it is also able to analyze the performance of software by transformation technique to the LQN [5] [6] [7]. Therefore, UCM is useful for capturing the interaction between agents and their organizational or architectural structure, but it is not useful for the implementation in a programming language. UML is suitable for describing the internal operation of an agent, but it is not appropriate to present the external operation between Multi-Agent.

The special feature of Multi-Agent technology is communication with other agents. In the multi-Agent environment, agents interact with other agents, and the message exchange between agents is described by means of a diagram which is similar to the Message Sequence Diagram used in many documents, such as FIPA Agent Specifications. So it is useful to employ Message Sequence Diagram, however the current Message Sequence Diagram have several defects, such as their inability to represent external operations such as "and", "fork", "branch" and so on. Consequently, a new notation is required to represent the external operation among agents, and it is necessary to support the use of modularized code in order to reduce the implementation time and to encapsulate the expert developer's skill.

In this paper, we propose a support tool for Multi-Agent development which is designed to reduce implementation time. The Agent designed by proposed scheme supports performance analysis at the design stage, and provides an automated technique for the generation of java codes which are consists of JADE API and java expression templates.

3 Proposed Scheme

In this section, we describe the design tool used to develop Multi-Agent. The scenario used for the interaction of the Multi-Agent agents is described at the stage when user's requirements are analyzed. UCM is useful for scenario design. The abstract design based on UCM is able to be used to estimate the performance with regard to the interaction between the agents. When the abstract design is completed, the developer designs the external operation between Multi-Agent and defines the components which make up an agent. The developer is able to obtain an optimized design, because proposed scheme supports performance analysis at the design stages.

In this paper, we use UCM to design the scenario regarding interactions between the Multi-Agent. Although UCM allows for the use of various notations, the full notation of UCM is not needed in this particular case. Fig. 1 shows the subset of the UCM notation which is used in this paper and which is sufficient to design the Multi-Agent [4]. A Start point represents the beginning of a causal path and one should imagine this point as being a source of "tokens" that follow this path. An end point terminates the causal path, while an *OR-fork* represents a probabilistic alternative at which a token may travel one way or another. Two or more paths may come together in an

OR-join. A token arriving at an *AND-fork* generates multiple, concurrent tokens, one for each output path. An *AND-join* requires the token to wait until another token arrives at each of the other joining paths. Finally, a token traveling along a path may reach a *Waiting Place* which cause it to halt a token until another token arrives along a trigger path.

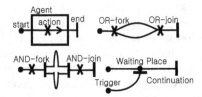

Fig. 1. UCM notation for Multi-Agent Design

name	notation
AND-fork	
OR-join	
N-way	PERFORMATIVE (N:M)
reply to	< >
reply-with (in reply to)	< >
reply by	
internal operation	int:methodName()
external operation	ext:PERFORMATIVE
envrionment	env:methodName()
DF publishing	dfp
DF searching	dfs

Fig. 2. The notation used for an extended Message Sequence Diagram

When the abstract design is completed using UCM, we can design the interaction and interoperation among Multi-Agent. The Message Sequence Diagram developed UML is used to present the flow chart of the message exchange between the Multi-Agent. However, the implementation should be bridged by the developer. In this paper, we use an extended notation to complement the Message Sequence Diagram to present the operation of Multi-Agent. The extended notation is described in Fig. 2.

Additionally, we propose a general architecture which consists of External and Internal operations of an agent, the Environmental interface and the knowledge required for its internal operation. All parts of an agent are reusable because of component based development. Fig. 3 shows the overall architecture provided by our tool. Each of the components is reusable, and the External Operation component provides the interface to use other components. The External Operation component has the functions which interact with other Agents and control other component. The Internal Operation Component is to operation of an inner operation such as learning or reasoning. The Agent-Environment Interface component is to interact with environment like non-Agent software and user. The Knowledge is used by Internal Operation component. When abstract design is completed, developers perform easily the modeling of a certain agent through this Architecture in Fig.3. And then the developers design the operation of Multi-Agent through extended Message Sequence Diagram in Fig.2.

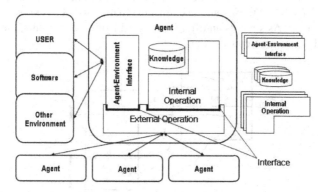

Fig. 3. Architecture of an Agent

```
● ⊢ or N-way

sender :
  private AID[] Agents =
    {new AID("Agnet1", AID.ISLOCALNAME),
      new AID("Agnet2", AID.ISLOCALNAME)};
  for (int i = 0; i < Agents.length; ++i) {
    PERFORMATIVE.addReceiver(sellerAgents[i]);
  }
  myAgent.send(msg);
receiver :
  ACLMessage msg = myAgent.receive(mt);
  if (msg != null) {
  }


● <?>

reply-with(send) :
  ACL fwd = new ACL();
  fwd.setReplyWith(msg.getReplyWith());
in-reply-to(receiver) :
  response.setInReplyTo(receivedMsg.getReplyWith());

● DF search

  DF AgentDescription template = new DF AgentDescription();
  ServiceDescription sd = new ServiceDescription();
  sd.setType("");
  template.addServices(sd);
  try {
    DF AgentDescription[] result = DF Service.search(myAgent, template);
    sellerAgents = new AID[result.length];
    for (int i = 0; i < result.length; ++i) {
      sellerAgents [i] = result.getName();
    }
  }
  catch (FIPAException fe) {
    fe.printStackTrace();   }
```

```
● Agent
import jade.core.*;
import jade.core.behaviours.*;
import jade.lang.acl.*;

public class BuyerAgent extends Agent {

  // Put agent initializations here
  protected void setup() {
  }

  // Put agent clean-up operations here
  protected void takeDown() {
  }

  public void action() {
  }

  public boolean done() {
  }

  protect void internalOPO {
    InternalOperation in = new InternalOperation();
  }

  protect void environmentInterfaceO {
    Environment Interface ei = new Environment Interface();
  }

● env methodNameO
  protected void request() {
  }

● —()→
reply-by(send) :
  msg.setReplyByDate(new Date
    (System.currentTimeMillis()+timeout));
reply-by(receive) :
  msg.getReplyByDate(new Date
    (System.currentTimeMillis()+timeout));
```

Fig. 4. Examples of the Modularized Code

We modularize the general expressions of the JADE code used for the conversion of the extended Message Sequence Diagram into actual code. Therefore, the developers are able to generate the codes based on the design. Several examples of modularized code are given in Fig. 4.

4 Evaluation

In this section, we explain the application of our approach, and we evaluate the capability of the code generation process. The scenario considered in this example includes Multi-Agent whose role is to sell books and CDs and other agents whose role is to purchase books and CDs on behalf of their users. The buyer agent is given the title of a book and a CD to buy and use this information to ask all known seller agents to request an offer. As soon as an offer is received from seller agents, the buyer agent accepts it and issues a purchase order.

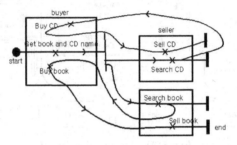

Fig. 5. UCM scenario design

Having bought the target book, the buyer agent terminates. The seller agents continuously wait for requests from buyer an agent. The abstract design used to represent the scenario is shown in Fig. 5, and the interaction design based on Fig. 5 is Fig. 6.

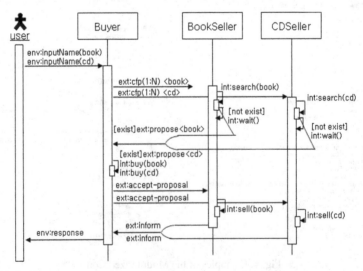

Fig. 6. Example of the Message Sequence Diagram

UCM and UML are able to estimate the performance, and the developer can design an optimized map through this performance evaluation. After the optimized Map is designed, the developer can rapidly implement Multi-Agent by assembling the modularized codes. The Fig.7 shows an example of the buyer agent implemented by the assembling technique. This example is implemented using Jade API and the Java programming expression. We can also implement the BookSeller agent and the CDSeller agent using this approach. If there are the available components for these-Multi-Agent, we can add the components for reduce development time. Although we have not the components, we can design the abstract of an Internal Operation component and a user interface component based on the design of External Operation component.

```
import jade.core.*;                                  for (int i = 0; i < Agents2.length; ++i) {
import jade.core.behaviours.*;
import jade.lang.acl.*;                                  CFP.addReceiver(sellerAgents[i]);
                                                         ACLMessage msg = new ACLMessage(ACLMessage.CFP)
public class BuyerAgent extends Agent {                  msg.setReplyWith(cd);
                                                         send(msg);
    protected void setup() {                         }
    }
                                                     MessageTemplate mt
    protected void takeDown() {                         = MessageTemplate.MatchPerformative(ACLMessage.PROPOSE);
    }                                                ACLMessage msg = BuyerAgent.receive(mt);
                                                     if (msg != null) {
    public void action() {                           }
        ACLMessage msg = new ACLMessage(ACLMessage.CFP)
                                                     ACLMessage msg = new ACLMessage(ACLMessage.ACCEPT-PROPOSAL);
    private AID[] Agents1 = ();                       send(msg);

    for (int i = 0; i < Agents1.length; ++i) {       ACLMessage msg1 = new ACLMessage(ACLMessage.ACCEPT-PROPOSAL);
                                                      send(msg1);
        CFP.addReceiver(sellerAgents[i]);        }
        ACLMessage msg = new ACLMessage(ACLMessage.CFP)
        msg.setReplyWith(book);              public boolean done() {
                                                 return true;
        send(msg);                           }
    }
                                             protected void buy() {
    private AID[] Agents2 = ();              }
```

Fig. 7. Implementation of the BuyerAgent

The level of the code generation is described by table 1 and table 2 and table 3. The classes and the methods and the codes for the External Operation are considerably implemented, however only the main classes and methods of the methods of the components are implemented for the internal operations and user's interface.

Table 1. Capability of the Code generation of Buyer Agent

⟨Buyer⟩		External Operation			Internal Operation			Agent–Environment Interface		
		CbH	PT	UML	CbH	PT	UML	CbH	PT	UML
Class	P	1	1	1	2	1	2	2	1	2
	M									
Method	P	6	6	6	4	1		3	2	
	M						4			3
Expression (LoC)	P		9(LoC)							
	M	47(LoC)	12(LoC)		30(LoC)			32(LoC)		
	N		5(LoC)							
PT: Proposed Tool P: Perfection M: Modification N: can Not use CbH: Coded by Human										
LoC: Line of Code										

Table 2. Capability of the Code generation of CDSeller Agent

<CDSeller>		External Operation			Internal Operation		
		CbH	PT	UML	CbH	PT	UML
Class	P	1	1	1	2	1	2
	M						
Method	P	7	6	6	4	2	
	M		1	1			4
Expression (LoC)	P		8(LoC)				
	M	29(LoC)	11(LoC)		30(LoC)		
	N		4(LoC)				

Table 3. Capability of the Code generation of BookSeller Agent

<BookSeller>		External Operation			Internal Operation		
		CbH	PT	UML	CbH	PT	UML
Class	P	1	1	1	2	1	2
	M						
Method	P	7	6	6	4	2	
	M		1	1			4
Expression (LoC)	P		8(LoC)				
	M	29(LoC)	11(LoC)		30(LoC)		
	N		4(LoC)				

We evaluate the proposed tool compared with implemented code by human, and we also compare the proposed tool with the generated code by UML. We realize that proposed tool is useful for modeling External Operation but we can use more usefully UML for modeling Internal Operation.

5 Conclusion

In this paper, we proposed a support tool for the Multi-Agent development. The advantages of this system are as follows. Firstly, developers who have little knowledge of the Agent development API can implement Multi-Agent easily based on the extended Message Sequence Diagram. Secondly, overall development time is reduced by component integration and source code generation. Finally, when no existing components are available, the proposed architecture supports the abstract design through defining required function for an Internal Operation component and an Environment Interface in External Operation component. Therefore, the developers do not require a high level of skill and the overall development time is reduced as a result of the code generation process.

However, further research is needed in order to design and implement the components, except for the External Operation component. To design these components, it is currently necessary to use UML, because the proposed scheme does not define all of the functions in the components. In short, the tool proposed in this paper helps to design the internal functions and external communication modules of Multi-Agent, before carrying out the detailed design of the Internal Operation and the Environment Interface using UML.

References

1. M. Younas, K-M Chao, R. Anane: The M-Commerce Transaction Management with Multi-Agent Support. Proceedings of the17th IEEE International Conference on Advanced Information Networking and Applications (AINA'03) (2003)

2. J. P. Bigus, D. A. Schlosnagle, J. R. Pilgrim, W. N. Mills III, Y. Diao: ABLE: A toolkit for building multiagent autonomic systems. IBM SYSTEMS JOURNAL, VOL 41, NO 3, (2002)
3. Buhr, R.J.A. and Casselman, R.S.: Use Case Maps for Object-Oriented Systems, Prentice-Hall, USA, (1995). http://www.UseCaseMaps.org/UseCaseMaps/pub/UCM_book95.pdf
4. Edward A. Billard.: Patterns of Agent Interaction Scenarios as Use Case Maps. IEEE TRANSACTIONS ON SYSTEMS, MAN, AND CYBERNETICS–PART B: CYBERNETICS, VOL. 34, NO. 4, (2004)
5. J. A. Rolia, K. C. Sevcik.: The Method of Layers. IEEE Transactions on Software Engineering, Volume 21, Issue 8, August (1995)
6. Hesham El-Sayed, Don Cameron, Murray Woodside.: Automation Support for Software Performance. ACM SIGMETRICS Performance Evaluation Review, Volume 29, Issue 1, June (2001)
7. Simonetta Balsamo, Antinisca Di Marco, Paola Inverardi, Member, IEEE, and Marta Simeoni.: Model-Based Performance Prediction in Software Development: A Survey. IEEE TRANSACTIONS ON SOFTWARE ENGINEERING, VOL. 30, NO. 5, MAY (2004)
8. Giovanni Caire (TILAB, formerly CSELT).: JADE TUTORIAL JADE PROGRAMMING FOR BEGINNERS, 04 December (2003)

A Hybrid Agent Architecture
for Modeling Autonomous Agents in SAGE

Amina Tariq[1], Amna Basharat[1], H. Farooq Ahmad[2], Hiroki Suguri[2], and Arshad Ali[3]

[1] National University of Science and Technology, Pakistan
{amina_tariq,aam_naa}@hotmail.com
[2] Communication Technologies, Japan
{farooq,suguri}@comtec.co.jp
[3] NUST Institute of Information Technology, Pakistan
arshad.ali@niit.edu.pk

Abstract. This paper highlights the Hybrid agent construction model being developed that allows the description and development of autonomous agents in SAGE (Scalable, fault Tolerant Agent Grooming Environment) – a second generation FIPA-Compliant Multi-Agent system. We aim to provide the programmer with a generic and well defined agent architecture enabling the development of sophisticated agents on SAGE, possessing the desired properties of autonomous agents – reactivity, pro-activity, social ability and knowledge based reasoning.

Keywords: Autonomous agents, MAS, Intelligent Agent, Agent Architecture, Hybrid Agent

1 Introduction

Multi-Agent Systems (MASs) are based on the idea that a cooperative working environment comprising synergistic software components can cope with problems which are hard to solve using the traditional centralized approach to computation [12]. Smaller software entities – software agents – with special capabilities (autonomous, reactive, pro-active and social) are used instead to interact in a flexible and dynamic way to solve problems more efficiently [24]. Agent architectures are the fundamental engines underlying the autonomous components that support effective behavior in real-world, dynamic and open environments. Initial efforts in the field of agent-based computing focused on the development of intelligent agent architectures, and the early years established several lasting styles of architecture. These range from purely *reactive* agents that operate in a simple stimulus-response fashion, at one extreme, to more *deliberative* agents that reason about their actions, such as the class of belief desire intention (BDI) agents [23] that are increasingly prevalent, at the other extreme. In between the two lie *hybrid* combinations of both, or *layered* architectures, which attempt to involve both reaction and deliberation in an effort to adopt the best of each approach. Increasingly more sophisticated agents than the traditional BDI kind are have also been developed, but the benefits of the increased sophistication is largely confined to well-defined areas of need rather than offering general solutions [15].

M. Gallagher, J. Hogan, and F. Maire (Eds.): IDEAL 2005, LNCS 3578, pp. 478–485, 2005.

MAS frameworks attempt to provide programmer with reusable agent-oriented classes which share useful relationships. FIPAOS [7], JADE [4], and Zeus [6] are all open source Java based First generation MAS frameworks implementing to varying degrees, FIPA (Foundation for Intelligent Physical Agents) [5] compliant agent Systems. They all have a core behavior subsystem that includes an execution process, ACL message interface agent behavior engine, and corresponding primitive processing objects [13].

SAGE [1, 2], a second generation FIPA-compliant MAS is being developed at the NUST-COMTEC labs. The SAGE supports a modular and extensible approach to design complex information systems, which require services of multiple autonomous agents having diverse capabilities and needs. These capabilities of agents are to be defined in agent's internal architecture. The challenge is to provide an agent API that is equipped with fundamental capabilities that an autonomous agent must possess to participate in the default society chosen by the MAS developers. The aim is to provide features for developing intelligent, distributed, and autonomous software using agents as the unit of encapsulation.

The remainder of this paper is organized as follows: Section 2 begins by giving the conceptualization of our Agent Architecture and the design of our proposed model. Section 3 and Section 4 discuss the design of its key components in detail, followed by concluding remarks in Section 5.

2 Conceptualization of Agent Architecture

For the agents in SAGE the strong notion of agency suggested in [8, 15] was adapted. It was analyzed that the agents must possess reactivity, proactivity, social ability, self-learning and adaptability. Thus a complete notion of a hybrid agent [15] was conceived. To incorporate these skills in SAGE agents such an agent architecture was required that should be enable the agents to carry out their tasks in a concurrent manner efficiently. To enable the agent reactivity it was realized that certain minimal behavioral support is also required at the architecture level. Since agents are highly social entities, the support for high level agent conversations was also taken as a must to be provided by the Agent Architecture. Furthermore, in order to endow the SAGE Agents with the capability of reasoning and adaptation, it was conceived that a reasoning engine should be provided as an ingredient of the Agent Architecture. As a consequence, it the Agent Architecture for SAGE was designed be a hybrid architecture – mix of deliberative and reactive architectures.

The high-level functional architecture on which the actual agent architecture for SAGE is based on is pictured in Figure 1, inspired by Bell's model of Rational Agent suggested in [10].

A Hybrid agent is embedded in the real world, and consists of two connected modules: a low-level (procedural) action sub-system termed Behaviour Engine and a high-level (symbolic) reasoning system termed Reasoning Engine. The Behaviour Engine theoretically consists of Execution and communication controllers along with sensors and effectors. This system represents the agent's functional and non-functional capacities and skills ("know how"). They receive high-level action commands from the practical reasoning system, expand the actions to the appropriate level of detail and then execute them. The Reasoning Engine is composed of a module for theoretical reasoning – Theoretical Reasoning Controller and a module for practical reasoning-The Practical Reasoning Controller, each with an associated database. Theoretical Reasoning Controller is responsible for agent reasoning that is based on its beliefs only. Where as The Practical Reasoning Controller represents the agent's reasoning about what it should do and consists of a high-level AI planning system. In the next two sections we present the design and component level detail of these two engines.

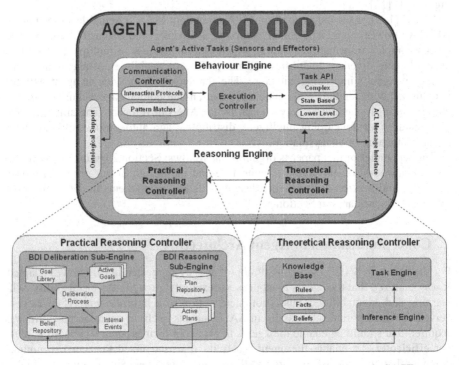

Fig. 1. Hybrid Agent Construction Model for Autonomous Agents in SAGE

3   The Behaviour Engine

The Behaviour Engine is responsible for reactive behaviour management for SAGE Agents by defining their range of internal behaviors and relationships with other agents. This section presents the complete conceptualization and design of the necessary modules of the behaviour engine namely the Task API, the Execution controller and the Communication Controller.

SAGE Agents are designed to possess complex life cycles, continually carrying on multiple threads of activity, and continually sensing and responding to the environment in which they are situated. The sensors are responsible for sensing the environment or receiving input from the environment, be it in the form of ACLMessages or any command generated by the system. Each SAGE Agent responds to the environment and carries out its actions through the set of effectors that it is equipped with.

The unit of abstraction used to model these sensors and effectors is termed "TaskUnit". TaskUnits provide the ability to perform lower level tasks to SAGE Agents where various TaskUnits basically encapsulate the actual role an agent has to perform Task Units provide means for multiple threads of activity and provide lower-level functional and non-functional behavioral support to the SAGE Agents. These are modeled as a user-level package termed as Task API, based on co-operative scheduling [3]. Task API- a library of tasks, provides the agent programmer with a set of Tasks that may be needed commonly by every agent in a society. The design of the Task API was based on the strong need for providing the support for lower level generic task management support to the SAGE Agents.

We have described Agent behavior for SAGE Agents by a set of Complex tasks each of which is accomplished when SAGE Agents execute certain State-based tasks which basically treat behavior execution in form of Finite State Machines (FSMs) or Hierarchical State Machines (HSMs). These further may be involved in the execution of more than one lower level Agent tasks which cannot be decomposed further and form the foundation of the agent behavior. These various task types are implemented hierarchically within the TaskAPI depicted in Figure 1. State-Based Task Modeling enables the SAGE Agents to respond to dynamic conditions of their environment. This notion not only necessary to embed reactivity and proactive-ness into the SAGE Agents, it is also seen as means to achieve high-level and enhanced social ability and the communication infrastructure for the agents.

SAGE Agents will typically be engaged in many activities simultaneously: participating in one or more negotiations at various phases of completion, proactively seeking inputs from other elements, and so on. In order to schedule their myriad activities, an Execution controller has been designed. The main objective of execution controller is to provide SAGE Agents with a strong execution framework allowing them to carry out concurrent task execution both at inter- and intra-agent levels. We have previously described a light weight multitasking model for the core design of the execution controller for SAGE in [3]. The execution controller directly interacts with the Task API and the communication controller. It is responsible for scheduling of active agents tasks efficiently at the user level in a cooperative manner [3].

An important contribution for independent and autonomous behaviour of agents is the ability to communicate with other agents and software components. To facilitate this ability a communication controller was designed as shown in Figure 1. FIPA-ACL and its complete semantics has been implemented as part of the system framework of SAGE [1]. The ACLMessage Interface as shown in Figure 1 has been designed to provide a dynamic interface to the programmer to utilize the features of ACL Module. The ACLMessage interface provides reusable TaskUnits for sending and receiving messages to alleviate programmers from writing tedious and redundant code. The prime purpose of the Communication Controller is to provide high-level conversation management support to the SAGE Agents. A library of Interaction Protocols has been provided allowing SAGE Agents to communicate in a one-to-one or one-to-many mode based on FIPA-Interaction Protocol library specifications [18]. The protocols range from simple query and request protocols, to more complex ones, such as the well-known negotiation protocols e.g. contract net negotiation protocol or the market based English and Dutch auctions. The protocols are modeled based on the notion of State-Based Modeling for Conversation Protocols [17] modeled on top of UML representation of Interaction Protocols specified by Odell in [19]. Complex knowledge management domain may lead to complex interactions between SAGE

Agents. In order to support this complexity it is necessary to have a good support for content language and ontology. General support for ontologies based on a model of the FIPA-SL content language has also been made to facilitate programmer and also allow for intelligible and more meaningful interactions. The importance of Ontologies for interaction protocols has been previously highlighted in [20]. The FIPA-specified support for content and ontologies and interactions allow for content based nature of inter-agent communication. The content-based nature of the communication decouples the sender of a message from its receivers, and promotes a context aware and autonomous behaviour of SAGE Agents in the system.

The messages received through the Execution Controller are recognized and analyzed through the pattern matcher before being passed onto the Reasoning Engine for reasoning purposes. The Pattern Matcher also allows for Message Template building and customized message patterns for utilization in Interaction Protocols and for their semantic interpretation.

4 The Reasoning Engine

This section presents the complete conceptualization, design and implementation of the necessary modules of the Reasoning Engine namely the Theoretical Reasoning controller and the Practical Reasoning Controller designed to embed autonomy and intelligence into the agent.

4.1 The Theoretical Reasoning Controller

Theoretical reasoning is the reasoning of the agents that is directed towards their beliefs. Agents with the capability of theoretical reasoning of are often reactive, having the added capability of making inferences. Capability of theoretical Reasoning can be easily embedded with in the agents by making them to follow a chain of rules [26]. Rules are needed for expressing participant agent's individual decision making as well as the contracts that bind it to other agents. Nailing down the desired decisions is nontrivial and often involves incrementally augmenting a given specification. Likewise, contracts are frequently partial, especially early in the process of being designed [16]. This is the reason that rules are highly suited to specifying such decision making and contracts in the agent domain. Realizing the importance of Theoretical Reasoning with in the agents, a Theoretical Reasoning Controller was conceived for SAGE's Agent Architecture whose design was based on the concept of integrating the Agent Architecture with a rule based expert system. The main idea was to encapsulate expert system rules within the agents. Rule based Expert systems are well suited for the purpose of theoretical reasoning in SAGE agents because Rules make a compact definition of behavior possible as described above. Integrating an MAS with an Expert System (ES) allows building of such agents that have the capacity to "reason" using knowledge supplied in the form of declarative rules. For example agent toolkits such as FIPA-OS, JADE and JATLite have integrated expert systems to support complex reasoning [9].

The expert system chosen for the design of Theoretical reasoning Controller for SAGE is the Java Expert System Shell (JESS) [27]. JESS is a rule-based expert system which in its simplest terms, means that Jess's purpose is it to continuously apply a set of if-then statements (*rules*) to a set of data (the *knowledge base*). JESS is one of the efficient expert Systems as it uses a very efficient method known as the Rete algorithm, which alleviates the inefficiency generally associated with expert systems by remembering past test results across iterations of the rule loop [27].

For SAGE Theoretical Reasoning Controller is designed as a built-in Task Unit to, this Task Unit is designed to work in manner that for each received message, it asserts a fact in the JESS engine that describes the message. This allows a JESS program to control sending or receiving messages and creating or destroying Task Units in response to the message received.

4.2 The Practical Reasoning Controller

Moving ahead in the journey towards development of the fully autonomous SAGE Agents, we analyzed that autonomy of agents is directly related to their capacity to make decisions without intervention of the human users. We aim to endow the SAGE users with the need only to make relatively less frequent predominantly higher level decisions, which the system will carry out automatically via more numerous ,lower level decisions and actions. We see Practical Reasoning as the most prospective means of achieving self-adaptation for SAGE Agents which involves Planning, Deliberation and Goal-Directed behaviour [23].

The Belief-Desire-Intention (BDI) Model [21, 22] is seen as a preliminary means to provide a base for practical reasoning and thus self-adaptation. The relevance of the BDI model can be explained in terms of: i) Its philosophical grounds on intentionality and practical reasoning; ii) Its elegant abstract logical semantics and different implementations, e.g., IRMA, and the PRS-like systems, including PRS, dMARS, and iii) Successful applications, e.g., diagnosis for space shuttle, factory process control, business process management as suggested in [14]. The BDI model as shown in Figure 1, for SAGE Agents has been designed to support the event-based reactive behaviour as well as pro-active behaviour. This BDI incorporation within the SAGE Agents can further be extended with learning competencies for MAS situations. We have designed the BDI based Practical Reasoning controller as composed of two sub-engines. BDI-Deliberation sub-engine includes a deliberation process (as shown in) contains the deliberation process responsible for the analysis and processing of agents goals and beliefs. The Deliberation process has been designed keeping in view all the factors and considerations mentioned in [25]. Incoming messages, as well as internal events and new goals serve as input to the Deliberation process. Based on the results of the deliberation process these events are dispatched to already running plans, or to new plans instantiated from the plan library. The BDI Reasoning Engine is responsible for determining the deliberative attitudes, defined as plans. The Reasoning Engine determines these plans on the basis of the goals selected by the BDI Deliberative Engine. Running plans may access and modify the belief base, send messages to other agents, create new top-level or sub-goals, and cause internal events. SAGE Agents use the plan-library approach to represent the plans of an agent, instead of performing adhoc planning. The execution model for Practical Reasoning Controller is event-based. Everything happening inside a SAGE Agent is represented as event. Message events denote the reception of an ACL message. Goal events announce the emergence and the achievement of goals, and internal events report e.g., changes of beliefs, timeouts, or that conditions are satisfied.

5 Conclusions

In this paper we presented hybrid architecture for Agents in SAGE, a software framework to aid the development of agent applications in compliance with the FIPA-2002 specifications for interoperable intelligent multi-agent systems.

The Agent architecture of SAGE is written in Java language and comprises various Java packages, giving application programmers both ready-made pieces of functionality and abstract interfaces for custom, application dependent tasks. Java was the chosen programming language because of its many attractive features, which are particularly geared towards object-oriented programming in distributed heterogeneous environments.

This paper presents a coherent framework for the agent model for which FIPA makes no assumptions. It provides a coherent implementation of reactive and deliberative architecture. The architecture is aimed to serve as a useful basis to implement autonomous agents, The Theoretical reasoning Controller of our agent model permits an easy integration of external software e.g. that makes it possible to use JESS as agent reasoning engine. Such an agent model is more cohesive than the agent models offered by JADE, FIPA-OS or Zeus or JACK. In addition, we have given a generic implementation for more sophisticated agent models such as BDI and reactive architectures. The development of Agent architecture for SAGE has not yet terminated. Our intention is to enhance the high level agent architecture and test it with real world applications.

References

1. Abdul Ghafoor, Mujahid ur Rehman, Zaheer Abbas Khan, H. Farooq Ahmad, Arshad Ali, "SAGE: Next Generation Multi-Agent System", PDPTA'04, pp.139-145, Vol. 1, (2004).
2. Zaheer Abbas Khan, H. Farooq Ahmad, Arshad Ali, Hiroki Suguri, "Decentralized Architecture for Fault Tolerant Multi Agent System", ISADS, 04, China, April 5-7, 2005 (2004) (accepted).
3. Amina Tariq, Amna Basharat, H. Farooq Ahmad, Ahmad R. Shahid, Arshad Ali, Hiroki Suguri, "An efficient and light-weight Multi-Tasking model to achieve Intra-Agent Concurrency for SAGE", INMIC 2004, Pakistan, pp. 611-617.
4. F. Bellifemine, A. Poggi & G. Rimassi, "JADE: A FIPA-Compliant agent framework", Proc. Practical Applications of Intelligent Agents and Multi-Agents, April 1999, pg 97-108.
5. Foundation for Intelligent Physical Agents (FIPA). http://www.fipa.org
6. H. Nwana, D. Nduma, L. Lee, J. Collis, "ZEUS: a toolkit for building distributed multi-agent systems", in Artificial Intelligence Journal, Vol. 13, No. 1, 1999, pp. 129-186.
7. Poslad, Stefan et al. The FIPS-OS agent Platform: Open Source for Open standards. Nortel Networks-Manchester UK.(2000).
8. M. Wooldridge and N. R. Jennings, Intelligent agents: Theory and practice, Knowledge Engineering Review, Vol.10, No.2, 1995
9. Singh, M.P.: Know-how. In Wooldridge, M., Rao, A., eds.: Foundations of Rational Agency. Kluwer Academic, Dordrecht (1999) 81–104
10. Bell, J. 1995. "A Planning Theory of Practical Rationality". *Proceedings of AAAI'95 Fall Symposium on Rational Agency*. 1-4.
11. Allen, J. 1984. Towards a General Theory of Action and Time. Artificial Intelligence 23: 123-154.
12. N. R. Jennings. On agent-based software engineering. Artificial Intelligence, 117:277–296, 2000.

13. Steven P. Fonseca1, Martin L. Griss, Reed Letsinger Agent Behavior Architectures, A MAS Framework Comparison, Hewlett-Packard Laboratories, Technical Report, HPL-2001-332
14. G. Hernandez, A. El Fallah-Seghrouchni and H. Soldano. Learning in BDI Multi-agent Systems. Fourth International Workshop on Computational Logic in Multi-Agent Systems (CLIMA IV) Florida, USA, January 6–7, 2004. pp 185-200.
15. Wooldridge, Micheal J: An Introduction to Multi-Agent Systems. John Wiley & Sons, 2002.
16. Munindar P. Singh and Michael N. Huhns, Service-Oriented Computing, Wiley, 2005.
17. Griss, M.L., Fonseca, S., Cowan, D., and Kessler, R. Using UML State Machine Models for More Precise and Flexible JADE Agent Behaviors. In Proceedings of the Third Int. Workshop on Agent-Oriented Software Engineering. Volume 2585 LNCS. Springer-Verlag, Berlin, 2002.
18. FIPA interaction protocol library. http://www.fipa.org/repository/ips.html, 2001.
19. Odell, J., Van Dyke Parunak, H., and Bauer, B. Representing Agent Interaction Protocols in UML. In First international workshop, AOSE 2000 on Agentoriented software engineering, p.121-140, Springer- Verlag, Berlin, 2001.
20. Stephen Cranefield, Martin Purvis, Mariusz Nowostawski and Peter Hwang. Ontologies for Interaction Protocols. Proceedings of the Second International *Workshop on Ontologies in Agent Systems,* Bologna, Italy, 15-19 July 2002
21. Rao and M. Georgeff, "BDI agents: From theory to practice," Proceedings of the First International Conference on Multi-Agent Systems (ICMAS-95), San Francisco, pp. 312-319.
22. Rao and M. Georgeff, "Modeling rational agents within a BDI architecture," Proceedings of the Second International Conference on Principles of Knowledge Representation and Reasoning, Cambridge, MA, 1991, pp. 473-484.
23. Bratman, M.: Intention, Plans, and Practical Reasoning. Harvard University Press, Cambridge MA., USA (1987)
24. E. Mangina, Review of Software Products for Multi-Agent Systems, AgentLink, software report 2002.
25. Dastani, M.M., Dignum, F.P.M., & Meyer, J-J.Ch. Autonomy and Agent Deliberation. Proceedings of The First International Workshop on Computational Autonomy (Autonomy 2003-AAMAS-2003).
26. Adaptive Agents : http://c2.com/cgi/wiki?AdaptiveAgent
27. Friedman Hill JESS- Java Expert System Shell. http://herzberg.ca.sandia.gov/jess/

Toward Transitive Dependence in MAS

Bo An[1], Chunyan Miao[2], Lianggui Tang[1],
Shuangqing Li[1], and Daijie Cheng[1]

[1] College of Computer Science, Chongqing University, China
anbolangzhong@sohu.com, tlg@ctbu.edu.cn,
sqlee@cqu.edu.cn, djcheng@cqu.edu.cn
[2] School of Computer Engineering, Nanyang Technological University, Singapore
ascymiao@ntu.edu.sg

Abstract. This research investigates transitive dependence relations, an extension of direct dependence relations, in multi-agent systems. In this paper, action dependence relations are employed to deduct transitive dependence relations from direct dependence relations. Transitive dependence is useful in representation, analysis, and social relations reasoning between agents, groups, organizations, etc. Furthermore, in this paper, dependence relations are differentiated by both dependence property and dependence degree, which is useful in quantitative social reasoning.

1 Introduction

Socially intelligent agents are autonomous problem solvers that have to achieve their objectives by interacting with other similarly autonomous entities. Social reasoning mechanisms have been successfully used to design and build such intelligent agents. Dependence relations are believed to be the most crucial kind of relations in MAS. Dependence relations allow an agent to know which of his goals are achievable and which of his plans are feasible at any moment. This way, an agent may dynamically choose a goal to pursue and a plan to achieve, being sure that every skill needed to accomplish the selected plan is available in the society. Most social reasoning mechanisms are based on dependence relations. Dependence networks [3, 5]and dependence graphs [4] are employed to represent social structures and reason about goals, intentions, and actions.

Although there is much related work addressing the crucial and difficult issues of social reasoning mechanisms with dependence relations (called direct dependence relations in this paper)[3–5], transitive dependence has not been considered in the existing research. For instance, if an agent ag_i depends on an agent ag_j about an action a_1, and the agent ag_j depends on an agent ag_k about an action a_2, is there a dependence relation between the agent ag_i and the agent ag_k can be deduced from the former two dependence relations? The answer is definitely not. Then under what condition will there exist dependence between the agent ag_i and the agent ag_k? If there is a dependence relation derived from the two direct dependence relations, this kind of dependence is called transitive dependence. To overcome the limitations in current research work, this research

M. Gallagher, J. Hogan, and F. Maire (Eds.): IDEAL 2005, LNCS 3578, pp. 486–493, 2005.

advocates the importance of transitive dependence in representation and analysis of social relations, and addresses the crucial notions of transitive dependence and utilizes it in representing and reasoning about the dependence relations between agents, organizations, groups, etc.

Moreover, concerning there are various kinds of dependence relations in MAS, how to differentiate these dependence relation is an important issue in dependence based social reasoning, especially in a quantitative way. To meet this end, this research gives a definition of dependence degree, which is used to define dependence intensity (the higher the dependence degree, the stronger the dependence relation is). Dependence degree is a quantitative characteristic of dependence relations, which can be used in quantitative social reasoning.

The remainder of this paper is organized as follows. Section 2 proposes the original dependence theory and the definition of dependence degree. Transitive dependence will be discussed in section 3. A simple example of transitive dependence will be described with dependence graphs in section 4. In the final section, some conclusions are presented and ideas for future work are outlined.

2 Dependence Theory

A multi-agent system is composed of agents, agent environments, agent organizations, agent interaction and relationships between agents. As social reasoning mechanisms are based on agents' information about the others. Here we use a data structure kno_{ag_i} to store information of the agent ag_i.

Definition 1 *The data structure used by an agent to store information is:* kno_{ag_i} $=_{def} \cup_{j=1}^{n} kno_{ag_i}(ag_j)$, *where* $kno_{ag_i}(ag_j)$ $=_{def}$ $\{\{D_{ag_i}(ag_j)\}, \{A_{ag_i}(ag_j)\},$ $\{R_{ag_i}(ag_j)\}, \{P_{ag_i}(ag_j)\}, \{DP_{ag_i}(ag_j)\}\}$ *where* $D_{ag_i}(ag_j)$ *is the set of desires,* $A_{ag_i}(ag_j)$ *is the set of actions,* $R_{ag_i}(ag_j)$ *is the set of resources,* $P_{ag_i}(ag_j)$ *is the set of plans the agent* ag_i *believes the agent* ag_j *has. A plan consists of a sequence of actions with its associated resources needed to accomplish them.* $DP_{ag_i}(ag_j)$ *is the set of action dependence relations the agent* ag_i *believes the agent* ag_j *has. Each action dependence relation in* $DP_{ag_i}(ag_j)$ *is an ordered triple* (ag_i, a_i, a_j). *The definition of action dependence will be discussed later.*

It's obvious that agents must have some information about other members in the multi-agent system before reasoning about possible coalition partners. The information can be acquired in three ways: 1) *Passive receiving*. When an agent joins a multi-agent system, he must present himself to the others, sending some information to introduce himself, e.g., capabilities, resources, goals, etc. While an agent leaves the multi-agent system, he has to tell the other members about this. 2) *Active inquiring*. When an agent wants to know some information about a member in agent society, he can inquire directly about the member or ask for other members' help. 3) *Internal reasoning*. Agents also can get information about the other members by internal reasoning.

We call a depending agent the depender, and the agent who is depended upon the dependee. The object around which the dependence relationship centres is called the dependum [2]. According to dependence property, we divide dependence relations into strong dependence and weak dependence [7].

Definition 2 *(Strong dependence) Suppose an agent ag_i tries to achieve a goal g. $p(ag_k, g) = a_1, a_2, \ldots, a_n$ is a plan of the agent ag_k for the goal g. The agent ag_i has no ability to achieve an action $a_i \in p(ag_k, g)$, but he believes that the agent ag_j has ability to achieve the action a_i, then we call the agent ag_i strongly depends on the agent ag_j about the action a_i, i.e., $Sdep(ag_i, ag_j, p(ag_k, g), a_i)$.*

Definition 3 *(Weak dependence) An agent ag_i tries to achieve a goal g. There is a plan of an agent ag_k for the goal g, $p(ag_k, g) = a_1, a_2, \ldots, a_n$. The agent ag_i can achieve the action $a_i \in p(ag_k, g)$ by himself, but he also believes that the agent ag_j has ability to achieve the action a_i if he pays $offer_{ag_i \rightarrow ag_j}(a_i)$ to the agent ag_j. If the agent ag_i achieves the action a_i by himself, he should cost $cost_{ag_i}(a_i)$, and $cost_{ag_i}(a_i) > offer_{ag_i \rightarrow ag_j}(a_i)$, then the agent ag_i weakly depends on the agent ag_j about the action a_i, i.e., $Wdep(ag_i, ag_j, p(ag_k, g), a_i)$.*

The definition of strong dependence is the same as it is in most related work. Although weak dependence relation has not been addressed in previous research, weak dependence relations exist in multi-agent systems, as well as in real society. For example, a robot who is good at washing clothes can also wash dishes. Nevertheless it has to spend much more time than letting a dishwasher robot do it. Therefore, the clothes-washer robot can request the dishwasher robot to wash dishes, and it can wash clothes for the dishwasher robot. In this way, it helps to save the cost and to increase efficiency through cooperation between the dishwasher robot and the robot who is good at washing clothes. Another simple example is the Tireworld [1], where every agent can move tiles. After analysis of weak dependence, agents can save cost through cooperation.

As discussed above, it is desired to differentiate various dependence relations in quantitative ways, rather than only from the dependence property. For instance, in case 1, the agent ag_1 strongly depends on the agent ag_2 about the action a_1 (i.e., only the agent ag_2 has ability to achieve the action a_1); in case 2, the agent ag_1 strongly or-depends on the agent ag_2 and the agent ag_3 about the action a_1 (i.e., both the agent ag_2 and the agent ag_3 can achieve the action a_1). It's obviously that the dependence relations between the agent ag_1 and the agent ag_2 in the two cases are different, although in both cases, the agent ag_1 strongly depends on the agent ag_2. The reason is: in case 1, if the agent ag_2 declines to achieve the action a_1 for the agent ag_1, the agent ag_1 would fail to achieve the action a_1. But in case 2, if the agent ag_2 declines to achieve the action a_1 for the agent ag_1, the agent ag_1 still could ask for the agent ag_3's help with the action a_1. Thus, the agent ag_1's dependence on the agent ag_2 about the action a_1 in case 1 is much stronger than that in case 2.

We utilize dependence degree to differentiate dependence relations in a qualitative way. Suppose an agent ag_i tries to achieve a goal g. There is a plan of an agent ag_k for the goal g, $p(ag_k, g) = a_1, a_2, \ldots, a_n$. For the sake of simplicity, we assume the agent ag_i depends on the agent ag_j about the action a_i, i.e., $Dep(ag_i, ag_j, p(ag_k, g), a_i)$, and the dependence can be strong dependence or weak dependence. Let $Sdependee(ag_i, p(ag_k, g), a_i)$ be the set of agents the agent ag_i depends on about the action a_i that belongs to the plan $p(ag_k, g)$, and we have: $\forall ag_j \in Sdependee(ag_i, p(ag_k, g), a_i) \Rightarrow Dep(ag_i, ag_j, p(ag_k, g), a_i)$

Definition 4 *(Dependence degree) Dependence degree is used to describe how strong a dependence relation is. $Dd : Dep_1 \rightarrow [0, 1]$ represents the dependence degree of the dependence relation Dep_1.*

The main factors that have influence on the dependence degree include (take the agent ag_i's dependence on the agent ag_j about the action a_i as an example, i.e., $Dep(ag_i, ag_j, p(ag_k, g), a_i)$) [1]:

- Dependence property, i.e., strong dependence or weak dependence.
- Number of agents that the agent ag_i can depend on about the action a_i, i.e., the number of dependence partners: $|Sdependee(ag_i, p(ag_k, g), a_i)|$. The dependence degree decreases with the increase of dependence partners.
- Number of dependence competitors, i.e., the number of agents which also depend on other agents about the action a_i.

3   Transitive Dependence Theory

Here we propose a set of formal definitions related to transitive dependence.

Definition 5 *(Action dependence) Suppose the agent ag_i can achieve the action a_i, but he wants any other agent who depends on him about the action a_i to do an action a_j for him, and he has no ability to achieve the action a_j, then the agent ag_i has an action dependence on the action a_j about the action a_i, i.e., $Adep(ag_i, a_i, a_j)$.*

Let A be a set of actions. The agent ag_i can achieve the action a_i. If he wants any other agent who depends on him about the action a_i to do all the actions in A, we call this kind of action dependence *and-action dependence*. If he wants any other agent who depends on him about the action a_i to do any one action in A, we call this kind of action dependence *or-action dependence*.

Now we discuss transitive dependence. For the agents ag_i, ag_j and ag_k, $Dep(ag_i, ag_j, p(ag_m, g_a), a_i)$ and $Dep(ag_j, ag_k, p(ag_q, g_b), a_j)$. Although the agent ag_j can achieve the action a_i, but he has an action dependence on the action a_j about the action a_i, i.e., $Adep(ag_j, a_i, a_j)$. We can find that the agent ag_i transitively depends on the agent ag_k about the action a_j.

In contrast to the transitive dependence, we call the dependence relations defined in definition 2 and definition 3 direct dependence.

Definition 6 *(Dependence chain) Dependence chain is used to describe the transition process of transitive dependence relations. A dependence chain has a head and a tail. For the agents ag_i, ag_j and ag_k, $Dep(ag_i, ag_j, p(ag_m, g_a), a_i)$, $Dep(ag_j, ag_k, p(ag_q, g_b), a_j)$, and $Adep(ag_j, a_i, a_j)$, the dependence chain from the agent ag_i to the agent ag_k is $Dpc = ag_i \xrightarrow{p(ag_m, g_a), a_i} ag_j \xrightarrow{p(ag_q, g_b), a_j} ag_k$.*

---

[1] It's not the main intention of this paper to discuss how to calculate the dependence degree, which will be reported in future paper

For a dependence chain Dpc, $Head(Dpc)$ represents the agent at the head of the dependence chain, and $Tail(Dpc)$ represents the agent at the tail of the dependence chain. For an agent ag_i in a dependence chain Dpc, $ToDep\_act$ (ag_i, Dpc) and $Deped\_act(ag_i, Dpc)$ represent the actions that the agent ag_i depends on and is depended upon respectively[2]. For the dependence chain Dpc in the last paragraph, $Head(Dpc) = ag_i$, $ToDep\_act(ag_i, Dpc) = a_i$, $Tail(Dpc) = ag_k$, and $Deped\_act(ag_k, Dpc) = a_j$.

Definition 7 *Transitive dependence can be described as $Tdep(Depender, Dependee, Dependencechain)$. For the sake of simplicity, we regard the direct dependence as a kind of special transitive dependence, i.e., the agent ag_i's dependence on the agent ag_j about the action a_i that belongs to the plan $p(ag_k, g)$ can be described as $Tdp(ag_i, ag_j, ag_i \xrightarrow{p(ag_k,g), a_i} ag_j)$. Transitive dependence can be recursively defined as:*

For the agents ag_i, ag_j and ag_k, $Tdep(ag_i, ag_j, Dpc_1) \wedge Tdep(ag_j, ag_k, Dpc_2) \wedge ADep(ag_j, Deped\_act(ag_j, Dpc_1)), ToDep\_act(ag_j, Dpc_2)) \Rightarrow Tdep(ag_i, ag_k, Dpc_1 + Dpc_2)$, where $Dpc_1 + Dpc_2$ represents the connection of Dpc_1 and Dpc_2.

Definition 8 *According to dependence property, transitive dependence can be divided into strong transitive dependence and weak transitive dependence. $TSdep$ (ag_i, ag_j, Dpc) means the agent ag_i strongly transitively depends on the agent ag_j and $TWdep(ag_i, ag_j, Dpc)$ represents the agent ag_i weakly transitively depends on the agent ag_j.*

According to definition 4, the transitive dependence relation $Tdep(ag_j, ag_k, Dpc_2)$ in definition 6 should be strong transitive dependence relation.

As we regard direct dependence as a kind of special transitive dependence, accordingly, we regard the strong direct dependence as strong transitive dependence, and the weak direct dependence can be regarded as weak transitive dependence. Furthermore, the dependence degree of a direct dependence relation can be regarded as its transitive dependence degree.

Definition 9 *For the agents ag_i, ag_j, ag_k, $Tdep(ag_i, ag_j, Dpc_1)$, $Tdep(ag_j, ag_k, Dpc_2)$ and $Tdep(ag_i, ag_k, Dpc_1 + Dpc_2)$. If the agent ag_i strongly transitively depends on the agent ag_j, the agent ag_i strongly transitively depends on the agent ag_k, otherwise the agent ag_i weakly transitively depends on the agent ag_k.*

Definition 10 *(Transitive dependence degree) Transitive dependence degree is used to describe how strong a transitive dependence relation is. If the agent ag_i transitively depends on the agent ag_j through dependence chain Dpc_1, the transitive dependence degree of the transitive dependence relation $Tdep_1 = Tdep(ag_i, ag_j, Dpc_1)$ is $TDp(Tdep_1)$.*

Definition 11 *For the agents ag_i, ag_j, ag_k, the agent ag_i transitively depends on the agent ag_j, $Tdep_1 = Tdep(ag_i, ag_j, Dpc_1)$, and its transitive dependence degree is $TDp(Tdep_1)$. The agent ag_j strongly transitively depends on the agent*

---

[2] An agent may appear more than once in a dependence chain

ag_k, $Tdep_2 = Tdep(ag_j, ag_k, Dpc_2)$, *and its transitive dependence degree is* $TDp($ $Tdep_2)$. *If the agent* ag_i *transitively depends on the agent* ag_k, *i.e.,* $Tdep_3 = Tdep(ag_i, ag_k, Dpc_1 + Dpc_2)$, *its transitive dependence degree can be got by*[3]:

$$TDp(Tdep_3) = TDp(Tdep_1) \times TDp(Tdep_2)$$

Transitive dependence makes the following situation possible: if the agent ag_i transitively depends on the agent ag_j about the action a_i, the agent ag_j transitively depends on the agent ag_i about the action a_j, and there is an action dependence relation $ADep(ag_j, a_i, a_j)$, then the agent ag_i transitively depends on himself about the action a_j.

Definition 12 *(Self-dependence) For the agent* ag_i, *transitive dependence relation* $Tdep(ag_i, ag_i, Dpc)$ *is called transitive self-dependence.*

4 An Example

In this section, a simple example is given. Here we utilize dependence graphs to represent direct and transitive dependence. Firstly, some definitions are introduced, more detailed introduction of dependence graphs can be found in [4].

Definition 13 *A dependence graph* DPG *is an ordered triple* $(V(DPG), E(DPG), \Psi_{DPG})$ *consisting of a nonempty set* $V(DPG)$ *of nodes, a set* $E(DPG)$ *of edges and an incidence function* Ψ_{DPG} *that associates with each edge of* DPG *an ordered pair of (not necessarily distinct) vertices of* DPG.

1. *The set* $V(DPG) = V_{ag}(DPG) \cup V_g(DPG) \cup V_p(DPG) \cup V_a(DPG)$ *is the union of four disjoint sets.* $V_{ag}(DPG)$ *is the set of agents,* $V_g(DPG)$ *is the set of the possible goals these agents may want to achieve,* $V_p(DPG)$ *is the set of plans the agents may use to achieve their goals, and* $V_a(DPG)$ *is the set of actions that can be performed by these agents.*
2. *The set* $E(DPG)$ *is a set of edges.*
3. *The function* $\Psi_{DPG} : E(DPG) \to V(DPG) \times V(DPG)$ *is defined as follows:*
   (a) $\Psi_{DPG}(e) = (ag_i, g_i)$ *associates an edge* e *with an ordered pair of vertices* (ag_i, g_i), *and represents the fact that the agent* ag_i *has the goal* g_i.
   (b) $\Psi_{DPG}(e) = (g_i, p_i)$ *represents the fact that the goal* g_i *can be achieved by the plan* p_i.
   (c) $\Psi_{DPG}(e) = (p_i, a_i)$ *represents the fact that the plan* p_i *needs the action* a_i *and the action can't be achieved by the depender or the depender can achieve it but has to cost more.*
   (d) $\Psi_{DPG}(e) = (a_i, ag_i)$ *represents the fact that the action* a_i *can be performed by the agent* ag_i.
   (e) $\Psi_{DPG}(e) = (ag_i, a_i)$ *represents the fact that the agent* ag_i *has an action dependence on the action* a_i, *i.e.,* $ADep(ag_i, a_k, a_i)$, *where the action* a_k *is the origin action node of the agent* ag_i.

---

[3] Actually, there are many methods to get the transitive dependence degree, and the detailed discussion of this is omitted due to lack of space

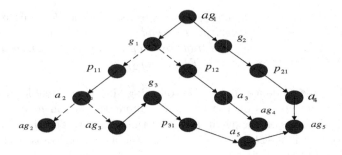

Fig. 1. A simple example of dependence graph

An simple example of a dependence graph is showed in Figure 1[4]. An agent ag_1 has two goals g_1 and g_2. For the first goal g_1, he has two alternative plans, $p_{11} = a_1, a_2$ and $p_{12} = a_1, a_3$. For the goal g_2, he has only one plan $p_{21} = a_1, a_4$. Suppose that the agent ag_1 can perform the actions a_1 and a_4, and the actions a_2 and a_3 can be performed respectively by the set of agents $\{ag_2, ag_3\}$ and $\{ag_4\}$. The agent ag_5 can also achieve the action a_4. If the agent ag_1 do the action a_4 by himself, he would cost more than the payoff to the agent ag_5 if he asks for the agent ag_5's help. The agent ag_3 has a goal g_3 and has a plan $p_{31} = a_2, a_5$ for the goal. Suppose that the agent ag_3 can only perform the action a_2, and the action a_5 can be performed by the agent ag_5. An action dependence relation of the agent ag_3 is $ADep(ag_3, a_2, a_5)$. In the above scenario, the following basic dependence relations hold:

$dp_1 = Sdep(ag_1, ag_2, \{p_{11} = a_1, a_2\}, a_2)$
$dp_2 = Sdep(ag_1, ag_3, \{p_{11} = a_1, a_2\}, a_2)$
$dp_3 = Sdep(ag_1, ag_4, \{p_{12} = a_1, a_3\}, a_3)$
$dp_4 = Wdep(ag_1, ag_5, \{p_{21} = a_1, a_4\}, a_4)$
$dp_5 = Sdep(ag_3, ag_5, \{p_{31} = a_2, a_5\}, a_5)$
$dp_6 = ADep(ag_3, a_2, a_5)$

According to dp_2, dp_5 and dp_6, we get a transitive dependence relation: $dp_7 = TDep(ag_1, ag_5, depchain)$, where $depchain = ag_1 \xrightarrow{p_{11}, a_2} ag_3 \xrightarrow{p_{31}, a_5} ag_5$. Because both the dependence relations dp_2 and dp_5 are strong dependence relations, according to definition 9, the transitive dependence relation dp_7 is strong. Suppose the dependence degrees of dp_2 and dp_5 are 0.8 and 0.7 respectively, according to definition 11, the dependence degree of dp_7 is 0.56.

5   Conclusions and Future Work

The transitive dependence is an important and useful phenomenon in the field of multi-agent systems, but it's ignored in the related work. To meet this gap, in this paper, we have addressed the crucial issues about transitive dependence relations in MAS.

---

[4] The or-dependence relations are represented with doted lines, and the and-dependence relations are represented with solid lines

As very first steps for computing transitive dependence and degrees of dependence, this research focusing on transitive dependence relations in MAS is far from being complete and formalized, and it's also a non-experimental (simulative) study. However, we believe that it might be inspiring for: 1) representation, analysis, and social structures reasoning in the field of multi-agent systems, 2) coalition formation in muiti-agent systems [1] and service oriented grid [8], and 3) quantitative social reasoning with the utilization of dependence degree, such as, cooperation partner selection, decision making of the order of actions, utility optimization, etc.

Future research concerning transitive dependence relations includes: 1) further analysis of the characteristics of transitive dependence; 2) transitive dependence based coalition formation; and 3) transitive dependence based quantitative reasoning.

Acknowledgments

The authors would like to thank Guido Boella, Leon van der Torre, Tom Mitchell and Luigi Sauro for their helpful suggestions on this research.

References

1. Zlotkin. G., Rosenschein. J. S.: Coalition, cryptography, and stability: mechanisms for coalition formation in task oriented domains. In Proc. of AAAI 94, (1994)432-437
2. Yu. E., Mylopoulos J.: Understanding "why" in software process modeling, analysis, and design. In Proc. of the 16th IEEE International Conference on Software Engineering, Sorrento, Italy, California, (1994)159-168
3. Sichman. J. S., Conte. R., Demazeau. Y., Castelfranchi. C.: A social reasoning mechanism based on dependence networks. In Proc. of the 16th European Conference on Artificial Intelligence, (1994)188-192
4. Sichman. J. S., Conte. R.: Multi-sgent dependence by dependence graphs. In Proc. of the 1st International Joint Conference on Autonomous Agents and Multi-Agent Systems (AAMAS'02), (2002)483-492
5. Inverno. M., Luck. M.: A formal view of social dependence networks. In Proc. of the First Australian Workshop on Distributed Artificial Intelligence, Lecture Notes in Artificial Intelligence, (1996)115-129
6. Boella. G. et al.: Power and dependence relations in groups of agents. In Proc. of IAT'04, (2004)246-252
7. Alonso. E.: An individualistic approach to social action in Multi-Agent Systems. Journal of Experimental and Theoretical Artificial Intelligence, 11(4)519-530
8. Foster. I., Jennings. N. R., Kesselman. C.: Brain meets brawn: why Grid and agents need each other. In Proc. of the 3rd International Joint Conference on Autonomous Agents and Multi- Agent Systems, (2004)8-15

494

An Architecture for Multi-agent
Based Self-adaptive System in Mobile Environment*

Seunghwa Lee, Jehwan Oh, and Eunseok Lee

School of Information and Communication Engineering, Sungkyunkwan University
300 Chunchun jangahn Suwon, 440-746, Korea
{jbmania,hide7674,eslee}@selab.skku.ac.kr

Abstract. Conventional adaptive systems have common well-known constraints when attempting to normalize environment. An adaptive system must contain a certain number of rules allowing such a system to adapt to specific situations. If there is an absence of a rule in a new situation, the system cannot take appropriate action. Building and managing such complex static adaptive systems places an enormous burden on system developers. In this paper, we propose a multi-agent based intelligent adaptive system with a self-growing engine. In this system, the *inference agent* evaluates input context with specific factors and analyzes the results. The *decision agent* selects the most appropriate action among alternatives available for a specific context and intelligently evolves and adapts by means of a self-growing engine (SGE). The SGE can evaluate actions and generate new rules by applying it to a practical situation using remote video conferencing with mobile devices such as PDAs, and PCs.

1 Introduction

Wireless Internet provides users with the possibility of accessing information wherever and whenever they want. Thanks to the continuous technological development of wireless Internet, we are now able to use high-speed broadband mobile communication services and global services, as well as the transmission of various types of information, including video. The development of mobile communication technology and the associated concept of *ubiquitous computing* have led to an increase in the use of handheld devices. However, these wireless devices have limited performance, such as a small display size, limited CPU and limited memory capacity. In addition, the environment in which these devices operate changes dynamically as the user migrates through various physical locations. In contrast to fixed networks, the performance of a device in wireless environments fluctuates often depending on where the user is located. Thus, research into adaptive middleware, which maintains an appropriate level of service in dynamically changing environment where resources are limited, is currently being conducted in a number of different institutions [1][2][3][4]. Most of these middleware systems operate between the media contents (image, text, video, etc.) provider and the end user, playing the role of analyzing a user's immediate environ-

---

* This work was supported by the Ubiquitous Autonomic Computing and Network Project, 21st Century Frontier R&D Program in Korea and the Brain Korea 21 Project in 2004. Dr. E. Lee is the corresponding author

M. Gallagher, J. Hogan, and F. Maire (Eds.): IDEAL 2005, LNCS 3578, pp. 494–500, 2005.

ment and controlling the service quality through the provision of various rules. However, most of these systems suffer from the drawback that they cannot cope with unforeseen situations for which no rule has been defined.

In this paper, we propose an intelligent adaptive system, which includes a self-growing function, allowing it to deal with unforeseen situations automatically by developing new rules based on the existing rules. This system abstracts the proper rule from among several candidate services depending on the context, and controls the content and intensity of the service as a function of the user's current tasks and device performance. Also, the system has a self-growing engine, updating existing rules, creating new rules and determining their suitability through feedback by observing changes in the system resources and the user's behavior.

This paper includes 5 sections. The comprehensive structure and modules of the system are described in Section 2, Details of the operational process and algorithm are provided in Section 3. The evaluation of the system through the implementation of a prototype is described in Section 4. Conclusions are made in Section 5.

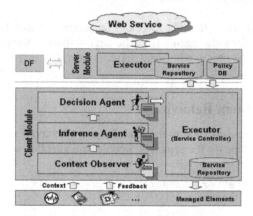

Fig. 1. Architecture of the Proposed System

2 Proposed System Structure

The adaptation in the proposed system is divided into two specific areas, media contents adjusting and system component reconfiguration. The overall architecture of the proposed system is shown in Fig.1, and consists two parts: the *Client Module* that is embedded in the client device and the *Server Module,* which operates on the server. Each module is composed of several components, as follows.

- *Context Observer (CO)*: The context observer acts as both an *aggregator* of the unique capacity and characteristics of the devices in order to create/manage system profiles, and as an inspector of the dynamically changing context information, i.e., CPU usage, network throughput, etc, so as to perceive the environmental variations. These profiles are described using W3C CC/PP[5].
- *Inference Agent*: The inference agent analyzes and infers the current situation based on the information collected by the *CO*.

- *Decision Agent*: The decision agent decides the appropriate countermeasures, based on predefined rules and analysis of the current situation conducted by the *IA*. It also has the ability to learn allowing the creation of adaptive rules as a result of process feedback.
- *Executor* (Client): The executor on the client side provides internal services required to execute applications and various environmental parameters according to the *DA*'s decision.
- *Executor* (Server): If an external service is needed by the client, in order to control its content, e.g. *page reformatting*, the *Executor* located in the middle stage server module provides this service upon receiving a request from the *Executor* on the client side.
- *Service Repository*: The service repository stores the various applications required to adjust the quality of the content, such as *image compression*.
- *Policy DB*: The countermeasures required for each complex context set are created and stored automatically in the *policy DB*. They are updated based on user feedback.
- *Directory Facilitator (DF)*: The directory facilitator acts as a *Yellow Pages* for the services supplied by the agents [6]. The agents register their services in the *DF* and use the *DF* to obtain additional services provided by external agents, whenever necessary.

3   Proposed System Behavior

The pseudo code corresponding to the overall system behavior is shown in Fig.2, and the behavior algorithms for the principal modules are as follows.

```
Step 1. Context Observer: Subscribe interest entities
Step 2. Perform monitoring
  Step 2.1. Collect system information, Creation of the Profile
    Step 2.1.1. if(change = true) then update the Profile
  Step 2.2. Collect dynamically changing environmental information
Step 3. Inference Agent: Interpret and infer the current state by
        analyzing various context information
Step 4. Decision Agent: Request the appropriate plan from the Policy
        DB
  Step 4.1. if(Plan = exist) then go to Step 5.
  Step 4.2. if(plan != exist) then find the most appropriate plan and
            adjust its intensity via various computations
Step 5. Executor: Executes the selected/computed countermeasure(=
        plan)
  Step 5.1. if(Plan = internal control) then the Executor in the cli-
            ent module adjusts the application/system parameters, or
            reconfigures system components
  Step 5.2. if(Plan = external control) then the Executor in the
            (proxy)server module adjusts the quality of the media
            content objects
Step 6. Creates/adjusts the plan in the Policy DB by monitoring the
        user behavior and changes in the system resources
```

Fig. 2. Pseudo Code for Overall System Behavior

1) Inference Phase

The *IA* periodically obtains the dynamically changing current context information from the *CO* and calculates various scores using the associated formulae, as shown in Table 2.

These scores are determined based on Table 1. To assess the dynamically changing environmental information, the event names defined in a related study [1] are employed, such as '*CPU_loading*(Float,%)' for CPU usage, '*RAM_freeSpace*(Int,MB)' for the remaining RAM capacity, '*Network_maxRate*(Int,bit/s)' for the current maximum transmission rate and '*Power_battery_Level*(Float,%)' for the remaining battery capacity in the device. An example of the result of the calculation is *Score set = {int CPU, int RAM, int Network, int Battery, ...}* and each device has a different score, even if the same values are collected, since most of the scores are calculated based on the specific characteristics of the device.

Table 1. Mapping Table used for Scoring

SCORE	Range of values
10	0.91~1.00
9	0.81~0.90
8	0.71~0.80
7	0.61~0.70
6	0.51~0.60
5	0.41~0.50
4	0.31~0.40
3	0.21~0.30
2	0.11~0.20
1	0.01~0.10

Table 2. Example of the interpretation of the Context by Scoring

Context type	Formula	Example	Score
CPU_loading	$1 - \dfrac{CPU_{loading}}{100} = CPU_{level}$	$1 - \dfrac{80}{100} = 0.2$	2
RAM_freeSpace	$\dfrac{RAM_{freeSpace}}{RAM_{size}} = RAM_{level}$	$\dfrac{20}{64} = 0.312$	4
:	:		:

2) Decision Phase

The *DA* searches the policy database for countermeasure corresponding to the score received from the *IA*. The policy database is located on the server side, increasing the response time, this is necessary because of the limited resources contained in handheld devices. If the countermeasure exists then the *DA* executes the countermeasure, if it does not exist then an additional procedure is executed to automatically create the required rule, as described below.

4 System Evaluation

Each module of the prototype developed for the system evaluation was developed mainly with C++ and Java, and WindowsCE on the two differently resourced PDA. Each PDA executed a '*Remote video conference*' application via the Web and a '*Ran-*

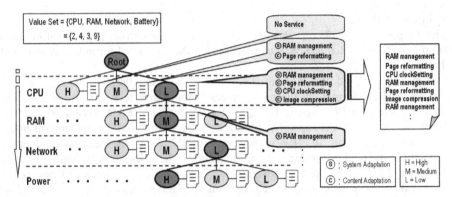

Fig. 3. Example for finding proper services using Decision tree

Step 1.	By following the tree, finds the list of 'currently available candidate service' described in each node
Step 2.	Removes the duplicate candidate services based on *resource priority* of running application.
Step 3.	Controls the intensity of the service based on the user preference
Step 4.	Finds services related with device characteristics
Step 5.	Adjusts the contents of the service according to the device profile
Step 6.	Executes the final countermeasure
Step 7.	Observes the system resources and the user behavior and receives their feedback
Step 7.1.	if (system resource = positive || user_action = positive) then stores current countermeasure to *Policy DB*, and add score 1 for this countermeasure
Step 7.2.	if (system resource = negative || user_action = negative) then searches for alternative countermeasures by re-executing Step 4 and Step 5, and subtract score 1 for previous countermeasure

Fig. 4. Pseudo Code for Decision Phase

dom process generator' to achieve system overload. After 10 minutes, according to the overload threshold of the CPU and RAM, '*RAM management*' and '*CPU_clocksetting*' were performed on the client side and '*Page_reformatting*' and '*Image_compression*' was performed on the server side for the *candidate service*. The final adaptive service shows different types and intensities according to each PDA's resource. PDA A, which had sufficient resources, performed '*Page_reformatting*', changing the video output from color to gray scale, PDA B, which had insufficient resources, performed '*RAM_management*' and high level control simultaneously, changing the video image to *Link* sentence. The corresponding rule was created in the *policy DB* for the current situation (i.e. *Score set = {2, 4, 3, 9}*) and for each device.

When subsequent, overload occurred, PDA A performed '*RAM_management*' and the contents of the policy ware modified (Learning from the observation of the result).

In this operational test, it is observed that the proposed system reduces the developer's workload by automatically creating countermeasures for unforeseen situations through a combination of the basic rules and calculations. In this way, the system is able to adapt to new complex contexts without any intervention from the developer. In addition, thanks to its learning ability, the system evolves in order to align itself to the user's preferences and device characteristics, by re-adjusting its rules based on feedback from the different tasks.

PDA A, which has sufficient resources   **PDA B, which has insufficient resources**

Fig. 5. The result for each different adaptive service depending on context

In this operational test, it was observed that the proposed system reduced the developer's workload by automatically creating countermeasures under unforeseen situations though a combination of basic rules and calculations. In this way, the system was able to adapt to new complex contextual information without intervention. In addition, the system evolved in order to align itself to the user's preferences and device characteristics, re-adjusting rules based on feedback from different tasks.

5   Conclusion

In this paper, we propose a *Self-Adaptive system* incorporating a *self-growing engine*, which selects and controls the most appropriate countermeasure automatically based on the *DA* and the *IA*, which analyze and interpret the current situation, and establish scores relating to the context and possible countermeasures. The objective of the proposed system is to solve the problems associated with the limited wireless computing environment and provide a method to create more efficient adaptive services.

References

1. Alvin T.S. Chan, Siu-Nam Chuang, "MobiPADS: A Reflective Middleware for Context-Aware Mobile Computing", IEEE Transaction on Software Engineering. Vol. 29, No.12 pp.1072-1085, Dec.2003
2. A. Friday, N. Davies, G.S. Blair and K.W.J. Cheverst, "Developing Adaptive Applications: The MOST Experience", Journal of Integrated Computer-Aided Engineering, 6(2), pp.143-157, 1999
3. Brian Noble, "System Support for Mobile, Adaptive Applications", IEEE Personal Communications Vol.7 No.1, Feb.2000

4. Wai Yip Lum, Francis C. M. Lau, "User-Centric Content Negotiation for Effective Adaptation Service in Mobile Computing", IEEE Transaction on Software Engineering. Vol. 29, No.12 pp.1100-1111, Dec.2003
5. W3C – Composite Capability/Preference Profiles (CC/PP), http://www.w3.org/Mobile, 2004
6. http://www.fipa.org/specs/fipa00023
7. Vahe Poladian, João Pedro Sousa, David Garlan, Mary Shaw, "Dynamic Configuration of Resource-Aware Services", 26th International Conference on Software Engineering (ICSE'04), pp.604-613, May.2004
8. Schilit, B.N., Hilbert, D.M., and Trevor, J. "Context-aware communication", In IEEE Wireless Communications, 9, 5, 46-54. Oct. 2002
9. Paolo Bellavista, Antonio Corradi, Rebecca Montanari, Cesare Stefanelli, "Context-Aware Middleware for Resource Management in the Wireless Internet", IEEE Transactions on Software Engineering, Vol.29, No.12, Dec.2003
10. Richard S. Sutton, Andrew G. Barto, 'Reinforcement Learning: An Introduction (Adaptive Computation and Machine Learning)', The MIT Press, Mar.1998
11. http://www.microsoft.com/windowsmobile/default.mspx

Autonomous and Dependable Recovery Scheme in UPnP Network Settings*

Youngsoo Choi[1], Sanguk Noh[2], Kyunghee Choi[1], and Gihyun Jung[3]

[1] Graduate School of Information and Communication, Ajou University, Suwon, Korea
{drabble,khchoi}@ajou.ac.kr
[2] School of Computer Science and Information Engineering,
The Catholic University of Korea, Bucheon, Korea
sunoh@catholic.ac.kr
[3] Division of Electronics Engineering, Ajou University, Suwon, Korea
khchung@ajou.ac.kr

Abstract. Resources or devices on the network might be unavailable due to serious network partitioning. To provide a robust network connectivity, this paper presents an autonomous and dependable recovery scheme using teamwork in UPnP network settings. For our scheme, we introduce a team of recoverable control points and corresponding recovery device, and, in case of network failures among devices, the recoverable control points autonomously take care of the devices to achieve their mutual goal as a team member. In the experiments, we tested our recovery scheme in terms of the recovery effectiveness. It turned out that the recoverable control point agent in our scheme successfully handled the events from the devices, regardless of one of recoverable control points being killed. We argue that our recovery scheme is fairly consistent, and the control point agents can recover from failures as quickly as possible.

1 Introduction

The Internet, the world's end-to-end communications network, is now pervasive in everyday's life. The users communicate with each other on the Internet, and also control any device through the Internet, if it is accessible. However, the machines or devices may crash due to hardware faults, for example, the breakdown of communication channels, or software faults, for example, the deadlock of protocols. These problems motivate us to develop an autonomous and dependable recovery scheme preventing catastrophic network partitioning.

To provide a robust network connectivity, we suggest a recovery scheme using teamwork [2, 5, 6, 8], particularly in an UPnP [10] network setting, which is a popular network architecture built on the top of TCP/IP. The control point of the UPnP is to maintain the network connectivity among devices, hence, it should be recoverable from network failures. In related work, Dabrowski et al. [3] simply presented the performances of UPnP and Jini [4] in case of communication failure. The critical issue is that the service-discovery protocols, such as UPnP and Jini, do not provide any recovery scheme. It is apparent, therefore, that we might need a robust recovery mechanism to improve the dependability of UPnP network.

---

* This work has been supported by the Catholic University of Korea, Research Fund, 2005, and by the KISTEP under National Research Laboratory program

M. Gallagher, J. Hogan, and F. Maire (Eds.): IDEAL 2005, LNCS 3578, pp. 501–506, 2005.

For our recovery scheme, we introduce new device type of recovery device and re-coverable agent of control point. The recovery device keeps track of the status of its control point, and the recoverable agent of control point replaces primary control point, if failed. Our scheme enables the recoverable control point agent in a team to autonomously get back from failures, and provides better dependability as more control points are actively working in the UPnP.

In the following section of this paper, we will describe the UPnP network environment and the details of our framework for autonomously constituting a dependable team to be recoverable in case of the failure of control point. Section 3 describes experimental results to evaluate our recovery scheme in UPnP settings. In conclusions we summarize our work and mention further research issues.

2   Recovery from Control Point Failure

Our online recovery scheme is based on a dynamic teamwork formation [2, 5, 6, 8], and built on UPnP settings. First, we will address the UPnP network architecture.

2.1   Components of UPnP Architecture

The components of UPnP consist of devices, services, and control points [9]. The devices provide services, and further could contain another device called 'embedded device.' In a UPnP architecture, the devices can be classified into several categories, according to their functions. The working group of the devices is equipped with standard interfaces to basically define the items of their tasks, which are stored in an XML device description document. The control points search the devices in the UPnP network, get the information of the services from the XML device description document of the devices, and register themselves into the event server of the services. The services use state variables to represent their states, and then they can be invoked through an action committed by a control point. Whenever the states of the services are updated, the event server of the services informs the subscribed control points of their changes as an event.

2.2   Autonomous and Dependable Recovery Scheme

We introduce a new type of recovery device and dependable agents which mean re-coverable control points in UPnP network settings. The recovery device keeps track of the status of its control point, and the dependable agents autonomously recover using teamwork [2, 5, 6, 8] in case that some of them unnoticeably fail.

In our recovery scheme, a group of control points keep monitoring their devices, and replace a failed control point with another control point. Thus, the goal of control point team is to maintain robust connectivity between themselves and their devices. For example, when a primary control point gets killed, any other agent in a team tries to make a connection to take care of the devices. If one of the other agents succeeds in forming a connection, the other control points perceive that their goal has been achieved, and then stop their trials. This recovery scheme, therefore, can autonomously proceed, and control points can robustly work on the UPnP setting in the face of their failure.

In the meantime, a recovery device informs the other control point agents in a team of an event in order to let the other control points know (1) the status of a primary control point and (2) the information of newly inserted or deleted devices. When the other control points have been informed that the primary control point is dead, one of them should be new primary control point to achieve the goal of the team. And also, the recoverable control point agent needs to let its recovery device know (1) its status, and (2) a list of devices.

In an example scenario, as depicted in Fig. 1, we assume that there are two pairs of recoverable control points (CP1 and CP2) and recovery devices (RD1 and RD2)[1].

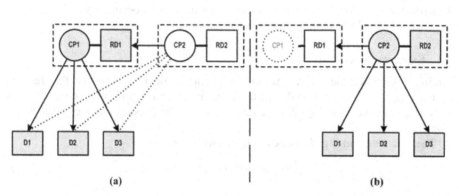

(a)   (b)

Fig. 1. Two pairs of recoverable control points (CP1 and CP2) and recovery devices (RD1 and RD2). In this example scenario, (a) the control point CP1 checks out the status of three devices D1, D2 and D3, and (b) immediately after the CP1 gets killed, the CP2, in lieu of the CP1, is capable of taking care of D1, D2 and D3

The primary control point CP1 receives the messages from the devices D1, D2 and D3, and passes its status and a list of the devices into the recovery device RD1. The CP2 in a team is another control point, and similarly, maintains the recovery device RD2. The CP2 searches only the type of recovery devices, and succeeds in finding the RD1, and constitutes a team. The RD1 repeatedly checks out the status of the CP1, and sends an event to notify the CP1's status to the CP2. As a result, the CP2 understands the current status of the CP1 and, due to the list of devices, knows that three devices are under the control of the CP1. When the RD1 notices that the CP1 gets killed, as depicted in Fig. 1 (b), the RD1 sends an event to a number of recoverable control points registered in a team. In our scenario, the only recoverable control point agent, the CP2, receives the message from the RD1. Even if the machine containing the CP1 and the RD1 fails, further, the CP2 can realize the catastrophic failure of the CP1 since the CP2 cannot receive any messages from the RD1 given a specific interval. To achieve their mutual goal formulated by their joint intention, for both cases, the CP2 autonomously contacts with the disconnected devices D1, D2 and D3, and returns to an original connectivity. Whenever the CP1 wakes up from its failure, the CP1 and the CP2 form a robust team as above.

---

[1] We made a scaled-up scenario simple for the clarity of presentation here

3 Evaluation

We tested our autonomous and dependable recovery scheme in terms of its recovery effectiveness. Intuitively, the recovery effectiveness presents how autonomously our scheme handles events occurred while control points get killed. We define the recovery effectiveness as a ratio of (the number of events normally processed/the total number of events occurred).

In the experiments, we measured the recovery effectiveness with two parameters: (1) the interval which the events of devices (D1, D2 and D3 in Fig. 1) occurred varied, while the duration which the control points (CP1 and CP2 in Fig. 1) got killed was fixed; and (2) the interval which the events of devices occurred was fixed, while the duration which the control points got killed varied.

3.1 Experimental Setup

During T seconds, the interval which the events of devices occurred, the duration which control points got killed, and the interval which the failures of control points occurred, as depicted in Fig. 2, were determined by the Poisson exponential distribution.

The parameters in Fig. 2 can be computed as follows:

$$F(x) = \frac{1}{\lambda}\ln(1-x), \tag{1}$$

where
- x is a random variable between 0 and 1;
- λ is a constant depending on the generation of each parameter.

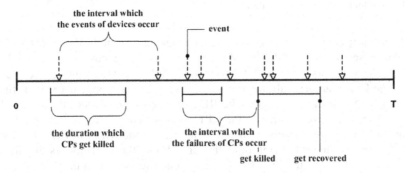

Fig. 2. During T seconds, a tapestry of events from devices occurs and a control point turns on and off

We benchmarked the performance of our recovery scheme with that of control point with no recovery scheme. Since our recovery scheme needs two control points, i.e., a primary control point agent and a recoverable control point agent, the above parameters were generated twice using the equation (1). For the following experiments, the interval which the failures of control points occurred was T/10 [1].

Our simulator was programmed using Linux SDK^{TM} for UPnP^{TM} Devices Version 1.2 [7], and was built on a single-CPU machine of 600MHz Intel Pentium^{TM} III with 256MB RAM. The machine was running Debian^{TM} Linux with kernel version 2.6.8.

3.2 Experimental Results

For the experiment in Fig. 3, we measured the recovery effectiveness, when the intervals which the events of devices occurred varied, i.e., ranging from T/50 to T/500, with the duration which the control points got killed fixed, i.e., T/40. When T was 1000 seconds, the performances of recovery effectiveness using our scheme and without recovery scheme were measured after 10 runs, respectively, as depicted in Fig. 3.

We could observe that the recovery effectiveness using our recovery scheme showed, on the average, 95% of the performance in case that all of the events were perfectly processed. On the other hand, the recovery effectiveness without recovery scheme presented from 55% to 76%. Thus, it turned out that the recoverable control point agent in our scheme successfully handled the events from the devices, regardless of one of recoverable control points being killed. The experimental results, further, prove that our recovery scheme is fairly consistent, and the recoverable agents have restored from failures as quickly as possible.

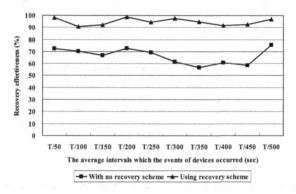

Fig. 3. The recovery effectiveness using our recovery scheme vs. without recovery scheme, when the average intervals which the events of devices occurred, on the x axis, varied

For the second experiment in Fig. 4, we measured the recovery effectiveness with the intervals which the events of devices occurred was fixed, i.e., T/200, while the duration which the control points got killed varied, i.e., ranging from T/100 to T/10.

In the experiment in Fig. 4, we changed the average duration which the control points got killed, varying from T/100 to T/10, while the duration in the experiment in Fig. 3 was fixed as T/40. As the duration which the control points got killed increased, the recovery effectiveness went down. However, while the performance using our scheme was around 80%, the performance without recovery scheme was below 40%, as depicted in Fig. 4. If more recoverable control point agents were registered in the network, the probability of becoming the agents available should increase, and then the performance of our recovery scheme should be improved.

4 Conclusion

To provide a robust network connectivity, we suggest an autonomous and dependable recovery scheme using teamwork in UPnP network settings. Our recovery scheme enables the recoverable control point agent in a team to autonomously recover from failures, and provides better dependability as more control points are actively working in the UPnP. In the experiments, we tested our recovery scheme in terms of the recovery effectiveness. The recovery effectiveness using our recovery scheme showed, on the average, 95% of the performance in case that all of the events were perfectly processed. The experimental results support that our recovery scheme is fairly consistent, and the recoverable agents have got back from failures as quickly as possible. For future research, we will expand our recovery scheme with much more control points to verify its soundness, and continuously apply our recovery scheme to various network settings.

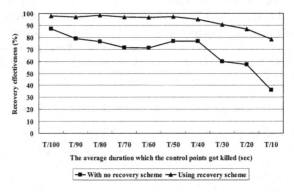

Fig. 4. The recovery effectiveness using our recovery scheme vs. without recovery scheme, when the average duration which the control points got killed, on the x axis, varied

References

1. Butler, R. W. and Finelli, G. B.: The Infeasibility of Quantifying the Reliability of Life-Critical Real-Time Software. IEEE Transactions on Software Engineering (1993).
2. Cohen, P. R and Levesque. H. J.: Confirmations and Joint Action. In Proceedings of the 12th International Joint Conference on Artificial Intelligence, Morgan Kaufman Publishers, Inc., San Mateo, California (1991) 951-957.
3. Dabrowski, C., Mills, K., and Elder, J.: Understanding Consistency Maintenance in Service Discovery Architectures during Communication Failure. In Proceedings of the 3rd International Workshop on Software and Performance (2002).
4. Ken, Arnold et al, The Jini Specification, V1.0, Addison Wesley (1999).
5. Kumar, S. and Cohen, P. R.: Towards a Fault-Tolerant Multi-Agent System Architecture. In Proceedings of the 4th International Conference on Autonomous Agents (Agents 2000), ACM Press, Barcelona, Spain (2000) 459-466.
6. Kumar, S., Cohen, P. R., and Levesque, H. J.: The Adaptive Agent Architecture: Achieving Fault-Tolerance Using Persistent Broker Teams. In Proceeding of the 4th International Conference on Multi-Agent Systems (ICMAS 2000), Boston MA, USA (2000).
7. Linux SDK for UPnP Devices Version 1.2.: http://intel.com/technology/upnp/, Intel (2003).
8. Tambe, M.: Towards flexible teamwork, Journal of Artificial Intelligence Research, vol. 7, (1997) 83-124.
9. Understanding UPnP™: A White Paper, Microsoft (2000).
10. Universal Plug and Play Device Architecture, Version 1.0.: http://www.upnp.org/download/UPnPDA10_20000613.htm, Microsoft (2000).

A Transitive Dependence Based Social Reasoning Mechanism for Coalition Formation

Bo An[1], Chunyan Miao[2], Lianggui Tang[1],
Shuangqing Li[1], and Daijie Cheng[1]

[1] College of Computer Science, Chongqing University, China
anbolangzhong@sohu.com, tlg@ctbu.edu.cn,
sqlee@cqu.edu.cn, djcheng@cqu.edu.cn
[2] School of Computer Engineering, Nanyang Technological University, Singapore
ascymiao@ntu.edu.sg

Abstract. Coalition formation in multi-agent systems (MAS) is becoming increasingly important as it increases the ability of agents to execute tasks and maximize their payoffs. This paper proposes a novel dependence theory namely transitive dependence theory for dynamic coalition formation in multi-agent system. Based on the proposed transitive dependence theory, a reasoning mechanism for searching coalition partners has been worked out which includes dependence tree generation, dependence tree reduction, plan optimization and action optimization.

1   Introduction

Cooperation among autonomous agents may be mutually beneficial even if the agents are selfish and try to maximize their own expected payoffs. Mutual benefit may arise from resource sharing and task redistribution. Coalition formation is important for agent cooperation in multi-agent environment. A number of coalition mechanisms have been successfully proposed and applied into many areas (e.g., [1–4]).

Social reasoning refers to agents' reasoning about others. The social reasoning mechanism is considered to be an essential building block of really autonomous agents. Although there are various kinds of relations in MAS as what in real society, the dependence relation is believed to be the most crucial one. Dependence relations allow an agent to know which of his goals are achievable and which of his plans are feasible at any moment.

Social reasoning mechanisms, especially dependence based methods, play an important role in coalition formation in MAS. Dependence relations are regarded as the foundation of coalition formation [6]. There have been some research efforts with respect to dependence based coalition formation (e.g., [5, 7]). However, transitive dependence has not been considered in the existing research. Moreover, search for potential partners is a crucial problem in dynamic coalition formation, which has not been clearly and completely addressed in the related work. This research advocates the importance of transitive dependence, an extension of direct dependence, in social reasoning and proposes a transitive dependence based

M. Gallagher, J. Hogan, and F. Maire (Eds.): IDEAL 2005, LNCS 3578, pp. 507–514, 2005.

method for searching coalition partners including dependence tree generation, dependence tree reduction, plan optimization and action optimization.

The remainder of this paper is organized as follows. Section 2 introduces the original transitive dependence theory. The transitive dependence based reasoning mechanism for coalition formation is proposed in section 3. In the final section, some conclusions are presented and ideas for future work are outlined.

2   Transitive Dependence Theory

A multi-agent system is composed of agents, agent environments, agent organizations, agent interaction and various relationships between agents. For the sake of simplicity, we regard all the social members as agents. As social reasoning mechanisms are based on agents' information about the others. Here we use a data structure kno_{ag_i} to store information of the agent ag_i.

Definition 1 *The data structure used by an agent to store information is:* kno_{ag_i} $=_{def} \cup_{j=1}^{n} kno_{ag_i}(ag_j)$, *where* $kno_{ag_i}(ag_j)$ $=_{def}$ $\{\{D_{ag_i}(ag_j)\}, \{A_{ag_i}(ag_j)\},$ $\{R_{ag_i}(ag_j)\}, \{P_{ag_i}(ag_j)\}, \{DP_{ag_i}(ag_j)\}\}$ *where* $D_{ag_i}(ag_j)$ *is the set of desires,* $A_{ag_i}(ag_j)$ *is the set of actions,* $R_{ag_i}(ag_j)$ *is the set of resources,* $P_{ag_i}(ag_j)$ *is the set of plans the agent* ag_i *believes the agent* ag_j *has. A plan consists of a sequence of actions with its associated resources needed to accomplish them.* $DP_{ag_i}(ag_j)$ *is the set of action dependence relations the agent* ag_i *believes the agent* ag_j *has. The definition of action dependence will be discussed later.*

According to dependence property, we divide dependence relations into strong dependence and weak dependence.

Definition 2 *(Strong dependence) Suppose an agent* ag_i *tries to achieve a goal* g. $p(ag_k, g) = a_1, a_2, \ldots, a_n$ *is a plan of the agent* ag_k *for the goal* g. *The agent* ag_i *has no ability to achieve an action* $a_i \in p(ag_k, g)$, *but it believes that the agent* ag_j *has ability to achieve the action* a_i, *then we call the agent* ag_i *strongly depends on the agent* ag_j *about the action* a_i, *i.e.,* $Sdep(ag_i, ag_j, p(ag_k, g), a_i)$.

Definition 3 *(Weak dependence) An agent* ag_i *tries to achieve a goal* g. *There is a plan of an agent* ag_k *for the goal* g, $p(ag_k, g) = a_1, a_2, \ldots, a_n$. *The agent* ag_i *can achieve the action* $a_i \in p(ag_k, g)$ *by itself, but it also believes that the agent* ag_j *has ability to achieve the action* a_i *if it pays* $offer_{ag_i \to ag_j}(a_i)$ *to the agent* ag_j. *If the agent* ag_i *achieves the action* a_i *by itself, it should spend* $cost_{ag_i}(a_i)$, *and* $cost_{ag_i}(a_i) > offer_{ag_i \to ag_j}(a_i)$, *then the agent* ag_i *weakly depends on the agent* ag_j *about the action* a_i, *i.e.,* $Wdep(ag_i, ag_j, p(ag_k, g), a_i)$.

The definition of strong dependence is the same as it is in most related work. Although weak dependence relation has not been addressed in previous research, weak dependence relations exist in multi-agent systems, as well as in real society. A simple example is the Tireworld [1], where every agent can move tiles. After analysis of weak dependence, agents can save cost through cooperation.

Definition 4 *(Action dependence) Suppose the agent ag_i can achieve the action a_i, but he wants any other agent who depends on him about the action a_i to do an action a_j for him, and he has no ability to achieve the action a_j, then the agent ag_i has an action dependence on the action a_j about the action a_i, i.e., $Adep(ag_i, a_i, a_j)$.*

Let A be a set of actions. The agent ag_i can achieve the action a_i. If he wants any other agent who depends on him about the action a_i to do all the actions in A, we call this kind of action dependence *and-action dependence*. If he wants any other agent who depends on him about the action a_i to do any one action in A, we call this kind of action dependence *or-action dependence*.

Now we discuss transitive dependence. For the agents ag_i, ag_j and ag_k, $Dep(ag_i, ag_j, p(ag_m, g_a), a_i)$ and $Dep(ag_j, ag_k, p(ag_q, g_b), a_j)$. Although the agent ag_j can achieve the action a_i, but he has an action dependence on the action a_j about the action a_i, i.e., $Adep(ag_j, a_i, a_j)$. We can find that the agent ag_i transitively depends on the agent ag_k about the action a_j.

In contrast to the transitive dependence, we call the dependence relations defined in definition 2 and definition 3 direct dependence.

Definition 5 *(Dependence chain) Dependence chain is used to describe the transition process of transitive dependence relations. A dependence chain has a head and a tail. For the agents ag_i, ag_j and ag_k, $Dep(ag_i, ag_j, p(ag_m, g_a), a_i)$, $Dep(ag_j, ag_k, p(ag_q, g_b), a_j)$, and $Adep(ag_j, a_i, a_j)$, the dependence chain from the agent ag_i to the agent ag_k is $Dpc = ag_i \xrightarrow{p(ag_m, g_a), a_i} ag_j \xrightarrow{p(ag_q, g_b), a_j} ag_k$.*

For a dependence chain Dpc, $Head(Dpc)$ represents the agent at the head of the dependence chain, and $Tail(Dpc)$ represents the agent at the tail of the dependence chain. For an agent ag_i in a dependence chain Dpc, $ToDep\_act(ag_i, Dpc)$ and $Deped\_act(ag_i, Dpc)$ represent the actions that the agent ag_i depends on and is depended upon respectively[1]. For the dependence chain Dpc in the last paragraph, $Head(Dpc) = ag_i$, $ToDep\_act(ag_i, Dpc) = a_i$, $Tail(Dpc) = ag_k$, and $Deped\_act(ag_k, Dpc) = a_j$.

Definition 6 *Transitive dependence can be described as $Tdep(Depender, Dependee, Dependencechain)$. For the sake of simplicity, we regard the direct dependence as a kind of special transitive dependence, i.e., the agent ag_i's dependence on the agent ag_j about the action a_i that belongs to the plan $p(ag_k, g)$ can be described as $Tdp(ag_i, ag_j, ag_i \xrightarrow{p(ag_k, g), a_i} ag_j)$. Transitive dependence can be recursively defined as:*

For the agents ag_i, ag_j and ag_k, $Tdep(ag_i, ag_j, Dpc_1) \wedge Tdep(ag_j, ag_k, Dpc_2) \wedge ADep(ag_j, Deped\_act(ag_j, Dpc_1)), ToDep\_act(ag_j, Dpc_2)) \Rightarrow Tdep(ag_i, ag_k, Dpc_1 + Dpc_2)$, where $Dpc_1 + Dpc_2$ represents the connection of Dpc_1 and Dpc_2.

Definition 7 *According to dependence property, transitive dependence can be divided into strong transitive dependence and weak transitive dependence. $TSdep$*

---

[1] An agent may appear more than once in a dependence chain

(ag_i, ag_j, Dpc) means the agent ag_i strongly transitively depends on the agent ag_j and $TWdep(ag_i, ag_j, Dpc)$ represents the agent ag_i weakly transitively depends on the agent ag_j.

According to definition 4, the transitive dependence relation $Tdep(ag_j, ag_k, Dpc_2)$ in definition 6 should be strong transitive dependence relation.

Definition 8 *For the agents ag_i, ag_j, ag_k, $Tdep(ag_i, ag_j, Dpc_1)$, $Tdep(ag_j, ag_k, Dpc_2)$ and $Tdep(ag_i, ag_k, Dpc_1 + Dpc_2)$. If the agent ag_i strongly transitively depends on the agent ag_j, the agent ag_i strongly transitively depends on the agent ag_k, otherwise the agent ag_i weakly transitively depends on the agent ag_k.*

3   Transitive Dependence Based Reasoning for Coalition Formation

In order to enable an agent to co-ordinate its activities with other agents and to participate in coalitions, one of the elements to take into account in its conception should be a social reasoning mechanism that allows the agent to reason about the other agents. In order to make the creation of mutually beneficial coalitions possible, we make the following two assumptions:

1) Complete information: We assume that agents'information about the other members in MAS is complete. The information is stored in the data structure described in section 2.

2) Personal rationality: We assume that each agent in the environment has personal rationality, i.e., it joins a coalition only if it can benefit at least as much within the coalition as it could benefit by itself or by joining in other coalitions. For instance, an agent ag_i can do an action a_i, if another agent ag_j ask for its help with the action a_i, and the agent ag_j can pay more than it wants and other agents will pay, the agent ag_i will join the coalition to do the action for the agent ag_j.

It's obvious that agents must have some information about other members in the multi-agent system before reasoning about possible coalition partners. This kind of information is acquired during an initial information gathering phase and can be acquired and updated dynamically. The information can be acquired in three ways: passive receiving, active inquiring and internal reasoning.

The dependence relation is got by analysis of the information about other members gathered. In the transitive dependence based reasoning mechanism, after analysis of the dependence relations, the reasoning process for potential coalition partners includes the three steps: *dependence tree generation, dependence tree reduction, plan optimization* and *action optimization*.

In this paper, dependence trees are employed to described the direct dependence and transitive dependence in achieving a goal.

Definition 9 *A dependence tree DPT is an ordered triple $(V(DPT), E(DPT), \Psi(DPT))$ consisting of a nonempty set $V(DPT)$ of nodes, a set $E(DPT)$ of edges and an incidence function $\Psi(DPT)$ that associates with each edge of DPT an ordered pair of (not necessarily distinct) vertices of DPT.*

1. *The set $V(DPT) = Root \cup V_{plan}(Root) \cup V_{ag}(DPT) \cup V_{act}(DPT)$ is the union of four disjoint sets. Root is the root of the dependence tree, i.e., the depender and his goal to achieve, $V_{plan}(Root)$ is the set of plans the agents may use to achieve the goal in the root node Root, $V_{ag}(DPT)$ is the set of agents, and $V_{act}(DPT)$ is the set of actions.*
2. *The set $E(DPT)$ is a set of edges.*
3. *The function $\Psi_{DPT} : E(DPT) \rightarrow V(DPT) \times V(DPT)$ is defined as follows:*
    (a) *$\Psi_{DPT}(e) = (Root, p_i)$ represents the fact that the goal in the root node Root can be achieved by the plan p_i.*
    (b) *$\Psi_{DPT}(e) = (p_i, a_i)$ represents the fact that the plan p_i needs the action a_i and the action can't be achieved by the depender or the depender can achieve it but has to cost more.*
    (c) *$\Psi_{DPT}(e) = (a_i, ag_i)$ represents the fact that the action a_i can be performed by the agent ag_i.*
    (d) *$\Psi_{DPT}(e) = (ag_i, a_i)$ represents the fact that the agent ag_i has an action dependence on the action a_i, i.e., $ADep(ag_i, a_k, a_i)$, where the action a_k is the origin action node of the agent ag_i.*

Here we define two notations for the dependence tree. Let a node x be any node but the *Root* node in a dependence tree DPT. $father(x)$ represents the father node of the node x, and $sons(x)$ represents the set of nodes whose father node is the node x. Each node x has only a father node $father(x)$, and may has more than one son node, i.e., $|sons(x)| \geq 0$.

A dependence tree has the following characteristics:

1) For an agent node x in a dependence tree, his father node, an action node, $a_i = father(x)$ and any son node $a_j \in sons(x)$ (if $|sons(x)| \geq 1$) belongs to an action dependence relation $ADep(x, a_i, a_j)$.

2) Let the node x is an action node in a dependence tree, for his father node $ag_i = father(x)$(if it's an agent node) and any son node, an agent node, $ag_j \in sons(x)$ (if $|sons(x)| \geq 1$), it's obvious that the maximum offer of the agent ag_i about the action x is no less than the reserve price of the agent ag_j.

3) For an agent node x in a dependence tree, his father node is $a_i = father(x)$ and the set of his son nodes is $sons(x)$ ($|sons(x)| \geq 1$). The node x is an "or" node if the agent x or-depends on the set $sons(x)$ of actions about the action a_i, and the node x is an "and" node if the agent and-depends on the set $sons(x)$ of actions about the action a_i.

An example of a dependence tree is in Figure 1[2]. An agent ag_1 has a goal g_1 and it has two alternative plans, $p_{11} = a_0, a_1, a_2$ and $p_{12} = a_0, a_3$ for the goal. Suppose that the agent ag_1 can only perform the action a_0, and the actions a_1 and a_2 can be performed respectively by the set of agents $\{ag_2, ag_3\}$ and $\{ag_4\}$. The agent ag_5 can achieve the action a_3. An action dependence relation of the agent ag_2 is $ADep(ag_2, a_1, a_4)$. An or-action dependence relation of the agent ag_3 is $ADep(ag_3, a_1, a_5 \vee a_6)$. An and-action dependence relation of the agent

---

[2] The or-dependence relations are represented with doted lines, and the and-dependence relations are represented with solid lines

ag_5 is $ADep(ag_5, a_3, a_7 \wedge a_8)$. The action a_5 can be performed by the agent ag_6. The action a_7 can be performed by the agents ag_7 and ag_8. The action a_8 can be performed by the agent ag_9. The actions a_4 and a_6 can't be performed by any agent.

Definition 10 *(Feasible action) For an action node a_i in a dependence tree, it's a feasible action if it can be achieved, which can be defined by:*

If the prior node of the action node a_i is a plan node, and the depending agent in the root node has ability to achieve the action a_i, the action a_i is a feasible action.

An edge e associates with an ordered pair of vertices (a_i, ag_j) and the node ag_j is a leaf node, the action a_i is feasible.

An edge e associates with an ordered pair of vertices (a_i, ag_j), if the node ag_j is an "or" node, and there is more than one ordered pair of vertices (ag_j, a_k), in which the action a_k is feasible, then the action a_i is a feasible action.

An edge e associates with an ordered pair of vertices (a_i, ag_j), if the node ag_j is an "and" node, and for every ordered pair of vertices (ag_j, a_k), the action a_k is feasible, then the action a_i is a feasible action.

Definition 11 *(Feasible plan) For a plan p_i in a dependence tree, if for every ordered pair of vertices (p_i, a_i), the action a_i is feasible, the plan p_i is feasible.*

Definition 12 *After deletion of the all actions and plans that are not feasible from a dependence tree, the reduced tree is called a reduced dependence tree.*

Take the dependence tree in Figure 1 as an example. Assume that the agent ag_2 has no ability to achieve the action a_4, and the agent ag_3 has no ability to achieve the action a_6. Figure 2 shows the reduced dependence tree after dependence tree reduction.

Definition 13 *For a reduced dependence tree, if the node Root is a leaf node, then the goal is not achievable; otherwise, it's a feasible goal.*

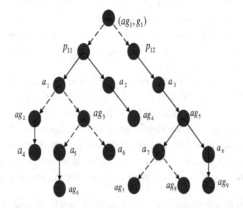

Fig. 1. A simple example of dependence tree

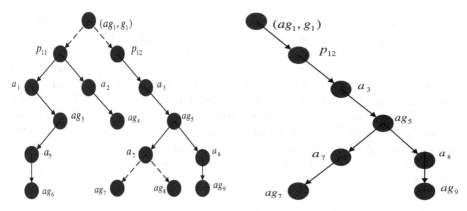

Fig. 2. A reduced dependence tree   **Fig. 3.** A coalition tree

Definition 14 *(Plan optimization) For a feasible goal, there may be more than one feasible plan, and we choose the most favorable plan to form coalition.*

Definition 15 *(Action optimization) Similarly, for a feasible action, there may be more than one agent can achieve it, and we choose an agent to achieve it that will result in the most favorable outcome.*

Definition 16 *(Coalition tree) For a reduced dependence tree, after plan optimization and action optimization, the reduced dependence tree is called a coalition tree.*

Definition 17 *(Dependence based coalition formation) Given a framework $F = < AG, G, Plan, Can, Dp >$, an agent $ag_i \in AG$ has a goal $g \in G$, according to the set of agents' ability Can and the set of dependence relations Dp, does there exists a coalition tree over F that is feasible for the goal g?*

Theorem 1 *The Dependence based coalition formation problem is NP-complete.*
Proof: *The detailed proof is omitted due to lack of space.*   □

Take the reduced dependence tree is in Figure 2 as an example. Let us assume that the agent ag_1 has to pay much more if he adopts the plan p_{11} than that if he adopts the plan p_{12}, and the reserve price of the agent ag_7 is less than that of the agent ag_8 for the action a_7. Figure 3 shows the coalition tree after plan optimization and action optimization. After reasoning the potential cooperation partners, the depending agent invites all the agents in the coalition tree to form a coalition. According to assumption 1 and assumption 2, all the agents in the coalition tree will agree to join in the coalition for cooperative problem solving.

4   Conclusions and Future Work

There are two major questions concerning coalition formation [2]: 1) how should a group of autonomous agents form a coalition? and 2) among all possible coalitions, what coalition will form, and what reasons and processes will lead the agents to form that particular coalition? The theory of direct dependence and transitive dependence tries to answer the first question, and it has been the direction followed by some previous works like those presented in [5, 7].

In this paper, we extend the related research work in a significant way by introducing a new theory transitive dependence theory in coalition formation. The transitive dependence based reasoning for potential partners is proposed for the second question. The coalition formation process is divided into three phases. Dependence tree, reduced dependence tree and coalition tree are employed in the reasoning about potential coalition partners. Our on-going research is focused on solving the large complexity of the transitive dependence based reasoning, which will be reported in the future papers.

Acknowledgments

The authors would like to thank Guido Boella, Leon van der Torre, Tom Mitchell and Luigi Sauro for their helpful suggestions on this research.

References

1. Zlotkin. G., Rosenschein. J. S.: Coalition, cryptography, and stability: Mechanisms for coalition formation in task oriented domains. In Proc. of AAAI 94, (1994)432-437

2. Shehory. O., Kraus. S.: Coalition Formation among Autonomous Agents: Strategies and Complexity. In From Reaction to Cognition, C. Castelfranchi and J. Muller, eds., Springer Verlag, Heidelberg, (1995)57-72

3. Sandholm. T., Lesser. V.: Coalitions among Computationally Bounded Agents. Artificial Intelligence, Special Issue on Economic Principles of Multi-Agent Systems, 94(1997)99-137,

4. Sandholm. T., Larson. K., Andersson. M., Shehory. O., Tohme. F.: Coalition Structure Generation with Worst Case Guarantees. Artificial Intelligence, 111(1999)209-238

5. Sichman. J. S.: DEPINT: Dependence-Based Coalition Formation in an Open Multi-Agent Scenarios. Journal of Artificial Societies and Social Simulation, vol. 1, no. 2, Available at http://www.soc.surrey.ac.uk/ JASS/1/2/3.html, 1998

6. Boella. G., Sauro. L., Van Der Torre. L.: Social viewpoints on multiagent systems. In Proc. of the 3rd International Joint Conference on Autonomous Agents and Multiagent Systems, (2004)1358-1359

7. David. N., Sichman. J. S., Coelho. H.: Extending Social Reasoning to Cope with Multiple Partner Coalitions. In Proc. of the 9th European Workshop on Modelling Autonomous Agents in a Multi-Agent World, 1647(1999)175-187

A Multi-agent Based Context Aware Self-healing System*

Jeongmin Park, Hyunsang Youn, and Eunseok Lee

School of Information and Communication Engineering Sungkyunkwan University
300 Chunchun Jangahn Suwon, 400-746, Korea
{jmpark,wizehack,eslee}@selab.skku.ac.kr

Abstract. There is increasing demand for the self-diagnosis and self-healing of problems or errors arising in systems operating in the ubiquitous computing environment. In this paper, we propose a self-healing system that monitors, diagnoses and heals its own problems. The proposed system consists of multi agents that analyze the log context in order to perform self-diagnosis and self-healing. To minimize the resources used by the *Adapters* in an existing system, we place a single process in memory. By this, we mean that a single *Monitoring Agent* monitors the context of the logs that are generated by the different components of the system. For rapid and efficient self-healing, we use a *6-step* process. The effectiveness of the proposed system is confirmed through experiments conducted with a prototype system.

1 Introduction

In today's distributed computing environment, there is a growing need for experts who can assure the efficient management of the various computer systems. However, management operations involving human intervention have clear limits in terms of their cost effectiveness and the availability of human resources [1]. Of all computer problems, about 40% are attributable to errors made by the system administrators [2]. Thus, the current system management method, which depends mainly on professional managers, needs to be improved.

In a ubiquitous environment, which involves an even greater number of computing devices whose mode of operation is more informal, this type of problem will have more serious consequences. To solve these problems when they do arise, there is a definite need for effective self-healing systems. A self-healing system allows the system or computing device itself to recognize, identify and heal the problems which arise, without depending on the administrators [3].

The existing self-healing systems consist of a 5-step process, including Monitoring, Translation, Analysis, Diagnosis and Feedback. This architecture has various drawbacks, such as the wastage of resources, increased log file sizes and numbers, and dependency on the administrator and vendor.

Consequently, in this paper, we propose *an Multi-Agent based self-healing system* which incorporates several functions designed to resolve the above mentioned prob-

---

* This work was supported by the Ubiquitous Autonomic Computing and Network Project, 21st Century Frontier R&D Program in Korea and the Brain Korea 21 Project in 2004. Dr. E. Lee is the corresponding author

M. Gallagher, J. Hogan, and F. Maire (Eds.): IDEAL 2005, LNCS 3578, pp. 515–523, 2005.

lems, namely i) the minimization of the resources required through the use of a single process (Monitoring Agent), ii) the use of a Meta Policy which offers different healing strategies according to the log context of the component, viz. *"Normal"*, *"Emergency" and "Error"*. iii) For the sake of rapid and efficient self-healing, we use a 6-step process, in which the Component Agent first filters the context of the log that identifies whether the component is "error" and then translates the filtered log context into the CBE (Common Base Event) format. The proposed system is designed and implemented in the form of a prototype, in order to prove its effectiveness through experiment. In section 2, we summarize related works. In section 3, we describe the proposed system, and in section 4, we discuss its implementation and evaluation. Finally, in section 5, we present our conclusions.

2   Related Works

Self-adaptive software has the capability to modify its own actions in response to changes such as system faults, resource variability and the like. These self-adaptive behaviors are the essence of the self-healing system or, in other words, the self-healing system must contain self-adaptive behaviors [11]. Oreizy et. al. [4] proposed the following processes for self-adaptive software: Monitoring the system, Planning the changes, Deploying the change descriptions and Enacting the changes [5][6][7][8].

The Adaptive Service Framework (ASF) [10] proposed by IBM and CISCO consists of a 5-step process, including *Monitoring, Translation, Analysis, Diagnosis and Feedback*. These 5 processes are applied in the form of self-adaptive behaviors.

The functions of the ASF are as follows:

- Firstly, the *Adapters* monitor the logs from the various components (*Monitoring*).
- Secondly, the *Adapter* [9] translates the log generated by the component into the CBE (Common Based Event) format (*Translation*).
- Thirdly, the *Autonomic Manager* [9] analyzes the CBE log. This step identifies the relationship between the components through their dependency (*Analysis*)
- Fourthly, the *Autonomic Manager* [9] finds the appropriate healing method by means of the *Symptom Rule*[9] and *Policy Engine*[9] and then applies the healing method to the applicable component. The feedback from the *Resource Manager* [9] enables the system to heal itself (*Diagnosis and Feedback*)
- Finally, in the event that the component has a critical problem or one which cannot be solved easily, the Autonomic Manager sends a Call Home Format[1] message to the Support Service Provider (SSP)/Vendor, requesting them to find a solution.

However, the size of the log in the CBE format is larger than that of the untranslated log. The disk, CPU and memory usage drastically increase in the process of conversion, due to the complex calculations involved. In effect, the ASF has as many

---

[1] Call Home Format: This is the message transmission code between healing system and SSP/Vendor that IBM&CISCO are undertaken for standardization.
http://www.cisco.com/application/pdf/en/us/guest/partners/partners/c644/ccmigration_09186 a0080202dc7.pdf

Adapters [9, 10] as there are components, and this may cause a problem of insufficient resources, particularly in the case of handheld devices used in the ubiquitous
environment. Furthermore, in the event that the component does not generate the log,
it is impossible for the system to heal itself.

3 Proposed System

In this section, we describe how the problems inherent in the existing self-healing
systems are resolved using the proposed Multi-Agent based system. *Firstly,* the *Monitoring Agent*, which runs as a single process, provides real time monitoring of events,
in order to overcome the problem associated with the number of *Adaptors* [10], which
results in memory being wasted. *Secondly*, the System Agent using threshold values
of the system resources recognizes the system situation and chooses an applicable
policy on the Meta level. *Thirdly*, before translating the original log into the log of the
CBE type, a filtering process is performed. These processes minimize the disk and
memory utilization. *Fourthly*, in the event that there is no applicable method of healing, the Searching Agent searches the web server of the vendor in an attempt to reduce the dependency on the administrator.

3.1 System Architecture

Fig. 1 shows the structure of the proposed system, which is composed of the *Monitor-
ing Agent, Component Agent, System Agent, Diagnosis Agent, Decision Agent and
Searching Agent*. The proposed system consists of 6 consecutive processes, viz.
Monitoring, Filtering, Translation, Analysis, Diagnosis, and Decision and Feed-back.

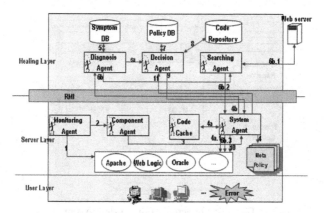

Fig. 1. The Multi-Agent based Self-healing system's architecture

(a) Monitoring Agent (*Monitoring*): the Monitoring Agent was designed to run as a
single process. It monitors the sizes of the log files, and if these are changed it executes the Component Agent. To deal with components that do not generate log, it
monitors events of a particular type arising in the event viewer of the operating system, in order to detect problems or errors concerning these components.

```
...
BufferedReader br = ReadeLineFromFile(logfile);
while((Line = br.readLine())!= null) {
        if((Line.indexOf("not") > 0)) {
                Line = Line + "ERROR"+"\n";
        }
        else if ((Line.indexOf("error") > 0)) {
                Line = Line + "ERROR"+"\n";
        }
        else if((Line.indexOf("reject") > 0)) {
                Line = Line + "ERROR"+"\n";
        }

        else
                Line = Line + "NORMAL"+"\n";
        log = log + Line;
}
WriteLineToFile(log, parsedfile);
...
```

Fig. 2. The Filtering source code

(b) Component Agent (*Filtering and Translation*): When the Monitoring Agent executes the Component Agent, the first action is to retrieve the path of the log. Next, the Component Agent extracts the logs needed for the healing process. Fig.2 shows that the Component Agent distinguishes error context from normal context in the log files. As can be seen, the error context is filtered by means of designated keywords, such as *"not"*, *"error"*, *"reject"*, *"notify"*, etc. Also, the Component Agent translates the filtered parts of the error context into the CBE format.

(c) System Agent (*Analysis*): The System Agent consists of the CBE Log Receiver, Resource Collector, Adaptation Module and Executor, as shown in Fig 3. When the System Agent receives the CBE log from the CBE Log Receiver, the Resource Collector gathers the CPU information, Memory information, process information and Job Schedule information, in order to deliver it to the Adaptation Module.

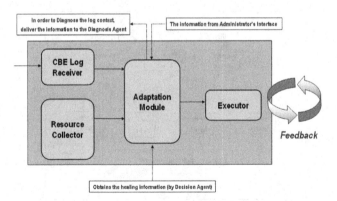

Fig. 3. Architecture of the System Agent

The Adaptation Module is in possession of the threshold values pertaining to the gathered resource information. According to the threshold value, a suitable policy is implemented. The Executor then executes the best healing method. In this step, we distinguish the dependency of the components. The collected information and CBE log are sent to the Diagnosis Agent. The System Agent handles emergency situations in accordance with the threshold value, and applies the best healing method.

(d) Diagnosis Agent (*Diagnosis*): The Diagnosis Agent analyzes the CBE log, resource information (received from the System Agent) and the dependency of the components, and then diagnoses the current problem (through the *Symptom DB*).

(e) Decision Agent (*Decision and Feedback*): Through the information that was delivered by the Diagnosis Agent, The Decision Agent determines the appropriate healing method with the help of the *Policy DB* and *Code Repository*. It also will receive the feedback information from the System Agent that applies the best healing method.

(f) Searching Agent: The Searching Agent is used to search the vendor's website for the knowledge required to resolve the problem, This Agent uses search engines such as *Google* to search for the address of the web site at which the patch specified in the CBE Log can be obtained.

(g) Code Repository: The Cod Repository stores the mechanisms used for self-healing, by transferring the relevant healing code, and responds to errors that was generated by the components.

(h) Code Cache: The Code Cache is used to provide healing code to solve the error of the component arising in the *emergency situations*.

The various steps required to heal the problem on *the Server Layer* are discussed below.

Steps 1, 2 and 3. The Monitoring Agent monitors the size of the logs generated by the components (such as Apache, Web logic, Oracle, etc). If there is an error component hat do not generate log, it monitors particular types of event arising in the event viewer of the operating system.

This monitoring information is delivered to the Component Agent, and the Component Agent filters the context of the log and translates the filtered parts of the error context into the CBE format. This information is delivered to the System Agent.

Steps 4a, 4a.1 and 4b. The System Agent recognizes urgent situations by comparing the threshold value with *the Meta Policy (as shown in Fig. 3)*. If an urgent situation is detected, the System Agent applies the healing code that is held in the Code Cache.

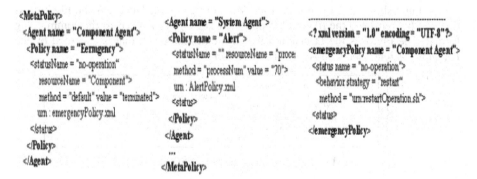

Fig. 4. The Meta Policy of the proposed system

Steps 5, 6a, 7, 8, 9, 10, 11. Using *the Symptom DB,* the Diagnosis Agent diagnoses the problem encountered by the component. The diagnostic information is delivered to the Decision Agent, in order to identify the appropriate Healing Method. Through the *Policy DB* and the *Code Repository*, the Decision Agent selects the possible Healing Methods and delivers them to the System Agent. The System Agent executes the Best Healing Method.

Steps 6b, 6b.1, 6b.2 and 6b.3. If the version of the component should be upgraded, the administrator has to patch the software for the component. In this case, the Searching agent autonomically obtains the patch file by retrieving it from the web server of the vendor.

4   Implementation and Evaluation

The implementation environment is as follows: we employed JAVA SDK1.4, and then used Oracle9i as the DBMS. Also we used JADE1.3 for the Agent development. The sample log used for the self-healing process was a log generated by *APACHE.*

We implemented *the Agents* of the proposed system (in the form of a JADE Agent Platform [13]). As shown in Fig 4 [13], each of the agents is registered with each of the containers, and the ACL(Agent Communication Launguage) is used to communicate among the agents. We performed the simulation using six agents.

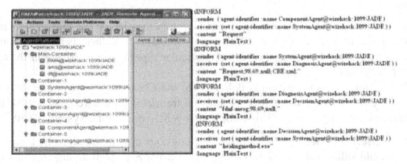

Fig. 5. Agent Platform & ACL

The Fig.5 shows that the result of the Monitoring Agent. The Fig.6 and Fig.7 illustrated to be translated the filtered log into the CBE log, which acts as the common log format. The Fig. 8 is the Decision Table, which is the result that is executed by the Diagnosis Agent, Decision Agent and Feedback.

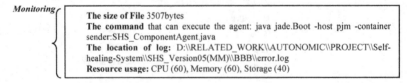

Fig. 6. The result of the Monitoring Agent

The proposed system was evaluated and compared qualitatively and quantitatively in terms of the Log Monitoring Module, the Filtering & Translating Efficiency, and ealing Time.

Filtering

> **date** : [Fri Mar 17 11:32:42 2005]
> **log_level** : [Alert]
> **client_ip** : [client 203.252.53.142]
> **log_description :**
> httpd: Could not determine the server's fully qualified domain name

Fig. 7. The filtered log (*"error context"*)

Translation

```
<situation reporterPriority=70 reporterSeverity=60 categoryName="DestroySituation">
    <situationType resoningScope="INTERNAL" successDisposition="UNSUCESSFULL">
    </situationType>
    <situationData localInstanceId="F0000001" msg="File does not exist:/usr/local/apache/htdocs/index.html
        <extendedDataElements name="CommonBaseEvent">
        </extendedDataElements>
    </situationData>
</situation>
```

Fig. 8. CBE(Common Base Event) Log

Diagnosis

Decision

Feedback

PROBLEM	TEMPORARY SOLUTION	ROOT SOLUTION	CURRENT JOB	FUTURE JOB	AVAILABLE MEMORY	DECISION	FEEDBACK INFORMATION
Connect	Change configuration	Reinstall	Null	Null	80%	T	Positive
Available	Null	Restart	Null	Null	80%	R	Positive
Overload	Allocate Memory	Reboot	BackUp	Null	80%	TR	Positive

Fig. 9. Decision Table

(a) Log Monitoring Test. In the existing system, if the number of components is Ω, the system has to have Ω processes to monitor the log. In the proposed system, however, only one process is needed to monitor the log, as shown in Fig. 9. In this figure, the proposed system demonstrates its ability to stay at a certain level of memory usage, even when the number of components is increased.

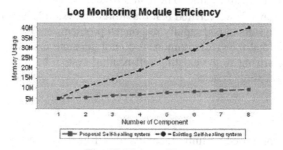

Fig. 10. Memory Usage

Table 1. Comparison of size and number of logs

Existing Self-healing system				
Created Logs	100	200	300	400	500
Translated Logs	100	200	300	400	500
Filtered Logs	26	87	90	103	106
Translated Log Size	260,400 byte	520,800 byte	781,200 byte	1,041,600 byte	1,302,000 byte
Proposal Self-healing system				
Created Log	100	200	300	400	500
Filtering Log	26	87	90	103	106
Translated Log	26	87	90	103	106
Translated Log Size	67,704 byte	226,548 byte	234,360 byte	268,212 byte	276,024 byte

(b) Filtering and Translation Efficiency Test. In the proposed system, the Component Agent searches for a designated keyword (such as *"not"*, *"reject"*, *"fail"*, *"error"*, etc.) in the log generated by the components. By using this approach, we were able to increase the efficiency of the system, in terms of the size of the log and the number of logs. We analyzed up to 500 logs, filtered out those logs not requiring any action to be taken, and evaluated the number and size of the logs in the case of both the existing and proposed system. As a result of the filtering process, only about 20% of the logs were needed for the healing process, as shown in **Table 1**. Therefore, the proposed system reduces the number and size of the logs needed to be converted into the CBE format.

Table 2. Comparison of the Healing time

Existing Self-healing Time			
Error Component (that generates log)		Error Component (that do not generate log)	
Remote	Local (urgent situation)	Remote	Local(urgent situation)
2022 ms	1880 ms	X	X
Proposed Self-healing Time			
Error Component (that generates log)		Error Component (that do not generate log)	
Remote	Local(urgent situation)	Remote	Local(urgent situation)
1652 ms	620 ms	1785 ms	752 ms

(c) Average Healing Time Measurement. We measured the *Average Healing Time* arising in the existing self-healing system and the proposed self-healing system. The detail evaluation was included below.

- We evaluated the healing time to heal an error component that generates log. Healing time to perform the healing method on remote (using the RMI) and local(we considered the problem on local into urgent situation.).
- We evaluated the healing time to heal an error component do not generate log.

As shown in Table 2, we verified that the proposed system's healing time is fastest than the existing system's, and rapidly responded problems arising in the urgent situation. In the event that the error component do not generate log, we couldn't measure the healing time arising in the existing self-healing system because the existing system is log-based healing system.

5   Conclusion

In this paper, we proposed a Multi-Agent based self-healing system, whose purpose is to enable a computer system to observe, diagnose and heal errors or problems in the ubiquitous environment. The advantages of this system are as follows. First, when prompt is required, the system can make an immediate decision and respond right away. Second, the Monitoring Agent monitors the generation of the log on the fly, thus improving the memory usage. Third, before converting the log into the CBE (Common Base Event) format, filtering is performed in order to minimize the memory and disk space used in the conversion of the log. Fourth, it provides the fast healing time. Fifth, using the *Meta Policy*, the appropriate adaptation policy is selected. However, further study is needed in order to develop an algorithm which is able to make accurate and general inferences when prompt based responses employed in the system proposed in this study. It is also necessary to examine the problems associated with the dependency on the vendor and manager.

References

1. http://www.ibm.com/autonomic
2. IBM: Autonomic Computing: IBM's Perspective on the State of Information Technology, http://www-1.ibm.com/industries/government/doc/content/resource/thought/278606109.html
3. J. O. Kephart and D. M. Chess: The Vision of Autonomic Computing, IEEE Computer Society, January (2003)
4. P. Oreizy, M. M. Gorlick, R. N. Taylor, D. Heimbigner, G. Hohnson, N. Medvidovic, A. Quilici, D. S. Rosenblum and A. L. Wolf: An Architecture-Based Approach to Self-Adaptive Software, IEEE Intelligent Systems, Vol. 14, No. 3, May/June (1999) 54-62.
5. Garlan, D. and Schmerl, B.: Model-based Adaptation for Self-Healing Systems, Proceedings of the First ACM SIGSOFT Workshop on Self-Healing Systems (WOSS), South Carolina, November (2002) 27-32.
6. G. D. Abowd, R. Allen and D. Garlan.: Formalizing style to understand descriptions of software architecture, ACM Transactions on Software Engineering and Methodology, Vol. 4, No. 4, October (1995) 319-364.
7. D. Batory and S. O'Malley: The Design and Implementation of Hierarchical Software Systems with Reusable Components, ACM Transactions on Software Engineering and Methodology, Vol. 1, No. 4, October (1992) 355-398.
8. M. Bernardo, P. Ciancarni and L. Donatiello: On the formalization of architectural types with process algebras, Proceedings of the 8th International Symposium on Foundations of Software Engineering, November (2000) 140-148
9. B. Topol, D. Ogle, D. Pierson, J. Thoensen, J. Sweitzer, M. Chow, M. A. Hoffmann, P. Durham, R. Telford, S. Sheth, T. Studwell: Automating problem determination: A first step toward self-healing computing system, IBM white paper, October (2003)
10. J. Baekelmans, P. Brittenham, T.Deckers, C.DeLaet, E.Merenda, BA. Miller, D.Ogle, B.Rajaraman, K.Sinclair, J. Sweitzer: Adaptive Services Framework CISCO white paper, October (2003)
11. Hillman, J. and Warren, I. Meta-adaptation in Autonomic systems, In Proceedings of the 10th International Workshop on Future Trends in Distributed Computer Systems (FTDCS), Sozhou, China, May 26-28 2004
12. D. Garlan, S. Cheng and B. Schmerl: Increasing System Dependability through Architecture-based Self-repair, Appears in Architecting Dependable Systems, de Lemos, Gacek, Romanovsky (eds) 2003, © Springer-Verlag.
13. F. Bellifemine, G. Caire and T. Trucco (TILAB, formerly CSELT) Giovanni Rimassa (University of Parma): JADE PROGRAMMER'S GUIDE

Combining Influence Maps and Cellular Automata
for Reactive Game Agents

Penelope Sweetser and Janet Wiles

School of ITEE, The University of Queensland, St Lucia 4072, Brisbane, Australia
{penny,j.wiles}@itee.uq.edu.au
http://www.itee.uq.edu.au/~penny

Abstract. Agents make up an important part of game worlds, ranging from the characters and monsters that live in the world to the armies that the player controls. Despite their importance, agents in current games rarely display an awareness of their environment or react appropriately, which severely detracts from the believability of the game. Some games have included agents with a basic awareness of other agents, but they are still unaware of important game events or environmental conditions. This paper presents an agent design we have developed, which combines cellular automata for environmental modeling with influence maps for agent decision-making. The agents were implemented into a 3D game environment we have developed, the EmerGEnT system, and tuned through three experiments. The result is simple, flexible game agents that are able to respond to natural phenomena (e.g. rain or fire), while pursuing a goal.

1 Introduction

Agents are an important part of game environments as they give the game life, story and atmosphere. Agents serve many different purposes and hold many different positions in games, which contributes to making the game world rich, interesting and complex. For example, strategy games include units (e.g. marines) that the player controls and role-playing games include agents that fill a wide range of different roles in society, from kings to cobolds. Game-players expect agents to behave intelligently by being cunning, flexible, unpredictable, challenging to play against and able to adapt and vary their strategies and responses [5]. However, players often find that agents in games are unintelligent and predictable [5]. Furthermore, players believe that agents' actions and reactions in games should demonstrate an awareness of events in their immediate surroundings [1]. However, many games are proliferated with agents that do not demonstrate even a basic awareness of the situation around them. These agents often occupy the landscape as glorified pieces of scenery and behave in exactly the same way in any number of situations, ranging from rain to open gun fire.

The question that arises is how can game agents be made to appear intelligent to the player by reacting sensibly to the game environment? First, we review various techniques that can be used for agents in games and identify influence maps as a potential solution. Then we describe a study in which we designed, implemented and tested reactive agents in the Emergent Games Engine Technology (EmerGEnT) system, a system we have developed that is based on cellular automata. Three structured

M. Gallagher, J. Hogan, and F. Maire (Eds.): IDEAL 2005, LNCS 3578, pp. 524–531, 2005.

experiments were conducted with the reactive agents in the EmerGEnT system to determine the design that would achieve the most appropriate agent behaviour, as indicated by criteria for efficiency, effectiveness and visible behaviour. The aim of the study was to assess the extent to which agents based on influence maps and cellular automata can exhibit behaviour that is appropriate, intelligent and realistic.

2 Reactive Agents in Current Games

The agents in most games are hard-coded, relying heavily on the prior knowledge of their designers and little on their current situation. Furthermore, many agents in current games simply do not react to the environment in any way. There are some games, however, in which the agents demonstrate situational awareness by actively sensing and reacting to other agents in their environment. For example, the agents in *Half-Life* and *Thief: The Dark Project* have sight and hearing and periodically "look" at and "listen" to the world [2]. However, the agents in these games are still hard-coded, as they periodically run through a list of rules to determine whether they sense an opponent. Also, as these agents must actively check to determine whether they can sense something periodically (real vision and hearing arrive at the senses continuously [2]), it is likely that events and actions will be missed.

Another game that requires the agents to sense and react to information in the environment is *The Sims*. Unlike *Half-Life* and *Thief*, the agents in *The Sims* constantly receive information from the environment. In *The Sims*, the AI is embedded in the objects in the environment, known as "Smart Terrain". Each agent has various motivations and needs and each object in the terrain broadcasts how it can satisfy those needs [7]. The agents in *The Sims* are not hard-coded like the agents in *Half-Life* and *Thief*. Instead, their behaviour is autonomous and emergent, based on their current needs and their environment.

Although the agents in each of these games are able to sense entities in the environment in some way, they are still unable to sense the state of the environment itself. The agents in *Thief* and *Half-Life* are limited to sensing other agents in the environment and the agents in *The Sims* are limited to sensing other agents and objects in the environment. These agents would still be unable to react to events and states of the environment such as rain, fire, gunfire and so on. Another approach that is more applicable to the problem of agents reacting to the game environment is a technique used in many strategy games, influence maps.

3 Influence Maps

Influence maps divide the game map into a grid of cells, with multiple layers of cells that each contain different information about the game world (see [3,6]). The values for each cell in each layer are first calculated based on the current state of the game and then the values are propagated to nearby cells, spreading the influence of each cell. Currently, influence maps are used in games for strategic, high-level decision-making. However, it would also be possible to use them for tactical, low-level decision-making, such as individual agents or units reacting to the environment.

The advantage of influence maps over methods that are currently used in games, such as Smart Terrain in *The Sims*, is that the agent is presented with a single value (calculated using the weighted sum to combine all the factors) instead of numerous messages being sent to the agent about the environment. Also, this approach has further advantages over the method used in games such as *Half-Life* and *Thief* as the agent is continuously adapting its behaviour to the environment (rather than probing at given time intervals) and its behaviour is a function of its environment (rather than following a prescribed set of rules). Finally, the influence map structure fits nicely with the cellular automata that are already being used to model the environment in the EmerGEnT system (see Sect. 4). Both use the same data structure and the raw values for the influence map are supplied by the calculations of the cellular automata. Therefore, the approach of using an influence map for tactical decision-making is investigated in this study as it accommodates passive sensing of a continuous environment (as opposed to discrete entities), allows the agents' situational awareness to evolve as a function of the environment, gives rise to reactive and emergent behaviour and combines well with the cellular automata model of the environment in the EmerGEnT system.

4   The EmerGEnT System

The Emergent Games Engine Technology (EmerGEnT) system is a 3D game world we have developed that models natural phenomena, such as fluid flow, heat, fire, pressure and explosions. The system is based on cellular automata, which divide the game world into a grid of cells and contain rules for how the cells interact. Each cell has a set of variables, including height, heat, pressure, fluid and terrain. The rules of the cellular automata are loosely based on thermodynamics and physics and use the properties of each cell to determine how the cells will exchange heat, pressure and fluid, which gives rise to explosions, fire and floods. The EmerGEnT world also includes game objects (e.g. buildings) and game agents (e.g. villagers) that have similar properties to the cells of the environment, which determine how the objects and agents act and interact in the game world.

5   Agent Design

For a game agent to react sensibly to the environment it must have two things: a way to sense the environment and a way to choose a suitable reaction, based on what it has sensed. An agent's understanding of its situation in the EmerGEnT system is represented as a weighted sum of the factors affecting each cell on the map. Based on the utility value of each cell, the agent chooses a cell to move to and reacts at a level that reflects its current situation (e.g. if the agent's current cell is on fire then it panics). After the agent chooses a destination, its task is simply to move towards it. This section discusses the "comfort" function that determines the utility of each cell, the agent's level of reaction and the agent's choice of destination cell.

The utility function for the agents in the EmerGEnT system determines how comfortable each cell is for the agents and is therefore called a *comfort* function. The comfort function is a weighted sum of the factors that affect the agents' comfort in each cell and includes *fire*, *heat*, *pressure* and *wetness*. Each of these factors is weighted according to how distressing it is for the agent. Fire is the most distressing, followed by temperature, pressure and wetness. The weights (W_1, W_2, W_3, W_4) can be tuned to reflect different priorities of different agents. For example, an alien might find water far more dangerous than heat. The comfort function returns a real value between zero and one, with a lower value representing a more comfortable cell.

$$Comfort = \text{Min}\ ((fire*W_1) + (heat*W_2) + (pressure*W_3) + (wetness*W_4),\ 1)$$

The comfort function provides an efficient alternative to the environment sending the agent multiple messages about its state, such as "it's hot" or "it's raining". Instead, the relevant factors are weighted and combined into a single value that gives the agent an estimate of the safety and comfort of its current location. The purpose of the comfort value is twofold. First, it provides a means for the agents to determine how comfortable they are in the current cell and to react accordingly. Second, it provides a means for the agents to assess surrounding cells and find a suitable destination. These two tasks are discussed in this section.

The comfort function returns a real value which allows the agent to react with varying degrees of distress, providing for diverse and interesting behaviour (see Table 1). The agent's level of reaction is denoted by its speed of movement, as well as its animation and sound. Scaling the agents' reactions allows the agents to react in varying ways to different situations, while greatly simplifying the process of determining how the agents will react. Instead of the agents considering each element in the environment individually, the comfort function determines the agents' level of discomfort and the agents respond accordingly by choosing the reaction level that corresponds to their comfort value.

Table 1. Agent reaction levels. Agents react with varying degrees of distress to provide more diverse behaviour

Value	Level	Reaction
< 0.1	comfortable	no reaction
0.1 - 0.3	uncomfortable	calmly moves to more comfortable cell
0.3 - 0.6	distressing	runs from the cell
> 0.6	painful	panics and runs quickly from cell

If the agents are not comfortable in their current cell then they must locate and move to a more comfortable cell. Each agent reassesses its situation each timestep, by calculating the comfort value for the cell it is standing in or passing through and finding a destination cell based on the comfort of its neighbour cells. As long as the agent is not comfortable, it will keep reassessing its situation and finding a new destination, which means that agents can change destination while they are moving towards their current destination, if they find a better destination. Also, as the state of the environment is continuously changing, the destination the agent found last cycle may no longer be a comfortable cell. In choosing a destination, the agents evaluate the comfort values of the cells in a neighbourhood of a given size and choose the cell with the lowest comfort value.

6 Agent Experiments

Three experiments were conducted to investigate and tune the behaviour of the agents in the EmerGEnT system, in terms of efficiency, effectiveness and observable behaviour. Several conditions were investigated in each experiment and ten trials with ten agents were run in each condition. The criteria that were used to evaluate the performance of the agents included whether or not the agents converged on a solution (i.e. agents located and reached comfortable cells), the number of cycles the Emer-GEnT system ran before the agents converged, how efficiently the agents found a solution, what (if any) strategies or patterns agents exhibited and the number of local optima (comfortable cells) on which the agents converged. The initial state of each trial was randomly generated, including the position of the agents, the position of rain and the number and position of explosions (see Fig. 1). See [4] for detailed experiments.

Fig. 1. The initial state of each trial was randomly generated, including position of agents, rain and explosions

The aim of the first experiment was to determine the optimal neighbourhood size that agents should evaluate when choosing a destination (i.e. where to move to maximise comfort). Three conditions were tested, in which the agents evaluated neighbourhoods with a radius or one, two or three. Agents with each of these neighbourhood sizes demonstrated various advantages and drawbacks. The agents with a neighbourhood size of one performed the best at avoiding immediate danger. However, their short sight meant that they often ran towards more dangerous situations or became stuck in larger hazards as they were unable to find a way out. With a neighbourhood size of two, the agents were better at choosing safe destinations and appeared more organised, but still expressed the problems associated with short sight. The agents with a neighbourhood size of three were exceptional at picking particularly desirable cells and appeared organized, as many agents moved to similar locations. However, the problems for these agents were almost the opposite of the previous agents, as they performed the best at choosing a destination but were unable to avoid immediate hazards in getting to their destination. They would often put themselves in great danger (e.g. run through fire) to get to a safe destination cell.

From the first experiment, it was concluded that it would be desirable to combine the ability to find local optima of the longer-sighted agents with the ability to avoid immediate threats of the short-sighted agents. Consequently, the second experiment investigated whether a combination of immediate area (reactive) evaluation and greater area (goal) evaluation is more effective than either approach individually. The aim of the second experiment was to determine what combination of reactive (neighbourhood size = 1) and goal (neighbourhood size = 3) evaluation gave rise to the best agent behaviour. Three conditions were tested: evenly-weighted, goal-directed and reactive.

The agents in the second experiment displayed definite advantages over the agents in the first experiment. The agents in the evenly weighted and goal-directed conditions appeared far more intelligent, as they moved towards a goal rather than running back and forth randomly. Also, these agents appeared more realistic, as they moved around hazards on the way to their goal rather than simply running in a straight line, which made the agents in the previous experiment appear very flat and synthetic. Also, the agents in the evenly weighted condition displayed more depth as they did not always react in the same way, sometimes they would appear organised and at other times they would appear more independent, with their behaviour being heavily dependent on the current situation. The agents in the evenly weighted condition took the least amount of time to converge on safe cells. The agents in the goal-directed condition behaved in a similar way to the agents in the evenly weighted condition, but became stuck more often and still ran through hazards. The agents in the reactive condition had the least desirable behaviour as they often appeared to move randomly, did not appear organised and often became stuck. Therefore, it was concluded from the second experiment that the most suitable combination of reactive and goal-directed behaviour for the agents in the EmerGEnT system is approximately equal, where it is more desirable to err on the side of goal-directed than on reactive behaviour.

The first and second experiments gave rise to agents that efficiently, intelligently and realistically react to the environment by moving from danger to safety. However, in a computer game situation, it is also likely that agents will have greater goals or desires that they need to fulfil, apart from simply surviving and reacting sensibly to the environment. For example, marines in a strategy game might be on a mission to kill the enemy in a particular cell or a villager in a role-playing game might want to stay near its house or shop. Drawing on the notion of "desirability" values from influence maps, goal areas could be given high desirability values for the agents. Additionally, desirability values could then be propagated out to surrounding areas to indicate that these areas are more desirable as they are near the goal. Therefore, the aim of the third experiment was to combine the desire to reach a greater goal with the agents' current behaviour of reacting to the environment and avoiding hazards. The third experiment combined an influence map to propagate the desirability of the cells with the cellular automata to determine the comfort of the cells. The three conditions that were investigated in the third experiment were designed to test different influences of comfort and desirability on the agent's choice. The three conditions were evenly weighted, goal-oriented, and self-preserving.

The third experiment demonstrated that an equal weighting of desirability and comfort gave the agents the most acceptable observable behaviour, in terms of organisation, avoiding hazards and navigating the environment realistically and intelligently. When the weighting was tipped towards either comfort or desirability, the agents' behaviour appeared random, less organised and less intelligent. Only about half the equal-weighting agents found the goal as they opted for comfort over the goal. It is difficult to judge this as a success or a failure without a context for the agents. For example, it would be reasonable for villagers to prioritise their safety over achieving a specific goal, but marines would be expected to carry out the player's orders. It was concluded that the success of the agents must be judged with respect to the game situation, as different game types and scenarios have different requirements for successful agent behaviour. In general, agents should be able to reach their goal, while displaying appropriate behaviour (e.g. avoiding danger), but the relative importance of each of these aspects would be determined by the game situation. The third experiment produced an agent model that successfully integrates goal-directed behaviour (based on agent desires) with situation awareness (based on comfort), which enabled the agents to both react to the environment in an intelligent, realistic and organised way while simultaneously satisfying their desire to reach a goal.

7 Discussion and Conclusions

The outcome of the first two experiments was a model for agents that dynamically respond to the environment in an intelligent and realistic way, based on concepts from cellular automata and influence maps. The outcome of the third experiment was an extension of this model that also integrates goal-directed behaviour to enable the agents to respond to the environment while pursuing a goal. An advantage of the model developed through these experiments is extensibility, in that it can be extended to incorporate any aspects in the game world that are relevant to the agents' behaviour (e.g. other agents, terrain, events). It would also be possible to incorporate other models for agent behaviour, such as flocking, so that the agents also take into consideration the movement of other agents around them. The simplicity and flexibility of this model means that it can be used to govern the behaviour of almost any agent in any circumstance. The contribution of this research is a design that allows agents to dynamically react to the changing situation of their environment, as well as an intelligent pathfinding algorithm that allows agents to find a safe path to a goal, based on aspects of their environment. The agent parameters were tuned through the experiments discussed, but future work will be required to optimise their behaviour for specific game situations.

In conclusion, this research provides a possible solution for incorporating agents that appear intelligent to the player, by reacting sensibly to the game environment, into game worlds. First, reactive agents can be incorporated into game worlds by giving the agents a measure of comfort in their current situation (via cellular automata or other means), as well as a map for deciding where they might move to maximise their comfort. As this design closely resembles an influence map, it is also possible to integrate goal-directed behaviour and potentially personality, group movement and various other behaviours into the agent model. Whereas current agents in games do not demonstrate an awareness of their situation or react appropriately to events in their immediate surroundings, the reactive agents presented in this paper maintain a model of the comfort of their environment and react according to the changing state of their situation. The reactive agent model developed in this study allows agents to dynamically react to the changing situation of their environment and to intelligently find a path to a goal, increasing their visible level of intelligent, realistic and responsive behaviour.

References

1. Drennan, P., Viller, S. and Wyeth, P.: Engaging Game Characters: Informing Design with Player Perspectives. Entertainment Computing - ICEC 2004: Third International Conference, Lecture Notes in Computer Science, Vol. 3166. Springer-Verlag, Berlin Heidelberg New York (2004) 355-358
2. Leonard, T.: Building an AI Sensory System: Examining the Design of Thief: The Dark Project. Gamasutra (March 7, 2003). Available online 2 February, 2005, at http://www.gamasutra.com/gdc2003/features/20030307/leonard_pfv.htm (2003)
3. Sweetser, P.: Strategic Decision-Making with Neural Networks and Influence Maps. In: S. Rabin (ed.): AI Game Programming Wisdom 2. Charles River Media, Inc., Hingham, MA (2004) 439-446
4. Sweetser, P.: PhD Thesis Chapter 6: Reactive Agents. In: An Emergent Approach to Game Design – Development and Play (in preparation). Available online, 25 April, at http://www.itee.uq.edu.au/~penny/publications.htm
5. Sweetser, P., Johnson, D., Sweetser, J. and Wiles, J.: Creating Engaging Artificial Characters for Games. Proceedings of the Second International Conference on Entertainment Computing. Carnegie Mellon University, Pittsburgh, PA (2003) 1-8
6. Tozour, P.: Influence Mapping. In: M. Deloura (ed.): Game Programming Gems 2. Charles River Media, Inc., Hingham, MA (2001) 287-297
7. Woodcock, S.: Game AI: The State of the Industry. Gamasutra (November 1, 2000). Available online 2 February, 2005, at http://www.gamasutra.com/features/20001101/woodcock_01.htm (2000)

Patterns in Complex Systems Modeling

Janet Wiles and James Watson

ARC Centre for Complex Systems,
School of Information Technology and Electrical Engineering
The University of Queensland, Brisbane, 4072, Australia
{j.wiles,j.watson}@itee.uq.edu.au
http://www.itee.uq.edu.au/~patterns/

Abstract. The design, development, and use of complex systems models raises a unique class of challenges and potential pitfalls, many of which are commonly recurring problems. Over time, researchers gain experience in this form of modeling, choosing algorithms, techniques, and frameworks that improve the quality, confidence level, and speed of development of their models. This increasing collective experience of complex systems modellers is a resource that should be captured. Fields such as software engineering and architecture have benefited from the development of generic solutions to recurring problems, called *patterns*. Using pattern development techniques from these fields, insights from communities such as learning and information processing, data mining, bioinformatics, and agent-based modeling can be identified and captured. Collections of such 'pattern languages' would allow knowledge gained through experience to be readily accessible to less-experienced practitioners and to other domains. This paper proposes a methodology for capturing the wisdom of computational modelers by introducing example visualization patterns, and a pattern classification system for analyzing the relationship between micro and macro behaviour in complex systems models. We anticipate that a new field of *complex systems patterns* will provide an invaluable resource for both practicing and future generations of modelers.

1 Introduction

While complex systems models are used by a wide variety of often experienced research groups, the development of such models is far from an exact science. The design of model architecture and algorithms, the choice of hardware and software infrastructure, and methods for tracking and analyzing results, are just some of the problems often faced and often re-solved. While each research project and each simulation within it is unique, there are many underlying commonalities which, once identified, can save much 'reinvention of the wheel'.

Established fields such as architecture [1] and software engineering [2] have captured much of the experience gained by their respected practitioners. These rules of thumb are known as *patterns* in architecture and software engineering (e.g. design patterns [3], process patterns [4]). They record both commonly-recurring problems, pertaining to any aspect of the work from global structure to specific detail, and their proven solutions. Libraries of such patterns are more than just collections of a field's heuristics. The context in which a solution is appropriate plays a critical part in the description of a pattern. Context is a recognized part of the background knowledge of

M. Gallagher, J. Hogan, and F. Maire (Eds.): IDEAL 2005, LNCS 3578, pp. 532–539, 2005.

any field, although in most areas it is rarely described as an integral part of a heuristic. For the field of machine learning, it is well known that no search technique will be optimal for all tasks, frequently expressed as 'no free lunch', however it is still rare for a new algorithm to be presented with an assessment of the tasks in which it is *in*appropriate. It is important to know in which contexts a heuristic is effective, and the consequences of their use, such as tradeoffs between accuracy versus time.

Capturing commonly-recurring problems, their contexts and consequences has had multiple benefits for software engineering and architecture. First, both beginning and experienced practitioners benefit from a rapidly accessible library of tested ideas, information about the situations where they should be used and the consequences or tradeoffs of their use. Second, an appropriate and tested format (building on 40 years of patterns research in a variety of fields) facilitates the ongoing community development of the library. This format provides a shared language of tools and methods agreed upon by the community, enabling rapid communication. Third, capturing the wisdom of the field in a practical and effective resource builds confidence in the quality of systems produced.

The field of complex systems currently lacks this library of experience. Shared libraries of algorithms and heuristics exist but they lack the experience of the complex systems modeler in when to apply them.

Using the patterns approach to capture experience in the field of complex systems modeling would provide a further benefit. The complex systems community is a unique collection of researchers from many disparate backgrounds (such as machine learning, complex adaptive systems, neural networks, gene expression analysis, multi-agent systems, etc.). However, the fundamental issues studied are common to all, such as the emergence of macro-level behaviour from micro-level interactions. Insights from one branch of complex systems science can often be applied to another when taken at an appropriate level of abstraction. Patterns can be used to capture knowledge unique to one branch of the field and effectively communicate these insights to other areas.

2 Software Patterns

The software engineering field has had decades of experience developing, maintaining and using complicated systems, advancing techniques such as problem decomposition, verification, validation and project management. Software engineering provides extensive experience in pattern development, with patterns spanning the problem space from global architecture to detailed programming language specific idioms. More than a heuristic or data structure, a pattern is the solution to a problem in a specific context, balancing inherent tradeoffs [5]. Software engineering patterns have defined characteristics including name, intent, motivation, consequences, known uses, and related patterns [2] (see Section 4).

A good software engineering pattern has the following key characteristics [6]:

- solves a particular problem (not just in principle);
- is a proven solution that has been successfully employed in at least three significant scenarios; and
- has a significant human component describing how and when it is useful.

In terms of the patterns development process, the following characteristics have become accepted in the software engineering community [6]:

- a strong focus on proven solutions to recurring problems;
- those writing patterns do *not* have to be the original inventor of the solution;
- non-anonymous review, where discussions focus on how patterns should be clarified or improved upon;
- development through discussions in workshops instead of solo presentations; and
- careful editing, through which the pattern authors can incorporate feedback gained through workshops and review before presenting the patterns in their final form.

These characteristics provide a useful guide for the development of patterns in complex systems science.

3 Complex Systems Patterns

As in software engineering, the field of complex systems consists of practitioners experienced with a wide range of solutions to common problems. Modeling techniques and implementation frameworks, methods of analysis and visualization, and the most effective ways of reporting results, are just some of the techniques that form the collective experience of the field. We propose that one of the most effective methods to capture and communicate complex systems knowledge is the proven technique of pattern development from software design.

Patterns from the complex systems community can be grouped into two classes. The first is collections of proven solutions to commonly recurring problems that occur in the development and use of complex systems models. Examples in this class of patterns include hardware and software platforms, model architectures and abstractions, and analysis and visualization techniques. The second source of potential patterns are the insights generated by the complex systems models themselves. Emergent robustness, evolvability, efficient connectivity, and modular design are some of the characteristics found in complex systems that can inform the development of solutions to certain problems, and communicate insights from one class of models, such as agent-based systems, to another, such as genetic regulatory networks.

Initial places to search for such classes of patterns include the visualization of network structure and dynamics such as expression patterns [7], [8], metrics for connectivity, diameter, and cluster coherency of networks [9], [10], and micro and macro scale, temporal and spatial structures [11], [12].

Patterns vary in their level of abstraction and granularity, and consequently there needs to be a way to classify them [2]. The micro and macro level characteristics of complex systems models can be at the level of structure, dynamics, or function. The structural level focuses on the static relationships between model entities, for example, a network of agent relationships or gene connectivity. The dynamic level is concerned with the interactions between these components, for example, a diagram of gene activations or the state space. The functional level focuses on the entire complex system functioning within an environment (e.g., a phenotype based on underlying component interactions placed within an evolutionary algorithm). A preliminary set of complex systems patterns, useful for modeling Boolean networks, and their classifications, is summarized in Table 1.

Table 1. Examples of visualizations that can inform development and use of Boolean network models

Pattern	Targeted Complex Systems Features					
	Structure	*Dynamics*	*Function*	*Micro Mechanics*	*Macro Behaviours*	......
Network Diagram	✓			✓		
Activation Diagram		✓		✓	✓	
State Space Diagram		✓			✓	
......						

4 Example Patterns

Consistent with best practice, refinements can be found at
http://www.itee.uq.edu.au/~patterns/repository/

4.1 Activation Diagram

One commonly-recurring problem in genetic regulatory network modeling is the visualization of system behaviour, where interesting behaviours span multiple levels in time and space. To provide a concrete feel for the nature and scope of a complex system pattern, this section illustrates a prototype pattern which solves this problem.

Name: Activation Diagram (Classification: Dynamics, Micro-Mechanics, Macro Behaviours)

Intent: Visualize micro level activation of components over time to see macro level characteristics.

Also Known as: Gene expression diagram, gene activation diagram, expression pattern, activation signature

Motivation: Understanding the effects over time of interactions between large numbers of nodes in a network can be difficult and time-consuming. Inferring macro-level classes of behaviour is easiest when the history of system-wide activations are presented as a single diagram. The idea of this pattern is to provide a visualization of node histories for a single initial condition, allowing macro-level features such as stable, cyclic, or chaotic behaviour to be identified, and characteristics such as the length of transient periods to be measured.

Applicability: Use the Activation Diagram pattern when you want to:

- visualize the characteristics of component activations over time when components have binary or real-valued states;
- visualize characteristics of macro level behaviour such as ordered, cyclic, or chaotic activity;
- visualize both the initial transient dynamics and the longer term behaviour;

- assess the life cycle of macro level behaviours (such as the number of steps before a network settles into a certain state); or
- (variation) manually investigate robustness of macro-level behaviour

Example Visualization:

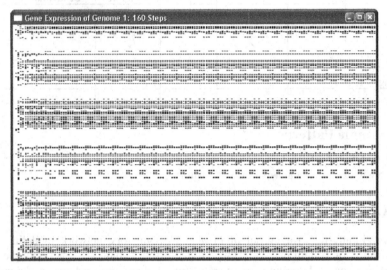

Fig. 1. Activation diagram. Time is shown along the *x* axis, and each component is positioned along the *y* axis. Active components are denoted by dark shading. This diagram shows the component activations falling into a cyclic state after a short transient period

Consequences: The Activation Diagram has the following consequences and inherent limitations:

- it provides a clean visualization of the dynamics from a single starting state but the inherent limitation is that only a single starting state and trajectory is shown per diagram;
- it requires access to the values of all components for each time step;
- large numbers of components can make viewing difficult;
- very long cycles can appear similar to chaotic trajectories;
- the two-dimensional representation maps time into space, consequently spatial information is lost (e.g., in random Boolean networks, neural networks); this can be mitigated by using the Activation Diagram pattern together with the Network Diagram pattern; and
- spatial information is preserved if a one-dimensional representation is used (e.g., cellular automata)

Implementation: The Activation Diagram has the following important implementation variations:

- time can be expressed along the *x* or *y* axis; and
- one-dimensional interactions (e.g., cellular automata) can be visualized by ordering nodes according to their interactions

Known Uses: Gene expression [13], random Boolean networks, cellular automata, neural network dynamics.

Related Patterns: State Space Diagram, Network Diagram

Sample Code:

This example visualizes the expression pattern of a Boolean network of gene regulation. A C++ source code listing is available at

http://www.itee.uq.edu.au/~patterns/repository/activation-diagram.html

```
e = expression data, indexed by [step number][gene number]
s = number of steps in e
g = number of genes in e

if (s > 0) and (g > 0):
    clear the screen
    xdist = screen-width / s
    ydist = screen-height / g
    xgap = 0.12 * xdist
    ygap = 0.12 * ydist

    x = 0   /* where 0 is leftmost screen coordinate */
    for i = 1 to s:
            y = 0   /* where 0 is topmost screen coordinate */
            for j = 1 to g:
                    if expression_data[i][j] is activated:
                            x1 = x + xgap
                            y1 = y + ygap
                            x2 = x + xdist - xgap
                            y2 = y + ydist - ygap
                            draw_rectangle(x1, y1, x2, y2)
                    y = y + ydist
            x = x + xdist
```

4.2 Network Diagram

Name and Classification: Network Diagram (Structure, Micro Mechanics)

Intent: Visualize micro-level interactions of components at a given point in time

Also Known as: Graph

Motivation: Understanding the relationships between nodes in a network, together with their spatial information, is most intuitive with a graphical depiction. The idea of this pattern is to visualize the nature and number of interactions between nodes in a network, and any spatial relationship these nodes may have with each other.

Applicability: Use the Network Diagram pattern when you want to

- visualize the interactions of components at a given point in time
- visualize spatial relationships between network components

Consequences: The Network Diagram has the following consequences and inherent limitations:

- interactions are only shown for a single point in time
- large numbers of nodes can make viewing difficult

Implementation: Implementation issues to consider for Network Diagram include:

- Spatial arrangement of nodes is very important when identifying certain network characteristics. A random layout is the simplest to implement, but is generally unsuitable for visualizing the giant component of the network. Increasingly sophisticated network layout algorithms can incur a cost in processor time (many optimal layouts are likely to be NP-complete).

Known Uses: Boolean network visualization and design, social network visualization, neural network visualization and design

Related Patterns: State Space Diagram, Activation Diagram

Sample Code:

```
n = network, indexed by node
p = position of each node

clear the screen
for i = 1 to (number of nodes in n):
    p[i] = random position
    draw sphere at p[i]

for i = 1 to (number of nodes in n):
    r = list of nodes regulated by n[i]
    for j = 1 to (number of nodes in r):
        draw arrow from p[i] to p[r[j]]
```

A C++ source code listing is available at
http://www.itee.uq.edu.au/~patterns/repository/network-diagram.html

5   Conclusions

Patterns are proven solutions to commonly-recurring problems. Using the extensive pattern development experience of the software engineering field, the complex systems community can capture its collective experience. Patterns provide a framework that asks the right questions to extract and document knowledge gained through experience, and offer a standardized language with which to discuss this captured knowledge. This paper is an initial step towards a community-driven library of complex systems patterns. Updates and pattern contributions are available online at http://www.itee.uq.edu.au/~patterns/.

Acknowledgments

This work was funded by the ARC Centre for Complex Systems and an Australian Research Council grant to the first author.

References

1. Alexander, C., et al., *A Pattern Language*. 1977, New York: Oxford University Press.
2. Gamma, E., et al., *Design Patterns: Elements of Reusable Object-Oriented Software*. Addison-Wesley Professional Computing Series. 1994: Addison-Wesley.
3. Srinivasan, S., *Design patterns in object-oriented frameworks*. Computer, 1999. **32**(2): p. 24-32.

4. Moore, J., et al. *Combining and adapting process patterns for flexible workflow*. in *11th International Workshop on Database and Expert Systems Applications*. 2000.
5. Coplien, J.O., *Software design patterns: common questions and answers*, in *The Patterns Handbook: Techniques, Strategies, and Applications*, L. Rising, Editor. 1998, Cambridge University Press, New York. p. 311-320.
6. Appleton, B., *Patterns and software: essential concepts and terminology*. 2000. http://www.cmcrossroads.com/bradapp/docs/patterns-intro.html
7. Wuensche, A. *Genomic regulation modeled as a network with basins of attraction*. in *Pacific Symposium on Biocomputing '98*. 1998. Singapore: World Scientific.
8. Solé, R.V., P. Fernández, and S.A. Kauffman, *Adaptive walks in a gene network model of morphogenesis: insights into the Cambrian explosion*. International Journal of Developmental Biology, 2003. **47**(7/8): p. 685-693.
9. Strogatz, S.H., *Exploring complex networks*. Nature, 2001. **410**: p. 268-276.
10. Newman, M.E.J., *The structure and function of complex networks*. SIAM Review, 2003. **45**(2): p. 167-256.
11. Raff, R.A., *Evo-Devo: The evolution of a new discipline*. Nature Reviews Genetics, 2000. **1**(1): p. 74-79.
12. Hasty, J., et al., *Computational studies of gene regulatory networks: In numero molecular biology*. Nature Reviews Genetics, 2001. **2**(4): p. 268-279.
13. Reil, T. *Dynamics of gene expression in an artificial genome - implications for biological and artificial ontogeny*. in *The 5th European Conference on Artificial Life*. 1999: Springer Verlag.

Global Optimization Using Evolutionary Algorithm Based on Level Set Evolution and Latin Square[*]

Yuping Wang[1], Jinling Du[1], and Chuangyin Dang[2]

[1] School of Computer, Xidian University, Xi'an, 710071, China
[2] Department of Manufacturing Engineering and Engineering Management
City University of Hong Kong, Hong Kong

Abstract. In this paper, a new crossover operator based on Latin square design is presented at first. This crossover operator can generate a set of uniformly scattered offspring around their parents, and it is of the ability of local search and thus can explore the search space efficiently. Then the level set of the objective function is evolved successively by crossover and mutation operators such that it gradually approaches to global optimal solution set. Based on these, a new evolutionary algorithm for nondifferentiable unconstrained global optimization is proposed and its global convergence is proved. At last, the numerical simulations are made for some standard test functions. The performance of the proposed algorithm is compared with that of two widely-cited algorithms. The results indicate the proposed algorithm is effective and has better performance than the compared algorithms for these test functions.

1 Introduction

Global optimization problems have been arisen in many fields such as computer science, engineering design and decision making, etc. They can be divided into two categories: differentiable global optimization problems and nondifferentiable global optimization problems. The objective functions of the former are differentiable while the objective functions of the later are nondifferentiable. Based on these two kinds of problems, the algorithms for global optimization problems are accordingly classified into two categories: differentiable global optimization algorithms and nondifferentiable global optimization algorithms. examples of the former are such as filled function algorithms (e.g., [1], [2]) and tunneling algorithms (e.g., [3]), etc, which make use of the derivatives of the objective functions and can not be applicable to nondifferentiable problems. While neural networks (e.g., [8]), evolutionary algorithms (e.g., [4], [5], [6], [7]) and simulated annealing (e.g., [9]) are examples of the later, which usually do not need to use derivatives of the objective functions and can be applicable to the nondifferentiable problems.

[*] This work was supported by the National Natural Science Foundation of China (60374063) and CERG (No.: 9040870 of Hong Kong Government)

The most of the recently developed evolutionary algorithms can be seen as the improvements of the classical evolutionary algorithms by improving genetic operators (crossover and mutation operators) and selection scheme, but the framework of the classical evolutionary algorithms is kept unchanged. However, in this paper, a different model of algorithm is proposed, in which the global optimization problem is solved by evolving the level set of the objective function consecutively such that the level set gradually becomes smaller and smaller and until the measure of it is zero. As a result, each point in it is a global optimal solution.

2   Concepts, Assumptions and Related Results

We consider the following global optimization problem

$$\min_{x \in G} f(x), \tag{1}$$

Where $G \subseteq R^n$. First, we introduce the following concepts

Definition 1. *Suppose that c is a constant satisfying $c \geq f^* = \min_{x \in G} f(x)$, then the set $H_c = \{x \in R^n | f(x) \leq c\}$ is called a level set of $f(x)$, and $M(f,c) = \frac{\int_{H_c} f(x)dx}{\mu(H_c)}$ is called mean of $f(x)$ on H_c, where $\mu(H_c)$ is the Lebesque measure of H_c. If $\{c_k\} \to f^*$ for $k \to \infty$ and $c_k > f^*$, define $M(f, f^*) = \lim_{k \to \infty} \frac{\int_{H_{c_k}} f(x)dx}{\mu(H_{c_k})}$.*

In order to guarantee the problem (1) is well-defined, i.e., there must exists global optimal solution, we make the following assumptions: (A1). $f(x)$ is continuous on G. (A2). There exists a real number c such that $G \cap H_c$ is a nonempty and compact set. Now we introduce some related results:

Lemma 1[10] *Under the assumptions (A1) and (A2), if $G \cap H_c \neq \emptyset$ and $\mu(G \cap H_c) = 0$, then c is the global optimal function value of $f(x)$ and $G \cap H_c$ is the set of global optimal solutions.*

Lemma 2[10] *Under the assumptions (A1) and (A2), we have*

- *If $c > f^*$, then $M(f,c) \leq c$. If $c_1 \geq c_2 \geq f^*$, then $M(f,c_1) \geq M(f,c_2) \geq f^*$.*
- *$\bar{f}$ is global optimal function value if and only if $M(f,\bar{f}) = \bar{f}$.*
- *If $\lim_{k \to \infty} f^k = \bar{f}$, then $\lim_{k \to \infty} M(f, f^k) = M(f, \bar{f})$.*

3   A New Evolutionary Algorithm
Based on Level Set Evolution and Latin Square

In the following we use real number encode, i.e., each individual is represented by its original real vector form x.

Latin square design: First, we introduce the concept of Latin square. Let $(x_1, x_2, \cdots, x_q) \in R^q$, a shift mapping $S : R^q \to R^q$ is defined as $S(x_1, x_2, \cdots, x_q) = (x_2, x_3, \cdots, x_q, x_1)$.

Definition 2. *If a $q \times q$ matrix satisfies the conditions: (I). Its first row $a = (x_1, x_2, \cdots, x_q)$, denoted as V_1, is a permutation of $(1, 2, \cdots, q)$. (II). Its i-th row, denoted as V_i, is defined by shift mapping $V_i = S(V_{i-1})$ for $i = 2 \sim q$. Then the matrix is called a Latin square of order q. A Latin square of order q with the first row a is denoted as $Ls(q, a)$, and its the i-th row and the j-th column element is denoted as v_{ij}.*

Latin square design is one of the uniform design methods ([11]). It can generate a uniformly scattered points in a domain. Since initially we do not know where the optimal solution is, it is better to generate the initial population which approximately uniformly scatter in the search space. We use Latin square design to generate the initial population. The idea of Latin square design is as follows. Suppose the domain considered is

$$[L, U] = \{x \in R^n | \, l_j \le x_j \le u_j, \, j = 1 \sim n\},$$

where x_j, l_j and u_j are the j-th component of x, L and U, respectively. Choose a row vector $a \in R^n$ and generate an order n Latin square $Ls(n, a) = (v_{ij})_{n \times n}$, then Latin square design generates a set of uniformly scattered points in $[L, U]$ as follows: $\{W^i | W^i = (w_{i1}, w_{i2}, \cdots, w_{in}), i = 1 \sim n\}$, where $w_{ij} = l_j + \frac{2v_{ij}-1}{2n}(u_j - l_j)$, $i, j = 1 \sim n$.

Initial population: Given the population size *pop*. Divide the search space into several smaller domains and use Latin square design to generate a set of points in each domain such that the total number of points generated is larger than or equal to the population size, then the initial population consist of the *pop* best points among these points.

Crossover operator: For two parents $X^i = (x_{i1}, x + i2, \cdots, x_{in})$, $i = 1, 2$, let $l_j = \min\{x_{1j}, x_{2j}\}$, $u_j = \max\{x_{1j}, x_{2j}\}$, $j = 1 \sim n$, $\bar{L} = (l_1, l_2, \cdots, l_n)$, $\bar{U} = (u_1, u_2, \cdots, u_n)$, and define domain $[\bar{L}, \bar{U}] = \{x \in R^n | l_j \le x_j \le u_j, j = 1 \sim n\}$. Choose a proper Latin square $Ls(q, a) = (v_{ij})$ of order q. If $q \ge n$, the i-th offspring $O^i = (o_{i1}, o_{i2}, \cdots, o_{in})$ can be generated by $o_{ij} = l_j + \frac{2v_{ij}-1}{2n}(u_j - l_j)$, $j = 1 \sim n$ for $i = 1 \sim q$. If $q < n$, divide the components of X^1, X^2, $\bar{L}$ and $\bar{U}$ into q sub-vectors in the same way as follows: $X^1 = (A^1, A^2, \cdots, A^q)$, $X^2 = (B^1, B^2, \cdots, B^q)$, $\bar{L} = (L^1, L^2, \cdots, L^q)$ and $\bar{U} = (U^1, U^2, \cdots, U^q)$, where A^j, B^j, L^j and U^j are same dimensional sub-vectors and the dimensions of q sub-vectors are randomly assigned. The i-th offspring $O^i = (O_1^i, O_2^i, \cdots, O_q^i)$ can be generated by $O_j^i = L^j + \frac{2v_{ij}-1}{2q}(U^j - L^j)$, $j = 1 \sim q$ for $i = 1 \sim q$.

Adaptive mutation operator: Suppose that x is an individual to undergo the mutation. Its offspring $\bar{O}$ generated by adaptive mutation can be given by $\bar{O} = x + \sigma(T, \bar{U} - x)$ if $r > 0$ and $\bar{O} = x - \sigma(T, x - \bar{L})$ if $r \le 0$, where r is a random number in $[-1, 1]$, $\sigma(T, y) = y(1 - t)^{\lambda T}$ with $t \in [0, 1]$ is a random number, λ is a parameter in $[2, 5]$, $T = \frac{f(x)-f_{min}}{f_{max}-f_{min}}$, f_{min} and f_{max} are the minimal and maximal fitness values in current population.

Selection scheme: The best individuals of 70% population size among the current population and all offspring generated in the current generation are selected to the next generation population, the remaining individuals of 30%

population size are selected among those which are as far as possible from the 70% selected individuals. Selection in this way is helpful to the diversity of the population.

Algorithm 1: (A new evolutionary algorithm based on level set evolution and Latin square)

1. (Initialization) Generate initial population $P(0) = \{x^1, x^2, \cdots, x^{pop}\}$, given crossover and mutation probabilities p_c and p_m, and a large positive integer $\bar{N}$. Let $k = 0$, $s = 0$ and $c_k = [f(x^1) + \cdots + f(x^{pop})]/pop$, where x^i is required to be in G for $i = 1 \sim pop$. Let $f_k = c_k$ and $L_k = \{x \in G | f(x) \leq f_k\}$. Find the points from $P(k)$ which are in L_k and denoted by $x^1, x^2, \cdots, x^{N_k}$ without loss of generality. Let $d_k = [f(x^1) + \cdots + f(x^{N_k})]/N_k$.

2. If $\mu(L_k) = 0$, f_k is the optimal fitness value and L_k is the global optimal solution set. Stop. Otherwise, go to step 3.

3. (Crossover) Select parents from $P(k)$ for crossover with probability p_c. Randomly match every two parents and use the crossover operator to each pair of matched parents to generate offspring. The set of all offspring generated is denoted as $O1$.

4. (Mutation) Select parents from $P(k)$ for mutation with probability p_m. Each selected parent generates an offspring and the set of all these offspring is denoted as $O2$.

5. (Selection) Estimate $d_{k+1} = \int_{L_k} f(x)dx/\mu(L_k)$ as follows: suppose that o^1, $o^2, \cdots, o^{m_k}$ are the offspring in both $O1 \cup O2$ and L_k. Let $d_k = [d_k \times N_k + f(o^1) + \cdots + f(o^{m_k})]/(N_k + m_k)$ and set $N_k = N_k + m_k$. If there exists $\xi^k \in O1 \cup O2 \cup P(k)$ such that $f_{k+1} = f(\xi^k) < d_k$, then $P(k+1)$ consist of the best pop individuals in $O1 \cup O2 \cup P(k)$. Let $L_{k+1} = \{x | f(x) \leq f_{k+1}, x \in G\}$. Suppose $x^1, x^2, \cdots, x^{N_{k+1}} \in P(k+1) \cap L_{k+1}$ without loss of generality. Define $d_{k+1} = [f(x^1) + \cdots + f(x^{N_{k+1}})]/N_{k+1}$, let $k = k + 1$. Go to step 2; otherwise, $f(\xi^k) \geq d_k$ for any $\xi^k \in O1 \cup O2 \cup P(k)$. Set $s = s + 1$. If $s \leq \bar{N}$, select pop individuals from $O1 \cup O2 \cup P(k)$ as temporary population $P_s(k)$ according to the selection scheme. Go to step 3; if $s > \bar{N}$, let $f_{k+1} = d_k$, go to step 6.

6. f_{k+1} is optimal fitness value and L_{k+1} is the set of global optimal solutions.

4   Global Convergence

Theorem 1 *Suppose that $\bar{N}$ is large enough such that there exists ξ^k satisfying $f(\xi^k) < d_k$ when $s \leq \bar{N}$ in step 5 of algorithm 1, then under assumptions (A1) and (A2) in section 2, $\{f^k\}$ and $\{L_k\}$ have the following properties:*

1. *If algorithm 1 stops in generation k, then f^k is the optimal fitness value and L_k is the set of global optimal solutions.*

2. *Otherwise, we have: (I). For $\forall k$, $f^k > f^{k+1} > f^*$ and $L_k \supset L_{k+1} \supset L_*$, where f^* is the optimal fitness value and $L_* = \{x | f(x) = f^*, x \in G\}$. (II).*
$$\lim_{k \to \infty} f^k = f^* \text{ and } \lim_{k \to \infty} L_k = L_* = \bigcap_{k=1}^{\infty} L_k.$$

Proof If algorithm 1 stops in generation k, then it must stops in step 2 or 6. In the former case, $\mu(L_k) = 0$. Conclusion 1 is true by Lemma 1. In the later case, for $\forall x \in G$, $f(x) \geq f^k$. Conclusion 1 ia also true.

If algorithm 1 does not stop in finite generations, by step 5 of algorithm 1, we have $f^{k+1} < f^k$ and $L_k \supset L_{k+1}$ for $\forall k$. Note that $f^k \geq f^*$ for $\forall k$, Thus there exists $\bar{f}$ such that $\lim_{k \to \infty} f^k = \bar{f}$. Now we prove $\bar{f} = f^*$. In fact, it can be seen from step 5 that $f^{k+1} \leq d_k = M(f, f^k)$, and it can be obtained by the first conclusion of Lemma 2 that $M(f, f^k) \leq f^k$. Thus $f^{k+1} \leq M(f, f^k) \leq f^k$. From $\lim_{k \to \infty} f^k = \bar{f}$ and the third conclusion of Lemma 2, we have $\bar{f} \leq M(f, \bar{f}) \leq \bar{f}$. Thus $\bar{f} = M(f, \bar{f})$. It can be seen from the second conclusion of Lemma 2 that $f^* = \bar{f}$. From $\lim_{k \to \infty} f^k = f^*$ we know $\lim_{k \to \infty} L_k = L_* = \bigcap_{k=1}^{\infty} L_k$.

5   Simulation Results

Five widely used test functions are chosen ([6]) and the proposed algorithm (denoted as LEA for short) is executed for these functions.

$F1 = 4x_1^2 - 2.1x_1^4 + (1/3)x_1^6 + x_1 x_2 - 4x_2^2 + 4x_2^4$, $x_i \in [-5, 5]$, $i = 1, 2$, $f^* = -1.0316285$.

$F2 = [x_2 - 5.1/(4\pi^2) + (5/\pi)x_1 - 6]^2 + 10(1 - 1/(8\pi)) \cos x_1 + 10$, $x_1 \in [-5, 10]$, $x_2 \in [0, 15]$, $f^* = 0.398$.

$F3 = \sum_{i=1}^{30} -x_i \sin(\sqrt{|x_i|})$, $x_i \in [-500, 500]$, $1 \leq x_i \leq 30$, $f^* = -12569.5$.

$F4 = \max\{|x_i|, 1 \leq i \leq 30\}$, $x_i \in [-100, 100]$, $1 \leq x_i \leq 30$, $f^* = 0$.

$F5 = \sum_{i=1}^{29} [100(x_{i+1} - x_i^2)^2 + (x_1 - 1)^2]$, $x_i \in [-30, 30]$, $1 \leq x_i \leq 30$, $f^* = 0$.

In simulation, we take the following parameters: $pop = 40$, $p_c = 0.2$, $p_m = 0.1$, $q = 5$, $\bar{N} = 500$ and $\lambda = 2$. We execute the proposed algorithm 50 independent runs for each test function and record the following data: Mean best fitness value (denoted as M-best) on 50 runs, standard deviation (denoted as Std) of best fitness values on 50 runs, and mean generations (denoted as M-gen) on 50 runs. For each run the algorithm 1 stops if the best solution found in 20 successive generations can not be improved. We compare the results with those obtained by two algorithms (denoted as FEP and CEP) in ([6]) in Table 1.

It can be seen from Table 1 that for each test function the mean best fitness value found by LEA is very close to the true optimal fitness value, and better or much better than those found by FEP and CEP. Moreover, the standard deviation obtained by LEA for each function is much smaller than those obtained by FEP and CEP. Furthermore, in the simulation, the mean number of function evaluations used in each generation by LEA is about 84, while the mean number of function evaluations used in each generation by FEP and CEP are 100. It can be seen from Table 1 that the Mean generations used by LEA are fewer than those used by FEP and CEP. Thus function evaluations used by LEA are fewer than those used by FEP and CEP. From above discussion we can conclude that

Table 1. Comparison of mean best solution, standard deviation and mean generation for LEA and FEP

	M-gen			M-best			Std		
	LEA	FEP	CEP	LEA	FEP	CEP	LEA	FEP	CEP
$F1$	80	100	100	-1.0315	-1.03	-1.03	2.7×10^{-15}	4.9×10^{-7}	4.9×10^{-7}
$F2$	80	100	100	0.3979	0.398	0.398	0	1.5×10^{-7}	1.5×10^{-7}
$F3$	2000	9000	9000	-12564.8	-12554.5	-7917.1	5.72	52.6	634.5
$F4$	5000	5000	5000	7.1×10^{-8}	0.3	2.0	8.2×10^{-7}	0.5	1.2
$F5$	5000	20000	20000	7.3×10^{-7}	5.06	577.76	6.3×10^{-6}	5.87	11125.76

LEA used less computation to find more precise solutions for all test functions than FEP and CEP did.

References

1. S.Lucidi, V. Piccialli.: New Classes of Globally Convexized Filled Functions for Global Optimization. J. of Global Optimization. **24** (2002) 219-236.
2. R.P. Ge, Y. F. Qin.: Globally Convexized Filled Functions for Global Optimization. Applied Mathematics and Computation. **35** (1999) 131-158.
3. E.M. Oblow.: Stochastic Tunneling Algorithm for Global Optimization. J. of Global Optimization. **20** (2001) 195-212.
4. C.Y. Lee, X. Yao.: Evolutionary Programming Using Mutations Based on the Levy Probability Distribution. IEEE Trans. Evol. Comput. **8** (2004) 1-13.
5. Y.W.Leung, Yuping Wang.: An Orthogonal Genetic Algorithm with Quantization for Global Numerical Optimization. IEEE Trans. Evol. Comput. **5** (2001) 41-53.
6. X. Yao, Y. Liu, G. Lin.: Evolutionary Programming Made Faster. IEEE Trans. Evol. Comput. **3** (1999) 82-102.
7. D.B. Fogel. *Evolutionary computation: toward a new philosophy of machine intelligence.* New York: IEEE Press, 1995.
8. K. Gurney, *An introduction to neural networks.* London : UCL Press, 1997.
9. S. Kirkpatrick, C.D. Gelatt and M.P. Vecchi.: Optimization by simulated annealing. Science, **220** (1983) 671-680.
10. C. S. Hong and Z. Quan, *Integral Global Optimization: Theory, Implementation and Applications.* Berlin Heidelberg: Springer-Verlag, 1988.
11. F.T.Fang, Y.Wang. *Number-theoretic methods in statistics.* London, UK, Chapman & Hall, 1994.

Co-evolutionary Rule-Chaining
Genetic Programming

Wing-Ho Shum[1], Kwong-sak Leung[1], and Man-Leung Wong[2]

[1] Department of Computer Science and Engineering, The Chinese University of Hong
Kong, Shatin, Hong Kong
{whshum,ksleung}@cse.cuhk.edu.hk
[2] Department of Information Systems, Lingnan University, Tuen Mun, Hong Kong
mlwong@ln.edu.hk

Abstract. A novel Genetic Programming (GP) paradigm called Co-
evolutionary Rule-Chaining Genetic Programming (CRGP) has been
proposed to learn the relationships among attributes represented by a
set of classification rules for multi-class problems. It employs backward
chaining inference to carry out classification based on the acquired acyclic
rule set. Its main advantages are: 1) it can handle more than one class
at a time; 2) it avoids cyclic result; 3) unlike Bayesian Network (BN),
the CRGP can handle input attributes with continuous values directly;
and 4) with the flexibility of GP, CRGP can learn complex relationship.
We have demonstrated its better performance on one synthetic and one
real-life medical data sets.

1 Introduction

GP is a branch of evolutionary computation (EC). It has been applied on different areas, like shortest path finding and classification[5]. Wilson's XCS [12]
and XCSI [13] are well-known classification algorithms based on learning classifier system. However, the classification problems currently being addressed are
single class problem.

BN is a network model, which represents a set of attributes for a given multi-
class problem, and provides the probabilistic relationship among them. However,
BN cannot handle continuous values directly; and the continuous values must
be discretized first [6]. Heckerman et al. proposed methods of learning a network
that contains Gaussian distributions [7]. Monti et al. use neural networks to
represent the conditional densities [10].

In this paper, we propose the CRGP to handle the multi-class problem. It
learns a set of classification rules, which represent the relationships among the
attributes. It avoids cyclic rules; and it can handle input attributes with continuous values directly. The remaining parts of the paper are organized as follows.
We describe the proposed algorithm in the next section. The experimental results
are presented in Section 3. The summary appears in the last section.

M. Gallagher, J. Hogan, and F. Maire (Eds.): IDEAL 2005, LNCS 3578, pp. 546–554, 2005.
© Springer-Verlag Berlin Heidelberg 2005

2   Co-evolutionary Chaining Genetic Programming

The problem addressed in this study is to learn classification rules and the relationships among attributes without cycle in the inference process for multi-class problem, in which one or more than one attributes are regarded as classes. Each attribute of the problem is regarded as either an input attribute or a class. The relationships among the attributes will be represented by rules.

The CRGP is a novel coarse grained multi-population GP based on backward chaining. Multi-population maintain the diversity of rules. Backward chaining can perform classification through the inference process and cyclic rules have to be avoided.

2.1   Initialization of Populations

The CRGP uses the Michigan approach. It starts with n populations of rules, where n is equivalent to the number of classes. Each population is assigned to learn a different class, which is considered as the local class of the corresponding population. The other classes are referred to as foreign classes.

The rules represent the relationships among attributes. They are of the form, $< antecedent >\rightarrow< consequent >$. The rules are in the prefix form. The function set is defined as $F = \{\wedge, >, <=, =, \neq\}$.

Each population has a different copy of the data set, which contains the values of the input attributes and local class only. The foreign classes' values are omitted, i.e. the populations cannot access their foreign classes' values.

The training process is divided into a number of epochs, which in turn consists of a number of generations. The number of rules in each population is the same and static. The populations are initialized randomly.

2.2   Backward Chaining

The populations in the CRGP cooperate through rule migration. Migration occurs in the beginning of each epoch. During migration, the populations send a copy of their rules to the others. In other words, the populations would get a set of rules from the rest and they are referred to as migrated rules. To make it clear, hereafter, we refer to the populations' own rules as local rules. The new migrated rules always replace the existing migrated ones of previous epoch.

Backward chaining is a well-known inferential methodology. Given a class, some facts and rules, it forms a backward chain of rules and proves if the class can be satisfied. The CRGP employs backward chaining in the fitness evaluation and the cyclic relationship in the rules will be detected and eliminated.

Tables 1 show the pseudocodes of the fitness evaluation and backward chaining procedures respectively. The populations cannot access the foreign classes' values. During the fitness evaluation, if the local rule being evaluated contains foreign class in its antecedent part, the backward chaining procedure would be invoked, for each of these foreign classes.

Table 1. (Top) The pseudocode of the Fitness Evaluation Procedure. (Bottom) The pseudocode of the Backward Chaining Procedure

1. Set $i = 0$.
2. while $i <$ the number of local rules,
• if the ith local rule contains one or more foreign classes in its $< antecedent >$,
◇ the ith local rule becomes the first rule in the backward chain of rules.
◇ the backward chaining procedure is invoked for each of these foreign classes.
• evaluate the ith rule's fitness by the fitness function.

input: a foreign class being looking for a backward chain of rules
1. Set $j = 0$ and $k = 0$.
2. while $j <$ the number of migrated rules,
• if the jth migrated rule infers the values of the foreign class, which is being looking for,
◇ if the jth migrated rule form no cycle with the others in the backward chain of rules
○ the jth migrated rule is selected.
3. Sort the selected migrated rules, according to their fitness values.
4. while $k <$ the number of selected migrated rules,
• if the kth selected migrated rule contains one or more foreign classes in its $< antecedent >$,
◇ the kth selected migrated rule is appended to the backward chain of rules.
◇ another copy of backward chaining procedure is invoked for each of these foreign classes
• fire the kth selected migrated rule.
5. remove the last rule from the backward chain of rules.

The backward chaining procedure selects suitable migrated rules to infer the foreign class's values. The migrated rules with the following characteristics are selected: 1) it is a migrated rule inferring that foreign class's values; and 2) it will not form cycles with the others in the backward chain of the relevant rules.

The backward chaining procedure then fires the selected migrated rules one by one to infer the foreign class's values. The firing order is based on their fitness values, the one with the highest fitness value is fired first. The fitness values are brought from their original populations during migration. If a selected migrated rule does further contain foreign class in its antecedent part, another round of the backward chaining procedure would be invoked, for each of these foreign classes forming a backward chain in the inference process.

The migrated rules, which would form cycle with the others in the backward chain of rules are excluded from the selection and the corresponding foreign class's values remain unknown. The rules referring to these unknown values become unfit and difficult to survive and hence the cyclic rules can be avoided.

After the backward chaining procedure fired all of the selected migrated rules, the local rule being considered would be evaluated, and a fitness value is assigned according to its classification accuracy.

2.3 Fitness Evaluation, Selection and Genetic Operators

The CRGP uses a support-confidence based fitness function and token competition to evaluate the local rules' fitness [1]. It employs three canonical genetic operators for evolution; they are the crossover, mutation and dropping conditions [9]. It selects local rules by the Roulette Wheel method. Fitter local rules, higher chance to be selected. The selected local rules are applied with one of the genetic operators, to produce the offspring. Then, all the local rules and the offspring compete with each other. The best half of them would be selected as the new population for the next generation.

When the maximum number of epochs is met, the training process is terminated and all of the local rules of all the populations are collected together as the resultant rule set.

3 Experiments

The CRGP has been compared with the Multi-population Genetic Programming (MGP), C5.0, Belief Network PowerConstructor (PC), WinMine (WM) and B-Course (BC). The MGP is a canonical GP with multi-population. It has no migration, no backward chaining and all of the populations can access all of classes' values directly. We have implemented the CRGP and the MGP in C++. They have the same implementation details. The C5.0, PC, WM and BC are downloaded from their web sites [2–4, 8].

We have evaluated the CRGP on a synthetic and a real-life medical data set, a Fracture medical data set. The synthetic data set is a multi-class problem with 400 data items. Table 2 and figure 1(left) show the pseudocode used to generate the synthetic data set and the corresponding relationships among the attributes respectively. It has 6 input attributes, 5 classes and 400 data items. Classes 3 and 4 are generated by the same set of rules. They are used to evaluate if the algorithm can produce an acyclic rule set. The real-life data set, "Fracture", is from the Orthopaedie Department of the Prince of Wales Hospital of Hong Kong. It consists of records of children with limb fractures admitted to the hospital in the period 1984-1996. "Fracture" has been used in [11]. It has 1 input attribute, 5 classes and 6574 data items.

The data sets are split into two parts. 66% of the data items are used for the training, the rest of them are used for the testing. For all of the algorithms, we have specified the input attributes. The values of the number of epochs, the

Table 2. The pseudocode of the synthetic data set generation

$attribute\ 0\ =\ random();$	$else$
$attribute\ 1\ =\ random();$	$\quad class\ 2\ =\ 0;$
$attribute\ 2\ =\ random();$	$if\ (class\ 0\ \neq\ class\ 1)$
$attribute\ 3\ =\ random();$	$\quad class\ 3\ =\ 0;$
$attribute\ 4\ =\ random();$	$else\ if\ (class\ 0\ \neq\ class\ 2)$
$attribute\ 5\ =\ random();$	$\quad class\ 3\ =\ 1;$
$if\ (attribute\ 0\ >\ attribute\ 1)$	$else$
$\quad class\ 0\ =\ 1;$	$\quad class\ 3\ =\ 2;$
$else$	$if\ (class\ 0\ \neq\ class\ 1)$
$\quad class\ 0\ =\ 0;$	$\quad class\ 4\ =\ 0;$
$if\ (attribute\ 2\ >\ attribute\ 3)$	$else\ if\ (class\ 0\ \neq\ class\ 2)$
$\quad class\ 1\ =\ 1;$	$\quad class\ 4\ =\ 1;$
$else$	$else$
$\quad class\ 1\ =\ 0;$	$\quad class\ 4\ =\ 2;$
$if\ (attribute\ 4\ >\ attribute\ 5)$	$where:$
$\quad class\ 2\ =\ 1;$	$\quad random()\ returns\ a\ real\ number\ between\ 0\ and\ 999$

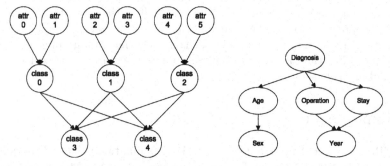

Fig. 1. (Left) The relationships among attributes in the synthetic data set. (Right) The relationships in Fracture learnt by the CRGP

maximum number of generations, the number of local rules in a population, the maximum depth, the crossover rate, the mutation rate and the dropping condition rate are 40, 10, 15, 0.5, 0.4 and 0.1 respectively.

3.1 Synthetic Data Set Results

We construct the relationships learnt by the CRGP and MGP by, 1) evaluating the resultant rule set by the typical testing methodology of GP and removing the redundant rules [11]; and 2) collecting the remaining rules as the learnt relationships. Since GP is a stochastic algorithm, it produces slightly different result in each run and the results are likely to have some redundant codes. To remove the stochastic effect, we consider only the relationships exist in all of the runs as the actual results learnt.

Since the C5.0 can handle only one class at a time, in the experiment, it is executed several times, once for each class. The relationships learnt by the C5.0 are derived by combining the trees it learnt in each run.

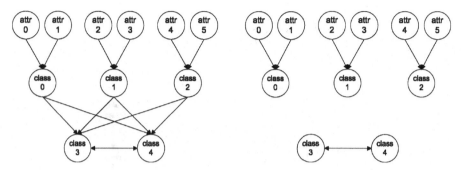

Fig. 2. (Left) The relationships learnt by the CRGP. (Right) The relationships learnt by the MGP

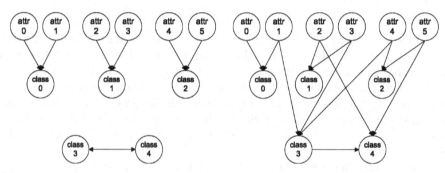

Fig. 3. (Left)The relationships learnt by the C5.0. (Right) The relationships learnt by the PC

The BN learning algorithms cannot handle continuous values directly. The continuous values are discretized first. The BC is a stochastic BN learning algorithm, we have evaluated it ten times and selected the best result.

Figure 2(left) shows the relationships learnt by the CRGP. The relationships are the same as the real relationships shown in figure 1(left). The additional relationship between classes 3 and 4 representing their values are generated by the same set of rules. The CRGP has learnt the relationships successfully. Figures 2(right), 3 and 4 show the relationships learnt by the MGP, PC, WM and BC respectively. They show that only the BC can learn very similar relationships. The MGP, C5.0 and WM cannot learn the relationships among class 3, attributes 0, 1 and 2, and the one among class 4, attributes 0, 1 and 2. The PC cannot learn the relationship between classes 3 and 1, and the one between class 4 and 1; It has also learnt three incorrect relationships.

Tables 3(top-left) and 3(top-right) illustrates the cyclic rules and trees produced by the MGP and C5.0 respectively. They show only the rules and trees with classes 3 and 4 of value 1. The rules and trees state that if class 3 is 1, then class 4 is 1, and vice versa. This is a cyclic phenomenon and we cannot infer anything for the classes given the input attributes' values.

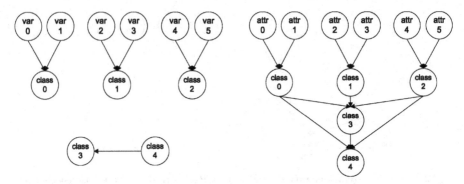

Fig. 4. (Left) The relationships learnt by the WM. (Right) The relationships learnt by the BC

Table 3(bottom) shows the corresponding rules produced by the CRGP, which are not cyclic. Besides the relationship between classes 3 and 4, the rules also represent inferences with classes 3 and 4 equaling to 1. The rules formed an acyclic inference chain and produces meaningful result. Also, the most important point is that the rules and the inference chains provide the relationships amongst the inputs and class attributes. It is the advantage of using the backward chaining rather than inferring all of the classes' values directly from the given inputs.

The results show only the CRGP and BC can learn the relationships; the result of the MGP shows the multi-class problem cannot be solved by accessing

Table 3. (Top-Left)The rules produced by the MGP. (Top-Right) The decision trees produced by the C5.0. (Bottom) The rules produced by the CRGP

(= class4 1)→(= class3 1). (= class3 1)→(= class4 1). (= class4 1)→(= class3 1). (= class4 1)→(= class3 1). (= class4 1)→(= class3 1). (= class3 1)→(= class4 1). (= class3 1)→(= class4 1). (= class3 1)→(= class4 1).	Decision tree for Class 3: Class 4 = 0: 0 (122) Class 4 = 1: 1 (68) Class 4 = 2: 2 (74) Decision tree for Class 4: Class 3 = 0: 0 (129) Class 3 = 1: 1 (69) Class 3 = 2: 2 (66)

(∧ (≠ class2 class0)(= class1 class0))→(= class4 1). (= class4 1)→(= class3 1). (≠ class0 class2)→(= class3 1). (∧ (≠ class2 class0)(= class1 class0))→(= class4 1). (∧ (> attr2 attr3)(≠ class2 class0)→(= class4 1). (∧ (> attr2 attr3)(≠ class2 class0)→(= class4 1). (∧ (> attr2 attr3)(≠ class2 class0)→(= class4 1). (∧ (> attr2 attr3)(≠ class2 class0)→(= class4 1).

all of classes' values directly; and the result of the C5.0 shows the multi-class problem cannot be solved by simply executing the algorithm several times.

3.2 Fracture Results

Wong et al have learnt the relationships represented by BN in the Fracture data set [11]. The result is confirmed by the medical experts.

Figure 1(right) shows the relationships learnt by the CRGP. The network is exactly the same as the one learnt by Wong. It shows: 1) The Diagnosis affects the Operation and Stay, different fractures are treated with different operations and need different time for recovery; 2) The Diagnosis affects the Age. Some fractures occur more often in particular age groups; 3) There is a relationship between the Age and Sex. It is observed that the young patients are more likely to be female; and 4) The Operation and Stay affect the Year. It is observed that the length of stay in hospital is different in different periods. The CRGP has learnt the relationships successfully.

4   Summary

We have described a novel algorithm, CRGP. It learns a set of classification rules and the relationships among attributes for multi-class problem. Unlike BN, it can handle input attributes with continuous values directly. We have evaluated its performance on a synthetic and a real-life medical data sets. The experimental results have shown the CRGP outperforms the MGP, C5.0, PC and WM; and it has the comparable result as the BC in relationship learning. With the flexibility of GP, we believe the CRGP can learn complex relationships amongst attributes with discrete or continuous values that cannot be handled by BN.

References

1. R. Agrawal, T. Imielinski, and A. Swami. Mining association rules between sets of otems in large databases. In *Proceedings of the 1993 International Conference on Management of Data*, pages 207–216, 1993.
2. Jie Cheng. Belief network powerconstructor. http://www.cs.ualberta.ca/~jcheng/bnpc.htm, 1998.
3. David Maxwell Chickering. The winmine toolkit. http://research.microsoft.com/~dmax/winmine/tooldoc.htm, 2002.
4. Helsinki Institute for Information Technology Complex Systems Computation Group. B-course. http://b-course.hiit.fi/, 2002.
5. Alex A. Freitas, editor. *Data Mining and Knowledge Discovery with Evolutionary Algorithms.* Springer, 2002.
6. N. Friedman, D. Geiger, and M. Goldszmidt. Bayesian network classifiers. In *Machine Learning*, pages 131–163, 1998.
7. D. Heckerman and D. Geiger. Learning bayesian networks: a unification for discrete and gaussian domains. In *Proceedings of the eleventh conference on uncertainty in artificial intelligence*, pages 274–284, 1995.

8. RuleQuest Research Pty Ltd. Data mining tools see5 and c5.0. http://www.rulequest.com/see5-info.html, 2003.

9. R.S. Michalski. A theory and methodology of inductive learning. In J.G. Carbonell R.S. Michalski and T.M. Mitchell, editors, *Machine Learning - An Artificial Intelligence Approach*, chapter 4. Los Altos, Calif., 1983.

10. S. Monti and G. F. Cooper. Learning bayesian belief networks with neural network estimators. In *Advances in Neural Information Processing Systems*, pages 579–584, 1997.

11. Wong M. L. Lam W. Leung K. S. Ngan, P. S. and J. C. Y. Cheng. Medical data mining using evolutionary computation. In *Artificial Intelligent in Medicine, Special Issue On Data Mining Techniques and Applications in Medicine*, pages 73–96, 1999.

12. S.W. Wilson. Generalization in the xcs classifier system. In *Genetic Programming: Proceedings of the Third Annual Conference*, pages 665–674, 1998.

13. S.W. Wilson. Mining oblique data with xcs. In *International Workshop on Learning Classifier Systems*, page Extended Abstract, 2000.

A Dynamic Migration Model
for Self-adaptive Genetic Algorithms

K.G. Srinivasa[1], K. Sridharan[2], P. Deepa Shenoy[1],
K.R. Venugopal[1], and Lalit M. Patnaik[3]

[1] Department of Computer Science and Engineering
University Visvesvaraya College of Engineering, Bangalore 560001
kgsrinivas@msrit.edu, shenoypd@yahoo.com, vkrajuk@vsnl.com
[2] Department of CSE, Sunny Buffalo
ks236@buffalo.edu
[3] Microprocessor Applications Laboratory, Indian Institute of Science, India
lalit@micro.iisc.ernet.in

Abstract. In this paper, we propose a self Adaptive Migration Model for Genetic Algorithms, where parameters of population size, the number of points of crossover and mutation rate for each population are fixed adaptively. Further, the migration of individuals between populations is decided dynamically. This paper gives a mathematical schema analysis of the method stating and showing that the algorithm exploits previously discovered knowledge for a more focused and concentrated search of heuristically high yielding regions while simultaneously performing a highly explorative search on the other regions of the search space. The effective performance of the algorithm is then shown using standard testbed functions, when compared with Island model GA(IGA) and Simple GA(SGA).

1 Introduction

In this paper, the proposed adaptive migration(island) model of GA is built such that, given a search space, the number of individuals in the population that resides in a relatively high fitness region of the search space increases thus improving exploitation. For these high fitness population, the mutation rate and number of points of crossover are decreased thus making the search more focused. On the other hand, for populations in a relatively low fitness zone of search space, the number of individuals is decreased but the mutation rates and number of points of crossover are increased to make the search of these regions more explorative [6].

2 Algorithm

Let S be made up of all the 2^k, k bit binary numbers representing the entire search space. Given the objective function f which is a mapping $f : S \rightarrow R$ where R is a set of real numbers, the problem is to find an $x^* \in S$ such that $f(x^*) \geq f(x) \ \forall \ x \in S$.

M. Gallagher, J. Hogan, and F. Maire (Eds.): IDEAL 2005, LNCS 3578, pp. 555–562, 2005.

2.1   Pseudocode for Self-adaptive Migration GA(SAMGA)

Let $E = \{P_1, P_2...P_{np}\}$ be an ecosystem with np populations in it. Populations $P_1, P_2...P_{np} \subset S$. $P_i[j]$ stands for the jth individual of population P_i, clearly $P_i[j] \in S$. Let n_i be the size of population P_i and nc_i be the number of points of crossover used for reproduction in population P_i. Let $\bar{f}_i$ be the average fitness of a population P_i. Let $f(P_i)$, the fitness of population P_i be the fitness of the best individual of that population. Let $\bar{f}$ be the average fitness of the ecosystem. Let $\bar{n}$ be the average number of individuals per population. Let pm_i be the rate of mutation used for population P_i. The rate of crossover being one. Then, the pseudo code for the adaptive GA can be given as below

1. **begin**
2. *var* prev = 0;
3. **for** i = 1 : np, **do**
   (a) Set n_i, the number of individuals in the population P_i to some arbitrary value n_0
   (b) Initialize all individuals of population P_i to some random bit strings
   (c) Set number of crossover points used for population P_i, nc_i to one
   (d) Set mutation rate used for population P_i, pm_i to 0.01
4. **for** gen = 1 : maximum generation limit, **do**
   (a) *var* nsum = 0;
   (b) *var* fsum = 0;
   (c) **for** i = 1 : np, **do**
      i. Evaluate fitness of all the individuals of the population P_i and find $f(P_i)$ the best fitness of the population
      ii. $nsum = nsum + n_i$
      iii. $fsum = fsum + f(P_i)$
   (d) prev $= \bar{f}$
   (e) $\bar{f} = \frac{fsum}{np}$
   (f) $\bar{n} = \frac{nsum}{np}$
   (g) **for** i = 1 : np, **do**
      i. $nc_i = nc_i + \frac{\bar{n}}{n} - 1$
      ii. $pm_i = pm_i + (\frac{\bar{n}}{n} - 1) * 0.0001$
      iii. $n_i = n_i + \frac{f(P_i)}{f} - 1$
      iv. **if** $(n_i == 0)$, Delete population P_i (extinction)
   (h) **for** i = 1 : np, **do**
      i. Perform *elitist* selection for population P_i with the modified population size n_i
      ii. Perform nc point non-uniform crossover on the selected individuals of population P_i
      iii. Perform mutation on the individuals of population P_i with mutation probability pm_i
   (i) **if** prev $== \bar{f}$
      Exchange or migrate best individuals between populations.
5. **end**

The algorithm shown above is adaptive in four respects. First, the size of the population is adaptively changed for each population. The size of the population is varied dynamically based on the fitness of the best individual of that population compared to the mean fitness of the population. The number of individuals in population P_i is updated as,

$$n_{i,t+1} = n_{i,t} + \frac{f(P_i)}{\bar{f}} - 1 \tag{1}$$

where t is used to represent time in generations. Using this update, the fitness grows when the size of the population with fitness greater than the mean population and vice versa. Thus, it can be visualized that more number of individuals are concentrated in the heuristically better promising region of search space (exploitation).

The second parameter that is dynamically adapted is the number of points of crossover. The update used for number of crossover points is given by,

$$nc_{i,t+1} = nc_{i,t} + \frac{\bar{n}}{n_i} - 1 \tag{2}$$

Using this update the number of points of crossover is increased, if the number of individuals in a population is less compared to the mean number of individuals in a population. Thus, the number of points of crossover is linked to fitness of population. It is clear that update of population size increases with fitness of population while the number of crossover points is increased for relatively low population size, thereby making search more explorative.

The significance of update of mutation rate is similar that of the number of crossover points and is given by,

$$pm_{i,t+1} = pm_{i,t} + (\frac{\bar{n}}{n_i} - 1) * 0.0001 \tag{3}$$

Obviously, higher the mutation rate, more explorative is the search. The factor of 0.0001 is arbitrarily chosen as it is a considerably small factor to update probability of mutation.

The final parameter that is adaptive in the algorithm is the rate of migration. Migration refers to copying individuals from one population to another. Migration helps in discovering new schemas generated by crossover of schemas of two populations. In the algorithm, there is no exact parameter for migration rate. Migration occurs when the average fitness of the populations remains unchanged between two generations. Thus, when populations have attained a steady state, migration occurs that will try to discover a new schema.

The selection scheme used in the genetic algorithm is the elitist scheme. The best individuals of each population are copied unaltered to the next generation population. The remaining individuals are selected based on their fitness. The use of elitistic selection guarantees that the best individual of any generation is atleast as good as the best individual of the previous generation. It helps in achieving global convergence.

3   Mathematical Analysis

The Holland's schema theorem for a general case can be given as,

$$M(H, t+1) \geq ((1 - p_c)M(H,t)\frac{f(H)}{f_{avg}}$$

$$+p_c[M(H,t)\frac{f(H)}{f_{avg}}(1 - losses) + gains])(1 - p_m)^{O(H)}$$

Where $M(H,t)$ is the number of individuals in a population with schema H are present in the current generation, f_{avg} is average fitness of population, $O(H)$ is order of schema H and p_c and p_m are rates of crossover and mutation respectively. In our algorithm, we consider p_c to be one. Hence the Schema theorem becomes,

$$M(H, t+1) \geq [M(H,t)\frac{f(H)}{f_{avg}}(1 - losses) + gains](1 - p_m)^{O(H)}$$

In the proposed algorithm, as the population size varies each generation, the schema lower bound becomes,

$$M(H, t+1) \geq [\frac{M(H,t)}{n_t}n_{t+1}\frac{f(H)}{f_{avg}}(1 - losses) + gains](1 - p_m)^{O(H)} \qquad (4)$$

where n_t is population size at generation t.

If we consider loss to be any crossover that disrupts the schema, then our calculation of gain must account for the preservance of the schema when both parents are of the schema H. Now for an n point crossover to be non-disruptive, even number of crossover points can occur only between fixed bits of schema [4]. The remaining crossover points must be outside the defining length. Hence the probability of n point crossover generating only even number of crossovers between fixed bits for a schema of k order hyperplane is $P_{k,even}$. Probability of disruption P_d of n point crossover is bounded by,

$$P_d(n, H_k) \leq 1 - P_{k,even}(n, H_k)$$

In this paper, we consider a n point non disruptive crossover. Let d_1, d_2 and d_3 are fixed bits, L_1 and L_2 are distances of d_3 and d_2 from d_1 respectively and L is the string length. As a special case, probability of even number of crossover points falling between fixed bits for a second order hyperplane is given by [5]

$$P_{2,even}(n, L, L_1) = \sum_{i=0}^{\frac{n}{2}} {}^nC_{2i}\frac{L_1}{L}^{2i}\frac{L - L_1}{L}^{n-2i} \qquad (5)$$

That is, the probability is given by the product of number of ways of choosing an even number of points from an n point crossover, the probability of placing an even number of points between the two defining points and the probability of placing the other points outside the defining points. L here is the string length and L_1 is the defining length.

We can extend the probability of disruption for a kth order hyperplane as

$$P_{k,even}(n, L, L_1, ..., L_{k-1})$$

$$= \sum_{i=0}^{\frac{n}{2}} {}^nC_{2i} \frac{L_1}{L}^{2i} \frac{L - L_1}{L}^{n-2i} P_{k-1,even}(n, L_1, L_2, ..., L_{k-1}) \qquad (6)$$

That is, probability that an even number of crossover points fall between k defining bits $P_{k,even}$ is given by the probability that even number of crossover points fall between the first two defining bits and the rest of the points fall outside the defining bits into $P_{k-1,even}$. Hence, taking bound on the probability of disruption

$$P_d(H_k) \leq 1 - \sum_{i=0}^{\frac{n}{2}} {}^nC_{2i} \frac{L_1}{L}^{2i} \frac{L - L_1}{L}^{n-2i} P_{k-1,even}(n, L_1, ..., L_{k-1}) \qquad (7)$$

Now, as mentioned earlier, the lower bound on the gain is given by the preservance of schema when disruptive crossover occurs between two parents both following the same schema. Hence, gain is given by

$gains \geq n * P_d *$ Probability that P_1 and P_2 are in schema H

After selection, the number of individuals in schema H is given by $M(H,t)\frac{f(H)}{f_{avg}}$. Total number of individuals in a population is n. Hence probability that given a parent, it is in schema H is given by $\frac{M(H,t)}{n}\frac{f(H)}{f_{avg}}$. Hence the gain is as follows,

$$gains \geq n_{t+1}P_d \frac{M(H,t)}{n_t} \frac{f(H)}{f_{avg}} \frac{M(H,t)}{n_t} \frac{f(H)}{f_{avg}} \qquad (8)$$

Using this lower bound on $gains$ in Equation (4) and replacing loss with disruption

$$M(H,t+1) \geq [\frac{M(H,t)}{n_t}n_{t+1}\frac{f(H)}{f_{avg}}(1-P_d)+n_{t+1}P_d(\frac{M(H,t)}{n_t}\frac{f(H)}{f_{avg}})^2](1-p_m)^{O(H)}$$

Simplifying,

$$M(H,t+1) \geq \frac{M(H,t)}{n_t}n_{t+1}\frac{f(H)}{f_{avg}}[1 - P_d + P_d(\frac{M(H,t)}{n_t}\frac{f(H)}{f_{avg}})](1 - p_m)^{O(H)}$$

But $n_t f_{avg} = \sum f$ for generation t. Therefore we get the schema theorem as

$$M(H,t+1) \geq \frac{M(H,t)}{n_t}n_{t+1}\frac{f(H)}{f_{avg}}[1 - P_d(1 - \frac{M(H,t)f(H)}{\sum f})](1 - p_m)^{O(H)} \quad (9)$$

This is the schema theorem that deals with a single population. An ecosystem of population where populations with better fitness have more number of individuals than those with low fitness population is considered in our algorithm.

Consider a low fitness population in the low yielding region of the search space. Consider the case when this population comes accross a high fitness point in the search space. Let $\bar{H}$ be the schema with high fitness that has come across a low fitness population. All other individuals in population have a low fitness compared to this high fitness point and hence

$$f(\bar{H}) = \sum f$$

Applying this to Equation (9) we get

$$M(\bar{H}, t+1) \geq \frac{M(\bar{H}, t)}{n_t} n_{t+1} \frac{f(\bar{H})}{f_{avg}} [1 - P_d(1 - M(\bar{H}, t))](1 - p_m)^{O(\bar{H})}$$

Since we have found only a single point with high fitness, $M(\bar{H}, t) = 1$. Therefore

$$M(\bar{H}, t+1) \geq \frac{M(\bar{H}, t)}{n_t} n_{t+1} \frac{f(\bar{H})}{f_{avg}} (1 - p_m)^{O(\bar{H})}$$

Thus, there is no disruption. $f_{avg} = \sum f/n_t$ and $f(\bar{H}) = \sum f$, Therefore

$$M(\bar{H}, t+1) \geq \frac{M(\bar{H}, t)}{n_t} n_t n_{t+1} (1 - p_m)^{O(\bar{H})}$$

But $M(\bar{H}, t) = 1$. Therefore

$$M(\bar{H}, t+1) \geq n_{t+1} (1 - p_m)^{O(\bar{H})}$$

Thus, if a population P_i in the low fitness region comes across even one high fitness solution then in the very next generation, aproximately $n_{i,t+1}(1 - p_m)^{O(\bar{H})}$ of the $n_{i,t+1}$ individuals of the population are finds place in schema $\bar{H}$. This immediate drift towards high fitness region of a low fitness population, suggests the robust performance of the method. The assumption that the fitness of the best solution is approximately equal to sum of fitness of all individuals in the population is used to display the power of the algorithm when the entire population is in a very low fitness area of search space. This analysis is a proof for the performance of the algorithm in the worst case. In general, the drift towards high fitness region is faster when the population lies in a low fitness region. The high fitness populations of the ecosystem drive the low fitness populations to perform a more explorative search while the high fitness populations perform a concentrated exploitational search in the high yielding regions. As soon as the low fitness populations find a better region, the individuals in the population crowd this region of the search space. This competitive nature of populations ensures robust performance. The search conducted by the genetic algorithm can thus be explained as exploitational with respect to high yielding regions of the search space and explorative with respect to other regions. The adaptive updates to the parameters of number of points of crossover and rate of mutation for each population are responsible for the explorative nature of the low fitness population. The adaptive parameter of population size helps in concentrated search in high fitness region of search space. The term explorative indicates that larger area of search space is covered by the search. There is no doubt that as mutation rate increases, the search is more explorative.

4   Experiments

To evaluate the performance of the algorithm, it was used to find the minimal points of complex high dimensional landscapes obtained using the different testbed functions. Function F1 ($f(x) = \sum_1^{10} x_i^2 - 5.12 \le x_i \le 5.12$), which is the De Jong's function 1, is a unimodal function with one distinct peak. Function F2 ($f(x) = 100(x_1^2 - x_2^2) + (1 - x_1)^2 - 2.048 \le x_i \le 2.048$), is a Rosenberg function which is basically an almost flat valley and hence finding the minimal point becomes a difficult problem. Function F3 ($f(x) = 200 + \sum_{i=1}^{10} x_i^2 - 10cos(2\pi x_i) - 5.12 \le x_i \le 5.12$) is a Rastragin multimodal function with many peaks. The function is a good testbed function as any algorithm has a good chance of getting stuck at one of the peaks which is a local minima. Function F4 ($f(x) = \sum_{i=1}^{10} x * sin(x) - 5.12 \le x_i \le 5.12$) is again a multimodal function. In the experiments conducted, the IGA and SAMGA both had ten populations of sixty individuals each. The SGA had 600 individuals in its population. For SGA and IGA the crossover rate chosen was one and mutation rate 0.01. The plot in Figure 1(a) shows the convergence of our algorithm(SAMGA), island model(IGA) and simple genetic algorithm(SGA) for the function F1. It is observed that the Self - Adaptive Migration GA(SAMGA) converges much faster than the other algorithms. The plot in Figure 1(b) shows the convergence

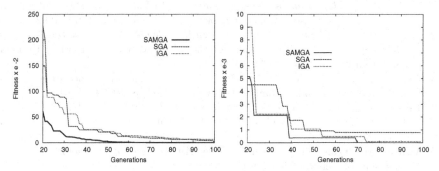

Fig. 1. (a): Convergence for function F1; (b): Convergence for function F2

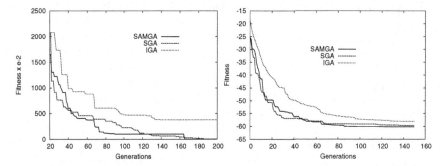

Fig. 2. (a): Convergence for function F3; (b): Convergence for function F4

of the three algorithms for Rosenberg function. As our function is low dimensional, the fitness was multiplied by a factor of 1000. Similarly, the plot in Figure 2(a) shows the convergence for Rastragin function. This is a multimodal function with many peaks of almost equal heights. In both the cases, SAMGA outperforms IGA and SGA. The plot in Figure 2(b) shows the convergence for function F4. Here SAMGA and SGA have similar performance and both outperform IGA. In all these cases, the performance of SAMGA is most significant in the later generations nearer to convergence.

5   Conclusions

In this paper we have proposed a Self-Adaptive Migration GA search techniques, that have two central but competing concepts of exploitation and exploration. The proposed algorithm can be characterized by focused and deeper exploitation of the heuristically promising regions of the search space and wider exploration of other regions of the search space. Our algorithm SAMGA converges much faster than other models and out performs IGA and SGA.

References

1. Back .T, *Self Adaptation in Genetic Algorithms* In F.J. Varela, P.B. editor, Proceedings of First European Conference on Artificial Life, pp 263-271, 1992
2. R Hinterding, Z Michalewicz and T C Peachey, *Self Adaptive Genetic Algorithm for Neumeric Functions* Proceedings of the 4th Conference on Parallel Problem Solving from Nature, pp 420-429, 1996
3. Kee E., Aiery S. and Cye W, *An Adaptive Genetic Algorithm* Proceedings of The Genetic and Evolutionary Computation Conference, pp 391-397, 2001
4. De Jong K.A, *An Analysis of the Behaviour of A Class of Genetic Adaptive Systems* PhD Thesis, Department of Computer and Communication Sciences, University of Michigan, Ann Arbor.
5. William M. Spear and Kenneth De Jong, *An Analysis of Multipoint Crossover*, Foundations of Genetic Algorithms.
6. Srinivasa K G, Venugopal K R, L M Patnaik, *Self Adaptive Migration Model Genetic Algorithms for Data Mining Applications*, Technical Report, University Visvesvaraya College of Engineering, Bangalore University, August 2004.

A Multicriteria Sorting Procedure
for Financial Classification Problems:
The Case of Business Failure Risk Assessment

Ceyhun Araz and Irem Ozkarahan

Dokuz Eylul University, Department of Industrial Engineering,
35100 Bornova-Izmir, Turkey
{ceyhun.araz,irem.ozkarahan}@deu.edu.tr

Abstract. This paper presents a new multicriteria sorting procedure in financial classification problems, based on the methodological framework of PRO-METHEE method. The proposed procedure, called as PROMSORT, is applied to the business failure risk problem and compared to PROMETHEE TRI and ELECTRE TRI. The proposed methodology also identifies the differences in performances across risk groups, and assists in monitoring the firms' financial performances. The results showed that the proposed procedure can be considered as an effective alternative to existing methods in financial classification problems.

1 Introduction

During the past decades the uncertainty and complexity in the financial environment have increased due to the effects of the globalization of financial markets and the rapid economic and technological changes. Therefore many researchers have been dedicated to develop efficient and realistic approaches for financial decision problems.

Financial decision making generally includes three types of decisions: choosing, ranking and sorting. In the field of finance choosing the best alternative or ranking the alternatives from the best to the worst do not always provide a solution to the problems such as business failure risk assessment, credit scoring, country risk assessment, portfolio selection and management, etc.. These problems are better addressed through the sorting problematic [1]. Sorting problematic involves the assignment of a set of alternatives in homogenous groups defined in a preference order.

The techniques traditionally applied in financial classification problems include mainly statistical and econometric methods like discriminant analysis [2], logit analysis [3], probit analysis [4] etc.. However, they are several shortcomings due to the restrictive statistical assumptions. A significant drawback of all these methods is the exclusion of qualitative criteria such as quality of management, market position, etc. [5].

In order to overcome these shortcomings alternative sorting approaches have been developed by researchers working in other fields such as operations research and artificial intelligence. A significant part is devoted on the development of multicriteria sorting (MCS) methods. MCS problem consists in assigning a set of alternatives A evaluated on n criteria to one of the predefined categories. Most known MCS methods are ELECTRE TRI [6], which is based on an outranking approach ELECTRE [7], UTADIS [8], which employs preference disaggregation analysis framework and

M. Gallagher, J. Hogan, and F. Maire (Eds.): IDEAL 2005, LNCS 3578, pp. 563–570, 2005.

M.H.DIS [9] which employs a hierarchical discrimination procedure to determine the classes. These methods have already been applied in financial classification problems (see [5],[10], [11], [12]). A complete survey of all the methods that have been applied in this field of financial management can be found in Dimitras et al. [13].

In the earlier eighties another outranking method, PROMETHEE, was created. PROMETHEE has not been adapted to MCS problems until very recently. A recent work [14] suggested an extension of PROMETHEE for sorting problems, which employs pairwise comparisons. Finally, Figueira et al. [15] proposed a new approach, called as PROMETHEE TRI. When assigning an alternative to a certain category, PROMETHEE TRI makes use of the concept of "central alternatives" instead of profile limits as in ELECTRE TRI and UTADIS methods. They applied PROMETHEE TRI to business failure risk problem to assign the alternatives different risk classes.

Many of the approaches proposed assume that a set of training sample exists. However, in some cases, it may not be possible. Furthermore, up to date, relative evaluation methods that compare firms, asset financial risks and identify potential reasons for differences in firms' risk level have not been fully explored in the literature. The main aim of this paper is to propose a new multicriteria sorting method in financial classification problems, based on the methodological framework of PROMETHEE method. PROMSORT assigns alternatives to predefined ordered categories. The assignment of an alternative a results from the comparison of a with the profiles defining the limits of the categories. This method is applied to the business failure risk problem, which is one of the major problems in the field of finance. The method is compared to PROMETHEE TRI and ELECTRE TRI using a real world application presented in [10]. Additionally, the proposed methodology identifies the differences in performances across risk groups, and assists in monitoring the firms' financial performances.

The rest of the paper is organized as follows. In section 2, a brief description of the PROMETHEE methodology will be given. A presentation of the methodology adopted in this paper is given in section 3. Section 4 is devoted to a numerical application. Finally the conclusions and further research will be given in section 5.

2   Brief Overview of PROMETHEE Methodology

PROMETHEE is a multicriteria decision making method developed by Brans et al., [16]. Let A be a set of alternatives and $g_j(a)$ represent the value of criterion g_j $(j=1,2,...,J)$ of alternative $a \in A$. A preference function $F_j(a,b)$ is defined for each pair of actions for criterion g_j. Assuming that more is preferred to less,

$$
\begin{aligned}
F_j(a,b) = 0 & \qquad iff \ g_j(a) - g_j(b) \le q_j \\
F_j(a,b) = 1 & \qquad iff \ g_j(a) - g_j(b) \ge p_j \qquad (1)\\
0 < F_j(a,b) < 1 & \qquad iff \ q_j < g_j(a) - g_j(b) < p_j
\end{aligned}
$$

Where q_j and p_j are indifference and preference thresholds for j^{th} criterion, respectively. Using the weights w_j assigned to each criterion (where $\sum wj=1$), one can determine the aggregated preference indicator as follows.

$$\Pi(a,b) = \sum w_j F_j(a,b) \qquad (2)$$

For each alternative $a \in A$, the following three outranking dominance flows can be obtained with respect to all the other alternatives $x \in A$.

$$\varphi^+(a) = \frac{1}{n-1}\sum_{x\in A}\Pi(a,x) \quad leaving \;\; flow$$

$$\varphi^-(a) = \frac{1}{n-1}\sum_{x\in A}\Pi(x,a) \quad entering \;\; flow \tag{3}$$

$$\varphi(a) = \varphi^+(a) - \varphi^-(a) \quad net \; flow$$

For each alternative a, it can also be determined the net flow for each criterion separately. Let us define the net flow for criterion g_j as follows,

$$\phi_j(a) = \frac{1}{n-1}\sum_{x\in A}(F_j(a,x) - F_j(x,a)) \tag{4}$$

The larger the single criterion net flow $\phi_j(a)$ the better alternative a on criterion g_j. According to PROMETHEE I, action a is superior to b (aPb) if the leaving flow of a is greater than the leaving flow of b and entering flow of a is smaller than the entering flow of b. Equality in $\phi+$ and $\phi-$ indicates indifference (aIb) among the two compared alternatives. In the case where the leaving flows indicate a is better than b, while the entering flows indicate the reverse the two actions are considered incomparable (aRb). If PROMETHEE I gives incomplete ranking, complete ranking can be obtained by the net flows in PROMETHEE II. The higher net flow, the better alternative.

3 Proposed MCS Method: PROMSORT

PROMSORT is a MCS method, i.e. a method that assigns alternatives to predefined ordered categories. The assignment of an alternative a results from the comparison of a with the profiles defining the limits of the categories. Let F denote the set of criteria ($F=\{g_1, g_2, ...,g_j\}$), B the set of profiles defining $k+1$ categories ($B=\{b_1,b_2,...,b_k\}$), and b_h being the upper limit of category C_h and the lower limit of category C_{h+1}, $h=1,2,...k$. PROMSORT assigns alternatives to categories following three consecutive steps: *i.* Construction of an outranking relation using PROMETHEE I, *ii.* Exploitation of the outranking relation in order to assign alternatives to specific categories except the incomparability and indifference situations, *iii.* Final assignment of the alternatives based on pairwise comparison.

3.1 Construction of an Outranking Relation Using PROMETHEE I

In PROMSORT, categories are defined by lower and upper limits like ELECTRE TRI. The comparison of an action a with the profile limit b_h, which distinguishes the categories C_h and C_{h+1}, is defined in the following way:

$$\begin{cases} aPb_h & iff & \begin{cases} \Phi^+(a) > \Phi^+(b_h) \, and \, \Phi^-(a) < \Phi^-(b_h), or \\ \Phi^+(a) = \Phi^+(b_h) \, and \, \Phi^-(a) < \Phi^-(b_h), or \\ \Phi^+(a) > \Phi^+(b_h) \, and \, \Phi^-(a) = \Phi^-(b_h) \end{cases} \\ aIb_h & iff & \Phi^+(a) = \Phi^+(b_h) \, and \, \Phi^-(a) = \Phi^-(b_h) \\ aRb_h & iff & \begin{cases} \Phi^+(a) > \Phi^+(b_h) \, and \, \Phi^-(a) > \Phi^-(b_h), or \\ \Phi^+(a) < \Phi^+(b_h) \, and \, \Phi^-(a) < \Phi^-(b_h) \end{cases} \end{cases} \tag{5}$$

3.2 Assignment of the Alternatives

The assignment of alternatives to categories results directly from the outranking relation. (Assume that $C_2 > C_1$ means that Category 2 outranks Category 1)

- Compare alternative a successively to b_i, for $i=k, k-1,...,1$,
- b_h being the first profile such that aPb_h
- b_t being the first profile such that aRb_t or aIb_t
- If $h>t$, assign a to category C_{h+1}
- Otherwise do not assign a to any category (it is not certain that alternative a
  would be assigned to category t or $t+1$)

After the second phase, it is possible that some alternatives could not have been
assigned to a category, since outranking relation indicates that these alternatives are
indifferent or incomparable to a profile limit and could not be assigned to a category
directly. On the other hand, some alternatives could be assigned to the categories. In
the third stage, we will use these alternatives as the reference actions of the categories
to be able to assign the alternatives which have not yet been assigned.

3.3 Final Assignment

In second phase, some alternatives are assigned in $h+1$ ordered categories
$C_{h+1}>C_h>....C_1$. Now, these alternatives are the reference alternatives for ordered
categories. Suppose that a reference set X_h consisting of m alternatives for category h,
i.e., $X=\{x_1, x_2,...., x_m\}$ and an alternative a which has not yet been assigned to a category,

- determine a distance (similar as Doumpos and Zapounidis [14])

$$d_k = \frac{1}{n_t}d^+_k - \frac{1}{n_{t+1}}d^-_k$$

$$d^+_k = \sum_{x \in X_t}(\Phi(a)-\Phi(x)) \tag{6}$$

$$d^-_k = \sum_{x \in X_{t+1}}(\Phi(x)-\Phi(a))$$

Where d_k^+ represent the outranking character of a over all alternatives assigned to
category C_t, d_k^- represents the outranked character of a by all alternatives belong
to category C_{t+1}, n_t is the number of reference alternatives of category C_t,
and $\Phi(a)$ is the net flow of alternative a.

- assign a cut-off point s (s can be specified by the decision maker and reflects the
  DMs point of view: pessimistic or optimistic). if the distance is greater than the
  cut-off point, assign alternative a to the category C_{t+1}, otherwise assign to the C_t.

$$\begin{cases} If & d_k \geq s & a \in C_{t+1} \\ If & d_k < s & a \in C_t \end{cases} \tag{7}$$

It is obvious that the classification rule cannot classify two identical alternatives in
different classes. Since identical alternatives have the same net flow value.

4 Business Failure Risk Application

The PROMSORT method has been applied in a real world classification problem concerning the evaluation of business failure risk presented in the study of Dimitras et al., [10]. This problem was also studied by Figueria et al. [15] to test PROMETHEE TRI. The application involves 40 firms that were classified in five predefined classes (instead of the three in the original paper, the number of categories is equal to five as in [15]): *i.* Class 1: Very high risk [worst category]; *ii.* Class 2: High risk; *iii.* Class 3: Medium risk; *iv.* Class 4: Low risk; *v.* Class 5: Very low risk [best category].The firms were evaluated on the basis of a set of 7 criteria. The evaluation criteria included five quantitative criteria (financial ratios) and two qualitative criteria. Parameters, the weights and the indifference and preference thresholds of a linear preference function, and profile limits for PROMSORT were given in Table 1. Following the methodology described above, PROMSORT assignments both pessimistic and optimistic were given in Table 2. PROMSORT assignments are compared with ELECTRE TRI and PROMETHEE TRI. The same set of parameters and profile limits was used when running ELECTRE TRI. However, in PROMETHEE TRI, the reference actions were built as the mid action of each category. ELECTRE TRI and PROMETHEE TRI assignments are given in Table 3.

Table 1. Parameters for PROMETHEE and Profile Limits for PROMSORT

Code	Evaluation criteria	Obj.	Weight	q	p	b_1	b_2	b_3	b_4
g_1	Earning before interest / Total assets	Max.	0.01	1	2	-10	0	8	25
g_2	Net income / Net worth	Max.	0.295	4	6	-60	-40	-20	30
g_3	Total liabilities / Total assets	Min.	0.225	1	3	90	75	60	35
g_4	Interest expenses / Sales	Min.	0.01	1	2	28	23	18	10
g_5	General and administrative expenses/Sales	Min.	0.225	3	4	40	32	22	14
g_6	Managers work experience	Max.	0.01	0	0	1	2	4	5
g_7	Market niche / Position	Max	0.225	0	0	0	2	3	4

Table 2. PROMSORT Assignments

Class	PROMSORT Optimistic ($s=0$)	PROMSORT Pessimistic ($s=1$)
C1	{}	{}
C2	{a_{35}}	{a_{35}}
C3	{$a_{24},a_{31},a_{34},a_{36},a_{37},a_{38},a_{39}$}	{$a_{14},a_{19},a_{21},a_{24},a_{26},a_{31},a_{34},a_{36},a_{37}, a_{38},a_{39}$}
C4	{$a_1,a_3,a_4,a_5,a_8,a_9,a_{10},a_{11},a_{13},a_{14},a_{16},$ $a_{18},a_{19},a_{20},a_{21},a_{22},a_{23},a_{25},a_{26},a_{27},a_{28}, a_{30},a_{32},a_{33}$}	{$a_1,a_2,a_3,a_4,a_5,a_6,a_8,a_9,a_{10},a_{11},a_{12},a_{13},a_{15},a_{16},$ $a_{17},a_{18},a_{20},a_{22},a_{23},a_{25},a_{27},a_{28},a_{30},a_{32},a_{33}$}
C5	{$a_0,a_2,a_6,a_7,a_{12},a_{15},a_{17},a_{29}$}	{a_0,a_7,a_{29}}

According to the result, it should be noted that no assignment done by PROMETHEE TRI and PROMSORT is outside the range of ELECTRE TRI assignments. Both PROMETHEE TRI and PROMSORT are based on the methodological framework of PROMETHEE method. Therefore it is expected that the assignments should be consistent with PROMETHEE rankings. If we use PROMETHEE in order to rank alternatives form the best to the worst, we obtain following ranking:

$$a_0,a_7,a_{29},a_{15},a_6,a_{17},a_2,a_{12},a_9,a_5,a_{16},a_{11},a_{30},a_1,a_3,a_{18},a_4,a_8,a_{22},a_{20},a_{10},$$

$$a_{32},a_{25},a_{27},a_{13},a_{33},a_{26},a_{19},a_{23},a_{21},a_{28},a_{14},a_{31},a_{36},a_{38},a_{34},a_{37},a_{39},a_{24},a_{35}$$

In PROMETHEE TRI, the use of single criterion net flow does not guarantee the ordered categories. For instance, according to the PROMETHEE results it should be noted that a_6 is ranked better than a_2, a_3, a_8, a_9, a_{11}, a_{12}, a_{16}, a_{17}, a_{18}, a_{20}. However, in PROMETHEE TRI, the all actions are assigned to the better category than a_6. Same conclusions can be derived for a_1, a_5, a_{14}, a_{36}, and a_{39}. In the lights of these results, we can say that PROMETHEE TRI may not assign the alternatives to the categories fully consistent with PROMETHEE results. On the other hand, assignments of PROMSORT are consistent with PROMETHEE results. Since PROMSORT uses preference relation to sort alternatives into ordered categories, whereas PROMETHEE TRI uses a kind of similarity based measurement. Therefore, PROMSORT seems to be a more reliable tool to assign the firms to the ordered risk categories.

ELECTRE TRI optimistic and pessimistic procedures assign the firms to the risk classes in wide range. For instance, in pessimistic procedure, a_{28} is assigned to the worst (Class 1) class. Contrarily, ELECTRE TRI optimistic procedure assigned it to the best class (Class 5). In ELECTRE TRI optimistic procedure, 85 % of the firms were assigned to the best category although there are huge differences in performances between some of them. On other hand, PROMSORT needs the decision maker's point of view only when the incomparability situation occurs. Both PROMSORT optimistic and pessimistic procedures are capable of assigning the firms, which have similar overall performance, to the same class.

Table 3. PROMETHEE TRI and ELECTRE TRI Assignments

Class	PROMETHEE TRI	ELECTRE TRI Pessimistic	ELECTRE TRI Optimistic
C1	{}	$\{a_{28},\}$	{}
C2	$\{a_{14},a_{24},a_{35},a_{36},a_{38},a_{39}\}$	$\{a_{14},a_{24},a_{31},a_{34},a_{35},a_{36},a_{38},a_{39}\}$	{}
C3	$\{a_{13},a_{19},a_{20},a_{21},a_{23},a_{25},a_{26},$ $a_{27},a_{28},a_{31},a_{33},a_{34},a_{37}\}$	$\{a_2,a_3,a_4,a_8,a_9,a_{10},a_{11},a_{12},a_{13},a_{16},a_{18},$ $a_{19},a_{20},a_{21},a_{23},a_{25},a_{26},a_{27},a_{32},a_{33},a_{37}\}$	$\{a_{35}\}$
C4	$\{a_1,a_4,a_5,a_6,a_{10},a_{22},\ a_{32}\}$	$\{a_1,a_5,a_6,a_7,a_{15},a_{17},a_{22},a_{29},a_{30}\}$	$\{a_{22},a_{24},a_{36},a_{37},a_{38}\}$
C5	$\{a_0,a_2,a_3,a_7,a_8,a_9,a_{11},a_{12},a_{15},$ $a_{16},a_{17},a_{18},a_{29},a_{30}\}$	$\{a_0\}$	$\{a_0,a_1,a_2,a_3,a_4,a_5,a_6,a_7,a_8,a_9,a_{10},a_{11},a_{12},a_{13}$ $a_{14},a_{15},a_{16},a_{17},a_{18},a_{19},a_{20},a_{21},a_{23},a_{25},a_{26},a_{27}$ $a_{28},a_{29},a_{30},a_{31},a_{32},a_{33},a_{34},a_{39}\}$

After assigning the firms to risk levels, PROMSORT methodology suggest using single criterion net flows in order to identify the differences among risk classes and to show the weak and strong features of the firms as compared with profile limits with regard to each criterion. Figure 1 (a) illustrates, for optimistic assignment, the comparison of the classes by means of average single criterion net flows and (b) illustrates the comparison of firm "a36" and profile limits by means of single criterion net flows. Based on the results in Figure 1 (a), for instance, one can conclude that the firms assigned to the fourth class, which represents the low risk category, have some weakness on "Market niche" criterion with respect to the firms assigned the fifth class. According to the results in Figure 1 (b), it can be concluded that firm "a36" was assigned to the medium risk category due to its weaknesses on criterion 1, 2, 6, and 7 although it is a good performer on criterion 3, 4 and 5. By the help of this analysis, PROMSORT can provide effective information in order to measure, monitor, manage and control financial risks.

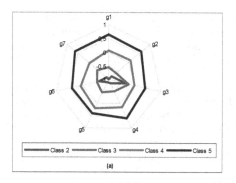
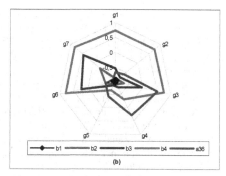

Fig. 1. Comparisons by means of single criterion net flows

5   Conclusion and Further Research

In this paper, a new multicriteria sorting procedure, called PROMSORT, in financial classification problems is presented. The assignment of the alternatives to the predefined ordered classes is based on an outranking relation obtained by PROMETHEE. PROMSORT was applied to the business failure risk problem and compared with two outranking based sorting methods, PROMETHEE TRI and ELECTRE TRI. The results showed that PROMSORT approach can be considered as an effective alternative to existing outranking based sorting methods in financial classification problems. However, the comparison with statistical methods and other multicriteria discrimination methods, like UTADIS and M.H.DIS, must be performed to investigate the potentials and efficiency of the proposed method. Furthermore it should be applied to other financial decision problems, such as credit scoring, credit cards assessment, country risk assessment, portfolio selection and management, etc.

References

1. Doumpos, M., Zopounidis, C.: Assessing financial risk using a multicriteria sorting procedure: the case of country risk assessment. Omega 29 (2001) 97–109.
2. Altman, E.I.: The success of business failure prediction models: an international survey. Journal of Banking and Finance 8(2) (1984) 171–198.
3. Keasey, K., McGuinness, P., Short, H: Multilogit approach to predicting corporate failure – further analysis and the issue of signal consistency. Omega 18(1) (1990) 85–94.
4. Skogsvik, K.: Current cost accounting ratios as predictors of business failure: The Swedish case. Journal of Business Finance and Accounting 17(1) (1990) 137–160.
5. Zopounidis, C., Doumpos, M.: A multicriteria decision aid methodology for sorting decision problems: The case of financial distress.Computational Economics 14(1999) 197–218.
6. Mousseau, R., Slowinski, R., Zielniewicz, P.: A user-oriented implementation of the ELECTRE TRI method integrating preference elicitation support. Computers and Operations Research 27(7-8) (2000) 757-777.
7. Roy, B.: The outranking approach and the foundations of ELECTRE methods. Theory and Decisions 31 (1990) 49-73.
8. Doumpos, M., Zanakis, S., Zapounidis, C.: Multicriteria preference disaggregation for classification problems with an application to global investing risk. Decision Sciences 32(2) (2001) 33-385.

9. Zopounidis,C., Doumpos, M.: Building additive utilities for multi-group hierarchical discrimination: The M.H.DIS method. Opt. Methods and Software 14(3) (2000)219–240.
10. Dimitras A.I., Zopounidis, C., Hurson, C.: A multicriteria decision aid method for the assessment of business failure risk. Foundations of Computing and Decision Sciences 20(2) (1995) 99-112.
11. Doumpos, M., Zopounidis, C.: Multi-criteria classification methods in financial and banking decisions. Intl. Trans. In Op. Res. 9 (2002) 567-581.
12. Zopounidis, C., Doumpos, M.: Business failure prediction using UTADIS multicriteria analysis. Journal of the Operational Research Society 50(11) (1999) 1138-1148.
13. Dimitras, A.I., Zanakis, S.H., Zopounidis, C.: A survey of business failures with an emphasis on prediction methods and industrial applications. European Journal of Operational Research 90 (1996) 487-513.
14. Doumpos, M., Zapounidis C.: A multicriteria classification approach based on pairwise comparisons. European Journal of Operational Research 158 (2004) 378-389.
15. Figueira, J., De Smet, Y., Brans, J.P.: MCDA methods for sorting and clustering problems: Promethee TRI and Promethee CLUSTER. Université Libre de Bruxelles, Service de Mathématiques de la Gestion, Working Paper 2004/02 (2004) (http://www.ulb.ac.be/polytech/smg/indexpublications.htm).
16. Brans, J.P., Vincke, P.H., Mareschal, B.: How to select and how to rank projects: The PROMETHEE method. European Journal of Operational Research 24 (1986) 228-238.

Volatility Modelling of Multivariate Financial Time Series by Using ICA-GARCH Models

Edmond H.C. Wu and Philip L.H. Yu

Department of Statistics & Actuarial Science, The University of Hong Kong
Pokfulam Road, Hong Kong
hcwu@graduate.hku.hk, plhyu@hku.hk

Abstract. Volatility modelling of asset returns is an important aspect for many financial applications, e.g., option pricing and risk management. GARCH models are usually used to model the volatility processes of financial time series. However, multivariate GARCH modelling of volatilities is still a challenge due to the complexity of parameters estimation. To solve this problem, we suggest using Independent Component Analysis (ICA) for transforming the multivariate time series into statistically independent time series. Then, we propose the ICA-GARCH model which is computationally efficient to estimate the volatilities. The experimental results show that this method is more effective to model multivariate time series than existing methods, e.g., PCA-GARCH.

Keywords: Financial Engineering, GARCH, ICA, Multivariate Time Series, Volatility

1 Introduction

One of the most important volatility models for time series is the autoregressive conditional heteroscedasticity (ARCH) model proposed by Engle [4] which also has been extended to GARCH model by Bollerslev [2]. Many studies show that the GARCH models are capable in capturing the dynamics of volatility from financial time series. Although univariate GARCH models are successful in volatility modelling, how to model volatility of multivariate time series is still a challenge in the field of financial engineering.

In this paper, we propose an ICA-GARCH model to solve this problem. The idea is that we first use the VAR model to find the residuals of return series. Then, we employ ICA to turn these residual series into statistically independent time series. After that, we can use univariate GARCH model to model the volatility of each independent time series. By some linear transformation of ICA, we can obtain the volatility of original multivariate time series. The most advantage of this method is that the computational cost is very low, as it is based on the univariate GARCH models of the independent components (ICs) obtained by ICA. The rest of this paper is organized as follows: In Section 2, we briefly introduce the AR, GARCH and ICA models. Then, we propose the ICA-GARCH model for multivariate volatilities modelling. Experimental results are given in Section 3. Finally, we conclude in Section 4.

M. Gallagher, J. Hogan, and F. Maire (Eds.): IDEAL 2005, LNCS 3578, pp. 571–579, 2005.

2   Volatility Modelling by Using ICA

2.1   AR Model

Autoregressive (AR) models are time series functions by its own lags. For instance, the autoregressive model of order 1, the $AR(1)$ model is:

$$r_t = \phi_0 + \phi_1 r_{t-1} + a_t \tag{1}$$

where a_t is assumed to be a white noise series with mean zero and variance σ^2. The constant ϕ_0 models a trend in the time series either upwards ($\phi_0 > 0$) or downwards ($\phi_0 < 0$). The lag coefficient ϕ_1 determines the stability of the process. Only when $|\phi_1| < 1$, the process will be stationary.

The extension of AR model to multivariate time series $\{\bar{r}_t\}$ is the vector autoregressive (VAR) model. The general $VAR(P)$ model is:

$$\bar{r}_t = \Phi_0 + \Phi_1 \bar{r}_{t-1} + \Phi_2 \bar{r}_{t-2} + ... + \Phi_p \bar{r}_{t-p} + \bar{a}_t \tag{2}$$

where $\Phi_0,...,\Phi_p$ are n-dimensional vectors, n is the time series number. $\{\bar{a}_t\}$ is a serially uncorrelated random vectors with mean zero and covariance Σ.

2.2   GARCH Model

It is well known that financial return volatility data is influenced by time dependent market information. Such time series can be parameterised using a generalized autoregressive conditional heteroscedasticity (GARCH) process to model and forecast the returns of financial indexes. In GARCH models, financial time series (e.g., stock returns) are assumed to be generated by a stochastic process with time-varying volatility. The GARCH(1,1) model is as follows:

$$y_t = \mu + \epsilon_t \tag{3}$$
$$\sigma_t^2 = \alpha_0 + \alpha_1 \epsilon_{t-1}^2 + \beta_1 \sigma_{t-1}^2 \tag{4}$$

where y_t consists of a conditional mean μ and a zero-mean error ϵ_t with conditional variance σ_t^2. To ensure a positive σ_t^2, we have $\alpha_0 > 0$, $\alpha_1 > 0$, and $\beta_1 > 0$. In most cases, GARCH(1,1) is adequate to model the volatility of an univariate time series. Also, the univariate GARCH models we use in this paper can fit time series with different data distributions, e.g., Gaussian, and Students' t distribution.

In order to check the predictability of a GARCH model for long-term volatility forecasts, we usually separate the in-sample and out-of-sample time series data. The in-sample data is used to train the GARCH models while the out-of-sample data is for the purpose of volatility forecasting based on the model estimation. The volatility forecasts can be obtained by the estimated GARCH parameters. For example, the 1-day ahead variance forecast in the GARCH(1,1) model is:

$$\hat{\sigma}_{t+1}^2 = \hat{\alpha_0} + \hat{\alpha_1} \epsilon_t^2 + \hat{\beta_1} \hat{\sigma}_t^2 \tag{5}$$

where $\hat{\alpha_0}$, $\hat{\alpha_1}$ and $\hat{\beta_1}$ are the estimation of GARCH(1,1) parameters α_0, α_1, and β_1, respectively.

2.3   ICA Model

Independent component analysis (ICA) [3] is a statistical method which aims to express the observed data in terms of a combination of underlying latent variables. For simplicity, we only consider linear combination in this article. The latent variables are assumed to be non-Gaussian and mutually independent. The task is to identify both the latent variables and the mixing process. A typical ICA model is:

$$X = AS \qquad (6)$$

where $X = (x_1, ..., x_n)$ is the vector of observed random variables, $S = (s_1, ..., s_m)$ is the vector of statistically independent latent variables called the independent components, and A is an unknown constant mixing matrix. The independent components s in the ICA model (1) are found by searching for a matrix W such that $S = WX$ up to some indeterminacies.

A fast fixed point algorithm (FastICA) for the separation of linearly mixed independent source signals was presented by Hyvarinen and Oja [5, 6]. The FastICA algorithm is a computationally efficient and robust fixed-point type algorithm for independent component analysis. The algorithm searches for the extrema of $E\{G(|wx|^2)\}$, where G is a nonquadratic function, e.g., $G(y) = log(cosh(y))$. We first need to transform the observed vector linearly so that we obtain a new vector $\bar{x}$ which is white, i.e. its components are uncorrelated and their variances equal unity. In other words, the covariance matrix of $\bar{x}$ equals the identity matrix $E(\bar{X}\bar{X}') = I$. Whitening can always be accomplished by e.g., principal component analysis.

The iterative fixed-point algorithm for finding one unit is:

$$\tilde{w}_{n+1} = E\{x(w_n x) * g(|w_n x|^2)\} - E\{g(|w_n x|^2) + |w_n x|^2 g'(|w_n x|^2)\}w_n \qquad (7)$$

where $w_{n+1} = \frac{\tilde{w}_{n+1}}{\|\tilde{w}_{n+1}\|}$. Getting the estimate of w, we can obtain an IC by $s = wx$. The above algorithm can be extended to the estimation of the whole ICA transformation $S = WX$. To prevent converging to the same ICs, the outputs $w_1 x, ..., w_n x$ are decorrelated after every iteration. When we have estimated n independent components, or n vectors $w_1, ..., w_n$, we run the one-unit fixed-point algorithm for w_{n+1}, and after every iteration step subtract from w_{n+1} the projections of the previously estimated n vectors, and then renormalize w_{n+1}:

$$\tilde{w}_{n+1} = \tilde{w}_{n+1} - \sum_{j=1}^{n} w_j w_j' \tilde{w}_{n+1}. \qquad (8)$$

where $w_{n+1} = \frac{\tilde{w}_{n+1}}{\|\tilde{w}_{n+1}\|}$. The above decorrelation scheme is suitable for deflationary separation of the ICs.

2.4   ICA-GARCH Model vs PCA-GARCH Model

The ICA-GARCH model works as follows: first find the residuals by AR model, then use ICA to capture the independent sources of information in the time series. Because the independent components are independent, such an approach will not significantly increase the computational complexity while retaining a very high accuracy. The ICA-GARCH model allows the multivariate volatilities of k time series to be generated from just m univariate GARCH models, where m is the number of independent components ($m \leq k$). Since only the univariate GARCH models are used to model volatilities, there is no dimensional restrictions for the ICA-GARCH model. However, for other multivariate GARCH models, when the number of time series increases, the computational difficulties occur in the multivariate parameterizations.

A similar method called orthogonal GARCH or principal component GARCH (PCA-GARCH) model was introduced by Alexander [1]. PCA-GARCH try to find W such that $\bar{y}_t = W\bar{r}_t$, $E(\bar{y}_t\bar{y}_t') \equiv V$ is diagonal. Both of the methods attempt to construct unconditionally linear combinations of the series $\bar{r}$. The main difference between ICA-GARCH and PCA-GARCH is that ICA makes the sources independent while PCA just makes the sources uncorrelated. The empirical study [7] showed that financial time series (e.g., asset returns) often demonstrate non-Gaussian distributions (e.g, fat-tails), in such cases, ICA is more suitable than PCA. In the following section, we will perform some experiments on ICA-GARCH model as well as PCA-GARCH model to compare their performance on real financial time series.

3   Experiments

The historical stock prices from New York and Hong Kong stock markets are used for experiments. The daily returns $r_i(t)$ are calculated by $r_i(t) = log(p_i(t)) - log(p_i(t-1))$, where $p_i(t)$ is the closing price of stock i on the trading day t. First, we choose the 1998-2003 stock prices of four U.S. IT stocks (HP, Dell, Microsoft and AMD) and use the ICA-GARCH and PCA-GARCH to model the volatilities of these stocks' return residuals.

Fig. 1 shows the results. The first column shows the return residuals of the four series obtained by VAR model. The left hand side of the vertical dotted lines denotes the in-sample data while the out-of-sample is on the right of the dotted lines. The second and third columns represent the volatilities estimated by PCA-GARCH and ICA-GARCH, respectively. The length of volatility forecasts is 250 days. Comparing the four figures in the second column, we can see that the volatilities obtained by PCA-GARCH are more volatile than ICA-GARCH, particularly when the changes of the residuals are unusual.

We also found that the volatilities of different series obtained by PCA-GARCH tend to be varying together even though the correlation coefficients of these time series are relatively small. What's more, this is not consistent with the changes of residual series we want to model. For example, in the 1st row, there is not significant changes in the beginning of the residual series, but the PCA-GARCH model misleads to indicate that the volatility at the beginning period is large. Also, the PCA-GARCH model overestimates the volatility around the No.1,100 observation of the 2nd series. However, ICA-GARCH model is capable in appropriately modelling the volatilities of these time series. For the last two series, both models identify that the average volatility of the 4th row is larger than the 3rd row, but ICA-GARCH model is better to model the magnitude of outliers. For instance, there is some smaller outliers in the middle of the 3rd residual series and in the beginning of the 4th residual series, however, PCA-GARCH treats these changes as large volatilities. ICA-GARCH seems to be more robust, which suggests two large volatilities in each of the series.

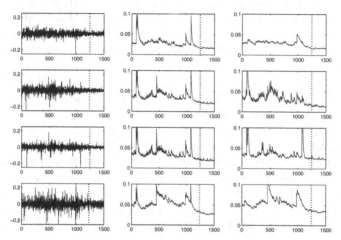

Fig. 1. Volatility modelling by PCA-GARCH and ICA-GARCH (1st row: HP, 2nd row: Dell, 3rd row: Microsoft, 4th row: AMD)

We also note that in Fig 1, there is not significant difference between the out-of-sample results of ICA-GARCH and PCA-GARCH. When we adjust the scales, we can see the difference of the predicting results more clear in Fig 2.

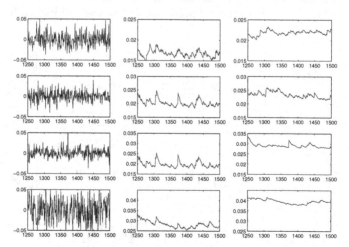

Fig. 2. Out-of-Sample Results by PCA-GARCH and ICA-GARCH (1st row: HP, 2nd row: Dell, 3rd row: Microsoft, 4th row: AMD)

ICA-GARCH can correctly forecast the peak around the No.1375 observation for the stock Microsoft, however, PCA-GARCH incorrectly forecasts some peaks in this time series. What's more, the last time series has the largest fluctuation, but PCA-GARCH underestimates the volatility. Therefore, the volatility prediction power of ICA-GARCH seems to be better than PCA-GARCH.

We further discover something interesting in the loadings of ICs. The A_I matrix below is the mixing matrix A in the ICA model $X = AS$. From the loadings (weights) of each IC, we can see that the dominant ICs (the IC with the significantly large weighting) for each residual series X_1, X_2, X_3, X_4 are S_4, S_3, S_2, and S_1, individually. We can also regard the dominant ICs as the main driven-forces of the series.

However, it is not the case for PCs. W_P below denotes the weights of the PCs derived from the residual time series X. From the loadings of the PCs, we find that the absolute values of the loadings are relatively closer. Hence, more than one series X_i will have significant influence on each PC. This may explain why the volatilities of multivariate time series by PCA-GARCH will tend to volatile together. ICs are statistically independent while PCs are just uncorrelated, ICs and PCs are equivalent only when the data strictly follows Gaussian distribution, however, we know that in most financial time series, it is not true. It is the reason why ICA-GARCH model can achieve better performance in modelling the volatilities than PCA-GARCH model.

$$A_I = \begin{pmatrix} 0.0048 & -0.0036 & -0.0033 & 0.027 \\ -0.0009 & -0.0027 & -0.035 & 0.006 \\ 0.0011 & 0.032 & -0.014 & 0.0048 \\ -0.046 & 0.0065 & -0.015 & 0.013 \end{pmatrix}; W_P = \begin{pmatrix} 0.028 & -0.012 & -0.63 & 0.77 \\ 0.40 & 0.56 & -0.56 & -0.46 \\ 0.29 & 0.67 & 0.53 & 0.43 \\ 0.87 & -0.48 & 0.098 & 0.041 \end{pmatrix}$$

We also calculate the dynamic correlations by using ICA-GARCH as well as PCA-GARCH. Fig 3 shows the results. The upper triangle matrix represents the time-varying correlations between the 4 US IT stock by using ICA-GARCH. The lower triangle matrix represents the time-varying correlations estimated by using PCA-GARCH. We can see that according to the two models' estimation, HP has

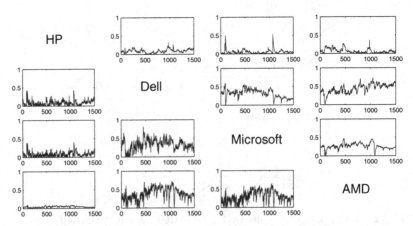

Fig. 3. The Dynamic Correlations by ICA-GARCH and PCA-GARCH

obviously smaller correlations with other stocks during the time horizon. More-over, the correlations estimated by ICA-GARCH seem to be more appropriate. For instance, the volatilities of Dell and Microsoft are relatively stable in the first 300 observations except one peak, the correlations estimated by ICA-GARCH correctly response to this. However, the correlations estimated by PCA-GARCH are much volatile which is not consistent with the fact.

To compare the results by using the data from other financial markets, we also employ the daily returns of three Hong Kong properties stocks (Sun Hung Kai Properties Ltd. (SHK), Henderson LD Co. Ltd. (HLD), Henderson Investment Ltd. (HIL)) during the period from Jan 2, 2001 to July 26, 2004. We also forecast the 150-days volatilities which plot on the right of the dotted lines in Fig 4. The volatilities of in-sample data are shown on the left of the dotted lines.

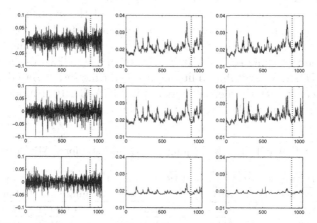

Fig. 4. Volatility modelling by PCA-GARCH and ICA-GARCH (1st row: SHK, 2nd row: HLD, 3rd row: HIL)

For the in-sample data, ICA-GARCH can correctly respond to the outliers in return residuals, e.g., the two peaks of the HIL series around the No. 500 obser-vation. However, PCA-GARCH exaggeratedly forecasts a large peak around the No. 800 observation. For out-of-sample data, ICA-GARCH model correctly pre-dicts that, for the HLD residual series, there is a volatility as large as the previous peak will occur while PCA-GARCH predicts a smaller volatility. In summary, ICA-GARCH has superior modelling performance than PCA-GARCH.

To further validate the effectiveness of the ICA-GARCH model, we use ARCH tests to test the presence of ARCH effects. The null hypothesis of ARCH test is that a time series of sample residuals consists of independent identically dis-tributed disturbances. Because we have used the GARCH models to estimate σ^2. Therefore, if the GARCH models are correctly specified, the series $\hat{\epsilon}_t = \epsilon_t / \sigma_t$ should have no autocorrelation. We also employ the Ljung-Box lack-of-fit hy-pothesis test for model misspecification by the Q-statistic, which is defined as:

$$Q = N(N+2) \sum_{k=1}^{L} \frac{r_k^2}{(N-K)} \qquad (9)$$

where N is the sample size, L is the number of autocorrelation lags, and r_k^2 is the squared sample autocorrelation at lag k.

In the tests, we set $\alpha = 0.05$, where α is the significance level of the hypothesis test. The corresponding critical value of the χ^2 distribution is 31.41 where $L = 20$. We use GARCH with t distribution to fit the time series. The estimated degree of freedom is in the range of 5.1 to 6.3, which suggests that these time series data exhibit non-Gaussian distribution. The test results are shown in Table 1. There are two values for each time series under two GARCH models and two tests. The left value is the test value of in-sample data. The values in the brackets are the test values for out-of-sample data.

In Table 1, we can see that, both models accept the hypothesis that there is no serial correlation or ARCH effect in the US stock data. However, for the three Hong Kong properties stocks, PCA-GARCH rejects two in-sample tests and one out-of sample test while ICA-GARCH accepts all tests. This result suggests that ICA-GARCH is more suitable to fit the financial time series. Based on the above studies, it seems that the better model is the ICA-GARCH model since it has fewer rejections and smaller test statistic values in most cases.

Table 1. ARCH Test and Ljung-Box Q-Statistic for GARCH models

GARCH Models	ICA-GARCH	PCA-GARCH	ICA-GARCH	PCA-GARCH
Stocks/Test Statistic	ARCH	ARCH	Ljung-Box	Ljung-Box
HP	3.96 (10.54)	4.25 (12.22)	15.74 (28.63)	17.00 (27.23)
Dell	1.46 (19.95)	1.40 (19.65)	18.17 (22.95)	21.23 (25.75)
Microsoft	0.33 (9.27)	0.34 (10.38)	13.80 (17.09)	15.73 (17.51)
AMD	1.09 (10.01)	1.17 (10.64)	17.15 (18.48)	17.76 (18.40)
SHK	25.39 (12.18)	**39.88** (13.09)	29.98 (27.54)	**35.02 (32.04)**
HLD	15.40 (8.63)	12.84 (8.39)	21.03 (18.56)	21.60 (19.41)
HIL	1.61 (14.67)	1.65 (14.87)	13.63 (22.05)	13.82 (22.90)

4   Conclusions

In this article, we propose an alternative multivariate GARCH model called ICA-GARCH for modelling the volatilities of time series. The ICA-GARCH model is computationally simple and efficient. The empirical studies demonstrate that the ICA-GARCH is effective in capturing the time-varying features of volatilities and it is more robust than comparable methods, e.g., PCA-GARCH. The ICA-GARCH model also provides a better volatility forecasting method for financial time series. In the future, we intend to employ the volatility model in practical financial engineering applications, e.g., portfolio management.

References

1. Alexander C.O., 'Orthogonal GARCH' in C.O.Alexander (ed.), Mastering Risk Volume 2. Financial Times- Prentice Hall, 2001.
2. Bollerslev, T., 1986, Generalized autoregressive conditional heteroscedasticity, Journal of Econometrics, 31(3), 307–327.
3. P. Comon, Independent component analysis: a new concept?" Signal Processing 36, 287-314, 1994.
4. Engle, R.F., 1982, Autoregressive conditional heteroscedasticity with estimates of the variance of the U. K. inflation, Econometrica, 50(4), 987–1008
5. A. Hyvarinen 1999,Fast and robust fixed-point algorithms for independent component analysis, IEEE Transactions on Neural Networks 10(3), 626-634.
6. A. Hyvarinen and E. Oja, A fast fixed-point algorithm for independent component analysis, Neural Computation 9, 1483-1492, 1997.
7. A.S.K. Wong, P.J.G. Vlaar, modelling time-varying correlations of financial markets, WO Research Memoranda (discontinued) 739, Netherlands Central Bank, Research Department, 2003.

Volatility Transmission Between Stock and Bond Markets: Evidence from US and Australia

Victor Fang[1], Vincent C.S. Lee[1,2], and Yee Choon Lim[1]

[1] Department of Accounting and Finance, Monash University,
Clayton, Australia 3800
Fax: +613 99055159, Tel: +613 990{32183, 52360}
victor.fang@buseco.monash.edu.au
vincent.lee@infotech.monash.edu.au
http://www.aaf.monash.edu.au
http://www.bsys.monash.edu.au
[2] School of Business Systems, Monash University,
Clayton, Australia 3800
Fax: +613 99055159, Tel: +613 990{32183, 52360}

Abstract. This paper investigates the cross-market informational dependence between these assets under disparate interest rate conditions of the U.S and Australia. With conditional variance as a proxy for volatility, we use the BEKK – a matricular decomposition of the bivariate GARCH (1,1) model to examine the cross-market contemporaneous effect of information arrival. Applying the model to the stock and bond indices of both countries, we find evidence of volatility spillover, thereby supporting the notion of informational dependence between each market.

Keywords: Comovement, volatility transmission, conditional varaince, GARCH (1,1)

JEL Classification: G11, G12

1 Introduction

Sufficient theory and evidence (Campbell and Ammer, 1993; Bollerslev and Wooldrige, 1990; Kwan, 1996) about comovement between stocks and bonds are documented in the past to suggest that volatility transmission exists, although a consensus to causation and prediction has yet to be reached. The portfolio theory accords both assets with complimentary characteristics, thus being a premise to our conjectures about cross-market linkages.Recent evidence of linkages between markets has been demonstrated through the causality in variance approach. Caporale *et al.* (2002) applies the test to East Asian markets[1] and find a causal relationship between stock prices and exchange rates volatility. Alaganar and Bhar (2003) use a slightly different methodology and find that the stock markets for all countries in the G7[2] are

---

[1] They are Indonesia, Korea Thailand and Japan
[2] They are essentially the G8 OECD countries, excluding Australia

M. Gallagher, J. Hogan, and F. Maire (Eds.): IDEAL 2005, LNCS 3578, pp. 580–587, 2005.

related to the U.S. Most interestingly, Japan causes other countries in mean and these countries reciprocate in variance, implying that, volatility spillovers are bi-directional, albeit unconvincing[3]. Stronger evidence emanate from Alaganar and Bhar (2003) as they observe causality in both mean and variance of the financial sector returns and short-term interest rates of the G7.

This paper investigates the cross-market informational dependence between these assets under disparate interest rate conditions of the U.S and Australia.

2 The Data

To obtain an unbiased representation of confounding informational effects, we employ daily data of the stock and bond indices for both the U.S. and Australia over the period[4] of 6/30/1998 to 11/14/2003. This sample period encapsulates volatility inducing events such as the devaluation of the rubble, the technology bubble, September 11th and the Middle-Eastern political uncertainty. The sample period also captures the disparity in interest rates, which may lead to the increased awareness of the benchmark rates in Australia. The cash rates of both countries are in tandem prior to May 2001, and start to diverge thereafter. By September 2003, the interest rate differential was higher than 4 per cent. However, due to the availability of data control measures, we are unable to extend the sample period.

The stock and bond index data for the U.S is available from Dow Jones: Dow Jones Industrial (DJI) and the Dow Jones Corporate Bond Index (DJBI). The DJI is a value weighted market aggregate index, while DJCI is a composition of investment grade bonds issued by 96 corporations in the U.S. For Australia, we use the Australia Stock Exchange All Ordinaries Price Index (ASX-200) and Australian Bond Index (ABI) available in Datastream. By construction and composition, all four indexes used in our analysis are able to capture volatility arising from systematic influences as they consist of firms from different industries, and thus are able to reflect general informational effects. Nonetheless, we observe a caveat in the use of bond indexes owing to the nature of the security. Returns are dependent on various characteristics such as duration and convexity. Therefore, it is ideal that corporate bond of differing maturities are well distributed in the index. The construction of the DJBI and ABI satisfies these conditions.

Cursorily, volatility for stocks is much higher than bonds for both countries while U.S stocks series display more clustering than the Australian counterpart. Table 1 presents a summary of the descriptive statistics of all four series. The sample size of 1402 is relatively small for modelling volatility thus explaining the low Ljung-Box statistics for the standardized squared residuals. The sample moments for all four series show heavy skewness while the distributions are leptokurtic.

---

[3] The use of monthly data and Markov method of extrapolating variance may not truly represent market movement

[4] The Australian Bond Index was initiated in 30th of June 1998, and thus it forbids us from obtaining a desirable (larger) sample size. Nonetheless, this should not prevent us from drawing reasonable inferences since any biasness inherent from distributional complications can be compensated by strict rejection criterion

Table 1.

Descriptive Statistics

	US DJI	US DJBI	Australia ASX-200	ABI
Mean	0.00006	0.00015	0.00013	0.00021
Median	0.00000	0.00019	0.00003	0.00001
Maximum	0.06155	0.01110	0.03387	0.02892
Minimum	-0.07396	-0.01767	-0.05853	-0.02690
Std. Dev.	0.01294	0.00273	0.00776	0.00316
Skewness	-0.09364	-0.36638	-0.51711	0.30152
Kurtosis	5.63168	6.11326	7.17430	14.41433
Jarque-Bera	406.916[b]	597.9893[b]	1081.149[b]	7637.622[b]
LB(SSR)	56.4[a]	160.7[b]	67.7792[a]	304.4624[b]

Sample period from 7/01/1998 to 11/14/2003

[a] indicates significant art 10%

[b] indicates significance at 5%

3 Methodology

We follow the methods of Karolyi (1995) and Caporale et al. (2002). They incorporated simple Granger causality tests through a multivariate GARCH (1,1) framework within the BEKK representation of Baba et al. (1987). They have also provided evidence to the robustness of this test, although applications were made to other financial assets: currencies and stock returns respectively. For scope of discussion, we shall summarize the relevant methods that may be applied to our study. Cheung and Ng (1996) use the residual cross-correlation function (CCF) on conditional mean and conditional variance estimates obtained from univariate time-series models. This simple approach allows the orthogonal relations in both variables to be tested, *per se;* a probable relation exists in either moment. This method is particularly appealing because it allows an analysis to various lag lengths. However, if more than one asset and market is to be introduced, a decomposition approach alike that of BEKK will be required to parameterize the relation. On the other hand, the BEKK is not able to parameterize possible lagged relations; instead, time varying volatility is being modeled based on the second-order nonlinear dependence of the GARCH (1,1).

Instead of undertaking the GARCH (1,1), Alaganar and Bhar (2003) employed the Markov Switching process to model conditional variances (on stock returns) based on the unobserved state of future information. The model estimation relies on a probability weighted maximum likelihood function, and generates a smooth distribution of conditional variances that are appropriate for a causality-in-variance test. Although the model is theoretically appealing as it addresses the martingale nature of financial markets, however, its estimates discard informational effects that represent daily volatility in the process of aggregation.

Given the properties of the techniques discussed, we employ the multivariate GARCH (1,1) – BEKK representation (Baba, Engle, Kraft and Kroner, 1990; Engle and Kroner, 1995) to model the relationship. Suitably, the model is applicable to two or more variables in both moments while not requiring excessive estimation of parameters; and alleviates complications arising from re-parameterization (inherent of the VAR). In addition, the quadratic specification allows us to treat problematic negative covariance matrices faced by other specifications (such as the VECH) without difficulty. First, it requires an estimate of the conditional variances from the GARCH (1,1) model[5]:

$$x_t = \gamma + \beta x_{t-1} + \varepsilon_t \tag{1}$$

Where x_t denotes the returns on the stock index SI_t as well as bond index BI_t. The residual vector $\varepsilon_t = (e_{1,t}, e_{2,t})$ is bivariate and normally distributed $\varepsilon_t \mid \Phi_{t-1} \sim (0, H_t)$ with its corresponding conditional variance covariance matrix given by:

$$H_t = \begin{bmatrix} h_{11t} & h_{12t} \\ h_{21t} & h_{22t} \end{bmatrix}$$

In a univariate GARCH (1,1) process, the conditional variance $\sigma_t^2 \mid \Phi_{t-1}$ is obtained from the variance equation (2). We adopt the BEKK representation, which is essentially a spectral decomposition of the conditional variance-covariance matrix. A multivariate GARCH(1,1) model (3) is resultant of the operation.

$$\sigma_t^2 = \mu + \alpha_1 \varepsilon_{t-1} + \beta \sigma_{t-1}^2 \tag{2}$$

$$H_t = \Omega'\Omega + \alpha' \varepsilon_{t-1}\varepsilon'_{t-1} \alpha + \beta' H_{t-1} \beta \tag{3}$$

The spectral decomposition follows:

$$H_t = \Omega_0{}'\Omega_0 + \begin{bmatrix} \alpha_{11} & \alpha_{12} \\ \alpha_{21} & \alpha_{22} \end{bmatrix}' \begin{bmatrix} e_{1,t-1}^2 & e_{1,t-1}e'_{2,t-1} \\ e_{1,t-1}e'_{2,t-1} & e_{2,t-1}^2 \end{bmatrix} \begin{bmatrix} \alpha_{11} & \alpha_{12} \\ \alpha_{21} & \alpha_{22} \end{bmatrix}$$
$$+ \begin{bmatrix} \beta_{11} & \beta_{12} \\ \beta_{21} & \beta_{22} \end{bmatrix}' H_{t-1} \begin{bmatrix} \beta_{11} & \beta_{12} \\ \beta_{21} & \beta_{22} \end{bmatrix} \tag{4}$$

The BEKK representation decomposes the GARCH (1,1) process into its multivariate constituents and models the time-varying process of H_t conditional on the lag values of the residuals of the mean and variance equation. The model facilitates the interaction between the conditional variances and covariances thus allowing us to observe the impact of information arrival upon two different markets. The matrix is restricted to the upper triangle to observe the unidirectional causality as shown in equation (5):

$$H_{2t} = \Omega_{12}^2 + \Omega_{22}^2 + \alpha_{12}^2 e_{1t-1}^2 + 2\alpha_{12}\alpha_{22}e_{1t-1}e_{2t-1} + 2\beta_{12}\beta_{22}h_{12t-1}$$
$$+ \alpha_{22}^2 e_{2t-1}^2 + \beta_{12}^2 h_{1t-1} + \beta_{22}^2 h_{2t-1} \tag{5}$$

Following the above, we test for the hypothesis of causality in conditional variances between the bond and stock markets within the country and between the individual assets of both countries in a pair-wise fashion. Restricting the matrix to the

---

[5] Bivariate Garch (1,1) representation in Engle and Kroner (1995)

upper triangle[6], allows us to investigate the causality effect of h_{1t} on h_{2t}. Thus, the null hypothesis $\mathbf{H_0}$: $\alpha_{12}=\beta_{12}=0$ is established due to the restriction; implying that h_{1t} does not have a causal effect on h_{2t}. To test for a bidirectional relation, we run the restricted model twice on each pair of asset, with each asset being the independent variable on each run. This simulates a full model without unnecessary parameterization.

Given a sample of T observations of the return vector, x_t, the parameters, θ of the model are obtained from the conditional density function as:

$$f(x_t \mid \Phi_{t-1};\theta)=(2\pi)^{-1}|H_t|^{-1/2}\exp\left(-\frac{\varepsilon_t^{'}(H_t^{-1})\varepsilon_t}{2}\right) \tag{6}$$

The log likelihood function is:
$$L = \sum \log f(x_t \mid \Phi_{t-1};\theta) \tag{7}$$
where θ is the vector of parameters and standard errors are calculated from the quasi-maximum likelihood method by Bollerslev and Wooldridge (1992) which are robust to the density function underlying the residuals.

4 Empirical Results

Table 2 presents the co-influences of mean and conditional variances of both assets in the U.S. and Australia. We are aware of the distributional complications arising from a relatively small sample size, which is a circumscription of the unavailability of an appropriate bond index. As such, to account for distributional complications, we take the population of the ABI and restrict our inferences to 1 per cent significance in order to compensate for any biasness that may arise.

Table 2. Summary of Estimates for Bidirectional Volatility Spillover for Individual Countries. The table presents the coefficient estimates from the bivariate GARCH (1,1) – BEKK representation. The co-efficient estimates are obtained from the maximum likelihood function of the bivariate model. Coefficient α_{12} denotes volatility transmission from the stock market to the bond market, while α_{21}, vice versa

| | U.S. | | Australia | |
	Coefficient	t-Statistic	Coefficient	t-Statistic
μ_{11}	0.00031	0.967221	0.0003	1.6974
μ_{22}	0.000203	2.883744	0.0002	2.7433
Ω_{11}	0.002058	6.782009	0.0014	7.1155
Ω_{12}	0.0007	0.7573	-0.0003	-3.2134
Ω_{21}	0.00043	1.53712	-0.000426	-2.004658
Ω_{22}	0.0023	7.5841	0.0008	8.0953
α_{11}	0.2552	13.2005	0.2664	15.9002
α_{12}	0.0052	0.5642	-0.0001	-0.0156
α_{21}	0.16298	2.35298	-0.071154	-1.56105
α_{22}	0.4409	15.3350	0.2525	20.2635
β_{11}	0.9540	129.7735	0.9485	112.8578
β_{12}	-0.0124	-0.8663	0.0066	1.7966
β_{21}	-0.05340	-2.06527	0.05008	1.713663
β_{22}	0.1455	0.8713	0.9272	72.5977

* indicates significance at 1%

---

[6] The procedure is similar to Caporale et al. (2002)

In contrast to *a priori* knowledge, the coefficient estimates of bidirectional causation in the conditional variances of both assets in the U.S indicating that volatility spillover does not occur between stocks and bonds on the aggregate, albeit some evidence is present if we lower the rejection criterion to 5 per cent. The interaction terms are significant under the 10 per cent rejection region, suggesting that bidirectional volatility transmission is palpable although we are inclined not to make any inferences. Given that the Australian economy has been operating in a relatively high interest rate environment, international investors are likely to be more sensitive to the available benchmark rates (Australian treasury securities and investment grade bonds), thus explaining the possibility of bidirectional causation.

The cross-market analysis presents a more comprehensive account of information transmission. We find strong evidence of interaction between the stock and bond markets of both the U.S. and Australia. The significant positive coefficients of unidirectional volatility transmission from the U.S. to Australia shown in Table 3 and Table 4 are consistent with our proposition.

Table 3. Summary of Pairwise Estimates for Unidirectional Volatility Spillover from DJI (US) to ASX-200 (Australia).β_{12} denotes volatility transmission from DJI to ASX-200; and DJI and ABI

DJI and ASX-200			DJI and ABI	
	Coefficient	t-Statistic	Coefficient	t-Statistic
μ_{11}	0.0003	0.9870	0.0004	1.2580
μ_{22}	0.0003	1.2907	0.0002	2.7216
Ω_{11}	0.0023	7.4825	0.0019	6.7094
Ω_{12}	0.0005	1.8353	0.0002	1.3787
Ω_{22}	0.0013	6.3192	0.0010	8.9249
α_{11}	0.2441	13.7548	0.2494	13.7784
α_{12}	-0.0603	-4.3942	0.0033	0.4991
α_{22}	0.3065	14.8242	0.2777	17.0565
β_{11}	0.9530	131.9807	0.9576	145.2375
β_{12}	0.0201	3.2674	-0.0080	-2.6675
β_{22}	0.9303	90.6807	0.8879	43.9753
Log LL	9273.725		10401.11	
Ave. Log LL	6.619361		7.424065	
AIC	-13.22302		-14.83243	
Schwarz criterion	-13.18184		-14.79125	
Hannan-Quinn criter.	-13.20763		-14.81703	

* indicates significance at 1%

The most interesting aspect of our study lies in the evidence of "flight to quality" from the U.S stock market to the Australian bond market. The statistically significant negative coefficient β_{12} (Table 4) of volatility transmission from the U.S stock provides for our conjecture of international diversification of substitute assets. It is apparent that investors are outweighing U.S stocks with Australian bonds in anticipation of uncertainty. The negative relation suggests that higher uncertainty in the U.S stock market within the sample period transmits information that leads to lower uncertainty in the Australian Bond market. The fact that Australian investors face a relatively higher benchmark rate compared to U.S. over the sample period supports our findings since it is reasonable to expect international investors to be actively seeking higher foreign benchmark rates that the domestic markets are not able to provide for. Laterally speaking, Australian bond portfolio holders may also short sell U.S. stocks during times of uncertainty.

Table 4. Summary of Pairwise Estimates for Unidirectional Volatility Spillover from DJBI(US) to Australia, β_{12} denotes volatility transmission from DJCI to ABI

DJBI and ABI		DJBI and ASX-200		
	Coefficient	t-Statistic	Coefficient	t-Statistic
μ_{11}	0.0002	2.6745	0.0002	2.1352
μ_{22}	0.0002	2.9153	0.0003	1.7430
Ω_{11}	0.0024	29.5791	0.0005	6.9286
Ω_{12}	0.0000	-0.2490	-0.0002	-0.4507
Ω_{22}	0.0000	-0.0004	0.0015	5.2113
α_{11}	0.4426	16.0616	0.1966	14.2367
α_{12}	-0.0851	-2.0406	-0.1692	-2.4762
α_{22}	0.2661	16.8288	0.2946	11.7945
β_{11}	0.1434	0.8578	0.9663	159.7531
β_{12}	0.3729	3.1196	0.0466	1.2658
β_{22}	0.8974	43.7394	0.9342	68.4297
Log LL	12485.949		11202.46	
Ave. Log LL	8.9121694		7.996044	
AIC	-17.8086		-15.97638	
Schwarz criterion	-17.7675		-15.9352	
Hannan-Quinn criter.	-17.7932		-15.96099	

* indicates significance at 1%

5   Conclusion

Our study elucidates the herding behaviour of investors given both complimentary assets. The high (rising) interest rate environment and the perceived resilience of the Australian economy provide us with a unique opportunity to investigate the informational dependence between stock and bond investors in both countries. As bond returns represent benchmark rates, it is reasonable to contend that a noticeable number of informed investors will fashion their portfolios to capitalize on the bond market of Australia. Therefore, we conduct an analysis in the given circumstance. Further tests on markets between both countries yield interesting results. Statistics reveal the spillovers between the stock markets of the U.S. and Australia, and the same effects are present in the bond markets of both countries.

References

1. Alaganar, V., and Ramaprasad Bhar, 2003, An International Study of Causality-in-Variance: Interest Rate and Financial Sector Returns, *Journal of Economics and Finance* 27, Issue 1, 39-56.
2. Baba, Y., Engle, R.F., Kraft, D., and Kroner, K. (1990), Multivariate simultaneous generalized ARCH, unpublished manuscript, University of California, San Diego.
3. Board of Governors of the Federal Reserve System, 1913, Effective Federal Funds Rate, Washington DC.

4. Bollerslev T., P., Wooldridge J., M., 1990, Quasi-maximum Likelihood Estimation and Inference in Dynamic Models with Time-varying Covariances, *Econometric Reviews* 11: 143-172.

5. Campbell, John Y., and John Ammer, 1993, What Moves the Stock and Bond Markets? A Variance Decomposition for Long Term Asset Returns, *Journal of Finance 48*, Issue 1, 3-37.

6. Caporale, Maria, G., Nikitas Ptittas and Nicola Spagnolo, 2002, Testing for Causality in Variance: An application to the East Asian Markets, *International Journal of Finance and Economics* 7, 235-245.

7. Cheung and Ng (1996), A Causality-in-variance test and its application to financial market prices, *Journal of Econometrics,* Vol 72, 33-48

8. Engle R. F, and Kroner, K. F. (1995), Multivariate simultaneous generalized ARCH, *Econometric Theory*, Vol. 11, 122-150

9. Karolyi, Andrew G., 1995, A multivariate GARCH model of international transmissions of stock returns and volatility: The case of the United States and Canada, *Journal of Business and Economics Statistics* 13, 11-25

10. Kwan, Simon, 1996, Firm-specific Information and the Correlation Between Individual Stocks and Bonds, *Journal of Financial Economics* 40, 63-80.

11. Reserve Bank of Australia, 1959, Cash Target Rate, Sydney, Australia

12. Shiller, Robert J., and Andrea E. Beltratti, 1992, Stock Prices and Bond Yields, *Journal of Monetary Economics* 30, 25-46.

A Machine Learning Approach to Intraday Trading on Foreign Exchange Markets

Andrei Hryshko and Tom Downs

University of Queensland, School of ITEE, QLD, St. Lucia, 4071, Australia
{dushenka,td}@itee.uq.edu.au

Abstract. Foreign Exchange trading has emerged in recent times as a significant activity in many countries. As with most forms of trading, the activity is influenced by many random parameters so that the creation of a system that effectively emulates the trading process will be very helpful. In this paper we try to create such a system using Machine learning approach to emulate trader behaviour on the Foreign Exchange market and to find the most profitable trading strategy.

1 Introduction

Trading on financial markets usually takes place through a broker who provides software that gives information to a trader, such as current and past share prices, exchange rate, market indicators etc. Based on this data, the trader can decide when to sell and when to buy a particular stock or currency. Choosing these actions in such a way as to maximize profit is difficult, not just for beginners, but also for experienced traders. The market is constantly changing so that different rules and concepts apply in different situations, and it is not uncommon that a trader's strategy that works well at a given time performs poorly two hours later. Hence the trader has to determine the times at which a strategy should be changed and to identify the changes that should be made.

Some related studies have previously been carried out but the question of how to combine theoretical investigations with practical trading requires further attention.

In this paper, we describe a on-line machine learning system that we have developed to deal with these problems and compare its performance with that of other systems that have been described elsewhere.

2 Statistical Approach to Technical Analysis

A widely used technique for predicting price movements is known as technical analysis, which draws upon a set of *indicators* that assist in identifying trends and other market fluctuations. An indicator makes use of a set of mathematical formulae which may, for instance, be derived from past prices or from other market data such as trade volumes. Different indicators play different roles in the analysis. Some indicators work better when the market has a strong trend, and some when the market is neutral. An example of a simple indicator is the Moving Average (MA) which shows the average value of prices during a defined period of time. The n-day MA is calculated using the simple formula:

M. Gallagher, J. Hogan, and F. Maire (Eds.): IDEAL 2005, LNCS 3578, pp. 588–595, 2005.

$$MA = \frac{P_1 + \ldots + P_n}{n} \qquad (1)$$

where P_i is the price $i-1$ days previously.

Buy and sell signals are generated according to behaviour of moving averages in the short and longer term. A buy signal is produced when the short average crosses above the longer one. When the short average moves below, this generates a sell signal.

The Machine Learning system described here makes use of 10 commonly-used indicators and these are listed in the Appendix.

3 Methodology

3.1 Genetic Algorithms

In the standard genetic algorithm (GA) formulation, a population of possible solutions is encoded as a set of bit strings, each having the same fixed length. In applying a GA to FX trading, each string represents a possible solution for the trader – adopt a short, long or neutral position. Decisions made by the trader are based upon the values of a set of market indicators. These values can be incorporated into the GA bit strings as binary variables. For instance, in the case of the moving average method mentioned in the previous section, the indicator generates a sell signal when the short average moves below the longer one. The indicator corresponding to this signal is called "MASell" and it takes on the binary value 1 when the condition for the sell signal is met. It has the value 0 otherwise.

An example of a rule employing this and two other indicators (see Appendix) is shown in Table 1. This rule instructs the trader to adopt a short position (ie sell) and is encoded as a bit string in the table. The rule states "IF MASell = 1 OR (MomentumSell =1 AND StochasticBuy = 0) THEN adopt a short position". Thus the connectives in the table are the Boolean operators AND and OR which have binary values 1 and 0 respectively.

Table 1. A Sell rule and its associated bit string

MASell	Connective	MomSel	Connective	StochBuy	Sell
1	0	1	1	0	0

Note that the instruction to sell in this rule is encoded as a zero at the right-hand end of the bit string. Rules that instruct the trader to adopt a long position (ie to buy) have a '1' in this position.

Rules for adopting a short or long position are called entry rules because they instruct the trader to participate actively in the market. There are also exit rules under which the trader returns to a neutral position. An example is shown in Table 2. Note that there is no explicit binary value for the instruction to exit. No such value is necessary because the exit action is always the same – that is, to return to a neutral position.

Table 2. An example of an exit rule

RSIBuy	Connect	MomSell	Connect	LWSell	Connect	POSell
1	0	1	0	1	1	0

The rule in Table 2 rule states "IF RSIBuy = 1 OR (MomentumSell = 1 OR (Larry WilliamsSell = 1 AND Price OscillatorSell = 0)) THEN adopt a neutral position.

The rules and their binary strings are obviously significantly longer than these when a large number of indicators have to be coded.

The rules in Tables 1 and 2 together can be considered as a *strategy*. This strategy states that if the trader enters under the rule in Table 1, the rule for exiting is the one in Table 2. Our objective is to use machine learning methods to determine the best possible such strategy for given market conditions.

In a typical implementation, a population of 150 rules of each type (entry and exit) is generated randomly. Then out of these 300 rules we randomly combine 150 pairs consisting of one entry rule and one exit rule. This therefore gives us 150 trading strategies. These strategies are ranked according to their profitability and are then stochastically chosen to participate in the creation of a new population. Those strategies with greater profitability (or *fitness*) are more likely to be selected to participate. Crossover and mutation (with low probability) are applied only to rules of the same type (entry or exit). If rules derived in this way are unique (differing from all other rules in the population) they are used to replace lower-ranked rules. This is done in such a way that the number of rules in the population remains constant.

The process is continued until a stopping criterion is met upon which the best pair of rules (the best strategy) is chosen to be the output of the genetic algorithm. The best strategy is the one that gives maximum profitability.

3.2 Reinforcement Learning

The general reinforcement learning problem addresses the following: an agent must explore its environment and make decisions in different situations based on incomplete knowledge about this environment. The only feedback that the agent receives from the environment is a scalar reinforcement signal which is positive if its actions are beneficial and negative otherwise. The objective of the agent is to choose its actions so as to increase the long-term sum of the reinforcement signals [8]. Besides the reinforcement signal, the agent also receives information on the current state of the environment (in the form of a vector of observations). On the FX market a trader (machine or human) has insufficient knowledge about the environment to choose the times at which buy and sell decisions should be made in order to maximize profit. The only information available is the gain (positive or negative) generated by trading decisions and this provides the reinforcement signal that drives our system and this provides the reinforcement signal that drives our system.

For our software implementation, we have developed an RL-engine based on the Q-learning algorithm proposed by Watkins in [12] for partially-observable Markov decision processes. The Q-learning algorithm, which can be used on-line, was developed for the optimization of a strategy based upon experience gained from the unknown environment.

In general, the Q-learning algorithm works as follows. The value $Q(s, a)$ is defined to be the expected discounted sum of future reinforcement signals when action a is taken in state s and an optimal policy is then followed. The state s belongs to S, the discrete set of states of the environment and the action a belongs to the set A of possible agent actions. Once we have the $Q(s, a)$ values, the optimal action from any state is the one with the highest Q-value. At the first step we initialise $Q_0(s_0, a_0)$ by arbitrary numbers and improved estimates of the Q-values are then obtained from incoming signals using the following procedure:

1. From the current state s_t, select an action a_t. This takes us to the next state s_{t+1} and provides the reinforcement signal r_{t+1}.
2. Update $Q_t(s_t, a_t)$ based on this outcome:

$$Q_{t+1}(s_t, a_t) := Q_t(s_t, a_t) + \alpha \left(r_{t+1} + \gamma \max_a Q_t(s_{t+1}, a) - Q_t(s_t, a_t) \right) \quad (2)$$

where α $(0 < \alpha \leq 1)$ is a learning-rate parameter and $0 < \gamma < 1$ is the discount factor used to place more emphasis on reinforcement signals that are received earlier.
3. Go to 1.

Note that we have to store each value $Q(s, a)$ for all $s \in S$ and $a \in A$. They are stored in a table called a Q-table.

The objective of the agent is to find the optimal policy $\pi(s) \in A$ for each state of the environment to maximise the long-run total reward. The Q-learning algorithm uses optimal Q-values $Q^*(s_t, a_t)$ for states s and actions a. The optimal Q-value function satisfies Bellman's optimality equation:

$$Q^*(s_t, a_t) := \sum_{s_{t+1}} P(s_t, a_t, s_{t+1}) \left[R(s_t, a_t, s_{t+1}) + \gamma \max_{a'} Q^*(s_{t+1}, a') \right] \quad (3)$$

where $P(s_t, a_t, s_{t+1})$ is the probability of a transition from state s_t to s_{t+1} with action a_t is taken; $R(s_t, a_t, s_{t+1})$ is an immediate reward obtained from taking action a_t when the environment state changes s_t to s_{t+1}; $\gamma (0 \leq \gamma \leq 1)$ is a discount factor to weight future rewards.

Given the optimal Q-values $Q^*(s, a)$ it is possible to choose the best action:

$$a^* = \arg \max_a (Q^*(s, a))$$

A major advantage of using Q-learning is that there is no need to know the transitive probabilities $P(s_t, a_t, s_{t+1})$. The algorithm can find the $Q^*(s, a)$ in a recursive manner. The Q-values are adjusted according to equation (2). If equation (2) is repeatedly applied for each pair (s_t, a_t) and the learning rate α is gradually reduced toward 0 over time, then $Q(s, a)$ converges with probability 1 to $Q^*(s, a)$.

On the FX market a trader (man or machine) has insufficient knowledge about the environment to choose the times at which buy and sell decisions should be made in order to maximize profit. The only information available is the gain (positive or negative) generated by trading decisions and this provides the reinforcement signal that drives our system.

3.3   Combining the Two Techniques

It is important to realize that, because of the vast number of combinations of indicator values and connectives, the GA is unable to search the whole space of strategies to find the optimum. To see this, note that if we have m indicators per rule and N indicators in total, the number of possible rules is $P(N, m)*2^{m-1}$, where $P(N, m)$ is the number of permutations of N objects taken m at a time. In our system, the 10 indicators we use are applied to both buying and selling, giving a total of 20 indicators in all. Our average rule length is 8 indicators, so the above formula gives the approximate number of possible rules as 6.5×10^{11}.

To illustrate our procedure a little further, suppose that the strategy given by Tables 1 and 2 has been selected by the GA as the most profitable one. (Note that this could only occur in a market where prices are falling.) Because of the combinatorial complexity, the GA will, with very high probability, have only considered one set of instantiations for the indicators and connectives making up this rule (ie the ones in Tables 1 and 2).

The fact that the GA identified this strategy as a profitable one shows that the indicators used in the strategy are capable of making useful market predictions. The role of the Q-learning algorithm is to choose the most profitable action based on other possible instantiations of the rule values.

3.4   Related Methods

Previous work with similar objectives includes Dunis et al. [6] who used a genetic algorithm (GA) to optimise indicator parameters and their trading model was based on two indicators only. Yao and Tan in [13] used Neural Networks to perform technical forecasting on the FX. The indicators they used were moving averages of different orders and these were employed as inputs to the neural network. Moody and Saffell in [9] proposed the use of recurrent reinforcement learning to optimise risk-adjusted investment returns. Their system is based on price series returns rather than technical indicators. The best results obtained from these systems were obtained by the recurrent RL trading system which achieved an annualised 15% return on the USD/GBP exchange rate. Dempster and Jones in [5] also applied GAs to trading on the Foreign Exchange market. The best result achieved for trading over a 15 minute interval was at around a 7% return.

The method most similar to our own is due to Dempster and Romahi in [3]. They described a method in which a GA is used to choose an optimal subset of indicators which is then fed to an RL module. But their method used the RL algorithm itself to determine which of the indicators have the greatest fitness. This is computationally much more demanding than our method in which the fitness function is simply calculated in terms of the Sharpe ratio [11].

A second major distinguishing feature of the work of Dempster and his colleagues in relation to ours is that they employ only an entry model for the GA system and therefore do not have a neutral position for the trader (unless the trader has lost more than 100 points and the position is closed by default). Our use of trading strategies, as described in Section 3.1, allows us to include a neutral position in our scheme. We consider our approach to be more realistic since in some situations when the market tendency is unclear, the trader does not have any position in the market and prefers not to trade.

The annualised return obtained by Dempster and Romahi in [3] varied from 5% to 15% at a 15 minute trading frequency.

4 The Software

When a trader uses our system, the software automatically connects to the broker's server, downloads data from the server and analyses the market situation. When using the 'on-line trading' mode the trader does not require any knowledge of the state of the market – the software system automatically sells and buys assets and follows the market whilst updating system parameters. In the 'off-line trading' mode, the traders can themselves place orders to sell or buy based upon analysis and advice provided by the system.

The software engine consists of a genetic algorithm module and a reinforcement learning module based on Q-learning as described above. This system draws upon available information to determine the optimum strategy for the trader. Unlike the human trader, it is capable of working on-line and around the clock so its parameters are updated continuously over time to achieve the highest returns. It recognizes the state of the market by simultaneously examining signals from each market indicator (rather than examining indicator signals one by one).

The fitness evaluation, crossover and mutation mechanisms are repeated until the fitness function cannot be improved any longer or a maximum number of iterations is reached. The fitness function is considered maximized if the average performance of the most profitable 10 pairs of rules does not change more than 3% over several iterations. When the GA module is finished we feed the indicators from the most profitable strategy to the RL module.

In the RL module the chosen indicators represent the FX market states so if M indicators have been provided by the GA then 2^M possible states have to be considered. Different market states are represented by Q-table columns. When new information comes from the market it activates one of these columns and the best action is chosen as the maximum row-value in the activated column.

5 Main Results

The data employed for testing our system is the intraday Foreign Exchange (FX) rate EUR/USD. This currency pair is highly liquid since it is traded by a large number of market participants in all time zones. The data we employ relate to the period from 02 June 2002 to 31 December 2002 with a 5 minute frequency 'off-line trading' mode and were obtained from the CQG Data Factory (www.cqg.com). They consist of 43700 intraday records with each daily record containing seven data fields. Figure 1 illustrates a sample of this data.

Date	Time	Open	High	Low	Close	#Ticks
20020602	1600	9328	9335	9322	9331	41
20020602	1605	9324	9334	9320	9330	30
20020602	1610	9326	9334	9320	9333	32
20020602	1615	9323	9334	9320	9330	46

Fig. 1. Samples of 5 minute EUR/USD data extracted from 2 June 2002

The first row of entries in the table in figure 1 indicates that in the 5 minute period commencing 16.00 on 02 June 2002 the rate was 1 EURO = 0.9238 USD and at 1605 it was 1 EURO = 0.9331 USD. The highest and lowest rates in this period were 0.9335 USD and 0.9222 USD respectively. There were 41 trades between 1600 and 1605. Using historical data our system learns to implement on-line trading. New training data is provided every five minutes and using this, the system learns to take a position, either buy, sell or neutral.

Transaction cost here is 2 pips per trade where a pip is the minimum unit of currency movement in the FX market. The initial trading capital was 10000 Euros. Following training on 2.5 months of data the system achieved a profitability of about 6% on 3.5 months of test data. The annualised return achieved was therefore about 20%, which is clearly superior to the results quoted above for other approaches.

6   Concluding Remarks

A hybrid GA-RL system has been described that is aimed at optimizing trading strategies in the FX market. The system was trained and tested on historical data and was shown to be capable of achieving moderate gains over the tested period. Based on this system, real-time software has been designed that is capable of replacing a human trader. There are still some important features that are to be designed in future versions of the system. They include stop-losses, different contract sizes, the possibility of trading through different brokers simultaneously and others.

References

1. Bertsekas, D., Tsitsiklis, J.: Neuro-Dynamic Programming. Mass. Athena Scientific (1996)
2. Carew, E., Slatyer, W.: Forex: The Techniques of Foreign Exchange. Allen & Unwin. (1989)
3. Dempster, M., Romahi, Y.: Intraday FX trading: An evolutionary reinforcement learning approach. Intelligent data engineering and automated learning. Proceedings of the IDEAL 2002 International Conference, 3rd, (2002) 347-358
4. Dempster, M., Payne, T., Romahi, Y., Thompson, G.: Computational Learning Techniques for Intraday FX Trading Using Popular Technical Indicators. IEEE Transactions on Neural Networks, 4, (12), (2001) 744-754.
5. Dempster, M., Jones, C.: A real-time adaptive trading system using genetic programming, Quantitative Finance, 1, (2001) 397-413
6. Dunis, C., Gavridis, M., Harris, A., Leong, S., Nacaskul, P. (1998). An Application of Genetic Algorithms to High Frequency Trading Models: A Case Study. In C. Dunis and B. Zhou (ed.) Nonlinear Modelling of High Frequency Financial Time Series, (pp. 247-278). Wiley

7. Hryshko, A., Downs, T.: An Implementation of Genetic Algorithms as a Basis for a Trading System on the Foreign Exchange Market. CEC 2003, Proceedings of the 2003 Congress on Evolutionary Computation, (2003) 1695-1701
8. Kaelbling, L., Littman, M.: Reinforcement Learning: A Survey. Journal of Artificial Intelligence Research, 4, (1996) 237-285
9. Moody, J., Wu, L., Liao, Y., Saffell., M: Performance Functions and Reinforcement Learning for Trading Systems and Portfolios. Journal of Forecast, 17, (1998) 441-470
10. Murphy, J.: Technical Analysis of the Financial Markets: A Comprehensive Guide to Trading Methods and Applications, Prentice Hall Press (1999)
11. Sharpe, W.: Mutual fund performance. Journal of Business, 39, (1966) 119-138
12. Watkins, C., Dayan P.: Technical Note. Q-learning. Machine Learning, 8, (1992) 279-292
13. Yao, J., Tan, C.: A case study on using neural networks to perform technical forecasting of forex. Neurocomputing, 34, (2000) 79-98

Appendix 1: The Indicators

The indicators used in our experiments are: Moving Average (MA), Moving Average Convergence/Divergence (MACD), The Stochastic (slow Stochastic), Relative Strength Index (RSI), Commodity Channel Index (CCI), Momentum Oscillator, Price Oscillator, Larry Williams, Bollinger Bands, On Balance Volume. A detailed description of these indicators can be found in [10].

Author Index

Adewale, Idowu O.   117
Ahmad, H. Farooq   478
Akbas, Ahmet   272
Akutagawa, Masatake   171
Alhajj, Reda   117
Ali, Arshad   478
Ali, Mohsin   294
An, Bo   486, 507
Araz, Ceyhun   563

Bae, Hae-Young   25
Bao, Yongguang   133
Basharat, Amna   478
Bean, Richard   302, 422
Berglund, Erik   343
Bhatt, Mehul   9
Bodén, Mikael   454
Botelho, Silvia S.C.   125
Bozic, Ivana   375
Brunner, Gerd   63
Brusic, Vladimir   375, 398, 440
Burkhardt, Hans   63

Campbell, Alexander   343
Carrasco-Ochoa, J. Ariel   280
Carreira-Perpiñán, Miguel Á.   335
Chan, Samuel W.K.   78
Chang, Shou-Chih   32
Chen, Lian   86
Chen, Shanben   155
Chen, Songcan   351
Cheng, Daijie   486, 507
Cheng, Qiansheng   250
Chetty, Madhu   432
Cho, Sungzoon   359
Cho, Woo-Jin   102
Choi, Joongmin   94
Choi, Kyunghee   501
Choi, Youngsoo   501
Christen, Peter   109
Corchado, Emilio   187

Dang, Chuangyin   540
Dayan, Peter   335
de Figueiredo, Matheus Bacelo   125
Deepa Shenoy, P.   555

Dong, Zhao Yang   294
Downs, Tom   588
Du, Jinling   540
Du, Xiaoyong   133

Fang, Victor   580
Farkaš, Igor   327
Fotouhi, Farshad   1
Frean, Marcus   195

Gallagher, Marcus   220
Goodhill, Geoffrey J.   335
Gordon, James   448

Hallinan, Jennifer   382
Hawkins, John   454
He, Qicai   203
Herrero, Álvaro   187
Hong, Jinkeun   141
Hryshko, Andrei   588
Huang, Xixia   155
Hubbard, S.   390
Hui, Kin-Ping   228
Hwang, Sungwook   470

Ishii, Naohiro   133

Jalili-Kharaajoo, Mahdi   164, 179
Jiang, Nan   462
Jones, Liat Ben-Tovim   422
Jung, Gihyun   501

Kabán, Ata   40
Kang, Jinbeom   94
Keeratipranon, Narongdech   286
Kim, Donghyun   149
Kim, Kihong   141
Kim, Ung Mo   1
Kim, Yu-Seop   102
Kinouchi, Yohsuke   171
Kokol, Peter   242
Kroese, Dirk P.   228

Lau, K.W.   390
Lautenschlger, Willian   125
Lee, Eunseok   470, 494, 515

Lee, Hyoung-joo   359
Lee, Jae-Young   102
Lee, Seunghwa   494
Lee, Vincent C.S.   580
Lee, Yuh-Jye   32
Lenič, Mitja   242
Leung, Kwong-sak   264, 546
Li, Shuangqing   486, 507
Li, Wenhui   17
Li, Xue   294
Li, Xueyao   258
Li, Zhuoming   171
Lilley, Matthew   195
Lim, Jongin   141
Lim, Yee Choon   580
Lin, Pan   71
Liu, Jun   351
Lu, Guojun   56
Lu, Zhiwu   250
Luo, Jun   406

Ma, Jinwen   203, 250, 406
Maetschke, Stefan   454
Maire, Frederic   286
Mao, Kezhi   414
Martínez-Trinidad, José Fco.   280
Mata, Mauricio M.   125
McLachlan, Geoff   302, 422
Mei, Lin   63
Mezzadri Centeno, Tania   125
Miao, Chunyan   486, 507
Miotto, Olivo   398
Mitchell, Ian   462
Möller-Levet, Carla S.   319

Nagashino, Hirofumi   171
Nariai, Sho   228
Nayak, Richi   234
Ng, Sai-cheong   264
Nikulin, Vladimir   311
Noh, Sanguk   501

Oh, Jehwan   494
Oh, Yu-Jin   102
Olvera-López, José A.   280
Ooi, Chia Huey   432
Ozkarahan, Irem   563

Paik, Juryon   1
Pao, Hsing-Kuo   32

Park, Jeongmin   515
Park, Soon-Young   25
Patnaik, Lalit M.   555
Pei, Xiaobing   48
Povalej, Petra   242

Qi, Tian   56

Rahayu, Wenny   9
Rajapakse, Menaka   440

Sáiz, José Manuel   187
Sajjanhar, Atul   56
Schmidt, Bertil   440
Setia, Lokesh   63
Shen, Liran   258
Shi, Baile   86
Shichijo, Fumio   171
Shum, Wing-Ho   546
Sridharan, K.   555
Srinivasa, K.G.   555
Stapley, B.   390
Sterling, Gerald   9
Streit, Alexander   343
Suguri, Hiroki   478
Sun, Haibin   17
Sweetser, Penelope   524

Tan, Tin Wee   398
Tan, Xiaoyang   351
Tang, Lianggui   486, 507
Tariq, Amina   478
Tiňo, Peter   327
Towsey, Michael   448
Tsuchiya, Eisuke   133

van Mourik, Jort   327
Venugopal, K.R.   555

Wakabayashi, Mark   454
Wang, Xin   40
Wang, Yuanzhen   48
Wang, Yuping   540
Watson, James   532
Wiles, Janet   524, 532
Won, Dongho   1
Wong, Man-Leung   546
Wu, Edmond H.C.   571
Wu, Wendy Xinyu   462
Wyse, Lonce   440

Yang, Jaeyoung   94
Yang, Yong   71
Yang, Zheng Rong   211
Ye, Huilin   367
Ye, Jianye   86
Yeh, Flora Yu-Hui   220
Yin, H.   390
Yin, Hujun   319
Yin, Qingbo   258
Yook, Dongsuk   149
Youn, Heeyong   470
Youn, Hyunsang   470, 515
Yu, Philip L.H.   571

Zhang, Dengsheng   56
Zhang, Feng   71
Zhang, Fuyan   351
Zhang, Guang Lan   375
Zhang, Liang   86
Zhang, Qinyu   171
Zhang, Rubo   258
Zhang, Yu   171
Zheng, Chongxun   71
Zhou, Xiangdong   86
Zhou, Xin   414
Zhu, Justin   422

Lecture Notes in Computer Science

For information about Vols. 1–3474

please contact your bookseller or Springer

Vol. 3578: M. Gallagher, J. Hogan, F. Maire (Eds.), Intelligent Data Engineering and Automated Learning - IDEAL 2005. XVI, 599 pages. 2005.

Vol. 3576: K. Etessami, S.K. Rajamani (Eds.), Computer Aided Verification. XV, 564 pages. 2005.

Vol. 3574: C. Boyd, J.M. González Nieto (Eds.), Information Security and Privacy. XIII, 586 pages. 2005.

Vol. 3573: S. Etalle (Ed.), Logic Based Program Synthesis and Transformation. VIII, 279 pages. 2005.

Vol. 3572: C. De Felice, A. Restivo (Eds.), Developments in Language Theory. XI, 409 pages. 2005.

Vol. 3570: A. S. Patrick, M. Yung (Eds.), Financial Cryptography and Data Security. XII, 376 pages. 2005.

Vol. 3569: F. Bacchus, T. Walsh (Eds.), Theory and Applications of Satisfiability Testing. XII, 492 pages. 2005.

Vol. 3567: M. Jackson, D. Nelson, S. Stirk (Eds.), Database: Enterprise, Skills and Innovation. XII, 185 pages. 2005.

Vol. 3565: G.E. Christensen, M. Sonka (Eds.), Information Processing in Medical Imaging. XXI, 777 pages. 2005.

Vol. 3562: J. Mira, J.R. Álvarez (Eds.), Artificial Intelligence and Knowledge Engineering Applications: A Bioinspired Approach, Part II. XXIV, 636 pages. 2005.

Vol. 3561: J. Mira, J.R. Álvarez (Eds.), Mechanisms, Symbols, and Models Underlying Cognition, Part I. XXIV, 532 pages. 2005.

Vol. 3560: V.K. Prasanna, S. Iyengar, P.G. Spirakis, M. Welsh (Eds.), Distributed Computing in Sensor Systems. XV, 423 pages. 2005.

Vol. 3559: P. Auer, R. Meir (Eds.), Learning Theory. XI, 692 pages. 2005. (Subseries LNAI).

Vol. 3557: H. Gilbert, H. Handschuh (Eds.), Fast Software Encryption. XI, 443 pages. 2005.

Vol. 3556: H. Baumeister, M. Marchesi, M. Holcombe (Eds.), Extreme Programming and Agile Processes in Software Engineering. XIV, 332 pages. 2005.

Vol. 3555: T. Vardanega, A. Wellings (Eds.), Reliable Software Technology – Ada-Europe 2005. XV, 273 pages. 2005.

Vol. 3554: A. Dey, B. Kokinov, D. Leake, R. Turner (Eds.), Modeling and Using Context. XIV, 572 pages. 2005. (Subseries LNAI).

Vol. 3553: T.D. Hämäläinen, A.D. Pimentel, J. Takala, S. Vassiliadis (Eds.), Embedded Computer Systems: Architectures, Modeling, and Simulation. XV, 476 pages. 2005.

Vol. 3552: H. de Meer, N. Bhatti (Eds.), Quality of Service – IWQoS 2005. XV, 400 pages. 2005.

Vol. 3551: T. Härder, W. Lehner (Eds.), Data Management in a Connected World. XIX, 371 pages. 2005.

Vol. 3548: K. Julisch, C. Kruegel (Eds.), Intrusion and Malware Detection and Vulnerability Assessment. X, 241 pages. 2005.

Vol. 3547: F. Bomarius, S. Komi-Sirviö (Eds.), Product Focused Software Process Improvement. XIII, 588 pages. 2005.

Vol. 3543: L. Kutvonen, N. Alonistioti (Eds.), Distributed Applications and Interoperable Systems. XI, 235 pages. 2005.

Vol. 3541: N.C. Oza, R. Polikar, J. Kittler, F. Roli (Eds.), Multiple Classifier Systems. XII, 430 pages. 2005.

Vol. 3540: H. Kalviainen, J. Parkkinen, A. Kaarna (Eds.), Image Analysis. XXII, 1270 pages. 2005.

Vol. 3537: A. Apostolico, M. Crochemore, K. Park (Eds.), Combinatorial Pattern Matching. XI, 444 pages. 2005.

Vol. 3536: G. Ciardo, P. Darondeau (Eds.), Applications and Theory of Petri Nets 2005. XI, 470 pages. 2005.

Vol. 3535: M. Steffen, G. Zavattaro (Eds.), Formal Methods for Open Object-Based Distributed Systems. X, 323 pages. 2005.

Vol. 3533: M. Ali, F. Esposito (Eds.), Innovations in Applied Artificial Intelligence. XX, 858 pages. 2005. (Subseries LNAI).

Vol. 3532: A. Gómez-Pérez, J. Euzenat (Eds.), The Semantic Web: Research and Applications. XV, 728 pages. 2005.

Vol. 3531: J. Ioannidis, A. Keromytis, M. Yung (Eds.), Applied Cryptography and Network Security. XI, 530 pages. 2005.

Vol. 3530: A. Prinz, R. Reed, J. Reed (Eds.), SDL 2005: Model Driven. XI, 361 pages. 2005.

Vol. 3528: P.S. Szczepaniak, J. Kacprzyk, A. Niewiadomski (Eds.), Advances in Web Intelligence. XVII, 513 pages. 2005. (Subseries LNAI).

Vol. 3527: R. Morrison, F. Oquendo (Eds.), Software Architecture. XII, 263 pages. 2005.

Vol. 3526: S.B. Cooper, B. Löwe, L. Torenvliet (Eds.), New Computational Paradigms. XVII, 574 pages. 2005.

Vol. 3525: A.E. Abdallah, C.B. Jones, J.W. Sanders (Eds.), Communicating Sequential Processes. XIV, 321 pages. 2005.

Vol. 3524: R. Barták, M. Milano (Eds.), Integration of AI and OR Techniques in Constraint Programming for Combinatorial Optimization Problems. XI, 320 pages. 2005.

Vol. 3523: J.S. Marques, N. Pérez de la Blanca, P. Pina (Eds.), Pattern Recognition and Image Analysis, Part II. XXVI, 733 pages. 2005.

Vol. 3522: J.S. Marques, N. Pérez de la Blanca, P. Pina (Eds.), Pattern Recognition and Image Analysis, Part I. XXVI, 703 pages. 2005.

Vol. 3521: N. Megiddo, Y. Xu, B. Zhu (Eds.), Algorithmic Applications in Management. XIII, 484 pages. 2005.

Vol. 3520: O. Pastor, J. Falcão e Cunha (Eds.), Advanced Information Systems Engineering. XVI, 584 pages. 2005.

Vol. 3519: H. Li, P. J. Olver, G. Sommer (Eds.), Computer Algebra and Geometric Algebra with Applications. IX, 449 pages. 2005.

Vol. 3518: T.B. Ho, D. Cheung, H. Liu (Eds.), Advances in Knowledge Discovery and Data Mining. XXI, 864 pages. 2005. (Subseries LNAI).

Vol. 3517: H.S. Baird, D.P. Lopresti (Eds.), Human Interactive Proofs. IX, 143 pages. 2005.

Vol. 3516: V.S. Sunderam, G.D.v. Albada, P.M.A. Sloot, J.J. Dongarra (Eds.), Computational Science – ICCS 2005, Part III. LXIII, 1143 pages. 2005.

Vol. 3515: V.S. Sunderam, G.D.v. Albada, P.M.A. Sloot, J.J. Dongarra (Eds.), Computational Science – ICCS 2005, Part II. LXIII, 1101 pages. 2005.

Vol. 3514: V.S. Sunderam, G.D.v. Albada, P.M.A. Sloot, J.J. Dongarra (Eds.), Computational Science – ICCS 2005, Part I. LXIII, 1089 pages. 2005.

Vol. 3513: A. Montoyo, R. Muñoz, E. Métais (Eds.), Natural Language Processing and Information Systems. XII, 408 pages. 2005.

Vol. 3512: J. Cabestany, A. Prieto, F. Sandoval (Eds.), Computational Intelligence and Bioinspired Systems. XXV, 1260 pages. 2005.

Vol. 3510: T. Braun, G. Carle, Y. Koucheryavy, V. Tsaoussidis (Eds.), Wired/Wireless Internet Communications. XIV, 366 pages. 2005.

Vol. 3509: M. Jünger, V. Kaibel (Eds.), Integer Programming and Combinatorial Optimization. XI, 484 pages. 2005.

Vol. 3508: P. Bresciani, P. Giorgini, B. Henderson-Sellers, G. Low, M. Winikoff (Eds.), Agent-Oriented Information Systems II. X, 227 pages. 2005. (Subseries LNAI).

Vol. 3507: F. Crestani, I. Ruthven (Eds.), Information Context: Nature, Impact, and Role. XIII, 253 pages. 2005.

Vol. 3506: C. Park, S. Chee (Eds.), Information Security and Cryptology – ICISC 2004. XIV, 490 pages. 2005.

Vol. 3505: V. Gorodetsky, J. Liu, V. A. Skormin (Eds.), Autonomous Intelligent Systems: Agents and Data Mining. XIII, 303 pages. 2005. (Subseries LNAI).

Vol. 3504: A.F. Frangi, P.I. Radeva, A. Santos, M. Hernandez (Eds.), Functional Imaging and Modeling of the Heart. XV, 489 pages. 2005.

Vol. 3503: S.E. Nikoletseas (Ed.), Experimental and Efficient Algorithms. XV, 624 pages. 2005.

Vol. 3502: F. Khendek, R. Dssouli (Eds.), Testing of Communicating Systems. X, 381 pages. 2005.

Vol. 3501: B. Kégl, G. Lapalme (Eds.), Advances in Artificial Intelligence. XV, 458 pages. 2005. (Subseries LNAI).

Vol. 3500: S. Miyano, J. Mesirov, S. Kasif, S. Istrail, P. Pevzner, M. Waterman (Eds.), Research in Computational Molecular Biology. XVII, 632 pages. 2005. (Subseries LNBI).

Vol. 3499: A. Pelc, M. Raynal (Eds.), Structural Information and Communication Complexity. X, 323 pages. 2005.

Vol. 3498: J. Wang, X. Liao, Z. Yi (Eds.), Advances in Neural Networks – ISNN 2005, Part III. XLIX, 1077 pages. 2005.

Vol. 3497: J. Wang, X. Liao, Z. Yi (Eds.), Advances in Neural Networks – ISNN 2005, Part II. XLIX, 947 pages. 2005.

Vol. 3496: J. Wang, X. Liao, Z. Yi (Eds.), Advances in Neural Networks – ISNN 2005, Part II. L, 1055 pages. 2005.

Vol. 3495: P. Kantor, G. Muresan, F. Roberts, D.D. Zeng, F.-Y. Wang, H. Chen, R.C. Merkle (Eds.), Intelligence and Security Informatics. XVIII, 674 pages. 2005.

Vol. 3494: R. Cramer (Ed.), Advances in Cryptology – EUROCRYPT 2005. XIV, 576 pages. 2005.

Vol. 3493: N. Fuhr, M. Lalmas, S. Malik, Z. Szlávik (Eds.), Advances in XML Information Retrieval. XI, 438 pages. 2005.

Vol. 3492: P. Blache, E. Stabler, J. Busquets, R. Moot (Eds.), Logical Aspects of Computational Linguistics. X, 363 pages. 2005. (Subseries LNAI).

Vol. 3489: G.T. Heineman, I. Crnkovic, H.W. Schmidt, J.A. Stafford, C. Szyperski, K. Wallnau (Eds.), Component-Based Software Engineering. XI, 358 pages. 2005.

Vol. 3488: M.-S. Hacid, N.V. Murray, Z.W. Raś, S. Tsumoto (Eds.), Foundations of Intelligent Systems. XIII, 700 pages. 2005. (Subseries LNAI).

Vol. 3486: T. Helleseth, D. Sarwate, H.-Y. Song, K. Yang (Eds.), Sequences and Their Applications - SETA 2004. XII, 451 pages. 2005.

Vol. 3483: O. Gervasi, M.L. Gavrilova, V. Kumar, A. Laganà, H.P. Lee, Y. Mun, D. Taniar, C.J.K. Tan (Eds.), Computational Science and Its Applications – ICCSA 2005, Part IV. LXV, 1362 pages. 2005.

Vol. 3482: O. Gervasi, M.L. Gavrilova, V. Kumar, A. Laganà, H.P. Lee, Y. Mun, D. Taniar, C.J.K. Tan (Eds.), Computational Science and Its Applications – ICCSA 2005, Part III. LXV, 1340 pages. 2005.

Vol. 3481: O. Gervasi, M.L. Gavrilova, V. Kumar, A. Laganà, H.P. Lee, Y. Mun, D. Taniar, C.J.K. Tan (Eds.), Computational Science and Its Applications – ICCSA 2005, Part II. LXV, 1316 pages. 2005.

Vol. 3480: O. Gervasi, M.L. Gavrilova, V. Kumar, A. Laganà, H.P. Lee, Y. Mun, D. Taniar, C.J.K. Tan (Eds.), Computational Science and Its Applications – ICCSA 2005, Part I. LXV, 1234 pages. 2005.

Vol. 3479: T. Strang, C. Linnhoff-Popien (Eds.), Location- and Context-Awareness. XII, 378 pages. 2005.

Vol. 3478: C. Jermann, A. Neumaier, D. Sam (Eds.), Global Optimization and Constraint Satisfaction. XIII, 193 pages. 2005.

Vol. 3477: P. Herrmann, V. Issarny, S. Shiu (Eds.), Trust Management. XII, 426 pages. 2005.

Vol. 3476: J. Leite, A. Omicini, P. Torroni, P. Yolum (Eds.), Declarative Agent Languages and Technologies II. XII, 289 pages. 2005. (Subseries LNAI).

Vol. 3475: N. Guelfi (Ed.), Rapid Integration of Software Engineering Techniques. X, 145 pages. 2005.